CHARLES W. CHESNUTT

Charles W. Chesnutt

STORIES, NOVELS, & ESSAYS

The Conjure Woman

The Wife of His Youth and Other Stories of the Color Line

The House Behind the Cedars

The Marrow of Tradition

Uncollected Stories

Selected Essays

THE LIBRARY OF AMERICA

The paper used in this publication meets the
minimum requirements of the American National Standard for
Information Sciences—Permanence of Paper for Printed
Library Materials, ANSI Z39.48—1984.

Distributed to the trade in the United States
by Penguin Putnam Inc.
and in Canada by Penguin Books Canada Ltd.

Library of Congress Catalog Number: 2001038120
For cataloging information, see end of Notes.
ISBN 1–931082–06–5

First Printing
The Library of America—131

Manufactured in the United States of America

Werner Sollors

SELECTED THE CONTENTS AND WROTE THE NOTES FOR THIS VOLUME

Contents

THE CONJURE WOMAN

(1899)

CONTENTS

The Goophered Grapevine

SOME YEARS AGO my wife was in poor health, and our family doctor, in whose skill and honesty I had implicit confidence, advised a change of climate. I shared, from an unprofessional standpoint, his opinion that the raw winds, the chill rains, and the violent changes of temperature that characterized the winters in the region of the Great Lakes tended to aggravate my wife's difficulty, and would undoubtedly shorten her life if she remained exposed to them. The doctor's advice was that we seek, not a temporary place of sojourn, but a permanent residence, in a warmer and more equable climate. I was engaged at the time in grape-culture in northern Ohio, and, as I liked the business and had given it much study, I decided to look for some other locality suitable for carrying it on. I thought of sunny France, of sleepy Spain, of Southern California, but there were objections to them all. It occurred to me that I might find what I wanted in some one of our own Southern States. It was a sufficient time after the war for conditions in the South to have become somewhat settled; and I was enough of a pioneer to start a new industry, if I could not find a place where grape-culture had been tried. I wrote to a cousin who had gone into the turpentine business in central North Carolina. He assured me, in response to my inquiries, that no better place could be found in the South than the State and neighborhood where he lived; the climate was perfect for health, and, in conjunction with the soil, ideal for grape-culture; labor was cheap, and land could be bought for a mere song. He gave us a cordial invitation to come and visit him while we looked into the matter. We accepted the invitation, and after several days of leisurely travel, the last hundred miles of which were up a river on a sidewheel steamer, we reached our destination, a quaint old town, which I shall call Patesville, because, for one reason, that is not its name. There was a red brick market-house in the public square, with a tall tower, which held a four-faced clock that struck the hours, and from which there pealed out a curfew at nine o'clock. There were two or three hotels, a court-house, a jail, stores, offices, and all the appurtenances of a county seat and a commercial emporium; for while Patesville numbered only four or five thousand inhabitants, of all shades of complexion, it was one of the principal towns in North Carolina, and had a considerable trade in cotton and naval stores. This business activity was not immediately apparent to my unaccustomed eyes. Indeed, when I first saw the town, there brooded over it a calm that seemed almost sabbatic in its restfulness, though I learned later on that underneath its somnolent exterior the deeper currents of life—love and hatred, joy and despair, ambition and avarice, faith and friendship—flowed not less steadily than in livelier latitudes.

We found the weather delightful at that season, the end of summer, and were hospitably entertained. Our host was a man of means and evidently regarded our visit as a pleasure, and we were therefore correspondingly at our ease, and in a position to act with the coolness of judgment desirable in making so radical a change in our lives. My cousin placed a horse and buggy at our disposal, and himself acted as our guide until I became somewhat familiar with the country.

I found that grape-culture, while it had never been carried on to any great extent, was not entirely unknown in the neighborhood. Several planters thereabouts had attempted it on a commercial scale, in former years, with greater or less success; but like most Southern industries, it had felt the blight of war and had fallen into desuetude.

I went several times to look at a place that I thought might suit me. It was a plantation of considerable extent, that had formerly belonged to a wealthy man by the name of McAdoo. The estate had been for years involved in litigation between disputing heirs, during which period shiftless cultivation had well-nigh exhausted the soil. There had been a vineyard of some extent on the place, but it had not been attended to since the war, and had lapsed into utter neglect. The vines—here partly supported by decayed and broken-down trellises, there twining themselves among the branches of the slender saplings which had sprung up among them—grew in wild and unpruned luxuriance, and the few scattered grapes they bore were the undisputed prey of the first comer. The site was admirably adapted to grape-raising; the soil, with a little attention, could not have been better; and with the native grape, the luscious scuppernong, as my main reliance in the beginning, I felt sure that I could introduce and cultivate successfully a number of other varieties.

One day I went over with my wife to show her the place. We drove out of the town over a long wooden bridge that spanned a spreading mill-pond, passed the long whitewashed fence surrounding the county fair-ground, and struck into a road so sandy that the horse's feet sank to the fetlocks. Our route lay partly up hill and partly down, for we were in the sand-hill county; we drove past cultivated farms, and then by abandoned fields grown up in scrub-oak and short-leaved pine, and once or twice through the solemn aisles of the virgin forest, where the tall pines, well-nigh meeting over the narrow road, shut out the sun, and wrapped us in cloistral solitude. Once, at a cross-roads, I was in doubt as to the turn to take, and we sat there waiting ten minutes—we had already caught some of the native infection of restfulness—for some human being to come along, who could direct us on our way. At length a little negro girl appeared, walking straight as an arrow, with a piggin full of water on her head. After a little patient investigation, necessary to overcome the child's shyness, we learned what we wished to know, and at the end of about five miles from the town reached our destination.

We drove between a pair of decayed gateposts—the gate itself had long since disappeared—and up a straight sandy lane, between two lines of rotting rail fence, partly concealed by jimson-weeds and briers, to the open space where a dwelling-house had once stood, evidently a spacious mansion, if we might judge from the ruined chimneys that were still standing, and the brick pillars on which the sills rested. The house itself, we had been informed, had fallen a victim to the fortunes of war.

We alighted from the buggy, walked about the yard for a while, and then wandered off into the adjoining vineyard. Upon Annie's complaining of weariness I led the way back to the yard, where a pine log, lying under a spreading elm, afforded a shady though somewhat hard seat. One end of the log was already occupied by a venerable-looking colored man. He held on his knees a hat full of grapes, over which he was smacking his lips with great gusto, and a pile of grapeskins near him indicated that the performance was no new thing. We approached him at an angle from the rear, and were close to him before he perceived us. He respectfully rose as we drew near, and was moving away, when I begged him to keep his seat.

"Don't let us disturb you," I said. "There is plenty of room for us all."

He resumed his seat with somewhat of embarrassment. While he had been standing, I had observed that he was a tall man, and, though slightly bowed by the weight of years, apparently quite vigorous. He was not entirely black, and this fact, together with the quality of his hair, which was about six inches long and very bushy, except on the top of his head, where he was quite bald, suggested a slight strain of other than negro blood. There was a shrewdness in his eyes, too, which was not altogether African, and which, as we afterwards learned from experience, was indicative of a corresponding shrewdness in his character. He went on eating the grapes, but did not seem to enjoy himself quite so well as he had apparently done before he became aware of our presence.

"Do you live around here?" I asked, anxious to put him at his ease.

"Yas, suh. I lives des ober yander, behine de nex' san'-hill, on de Lumberton plank-road."

"Do you know anything about the time when this vineyard was cultivated?"

"Lawd bless you, suh, I knows all about it. Dey ain' na'er a man in dis settlement w'at won' tell you ole Julius McAdoo 'uz bawn en raise' on dis yer same plantation. Is you de Norv'n gemman w'at's gwine ter buy de ole vimya'd?"

"I am looking at it," I replied; "but I don't know that I shall care to buy unless I can be reasonably sure of making something out of it."

"Well, suh, you is a stranger ter me, en I is a stranger ter you, en we is bofe strangers ter one anudder, but 'f I 'uz in yo' place, I would n' buy dis vimya'd."

"Why not?" I asked.

"Well, I dunno whe'r you b'lieves in cunj'in 'er not,—some

er de w'ite folks don't, er says dey don't,—but de truf er de matter is dat dis yer ole vimya'd is goophered."

"Is what?" I asked, not grasping the meaning of this unfamiliar word.

"Is goophered,—cunju'd, bewitch'."

He imparted this information with such solemn earnestness, and with such an air of confidential mystery, that I felt somewhat interested, while Annie was evidently much impressed, and drew closer to me.

"How do you know it is bewitched?" I asked.

"I would n' spec' fer you ter b'lieve me 'less you know all 'bout de fac's. But ef you en young miss dere doan' min' lis'nin' ter a ole nigger run on a minute er two w'ile you er restin', I kin 'splain to you how it all happen'."

We assured him that we would be glad to hear how it all happened, and he began to tell us. At first the current of his memory—or imagination—seemed somewhat sluggish; but as his embarrassment wore off, his language flowed more freely, and the story acquired perspective and coherence. As he became more and more absorbed in the narrative, his eyes assumed a dreamy expression, and he seemed to lose sight of his auditors, and to be living over again in monologue his life on the old plantation.

"Ole Mars Dugal' McAdoo," he began, "bought dis place long many years befo' de wah, en I 'member well w'en he sot out all dis yer part er de plantation in scuppernon's. De vimes growed monst'us fas', en Mars Dugal' made a thousan' gallon er scuppernon' wine eve'y year.

"Now, ef dey's an'thing a nigger lub, nex' ter 'possum, en chick'n, en watermillyums, it 's scuppernon's. Dey ain' nuffin dat kin stan' up side'n de scuppernon' fer sweetness; sugar ain't a suckumstance ter scuppernon'. W'en de season is nigh 'bout ober, en de grapes begin ter swivel up des a little wid de wrinkles er ole age,—w'en de skin git sof' en brown,—den de scuppernon' make you smack yo' lip en roll yo' eye en wush fer mo'; so I reckon it ain' very 'stonishin' dat niggers lub scuppernon'.

"Dey wuz a sight er niggers in de naberhood er de vimya'd. Dere wuz ole Mars Henry Brayboy's niggers, en ole Mars Jeems McLean's niggers, en Mars Dugal's own niggers; den dey wuz a settlement er free niggers en po' buckrahs down by de Wim'l'ton Road, en Mars Dugal' had de only vimya'd in de naberhood. I reckon it ain' so much so nowadays, but befo' de wah, in slab'ry times, a nigger did n' mine goin' fi' er ten mile in a night, w'en dey wuz sump'n good ter eat at de yuther een'.

"So atter a w'ile Mars Dugal' begin ter miss his scuppernon's. Co'se he 'cuse' de niggers er it, but dey all 'nied it ter de las'. Mars Dugal' sot spring guns en steel traps, en he en de oberseah sot up nights once't er twice't, tel one night Mars Dugal'—he 'uz a monst'us keerless man—got his leg shot full er cow-peas. But somehow er nudder dey could n' nebber ketch none er de niggers. I dunner how it happen, but it happen des like I tell you, en de grapes kep' on a-goin' des de same.

"But bimeby ole Mars Dugal' fix' up a plan ter stop it. Dey wuz a cunjuh 'oman livin' down 'mongs' de free niggers on de Wim'l'ton Road, en all de darkies fum Rockfish ter Beaver Crick wuz feared er her. She could wuk de mos' powerfulles' kin' er goopher,—could make people hab fits, er rheumatiz, er make 'em des dwinel away en die; en dey say she went out ridin' de niggers at night, fer she wuz a witch 'sides bein' a cunjuh 'oman. Mars Dugal' hearn 'bout Aun' Peggy's doin's, en begun ter 'flect whe'r er no he could n' git her ter he'p him keep de niggers off'n de grapevimes. One day in de spring er de year, ole miss pack' up a basket er chick'n en poun'-cake, en a bottle er scuppernon' wine, en Mars Dugal' tuk it in his buggy en driv ober ter Aun' Peggy's cabin. He tuk de basket in, en had a long talk wid Aun' Peggy.

"De nex' day Aun' Peggy come up ter de vimya'd. De niggers seed her slippin' 'roun', en dey soon foun' out what she 'uz doin' dere. Mars Dugal' had hi'ed her ter goopher de grapevimes. She sa'ntered 'roun' 'mongs' de vimes, en tuk a leaf fum dis one, en a grape-hull fum dat one, en a grape-seed fum anudder one; en den a little twig fum here, en a little pinch er dirt fum dere,—en put it all in a big black bottle, wid a snake's toof en a speckle' hen's gall en some ha'rs fum a black cat's tail, en den fill' de bottle wid scuppernon' wine. W'en she got de goopher all ready en fix', she tuk 'n went out in de woods en buried it under de root uv a red oak tree, en den come back en tole one er de niggers she done goopher de grapevimes, en a'er a nigger w'at eat dem grapes 'ud be sho ter die inside'n twel' mont's.

"Atter dat de niggers let de scuppernon's 'lone, en Mars Dugal' did n' hab no 'casion ter fine no mo' fault; en de season wuz mos' gone, w'en a strange gemman stop at de plantation one night ter see Mars Dugal' on some business; en his coachman, seein' de scuppernon's growin' so nice en sweet, slip 'roun' behine de smoke-house, en et all de scuppernon's he could hole. Nobody did n' notice it at de time, but dat night, on de way home, de gemman's hoss runned away en kill' de coachman. W'en we hearn de noos, Aun' Lucy, de cook, she up 'n say she seed de strange nigger eat'n' er de scuppernon's behine de smoke-house; en den we knowed de goopher had b'en er wukkin'. Den one er de nigger chilluns runned away fum de quarters one day, en got in de scuppernon's, en died de nex' week. W'ite folks say he die' er de fevuh, but de niggers knowed it wuz de goopher. So you k'n be sho de darkies did n' hab much ter do wid dem scuppernon' vimes.

"W'en de scuppernon' season 'uz ober fer dat year, Mars Dugal' foun' he had made fifteen hund'ed gallon er wine; en one er de niggers hearn him laffin' wid de oberseah fit ter kill, en sayin' dem fifteen hund'ed gallon er wine wuz monst'us good intrus' on de ten dollars he laid out on de vimya'd. So I 'low ez he paid Aun' Peggy ten dollars fer to goopher de grapevimes.

"De goopher did n' wuk no mo' tel de nex' summer, w'en 'long to'ds de middle er de season one er de fiel' han's died; en ez dat lef' Mars Dugal' sho't er han's, he went off ter town fer ter buy anudder. He fotch de noo nigger home wid 'im. He wuz er ole nigger, er de color er a gingy-cake, en ball ez a hoss-apple on de top er his head. He wuz a peart ole nigger, do', en could do a big day's wuk.

"Now it happen dat one er de niggers on de nex' plantation, one er ole Mars Henry Brayboy's niggers, had runned away de day befo', en tuk ter de swamp, en ole Mars Dugal' en some er de yuther nabor w'ite folks had gone out wid dere guns en dere dogs fer ter he'p 'em hunt fer de nigger; en de han's on our own plantation wuz all so flusterated dat we fuhgot ter tell de noo han' 'bout de goopher on de scuppernon' vimes. Co'se he smell de grapes en see de vimes, an atter dahk de fus' thing he done wuz ter slip off ter de grapevimes 'dout sayin' nuffin ter nobody. Nex' mawnin' he tole some er de niggers 'bout de fine bait er scuppernon' he et de night befo'.

"W'en dey tole im 'bout de goopher on de grapevimes, he 'uz dat tarrified dat he turn pale, en look des like he gwine ter die right in his tracks. De oberseah come up en axed w'at 'uz de matter; en w'en dey tole 'im Henry be'n eatin' er de scuppernon's, en got de goopher on 'im, he gin Henry a big drink er w'iskey, en 'low dat de nex' rainy day he take 'im ober ter Aun' Peggy's, en see ef she would n' take de goopher off'n him, seein' ez he did n' know nuffin erbout it tel he done et de grapes.

"Sho nuff, it rain de nex' day, en de oberseah went ober ter Aun' Peggy's wid Henry. En Aun' Peggy say dat bein' ez Henry did n' know 'bout de goopher, en et de grapes in ign'ance er de conseq'ences, she reckon she mought be able fer ter take de goopher off'n him. So she fotch out er bottle wid some cunjuh medicine in it, en po'd some out in a go'd fer Henry ter drink. He manage ter git it down; he say it tas'e like whiskey wid sump'n bitter in it. She 'lowed dat 'ud keep de goopher off'n him tel de spring; but w'en de sap begin ter rise in de grapevimes he ha' ter come en see her ag'in, en she tell him w'at e's ter do.

"Nex' spring, w'en de sap commence' ter rise in de scuppernon' vime, Henry tuk a ham one night. Whar'd he git de ham? *I* doan know; dey wa'n't no hams on de plantation 'cep'n' w'at 'uz in de smoke-house, but *I* never see Henry 'bout de smoke-house. But ez I wuz a-sayin', he tuk de ham ober ter Aun' Peggy's; en Aun' Peggy tole 'im dat w'en Mars Dugal' begin ter prune de grapevimes, he mus' go en take 'n scrape off de sap whar it ooze out'n de cut een's er de vimes, en 'n'int his ball head wid it; en ef he do dat once't a year de goopher would n' wuk agin 'im long ez he done it. En bein' ez he fotch her de ham, she fix' it so he kin eat all de scuppernon' he want.

"So Henry 'n'int his head wid de sap out'n de big grapevime des ha'f way 'twix' de quarters en de big house, en de goopher nebber wuk agin him dat summer. But de beatenes' thing you eber see happen ter Henry. Up ter dat time he wuz ez ball ez a sweeten' 'tater, but des ez soon ez de young leaves begun ter come out on de grapevimes, de ha'r begun ter grow out on Henry's head, en by de middle er de summer he had de bigges' head er ha'r on de plantation. Befo' dat, Henry had tol'able good ha'r 'roun' de aidges, but soon ez de young grapes begun ter come, Henry's ha'r begun to quirl all up in little balls, des like dis yer reg'lar grapy ha'r, en by de time de grapes got ripe his head look des like a bunch er grapes. Combin' it did n' do no good; he wuk at it ha'f de night wid er Jim Crow,* en think he git it straighten' out, but in de mawnin' de grapes 'ud be dere des de same. So he gin it up, en tried ter keep de grapes down by havin' his ha'r cut sho't.

"But dat wa'n't de quares' thing 'bout de goopher. When Henry come ter de plantation, he wuz gittin' a little ole an stiff in de j'ints. But dat summer he got des ez spry en libely ez any young nigger on de plantation; fac', he got so biggity dat Mars Jackson, de oberseah, ha' ter th'eaten ter whip 'im, ef he did n' stop cuttin' up his didos en behave hisse'f. But de mos' cur'ouses' thing happen' in de fall, when de sap begin ter go down in de grapevimes. Fus', when de grapes 'uz gethered, de knots begun ter straighten out'n Henry's ha'r; en w'en de leaves begin ter fall, Henry's ha'r 'mence' ter drap out; en when de vimes 'uz bar', Henry's head wuz baller'n it wuz in de spring, en he begin ter git ole en stiff in de j'ints ag'in, en paid no mo' 'tention ter de gals dyoin' er de whole winter. En nex' spring, w'en he rub de sap on ag'in, he got young ag'in, en so soopl en libely dat none er de young niggers on de plantation could n' jump, ner dance, ner hoe ez much cotton ez Henry. But in de fall er de year his grapes 'mence' ter straighten out, en his j'ints ter git stiff, en his ha'r drap off, en de rheumatiz begin ter wrastle wid 'im.

"Now, ef you'd 'a' knowed ole Mars Dugal' McAdoo, you'd 'a' knowed dat it ha' ter be a mighty rainy day when he could n' fine sump'n fer his niggers ter do, en it ha' ter be a mighty little hole he could n' crawl thoo, en ha' ter be a monst'us cloudy night when a dollar git by him in de dahkness; en

*A small card, resembling a currycomb in construction, and used by negroes in the rural districts instead of a comb.

w'en he see how Henry git young in de spring en ole in de fall, he 'lowed ter hisse'f ez how he could make mo' money out'n Henry dan by wukkin' him in de cotton-fiel'. 'Long de nex' spring, atter de sap 'mence' ter rise, en Henry 'n'int 'is head en sta'ted fer ter git young en soopl, Mars Dugal' up 'n tuk Henry ter town, en sole 'im fer fifteen hunder' dollars. Co'se de man w'at bought Henry did n' know nuffin 'bout de goopher, en Mars Dugal' did n' see no 'casion fer ter tell 'im. Long to'ds de fall, w'en de sap went down, Henry begin ter git ole ag'in same ez yuzhal, en his noo marster begin ter git skeered les'n he gwine ter lose his fifteen-hunder'-dollar nigger. He sent fer a mighty fine doctor, but de med'cine did n' 'pear ter do no good; de goopher had a good holt. Henry tole de doctor 'bout de goopher, but de doctor des laff at 'im.

"One day in de winter Mars Dugal' went ter town, en wuz santerin' 'long de Main Street, when who should he meet but Henry's noo marster. Dey said 'Hoddy,' en Mars Dugal' ax 'im ter hab a seegyar; en atter dey run on awhile 'bout de craps en de weather, Mars Dugal' ax 'im, sorter keerless, like ez ef he des thought of it,—

" 'How you like de nigger I sole you las' spring?'

"Henry's marster shuck his head en knock de ashes off'n his seegyar.

" 'Spec' I made a bad bahgin when I bought dat nigger. Henry done good wuk all de summer, but sence de fall set in he 'pears ter be sorter pinin' away. Dey ain' nuffin pertickler de matter wid 'im—leastways de doctor say so—'cep'n' a tech er de rheumatiz; but his ha'r is all fell out, en ef he don't pick up his strenk mighty soon, I spec' I 'm gwine ter lose 'im.'

"Dey smoked on awhile, en bimeby ole mars say, 'Well, a bahgin 's a bahgin, but you en me is good fren's, en I doan wan' ter see you lose all de money you paid fer dat nigger; en ef w'at you say is so, en I ain't 'sputin' it, he ain't wuf much now. I 'spec's you wukked him too ha'd dis summer, er e'se de swamps down here don't agree wid de san'-hill nigger. So you des lemme know, en ef he gits any wusser I 'll be willin' ter gib yer five hund'ed dollars fer 'im, en take my chances on his livin'.'

"Sho 'nuff, when Henry begun ter draw up wid de

rheumatiz en it look like he gwine ter die fer sho, his noo marster sen' fer Mars Dugal', en Mars Dugal' gin him what he promus, en brung Henry home ag'in. He tuk good keer uv 'im dyoin' er de winter,—give 'im w'iskey ter rub his rheumatiz, en terbacker ter smoke, en all he want ter eat,—'caze a nigger w'at he could make a thousan' dollars a year off'n did n' grow on eve'y huckleberry bush.

"Nex' spring, w'en de sap ris en Henry's ha'r commence' ter sprout, Mars Dugal' sole 'im ag'in, down in Robeson County dis time; en he kep' dat sellin' business up fer five year er mo'. Henry nebber say nuffin 'bout de goopher ter his noo marsters, 'caze he know he gwine ter be tuk good keer uv de nex' winter, w'en Mars Dugal' buy him back. En Mars Dugal' made 'nuff money off'n Henry ter buy anudder plantation ober on Beaver Crick.

"But 'long 'bout de een' er dat five year dey come a stranger ter stop at de plantation. De fus' day he 'uz dere he went out wid Mars Dugal' en spent all de mawnin' lookin' ober de vimya'd, en atter dinner dey spent all de evenin' playin' kya'ds. De niggers soon 'skiver' dat he wuz a Yankee, en dat he come down ter Norf C'lina fer ter l'arn de w'ite folks how to raise grapes en make wine. He promus Mars Dugal' he c'd make de grapevimes b'ar twice't ez many grapes, en dat de noo winepress he wuz a-sellin' would make mo' d'n twice't ez many gallons er wine. En ole Mars Dugal' des drunk it all in, des 'peared ter be bewitch' wid dat Yankee. W'en de darkies see dat Yankee runnin' 'roun' de vimya'd en diggin' under de grapevimes, dey shuk dere heads, en 'lowed dat dey feared Mars Dugal' losin' his min'. Mars Dugal' had all de dirt dug away fum under de roots er all de scuppernon' vimes, an' let 'em stan' dat away fer a week er mo'. Den dat Yankee made de niggers fix up a mixtry er lime en ashes en manyo, en po' it 'roun' de roots er de grapevimes. Den he 'vise Mars Dugal' fer ter trim de vimes close't, en Mars Dugal' tuck 'n done eve'ything de Yankee tole him ter do. Dyoin' all er dis time, mind yer, dis yer Yankee wuz libbin' off'n de fat er de lan', at de big house, en playin' kya'ds wid Mars Dugal' eve'y night; en dey say Mars Dugal' los' mo'n a thousan' dollars dyoin' er de week dat Yankee wuz a-ruinin' de grapevimes.

"W'en de sap ris nex' spring, ole Henry 'n'inted his head ez yuzhal, en his ha'r 'mence' ter grow des de same ez it done eve'y year. De scuppernon' vimes growed monst's fas', en de leaves wuz greener en thicker dan dey eber be'n dyoin' my re-memb'ance; en Henry's ha'r growed out thicker dan eber, en he 'peared ter git younger 'n younger, en soopler 'n soopler; en seein' ez he wuz sho't er han's dat spring, havin' tuk in consid'able noo groun', Mars Dugal' 'cluded he would n' sell Henry 'tel he git de crap in en de cotton chop'. So he kep' Henry on de plantation.

"But 'long 'bout time fer de grapes ter come on de scup-pernon' vimes, dey 'peared ter come a change ober 'em; de leaves withered en swivel' up, en de young grapes turn' yaller, en bimeby eve'ybody on de plantation could see dat de whole vimya'd wuz dyin'. Mars Dugal' tuk 'n water de vimes en done all he could, but 't wa'n' no use: dat Yankee had done bus' de watermillyum. One time de vimes picked up a bit, en Mars Dugal' 'lowed dey wuz gwine ter come out ag'in; but dat Yankee done dug too close under de roots, en prune de branches too close ter de vime, en all dat lime en ashes done burn' de life out'n de vimes, en dey des kep' a-with'in' en a-swivelin'.

"All dis time de goopher wuz a-wukkin'. When de vimes sta'ted ter wither, Henry 'mence' ter complain er his rheuma-tiz; en when de leaves begin ter dry up, his ha'r 'mence' ter drap out. When de vimes fresh' up a bit, Henry 'd git peart ag'in, en when de vimes wither' ag'in, Henry 'd git ole ag'in, en des kep gittin' mo' en mo' fitten fer nuffin; he des pined away, en pined away, en fine'ly tuk ter his cabin; en when de big vime whar he got de sap ter 'n'int his head withered en turned yaller en died, Henry died too,—des went out sorter like a cannel. Dey did n't 'pear ter be nuffin de matter wid 'im, 'cep'n' de rheumatiz, but his strenk des dwinel' away 'tel he did n' hab ernuff lef' ter draw his bref. De goopher had got de under holt, en th'owed Henry dat time fer good en all.

"Mars Dugal' tuk on might'ly 'bout losin' his vimes en his nigger in de same year; en he swo' dat ef he could git holt er dat Yankee he 'd wear 'im ter a frazzle, en den chaw up de frazzle; en he 'd done it, too, for Mars Dugal' 'uz a monst'us brash man w'en he once git started. He sot de vimya'd out ober ag'in, but it wuz th'ee er fo' year befo' de vimes got ter b'arin' any scuppernon's.

"W'en de wah broke out, Mars Dugal' raise' a comp'ny, en went off ter fight de Yankees. He say he wuz mighty glad dat wah come, en he des want ter kill a Yankee fer eve'y dollar he los' 'long er dat grape-raisin' Yankee. En I 'spec' he would 'a' done it, too, ef de Yankees had n' s'picioned sump'n, en killed him fus'. Atter de s'render ole miss move' ter town, de niggers all scattered 'way fum de plantation, en de vimya'd ain' be'n cultervated sence."

"Is that story true?" asked Annie doubtfully, but seriously, as the old man concluded his narrative.

"It 's des ez true ez I 'm a-settin' here, miss. Dey 's a easy way ter prove it: I kin lead de way right ter Henry's grave ober yander in de plantation buryin'-groun'. En I tell yer w'at, marster, I would n' 'vise you to buy dis yer ole vimya'd, 'caze de goopher 's on it yit, en dey ain' no tellin' w'en it 's gwine ter crap out."

"But I thought you said all the old vines died."

"Dey did 'pear ter die, but a few un 'em come out ag'in, en is mixed in 'mongs' de yuthers. I ain' skeered ter eat de grapes, 'caze I knows de old vimes fum de noo ones; but wid strangers dey ain' no tellin' w'at mought happen. I would n' 'vise yer ter buy dis vimya'd."

I bought the vineyard, nevertheless, and it has been for a long time in a thriving condition, and is often referred to by the local press as a striking illustration of the opportunities open to Northern capital in the development of Southern industries. The luscious scuppernong holds first rank among our grapes, though we cultivate a great many other varieties, and our income from grapes packed and shipped to the Northern markets is quite considerable. I have not noticed any developments of the goopher in the vineyard, although I have a mild suspicion that our colored assistants do not suffer from want of grapes during the season.

I found, when I bought the vineyard, that Uncle Julius had occupied a cabin on the place for many years, and derived a respectable revenue from the product of the neglected grapevines. This, doubtless, accounted for his advice to me not to buy the vineyard, though whether it inspired the goopher story I am unable to state. I believe, however, that the wages I paid him for his services as coachman, for I gave him employment in that capacity, were more than an equivalent for anything he lost by the sale of the vineyard.

Po' Sandy

On the northeast corner of my vineyard in central North Carolina, and fronting on the Lumberton plank-road, there stood a small frame house, of the simplest construction. It was built of pine lumber, and contained but one room, to which one window gave light and one door admission. Its weather-beaten sides revealed a virgin innocence of paint. Against one end of the house, and occupying half its width, there stood a huge brick chimney: the crumbling mortar had left large cracks between the bricks; the bricks themselves had begun to scale off in large flakes, leaving the chimney sprinkled with unsightly blotches. These evidences of decay were but partially concealed by a creeping vine, which extended its slender branches hither and thither in an ambitious but futile attempt to cover the whole chimney. The wooden shutter, which had once protected the unglazed window, had fallen from its hinges, and lay rotting in the rank grass and jimson-weeds beneath. This building, I learned when I bought the place, had been used as a schoolhouse for several years prior to the breaking out of the war, since which time it had remained unoccupied, save when some stray cow or vagrant hog had sought shelter within its walls from the chill rains and nipping winds of winter.

One day my wife requested me to build her a new kitchen. The house erected by us, when we first came to live upon the vineyard, contained a very conveniently arranged kitchen; but for some occult reason my wife wanted a kitchen in the back yard, apart from the dwelling-house, after the usual Southern fashion. Of course I had to build it.

To save expense, I decided to tear down the old schoolhouse, and use the lumber, which was in a good state of preservation, in the construction of the new kitchen. Before demolishing the old house, however, I made an estimate of the amount of material contained in it, and found that I would have to buy several hundred feet of lumber additional, in order to build the new kitchen according to my wife's plan.

One morning old Julius McAdoo, our colored coachman,

harnessed the gray mare to the rockaway, and drove my wife and me over to the sawmill from which I meant to order the new lumber. We drove down the long lane which led from our house to the plank-road; following the plank-road for about a mile, we turned into a road running through the forest and across the swamp to the sawmill beyond. Our carriage jolted over the half-rotted corduroy road which traversed the swamp, and then climbed the long hill leading to the sawmill. When we reached the mill, the foreman had gone over to a neighboring farmhouse, probably to smoke or gossip, and we were compelled to await his return before we could transact our business. We remained seated in the carriage, a few rods from the mill, and watched the leisurely movements of the mill-hands. We had not waited long before a huge pine log was placed in position, the machinery of the mill was set in motion, and the circular saw began to eat its way through the log, with a loud whir which resounded throughout the vicinity of the mill. The sound rose and fell in a sort of rhythmic cadence, which, heard from where we sat, was not unpleasing, and not loud enough to prevent conversation. When the saw started on its second journey through the log, Julius observed, in a lugubrious tone, and with a perceptible shudder:—

"Ugh! but dat des do cuddle my blood!"

"What 's the matter, Uncle Julius?" inquired my wife, who is of a very sympathetic turn of mind. "Does the noise affect your nerves?"

"No, Mis' Annie," replied the old man, with emotion, "I ain' narvous; but dat saw, a-cuttin' en grindin' thoo dat stick er timber, en moanin', en groanin,' en sweekin', kyars my 'memb'ance back ter ole times, en 'min's me er po' Sandy." The pathetic intonation with which he lengthened out the "po' Sandy" touched a responsive chord in our own hearts.

"And who was poor Sandy?" asked my wife, who takes a deep interest in the stories of plantation life which she hears from the lips of the older colored people. Some of these stories are quaintly humorous; others wildly extravagant, revealing the Oriental cast of the negro's imagination; while others, poured freely into the sympathetic ear of a Northern-bred woman, disclose many a tragic incident of the darker side of slavery.

"Sandy," said Julius, in reply to my wife's question, "was a nigger w'at useter b'long ter ole Mars Marrabo McSwayne. Mars Marrabo's place wuz on de yuther side'n de swamp, right nex' ter yo' place. Sandy wuz a monst'us good nigger, en could do so many things erbout a plantation, en alluz 'ten' ter his wuk so well, dat w'en Mars Marrabo's chilluns growed up en married off, dey all un 'em wanted dey daddy fer ter gin 'em Sandy fer a weddin' present. But Mars Marrabo knowed de res' would n' be satisfied ef he gin Sandy ter a'er one un 'em; so w'en dey wuz all done married, he fix it by 'lowin' one er his chilluns ter take Sandy fer a mont' er so, en den ernudder for a mont' er so, en so on dat erway tel dey had all had 'im de same lenk er time; en den dey would all take him roun' ag'in, 'cep'n' oncet in a w'ile w'en Mars Marrabo would len' 'im ter some er his yuther kinfolks 'roun' de country, w'en dey wuz short er han's; tel bimeby it go so Sandy did n' hardly knowed whar he wuz gwine ter stay fum one week's een' ter de yuther.

"One time w'en Sandy wuz lent out ez yushal, a spekilater come erlong wid a lot er niggers, en Mars Marrabo swap' Sandy's wife off fer a noo 'oman. W'en Sandy come back, Mars Marrabo gin 'im a dollar, en 'lowed he wuz monst'us sorry fer ter break up de fambly, but de spekilater had gin 'im big boot, en times wuz hard en money skase, en so he wuz bleedst ter make de trade. Sandy tuk on some 'bout losin' his wife, but he soon seed dey want no use cryin' ober spilt merlasses; en bein' ez he lacked de looks er de noo 'oman, he tuk up wid her atter she 'd be'n on de plantation a mont' er so.

"Sandy en his noo wife got on mighty well tergedder, en de niggers all 'mence' ter talk about how lovin' dey wuz. W'en Tenie wuz tuk sick oncet, Sandy useter set up all night wid 'er, en den go ter wuk in de mawnin' des lack he had his reg'lar sleep; en Tenie would 'a' done anythin' in de worl' for her Sandy.

"Sandy en Tenie had n' be'n libbin' tergedder fer mo' d'n two mont's befo' Mars Marrabo's old uncle, w'at libbed down in Robeson County, sent up ter fin' out ef Mars Marrabo could n' len' 'im er hire 'im a good han' fer a mont' er so. Sandy's marster wuz one er dese yer easy-gwine folks w'at wanter please eve'ybody, en he says yas, he could len' 'im Sandy. En Mars Marrabo tol' Sandy fer ter git ready ter go down ter Robeson nex' day, fer ter stay a mont' er so.

"It wuz monst'us hard on Sandy fer ter take 'im 'way fum Tenie. It wuz so fur down ter Robeson dat he did n' hab no chance er comin' back ter see her tel de time wuz up; he would n' 'a' mine comin' ten er fifteen mile at night ter see Tenie, but Mars Marrabo's uncle's plantation wuz mo' d'n forty mile off. Sandy wuz mighty sad en cas' down atter w'at Mars Marrabo tol' 'im, en he says ter Tenie, sezee:—

" 'I 'm gittin' monst'us ti'ed er dish yer gwine roun' so much. Here I is lent ter Mars Jeems dis mont', en I got ter do so-en-so; en ter Mars Archie de nex' mont', en I got ter do so-en-so; den I got ter go ter Miss Jinnie's: en hit 's Sandy dis en Sandy dat, en Sandy yer en Sandy dere, tel it 'pears ter me I ain' got no home, ner no marster, ner no mis-tiss, ner no nuffin. I can't eben keep a wife: my yuther ole 'oman wuz sol' away widout my gittin' a chance fer ter tell her good-by; en now I got ter go off en leab you, Tenie, en I dunno whe'r I 'm eber gwine ter see you ag'in er no. I wisht I wuz a tree, er a stump, er a rock, er sump'n w'at could stay on de plantation fer a w'ile.'

"Atter Sandy got thoo talkin', Tenie did n' say naer word, but des sot dere by de fier, studyin' en studyin'. Bimeby she up'n' says:—

" 'Sandy, is I eber tol' you I wuz a cunjuh 'oman?'

"Co'se Sandy had n' nebber dremp' er nuffin lack dat, en he made a great 'miration w'en he hear w'at Tenie say. Bimeby Tenie went on:—

" 'I ain' goophered nobody, ner done no cunjuh wuk, fer fifteen year er mo'; en w'en I got religion I made up my mine I would n' wuk no mo' goopher. But dey is some things I doan b'lieve it 's no sin fer ter do; en ef you doan wanter be sent roun' fum pillar ter pos', en ef you doan wanter go down ter Robeson, I kin fix things so you won't haf ter. Ef you 'll des say de word, I kin turn you ter w'ateber you wanter be, en you kin stay right whar you wanter, ez long ez you mineter.'

"Sandy say he doan keer; he 's willin' fer ter do anythin' fer ter stay close ter Tenie. Den Tenie ax 'im ef he doan wanter be turnt inter a rabbit.

"Sandy say, 'No, de dogs mought git atter me.'

" 'Shill I turn you ter a wolf?' sez Tenie.

" 'No, eve'ybody 's skeered er a wolf, en I doan want nobody ter be skeered er me.'

" 'Shill I turn you ter a mawkin'bird?'

" 'No, a hawk mought ketch me. I wanter be turnt inter sump'n w'at 'll stay in one place.'

" 'I kin turn you ter a tree,' sez Tenie. 'You won't hab no mouf ner years, but I kin turn you back oncet in a w'ile, so you kin git sump'n ter eat, en hear w'at 's gwine on.'

"Well, Sandy say dat 'll do. En so Tenie tuk 'im down by de aidge er de swamp, not fur fum de quarters, en turnt 'im inter a big pine-tree, en sot 'im out 'mongs' some yuther trees. En de nex' mawnin', ez some er de fiel' han's wuz gwine long dere, dey seed a tree w'at dey did n' 'member er habbin' seed befo'; it wuz monst'us quare, en dey wuz bleedst ter 'low dat dey had n' 'membered right, er e'se one er de saplin's had be'n growin' monst'us fas'.

"W'en Mars Marrabo 'skiver' dat Sandy wuz gone, he 'lowed Sandy had runned away. He got de dogs out, but de las' place dey could track Sandy ter wuz de foot er dat pine-tree. En dere de dogs stood en barked, en bayed, en pawed at de tree, en tried ter climb up on it; en w'en dey wuz tuk roun' thoo de swamp ter look fer de scent, dey broke loose en made fer dat tree ag'in. It wuz de beatenis' thing de w'ite folks eber hearn of, en Mars Marrabo 'lowed dat Sandy must 'a' clim' up on de tree en jump' off on a mule er sump'n, en rid fur ernuff fer ter spile de scent. Mars Marrabo wanted ter 'cuse some er de yuther niggers er heppin' Sandy off, but dey all 'nied it ter de las'; en eve'ybody knowed Tenie sot too much sto' by Sandy fer ter he'p 'im run away whar she could n' nebber see 'im no mo'.

"W'en Sandy had be'n gone long ernuff fer folks ter think he done got clean away, Tenie useter go down ter de woods at night en turn 'im back, en den dey 'd slip up ter de cabin en set by de fire en talk. But dey ha' ter be monst'us keerful, er e'se somebody would 'a' seed 'em, en dat would 'a' spile' de whole thing; so Tenie alluz turnt Sandy back in de mawnin' early, befo' anybody wuz a-stirrin'.

"But Sandy did n' git erlong widout his trials en tribberlations. One day a woodpecker come erlong en 'mence' ter peck at de tree; en de nex' time Sandy wuz turnt back he had a little roun' hole in his arm, des lack a sharp stick be'n stuck in it. Atter dat Tenie sot a sparrer-hawk fer ter watch de tree; en w'en de woodpecker come erlong nex' mawnin' fer ter finish his nes', he got gobble' up mos' 'fo' he stuck his bill in de bark.

"Nudder time, Mars Marrabo sent a nigger out in de woods fer ter chop tuppentime boxes. De man chop a box in dish yer tree, en hack' de bark up two er th'ee feet, fer ter let de tuppentime run. De nex' time Sandy wuz turnt back he had a big skyar on his lef' leg, des lack it be'n skunt; en it tuk Tenie nigh 'bout all night fer ter fix a mixtry ter kyo it up. Atter dat, Tenie sot a hawnet fer ter watch de tree; en w'en de nigger come back ag'in fer ter cut ernudder box on de yuther side'n de tree, de hawnet stung 'im so hard dat de ax slip en cut his foot nigh 'bout off.

"W'en Tenie see so many things happenin' ter de tree, she 'cluded she 'd ha' ter turn Sandy ter sump'n e'se; en atter studyin' de matter ober, en talkin' wid Sandy one ebenin', she made up her mine fer ter fix up a goopher mixtry w'at would turn herse'f en Sandy ter foxes, er sump'n, so dey could run away en go some'rs whar dey could be free en lib lack w'ite folks.

"But dey ain' no tellin' w'at 's gwine ter happen in dis worl'. Tenie had got de night sot fer her en Sandy ter run away, w'en dat ve'y day one er Mars Marrabo's sons rid up ter de big house in his buggy, en say his wife wuz monst'us sick, en he want his mammy ter len' 'im a 'oman fer ter nuss his wife. Tenie's mistiss say sen' Tenie; she wuz a good nuss. Young mars wuz in a tarrible hurry fer ter git back home. Tenie wuz washin' at de big house dat day, en her mistiss say she should go right 'long wid her young marster. Tenie tried ter make some 'scuse fer ter git away en hide 'tel night, w'en she would have eve'ything fix' up fer her en Sandy; she say she wanter go ter her cabin fer ter git her bonnet. Her mistiss say it doan matter 'bout de bonnet; her head-hankcher wuz good ernuff. Den Tenie say she wanter git her bes' frock; her mistiss say no, she doan need no mo' frock, en w'en dat one got dirty she could git a clean one whar she wuz gwine. So Tenie had ter git in de buggy en go 'long wid young Mars Dunkin ter his plantation, w'ich wuz mo' d'n twenty mile away; en dey wa'n't no chance er her seein' Sandy no mo' 'tel she come back home. De po' gal felt monst'us bad 'bout de way things wuz gwine on, en she knowed Sandy mus' be a wond'rin' why she did n' come en turn 'im back no mo'.

"W'iles Tenie wuz away nussin' young Mars Dunkin's wife, Mars Marrabo tuk a notion fer ter buil' 'im a noo kitchen; en bein' ez he had lots er timber on his place, he begun ter look 'roun' fer a tree ter hab de lumber sawed out'n. En I dunno how it come to be so, but he happen fer ter hit on de ve'y tree w'at Sandy wuz turnt inter. Tenie wuz gone, en dey wa'n't nobody ner nuffin fer ter watch de tree.

"De two men w'at cut de tree down say dey nebber had sech a time wid a tree befo': dey axes would glansh off, en did n' 'pear ter make no progress thoo de wood; en of all de creakin', en shakin', en wobblin' you eber see, dat tree done it w'en it commence' ter fall. It wuz de beatenis' thing!

"W'en dey got de tree all trim' up, dey chain it up ter a timber waggin, en start fer de sawmill. But dey had a hard time gittin' de log dere: fus' dey got stuck in de mud w'en dey wuz gwine crosst de swamp, en it wuz two er th'ee hours befo' dey could git out. W'en dey start' on ag'in, de chain kep' a-comin' loose, en dey had ter keep a-stoppin' en a-stoppin' fer ter hitch de log up ag'in. W'en dey commence' ter climb de hill ter de sawmill, de log broke loose, en roll down de hill en in 'mongs' de trees, en hit tuk nigh 'bout half a day mo' ter git it haul' up ter de sawmill.

"De nex' mawnin' atter de day de tree wuz haul' ter de sawmill, Tenie come home. W'en she got back ter her cabin, de fus' thing she done wuz ter run down ter de woods en see how Sandy wuz gittin' on. W'en she seed de stump standin' dere, wid de sap runnin' out'n it, en de limbs layin' scattered roun', she nigh 'bout went out'n her min'. She run ter her cabin, en got her goopher mixtry, en den follered de track er de timber waggin ter de sawmill. She knowed Sandy could n' lib mo' d'n a minute er so ef she turnt him back, fer he wuz all chop' up so he 'd 'a' be'n bleedst ter die. But she wanted ter turn 'im back long ernuff fer ter 'splain ter 'im dat she had n' went off a-purpose, en lef' 'im ter be chop' down en sawed up. She did n' want Sandy ter die wid no hard feelin's to'ds her.

"De han's at de sawmill had des got de big log on de kerridge, en wuz startin' up de saw, w'en dey seed a 'oman runnin' up de hill, all out er bref, cryin' en gwine on des lack she wuz plumb 'stracted. It wuz Tenie; she come right inter de mill, en th'owed herse'f on de log, right in front er de saw, a-hollerin' en cryin' ter her Sandy ter fergib her, en not ter think hard er her, fer it wa'n't no fault er hern. Den Tenie 'membered de tree did n' hab no years, en she wuz gittin' ready fer ter wuk her goopher mixtry so ez ter turn Sandy back, w'en de mill-hands kotch holt er her en tied her arms wid a rope, en fasten' her to one er de posts in de sawmill; en den dey started de saw up ag'in, en cut de log up inter bo'ds en scantlin's right befo' her eyes. But it wuz mighty hard wuk; fer of all de sweekin', en moanin', en groanin', dat log done it w'iles de saw wuz a-cuttin' thoo it. De saw wuz one er dese yer ole-timey, up-en-down saws, en hit tuk longer dem days ter saw a log 'en it do now. Dey greased de saw, but dat did n' stop de fuss; hit kep' right on, tel fin'ly dey got de log all sawed up.

"W'en de oberseah w'at run de sawmill come fum breakfas', de han's up en tell him 'bout de crazy 'oman—ez dey s'posed she wuz—w'at had come runnin' in de sawmill, a-hollerin' en gwine on, en tried ter th'ow herse'f befo' de saw. En de oberseah sent two er th'ee er de han's fer ter take Tenie back ter her marster's plantation.

"Tenie 'peared ter be out'n her min' fer a long time, en her marster ha' ter lock her up in de smoke-'ouse 'tel she got ober her spells. Mars Marrabo wuz monst'us mad, en hit would 'a' made yo' flesh crawl fer ter hear him cuss, 'caze he say de spekilater w'at he got Tenie fum had fooled 'im by wukkin' a crazy 'oman off on him. W'iles Tenie wuz lock up in de smoke-'ouse, Mars Marrabo tuk 'n' haul de lumber fum de sawmill, en put up his noo kitchen.

"W'en Tenie got quiet' down, so she could be 'lowed ter go 'roun' de plantation, she up'n' tole her marster all erbout Sandy en de pine-tree; en w'en Mars Marrabo hearn it, he 'lowed she wuz de wuss 'stracted nigger he eber hearn of. He did n' know w'at ter do wid Tenie: fus' he thought he 'd put her in de po'-house; but fin'ly, seein' ez she did n' do no harm ter nobody ner nuffin, but des went 'roun' moanin', en groanin', en shakin' her head, he 'cluded ter let her stay on de plantation en nuss de little nigger chilluns w'en dey mammies wuz ter wuk in de cotton-fiel'.

"De noo kitchen Mars Marrabo buil' wuz n' much use, fer it had n' be'n put up long befo' de niggers 'mence' ter notice quare things erbout it. Dey could hear sump'n moanin' en groanin' 'bout de kitchen in de night-time, en w'en de win' would blow dey could hear sump'n a-hollerin' en sweekin' lack it wuz in great pain en sufferin'. En it got so atter a w'ile dat it wuz all Mars Marrabo's wife could do ter git a 'oman ter stay in de kitchen in de daytime long ernuff ter do de cookin'; en dey wa'n't naer nigger on de plantation w'at would n' rudder take forty dan ter go 'bout dat kitchen atter dark,—dat is, 'cep'n' Tenie; she did n' 'pear ter min' de ha'nts. She useter slip 'roun' at night, en set on de kitchen steps, en lean up agin de do'-jamb, en run on ter herse'f wid some kine er foolishness w'at nobody could n' make out; fer Mars Marrabo had th'eaten' ter sen' her off'n de plantation ef she say anything ter any er de yuther niggers 'bout de pine-tree. But somehow er 'nudder de niggers foun' out all erbout it, en dey all knowed de kitchen wuz ha'nted by Sandy's sperrit. En bimeby hit got so Mars Marrabo's wife herse'f wuz skeered ter go out in de yard atter dark.

"W'en it come ter dat, Mars Marrabo tuk en to' de kitchen down, en use' de lumber fer ter buil' dat ole school'ouse w'at you er talkin' 'bout pullin' down. De school'ouse wuz n' use' 'cep'n' in de daytime, en on dark nights folks gwine 'long de road would hear quare soun's en see quare things. Po' ole Tenie useter go down dere at night, en wander 'roun' de school'ouse; en de niggers all 'lowed she went fer ter talk wid Sandy's sperrit. En one winter mawnin', w'en one er de boys went ter school early fer ter start de fire, w'at should he fin' but po' ole Tenie, layin' on de flo', stiff, en col', en dead. Dere did n' 'pear ter be nuffin pertickler de matter wid her,—she had des grieve' herse'f ter def fer her Sandy. Mars Marrabo did n' shed no tears. He thought Tenie wuz crazy, en dey wa'n't no tellin' w'at she mought do nex'; en dey ain' much room in dis worl' fer crazy w'ite folks, let 'lone a crazy nigger.

"Hit wa'n't long atter dat befo' Mars Marrabo sol' a piece er his track er lan' ter Mars Dugal' McAdoo,—*my* ole marster,—en dat's how de ole school'ouse happen to be on yo' place. W'en de wah broke out, de school stop', en de ole school'ouse be'n stannin' empty ever sence,—dat is, 'cep'n' fer de ha'nts. En folks sez dat de ole school'ouse, er any yuther house w'at got any er dat lumber in it w'at wuz sawed out'n de tree w'at Sandy wuz turnt inter, is gwine ter be ha'nted tel de las' piece er plank is rotted en crumble' inter dus'."

Annie had listened to this gruesome narrative with strained attention.

"What a system it was," she exclaimed, when Julius had finished, "under which such things were possible!"

"What things?" I asked, in amazement. "Are you seriously considering the possibility of a man's being turned into a tree?"

"Oh, no," she replied quickly, "not that;" and then she murmured absently, and with a dim look in her fine eyes, "Poor Tenie!"

We ordered the lumber, and returned home. That night, after we had gone to bed, and my wife had to all appearances been sound asleep for half an hour, she startled me out of an incipient doze by exclaiming suddenly,—

"John, I don't believe I want my new kitchen built out of the lumber in that old schoolhouse."

"You would n't for a moment allow yourself," I replied, with some asperity, "to be influenced by that absurdly impossible yarn which Julius was spinning to-day?"

"I know the story is absurd," she replied dreamily, "and I am not so silly as to believe it. But I don't think I should ever be able to take any pleasure in that kitchen if it were built out of that lumber. Besides, I think the kitchen would look better and last longer if the lumber were all new."

Of course she had her way. I bought the new lumber, though not without grumbling. A week or two later I was called away from home on business. On my return, after an absence of several days, my wife remarked to me,—

"John, there has been a split in the Sandy Run Colored Baptist Church, on the temperance question. About half the members have come out from the main body, and set up for themselves. Uncle Julius is one of the seceders, and he came to me yesterday and asked if they might not hold their meetings in the old schoolhouse for the present."

"I hope you did n't let the old rascal have it," I returned, with some warmth. I had just received a bill for the new lumber I had bought.

"Well," she replied, "I could n't refuse him the use of the house for so good a purpose."

"And I 'll venture to say," I continued, "that you subscribed something toward the support of the new church?"

She did not attempt to deny it.

"What are they going to do about the ghost?" I asked, somewhat curious to know how Julius would get around this obstacle.

"Oh," replied Annie, "Uncle Julius says that ghosts never disturb religious worship, but that if Sandy's spirit *should* happen to stray into meeting by mistake, no doubt the preaching would do it good."

Mars Jeems's Nightmare

WE FOUND old Julius very useful when we moved to our new residence. He had a thorough knowledge of the neighborhood, was familiar with the roads and the water-courses, knew the qualities of the various soils and what they would produce, and where the best hunting and fishing were to be had. He was a marvelous hand in the management of horses and dogs, with whose mental processes he manifested a greater familiarity than mere use would seem to account for, though it was doubtless due to the simplicity of a life that had kept him close to nature. Toward my tract of land and the things that were on it—the creeks, the swamps, the hills, the meadows, the stones, the trees—he maintained a peculiar personal attitude, that might be called predial rather than proprietary. He had been accustomed, until long after middle life, to look upon himself as the property of another. When this relation was no longer possible, owing to the war, and to his master's death and the dispersion of the family, he had been unable to break off entirely the mental habits of a lifetime, but had attached himself to the old plantation, of which he seemed to consider himself an appurtenance. We found him useful in many ways and entertaining in others, and my wife and I took quite a fancy to him.

Shortly after we became established in our home on the sand-hills, Julius brought up to the house one day a colored boy of about seventeen, whom he introduced as his grandson, and for whom he solicited employment. I was not favorably impressed by the youth's appearance,—quite the contrary, in fact; but mainly to please the old man I hired Tom—his name was Tom—to help about the stables, weed the garden, cut wood and bring water, and in general to make himself useful about the outdoor work of the household.

My first impression of Tom proved to be correct. He turned out to be very trifling, and I was much annoyed by his laziness, his carelessness, and his apparent lack of any sense of responsibility. I kept him longer than I should, on Julius's account, hoping that he might improve; but he seemed to grow worse instead of better, and when I finally reached the limit of my patience, I discharged him.

"I am sorry, Julius," I said to the old man; "I should have liked to oblige you by keeping him; but I can't stand Tom any longer. He is absolutely untrustworthy."

"Yas, suh," replied Julius, with a deep sigh and a long shake of the head, "I knows he ain' much account, en dey ain' much 'pen'ence ter be put on 'im. But I wuz hopin' dat you mought make some 'lowance fuh a' ign'ant young nigger, suh, en gib 'im one mo' chance."

But I had hardened my heart. I had always been too easily imposed upon, and had suffered too much from this weakness. I determined to be firm as a rock in this instance.

"No, Julius," I rejoined decidedly, "it is impossible. I gave him more than a fair trial, and he simply won't do."

When my wife and I set out for our drive in the cool of the evening,—afternoon is "evening" in Southern parlance,—one of the servants put into the rockaway two large earthenware jugs. Our drive was to be down through the swamp to the mineral spring at the foot of the sand-hills beyond. The water of this spring was strongly impregnated with sulphur and iron, and, while not particularly agreeable of smell or taste, was used by us, in moderation, for sanitary reasons.

When we reached the spring, we found a man engaged in cleaning it out. In answer to an inquiry he said that if we would wait five or ten minutes, his task would be finished and the spring in such condition that we could fill our jugs. We might have driven on, and come back by way of the spring, but there was a bad stretch of road beyond, and we concluded to remain where we were until the spring should be ready. We were in a cool and shady place. It was often necessary to wait awhile in North Carolina; and our Northern energy had not been entirely proof against the influences of climate and local custom.

While we sat there, a man came suddenly around a turn of the road ahead of us. I recognized in him a neighbor with whom I had exchanged formal calls. He was driving a horse, apparently a high-spirited creature, possessing, so far as I could see at a glance, the marks of good temper and good breeding; the gentleman, I had heard it suggested, was slightly deficient in both. The horse was rearing and plunging, and the man was beating him furiously with a buggy-whip. When he saw us, he flushed a fiery red, and, as he passed, held the reins with one hand, at some risk to his safety, lifted his hat, and bowed somewhat constrainedly as the horse darted by us, still panting and snorting with fear.

"He looks as though he were ashamed of himself," I observed.

"I 'm sure he ought to be," exclaimed my wife indignantly. "I think there is no worse sin and no more disgraceful thing than cruelty."

"I quite agree with you," I assented.

"A man w'at 'buses his hoss is gwine ter be ha'd on de folks w'at wuks fer 'im," remarked Julius. "Ef young Mistah McLean doan min', he 'll hab a bad dream one er dese days, des lack 'is grandaddy had way back yander, long yeahs befo' de wah."

"What was it about Mr. McLean's dream, Julius?" I asked. The man had not yet finished cleaning the spring, and we might as well put in time listening to Julius as in any other way. We had found some of his plantation tales quite interesting.

"Mars Jeems McLean," said Julius, "wuz de grandaddy er dis yer gent'eman w'at is des gone by us beatin' his hoss. He had a big plantation en a heap er niggers. Mars Jeems wuz a ha'd man, en monst'us stric' wid his han's. Eber sence he growed up he nebber 'peared ter hab no feelin' fer nobody. W'en his daddy, ole Mars John McLean, died, de plantation en all de niggers fell ter young Mars Jeems. He had be'n bad 'nuff befo', but it wa'n't long atterwa'ds 'tel he got so dey wuz no use in libbin' at all ef you ha' ter lib roun' Mars Jeems. His niggers wuz bleedzd ter slabe fum daylight ter da'k, w'iles yuther folks's did n' hafter wuk 'cep'n' fum sun ter sun; en dey did n' git no mo' ter eat dan dey oughter, en dat de coa'ses' kin'. Dey wa'n't 'lowed ter sing, ner dance, ner play de banjo w'en Mars Jeems wuz roun' de place; fer Mars Jeems say he would n' hab no sech gwines-on,—said he bought his han's ter wuk, en not ter play, en w'en night come dey mus' sleep en res', so dey 'd be ready ter git up soon in de mawnin' en go ter dey wuk fresh en strong.

"Mars Jeems did n' 'low no co'tin' er juneseyin' roun' his plantation,—said he wanted his niggers ter put dey min's on dey wuk, en not be wastin' dey time wid no sech foolis'ness. En he would n' let his han's git married,—said he wuz n' raisin' niggers, but wuz raisin' cotton. En w'eneber any er de boys en gals 'ud 'mence ter git sweet on one ernudder, he 'd sell one er de yuther un 'em, er sen' 'em way down in Robeson County ter his yuther plantation, whar dey could n' nebber see one ernudder.

"Ef any er de niggers eber complained, dey got fo'ty; so co'se dey did n' many un 'em complain. But dey did n' lack it, des de same, en nobody could n' blame 'em, fer dey had a ha'd time. Mars Jeems did n' make no 'lowance fer nachul bawn laz'ness, ner sickness, ner trouble in de min', ner nuffin; he wuz des gwine ter git so much wuk outer eve'y han', er know de reason w'y.

"Dey wuz one time de niggers 'lowed, fer a spell, dat Mars Jeems mought git bettah. He tuk a lackin' ter Mars Marrabo McSwayne's oldes' gal, Miss Libbie, en useter go ober dere eve'y day er eve'y ebenin', en folks said dey wuz gwine ter git married sho'. But it 'pears dat Miss Libbie heared 'bout de gwines-on on Mars Jeems's plantation, en she des 'lowed she could n' trus' herse'f wid no sech a man; dat he mought git so useter 'busin' his niggers dat he 'd 'mence ter 'buse his wife atter he got useter habbin' her roun' de house. So she 'clared she wuz n' gwine ter hab nuffin mo' ter do wid young Mars Jeems.

"De niggers wuz all monst'us sorry w'en de match wuz bust' up, fer now Mars Jeems got wusser'n he wuz befo' he sta'ted sweethea'tin'. De time he useter spen' co'tin' Miss Libbie he put in findin' fault wid de niggers, en all his bad feelin's 'ca'se Miss Libbie th'owed 'im ober he 'peared ter try ter wuk off on de po' niggers.

"W'iles Mars Jeems wuz co'tin' Miss Libbie, two er de han's on de plantation had got ter settin' a heap er sto' by one ernudder. One un 'em wuz name' Solomon, en de yuther wuz a 'oman w'at wukked in de fiel' 'long er 'im—I fe'git dat 'oman's name, but it doan 'mount ter much in de tale nohow. Now, whuther 'ca'se Mars Jeems wuz so tuk up wid his own junesey dat he did n' paid no 'tention fer a w'ile ter w'at wuz gwine on 'twix' Solomon en his junesey, er whuther his own co'tin' made 'im kin' er easy on de co'tin' in de qua'ters, dey ain' no tellin'. But dey 's one thing sho', dat w'en Miss Libbie th'owed 'im ober, he foun' out 'bout Solomon en de gal monst'us quick, en gun Solomon fo'ty, en sont de gal down ter de Robeson County plantation, en tol' all de niggers ef he ketch 'em at any mo' sech foolishness, he wuz gwine ter skin 'em alibe en tan dey hides befo' dey ve'y eyes. Co'se he would n' 'a' done it, but he mought 'a' made things wusser 'n dey wuz. So you kin 'magine dey wa'n't much lub-makin' in de qua'ters fer a long time.

"Mars Jeems useter go down ter de yuther plantation sometimes fer a week er mo', en so he had ter hab a oberseah ter look atter his wuk w'iles he 'uz gone. Mars Jeems's oberseah wuz a po' w'ite man name' Nick Johnson,—de niggers called 'im Mars Johnson ter his face, but behin' his back dey useter call 'im Ole Nick, en de name suited 'im ter a T. He wuz wusser 'n Mars Jeems ever da'ed ter be. Co'se de darkies did n' lack de way Mars Jeems used 'em, but he wuz de marster, en had a right ter do ez he please'; but dis yer Ole Nick wa'n't nuffin but a po' buckrah, en all de niggers 'spised 'im ez much ez dey hated 'im, fer he did n' own nobody, en wa'n't no bettah 'n a nigger, fer in dem days any 'spectable pusson would ruther be a nigger dan a po' w'ite man.

"Now, atter Solomon's gal had be'n sont away, he kep' feelin' mo' en mo' bad erbout it, 'tel fin'lly he 'lowed he wuz gwine ter see ef dey could n' be sump'n done fer ter git 'er back, en ter make Mars Jeems treat de darkies bettah. So he tuk a peck er co'n out'n de ba'n one night, en went ober ter see ole Aun' Peggy, de free-nigger cunjuh 'oman down by de Wim'l'ton Road.

"Aun' Peggy listen' ter 'is tale, en ax' him some queshtuns, en den tol' 'im she 'd wuk her roots, en see w'at dey 'd say 'bout it, en ter-morrer night he sh'd come back ag'in en fetch ernudder peck er co'n, en den she 'd hab sump'n fer ter tell 'im.

"So Solomon went back de nex' night, en sho' 'nuff, Aun' Peggy tol' 'im w'at ter do. She gun 'im some stuff w'at look' lack it be'n made by poundin' up some roots en yarbs wid a pestle in a mo'tar.

" 'Dis yer stuff,' sez she, 'is monst'us pow'ful kin' er goopher. You take dis home, en gin it ter de cook, ef you kin trus' her, en tell her fer ter put it in yo' marster's soup de fus' cloudy day he hab okra soup fer dinnah. Min' you follers de d'rections.'

" 'It ain' gwineter p'isen 'im, is it?' ax' Solomon, gittin' kin' er skeered; fer Solomon wuz a good man, en did n' want ter do nobody no rale ha'm.

" 'Oh, no,' sez ole Aun' Peggy, 'it's gwine ter do 'im good, but he 'll hab a monst'us bad dream fus'. A mont' fum now you come down heah en lemme know how de goopher is wukkin'. Fer I ain' done much er dis kin' er cunj'in' er late yeahs, en I has ter kinder keep track un it ter see dat it doan 'complish no mo' d'n I 'lows fer it ter do. En I has ter be kinder keerful 'bout cunj'in' w'ite folks; so be sho' en lemme know, w'ateber you do, des w'at is gwine on roun' de plantation.'

"So Solomon say all right, en tuk de goopher mixtry up ter de big house en gun it ter de cook, en tol' her fer ter put it in Mars Jeems's soup de fus' cloudy day she hab okra soup fer dinnah. It happen' dat de ve'y nex' day wuz a cloudy day, en so de cook made okra soup fer Mars Jeems's dinnah, en put de powder Solomon gun her inter de soup, en made de soup rale good, so Mars Jeems eat a whole lot of it en 'peared ter enjoy it.

"De nex' mawnin' Mars Jeems tol' de oberseah he wuz gwine 'way on some bizness, en den he wuz gwine ter his yuther plantation, down in Robeson County, en he did n' 'spec' he 'd be back fer a mont' er so.

" 'But,' sezee, 'I wants you ter run dis yer plantation fer all it's wuth. Dese yer niggers is gittin' monst'us triflin' en lazy en keerless, en dey ain' no 'pen'ence ter be put in 'em. I wants dat stop', en w'iles I'm gone erway I wants de 'spenses cut 'way down en a heap mo' wuk done. Fac', I wants dis yer plantation ter make a reco'd dat 'll show w'at kinder oberseah you is.'

"Ole Nick did n' said nuffin but 'Yas, suh,' but de way he kinder grin' ter hisse'f en show' his big yaller teef, en snap' de rawhide he useter kyar roun' wid 'im, made col' chills run up and down de backbone er dem niggers w'at heared Mars

Jeems a-talkin'. En dat night dey wuz mo'nin' en groanin' down in de qua'ters, fer de niggers all knowed w'at wuz comin'.

"So, sho' 'nuff, Mars Jeems went erway nex' mawnin', en de trouble begun. Mars Johnson sta'ted off de ve'y fus' day fer ter see w'at he could hab ter show Mars Jeems w'en he come back. He made de tasks bigger en de rashuns littler, en w'en de niggers had wukked all day, he 'd fin' sump'n fer 'em ter do roun' de ba'n er som'ers atter da'k, fer ter keep 'em busy a' hour er so befo' dey went ter sleep.

"About th'ee er fo' days atter Mars Jeems went erway, young Mars Dunkin McSwayne rode up ter de big house one day wid a nigger settin' behin' 'im in de buggy, tied ter de seat, en ax' ef Mars Jeems wuz home. Mars Johnson wuz at de house, and he say no.

" 'Well,' sez Mars Dunkin, sezee, 'I fotch dis nigger ober ter Mistah McLean fer ter pay a bet I made wid 'im las' week w'en we wuz playin' kya'ds te'gedder. I bet 'im a nigger man, en heah's one I reckon 'll fill de bill. He wuz tuk up de yuther day fer a stray nigger, en he could n' gib no 'count er hisse'f, en so he wuz sol' at oction, en I bought 'im. He's kinder brash, but I knows yo' powers, Mistah Johnson, en I reckon ef anybody kin make 'im toe de ma'k, you is de man.'

"Mars Johnson grin' one er dem grins w'at show' all his snaggle teef, en make de niggers 'low he look lack de ole debbil, en sezee ter Mars Dunkin:—

" 'I reckon you kin trus' me, Mistah Dunkin, fer ter tame any nigger wuz eber bawn. De nigger doan lib w'at I can't take down in 'bout fo' days.'

"Well, Ole Nick had 'is han's full long er dat noo nigger; en w'iles de res' er de darkies wuz sorry fer de po' man, dey 'lowed he kep' Mars Johnson so busy dat dey got along better 'n dey 'd 'a' done ef de noo nigger had nebber come.

"De fus' thing dat happen', Mars Johnson sez ter dis yer noo man:—

" 'W'at 's yo' name, Sambo?'

" 'My name ain' Sambo,' 'spon' de noo nigger.

" 'Did I ax you w'at yo' name wa'n't?' sez Mars Johnson. 'You wants ter be pa'tic'lar how you talks ter me. Now, w'at is yo' name, en whar did you come fum?'

" 'I dunno my name,' sez de nigger, 'en I doan 'member whar I come fum. My head is all kin' er mix' up.'

" 'Yas,' sez Mars Johnson, 'I reckon I 'll ha' ter gib you sump'n fer ter cl'ar yo' head. At de same time, it 'll l'arn you some manners, en atter dis mebbe you 'll say "suh" w'en you speaks ter me.'

"Well, Mars Johnson haul' off wid his rawhide en hit de noo nigger once. De noo man look' at Mars Johnson fer a minute ez ef he did n' know w'at ter make er dis yer kin' er l'arnin'. But w'en de oberseah raise' his w'ip ter hit him ag'in, de noo nigger des haul' off en made fer Mars Johnson, en ef some er de yuther niggers had n' stop' 'im, it 'peared ez ef he mought 'a' made it wa'm fer Ole Nick dere fer a w'ile. But de oberseah made de yuther niggers he'p tie de noo nigger up, en den gun 'im fo'ty, wid a dozen er so th'owed in fer good measure, fer Ole Nick wuz nebber stingy wid dem kin' er rashuns. De nigger went on at a tarrable rate, des lack a wil' man, but co'se he wuz bleedzd ter take his med'cine, fer he wuz tied up en could n' he'p hisse'f.

"Mars Johnson lock' de noo nigger up in de ba'n, en did n' gib 'im nuffin ter eat fer a day er so, 'tel he got 'im kin'er quiet' down, en den he tu'nt 'im loose en put 'im ter wuk. De nigger 'lowed he wa'n't useter wukkin', en would n' wuk, en Mars Johnson gun 'im anudder fo'ty fer laziness en impidence, en let 'im fas' a day er so mo', en den put 'im ter wuk ag'in. De nigger went ter wuk, but did n' 'pear ter know how ter han'le a hoe. It tuk des 'bout half de oberseah's time lookin' atter 'im, en dat po' nigger got mo' lashin's en cussin's en cuffin's dan any fo' yuthers on de plantation. He did n' mix' wid ner talk much ter de res' er de niggers, en could n' 'pear ter git it th'oo his min' dat he wuz a slabe en had ter wuk en min' de w'ite folks, spite er de fac' dat Ole Nick gun 'im a lesson eve'y day. En fin'lly Mars Johnson 'lowed dat he could n' do nuffin wid 'im; dat ef he wuz his nigger, he 'd break his sperrit er break 'is neck, one er de yuther. But co'se he wuz only sont ober on trial, en ez he did n' gib sat'sfaction, en he had n' heared fum Mars Jeems 'bout w'en he wuz comin' back; en ez he wuz feared he 'd git mad some time er 'nuther en kill de nigger befo' he knowed it, he 'lowed he 'd better sen' 'im back whar he come fum. So he tied 'im up en sont 'im back ter Mars Dunkin.

"Now, Mars Dunkin McSwayne wuz one er dese yer easy-gwine gent'emen w'at did n' lack ter hab no trouble wid niggers er nobody e'se, en he knowed ef Mars Ole Nick could n' git 'long wid dis nigger, nobody could. So he tuk de nigger ter town dat same day, en sol' 'im ter a trader w'at wuz gittin' up a gang er lackly niggers fer ter ship off on de steamboat ter go down de ribber ter Wim'l'ton en fum dere ter Noo Orleens.

"De nex' day atter de noo man had be'n sont away, Solomon wuz wukkin' in de cotton-fiel', en w'en he got ter de fence nex' ter de woods, at de een' er de row, who sh'd he see on de yuther side but ole Aun' Peggy. She beckon' ter 'im,—de oberseah wuz down on de yuther side er de fiel',—en sez she:—

" 'W'y ain' you done come en 'po'ted ter me lack I tol' you?'

" 'W'y, law! Aun' Peggy,' sez Solomon, 'dey ain' nuffin ter 'po't. Mars Jeems went away de day atter we gun 'im de goopher mixtry, en we ain' seed hide ner hair un 'im sence, en co'se we doan know nuffin 'bout w'at 'fec' it had on 'im.'

" 'I doan keer nuffin 'bout yo' Mars Jeems now; w'at I wants ter know is w'at is be'n gwine on 'mongs' de niggers. Has you be'n gittin' 'long any better on de plantation?'

" 'No, Aun' Peggy, we be'n gittin' 'long wusser. Mars Johnson is stric'er 'n he eber wuz befo', en de po' niggers doan ha'dly git time ter draw dey bref, en dey 'lows dey mought des ez well be dead ez alibe.'

" 'Uh huh!' sez Aun' Peggy, sez she, 'I tol' you dat 'uz monst'us pow'ful goopher, en its wuk doan 'pear all at once.'

" 'Long ez we had dat noo nigger heah,' Solomon went on, 'he kep' Mars Johnson busy pa't er de time; but now he 's gone erway, I s'pose de res' un us 'll ketch it wusser 'n eber.'

" 'W'at 's gone wid de noo nigger?' sez Aun' Peggy, rale quick, battin' her eyes en straight'nin' up.

" 'Ole Nick done sont 'im back ter Mars Dunkin, who had fotch 'im heah fer ter pay a gamblin' debt ter Mars Jeems,' sez Solomon, 'en I heahs Mars Dunkin has sol' 'im ter a nigger-trader up in Patesville, w'at 's gwine ter ship 'im off wid a gang ter-morrer.'

"Ole Aun' Peggy 'peared ter git rale stirred up w'en Solomon tol' 'er dat, en sez she, shakin' her stick at 'im:—

" 'W'y did n' you come en tell me 'bout dis noo nigger bein' sol' erway? Did n' you promus me, ef I 'd gib you dat goopher, you 'd come en 'po't ter me 'bout all w'at wuz gwine on on dis plantation? Co'se I could 'a' foun' out fer myse'f, but I 'pended on yo' tellin' me, en now by not doin' it I 's feared you gwine spile my cunj'in'. You come down ter my house ter-night en do w'at I tells you, er I 'll put a spell on you dat 'll make yo' ha'r fall out so you 'll be bal', en yo' eyes drap out so you can't see, en yo teef fall out so you can't eat, en yo' years grow up so you can't heah. W'en you is foolin' wid a cunjuh 'oman lack me, you got ter min' yo' P's en Q's er dey 'll be trouble sho' 'nuff.'

"So co'se Solomon went down ter Aun' Peggy's dat night, en she gun 'im a roasted sweet'n' 'tater.

" 'You take dis yer sweet'n' 'tater,' sez she,—'I done goophered it 'speshly fer dat noo nigger, so you better not eat it yo'se'f er you 'll wush you had n',—en slip off ter town, en fin' dat strange man, en gib 'im dis yer sweet'n' 'tater. He mus' eat it befo' mawnin', sho', ef he doan wanter be sol' erway ter Noo Orleens.'

" 'But s'posen de patteroles ketch me, Aun' Peggy, w'at I gwine ter do?' sez Solomon.

" 'De patteroles ain' gwine tech you, but ef you doan fin' dat nigger, *I'm* gwine git you, en you 'll fin' me wusser 'n de patteroles. Des hol' on a minute, en I 'll sprinkle you wid some er dis mixtry out'n dis yer bottle, so de patteroles can't see you, en you kin rub yo' feet wid some er dis yer grease out'n dis go'd, so you kin run fas', en rub some un it on yo' eyes so you kin see in de da'k; en den you mus' fin' dat noo nigger en gib 'im dis yer 'tater, er you gwine ter hab mo' trouble on yo' han's 'n you eber had befo' in yo' life er eber will hab sence.'

"So Solomon tuk de sweet'n' 'tater en sta'ted up de road fas' ez he could go, en befo' long he retch' town. He went right 'long by de patteroles, en dey did n' 'pear ter notice 'im, en bimeby he foun' whar de strange nigger was kep', en he walked right pas' de gyard at de do' en foun' 'im. De nigger could n' see 'im, ob co'se, en he could n' 'a' seed de nigger in de da'k, ef it had n' be'n fer de stuff Aun' Peggy gun 'im ter rub on 'is eyes. De nigger wuz layin' in a co'nder, 'sleep, en Solomon des slip' up ter 'im, en hilt dat sweet'n' 'tater 'fo' de nigger's nose, en he des nach'ly retch' up wid his han', en tuk de 'tater en eat it in his sleep, widout knowin' it. W'en Solomon seed he 'd done eat de 'tater, he went back en tol' Aun' Peggy, en den went home ter his cabin ter sleep, 'way 'long 'bout two o'clock in de mawnin'.

"De nex' day wuz Sunday, en so de niggers had a little time ter deyse'ves. Solomon wuz kinder 'sturb' in his min' thinkin' 'bout his junesey w'at 'uz gone away, en wond'rin' w'at Aun' Peggy had ter do wid dat noo nigger; en he had sa'ntered up in de woods so 's ter be by hisse'f a little, en at de same time ter look atter a rabbit-trap he 'd sot down in de aidge er de swamp, w'en who sh'd he see stan'in' unner a tree but a w'ite man.

"Solomon did n' knowed de w'ite man at fus', 'tel de w'ite man spoke up ter 'im.

" 'Is dat you, Solomon?' sezee.

"Den Solomon reco'nized de voice.

" 'Fer de Lawd's sake, Mars Jeems! is dat you?'

" 'Yas, Solomon,' sez his marster, 'dis is me, er w'at 's lef' er me.'

"It wa'n't no wonder Solomon had n' knowed Mars Jeems at fus', fer he wuz dress' lack a po' w'ite man, en wuz bare-footed, en look' monst'us pale en peaked, ez ef he 'd des come th'oo a ha'd spell er sickness.

" 'You er lookin' kinder po'ly, Mars Jeems,' sez Solomon. 'Is you be'n sick, suh?'

" 'No, Solomon,' sez Mars Jeems, shakin' his head, en speakin' sorter slow en sad, 'I ain' be'n sick, but I 's had a monst'us bad dream,—fac', a reg'lar, nach'ul nightmare. But tell me how things has be'n gwine on up ter de plantation sence I be'n gone, Solomon.'

"So Solomon up en tol' 'im 'bout de craps, en 'bout de hosses en de mules, en 'bout de cows en de hawgs. En w'en he 'mence' ter tell 'bout de noo nigger, Mars Jeems prick' up 'is yeahs en listen', en eve'y now en den he 'd say, 'Uh huh! uh huh!' en nod 'is head. En bimeby, w'en he 'd ax' Solomon some mo' queshtuns, he sez, sezee:—

" 'Now, Solomon, I doan want you ter say a wo'd ter nobody 'bout meetin' me heah, but I wants you ter slip up ter de house, en fetch me some clo's en some shoes,—I fergot ter tell you dat a man rob' me back yander on de road en swap' clo's wid me widout axin' me whuther er no,—but you neenter say nuffin 'bout dat, nuther. You go en fetch me some clo's heah, so nobody won't see you, en keep yo' mouf shet, en I 'll gib you a dollah.'

"Solomon wuz so 'stonish' he lack ter fell ober in his tracks, w'en Mars Jeems promus' ter gib 'im a dollah. Dey su't'nly wuz a change come ober Mars Jeems, w'en he offer' one er his niggers dat much money. Solomon 'mence' ter 'spec' dat Aun' Peggy's cunj'ation had be'n wukkin' monst'us strong.

"Solomon fotch Mars Jeems some clo's en shoes, en dat same eb'nin' Mars Jeems 'peared at de house, en let on lack he des dat minute got home fum Robeson County. Mars Johnson was all ready ter talk ter 'im, but Mars Jeems sont 'im wo'd he wa'n't feelin' ve'y well dat night, en he 'd see 'im ter-morrer.

"So nex' mawnin' atter breakfus' Mars Jeems sont fer de oberseah, en ax' 'im fer ter gib 'count er his styoa'dship. Ole Nick tol' Mars Jeems how much wuk be'n done, en got de books en showed 'im how much money be'n save'. Den Mars Jeems ax' 'im how de darkies be'n behabin', en Mars Johnson say dey be'n behabin' good, most un 'em, en dem w'at did n' behabe good at fus' change dey conduc' atter he got holt un 'em a time er two.

" 'All,' sezee, ' 'cep'n' de noo nigger Mistah Dunkin fotch ober heah en lef' on trial, w'iles you wuz gone.'

" 'Oh, yas,' 'lows Mars Jeems, 'tell me all 'bout dat noo nigger. I heared a little 'bout dat quare noo nigger las' night, en it wuz des too redik'lus. Tell me all 'bout dat noo nigger.'

"So seein' Mars Jeems so good-nachu'd 'bout it, Mars Johnson up en tol' 'im how he tied up de noo han' de fus' day en gun 'im fo'ty 'ca'se he would n' tell 'im 'is name.

" 'Ha, ha, ha!' sez Mars Jeems, laffin' fit ter kill, 'but dat is too funny fer any use. Tell me some mo' 'bout dat noo nigger.'

"So Mars Johnson went on en tol' 'im how he had ter starbe de noo nigger 'fo' he could make 'im take holt er a hoe.

" 'Dat wuz de beatinis' notion fer a nigger,' sez Mars Jeems, 'puttin' on airs, des lack he wuz a w'ite man! En I reckon you did n' do nuffin ter 'im?'

" 'Oh, no, suh,' sez de oberseah, grinnin' lack a chessy-cat, 'I did n' do nuffin but take de hide off'n 'im.'

"Mars Jeems lafft en lafft, 'tel it 'peared lack he wuz des gwine ter bu'st. '*Tell* me some mo' 'bout dat noo nigger, oh, *tell* me some mo'. Dat noo nigger int'rusts me, he do, en dat is a fac'.'

"Mars Johnson did n' quite un'erstan' w'y Mars Jeems sh'd make sich a great 'miration 'bout de noo nigger, but co'se he want' ter please de gent'eman w'at hi'ed 'im, en so he 'splain' all 'bout how many times he had ter cowhide de noo nigger, en how he made 'im do tasks twicet ez big ez some er de yuther han's, en how he'd chain 'im up in de ba'n at night en feed 'im on co'n-bread en water.

" 'Oh! but you is a monst'us good oberseah; you is de bes' oberseah in dis county, Mistah Johnson,' sez Mars Jeems, w'en de oberseah got th'oo wid his tale; 'en dey ain' nebber be'n no nigger-breaker lack you roun' heah befo'. En you desarbes great credit fer sendin' dat nigger 'way befo' you sp'ilt 'im fer de market. Fac', you is sech a monst'us good oberseah, en you is got dis yer plantation in sech fine shape, dat I reckon I doan need you no mo'. You is got dese yer darkies so well train' dat I 'spec' I kin run 'em myse'f fum dis time on. But I does wush you had 'a' hilt on ter dat noo nigger 'tel I got home, fer I 'd 'a' lack ter 'a' seed 'im, I su't'nly should.'

"De oberseah wuz so 'stonish' he did n' ha'dly know w'at ter say, but fin'lly he ax' Mars Jeems ef he would n' gib 'im a riccommen' fer ter git ernudder place.

" 'No, suh,' sez Mars Jeems, 'somehow er 'nuther I doan lack yo' looks sence I come back dis time, en I'd much ruther you would n' stay roun' heah. Fac', I 's feared ef I 'd meet you alone in de woods some time, I mought wanter ha'm you. But layin' dat aside, I be'n lookin' ober dese yer books er yo'n w'at you kep' w'iles I wuz 'way, en fer a yeah er so back, en dere 's some figgers w'at ain' des cl'ar ter me. I ain' got no time fer ter talk 'bout 'em now, but I 'spec' befo' I settles wid you fer dis las' mont', you better come up heah ter-morrer, atter I 's look' de books en 'counts ober some mo', en den we 'll straighten ou' business all up.'

"Mars Jeems 'lowed atterwa'ds dat he wuz des shootin' in de da'k w'en he said dat 'bout de books, but howsomeber, Mars Nick Johnson lef' dat naberhood 'twix' de nex' two suns, en nobody roun' dere nebber seed hide ner hair un 'im sence. En all de darkies t'ank de Lawd, en 'lowed it wuz a good riddance er bad rubbage.

"But all dem things I done tol' you ain' nuffin 'side'n de change w'at come ober Mars Jeems fum dat time on. Aun' Peggy's goopher had made a noo man un 'im enti'ely. De nex' day atter he come back, he tol' de han's dey neenter wuk on'y fum sun ter sun, en he cut dey tasks down so dey did n' nobody hab ter stan' ober 'em wid a rawhide er a hick'ry. En he 'lowed ef de niggers want ter hab a dance in de big ba'n any Sad'day night, dey mought hab it. En bimeby, w'en Solomon seed how good Mars Jeems wuz, he ax' 'im ef he would n' please sen' down ter de yuther plantation fer his junesey. Mars Jeems say su't'nly, en gun Solomon a pass en a note ter de oberseah on de yuther plantation, en sont Solomon down ter Robeson County wid a hoss en buggy fer ter fetch his junesey back. W'en de niggers see how fine Mars Jeems gwine treat 'em, dey all tuk ter sweethea'tin' en juneseyin' en singin' en dancin', en eight er ten couples got married, en bimeby eve'ybody 'mence' ter say Mars Jeems McLean got a finer plantation, en slicker-lookin' niggers, en dat he 'uz makin' mo' cotton en co'n, dan any yuther gent'eman in de county. En Mars Jeems's own junesey, Miss Libbie, heared 'bout de noo gwines-on on Mars Jeems's plantation, en she change' her min' 'bout Mars Jeems en tuk 'im back ag'in, en 'fo' long dey had a fine weddin', en all de darkies had a big feas', en dey wuz fiddlin' en dancin' en funnin' en frolic'in' fum sundown 'tel mawnin'."

"And they all lived happy ever after," I said, as the old man reached a full stop.

"Yas, suh," he said, interpreting my remarks as a question, "dey did. Solomon useter say," he added, "dat Aun' Peggy's goopher had turnt Mars Jeems ter a nigger, en dat dat noo han' wuz Mars Jeems hisse'f. But co'se Solomon did n' das' ter let on 'bout w'at he 'spicioned, en ole Aun' Peggy would 'a' 'nied ef she had be'n ax', fer she 'd 'a' got in trouble sho', ef it 'uz knowed she 'd be'n cunj'in' de w'ite folks.

"Dis yer tale goes ter show," concluded Julius sententiously, as the man came up and announced that the spring was ready for us to get water, "dat w'ite folks w'at is so ha'd en stric', en doan make no 'lowance fer po' ign'ant niggers w'at ain' had no chanst ter l'arn, is li'ble ter hab bad dreams, ter say de leas', en dat dem w'at is kin' en good ter po' people is sho' ter prosper en git 'long in de worl'."

"That is a very strange story, Uncle Julius," observed my wife, smiling, "and Solomon's explanation is quite improbable."

"Yes, Julius," said I, "that was powerful goopher. I am glad, too, that you told us the moral of the story; it might have escaped us otherwise. By the way, did you make that up all by yourself?"

The old man's face assumed an injured look, expressive more of sorrow than of anger, and shaking his head he replied:—

"No, suh, I heared dat tale befo' you er Mis' Annie dere wuz bawn, suh. My mammy tol' me dat tale w'en I wa'n't mo' d'n knee-high ter a hopper-grass."

I drove to town next morning, on some business, and did not return until noon; and after dinner I had to visit a neighbor, and did not get back until supper-time. I was smoking a cigar on the back piazza in the early evening, when I saw a familiar figure carrying a bucket of water to the barn. I called my wife.

"My dear," I said severely, "what is that rascal doing here? I thought I discharged him yesterday for good and all."

"Oh, yes," she answered, "I forgot to tell you. He was hanging round the place all the morning, and looking so down in the mouth, that I told him that if he would try to do better, we would give him one more chance. He seems so grateful, and so really in earnest in his promises of amendment, that I 'm sure you 'll not regret taking him back."

I was seriously enough annoyed to let my cigar go out. I did not share my wife's rose-colored hopes in regard to Tom; but as I did not wish the servants to think there was any conflict of authority in the household, I let the boy stay.

The Conjurer's Revenge

SUNDAY was sometimes a rather dull day at our place. In the morning, when the weather was pleasant, my wife and I would drive to town, a distance of about five miles, to attend the church of our choice. The afternoons we spent at home, for the most part, occupying ourselves with the newspapers and magazines, and the contents of a fairly good library. We had a piano in the house, on which my wife played with skill and feeling. I possessed a passable baritone voice, and could accompany myself indifferently well when my wife was not by to assist me. When these resources failed us, we were apt to find it a little dull.

One Sunday afternoon in early spring,—the balmy spring of North Carolina, when the air is in that ideal balance between heat and cold where one wishes it could always remain,—my wife and I were seated on the front piazza, she wearily but conscientiously ploughing through a missionary report, while I followed the impossible career of the blonde heroine of a rudimentary novel. I had thrown the book aside in disgust, when I saw Julius coming through the yard, under the spreading elms, which were already in full leaf. He wore his Sunday clothes, and advanced with a dignity of movement quite different from his week-day slouch.

"Have a seat, Julius," I said, pointing to an empty rocking-chair.

"No, thanky, boss, I 'll des set here on de top step."

"Oh, no, Uncle Julius," exclaimed Annie, "take this chair. You will find it much more comfortable."

The old man grinned in appreciation of her solicitude, and seated himself somewhat awkwardly.

"Julius," I remarked, "I am thinking of setting out scuppernong vines on that sand-hill where the three persimmon-trees are; and while I 'm working there, I think I 'll plant watermelons between the vines, and get a little something to pay for my first year's work. The new railroad will be finished by the middle of summer, and I can ship the melons North, and get a good price for them."

"Ef you er gwine ter hab any mo' ploughin' ter do," replied Julius, "I 'spec' you 'll ha' ter buy ernudder creetur, 'ca'se hit 's much ez dem hosses kin do ter 'ten' ter de wuk dey got now."

"Yes, I had thought of that. I think I 'll get a mule; a mule can do more work, and does n't require as much attention as a horse."

"I would n' 'vise you ter buy no mule," remarked Julius, with a shake of his head.

"Why not?"

"Well, you may 'low hit 's all foolis'ness, but ef I wuz in yo' place, I would n' buy no mule."

"But that is n't a reason; what objection have you to a mule?"

"Fac' is," continued the old man, in a serious tone, "I doan lack ter dribe a mule. I 's alluz afeared I mought be imposin' on some human creetur; eve'y time I cuts a mule wid a hick-'ry, 'pears ter me mos' lackly I 's cuttin' some er my own re-lations, er somebody e'se w'at can't he'p deyse'ves."

"What put such an absurd idea into your head?" I asked.

My question was followed by a short silence, during which Julius seemed engaged in a mental struggle.

"I dunno ez hit 's wuf w'ile ter tell you dis," he said, at length. "I doan ha'dly 'spec' fer you ter b'lieve it. Does you 'member dat club-footed man w'at hilt de hoss fer you de yuther day w'en you was gittin' out'n de rockaway down ter Mars Archie McMillan's sto'?"

"Yes, I believe I do remember seeing a club-footed man there."

"Did you eber see a club-footed nigger befo' er sence?"

"No, I can't remember that I ever saw a club-footed col-ored man," I replied, after a moment's reflection.

"You en Mis' Annie would n' wanter b'lieve me, ef I wuz ter 'low dat dat man was oncet a mule?"

"No," I replied, "I don't think it very likely that you could make us believe it."

"Why, Uncle Julius!" said Annie severely, "what ridiculous nonsense!"

This reception of the old man's statement reduced him to silence, and it required some diplomacy on my part to induce him to vouchsafe an explanation. The prospect of a long, dull afternoon was not alluring, and I was glad to have the monotony of Sabbath quiet relieved by a plantation legend.

"W'en I wuz a young man," began Julius, when I had finally prevailed upon him to tell us the story, "dat club-footed nigger—his name is Primus—use' ter b'long ter ole Mars Jim McGee ober on de Lumbe'ton plank-road. I use' ter go ober dere ter see a 'oman w'at libbed on de plantation; dat 's how I come ter know all erbout it. Dis yer Primus wuz de livelies' han' on de place, alluz a-dancin', en drinkin', en runnin' roun', en singin', en pickin' de banjo; 'cep'n' once in a w'ile, w'en he 'd 'low he wa'n't treated right 'bout sump'n ernudder, he 'd git so sulky en stubborn dat de w'ite folks could n' ha'dly do nuffin wid 'im.

"It wuz 'gin' de rules fer any er de han's ter go 'way fum de plantation at night; but Primus did n' min' de rules, en went w'en he felt lack it; en de w'ite folks purten' lack dey did n' know it, fer Primus was dange'ous w'en he got in dem stubborn spells, en dey 'd ruther not fool wid 'im.

"One night in de spring er de year, Primus slip' off fum de plantation, en went down on de Wim'l'ton Road ter a dance gun by some er de free niggers down dere. Dey wuz a fiddle, en a banjo, en a jug gwine roun' on de outside, en Primus sung en dance' 'tel 'long 'bout two o'clock in de mawnin', w'en he start' fer home. Ez he come erlong back, he tuk a nigh-cut 'cross de cotton-fiel's en 'long by de aidge er de Min'al Spring Swamp, so ez ter git shet er de patteroles w'at rid up en down de big road fer ter keep de darkies fum runnin' roun' nights. Primus was sa'nt'rin' 'long, studyin' 'bout de good time he 'd had wid de gals, w'en, ez he wuz gwine by a fence co'nder, w'at sh'd he heah but sump'n grunt. He stopped a minute ter listen, en he heared sump'n grunt ag'in. Den he went ober ter de fence whar he heard de fuss, en dere, layin' in de fence co'nder, on a pile er pine straw, he seed a fine, fat shote.

"Primus look' ha'd at de shote, en den sta'ted home. But somehow er 'nudder he could n' git away fum dat shote; w'en he tuk one step for'ards wid one foot, de yuther foot 'peared ter take two steps back'ards, en so he kep' nachly gittin' closeter en closeter ter de shote. It was de beatin'es' thing! De shote des 'peared ter cha'm Primus, en fus' thing you know Primus foun' hisse'f 'way up de road wid de shote on his back.

"Ef Primus had 'a' knowed whose shote dat wuz, he 'd 'a' manage' ter git pas' it somehow er 'nudder. Ez it happen', de shote b'long ter a cunjuh man w'at libbed down in de free-nigger sett'ement. Co'se de cunjuh man did n' hab ter wuk his roots but a little w'ile 'fo' he foun' out who tuk his shote, en den de trouble begun. One mawnin', a day er so later, en befo' he got de shote eat up, Primus did n' go ter wuk w'en de hawn blow, en w'en de oberseah wen' ter look fer him, dey wa' no trace er Primus ter be 'skivered nowhar. W'en he did n' come back in a day er so mo', eve'ybody on de plantation 'lowed he had runned erway. His marster a'vertise' him in de papers, en offered a big reward fer 'im. De nigger-ketchers fotch out dey dogs, en track' 'im down ter de aidge er de swamp, en den de scent gun out; en dat was de las' anybody seed er Primus fer a long, long time.

"Two er th'ee weeks atter Primus disappear', his marster went ter town one Sad'day. Mars Jim was stan'in' in front er Sandy Campbell's bar-room, up by de ole wagon-ya'd, w'en a po' w'ite man fum down on de Wim'l'ton Road come up ter 'im en ax' 'im, kinder keerless lack, ef he did n' wanter buy a mule.

" 'I dunno,' says Mars Jim; 'it 'pen's on de mule, en on de price. Whar is de mule?'

" 'Des 'roun' heah back er ole Tom McAllister's sto',' says de po' w'ite man.

" 'I reckon I 'll hab a look at de mule,' says Mars Jim, 'en ef he suit me, I dunno but w'at I mought buy 'im.'

"So de po' w'ite man tuk Mars Jim 'roun' back er de sto', en dere stood a monst'us fine mule. W'en de mule see Mars Jim, he gun a whinny, des lack he knowed him befo'. Mars Jim look' at de mule, en de mule 'peared ter be soun' en strong. Mars Jim 'lowed dey 'peared ter be sump'n fermilyus 'bout de mule's face, 'spesh'ly his eyes; but he had n' los' naer mule, en did n' hab no recommemb'ance er habin' seed de mule befo'. He ax' de po' buckrah whar he got de mule, en de po' buckrah say his brer raise' de mule down on Rockfish Creek. Mars Jim was a little s'picious er seein' a po' w'ite man wid sech a fine creetur, but he fin'lly 'greed ter gib de man fifty dollars fer de mule,—'bout ha'f w'at a good mule was wuf dem days.

"He tied de mule behin' de buggy w'en he went home, en put 'im ter ploughin' cotton de nex' day. De mule done mighty well fer th'ee er fo' days, en den de niggers 'mence' ter notice some quare things erbout him. Dey wuz a medder on de plantation whar dey use' ter put de hosses en mules ter pastur'. Hit was fence' off fum de corn-fiel' on one side, but on de yuther side'n de pastur' was a terbacker-patch w'at wa'n't fence' off, 'ca'se de beastisses doan none un 'em eat terbacker. Dey doan know w'at 's good! Terbacker is lack religion, de good Lawd made it fer people, en dey ain' no yuther creetur w'at kin 'preciate it. De darkies notice' dat de fus' thing de new mule done, w'en he was turnt inter de pastur', wuz ter make fer de terbacker-patch. Co'se dey didn' think nuffin un it, but nex' mawnin', w'en dey went ter ketch 'im, dey 'skivered dat he had eat up two whole rows er terbacker plants. Atter dat dey had ter put a halter on 'im, en tie 'im ter a stake, er e'se dey wouldn' 'a' been naer leaf er terbacker lef' in de patch.

"Ernudder day one er de han's, name' 'Dolphus, hitch' de mule up, en dribe up here ter dis yer vimya'd,—dat wuz w'en ole Mars Dugal' own' dis place. Mars Dugal' had kilt a yearlin', en de naber w'ite folks all sont ober fer ter git some fraish beef, en Mars Jim had sont 'Dolphus fer some too. Dey wuz a wine-press in de ya'd whar 'Dolphus lef' de mule a-stan'in', en right in front er de press dey wuz a tub er grape-juice, des pressed out, en a little ter one side a bairl erbout half full er wine w'at had be'n stan'in' two er th'ee days, en had begun ter git sorter sha'p ter de tas'e. Dey wuz a couple er bo'ds on top er dis yer bairl, wid a rock laid on 'em ter hol' 'em down. Ez I wuz a-sayin', 'Dolphus lef' de mule stan'in' in de ya'd, en went inter de smoke-house fer ter git de beef. Bimeby, w'en he come out, he seed de mule a-stagg'rin' 'bout de ya'd; en 'fo' 'Dolphus could git dere ter fin' out w'at wuz de matter, de mule fell right ober on his side, en laid dere des' lack he was dead.

"All de niggers 'bout de house run out dere fer ter see w'at wuz de matter. Some say de mule had de colic; some say one thing en some ernudder; 'tel bimeby one er de han's seed de top wuz off'n de bairl, en run en looked in.

" 'Fo' de Lawd!' he say, 'dat mule drunk! he be'n drinkin' de wine.' En sho' 'nuff, de mule had pas' right by de tub er fraish grape-juice en push' de kiver off'n de bairl, en drunk two er th'ee gallon er de wine w'at had been stan'in' long ernough fer ter begin ter git sha'p.

"De darkies all made a great 'miration 'bout de mule gittin' drunk. Dey never had 'n seed nuffin lack it in dey bawn days. Dey po'd water ober de mule, en tried ter sober 'im up; but it wa'n't no use, en 'Dolphus had ter take de beef home on his back, en leabe de mule dere, 'tel he slep' off 'is spree.

"I doan 'member whe'r I tol' you er no, but w'en Primus disappear' fum de plantation, he lef' a wife behin' 'im,—a monst'us good-lookin' yaller gal, name' Sally. W'en Primus had be'n gone a mont' er so, Sally 'mence' fer ter git lonesome, en tuk up wid ernudder young man name' Dan, w'at b'long' on de same plantation. One day dis yer Dan tuk de noo mule out in de cotton-fiel' fer ter plough, en w'en dey wuz gwine 'long de tu'n-row, who sh'd he meet but dis yer Sally. Dan look' 'roun' en he did n' see de oberseah nowhar, so he stop' a minute fer ter run on wid Sally.

" 'Hoddy, honey,' sezee. 'How you feelin' dis mawnin'?'

" 'Fus' rate,' 'spon' Sally.

"Dey wuz lookin' at one ernudder, en dey did n' naer one un 'em pay no 'tention ter de mule, who had turnt 'is head 'roun' er wuz lookin' at Sally ez ha'd ez he could, en stretchin' 'is neck en raisin' 'is years, en whinnyin' kinder sof' ter hisse'f.

" 'Yas, honey,' 'lows Dan, 'en you gwine ter feel fus' rate long ez you sticks ter me. Fer I 's a better man dan dat low-down runaway nigger Primus dat you be'n wastin' yo' time wid.'

"Dan had let go de plough-handle, en had put his arm 'roun' Sally, en wuz des gwine ter kiss her, w'en sump'n ketch' 'im by de scruff er de neck en flung 'im 'way ober in de cotton-patch. W'en he pick' 'isse'f up, Sally had gone kitin' down de tu'n-row, en de mule wuz stan'in' dere lookin' ez ca'm en peaceful ez a Sunday mawnin'.

"Fus' Dan had 'lowed it wuz de oberseah w'at had cotch'

'im wastin' 'is time. But dey wa'n't no oberseah in sight, so he 'cluded it must 'a' be'n de mule. So he pitch' inter de mule en lammed 'im ez ha'd ez he could. De mule tuk it all, en 'peared ter be ez 'umble ez a mule could be; but w'en dey wuz makin' de turn at de een' er de row, one er de plough-lines got under de mule's hin' leg. Dan retch' down ter git de line out, sorter keerless like, w'en de mule haul' off en kick him clean ober de fence inter a brier-patch on de yuther side.

"Dan wuz mighty so' fum 'is woun's en scratches, en wuz laid up fer two er th'ee days. One night de noo mule got out'n de pastur', en went down to de quarters. Dan wuz layin' dere on his pallet, w'en he heard sump'n bangin' erway at de side er his cabin. He raise' up on one shoulder en look' roun', w'en w'at should he see but de noo mule's head stickin' in de winder, wid his lips drawed back over his toofs, grinnin' en snappin' at Dan des' lack he wanter eat 'im up. Den de mule went roun' ter de do', en kick' erway lack he wanter break de do' down, 'tel bimeby somebody come 'long en driv him back ter de pastur'. W'en Sally come in a little later fum de big house, whar she 'd be'n waitin' on de w'ite folks, she foun' po' Dan nigh 'bout dead, he wuz so skeered. She 'lowed Dan had had de nightmare; but w'en dey look' at de do', dey seed de marks er de mule's huffs, so dey could n' be no mistake 'bout w'at had happen'.

"Co'se de niggers tol' dey marster 'bout de mule's gwines-on. Fust he did n' pay no 'tention ter it, but atter a w'ile he tol' 'em ef dey did n' stop dey foolis'ness, he gwine tie some un 'em up. So atter dat dey did n' say nuffin mo' ter dey marster, but dey kep' on noticin' de mule's quare ways des de same.

"'Long 'bout de middle er de summer dey wuz a big camp-meetin' broke out down on de Wim'l'ton Road, en nigh 'bout all de po' w'ite folks en free niggers in de settlement got 'ligion, en lo en behol'! 'mongs' 'em wuz de cunjuh man w'at own' de shote w'at cha'med Primus.

"Dis cunjuh man wuz a Guinea nigger, en befo' he wuz sot free had use' ter b'long ter a gent'eman down in Sampson County. De cunjuh man say his daddy wuz a king, er a guv'ner, er some sorter w'at-you-may-call-'em 'way ober yander in Affiky whar de niggers come fum, befo' he was stoled erway en sol' ter de spekilaters. De cunjuh man had he'ped his marster out'n some trouble ernudder wid his goopher, en his marster had sot him free, en bought him a trac' er land down on de Wim'l'ton Road. He purten' ter be a cow-doctor, but eve'ybody knowed w'at he r'al'y wuz.

"De cunjuh man had n' mo' d'n come th'oo good, befo' he wuz tuk sick wid a col' w'at he kotch kneelin' on de groun' so long at de mou'ners' bench. He kep' gittin' wusser en wusser, en bimeby de rheumatiz tuk holt er 'im, en drawed him all up, 'til one day he sont word up ter Mars Jim McGee's plantation, en ax' Pete, de nigger w'at tuk keer er de mules, fer ter come down dere dat night en fetch dat mule w'at his marster had bought fum de po' w'ite man dyoin' er de summer.

"Pete did n' know w'at de cunjuh man wuz dribin' at, but he did n' daster stay way; en so dat night, w'en he 'd done eat his bacon en his hoe-cake, en drunk his 'lasses-en-water, he put a bridle on de mule, en rid 'im down ter de cunjuh man's cabin. W'en he got ter de do', he lit en hitch' de mule, en den knock' at de do'. He felt mighty jubous 'bout gwine in, but he was bleedst ter do it; he knowed he could n' he'p 'isse'f.

" 'Pull de string,' sez a weak voice, en w'en Pete lif' de latch en went in, de cunjuh man was layin' on de bed, lookin' pale en weak, lack he did n' hab much longer fer ter lib.

" 'Is you fotch' de mule?' sezee.

"Pete say yas, en de cunjuh man kep' on.

" 'Brer Pete,' sezee, 'I 's be'n a monst'us sinner man, en I 's done a power er wickedness endyoin' er my days; but de good Lawd is wash' my sins erway, en I feels now dat I 's boun' fer de kingdom. En I feels, too, dat I ain' gwine ter git up fum dis bed no mo' in dis wold', en I wants ter ondo some er de harm I done. En dat 's de reason, Brer Pete, I sont fer you ter fetch dat mule down here. You 'member dat shote I was up ter yo' plantation inquirin' 'bout las' June?'

" 'Yas,' says Brer Pete, 'I 'member yo' axin' 'bout a shote you had los'.'

" 'I dunno whe'r you eber l'arnt it er no,' says de cunjuh man, 'but I done knowed yo' marster's Primus had tuk de shote, en I wuz boun' ter git eben wid 'im. So one night I cotch' 'im down by de swamp on his way ter a candy-pullin', en I th'owed a goopher mixtry on 'im, en turnt 'em ter a mule, en got a po' w'ite man ter sell de mule, en we 'vided de money. But I doan want ter die 'tel I turn Brer Primus back ag'in.'

"Den de cunjuh man ax' Pete ter take down one er two go'ds off'n a she'f in de corner, en one er two bottles wid some kin' er mixtry in 'em, en set 'em on a stool by de bed; en den he ax' 'im ter fetch de mule in.

"W'en de mule come in de do', he gin a snort, en started fer de bed, des lack he was gwine ter jump on it.

" 'Hol' on dere, Brer Primus!' de cunjuh man hollered. 'I 's monst'us weak, en ef you 'mence on me, you won't nebber hab no chance fer ter git turn' back no mo'.'

"De mule seed de sense er dat, en stood still. Den de cunjuh man tuk de go'ds en bottles, en 'mence' ter wuk de roots en yarbs, en de mule 'mence' ter turn back ter a man,—fust his years, den de res' er his head, den his shoulders en arms. All de time de cunjuh man kep' on wukkin' his roots; en Pete en Primus could see he wuz gittin' weaker en weaker all de time.

" 'Brer Pete,' sezee, bimeby, 'gimme a drink er dem bitters out'n dat green bottle on de she'f yander. I 's gwine fas', en it 'll gimme strenk fer ter finish dis wuk.'

"Brer Pete look' up on de mantelpiece, en he seed a bottle in de corner. It was so da'k in de cabin he could n' tell whe'r it wuz a green bottle er no. But he hilt de bottle ter de cunjuh man 's mouf, en he tuk a big mouff'l. He had n' mo' d'n swallowed it befo' he 'mence' ter holler.

" 'You gimme de wrong bottle, Brer Pete; dis yer bottle 's got pizen in it, en I 's done fer dis time, sho'. Hol' me up, fer de Lawd's sake! 'tel I git th'oo turnin' Brer Primus back.'

"So Pete hilt him up, en he kep' on wukkin' de roots, 'tel he got de goopher all tuk off'n Brer Primus 'cep'n' one foot. He had n' got dis foot mo' d'n half turnt back befo' his strenk gun out enti'ely, en he drap' de roots en fell back on de bed.

" 'I can't do no mo' fer you, Brer Primus,' sezee, 'but I hopes you will fergib me fer w'at harm I done you. I knows de good Lawd done fergib me, en I hope ter meet you bofe in glory. I sees de good angels waitin' fer me up yander, wid a long w'ite robe en a starry crown, en I 'm on my way ter jine 'em.' En so de cunjuh man died, en Pete en Primus went back ter de plantation.

"De darkies all made a great 'miration w'en Primus come back. Mars Jim let on lack he did n' b'lieve de tale de two niggers tol'; he sez Primus had runned erway, en stay' 'tel he got ti'ed er de swamps, en den come back on him ter be fed. He tried ter 'count fer de shape er Primus' foot by sayin' Primus got his foot smash', er snake-bit, er sump'n, w'iles he wuz erway, en den stayed out in de woods whar he could n' git it kyoed up straight, 'stidder comin' long home whar a doctor could 'a' 'tended ter it. But de niggers all notice' dey marster did n' tie Primus up, ner take on much 'ca'se de mule wuz gone. So dey 'lowed dey marster must 'a' had his s'picions 'bout dat cunjuh man."

My wife had listened to Julius's recital with only a mild interest. When the old man had finished it she remarked:—

"That story does not appeal to me, Uncle Julius, and is not up to your usual mark. It is n't pathetic, it has no moral that I can discover, and I can't see why you should tell it. In fact, it seems to me like nonsense."

The old man looked puzzled as well as pained. He had not pleased the lady, and he did not seem to understand why.

"I 'm sorry, ma'm," he said reproachfully, "ef you doan lack dat tale. I can't make out w'at you means by some er dem wo'ds you uses, but I 'm tellin' nuffin but de truf. Co'se I did n' see de cunjuh man tu'n 'im back, fer I wuz n' dere; but I be'n hearin' de tale fer twenty-five yeahs, en I ain' got no 'casion fer ter 'spute it. Dey 's so many things a body knows is lies, dat dey ain' no use gwine roun' findin' fault wid tales dat mought des ez well be so ez not. F' instance, dey 's a young nigger gwine ter school in town, en he come out heah de yuther day en 'lowed dat de sun stood still en de yeath turnt roun' eve'y day on a kinder axletree. I tol' dat young nigger ef he did n' take hisse'f 'way wid dem lies, I 'd take a buggy-trace ter 'im; fer I sees de yeath stan'in' still all de time, en I sees de sun gwine roun' it, en ef a man can't b'lieve w'at 'e sees, I can't see no use in libbin'—mought 's well die en be whar we can't see nuffin. En ernudder thing w'at proves de tale 'bout dis ole Primus is de way he goes on ef anybody ax' him how he come by dat club-foot. I axed 'im one day, mighty perlite en civil, en he call' me a' ole fool, en got so mad he ain' spoke ter me sence. Hit 's monst'us quare. But dis is a quare worl', anyway yer kin fix it," concluded the old man, with a weary sigh.

"Ef you makes up yo' min' not ter buy dat mule, suh," he added, as he rose to go, "I knows a man w'at 's got a good hoss he wants ter sell,—leas'ways dat 's w'at I heared. I'm gwine ter pra'rmeetin' ter-night, en I 'm gwine right by de man's house, en ef you 'd lack ter look at de hoss, I 'll ax 'im ter fetch him roun'."

"Oh, yes," I said, "you can ask him to stop in, if he is passing. There will be no harm in looking at the horse, though I rather think I shall buy a mule."

Early next morning the man brought the horse up to the vineyard. At that time I was not a very good judge of horse-flesh. The horse appeared sound and gentle, and, as the owner assured me, had no bad habits. The man wanted a large price for the horse, but finally agreed to accept a much smaller sum, upon payment of which I became possessed of a very fine-looking animal. But alas for the deceitfulness of appearances! I soon ascertained that the horse was blind in one eye, and that the sight of the other was very defective; and not a month elapsed before my purchase developed most of the diseases that horse-flesh is heir to, and a more worthless, broken-winded, spavined quadruped never disgraced the noble name of horse. After worrying through two or three months of life, he expired one night in a fit of the colic. I replaced him with a mule, and Julius henceforth had to take his chances of driving some metamorphosed unfortunate.

Circumstances that afterwards came to my knowledge created in my mind a strong suspicion that Julius may have played a more than unconscious part in this transaction. Among other significant facts was his appearance, the Sunday following the purchase of the horse, in a new suit of store clothes, which I had seen displayed in the window of Mr. Solomon Cohen's store on my last visit to town, and had remarked on account of their striking originality of cut and pattern. As I had not recently paid Julius any money, and as he had no property to mortgage, I was driven to conjecture to account for his possession of the means to buy the clothes. Of course I would not charge him with duplicity unless I could prove it, at least to a moral certainty, but for a long time afterwards I took his advice only in small doses and with great discrimination.

Sis' Becky's Pickaninny

WE HAD not lived in North Carolina very long before I was able to note a marked improvement in my wife's health. The ozone-laden air of the surrounding piney woods, the mild and equable climate, the peaceful leisure of country life, had brought about in hopeful measure the cure we had anticipated. Toward the end of our second year, however, her ailment took an unexpected turn for the worse. She became the victim of a settled melancholy, attended with vague fore-bodings of impending misfortune.

"You must keep up her spirits," said our physician, the best in the neighboring town. "This melancholy lowers her tone too much, tends to lessen her strength, and, if it continue too long, may be fraught with grave consequences."

I tried various expedients to cheer her up. I read novels to her. I had the hands on the place come up in the evening and serenade her with plantation songs. Friends came in some-times and talked, and frequent letters from the North kept her in touch with her former home. But nothing seemed to rouse her from the depression into which she had fallen.

One pleasant afternoon in spring, I placed an armchair in a shaded portion of the front piazza, and filling it with pillows led my wife out of the house and seated her where she would have the pleasantest view of a somewhat monotonous scenery. She was scarcely placed when old Julius came through the yard, and, taking off his tattered straw hat, inquired, some-what anxiously:—

"How is you feelin' dis atternoon, ma'm?"

"She is not very cheerful, Julius," I said. My wife was ap-parently without energy enough to speak for herself.

The old man did not seem inclined to go away, so I asked him to sit down. I had noticed, as he came up, that he held some small object in his hand. When he had taken his seat on the top step, he kept fingering this object,—what it was I could not quite make out.

"What is that you have there, Julius?" I asked, with mild curiosity.

"Dis is my rabbit foot, suh."

This was at a time before this curious superstition had attained its present jocular popularity among white people, and while I had heard of it before, it had not yet outgrown the charm of novelty.

"What do you do with it?"

"I kyars it wid me fer luck, suh."

"Julius," I observed, half to him and half to my wife, "your people will never rise in the world until they throw off these childish superstitions and learn to live by the light of reason and common sense. How absurd to imagine that the fore-foot of a poor dead rabbit, with which he timorously felt his way along through a life surrounded by snares and pitfalls, beset by enemies on every hand, can promote happiness or success, or ward off failure or misfortune!"

"It is ridiculous," assented my wife, with faint interest.

"Dat 's w'at I tells dese niggers roun' heah," said Julius. "De fo'-foot ain' got no power. It has ter be de hin'-foot, suh,—de lef' hin'-foot er a grabeya'd rabbit, killt by a cross-eyed nigger on a da'k night in de full er de moon."

"They must be very rare and valuable," I said.

"Dey is kinder ska'ce, suh, en dey ain' no 'mount er money could buy mine, suh. I mought len' it ter anybody I sot sto' by, but I would n' sell it, no indeed, suh, I would n'."

"How do you know it brings good luck?" I asked.

"'Ca'se I ain' had no bad luck sence I had it, suh, en I 's had dis rabbit foot fer fo'ty yeahs. I had a good marster befo' de wah, en I wa'n't sol' erway, en I wuz sot free; en dat 'uz all good luck."

"But that does n't prove anything," I rejoined. "Many other people have gone through a similar experience, and probably more than one of them had no rabbit's foot."

"Law, suh! you doan hafter prove 'bout de rabbit foot! Eve'ybody knows dat; leas'ways eve'ybody roun' heah knows it. But ef it has ter be prove' ter folks w'at wa'n't bawn en raise' in dis naberhood, dey is a' easy way ter prove it. Is I eber tol' you de tale er Sis' Becky en her pickaninny?"

"No," I said, "let us hear it." I thought perhaps the story might interest my wife as much or more than the novel I had meant to read from.

"Dis yer Becky," Julius began, "useter b'long ter ole Kunnel Pen'leton, who owned a plantation down on de Wim'l'ton Road, 'bout ten miles fum heah, des befo' you gits ter Black Swamp. Dis yer Becky wuz a fiel'-han', en a monst'us good 'un. She had a husban' oncet, a nigger w'at b'longed on de nex' plantation, but de man w'at owned her husban' died, en his lan' en his niggers had ter be sol' fer ter pay his debts. Kunnel Pen'leton 'lowed he 'd 'a' bought dis nigger, but he had be'n bettin' on hoss races, en did n' hab no money, en so Becky's husban' wuz sol' erway ter Fuhginny.

"Co'se Becky went on some 'bout losin' her man, but she could n' he'p herse'f; en 'sides dat, she had her pickaninny fer ter comfo't her. Dis yer little Mose wuz de cutes', blackes', shiny-eyedes' little nigger you eber laid eyes on, en he wuz ez fon' er his mammy ez his mammy wuz er him. Co'se Becky had ter wuk en did n' hab much time ter was'e wid her baby. Ole Aun' Nancy, de plantation nuss down at de qua'ters, useter take keer er little Mose in de daytime, en atter de niggers come in fum de cotton-fiel' Becky 'ud git her chile en kiss 'im en nuss 'im, en keep 'im 'tel mawnin'; en on Sundays she 'd hab 'im in her cabin wid her all day long.

"Sis' Becky had got sorter useter gittin' 'long widout her husban', w'en one day Kunnel Pen'leton went ter de races. Co'se w'en he went ter de races, he tuk his hosses, en co'se he bet on 'is own hosses, en co'se he los' his money; fer Kunnel Pen'leton did n' nebber hab no luck wid his hosses, ef he did keep hisse'f po' projeckin' wid 'em. But dis time dey wuz a hoss name' Lightnin' Bug, w'at b'longed ter ernudder man, en dis hoss won de sweep-stakes; en Kunnel Pen'leton tuk a lackin' ter dat hoss, en ax' his owner w'at he wuz willin' ter take fer 'im.

" 'I 'll take a thousan' dollahs fer dat hoss,' sez dis yer man, who had a big plantation down to'ds Wim'l'ton, whar he raise' hosses fer ter race en ter sell.

"Well, Kunnel Pen'leton scratch' 'is head, en wonder whar he wuz gwine ter raise a thousan' dollahs; en he did n' see des how he could do it, fer he owed ez much ez he could borry a'ready on de skyo'ity he could gib. But he wuz des boun' ter hab dat hoss, so sezee:—

" 'I 'll gib you my note fer 'leven hund'ed dollahs fer dat hoss.'

"De yuther man shuck 'is head, en sezee:—

" 'Yo' note, suh, is better 'n gol', I doan doubt; but I is made it a rule in my bizness not ter take no notes fum nobody. Howsomeber, suh, ef you is kinder sho't er fun's, mos' lackly we kin make some kin' er bahg'in. En w'iles we is talkin', I mought 's well say dat I needs ernudder good nigger down on my place. Ef you is got a good one ter spar', I mought trade wid you.'

"Now, Kunnel Pen'leton did n' r'ally hab no niggers fer ter spar', but he 'lowed ter hisse'f he wuz des bleedzd ter hab dat hoss, en so he sez, sezee:—

" 'Well, I doan lack ter, but I reckon I 'll haf ter. You come out ter my plantation ter-morrer en look ober my niggers, en pick out de one you wants.'

"So sho' 'nuff nex' day dis yer man come out ter Kunnel Pen'leton's place en rid roun' de plantation en glanshed at de niggers, en who sh'd he pick out fum 'em all but Sis' Becky.

" 'I needs a noo nigger 'oman down ter my place,' sezee, 'fer ter cook en wash, en so on; en dat young 'oman 'll des fill de bill. You gimme her, en you kin hab Lightnin' Bug.' "

"Now, Kunnel Pen'leton did n' lack ter trade Sis' Becky, 'ca'se she wuz nigh 'bout de bes' fiel'-han' he had; en 'sides, Mars Dugal' did n' keer ter take de mammies 'way fum dey chillun w'iles de chillun wuz little. But dis man say he want Becky, er e'se Kunnel Pen'leton could n' hab de race hoss.

" 'Well,' sez de kunnel, 'you kin hab de 'oman. But I doan lack ter sen' her 'way fum her baby. W'at 'll you gimme fer dat nigger baby?'

" 'I doan want de baby,' sez de yuther man. 'I ain' got no use fer de baby.'

" 'I tell yer w'at I 'll do,' 'lows Kunnel Pen'leton, 'I 'll th'ow dat pickaninny in fer good measure.'

"But de yuther man shuck his head. 'No,' sezee, 'I 's much erbleedzd, but I doan raise niggers; I raises hosses, en I doan wanter be both'rin' wid no nigger babies. Nemmine de baby. I 'll keep dat 'oman so busy she 'll fergit de baby; fer niggers is made ter wuk, en dey ain' got no time fer no sich foolis'-ness ez babies.'

"Kunnel Pen'leton did n' wanter hu't Becky's feelin's,—fer Kunnel Pen'leton wuz a kin'-hea'ted man, en nebber lack' ter make no trouble fer nobody,—en so he tol' Becky he wuz gwine sen' her down ter Robeson County fer a day er so, ter he'p out his son-in-law in his wuk; en bein' ez dis yuther man wuz gwine dat way, he had ax' 'im ter take her 'long in his buggy.

" 'Kin I kyar little Mose wid me, marster?' ax' Sis' Becky.

" 'N-o,' sez de kunnel, ez ef he wuz studyin' whuther ter let her take 'im er no; 'I reckon you better let Aun' Nancy look atter yo' baby fer de day er two you 'll be gone, en she 'll see dat he gits ernuff ter eat 'tel you gits back.'

"So Sis' Becky hug' en kiss' little Mose, en tol' 'im ter be a good little pickaninny, en take keer er hisse'f, en not fergit his mammy w'iles she wuz gone. En little Mose put his arms roun' his mammy en lafft en crowed des lack it wuz monst'us fine fun fer his mammy ter go 'way en leabe 'im.

"Well, dis yer hoss trader sta'ted out wid Becky, en bimeby, atter dey 'd gone down de Lumbe'ton Road fer a few miles er so, dis man tu'nt roun' in a diffe'nt d'rection, en kep' goin' dat erway, 'tel bimeby Sis' Becky up 'n ax' 'im ef he wuz gwine ter Robeson County by a noo road.

" 'No, nigger,' sezee, 'I ain' gwine ter Robeson County at all. I 's gwine ter Bladen County, whar my plantation is, en whar I raises all my hosses.'

" 'But how is I gwine ter git ter Mis' Laura's plantation down in Robeson County?' sez Becky, wid her hea't in her mouf, fer she 'mence' ter git skeered all er a sudden.

" 'You ain' gwine ter git dere at all,' sez de man. 'You b'-longs ter me now, fer I done traded my bes' race hoss fer you, wid yo' ole marster. Ef you is a good gal, I 'll treat you right, en ef you doan behabe yo'se'f,—w'y, w'at e'se happens 'll be yo' own fault.'

"Co'se Sis' Becky cried en went on 'bout her pickaninny, but co'se it did n' do no good, en bimeby dey got down ter dis yer man's place, en he put Sis' Becky ter wuk, en fergot all 'bout her habin' a pickaninny.

"Meanw'iles, w'en ebenin' come, de day Sis' Becky wuz tuk 'way, little Mose 'mence' ter git res'less, en bimeby, w'en his mammy did n' come, he sta'ted ter cry fer 'er. Aun' Nancy fed 'im en rocked 'im en rocked 'im, en fin'lly he des cried en cried 'tel he cried hisse'f ter sleep.

"De nex' day he did n' 'pear ter be as peart ez yushal, en w'en night come he fretted en went on wuss'n he did de night befo'. De nex' day his little eyes 'mence' ter lose dey shine, en he would n' eat nuffin, en he 'mence' ter look so peaked dat Aun' Nancy tuk 'n kyared 'im up ter de big house, en showed 'im ter her ole missis, en her ole missis gun her some med'cine fer 'im, en 'lowed ef he did n' git no better she sh'd fetch 'im up ter de big house ag'in, en dey 'd hab a doctor, en nuss little Mose up dere. Fer Aun' Nancy's ole missis 'lowed he wuz a lackly little nigger en wu'th raisin'.

"But Aun' Nancy had l'arn' ter lack little Mose, en she did n' wanter hab 'im tuk up ter de big house. En so w'en he did n' git no better, she gethered a mess er green peas, and tuk de peas en de baby, en went ter see ole Aun' Peggy, de cunjuh 'oman down by de Wim'l'ton Road. She gun Aun' Peggy de mess er peas, en tol' her all 'bout Sis' Becky en little Mose.

" 'Dat is a monst'us small mess er peas you is fotch' me,' sez Aun' Peggy, sez she.

" 'Yas, I knows,' 'lowed Aun' Nancy, 'but dis yere is a monst'us small pickaninny.'

" 'You 'll hafter fetch me sump'n mo',' sez Aun' Peggy, 'fer you can't 'spec' me ter was'e my time diggin' roots en wukkin' cunj'ation fer nuffin.'

" 'All right,' sez Aun' Nancy, 'I 'll fetch you sump'n mo' nex' time.'

" 'You bettah,' sez Aun' Peggy, 'er e'se dey 'll be trouble. W'at dis yer little pickaninny needs is ter see his mammy. You leabe 'im heah 'tel ebenin' en I 'll show 'im his mammy.'

"So w'en Aun' Nancy had gone 'way, Aun' Peggy tuk 'n wukked her roots, en tu'nt little Mose ter a hummin'-bird, en sont 'im off fer ter fin' his mammy.

"So little Mose flewed, en flewed, en flewed away, 'tel bimeby he got ter de place whar Sis' Becky b'longed. He seed his mammy wukkin' roun' de ya'd, en he could tell fum lookin' at her dat she wuz trouble' in her min' 'bout sump'n, en feelin' kin' er po'ly. Sis' Becky heared sump'n hummin' roun' en roun' her, sweet en low. Fus' she 'lowed it wuz a hummin'-bird; den she thought it sounded lack her little Mose croonin' on her breas' way back yander on de ole plantation. En she des 'magine' it wuz her little Mose, en it made her feel bettah, en she went on 'bout her wuk pearter 'n she 'd done sence she 'd be'n down dere. Little Mose stayed roun' 'tel late in de ebenin', en den flewed back ez hard ez he could ter Aun' Peggy. Ez fer Sis' Becky, she dremp all dat night dat she wuz holdin' her pickaninny in her arms, en kissin' him, en nussin' him, des lack she useter do back on de ole plantation whar he wuz bawn. En fer th'ee er fo' days Sis' Becky went 'bout her wuk wid mo' sperrit dan she 'd showed sence she 'd be'n down dere ter dis man's plantation.

"De nex' day atter he come back, little Mose wuz mo' pearter en better 'n he had be'n fer a long time. But to'ds de een' er de week he 'mence' ter git res'less ag'in, en stop' eatin', en Aun' Nancy kyared 'im down ter Aun' Peggy once mo', en she tu'nt 'im ter a mawkin'-bird dis time, en sont 'im off ter see his mammy ag'in.

"It did n' take him long fer ter git dere, en w'en he did, he seed his mammy standin' in de kitchen, lookin' back in de d'rection little Mose wuz comin' fum. En dey wuz tears in her eyes, en she look' mo' po'ly en peaked 'n she had w'en he wuz down dere befo'. So little Mose sot on a tree in de ya'd en sung, en sung, en sung, des fittin' ter split his th'oat. Fus' Sis' Becky did n' notice 'im much, but dis mawkin'-bird kep' stayin' roun' de house all day, en bimeby Sis' Becky des 'magine' dat mawkin'-bird wuz her little Mose crowin' en crowin', des lack he useter do w'en his mammy would come home at night fum de cotton-fiel'. De mawkin'-bird stayed roun' dere 'mos' all day, en w'en Sis' Becky went out in de ya'd one time, dis yer mawkin'-bird lit on her shoulder en peck' at de piece er bread she wuz eatin', en fluttered his wings so dey rub' up agin de side er her head. En w'en he flewed away 'long late in de ebenin', des 'fo' sundown, Sis' Becky felt mo' better 'n she had sence she had heared dat hummin'-bird a week er so pas'. En dat night she dremp 'bout ole times ag'in, des lack she did befo'.

"But dis yer totin' little Mose down ter ole Aun' Peggy, en dis yer gittin' things fer ter pay de cunjuh 'oman, use' up a lot er Aun' Nancy's time, en she begun ter git kinder ti'ed. 'Sides dat, w'en Sis' Becky had be'n on de plantation, she had useter he'p Aun' Nancy wid de young uns ebenin's en Sundays; en Aun' Nancy 'mence' ter miss 'er monst'us, 'speshly sence she got a tech er de rheumatiz herse'f, en so she 'lows ter ole Aun' Peggy one day:—

" 'Aun' Peggy, ain' dey no way you kin fetch Sis' Becky back home?'

" 'Huh!' sez Aun' Peggy, 'I dunno 'bout dat. I 'll hafter wuk my roots en fin' out whuther I kin er no. But it 'll take a monst'us heap er wuk, en I can't was'e my time fer nuffin. Ef you 'll fetch me sump'n ter pay me fer my trouble, I reckon we kin fix it.'

"So nex' day Aun' Nancy went down ter see Aun' Peggy ag'in.

" 'Aun' Peggy,' sez she, 'I is fotch' you my bes' Sunday head-hankercher. Will dat do?'

"Aun' Peggy look' at de head-hankercher, en run her han' ober it, en sez she:—

" 'Yas, dat 'll do fus'-rate. I 's be'n wukkin' my roots sence you be'n gone, en I 'lows mos' lackly I kin git Sis' Becky back, but it 's gwine take fig'rin' en studyin' ez well ez cunj'in'. De fus' thing ter do 'll be ter stop fetchin' dat pickaninny down heah, en not sen' 'im ter see his mammy no mo'. Ef he gits too po'ly, you lemme know, en I 'll gib you some kin' er mixtry fer ter make 'im fergit Sis' Becky fer a week er so. So 'less'n you comes fer dat, you neenter come back ter see me no mo' 'tel I sen's fer you.'

"So Aun' Peggy sont Aun' Nancy erway, en de fus' thing she done wuz ter call a hawnet fum a nes' unner her eaves.

" 'You go up ter Kunnel Pen'leton's stable, hawnet,' sez she, 'en sting de knees er de race hoss name' Lightnin' Bug. Be sho' en git de right one.'

"So de hawnet flewed up ter Kunnel Pen'leton's stable en stung Lightnin' Bug roun' de laigs, en de nex' mawnin' Lightnin' Bug's knees wuz all swoll' up, twice't ez big ez dey oughter be. W'en Kunnel Pen'leton went out ter de stable en see de hoss's laigs, hit would 'a' des made you trimble lack a leaf fer ter heah him cuss dat hoss trader. Howsomeber, he cool' off bimeby en tol' de stable boy fer ter rub Lightnin' Bug's laigs wid some linimum. De boy done ez his marster tol' 'im, en by de nex' day de swellin' had gone down consid'able. Aun' Peggy had sont a sparrer, w'at had a nes' in one er de trees close ter her cabin, fer ter watch w'at wuz gwine on 'roun' de big house, en w'en dis yer sparrer tol' 'er de hoss wuz gittin' ober de swellin', she sont de hawnet back fer ter sting 'is knees some mo', en de nex' mawnin' Lightnin' Bug's laigs wuz swoll' up wuss 'n befo'.

"Well, dis time Kunnel Pen'leton wuz mad th'oo en th'oo, en all de way 'roun', en he cusst dat hoss trader up en down, fum *A* ter *Izzard*. He cusst so ha'd dat de stable boy got mos' skeered ter def, en went off en hid hisse'f in de hay.

"Ez fer Kunnel Pen'leton, he went right up ter de house en got out his pen en ink, en tuk off his coat en roll' up his sleeves, en writ a letter ter dis yer hoss trader, en sezee:—

" 'You is sol' me a hoss w'at is got a ringbone er a spavin er sump'n, en w'at I paid you fer wuz a soun' hoss. I wants you ter sen' my nigger 'oman back en take yo' ole hoss, er e'se I 'll sue you, sho 's you bawn.'

"But dis yer man wa'n't skeered a bit, en he writ back ter Kunnel Pen'leton dat a bahg'in wuz a bahg'in; dat Lightnin' Bug wuz soun' w'en he sol' 'im, en ef Kunnel Pen'leton did n' knowed ernuff 'bout hosses ter take keer er a fine racer, dat wuz his own fune'al. En he say Kunnel Pen'leton kin sue en be cusst fer all he keer, but he ain' gwine ter gib up de nigger he bought en paid fer.

"W'en Kunnel Pen'leton got dis letter he wuz madder 'n he wuz befo', 'speshly 'ca'se dis man 'lowed he did n' know how ter take keer er fine hosses. But he could n' do nuffin but fetch a lawsuit, en he knowed, by his own 'spe'ience, dat lawsuits wuz slow ez de seben-yeah eetch and cos' mo' d'n dey come ter, en he 'lowed he better go slow en wait awhile.

"Aun' Peggy knowed w'at wuz gwine on all dis time, en she fix' up a little bag wid some roots en one thing en ernudder in it, en gun it ter dis sparrer er her'n, en tol' 'im ter take it 'way down yander whar Sis' Becky wuz, en drap it right befo' de do' er her cabin, so she 'd be sho' en fin' it de fus' time she come out'n de do'.

"One night Sis' Becky dremp' her pickaninny wuz dead, en de nex' day she wuz mo'nin' en groanin' all day. She dremp' de same dream th'ee nights runnin', en den, de nex' mawnin' atter de las' night, she foun' dis yer little bag de sparrer had drap' in front her do'; en she 'lowed she 'd be'n cunju'd, en wuz gwine ter die, en ez long ez her pickaninny wuz dead dey wa'n't no use tryin' ter do nuffin nohow. En so she tuk 'n went ter bed, en tol' her marster she 'd be'n cunju'd en wuz gwine ter die.

"Her marster lafft at her, en argyed wid her, en tried ter 'suade her out'n dis yer fool notion, ez he called it,—fer he wuz one er dese yer w'ite folks w'at purten' dey doan b'liebe in cunj'in',—but hit wa'n't no use. Sis' Becky kep' gittin' wusser en wusser, 'tel fin'lly dis yer man 'lowed Sis' Becky wuz gwine ter die, sho' 'nuff. En ez he knowed dey had n' be'n nuffin de matter wid Lightnin' Bug w'en he traded 'im, he 'lowed mebbe he could kyo' 'im en fetch 'im roun' all right, leas'ways good 'nuff ter sell ag'in. En anyhow, a lame hoss wuz better 'n a dead nigger. So he sot down en writ Kunnel Pen'leton a letter.

" 'My conscience,' sezee, 'has be'n troublin' me 'bout dat ringbone' hoss I sol' you. Some folks 'lows a hoss trader ain' got no conscience, but dey doan know me, fer dat is my weak spot, en de reason I ain' made no mo' money hoss tradin'. Fac' is,' sezee, 'I is got so I can't sleep nights fum studyin' 'bout dat spavin' hoss; en I is made up my min' dat, w'iles a bahg'in is a bahg'in, en you seed Lightnin' Bug befo' you traded fer 'im, principle is wuth mo' d'n money er hosses er niggers. So ef you 'll sen' Lightnin' Bug down heah, I 'll sen' yo' nigger 'oman back, en we 'll call de trade off, en be ez good frien's ez we eber wuz, en no ha'd feelin's.'

"So sho' 'nuff, Kunnel Pen'leton sont de hoss back. En w'en de man w'at come ter bring Lightnin' Bug tol' Sis' Becky her pickaninny wa'n't dead, Sis' Becky wuz so glad dat she 'lowed she wuz gwine ter try ter lib 'tel she got back whar she could see little Mose once mo'. En w'en she retch' de ole plantation en seed her baby kickin' en crowin' en holdin' out his little arms to'ds her, she wush' she wuz n' cunju'd en did n' hafter die. En w'en Aun' Nancy tol' 'er all 'bout Aun' Peggy, Sis' Becky went down ter see de cunjuh 'oman, en Aun' Peggy tol' her she had cunju'd her. En den Aun' Peggy tuk de goopher off'n her, en she got well, en stayed on de plantation, en raise' her pickaninny. En w'en little Mose growed up, he could sing en whistle des lack a mawkin'-bird, so dat de w'ite folks useter hab 'im come up ter de big house at night, en whistle en sing fer 'em, en dey useter gib 'im money en vittles en one thing er ernudder, w'ich he alluz tuk home ter his mammy; fer he knowed all 'bout w'at she had gone th'oo. He tu'nt out ter be a sma't man, en l'arnt de blacksmif trade; en Kunnel Pen'leton let 'im hire his time. En bimeby he bought his mammy en sot her free, en den he bought hisse'f, en tuk keer er Sis' Becky ez long ez dey bofe libbed."

My wife had listened to this story with greater interest than she had manifested in any subject for several days. I had watched her furtively from time to time during the recital, and had observed the play of her countenance. It had expressed in turn sympathy, indignation, pity, and at the end lively satisfaction.

"That is a very ingenious fairy tale, Julius," I said, "and we are much obliged to you."

"Why, John!" said my wife severely, "the story bears the stamp of truth, if ever a story did."

"Yes," I replied, "especially the humming-bird episode, and the mocking-bird digression, to say nothing of the doings of the hornet and the sparrow."

"Oh, well, I don't care," she rejoined, with delightful animation; "those are mere ornamental details and not at all essential. The story is true to nature, and might have happened half a hundred times, and no doubt did happen, in those horrid days before the war."

"By the way, Julius," I remarked, "your story does n't establish what you started out to prove,—that a rabbit's foot brings good luck."

"Hit 's plain 'nuff ter me, suh," replied Julius. "I bet young missis dere kin 'splain it herse'f."

"I rather suspect," replied my wife promptly, "that Sis' Becky had no rabbit's foot."

"You is hit de bull's-eye de fus' fire, ma'm," assented Julius. "Ef Sis' Becky had had a rabbit foot, she nebber would 'a' went th'oo all dis trouble."

I went into the house for some purpose, and left Julius talking to my wife. When I came back a moment later, he was gone.

My wife's condition took a turn for the better from this very day, and she was soon on the way to ultimate recovery.

Several weeks later, after she had resumed her afternoon drives, which had been interrupted by her illness, Julius brought the rockaway round to the front door one day, and I assisted my wife into the carriage.

"John," she said, before I had taken my seat, "I wish you would look in my room, and bring me my handkerchief. You will find it in the pocket of my blue dress."

I went to execute the commission. When I pulled the handkerchief out of her pocket, something else came with it and fell on the floor. I picked up the object and looked at it. It was Julius's rabbit's foot.

The Gray Wolf's Ha'nt

IT WAS a rainy day at the vineyard. The morning had dawned bright and clear. But the sky had soon clouded, and by nine o'clock there was a light shower, followed by others at brief intervals. By noon the rain had settled into a dull, steady downpour. The clouds hung low, and seemed to grow denser instead of lighter as they discharged their watery burden, and there was now and then a muttering of distant thunder. Outdoor work was suspended, and I spent most of the day at the house, looking over my accounts and bringing up some arrears of correspondence.

Towards four o'clock I went out on the piazza, which was broad and dry, and less gloomy than the interior of the house, and composed myself for a quiet smoke. I had lit my cigar and opened the volume I was reading at that time, when my wife, whom I had left dozing on a lounge, came out and took a rocking-chair near me.

"I wish you would talk to me, or read to me—or something," she exclaimed petulantly. "It 's awfully dull here to-day."

"I 'll read to you with pleasure," I replied, and began at the point where I had found my bookmark:—

" 'The difficulty of dealing with transformations so many-sided as those which all existences have undergone, or are undergoing, is such as to make a complete and deductive interpretation almost hopeless. So to grasp the total process of redistribution of matter and motion as to see simultaneously its several necessary results in their actual interdependence is scarcely possible. There is, however, a mode of rendering the process as a whole tolerably comprehensible. Though the genesis of the rearrangement of every evolving aggregate is in itself one, it presents to our intelligence' "—

"John," interrupted my wife, "I wish you would stop reading that nonsense and see who that is coming up the lane."

I closed my book with a sigh. I had never been able to interest my wife in the study of philosophy, even when presented in the simplest and most lucid form.

Some one was coming up the lane; at least, a huge faded cotton umbrella was making progress toward the house, and beneath it a pair of nether extremities in trousers was discernible. Any doubt in my mind as to whose they were was soon resolved when Julius reached the steps and, putting the umbrella down, got a good dash of the rain as he stepped up on the porch.

"Why in the world, Julius," I asked, "did n't you keep the umbrella up until you got under cover?"

"It 's bad luck, suh, ter raise a' umbrella in de house, en w'iles I dunno whuther it 's bad luck ter kyar one inter de piazzer er no, I 'lows it 's alluz bes' ter be on de safe side. I did n' s'pose you en young missis 'u'd be gwine on yo' dribe ter-day, but bein' ez it 's my pa't ter take you ef you does, I 'lowed I 'd repo't fer dooty, en let you say whuther er no you wants ter go."

"I 'm glad you came, Julius," I responded. "We don't want to go driving, of course, in the rain, but I should like to consult you about another matter. I 'm thinking of taking in a piece of new ground. What do you imagine it would cost to have that neck of woods down by the swamp cleared up?"

The old man's countenance assumed an expression of unwonted seriousness, and he shook his head doubtfully.

"I dunno 'bout dat, suh. It mought cos' mo', en it mought cos' less, ez fuh ez money is consarned. I ain' denyin' you could cl'ar up dat trac' er lan' fer a hund'ed er a couple er hund'ed dollahs,—ef you wants ter cl'ar it up. But ef dat 'uz my trac' er lan', I would n' 'sturb it, no, suh, I would n'; sho's you bawn, I would n'."

"But why not?" I asked.

"It ain' fittin' fer grapes, fer noo groun' nebber is."

"I know it, but"—

"It ain' no yeathly good fer cotton, 'ca'se it 's too low."

"Perhaps so; but it will raise splendid corn."

"I dunno," rejoined Julius deprecatorily. "It 's so nigh de swamp dat de 'coons 'll eat up all de cawn."

"I think I 'll risk it," I answered.

"Well, suh," said Julius, "I wushes you much joy er yo' job. Ef you has bad luck er sickness er trouble er any kin', doan blame *me*. You can't say ole Julius did n' wa'n you."

"Warn him of what, Uncle Julius?" asked my wife.

"Er de bad luck w'at follers folks w'at 'sturbs dat trac' er lan'. Dey is snakes en sco'pions in dem woods. En ef you manages ter 'scape de p'isen animals, you is des boun' ter hab a ha'nt ter settle wid,—ef you doan hab two."

"Whose haunt?" my wife demanded, with growing interest.

"De gray wolf's ha'nt, some folks calls it,—but I knows better."

"Tell us about it, Uncle Julius," said my wife. "A story will be a godsend to-day."

It was not difficult to induce the old man to tell a story, if he were in a reminiscent mood. Of tales of the old slavery days he seemed indeed to possess an exhaustless store,—some weirdly grotesque, some broadly humorous; some bearing the stamp of truth, faint, perhaps, but still discernible; others palpable inventions, whether his own or not we never knew, though his fancy doubtless embellished them. But even the wildest was not without an element of pathos,—the tragedy, it might be, of the story itself; the shadow, never absent, of slavery and of ignorance; the sadness, always, of life as seen by the fading light of an old man's memory.

"Way back yander befo' de wah," began Julius, "ole Mars Dugal' McAdoo useter own a nigger name' Dan. Dan wuz big en strong en hearty en peaceable en good-nachu'd most er de time, but dange'ous ter aggervate. He alluz done his task, en nebber had no trouble wid de w'ite folks, but woe be unter de nigger w'at 'lowed he c'd fool wid Dan, fer he wuz mos' sho' ter git a good lammin'. Soon ez eve'ybody foun' Dan out, dey didn' many un 'em 'temp' ter 'sturb 'im. De one dat did would 'a' wush' he had n', ef he could 'a' libbed long ernuff ter do any wushin'.

"It all happen' dis erway. Dey wuz a cunjuh man w'at libbed ober t' other side er de Lumbe'ton Road. He had be'n de only cunjuh doctor in de naberhood fer lo! dese many yeahs, 'tel ole Aun' Peggy sot up in de bizness down by de Wim'l'ton Road. Dis cunjuh man had a son w'at libbed wid 'im, en it wuz dis yer son w'at got mix' up wid Dan,—en all 'bout a 'oman.

"Dey wuz a gal on de plantation name' Mahaly. She wuz a monst'us lackly gal,—tall en soopl', wid big eyes, en a small foot, en a lively tongue, en w'en Dan tuk ter gwine wid 'er eve'ybody 'lowed dey wuz well match', en none er de yuther nigger men on de plantation das' ter go nigh her, fer dey wuz all feared er Dan.

"Now, it happen' dat dis yer cunjuh man's son wuz gwine 'long de road one day, w'en who sh'd come pas' but Mahaly. En de minute dis man sot eyes on Mahaly, he 'lowed he wuz gwine ter hab her fer hisse'f. He come up side er her en 'mence' ter talk ter her; but she did n' paid no 'tention ter 'im, fer she wuz studyin' 'bout Dan, en she did n' lack dis nigger's looks nohow. So w'en she got ter whar she wuz gwine, dis yer man wa'n't no fu'ther 'long dan he wuz w'en he sta'ted.

"Co'se, atter he had made up his min' fer ter git Mahaly, he 'mence' ter 'quire 'roun', en soon foun' out all 'bout Dan, en w'at a dange'ous nigger he wuz. But dis man 'lowed his daddy wuz a cunjuh man, en so he 'd come out all right in de een'; en he kep' right on atter Mahaly. Meanw'iles Dan's marster had said dey could git married ef dey wanter, en so Dan en Mahaly had tuk up wid one ernudder, en wuz libbin' in a cabin by deyse'ves, en wuz des wrop' up in one ernudder.

"But dis yer cunjuh man's son did n' 'pear ter min' Dan's takin' up wid Mahaly, en he kep' on hangin' 'roun' des de same, 'tel fin'lly one day Mahaly sez ter Dan, sez she:—

" 'I wush you 'd do sump'n ter stop dat free nigger man fum follerin' me 'roun'. I doan lack him nohow, en I ain' got no time fer ter was'e wid no man but you.'

"Co'se Dan got mad w'en he heared 'bout dis man pest'rin' Mahaly, en de nex' night, w'en he seed dis nigger comin' 'long de road, he up en ax' 'im w'at he mean by hangin' 'roun' his 'oman. De man did n' 'spon' ter suit Dan, en one wo'd led ter ernudder, 'tel bimeby dis cunjuh man's son pull' out a knife en sta'ted ter stick it in Dan; but befo' he could git it drawed good, Dan haul' off en hit 'im in de head so ha'd dat he nebber got up. Dan 'lowed he 'd come to atter a w'ile en go 'long 'bout his bizness, so he went off en lef' 'im layin' dere on de groun'.

"De nex' mawnin' de man wuz foun' dead. Dey wuz a great 'miration made 'bout it, but Dan did n' say nuffin, en none er de yuther niggers had n' seed de fight, so dey wa'n't no way ter tell who done de killin'. En bein' ez it wuz a free nigger, en dey wa'n't no w'ite folks 'speshly int'rusted, dey wa'n't nuffin done 'bout it, en de cunjuh man come en tuk his son en kyared 'im 'way en buried 'im.

"Now, Dan hadn' meant ter kill dis nigger, en w'iles he knowed de man hadn' got no mo' d'n he desarved, Dan 'mence' ter worry mo' er less. Fer he knowed dis man's daddy would wuk his roots en prob'ly fin' out who had killt 'is son, en make all de trouble fer 'im he could. En Dan kep' on studyin' 'bout dis 'tel he got so he didn' ha'dly das' ter eat er drink fer fear dis cunjuh man had p'isen' de vittles er de water. Fin'lly he 'lowed he'd go ter see Aun' Peggy, de noo cunjuh 'oman w'at had moved down by de Wim'l'ton Road, en ax her fer ter do sump'n ter pertec' 'im fum dis cunjuh man. So he tuk a peck er 'taters en went down ter her cabin one night.

"Aun' Peggy heared his tale, en den sez she:—

" 'Dat cunjuh man is mo' d'n twice't ez ole ez I is, en he kin make monst'us powe'ful goopher. W'at you needs is a life-cha'm, en I'll make you one ter-morrer; it's de on'y thing w'at'll do you any good. You leabe me a couple er ha'rs fum yo' head, en fetch me a pig ter-morrer night fer ter roas', en w'en you come I'll hab de cha'm all ready fer you.'

"So Dan went down ter Aun' Peggy de nex' night,—wid a young shote,—en Aun' Peggy gun 'im de cha'm. She had tuk de ha'rs Dan had lef' wid 'er, en a piece er red flannin, en some roots en yarbs, en had put 'em in a little bag made out'n 'coon-skin.

" 'You take dis cha'm,' sez she, 'en put it in a bottle er a tin box, en bury it deep unner de root er a live-oak tree, en ez long ez it stays dere safe en soun', dey ain' no p'isen kin p'isen you, dey ain' no rattlesnake kin bite you, dey ain' no sco'pion kin sting you. Dis yere cunjuh man mought do one thing er 'nudder ter you, but he can't kill you. So you neenter be at all skeered, but go 'long 'bout yo' bizness en doan bother yo' min'.'

"So Dan went down by de ribber, en 'way up on de bank he buried de cha'm deep unner de root er a live-oak tree, en kivered it up en stomp' de dirt down en scattered leaves ober de spot, en den went home wid his min' easy.

"Sho' 'nuff, dis yer cunjuh man wukked his roots, des ez Dan had 'spected he would, en soon l'arn' who killt his son. En co'se he made up his min' fer ter git eben wid Dan. So he sont a rattlesnake fer ter sting 'im, but de rattlesnake say de nigger's heel wuz so ha'd he could n' git his sting in. Den he sont his jay-bird fer ter put p'isen in Dan's vittles, but de p'isen did n' wuk. Den de cunjuh man 'low' he 'd double Dan all up wid de rheumatiz, so he could n' git 'is han' ter his mouf ter eat, en would hafter sta've ter def; but Dan went ter Aun' Peggy, en she gun 'im a' 'intment ter kyo de rheumatiz. Den de cunjuh man 'lowed he 'd bu'n Dan up wid a fever, but Aun' Peggy tol' 'im how ter make some yarb tea fer dat. Nuffin dis man tried would kill Dan, so fin'lly de cunjuh man 'lowed Dan mus' hab a life-cha'm.

"Now, dis yer jay-bird de cunjuh man had wuz a monst'us sma't creeter,—fac', de niggers 'lowed he wuz de ole Debbil hisse'f, des settin' roun' waitin' ter kyar dis ole man erway w'en he 'd retch' de een' er his rope. De cunjuh man sont dis jay-bird fer ter watch Dan en fin' out whar he kep' his cha'm. De jay-bird hung roun' Dan fer a week er so, en one day he seed Dan go down by de ribber en look at a live-oak tree; en den de jay-bird went back ter his marster, en tol' 'im he 'spec' de nigger kep' his life-cha'm under dat tree.

"De cunjuh man lafft en lafft, en he put on his bigges' pot, en fill' it wid his stronges' roots, en b'iled it en b'iled it, 'tel bimeby de win' blowed en blowed, 'tel it blowed down de live-oak tree. Den he stirred some more roots in de pot, en it rained en rained 'tel de water run down de ribber bank en wash' Dan's life-cha'm inter de ribber, en de bottle went bobbin' down de current des ez onconsarned ez ef it wa'n't takin' po' Dan's chances all 'long wid it. En den de cunjuh man lafft some mo', en 'lowed ter hisse'f dat he wuz gwine ter fix Dan now, sho' 'nuff; he wa'n't gwine ter kill 'im des yet, fer he could do sump'n ter 'im w'at would hu't wusser 'n killin'.

"So dis cunjuh man 'mence' by gwine up ter Dan's cabin eve'y night, en takin' Dan out in his sleep en ridin' 'im roun' de roads en fiel's ober de rough groun'. In de mawnin' Dan would be ez ti'ed ez ef he had n' be'n ter sleep. Dis kin' er thing kep' up fer a week er so, en Dan had des 'bout made up his min' fer ter go en see Aun' Peggy ag'in, w'en who sh'd he come across, gwine 'long de road one day, to'ds sundown, but dis yer cunjuh man. Dan felt kinder skeered at fus'; but den he 'membered 'bout his life-cha'm, w'ich he had n' be'n ter see fer a week er so, en 'lowed wuz safe en soun' unner de live-oak tree, en so he hilt up 'is head en walk' 'long, des lack he did n' keer nuffin 'bout dis man no mo' d'n any yuther nigger. W'en he got close ter de cunjuh man, dis cunjuh man sez, sezee:—

" 'Hoddy, Brer Dan? I hopes you er well?'

"W'en Dan seed de cunjuh man wuz in a good humor en did n' 'pear ter bear no malice, Dan 'lowed mebbe de cunjuh man had n' foun' out who killt his son, en so he 'termine' fer ter let on lack he did n' know nuffin, en so sezee:—

" 'Hoddy, Unk' Jube?'—dis ole cunjuh man's name wuz Jube. 'I 's p'utty well, I thank you. How is you feelin' dis mawnin'?'

" 'I 's feelin' ez well ez a' ole nigger could feel w'at had los' his only son, en his main 'pen'ence in 'is ole age.

" 'But den my son wuz a bad boy,' sezee, 'en I could n' 'spec' nuffin e'se. I tried ter l'arn him de arrer er his ways en make him go ter chu'ch en pra'r-meetin'; but it wa'n't no use. I dunno who killt 'im, en I doan wanter know, fer I 'd be mos' sho' ter fin' out dat my boy had sta'ted de fuss. Ef I 'd 'a' had a son lack you, Brer Dan, I 'd 'a' be'n a proud nigger; oh, yas, I would, sho 's you bawn. But you ain' lookin' ez well ez you oughter, Brer Dan. Dey 's sump'n de matter wid you, en w'at 's mo', I 'spec' you dunno w'at it is.'

"Now, dis yer kin' er talk nach'ly th'owed Dan off'n his gya'd, en fus' thing he knowed he wuz talkin' ter dis ole cunjuh man des lack he wuz one er his bes' frien's. He tol' 'im all 'bout not feelin' well in de mawnin', en ax' 'im ef he could tell w'at wuz de matter wid 'im.

" 'Yas,' sez de cunjuh man. 'Dey is a witch be'n ridin' you right 'long. I kin see de marks er de bridle on yo' mouf. En I 'll des bet yo' back is raw whar she 's be'n beatin' you.'

" 'Yas,' 'spon' Dan, 'so, it is.' He had n' notice it befo', but now he felt des lack de hide had be'n tuk off'n 'im.

" 'En yo' thighs is des raw whar de spurrers has be'n driv' in you,' sez de cunjuh man. 'You can't see de raw spots, but you kin feel em.'

" 'Oh, yas,' 'lows Dan, 'dey does hu't pow'ful bad.'

" 'En w'at's mo',' sez de cunjuh man, comin' up close ter Dan en whusp'in' in his yeah, 'I knows who it is be'n ridin' you.'

" 'Who is it?' ax' Dan. 'Tell me who it is.'

" 'It 's a' ole nigger 'oman down by Rockfish Crick. She had a pet rabbit, en you cotch' 'im one day, en she 's been squarin' up wid you eber sence. But you better stop her, er e'se you 'll be rid ter def in a mont' er so.'

" 'No,' sez Dan, 'she can't kill me, sho'.'

" 'I dunno how dat is,' said de cunjuh man, 'but she kin make yo' life mighty mis'able. Ef I wuz in yo' place, I 'd stop her right off.'

" 'But how is I gwine ter stop her?' ax' Dan. 'I dunno nuffin 'bout stoppin' witches.'

" 'Look a heah, Dan,' sez de yuther; 'you is a good young man. I lacks you monst'us well. Fac', I feels lack some er dese days I mought buy you fum yo' marster, ef I could eber make money ernuff at my bizness dese hard times, en 'dop' you fer my son. I lacks you so well dat I 'm gwine ter he'p you git rid er dis yer witch fer good en all; fer des ez long ez she libs, you is sho' ter hab trouble, en trouble, en mo' trouble.'

" 'You is de bes' frien' I got, Unk' Jube,' sez Dan, 'en I 'll 'member yo' kin'ness ter my dyin' day. Tell me how I kin git rid er dis yer ole witch w'at 's be'n ridin' me so ha'd.'

" 'In de fus' place,' sez de cunjuh man, 'dis ole witch nebber comes in her own shape, but eve'y night, at ten o'clock, she tu'ns herse'f inter a black cat, en runs down ter yo' cabin en bridles you, en mounts you, en dribes you out th'oo de chimbly, en rides you ober de roughes' places she kin fin'. All you got ter do is ter set fer her in de bushes 'side er yo' cabin, en hit her in de head wid a rock er a lighterd-knot w'en she goes pas'.'

" 'But,' sez Dan, 'how kin I see her in de da'k? En s'posen I hits at her en misses her? Er s'posen I des woun's her, en she gits erway,—w'at she gwine do ter me den?'

" 'I is done studied 'bout all dem things,' sez de cunjuh man, 'en it 'pears ter me de bes' plan fer you ter foller is ter lemme tu'n you ter some creetur w'at kin see in de da'k, en w'at kin run des ez fas' ez a cat, en w'at kin bite, en bite fer ter kill; en den you won't hafter hab no trouble atter de job is done. I dunno whuther you'd lack dat er no, but dat is de sho'es' way.'

" 'I doan keer,' 'spon' Dan. 'I 'd des ez lief be anything fer a' hour er so, ef I kin kill dat ole witch. You kin do des w'at you er mineter.'

" 'All right, den,' sez de cunjuh man, 'you come down ter my cabin at half-past nine o'clock ter-night, en I 'll fix you up.'

"Now, dis cunjuh man, w'en he had got th'oo talkin' wid Dan, kep' on down de road 'long de side er de plantation, 'tel he met Mahaly comin' home fum wuk des atter sundown.

" 'Hoddy do, ma'm,' sezee; 'is yo' name Sis' Mahaly, w'at b'longs ter Mars Dugal' McAdoo?'

" 'Yas,' 'spon' Mahaly, 'dat's my name, en I b'longs ter Mars Dugal'.'

" 'Well,' sezee, 'yo' husban' Dan wuz down by my cabin dis ebenin', en he got bit by a spider er sump'n, en his foot is swoll' up so he can't walk. En he ax' me fer ter fin' you en fetch you down dere ter he'p 'im home.'

"Co'se Mahaly wanter see w'at had happen' ter Dan, en so she sta'ted down de road wid de cunjuh man. Ez soon ez he got her inter his cabin, he shet de do', en sprinkle' some goopher mixtry on her, en tu'nt her ter a black cat. Den he tuk 'n put her in a bairl, en put a bo'd on de bairl, en a rock on de bo'd, en lef' her dere 'tel he got good en ready fer ter use her.

"'Long 'bout half-pas' nine o'clock Dan come down ter de cunjuh man's cabin. It wuz a wa'm night, en de do' wuz stan'in' open. De cunjuh man 'vited Dan ter come in, en pass' de time er day wid 'im. Ez soon ez Dan 'mence' talkin', he heared a cat miauin' en scratchin' en gwine on at a tarrable rate.

" 'W'at 's all dat fuss 'bout?' ax' Dan.

" 'Oh, dat ain' nuffin but my ole gray tomcat,' sez de cunjuh man. 'I has ter shet 'im up sometimes fer ter keep 'im in nights, en co'se he doan lack it.

" 'Now,' 'lows de cunjuh man, 'lemme tell you des w'at you is got ter do. W'en you ketches dis witch, you mus' take her right by de th'oat en bite her right th'oo de neck. Be sho' yo' teef goes th'oo at de fus' bite, en den you won't nebber be bothe'd no mo' by dat witch. En w'en you git done, come back heah en I 'll tu'n you ter yo'se'f ag'in, so you kin go home en git yo' night's res'.'

"Den de cunjuh man gun Dan sump'n nice en sweet ter drink out'n a new go'd, en in 'bout a minute Dan foun' hisse'f tu'nt ter a gray wolf; en soon ez he felt all fo' er his noo feet on de groun', he sta'ted off fas' ez he could fer his own cabin, so he could be sho' en be dere time ernuff ter ketch de witch, en put a' een' ter her kyarin's-on.

"Ez soon ez Dan wuz gone good, de cunjuh man tuk de rock off'n de bo'd, en de bo'd off'n de bairl, en out le'p' Mahaly en sta'ted fer ter go home, des lack a cat er a 'oman er anybody e'se would w'at wuz in trouble; en it wa'n't many minutes befo' she wuz gwine up de path ter her own do'.

"Meanw'iles, w'en Dan had retch' de cabin, he had hid hisse'f in a bunch er jimson weeds in de ya'd. He had n' wait' long befo' he seed a black cat run up de path to'ds de do'. Des ez soon ez she got close ter 'im, he le'p' out en ketch' her by de th'oat, en got a grip on her, des lack de cunjuh man had tol' 'im ter do. En lo en behol'! no sooner had de blood 'mence' ter flow dan de black cat tu'nt back ter Mahaly, en Dan seed dat he had killt his own wife. En w'iles her bref wuz gwine she call' out:

" '*O* Dan! *O* my husban'! come en he'p me! come en sabe me fum dis wolf w'at 's killin' me!'

"W'en po' Dan sta'ted to'ds her, ez any man nach'ly would, it des made her holler wuss en wuss; fer she did n' knowed dis yer wolf wuz her Dan. En Dan des had ter hide in de weeds, en grit his teef en hol' hisse'f in, 'tel she passed out'n her mis'ry, callin' fer Dan ter de las', en wond'rin' w'y he did n' come en he'p her. En Dan 'lowed ter hisse'f he 'd ruther 'a' be'n killt a dozen times 'n ter 'a' done w'at he had ter Mahaly.

"Dan wuz mighty nigh 'stracted, but w'en Mahaly wuz dead en he got his min' straighten' out a little, it did n' take 'im mo' d'n a minute er so fer ter see th'oo all de cunjuh man's lies, en how de cunjuh man had fooled 'im en made 'im kill Mahaly, fer ter git eben wid 'im fer killin' er his son. He kep' gittin' madder en madder, en Mahaly had n' much mo' d'n drawed her' las bref befo' he sta'ted back ter de cunjuh man's cabin ha'd ez he could run.

"W'en he got dere, de do' wuz stan'in' open; a lighterd-knot wuz flick'rin' on de h'a'th, en de ole cunjuh man wuz settin' dere noddin' in de corner. Dan le'p' in de do' en jump' fer dis man's th'oat, en got de same grip on 'im w'at de cunjuh man had tol' 'im 'bout half a' hour befo'. It wuz ha'd wuk dis time, fer de ole man's neck wuz monst'us tough en stringy, but Dan hilt on long ernuff ter be sho' his job wuz done right. En eben den he did n' hol' on long ernuff; fer w'en he tu'nt de cunjuh man loose en he fell ober on de flo', de cunjuh man rollt his eyes at Dan, en sezee:—

" 'I 's eben wid you, Brer Dan, en you er eben wid me; you killt my son en I killt yo' 'oman. En ez I doan want no mo' d'n w'at 's fair 'bout dis thing, ef you 'll retch up wid yo' paw en take down dat go'd hangin' on dat peg ober de chimbly, en take a sip er dat mixtry, it 'll tu'n you back ter a nigger ag'in, en I kin die mo' sad'sfied 'n ef I lef' you lack you is.'

"Dan nebber 'lowed fer a minute dat a man would lie wid his las' bref, en co'se he seed de sense er gittin' tu'nt back befo' de cunjuh man died; so he clumb on a chair en retch' fer de go'd, en tuk a sip er de mixtry. En ez soon ez he 'd done dat de cunjuh man lafft his las' laf, en gapsed out wid 'is las' gaps:—

" 'Uh huh! I reckon I 's square wid you now fer killin' me, too; fer dat goopher on you is done fix' en sot now fer good, en all de cunj'in' in de worl' won't nebber take it off.

'Wolf you is en wolf you stays,
All de rest er yo' bawn days.'

"Co'se Brer Dan could n' do nuffin. He knowed it wa'n't no use, but he clumb up on de chimbly en got down de go'ds en bottles en yuther cunjuh fixin's, en tried 'em all on hisse'f, but dey did n' do no good. Den he run down ter ole Aun' Peggy, but she did n' know de wolf langwidge, en could n't 'a' tuk off dis yuther goopher nohow, eben ef she 'd 'a' unnerstood w'at Dan wuz sayin'. So po' Dan wuz bleedgd ter be a wolf all de rest er his bawn days.

"Dey foun' Mahaly down by her own cabin nex' mawnin', en eve'ybody made a great 'miration 'bout how she 'd be'n killt. De niggers 'lowed a wolf had bit her. De w'ite folks say no, dey ain' be'n no wolves 'roun' dere fer ten yeahs er mo'; en dey did n' know w'at ter make out'n it. En w'en dey could n' fin' Dan nowhar, dey 'lowed he 'd quo'lled wid Mahaly en killt her, en run erway; en dey did n' know w'at ter make er dat, fer Dan en Mahaly wuz de mos' lovin' couple on de plantation. Dey put de dawgs on Dan's scent, en track' 'im down ter ole Unk' Jube's cabin, en foun' de ole man dead, en dey did n' know w'at ter make er dat; en den Dan's scent gun out, en dey did n' know w'at ter make er dat. Mars Dugal' tuk on a heap 'bout losin' two er his bes' han's in one day, en ole missis 'lowed it wuz a jedgment on 'im fer sump'n he'd done. But dat fall de craps wuz monst'us big, so Mars Dugal' say de Lawd had temper' de win' ter de sho'n ram, en make up ter 'im fer w'at he had los'.

"Dey buried Mahaly down in dat piece er low groun' you er talkin' 'bout cl'arin' up. Ez fer po' Dan, he did n' hab nowhar e'se ter go, so he des stayed 'roun' Mahaly's grabe, w'en he wa'n't out in de yuther woods gittin' sump'n ter eat. En sometimes, w'en night would come, de niggers useter heah him howlin' en howlin' down dere, des fittin' ter break his hea't. En den some mo' un 'em said dey seed Mahaly's ha'nt dere 'bun'ance er times, colloguin' wid dis gray wolf. En eben now, fifty yeahs sence, long atter ole Dan has died en dried up in de woods, his ha'nt en Mahaly's hangs 'roun' dat piece er low groun', en eve'body w'at goes 'bout dere has some bad luck er 'nuther; fer ha'nts doan lack ter be 'sturb' on dey own stompin'-groun'."

The air had darkened while the old man related this harrowing tale. The rising wind whistled around the eaves, slammed the loose window-shutters, and, still increasing, drove the rain in fiercer gusts into the piazza. As Julius finished his story and we rose to seek shelter within doors, the blast caught the angle of some chimney or gable in the rear of the house, and bore to our ears a long, wailing note, an epitome, as it were, of remorse and hopelessness.

"Dat 's des lack po' ole Dan useter howl," observed Julius, as he reached for his umbrella, "en w'at I be'n tellin' you is de reason I doan lack ter see dat neck er woods cl'ared up. Co'se it b'longs ter you, en a man kin do ez he choose' wid 'is own. But ef you gits rheumatiz er fever en agur, er ef you er snake-bit er p'isen' wid some yarb er 'nuther, er ef a tree falls on you, er a ha'nt runs you en makes you git 'stracted in yo' min', lack some folks I knows w'at went foolin' 'roun' dat piece er lan', you can't say I neber wa'ned you, suh, en tol' you w'at you mought look fer en be sho' ter fin'."

When I cleared up the land in question, which was not until the following year, I recalled the story Julius had told us, and looked in vain for a sunken grave or perhaps a few weather-bleached bones of some denizen of the forest. I cannot say, of course, that some one had not been buried there; but if so, the hand of time had long since removed any evidence of the fact. If some lone wolf, the last of his pack, had once made his den there, his bones had long since crumbled into dust and gone to fertilize the rank vegetation that formed the undergrowth of this wild spot. I did find, however, a bee-tree in the woods, with an ample cavity in its trunk, and an opening through which convenient access could be had to the stores of honey within. I have reason to believe that ever since I had bought the place, and for many years before, Julius had been getting honey from this tree. The gray wolf's haunt had doubtless proved useful in keeping off too inquisitive people, who might have interfered with his monopoly.

Hot-Foot Hannibal

"I hate you and despise you! I wish never to see you or speak to you again!"

"Very well; I will take care that henceforth you have no opportunity to do either."

These words—the first in the passionately vibrant tones of my sister-in-law, and the latter in the deeper and more restrained accents of an angry man—startled me from my nap. I had been dozing in my hammock on the front piazza, behind the honeysuckle vine. I had been faintly aware of a buzz of conversation in the parlor, but had not at all awakened to its import until these sentences fell, or, I might rather say, were hurled upon my ear. I presume the young people had either not seen me lying there,—the Venetian blinds opening from the parlor windows upon the piazza were partly closed on account of the heat,—or else in their excitement they had forgotten my proximity.

I felt somewhat concerned. The young man, I had remarked, was proud, firm, jealous of the point of honor, and, from my observation of him, quite likely to resent to the bitter end what he deemed a slight or an injustice. The girl, I knew, was quite as high-spirited as young Murchison. I feared she was not so just, and hoped she would prove more yielding. I knew that her affections were strong and enduring, but that her temperament was capricious, and her sunniest moods easily overcast by some small cloud of jealousy or pique. I had never imagined, however, that she was capable of such intensity as was revealed by these few words of hers. As I say, I felt concerned. I had learned to like Malcolm Murchison, and had heartily consented to his marriage with my ward; for it was in that capacity that I had stood for a year or two to my wife's younger sister, Mabel. The match thus rudely broken off had promised to be another link binding me to the kindly Southern people among whom I had not long before taken up my residence.

Young Murchison came out of the door, cleared the piazza in two strides without seeming aware of my presence, and went off down the lane at a furious pace. A few moments later Mabel began playing the piano loudly, with a touch that indicated anger and pride and independence and a dash of exultation, as though she were really glad that she had driven away forever the young man whom the day before she had loved with all the ardor of a first passion.

I hoped that time might heal the breach and bring the two young people together again. I told my wife what I had overheard. In return she gave me Mabel's version of the affair.

"I do not see how it can ever be settled," my wife said. "It is something more than a mere lovers' quarrel. It began, it is true, because she found fault with him for going to church with that hateful Branson girl. But before it ended there were things said that no woman of any spirit could stand. I am afraid it is all over between them."

I was sorry to hear this. In spite of the very firm attitude taken by my wife and her sister, I still hoped that the quarrel would be made up within a day or two. Nevertheless, when a week had passed with no word from young Murchison, and with no sign of relenting on Mabel's part, I began to think myself mistaken.

One pleasant afternoon, about ten days after the rupture, old Julius drove the rockaway up to the piazza, and my wife, Mabel, and I took our seats for a drive to a neighbor's vineyard, over on the Lumberton plank-road.

"Which way shall we go," I asked,—"the short road or the long one?"

"I guess we had better take the short road," answered my wife. "We will get there sooner."

"It 's a mighty fine dribe roun' by de big road, Mis' Annie," observed Julius, "en it doan take much longer to git dere."

"No," said my wife, "I think we will go by the short road. There is a bay-tree in blossom near the mineral spring, and I wish to get some of the flowers."

"I 'spec's you 'd fin' some bay-trees 'long de big road, ma'm," suggested Julius.

"But I know about the flowers on the short road, and they are the ones I want."

We drove down the lane to the highway, and soon struck

into the short road leading past the mineral spring. Our route lay partly through a swamp, and on each side the dark, umbrageous foliage, unbroken by any clearing, lent to the road solemnity, and to the air a refreshing coolness. About half a mile from the house, and about half-way to the mineral spring, we stopped at the tree of which my wife had spoken, and reaching up to the low-hanging boughs, I gathered a dozen of the fragrant white flowers. When I resumed my seat in the rockaway, Julius started the mare. She went on for a few rods, until we had reached the edge of a branch crossing the road, when she stopped short.

"Why did you stop, Julius?" I asked.

"I did n', suh," he replied. "'T wuz de mare stop'. G' 'long dere, Lucy! W'at you mean by dis foolis'ness?"

Julius jerked the reins and applied the whip lightly, but the mare did not stir.

"Perhaps you had better get down and lead her," I suggested. "If you get her started, you can cross on the log and keep your feet dry."

Julius alighted, took hold of the bridle, and vainly essayed to make the mare move. She planted her feet with even more evident obstinacy.

"I don't know what to make of this," I said. "I have never known her to balk before. Have you, Julius?"

"No, suh," replied the old man, "I neber has. It 's a cu'ous thing ter me, suh."

"What 's the best way to make her go?"

"I 'spec's, suh, dat ef I 'd tu'n her 'roun', she 'd go de udder way."

"But we want her to go this way."

"Well, suh, I 'low ef we des set heah fo' er fibe minutes, she 'll sta't up by herse'f."

"All right," I rejoined; "it is cooler here than any place I have struck to-day. We 'll let her stand for a while, and see what she does."

We had sat in silence for a few minutes, when Julius suddenly ejaculated, "Uh huh! I knows w'y dis mare doan go. It des flash' 'cross my recommemb'ance."

"Why is it, Julius?" I inquired.

"'Ca'se she sees Chloe."

"Where is Chloe?" I demanded.

"Chloe 's done be'n dead dese fo'ty years er mo'," the old man returned. "Her ha'nt is settin' ober yander on de udder side er de branch, unner dat willer-tree, dis blessed minute."

"Why, Julius!" said my wife, "do you see the haunt?"

"No 'm," he answered, shaking his head, "I doan see 'er, but de mare sees 'er."

"How do you know?" I inquired.

"Well, suh, dis yer is a gray hoss, en dis yer is a Friday; en a gray hoss kin alluz see a ha'nt w'at walks on Friday."

"Who was Chloe?" said Mabel.

"And why does Chloe's haunt walk?" asked my wife.

"It 's all in de tale, ma'm," Julius replied, with a deep sigh. "It 's all in de tale."

"Tell us the tale," I said. "Perhaps, by the time you get through, the haunt will go away and the mare will cross."

I was willing to humor the old man's fancy. He had not told us a story for some time; and the dark and solemn swamp around us; the amber-colored stream flowing silently and sluggishly at our feet, like the waters of Lethe; the heavy, aromatic scent of the bays, faintly suggestive of funeral wreaths,—all made the place an ideal one for a ghost story.

"Chloe," Julius began in a subdued tone, "use' ter b'long ter ole Mars' Dugal' McAdoo,—my ole marster. She wuz a lackly gal en a smart gal, en ole mis' tuk her up ter de big house, en l'arnt her ter wait on de w'ite folks, 'tel bimeby she come ter be mis's own maid, en 'peared ter 'low she run de house herse'f, ter heah her talk erbout it. I wuz a young boy den, en use' ter wuk 'bout de stables, so I knowed eve'ythin' dat wuz gwine on 'roun' de plantation.

"Well, one time Mars' Dugal' wanted a house boy, en sont down ter de qua'ters fer ter hab Jeff en Hannibal come up ter de big house nex' mawnin'. Ole marster en ole mis' look' de two boys ober, en 'sco'sed wid deyse'ves fer a little w'ile, en den Mars' Dugal' sez, sezee:—

" 'We lacks Hannibal de bes', en we gwine ter keep him. Heah, Hannibal, you 'll wuk at de house fum now on. En ef you er a good nigger en min's yo' bizness, I 'll gib you Chloe fer a wife nex' spring. You other nigger, you Jeff, you kin go back ter de qua'ters. We ain' gwine ter need you.'

"Now Chloe had be'n stan'in' dere behin' ole mis' dyoin' all er dis yer talk, en Chloe made up her min' fum de ve'y fus' minute she sot eyes on dem two dat she did n' lack dat nigger Hannibal, en wa'n't neber gwine keer fer 'im, en she wuz des ez sho' dat she lack' Jeff, en wuz gwine ter set sto' by 'im, whuther Mars' Dugal' tuk 'im in de big house er no; en so co'se Chloe wuz monst'us sorry w'en ole Mars' Dugal' tuk Hannibal en sont Jeff back. So she slip' roun' de house en waylaid Jeff on de way back ter de qua'ters, en tol' 'im not ter be down-hea'ted, fer she wuz gwine ter see ef she could n' fin' some way er 'nuther ter git rid er dat nigger Hannibal, en git Jeff up ter de house in his place.

"De noo house boy kotch' on monst'us fas', en it wa'n't no time ha'dly befo' Mars' Dugal' en ole mis' bofe 'mence' ter 'low Hannibal wuz de bes' house boy dey eber had. He wuz peart en soopl', quick ez lightnin', en sha'p ez a razor. But Chloe did n' lack his ways. He wuz so sho' he wuz gwine ter git 'er in de spring, dat he did n' 'pear ter 'low he had ter do any co'tin', en w'en he 'd run 'cross Chloe 'bout de house, he 'd swell roun' 'er in a biggity way en say:—

" 'Come heah en kiss me, honey. You gwine ter be mine in de spring. You doan 'pear ter be ez fon' er me ez you oughter be.'

"Chloe did n' keer nuffin fer Hannibal, en had n' keered nuffin fer 'im, en she sot des ez much sto' by Jeff ez she did de day she fus' laid eyes on 'im. En de mo' fermilyus dis yer Hannibal got, de mo' Chloe let her min' run on Jeff, en one ebenin' she went down ter de qua'ters en watch', 'tel she got a chance fer ter talk wid 'im by hisse'f. En she tol' Jeff fer ter go down en see ole Aun' Peggy, de cunjuh 'oman down by de Wim'l'ton Road, en ax her ter gib 'im sump'n ter he'p git Hannibal out'n de big house, so de w'ite folks 'u'd sen' fer Jeff ag'in. En bein' ez Jeff did n' hab nuffin ter gib Aun' Peggy, Chloe gun 'im a silber dollah en a silk han'kercher fer ter pay her wid, fer Aun' Peggy neber lack ter wuk fer nobody fer nuffin.

"So Jeff slip' off down ter Aun' Peggy's one night, en gun 'er de present he brung, en tol' 'er all 'bout 'im en Chloe en Hannibal, en ax' 'er ter he'p 'im out. Aun' Peggy tol' 'im she 'd wuk 'er roots, en fer 'im ter come back de nex' night, en she 'd tell 'im w'at she c'd do fer 'im.

"So de nex' night Jeff went back, en Aun' Peggy gun 'im a baby doll, wid a body made out'n a piece er co'n-stalk, en wid splinters fer a'ms en laigs, en a head made out'n elderberry peth, en two little red peppers fer feet.

" 'Dis yer baby doll,' sez she, 'is Hannibal. Dis yer peth head is Hannibal's head, en dese yer pepper feet is Hannibal's feet. You take dis en hide it unner de house, on de sill unner de do', whar Hannibal 'll hafter walk ober it eve'y day. En ez long ez Hannibal comes anywhar nigh dis baby doll, he 'll be des lack it is,—light-headed en hot-footed; en ef dem two things doan git 'im inter trouble mighty soon, den I 'm no cunjuh 'oman. But w'en you git Hannibal out'n de house, en git all th'oo wid dis baby doll, you mus' fetch it back ter me, fer it 's monst'us powerful goopher, en is liable ter make mo' trouble ef you leabe it layin' roun'.'

"Well, Jeff tuk de baby doll, en slip' up ter de big house, en whistle' ter Chloe, en w'en she come out he tol' 'er w'at ole Aun' Peggy had said. En Chloe showed 'im how ter git unner de house, en w'en he had put de cunjuh doll on de sill, he went 'long back ter de qua'ters—en des waited.

"Nex' day, sho' 'nuff, de goopher 'mence' ter wuk. Hannibal sta'ted in de house soon in de mawnin' wid a armful er wood ter make a fire, en he had n' mo' d'n got 'cross de do'-sill befo' his feet begun ter bu'n so dat he drap' de armful er wood on de flo' en woke ole mis' up a' hour sooner 'n yushal, en co'se ole mis' did n' lack dat, en spoke sha'p erbout it.

"W'en dinner-time come, en Hannibal wuz help'n' de cook kyar de dinner f'm de kitchen inter de big house, en wuz gittin' close ter de do' whar he had ter go in, his feet sta'ted ter bu'n en his head begun ter swim, en he let de big dish er chicken en dumplin's fall right down in de dirt, in de middle er de ya'd, en de w'ite folks had ter make dey dinner dat day off'n col' ham en sweet'n' 'taters.

"De nex' mawnin' he overslep' hisse'f, en got inter mo' trouble. Atter breakfus', Mars' Dugal' sont 'im ober ter Mars' Marrabo Utley's fer ter borry a monkey wrench. He oughter be'n back in ha'f a' hour, but he come pokin' home 'bout dinner-time wid a screw-driver stidder a monkey wrench. Mars' Dugal' sont ernudder nigger back wid de screw-driver, en Hannibal did n' git no dinner. 'Long in de atternoon, ole mis' sot Hannibal ter weedin' de flowers in de front gya'den, en Hannibal dug up all de bulbs ole mis' had sont erway fer, en paid a lot er money fer, en tuk 'em down ter de hawg-pen by de ba'nya'd, en fed 'em ter de hawgs. W'en ole mis' come out in de cool er de ebenin', en seed w'at Hannibal had done, she wuz mos' crazy, en she wrote a note en sont Hannibal down ter de oberseah wid it.

"But w'at Hannibal got fum de oberseah did n' 'pear ter do no good. Eve'y now en den 'is feet 'd 'mence ter torment 'im, en 'is min' 'u'd git all mix' up, en his conduc' kep' gittin' wusser en wusser, 'tel fin'lly de w'ite folks could n' stan' it no longer, en Mars' Dugal' tuk Hannibal back down ter de qua'ters.

" 'Mr. Smif,' sez Mars' Dugal' ter de oberseah, 'dis yer nigger has done got so triflin' yer lately dat we can't keep 'im at de house no mo', en I 's fotch' 'im ter you ter be straighten' up. You 's had 'casion ter deal wid 'im once, so he knows w'at ter expec'. You des take 'im in han', en lemme know how he tu'ns out. En w'en de han's comes in fum de fiel' dis ebenin' you kin sen' dat yaller nigger Jeff up ter de house. I 'll try 'im, en see ef he 's any better 'n Hannibal.'

"So Jeff went up ter de big house, en pleas' Mars' Dugal' en ole mis' en de res' er de fambly so well dat dey all got ter lackin' 'im fus'rate; en dey 'd 'a' fergot all 'bout Hannibal, ef it had n' be'n fer de bad repo'ts w'at come up fum de qua'ters 'bout 'im fer a mont' er so. Fac' is, dat Chloe en Jeff wuz so int'rusted in one ernudder sence Jeff be'n up ter de house, dat dey fergot all 'bout takin' de baby doll back ter Aun' Peggy, en it kep' wukkin' fer a w'ile, en makin' Hannibal's feet bu'n mo' er less, 'tel all de folks on de plantation got ter callin' 'im Hot-Foot Hannibal. He kep' gittin' mo' en mo' triflin', 'tel he got de name er bein' de mos' no 'countes' nigger on de plantation, en Mars' Dugal' had ter th'eaten ter sell 'im in de spring, w'en bimeby de goopher quit wukkin', en Hannibal 'mence' ter pick up some en make folks set a little mo' sto' by 'im.

"Now, dis yer Hannibal was a monst'us sma't nigger, en w'en he got rid er dem so' feet, his min' kep' runnin' on is udder troubles. Heah th'ee er fo' weeks befo' he 'd had a' easy job, waitin' on de w'ite folks, libbin' off'n de fat er de lan', en promus' de fines' gal on de plantation fer a wife in de spring, en now heah he wuz back in de co'n-fiel', wid de oberseah a-cussin' en a-r'arin' ef he didn' get a ha'd tas' done; wid nuffin but co'n bread en bacon en merlasses ter eat; en all de fiel'-han's makin' rema'ks, en pokin' fun at 'im 'ca'se he'd be'n sont back fum de big house ter de fiel'. En de mo' Hannibal studied 'bout it de mo' madder he got, 'tel he fin'lly swo' he wuz gwine ter git eben wid Jeff en Chloe, ef it wuz de las' ac'.

"So Hannibal slipped 'way fum de qua'ters one Sunday en hid in de co'n up close ter de big house, 'tel he see Chloe gwine down de road. He waylaid her, en sezee:—

" 'Hoddy, Chloe?'

" 'I ain' got no time fer ter fool wid fiel'-han's,' sez Chloe, tossin' her head; 'w'at you want wid me, Hot-Foot?'

" 'I wants ter know how you en Jeff is gittin' 'long.'

" 'I 'lows dat 's none er yo' bizness, nigger. I doan see w'at 'casion any common fiel'-han' has got ter mix in wid de 'fairs er folks w'at libs in de big house. But ef it 'll do you any good ter know, I mought say dat me en Jeff is gittin' 'long mighty well, en we gwine ter git married in de spring, en you ain' gwine ter be 'vited ter de weddin' nuther.'

" 'No, no!' sezee, 'I wouldn' 'spec' ter be 'vited ter de weddin',—a common, low-down fiel'-han' lack *I* is. But I 's glad ter heah you en Jeff is gittin' 'long so well. I didn' knowed but w'at he had 'mence' ter be a little ti'ed.'

" 'Ti'ed er me? Dat 's rediklus!' sez Chloe. 'W'y, dat nigger lubs me so I b'liebe he 'd go th'oo fire en water fer me. Dat nigger is des wrop' up in me.'

" 'Uh huh,' sez Hannibal, 'den I reckon it mus' be some udder nigger w'at meets a 'oman down by de crick in de swamp eve'y Sunday ebenin', ter say nuffin 'bout two er th'ee times a week.'

" 'Yas, hit is ernudder nigger, en you is a liah w'en you say it wuz Jeff.'

" 'Mebbe I is a liah, en mebbe I ain' got good eyes. But 'less'n I *is* a liah, en 'less'n I *ain'* got good eyes, Jeff is gwine ter meet dat 'oman dis ebenin' 'long 'bout eight o'clock right down dere by de crick in de swamp 'bout half-way betwix' dis plantation en Mars' Marrabo Utley's.'

"Well, Chloe tol' Hannibal she didn' b'liebe a wo'd he said, en call' 'im a low-down nigger, who wuz tryin' ter slander Jeff 'ca'se he wuz mo' luckier 'n he wuz. But all de same, she couldn' keep her min' fum runnin' on w'at Hannibal had said. She 'membered she 'd heared one er de niggers say dey wuz a gal ober at Mars' Marrabo Utley's plantation w'at Jeff use' ter go wid some befo' he got 'quainted wid Chloe. Den she 'mence' ter figger back, en sho' 'nuff, dey wuz two er th'ee times in de las' week w'en she 'd be'n he'pin' de ladies wid dey dressin' en udder fixin's in de ebenin', en Jeff mought 'a' gone down ter de swamp widout her knowin' 'bout it at all. En den she 'mence' ter 'member little things w'at she hadn' tuk no notice of befo', en w'at 'u'd make it 'pear lack Jeff had sump'n on his min'.

"Chloe set a monst'us heap er sto' by Jeff, en would 'a' done mos' anythin' fer 'im, so long ez he stuck ter her. But Chloe wuz a mighty jealous 'oman, en w'iles she didn' b'liebe w'at Hannibal said, she seed how it *could* 'a' be'n so, en she 'termine' fer ter fin' out fer herse'f whuther it *wuz* so er no.

"Now, Chloe hadn' seed Jeff all day, fer Mars' Dugal' had sont Jeff ober ter his daughter's house, young Mis' Ma'g'ret's, w'at libbed 'bout fo' miles fum Mars' Dugal's, en Jeff wuzn' 'spected home 'tel ebenin'. But des atter supper wuz ober, en w'iles de ladies wuz settin' out on de piazzer, Chloe slip' off fum de house en run down de road,—dis yer same road we come; en w'en she got mos' ter de crick—dis yer same crick right befo' us—she kin' er kep' in de bushes at de side er de road, 'tel fin'lly she seed Jeff settin' on de bank on de udder side er de crick,—right unner dat ole willer-tree droopin' ober de water yander. En eve'y now en den he 'd git up en look up de road to'ds Mars' Marrabo's on de udder side er de swamp.

"Fus' Chloe felt lack she 'd go right ober de crick en gib Jeff a piece er her min'. Den she 'lowed she better be sho' befo' she done anythin'. So she helt herse'f in de bes' she could, gittin' madder en madder eve'y minute, 'tel bimeby she seed a 'oman comin' down de road on de udder side fum to'ds Mars' Marrabo Utley's plantation. En w'en she seed Jeff jump up en run to'ds dat 'oman, en th'ow his a'ms roun' her neck, po' Chloe did n' stop ter see no mo', but des tu'nt roun' en run up ter de house, en rush' up on de piazzer, en up en tol' Mars' Dugal' en ole mis' all 'bout de baby doll, en all 'bout Jeff gittin' de goopher fum Aun' Peggy, en 'bout w'at de goopher had done ter Hannibal.

"Mars' Dugal' wuz monst'us mad. He did n' let on at fus' lack he b'liebed Chloe, but w'en she tuk en showed 'im whar ter fin' de baby doll, Mars' Dugal' tu'nt w'ite ez chalk.

" 'W'at debil's wuk is dis?' sezee. 'No wonder de po' nigger's feet eetched. Sump'n got ter be done ter l'arn dat ole witch ter keep her han's off'n my niggers. En ez fer dis yer Jeff, I 'm gwine ter do des w'at I promus', so de darkies on dis plantation 'll know I means w'at I sez.'

"Fer Mars' Dugal' had warned de han's befo' 'bout foolin' wid cunju'ation; fac', he had los' one er two niggers hisse'f fum dey bein' goophered, en he would 'a' had ole Aun' Peggy whip' long ago, on'y Aun' Peggy wuz a free 'oman, en he wuz 'feard she'd cunjuh him. En w'iles Mars' Dugal' say he did n' b'liebe in cunj'in' en sich, he 'peared ter 'low it wuz bes' ter be on de safe side, en let Aun' Peggy alone.

"So Mars' Dugal' done des ez he say. Ef ole mis' had ple'd fer Jeff, he mought 'a' kep' 'im. But ole mis' had n' got ober losin' dem bulbs yit, en she neber said a wo'd. Mars' Dugal' tuk Jeff ter town nex' day en' sol' 'im ter a spekilater, who sta'ted down de ribber wid 'im nex' mawnin' on a steamboat, fer ter take 'im ter Alabama.

"Now, w'en Chloe tol' ole Mars' Dugal' 'bout dis yer baby doll en dis udder goopher, she had n' ha'dly 'lowed Mars' Dugal' would sell Jeff down Souf. Howsomeber, she wuz so mad wid Jeff dat she 'suaded herse'f she did n' keer; en so she hilt her head up en went roun' lookin' lack she wuz rale glad 'bout it. But one day she wuz walkin' down de road, w'en who sh'd come 'long but dis yer Hannibal.

"W'en Hannibal seed 'er, he bus' out laffin' fittin' fer ter kill: 'Yah, yah, yah! ho, ho, ho! ha, ha, ha! Oh, hol' me, honey, hol' me, er I 'll laf myse'f ter def. I ain' nebber laf' so much sence I be'n bawn.'

" 'W'at you laffin' at, Hot-Foot?'

" 'Yah, yah, yah! W'at I laffin' at? W'y, I 's laffin' at myse'f, tooby sho',—laffin' ter think w'at a fine 'oman I made.'

"Chloe tu'nt pale, en her hea't come up in her mouf.

" 'W'at you mean, nigger?' sez she, ketchin' holt er a bush by de road fer ter stiddy herse'f. 'W'at you mean by de kin' er 'oman you made?'

" 'W'at do I mean? I means dat I got squared up wid you fer treatin' me de way you done, en I got eben wid dat yaller nigger Jeff fer cuttin' me out. Now, he 's gwine ter know w'at it is ter eat co'n bread en merlasses once mo', en wuk fum daylight ter da'k, en ter hab a oberseah dribin' 'im fum one day's een' ter de udder. I means dat I sont wo'd ter Jeff dat Sunday dat you wuz gwine ter be ober ter Mars' Marrabo's visitin' dat ebenin', en you want 'im ter meet you down by de crick on de way home en go de rest er de road wid you. En den I put on a frock en a sunbonnet, en fix' myse'f up ter look lack a 'oman; en w'en Jeff seed me comin', he run ter meet me, en you seed 'im,—fer I'd be'n watchin' in de bushes befo' en 'skivered you comin' down de road. En now I reckon you en Jeff bofe knows w'at it means ter mess wid a nigger lack me.'

"Po' Chloe had n' heared mo' d'n half er de las' part er w'at Hannibal said, but she had heared 'nuff to l'arn dat dis nigger had fooled her en Jeff, en dat po' Jeff had n' done nuffin, en dat fer lovin' her too much en goin' ter meet her she had cause' 'im ter be sol' erway whar she 'd neber, neber see 'im no mo'. De sun mought shine by day, de moon by night; de flowers mought bloom, en de mawkin'-birds mought sing, but po' Jeff wuz done los' ter her fereber en fereber.

"Hannibal had n' mo' d'n finish' w'at he had ter say, w'en Chloe's knees gun 'way unner her, en she fell down in de road, en lay dere half a' hour er so befo' she come to. W'en she did, she crep' up ter de house des ez pale ez a ghos'. En fer a mont' er so she crawled roun' de house, en 'peared ter be so po'ly dat Mars' Dugal' sont fer a doctor; en de doctor kep' on axin' her questions 'tel he foun' she wuz des pinin' erway fer Jeff.

"W'en he tol' Mars' Dugal', Mars' Dugal' lafft, en said he 'd fix dat. She could hab de noo house boy fer a husban'. But ole mis' say, no, Chloe ain' dat kin'er gal, en dat Mars' Dugal' sh'd buy Jeff back.

"So Mars' Dugal' writ a letter ter dis yer spekilater down

ter Wim'l'ton, en tol' ef he ain' done sol' dat nigger Souf w'at he bought fum 'im, he'd lack ter buy 'im back ag'in. Chloe 'mence' ter pick up a little w'en ole mis' tol' her 'bout dis letter. Howsomeber, bimeby Mars' Dugal' got a' answer fum de spekilater, who said he wuz monst'us sorry, but Jeff had fell ove'boa'd er jumped off'n de steamboat on de way ter Wim'l'ton, en got drownded, en co'se he could n' sell 'im back, much ez he'd lack ter 'bleedge Mars' Dugal'.

"Well, atter Chloe heared dis, she wa'n't much mo' use ter nobody. She pu'tended ter do her wuk, en ole mis' put up wid her, en had de doctor gib her medicine, en let 'er go ter de circus, en all so'ts er things fer ter take her min' off'n her troubles. But dey did n' none un 'em do no good. Chloe got ter slippin' down here in de ebenin' des lack she 'uz comin' ter meet Jeff, en she 'd set dere unner dat willer-tree on de udder side, en wait fer 'im, night atter night. Bimeby she got so bad de w'ite folks sont her ober ter young Mis' Ma'g'ret's fer ter gib her a change; but she runned erway de fus' night, en w'en dey looked fer 'er nex' mawnin', dey foun' her co'pse layin' in de branch yander, right 'cross fum whar we 're settin' now.

"Eber sence den," said Julius in conclusion, "Chloe's ha'nt comes eve'y ebenin' en sets down unner dat willer-tree en waits fer Jeff, er e'se walks up en down de road yander, lookin' en lookin', en waitin' en waitin', fer her sweethea't w'at ain' neber, neber come back ter her no mo'."

There was silence when the old man had finished, and I am sure I saw a tear in my wife's eye, and more than one in Mabel's.

"I think, Julius," said my wife, after a moment, "that you may turn the mare around and go by the long road."

The old man obeyed with alacrity, and I noticed no reluctance on the mare's part.

"You are not afraid of Chloe's haunt, are you?" I asked jocularly.

My mood was not responded to, and neither of the ladies smiled.

"Oh, no," said Annie, "but I 've changed my mind. I prefer the other route."

When we had reached the main road and had proceeded

along it for a short distance, we met a cart driven by a young negro, and on the cart were a trunk and a valise. We recognized the man as Malcolm Murchison's servant, and drew up a moment to speak to him.

"Who 's going away, Marshall?" I inquired.

"Young Mistah Ma'colm gwine 'way on de boat ter Noo Yo'k dis ebenin', suh, en I 'm takin' his things down ter de wharf, suh."

This was news to me, and I heard it with regret. My wife looked sorry, too, and I could see that Mabel was trying hard to hide her concern.

"He 's comin' 'long behin', suh, en I 'spec's you 'll meet 'im up de road a piece. He 's gwine ter walk down ez fur ez Mistah Jim Williams's, en take de buggy fum dere ter town. He 'spec's ter be gone a long time, suh, en say prob'ly he ain' neber comin' back."

The man drove on. There were a few words exchanged in an undertone between my wife and Mabel, which I did not catch. Then Annie said: "Julius, you may stop the rockaway a moment. There are some trumpet-flowers by the road there that I want. Will you get them for me, John?"

I sprang into the underbrush, and soon returned with a great bunch of scarlet blossoms.

"Where is Mabel?" I asked, noting her absence.

"She has walked on ahead. We shall overtake her in a few minutes."

The carriage had gone only a short distance when my wife discovered that she had dropped her fan.

"I had it where we were stopping. Julius, will you go back and get it for me?"

Julius got down and went back for the fan. He was an unconscionably long time finding it. After we got started again we had gone only a little way, when we saw Mabel and young Murchison coming toward us. They were walking arm in arm, and their faces were aglow with the light of love.

I do not know whether or not Julius had a previous understanding with Malcolm Murchison by which he was to drive us round by the long road that day, nor do I know exactly what motive influenced the old man's exertions in the matter.

He was fond of Mabel, but I was old enough, and knew Julius well enough, to be skeptical of his motives. It is certain that a most excellent understanding existed between him and Murchison after the reconciliation, and that when the young people set up housekeeping over at the old Murchison place, Julius had an opportunity to enter their service. For some reason or other, however, he preferred to remain with us. The mare, I might add, was never known to balk again.

THE WIFE OF HIS YOUTH AND OTHER STORIES OF THE COLOR LINE

(1899)

CONTENTS

The Wife of His Youth

I

MR. RYDER was going to give a ball. There were several reasons why this was an opportune time for such an event.

Mr. Ryder might aptly be called the dean of the Blue Veins. The original Blue Veins were a little society of colored persons organized in a certain Northern city shortly after the war. Its purpose was to establish and maintain correct social standards among a people whose social condition presented almost unlimited room for improvement. By accident, combined perhaps with some natural affinity, the society consisted of individuals who were, generally speaking, more white than black. Some envious outsider made the suggestion that no one was eligible for membership who was not white enough to show blue veins. The suggestion was readily adopted by those who were not of the favored few, and since that time the society, though possessing a longer and more pretentious name, had been known far and wide as the "Blue Vein Society," and its members as the "Blue Veins."

The Blue Veins did not allow that any such requirement existed for admission to their circle, but, on the contrary, declared that character and culture were the only things considered; and that if most of their members were light-colored, it was because such persons, as a rule, had had better opportunities to qualify themselves for membership. Opinions differed, too, as to the usefulness of the society. There were those who had been known to assail it violently as a glaring example of the very prejudice from which the colored race had suffered most; and later, when such critics had succeeded in getting on the inside, they had been heard to maintain with zeal and earnestness that the society was a lifeboat, an anchor, a bulwark and a shield,—a pillar of cloud by day and of fire by night, to guide their people through the social wilderness. Another alleged prerequisite for Blue Vein membership was that of free birth; and while there was really no such requirement, it is doubtless true that very few of the members would have been unable to meet it if there had been. If there were one or two of the older members who had come up from the South and from slavery, their history presented enough romantic circumstances to rob their servile origin of its grosser aspects.

While there were no such tests of eligibility, it is true that the Blue Veins had their notions on these subjects, and that not all of them were equally liberal in regard to the things they collectively disclaimed. Mr. Ryder was one of the most conservative. Though he had not been among the founders of the society, but had come in some years later, his genius for social leadership was such that he had speedily become its recognized adviser and head, the custodian of its standards, and the preserver of its traditions. He shaped its social policy, was active in providing for its entertainment, and when the interest fell off, as it sometimes did, he fanned the embers until they burst again into a cheerful flame.

There were still other reasons for his popularity. While he was not as white as some of the Blue Veins, his appearance was such as to confer distinction upon them. His features were of a refined type, his hair was almost straight; he was always neatly dressed; his manners were irreproachable, and his morals above suspicion. He had come to Groveland a young man, and obtaining employment in the office of a railroad company as messenger had in time worked himself up to the position of stationery clerk, having charge of the distribution of the office supplies for the whole company. Although the lack of early training had hindered the orderly development of a naturally fine mind, it had not prevented him from doing a great deal of reading or from forming decidedly literary tastes. Poetry was his passion. He could repeat whole pages of the great English poets; and if his pronunciation was sometimes faulty, his eye, his voice, his gestures, would respond to the changing sentiment with a precision that revealed a poetic soul and disarmed criticism. He was economical, and had saved money; he owned and occupied a very comfortable house on a respectable street. His residence was handsomely furnished, containing among other things a good library, especially rich in poetry, a piano, and some choice engravings. He generally shared his house with some young couple, who looked after his wants and were company for him; for Mr. Ryder was a single man. In the early days of his connection with the Blue Veins he had been regarded as quite a catch, and young ladies and their mothers had manœuvred with much ingenuity to capture him. Not, however, until Mrs. Molly Dixon visited Groveland had any woman ever made him wish to change his condition to that of a married man.

Mrs. Dixon had come to Groveland from Washington in the spring, and before the summer was over she had won Mr. Ryder's heart. She possessed many attractive qualities. She was much younger than he; in fact, he was old enough to have been her father, though no one knew exactly how old he was. She was whiter than he, and better educated. She had moved in the best colored society of the country, at Washington, and had taught in the schools of that city. Such a superior person had been eagerly welcomed to the Blue Vein Society, and had taken a leading part in its activities. Mr. Ryder had at first been attracted by her charms of person, for she was very good looking and not over twenty-five; then by her refined manners and the vivacity of her wit. Her husband had been a government clerk, and at his death had left a considerable life insurance. She was visiting friends in Groveland, and, finding the town and the people to her liking, had prolonged her stay indefinitely. She had not seemed displeased at Mr. Ryder's attentions, but on the contrary had given him every proper encouragement; indeed, a younger and less cautious man would long since have spoken. But he had made up his mind, and had only to determine the time when he would ask her to be his wife. He decided to give a ball in her honor, and at some time during the evening of the ball to offer her his heart and hand. He had no special fears about the outcome, but, with a little touch of romance, he wanted the surroundings to be in harmony with his own feelings when he should have received the answer he expected.

Mr. Ryder resolved that this ball should mark an epoch in the social history of Groveland. He knew, of course,—no one could know better,—the entertainments that had taken place in past years, and what must be done to surpass them. His ball must be worthy of the lady in whose honor it was to be given, and must, by the quality of its guests, set an example for the future. He had observed of late a growing liberality, almost a laxity, in social matters, even among members of his own set, and had several times been forced to meet in a social way persons whose complexions and callings in life were hardly up to the standard which he considered proper for the society to maintain. He had a theory of his own.

"I have no race prejudice," he would say, "but we people of mixed blood are ground between the upper and the nether millstone. Our fate lies between absorption by the white race and extinction in the black. The one does n't want us yet, but may take us in time. The other would welcome us, but it would be for us a backward step. 'With malice towards none, with charity for all,' we must do the best we can for ourselves and those who are to follow us. Self-preservation is the first law of nature."

His ball would serve by its exclusiveness to counteract leveling tendencies, and his marriage with Mrs. Dixon would help to further the upward process of absorption he had been wishing and waiting for.

II

The ball was to take place on Friday night. The house had been put in order, the carpets covered with canvas, the halls and stairs decorated with palms and potted plants; and in the afternoon Mr. Ryder sat on his front porch, which the shade of a vine running up over a wire netting made a cool and pleasant lounging place. He expected to respond to the toast "The Ladies" at the supper, and from a volume of Tennyson—his favorite poet—was fortifying himself with apt quotations. The volume was open at "A Dream of Fair Women." His eyes fell on these lines, and he read them aloud to judge better of their effect:—

"At length I saw a lady within call,
  Stiller than chisell'd marble, standing there;
A daughter of the gods, divinely tall,
  And most divinely fair."

He marked the verse, and turning the page read the stanza beginning,—

"O sweet pale Margaret,
O rare pale Margaret."

He weighed the passage a moment, and decided that it would not do. Mrs. Dixon was the palest lady he expected at the ball, and she was of a rather ruddy complexion, and of lively disposition and buxom build. So he ran over the leaves until his eye rested on the description of Queen Guinevere:—

"She seem'd a part of joyous Spring;
A gown of grass-green silk she wore,
Buckled with golden clasps before;
A light-green tuft of plumes she bore
Closed in a golden ring.
* * * * * *
"She look'd so lovely, as she sway'd
The rein with dainty finger-tips,
A man had given all other bliss,
And all his worldly worth for this,
To waste his whole heart in one kiss
Upon her perfect lips."

As Mr. Ryder murmured these words audibly, with an appreciative thrill, he heard the latch of his gate click, and a light footfall sounding on the steps. He turned his head, and saw a woman standing before his door.

She was a little woman, not five feet tall, and proportioned to her height. Although she stood erect, and looked around her with very bright and restless eyes, she seemed quite old; for her face was crossed and recrossed with a hundred wrinkles, and around the edges of her bonnet could be seen protruding here and there a tuft of short gray wool. She wore a blue calico gown of ancient cut, a little red shawl fastened around her shoulders with an old-fashioned brass brooch, and a large bonnet profusely ornamented with faded red and yellow artificial flowers. And she was very black,—so black that her toothless gums, revealed when she opened her mouth to speak, were not red, but blue. She looked like a bit of the old plantation life, summoned up from the past by the wave of a magician's wand, as the poet's fancy had called into being the gracious shapes of which Mr. Ryder had just been reading.

He rose from his chair and came over to where she stood.

"Good-afternoon, madam," he said.

"Good-evenin', suh," she answered, ducking suddenly with a quaint curtsy. Her voice was shrill and piping, but softened somewhat by age. "Is dis yere whar Mistuh Ryduh lib, suh?" she asked, looking around her doubtfully, and glancing into the open windows, through which some of the preparations for the evening were visible.

"Yes," he replied, with an air of kindly patronage, unconsciously flattered by her manner, "I am Mr. Ryder. Did you want to see me?"

"Yas, suh, ef I ain't 'sturbin' of you too much."

"Not at all. Have a seat over here behind the vine, where it is cool. What can I do for you?"

"'Scuse me, suh," she continued, when she had sat down on the edge of a chair, "'scuse me, suh, I 's lookin' for my husban'. I heerd you wuz a big man an' had libbed heah a long time, an' I 'lowed you would n't min' ef I 'd come roun' an' ax you ef you 'd ever heerd of a merlatter man by de name er Sam Taylor 'quirin' roun' in de chu'ches ermongs' de people fer his wife 'Liza Jane?"

Mr. Ryder seemed to think for a moment.

"There used to be many such cases right after the war," he said, "but it has been so long that I have forgotten them. There are very few now. But tell me your story, and it may refresh my memory."

She sat back farther in her chair so as to be more comfortable, and folded her withered hands in her lap.

"My name 's 'Liza," she began, "'Liza Jane. W'en I wuz young I us'ter b'long ter Marse Bob Smif, down in ole Missoura. I wuz bawn down dere. W'en I wuz a gal I wuz married ter a man named Jim. But Jim died, an' after dat I married a merlatter man named Sam Taylor. Sam wuz freebawn, but his mammy and daddy died, an' de w'ite folks 'prenticed him ter my marster fer ter work fer 'im 'tel he wuz growed up. Sam worked in de fiel', an' I wuz de cook. One day Ma'y Ann, ole miss's maid, came rushin' out ter de kitchen, an' says she, ''Liza Jane, ole marse gwine sell yo' Sam down de ribber.'

" 'Go way f'm yere,' says I; 'my husban' 's free!'

" 'Don' make no diff'ence. I heerd ole marse tell ole miss he wuz gwine take yo' Sam 'way wid 'im ter-morrow, fer he needed money, an' he knowed whar he could git a t'ousan' dollars fer Sam an' no questions axed.'

"W'en Sam come home f'm de fiel' dat night, I tole him 'bout ole marse gwine steal 'im, an' Sam run erway. His time wuz mos' up, an' he swo' dat w'en he wuz twenty-one he would come back an' he'p me run erway, er else save up de money ter buy my freedom. An' I know he 'd 'a' done it, fer he thought a heap er me, Sam did. But w'en he come back he did n' fin' me, fer I wuz n' dere. Ole marse had heerd dat I warned Sam, so he had me whip' an' sol' down de ribber.

"Den de wah broke out, an' w'en it wuz ober de cullud folks wuz scattered. I went back ter de ole home; but Sam wuz n' dere, an' I could n' l'arn nuffin' 'bout 'im. But I knowed he 'd be'n dere to look fer me an' had n' foun' me, an' had gone erway ter hunt fer me.

"I 's be'n lookin' fer 'im eber sence," she added simply, as though twenty-five years were but a couple of weeks, "an' I knows he 's be'n lookin' fer me. Fer he sot a heap er sto' by me, Sam did, an' I know he 's be'n huntin' fer me all dese years,—'less'n he 's be'n sick er sump'n, so he could n' work, er out'n his head, so he could n' 'member his promise. I went back down de ribber, fer I 'lowed he 'd gone down dere lookin' fer me. I 's be'n ter Noo Orleens, an' Atlanty, an' Charleston, an' Richmon'; an' w'en I 'd be'n all ober de Souf I come ter de Norf. Fer I knows I 'll fin' 'im some er dese days," she added softly, "er he 'll fin' me, an' den we 'll bofe be as happy in freedom as we wuz in de ole days befo' de wah." A smile stole over her withered countenance as she paused a moment, and her bright eyes softened into a far-away look.

This was the substance of the old woman's story. She had wandered a little here and there. Mr. Ryder was looking at her curiously when she finished.

"How have you lived all these years?" he asked.

"Cookin', suh. I 's a good cook. Does you know anybody w'at needs a good cook, suh? I 's stoppin' wid a cullud fam'ly roun' de corner yonder 'tel I kin git a place."

"Do you really expect to find your husband? He may be dead long ago."

She shook her head emphatically. "Oh no, he ain' dead. De signs an' de tokens tells me. I dremp three nights runnin' on'y dis las' week dat I foun' him."

"He may have married another woman. Your slave marriage would not have prevented him, for you never lived with him after the war, and without that your marriage does n't count."

"Would n' make no diff'ence wid Sam. He would n' marry no yuther 'ooman 'tel he foun' out 'bout me. I knows it," she added. "Sump'n 's be'n tellin' me all dese years dat I 's gwine fin' Sam 'fo' I dies."

"Perhaps he 's outgrown you, and climbed up in the world where he would n't care to have you find him."

"No, indeed, suh," she replied, "Sam ain' dat kin' er man. He wuz good ter me, Sam wuz, but he wuz n' much good ter nobody e'se, fer he wuz one er de triflin'es' han's on de plantation. I 'spec's ter haf ter suppo't 'im w'en I fin' 'im, fer he nebber would work 'less'n he had ter. But den he wuz free, an' he did n' git no pay fer his work, an' I don' blame 'im much. Mebbe he 's done better sence he run erway, but I ain' 'spectin' much."

"You may have passed him on the street a hundred times during the twenty-five years, and not have known him; time works great changes."

She smiled incredulously. "I 'd know 'im 'mongs' a hund'ed men. Fer dey wuz n' no yuther merlatter man like my man Sam, an' I could n' be mistook. I 's toted his picture roun' wid me twenty-five years."

"May I see it?" asked Mr. Ryder. "It might help me to remember whether I have seen the original."

As she drew a small parcel from her bosom he saw that it was fastened to a string that went around her neck. Removing several wrappers, she brought to light an old-fashioned daguerreotype in a black case. He looked long and intently at the portrait. It was faded with time, but the features were still distinct, and it was easy to see what manner of man it had represented.

He closed the case, and with a slow movement handed it back to her.

"I don't know of any man in town who goes by that name," he said, "nor have I heard of any one making such inquiries. But if you will leave me your address, I will give the matter some attention, and if I find out anything I will let you know."

She gave him the number of a house in the neighborhood, and went away, after thanking him warmly.

He wrote the address on the fly-leaf of the volume of Tennyson, and, when she had gone, rose to his feet and stood looking after her curiously. As she walked down the street with mincing step, he saw several persons whom she passed turn and look back at her with a smile of kindly amusement. When she had turned the corner, he went upstairs to his bedroom, and stood for a long time before the mirror of his dressing-case, gazing thoughtfully at the reflection of his own face.

III

At eight o'clock the ballroom was a blaze of light and the guests had begun to assemble; for there was a literary programme and some routine business of the society to be gone through with before the dancing. A black servant in evening dress waited at the door and directed the guests to the dressing-rooms.

The occasion was long memorable among the colored people of the city; not alone for the dress and display, but for the high average of intelligence and culture that distinguished the gathering as a whole. There were a number of school-teachers, several young doctors, three or four lawyers, some professional singers, an editor, a lieutenant in the United States army spending his furlough in the city, and others in various polite callings; these were colored, though most of them would not have attracted even a casual glance because of any marked difference from white people. Most of the ladies were in evening costume, and dress coats and dancing pumps were the rule among the men. A band of string music, stationed in an alcove behind a row of palms, played popular airs while the guests were gathering.

The dancing began at half past nine. At eleven o'clock supper was served. Mr. Ryder had left the ballroom some little time before the intermission, but reappeared at the supper-table. The spread was worthy of the occasion, and the guests did full justice to it. When the coffee had been served, the toast-master, Mr. Solomon Sadler, rapped for order. He made a brief introductory speech, complimenting host and guests, and then presented in their order the toasts of the evening. They were responded to with a very fair display of after-dinner wit.

"The last toast," said the toast-master, when he reached the end of the list, "is one which must appeal to us all. There is no one of us of the sterner sex who is not at some time dependent upon woman,—in infancy for protection, in manhood for companionship, in old age for care and comforting. Our good host has been trying to live alone, but the fair faces I see around me to-night prove that he too is largely dependent upon the gentler sex for most that makes life worth living, —the society and love of friends,—and rumor is at fault if he does not soon yield entire subjection to one of them. Mr. Ryder will now respond to the toast,—The Ladies."

There was a pensive look in Mr. Ryder's eyes as he took the floor and adjusted his eyeglasses. He began by speaking of woman as the gift of Heaven to man, and after some general observations on the relations of the sexes he said: "But perhaps the quality which most distinguishes woman is her fidelity and devotion to those she loves. History is full of examples, but has recorded none more striking than one which only to-day came under my notice."

He then related, simply but effectively, the story told by his visitor of the afternoon. He gave it in the same soft dialect, which came readily to his lips, while the company listened attentively and sympathetically. For the story had awakened a responsive thrill in many hearts. There were some present who had seen, and others who had heard their fathers and grandfathers tell, the wrongs and sufferings of this past generation, and all of them still felt, in their darker moments, the shadow hanging over them. Mr. Ryder went on:—

"Such devotion and confidence are rare even among women. There are many who would have searched a year, some who would have waited five years, a few who might have hoped ten years; but for twenty-five years this woman has retained her affection for and her faith in a man she has not seen or heard of in all that time.

"She came to me to-day in the hope that I might be able to help her find this long-lost husband. And when she was gone I gave my fancy rein, and imagined a case I will put to you.

"Suppose that this husband, soon after his escape, had learned that his wife had been sold away, and that such inquiries as he could make brought no information of her whereabouts. Suppose that he was young, and she much older than he; that he was light, and she was black; that their marriage was a slave marriage, and legally binding only if they chose to make it so after the war. Suppose, too, that he made his way to the North, as some of us have done, and there, where he had larger opportunities, had improved them, and had in the course of all these years grown to be as different from the ignorant boy who ran away from fear of slavery as the day is from the night. Suppose, even, that he had qualified himself, by industry, by thrift, and by study, to win the friendship and be considered worthy the society of such people as these I see around me to-night, gracing my board and filling my heart with gladness; for I am old enough to remember the day when such a gathering would not have been possible in this land. Suppose, too, that, as the years went by, this man's memory of the past grew more and more indistinct, until at last it was rarely, except in his dreams, that any image of this bygone period rose before his mind. And then suppose that accident should bring to his knowledge the fact that the wife of his youth, the wife he had left behind him,—not one who had walked by his side and kept pace with him in his upward struggle, but one upon whom advancing years and a laborious life had set their mark,—was alive and seeking him, but that he was absolutely safe from recognition or discovery, unless he chose to reveal himself. My friends, what would the man do? I will presume that he was one who loved honor, and tried to deal justly with all men. I will even carry the case further, and suppose that perhaps he had set his heart upon another, whom he had hoped to call his own. What would he do, or rather what ought he to do, in such a crisis of a lifetime?

"It seemed to me that he might hesitate, and I imagined that I was an old friend, a near friend, and that he had come to me for advice; and I argued the case with him. I tried to discuss it impartially. After we had looked upon the matter from every point of view, I said to him, in words that we all know:—

> 'This above all: to thine own self be true,
> And it must follow, as the night the day,
> Thou canst not then be false to any man.'

Then, finally, I put the question to him, 'Shall you acknowledge her?'

"And now, ladies and gentlemen, friends and companions, I ask you, what should he have done?"

There was something in Mr. Ryder's voice that stirred the hearts of those who sat around him. It suggested more than mere sympathy with an imaginary situation; it seemed rather in the nature of a personal appeal. It was observed, too, that his look rested more especially upon Mrs. Dixon, with a mingled expression of renunciation and inquiry.

She had listened, with parted lips and streaming eyes. She was the first to speak: "He should have acknowledged her."

"Yes," they all echoed, "he should have acknowledged her."

"My friends and companions," responded Mr. Ryder, "I thank you, one and all. It is the answer I expected, for I knew your hearts."

He turned and walked toward the closed door of an adjoining room, while every eye followed him in wondering curiosity. He came back in a moment, leading by the hand his visitor of the afternoon, who stood startled and trembling at the sudden plunge into this scene of brilliant gayety. She was neatly dressed in gray, and wore the white cap of an elderly woman.

"Ladies and gentlemen," he said, "this is the woman, and I am the man, whose story I have told you. Permit me to introduce to you the wife of my youth."

Her Virginia Mammy

I

THE PIANIST had struck up a lively two-step, and soon the floor was covered with couples, each turning on its own axis, and all revolving around a common centre, in obedience perhaps to the same law of motion that governs the planetary systems. The dancing-hall was a long room, with a waxed floor that glistened with the reflection of the lights from the chandeliers. The walls were hung in paper of blue and white, above a varnished hard wood wainscoting; the monotony of surface being broken by numerous windows draped with curtains of dotted muslin, and by occasional engravings and colored pictures representing the dances of various nations, judiciously selected. The rows of chairs along the two sides of the room were left unoccupied by the time the music was well under way, for the pianist, a tall colored woman with long fingers and a muscular wrist, played with a verve and a swing that set the feet of the listeners involuntarily in motion.

The dance was sure to occupy the class for a quarter of an hour at least, and the little dancing-mistress took the opportunity to slip away to her own sitting-room, which was on the same floor of the block, for a few minutes of rest. Her day had been a hard one. There had been a matinée at two o'clock, a children's class at four, and at eight o'clock the class now on the floor had assembled.

When she reached the sitting-room she gave a start of pleasure. A young man rose at her entrance, and advanced with both hands extended—a tall, broad-shouldered, fair-haired young man, with a frank and kindly countenance, now lit up with the animation of pleasure. He seemed about twenty-six or twenty-seven years old. His face was of the type one instinctively associates with intellect and character, and it gave the impression, besides, of that intangible something which we call race. He was neatly and carefully dressed, though his clothing was not without indications that he found it necessary or expedient to practice economy.

"Good-evening, Clara," he said, taking her hands in his;

"I 've been waiting for you five minutes. I supposed you would be in, but if you had been a moment later I was going to the hall to look you up. You seem tired to-night," he added, drawing her nearer to him and scanning her features at short range. "This work is too hard; you are not fitted for it. When are you going to give it up?"

"The season is almost over," she answered, "and then I shall stop for the summer."

He drew her closer still and kissed her lovingly. "Tell me, Clara," he said, looking down into her face,—he was at least a foot taller than she,—"when I am to have my answer."

"Will you take the answer you can get to-night?" she asked with a wan smile.

"I will take but one answer, Clara. But do not make me wait too long for that. Why, just think of it! I have known you for six months."

"That is an extremely long time," said Clara, as they sat down side by side.

"It has been an age," he rejoined. "For a fortnight of it, too, which seems longer than all the rest, I have been waiting for my answer. I am turning gray under the suspense. Seriously, Clara dear, what shall it be? or rather, when shall it be? for to the other question there is but one answer possible."

He looked into her eyes, which slowly filled with tears. She repulsed him gently as he bent over to kiss them away.

"You know I love you, John, and why I do not say what you wish. You must give me a little more time to make up my mind before I can consent to burden you with a nameless wife, one who does not know who her mother was"—

"She was a good woman, and beautiful, if you are at all like her."

"Or her father"—

"He was a gentleman and a scholar, if you inherited from him your mind or your manners."

"It is good of you to say that, and I try to believe it. But it is a serious matter; it is a dreadful thing to have no name."

"You are known by a worthy one, which was freely given you, and is legally yours."

"I know—and I am grateful for it. After all, though, it is not my real name; and since I have learned that it was not, it seems like a garment—something external, accessory, and not a part of myself. It does not mean what one's own name would signify."

"Take mine, Clara, and make it yours; I lay it at your feet. Some honored men have borne it."

"Ah yes, and that is what makes my position the harder. Your great-grandfather was governor of Connecticut."

"I have heard my mother say so."

"And one of your ancestors came over in the Mayflower."

"In some capacity—I have never been quite clear whether as ship's cook or before the mast."

"Now you are insincere, John; but you cannot deceive me. You never spoke in that way about your ancestors until you learned that I had none. I know you are proud of them, and that the memory of the governor and the judge and the Harvard professor and the Mayflower pilgrim makes you strive to excel, in order to prove yourself worthy of them."

"It did until I met you, Clara. Now the one inspiration of my life is the hope to make you mine."

"And your profession?"

"It will furnish me the means to take you out of this; you are not fit for toil."

"And your book—your treatise that is to make you famous?"

"I have worked twice as hard on it and accomplished twice as much since I have hoped that you might share my success."

"Oh! if I but knew the truth!" she sighed, "or could find it out! I realize that I am absurd, that I ought to be happy. I love my parents—my foster-parents—dearly. I owe them everything. Mother—poor, dear mother!—could not have loved me better or cared for me more faithfully had I been her own child. Yet—I am ashamed to say it—I always felt that I was not like them, that there was a subtle difference between us. They were contented in prosperity, resigned in misfortune; I was ever restless, and filled with vague ambitions. They were good, but dull. They loved me, but they never said so. I feel that there is warmer, richer blood coursing in my veins than the placid stream that crept through theirs."

"There will never be any such people to me as they were,"

said her lover, "for they took you and brought you up for me."

"Sometimes," she went on dreamily, "I feel sure that I am of good family, and the blood of my ancestors seems to call to me in clear and certain tones. Then again when my mood changes, I am all at sea—I feel that even if I had but simply to turn my hand to learn who I am and whence I came, I should shrink from taking the step, for fear that what I might learn would leave me forever unhappy."

"Dearest," he said, taking her in his arms, while from the hall and down the corridor came the softened strains of music, "put aside these unwholesome fancies. Your past is shrouded in mystery. Take my name, as you have taken my love, and I 'll make your future so happy that you won't have time to think of the past. What are a lot of musty, mouldy old grandfathers, compared with life and love and happiness? It 's hardly good form to mention one's ancestors nowadays, and what 's the use of them at all if one can't boast of them?"

"It 's all very well of you to talk that way," she rejoined. "But suppose you should marry me, and when you become famous and rich, and patients flock to your office, and fashionable people to your home, and every one wants to know who you are and whence you came, you 'll be obliged to bring out the governor, and the judge, and the rest of them. If you should refrain, in order to forestall embarrassing inquiries about *my* ancestry, I should have deprived you of something you are entitled to, something which has a real social value. And when people found out all about you, as they eventually would from some source, they would want to know—we Americans are a curious people—who your wife was, and you could only say"—

"The best and sweetest woman on earth, whom I love unspeakably."

"You know that is not what I mean. You could only say—a Miss Nobody, from Nowhere."

"A Miss Hohlfelder, from Cincinnati, the only child of worthy German parents, who fled from their own country in '49 to escape political persecution—an ancestry that one surely need not be ashamed of."

"No; but the consciousness that it was not true would be

always with me, poisoning my mind, and darkening my life and yours."

"Your views of life are entirely too tragic, Clara," the young man argued soothingly. "We are all worms of the dust, and if we go back far enough, each of us has had millions of ancestors; peasants and serfs, most of them; thieves, murderers, and vagabonds, many of them, no doubt; and therefore the best of us have but little to boast of. Yet we are all made after God's own image, and formed by his hand, for his ends; and therefore not to be lightly despised, even the humblest of us, least of all by ourselves. For the past we can claim no credit, for those who made it died with it. Our destiny lies in the future."

"Yes," she sighed, "I know all that. But I am not like you. A woman is not like a man; she cannot lose herself in theories and generalizations. And there are tests that even all your philosophy could not endure. Suppose you should marry me, and then some time, by the merest accident, you should learn that my origin was the worst it could be—that I not only had no name, but was not entitled to one."

"I cannot believe it," he said, "and from what we do know of your history it is hardly possible. If I learned it, I should forget it, unless, perchance, it should enhance your value in my eyes, by stamping you as a rare work of nature, an exception to the law of heredity, a triumph of pure beauty and goodness over the grosser limitations of matter. I cannot imagine, now that I know you, anything that could make me love you less. I would marry you just the same—even if you were one of your dancing-class to-night."

"I must go back to them," said Clara, as the music ceased.

"My answer," he urged, "give me my answer!"

"Not to-night, John," she pleaded. "Grant me a little longer time to make up my mind—for your sake."

"Not for my sake, Clara, no."

"Well—for mine." She let him take her in his arms and kiss her again.

"I have a patient yet to see to-night," he said as he went out. "If I am not detained too long, I may come back this way—if I see the lights in the hall still burning. Do not wonder if I ask you again for my answer, for I shall be unhappy until I get it."

II

A stranger entering the hall with Miss Hohlfelder would have seen, at first glance, only a company of well-dressed people, with nothing to specially distinguish them from ordinary humanity in temperate climates. After the eye had rested for a moment and begun to separate the mass into its component parts, one or two dark faces would have arrested its attention; and with the suggestion thus offered, a closer inspection would have revealed that they were nearly all a little less than white. With most of them this fact would not have been noticed, while they were alone or in company with one another, though if a fair white person had gone among them it would perhaps have been more apparent. From the few who were undistinguishable from pure white, the colors ran down the scale by minute gradations to the two or three brown faces at the other extremity.

It was Miss Hohlfelder's first colored class. She had been somewhat startled when first asked to take it. No person of color had ever applied to her for lessons; and while a woman of that race had played the piano for her for several months, she had never thought of colored people as possible pupils. So when she was asked if she would take a class of twenty or thirty, she had hesitated, and begged for time to consider the application. She knew that several of the more fashionable dancing-schools tabooed all pupils, singly or in classes, who labored under social disabilities—and this included the people of at least one other race who were vastly farther along in the world than the colored people of the community where Miss Hohlfelder lived. Personally she had no such prejudice, except perhaps a little shrinking at the thought of personal contact with the dark faces of whom Americans always think when "colored people" are spoken of. Again, a class of forty pupils was not to be despised, for she taught for money, which was equally current and desirable, regardless of its color. She had consulted her foster-parents, and after them her lover. Her foster-parents, who were German-born, and had never become thoroughly Americanized, saw no objection. As for her lover, he was indifferent.

"Do as you please," he said. "It may drive away some other

pupils. If it should break up the business entirely, perhaps you might be willing to give me a chance so much the sooner."

She mentioned the matter to one or two other friends, who expressed conflicting opinions. She decided at length to take the class, and take the consequences.

"I don't think it would be either right or kind to refuse them for any such reason, and I don't believe I shall lose anything by it."

She was somewhat surprised, and pleasantly so, when her class came together for their first lesson, at not finding them darker and more uncouth. Her pupils were mostly people whom she would have passed on the street without a second glance, and among them were several whom she had known by sight for years, but had never dreamed of as being colored people. Their manners were good, they dressed quietly and as a rule with good taste, avoiding rather than choosing bright colors and striking combinations—whether from natural preference, or because of a slightly morbid shrinking from criticism, of course she could not say. Among them, the dancing-mistress soon learned, there were lawyers and doctors, teachers, telegraph operators, clerks, milliners and dressmakers, students of the local college and scientific school, and, somewhat to her awe at the first meeting, even a member of the legislature. They were mostly young, although a few light-hearted older people joined the class, as much for company as for the dancing.

"Of course, Miss Hohlfelder," explained Mr. Solomon Sadler, to whom the teacher had paid a compliment on the quality of the class, "the more advanced of us are not numerous enough to make the fine distinctions that are possible among white people; and of course as we rise in life we can't get entirely away from our brothers and our sisters and our cousins, who don't always keep abreast of us. We do, however, draw certain lines of character and manners and occupation. You see the sort of people we are. Of course we have no prejudice against color, and we regard all labor as honorable, provided a man does the best he can. But we must have standards that will give our people something to aspire to."

The class was not a difficult one, as many of the members were already fairly good dancers. Indeed the class had been formed as much for pleasure as for instruction. Music and hall rent and a knowledge of the latest dances could be obtained cheaper in this way than in any other. The pupils had made rapid progress, displaying in fact a natural aptitude for rhythmic motion, and a keen susceptibility to musical sounds. As their race had never been criticised for these characteristics, they gave them full play, and soon developed, most of them, into graceful and indefatigable dancers. They were now almost at the end of their course, and this was the evening of the last lesson but one.

Miss Hohlfelder had remarked to her lover more than once that it was a pleasure to teach them. "They enter into the spirit of it so thoroughly, and they seem to enjoy themselves so much."

"One would think," he suggested, "that the whitest of them would find their position painful and more or less pathetic; to be so white and yet to be classed as black—so near and yet so far."

"They don't accept our classification blindly. They do not acknowledge any inferiority; they think they are a great deal better than any but the best white people," replied Miss Hohlfelder. "And since they have been coming here, do you know," she went on, "I hardly think of them as any different from other people. I feel perfectly at home among them."

"It is a great thing to have faith in one's self," he replied. "It is a fine thing, too, to be able to enjoy the passing moment. One of your greatest charms in my eyes, Clara, is that in your lighter moods you have this faculty. You sing because you love to sing. You find pleasure in dancing, even by way of work. You feel the *joie de vivre*—the joy of living. You are not always so, but when you are so I think you most delightful."

Miss Hohlfelder, upon entering the hall, spoke to the pianist and then exchanged a few words with various members of the class. The pianist began to play a dreamy Strauss waltz. When the dance was well under way Miss Hohlfelder left the hall again and stepped into the ladies' dressing-room. There was a woman seated quietly on a couch in a corner, her hands folded on her lap.

"Good-evening, Miss Hohlfelder. You do not seem as bright as usual to-night."

Miss Hohlfelder felt a sudden yearning for sympathy. Perhaps it was the gentle tones of the greeting; perhaps the kindly expression of the soft though faded eyes that were scanning Miss Hohlfelder's features. The woman was of the indefinite age between forty and fifty. There were lines on her face which, if due to years, might have carried her even past the half-century mark, but if caused by trouble or ill health might leave her somewhat below it. She was quietly dressed in black, and wore her slightly wavy hair low over her ears, where it lay naturally in the ripples which some others of her sex so sedulously seek by art. A little woman, of clear olive complexion and regular features, her face was almost a perfect oval, except as time had marred its outline. She had been in the habit of coming to the class with some young women of the family she lived with, part boarder, part seamstress and friend of the family. Sometimes, while waiting for her young charges, the music would jar her nerves, and she would seek the comparative quiet of the dressing-room.

"Oh, I'm all right, Mrs. Harper," replied the dancing-mistress, with a brave attempt at cheerfulness,—"just a little tired, after a hard day's work."

She sat down on the couch by the elder woman's side. Mrs. Harper took her hand and stroked it gently, and Clara felt soothed and quieted by her touch.

"There are tears in your eyes and trouble in your face. I know it, for I have shed the one and known the other. Tell me, child, what ails you? I am older than you, and perhaps I have learned some things in the hard school of life that may be of comfort or service to you."

Such a request, coming from a comparative stranger, might very properly have been resented or lightly parried. But Clara was not what would be called self-contained. Her griefs seemed lighter when they were shared with others, even in spirit. There was in her nature a childish strain that craved sympathy and comforting. She had never known—or if so it was only in a dim and dreamlike past—the tender, brooding care that was her conception of a mother's love. Mrs. Hohlfelder had been fond of her in a placid way, and had given her every comfort and luxury her means permitted. Clara's ideal of maternal love had been of another and more romantic type; she had thought of a fond, impulsive mother, to whose bosom she could fly when in trouble or distress, and to whom she could communicate her sorrows and trials; who would dry her tears and soothe her with caresses. Now, when even her kind foster-mother was gone, she felt still more the need of sympathy and companionship with her own sex; and when this little Mrs. Harper spoke to her so gently, she felt her heart respond instinctively.

"Yes, Mrs. Harper," replied Clara with a sigh, "I am in trouble, but it is trouble that you nor any one else can heal."

"You do not know, child. A simple remedy can sometimes cure a very grave complaint. Tell me your trouble, if it is something you are at liberty to tell."

"I have a story," said Clara, "and it is a strange one,—a story I have told to but one other person, one very dear to me."

"He must be dear to you indeed, from the tone in which you speak of him. Your very accents breathe love."

"Yes, I love him, and if you saw him—perhaps you have seen him, for he has looked in here once or twice during the dancing-lessons—you would know why I love him. He is handsome, he is learned, he is ambitious, he is brave, he is good; he is poor, but he will not always be so; and he loves me, oh, so much!"

The other woman smiled. "It is not so strange to love, nor yet to be loved. And all lovers are handsome and brave and fond."

"That is not all of my story. He wants to marry me." Clara paused, as if to let this statement impress itself upon the other.

"True lovers always do," said the elder woman.

"But sometimes, you know, there are circumstances which prevent them."

"Ah yes," murmured the other reflectively, and looking at the girl with deeper interest, "circumstances which prevent them. I have known of such a case."

"The circumstance which prevents us from marrying is my story."

"Tell me your story, child, and perhaps, if I cannot help you otherwise, I can tell you one that will make yours seem less sad."

"You know me," said the young woman, "as Miss Hohlfelder; but that is not actually my name. In fact I do not know my real name, for I am not the daughter of Mr. and Mrs. Hohlfelder, but only an adopted child. While Mrs. Hohlfelder lived, I never knew that I was not her child. I knew I was very different from her and father,—I mean Mr. Hohlfelder. I knew they were fair and I was dark; they were stout and I was slender; they were slow and I was quick. But of course I never dreamed of the true reason of this difference. When mother—Mrs. Hohlfelder—died, I found among her things one day a little packet, carefully wrapped up, containing a child's slip and some trinkets. The paper wrapper of the packet bore an inscription that awakened my curiosity. I asked father Hohlfelder whose the things had been, and then for the first time I learned my real story.

"I was not their own daughter, he stated, but an adopted child. Twenty-three years ago, when he had lived in St. Louis, a steamboat explosion had occurred up the river, and on a piece of wreckage floating down stream, a girl baby had been found. There was nothing on the child to give a hint of its home or parentage; and no one came to claim it, though the fact that a child had been found was advertised all along the river. It was believed that the infant's parents must have perished in the wreck, and certainly no one of those who were saved could identify the child. There had been a passenger list on board the steamer, but the list, with the officer who kept it, had been lost in the accident. The child was turned over to an orphan asylum, from which within a year it was adopted by the two kind-hearted and childless German people who brought it up as their own. I was that child."

The woman seated by Clara's side had listened with strained attention. "Did you learn the name of the steamboat?" she asked quietly, but quickly, when Clara paused.

"The Pride of St. Louis," answered Clara. She did not look at Mrs. Harper, but was gazing dreamily toward the front, and therefore did not see the expression that sprang into the other's face,—a look in which hope struggled with fear, and yearning love with both,—nor the strong effort with which Mrs. Harper controlled herself and moved not one muscle while the other went on.

"I was never sought," Clara continued, "and the good people who brought me up gave me every care. Father and mother—I can never train my tongue to call them anything else—were very good to me. When they adopted me they were poor; he was a pharmacist with a small shop. Later on he moved to Cincinnati, where he made and sold a popular 'patent' medicine and amassed a fortune. Then I went to a fashionable school, was taught French, and deportment, and dancing. Father Hohlfelder made some bad investments, and lost most of his money. The patent medicine fell off in popularity. A year or two ago we came to this city to live. Father bought this block and opened the little drug store below. We moved into the rooms upstairs. The business was poor, and I felt that I ought to do something to earn money and help support the family. I could dance; we had this hall, and it was not rented all the time, so I opened a dancing-school."

"Tell me, child," said the other woman, with restrained eagerness, "what were the things found upon you when you were taken from the river?"

"Yes," answered the girl, "I will. But I have not told you all my story, for this is but the prelude. About a year ago a young doctor rented an office in our block. We met each other, at first only now and then, and afterwards oftener; and six months ago he told me that he loved me."

She paused, and sat with half opened lips and dreamy eyes, looking back into the past six months.

"And the things found upon you"—

"Yes, I will show them to you when you have heard all my story. He wanted to marry me, and has asked me every week since. I have told him that I love him, but I have not said I would marry him. I don't think it would be right for me to do so, unless I could clear up this mystery. I believe he is going to be great and rich and famous, and there might come a time when he would be ashamed of me. I don't say that I shall never marry him; for I have hoped—I have a presentiment that in some strange way I shall find out who I am, and who my parents were. It may be mere imagination on my part, but somehow I believe it is more than that."

"Are you sure there was no mark on the things that were found upon you?" said the elder woman.

"Ah yes," sighed Clara, "I am sure, for I have looked at them a hundred times. They tell me nothing, and yet they suggest to me many things. Come," she said, taking the other by the hand, "and I will show them to you."

She led the way along the hall to her sitting-room, and to her bedchamber beyond. It was a small room hung with paper showing a pattern of morning-glories on a light ground, with dotted muslin curtains, a white iron bedstead, a few prints on the wall, a rocking-chair—a very dainty room. She went to the maple dressing-case, and opened one of the drawers.

As they stood for a moment, the mirror reflecting and framing their image, more than one point of resemblance between them was emphasized. There was something of the same oval face, and in Clara's hair a faint suggestion of the wave in the older woman's; and though Clara was fairer of complexion, and her eyes were gray and the other's black, there was visible, under the influence of the momentary excitement, one of those indefinable likenesses which are at times encountered,—sometimes marking blood relationship, sometimes the impress of a common training; in one case perhaps a mere earmark of temperament, and in another the index of a type. Except for the difference in color, one might imagine that if the younger woman were twenty years older the resemblance would be still more apparent.

Clara reached her hand into the drawer and drew out a folded packet, which she unwrapped, Mrs. Harper following her movements meanwhile with a suppressed intensity of interest which Clara, had she not been absorbed in her own thoughts, could not have failed to observe.

When the last fold of paper was removed there lay revealed a child's muslin slip. Clara lifted it and shook it gently until it was unfolded before their eyes. The lower half was delicately worked in a lacelike pattern, revealing an immense amount of patient labor.

The elder woman seized the slip with hands which could not disguise their trembling. Scanning the garment carefully, she seemed to be noting the pattern of the needlework, and then, pointing to a certain spot, exclaimed:—

"I thought so! I was sure of it! Do you not see the letters—M. S.?"

"Oh, how wonderful!" Clara seized the slip in turn and scanned the monogram. "How strange that you should see that at once and that I should not have discovered it, who have looked at it a hundred times! And here," she added, opening a small package which had been inclosed in the other, "is my coral necklace. Perhaps your keen eyes can find something in that."

It was a simple trinket, at which the older woman gave but a glance—a glance that added to her emotion.

"Listen, child," she said, laying her trembling hand on the other's arm. "It is all very strange and wonderful, for that slip and necklace, and, now that I have seen them, your face and your voice and your ways, all tell me who you are. Your eyes are your father's eyes, your voice is your father's voice. The slip was worked by your mother's hand."

"Oh!" cried Clara, and for a moment the whole world swam before her eyes.

"I was on the Pride of St. Louis, and I knew your father—and your mother."

Clara, pale with excitement, burst into tears, and would have fallen had not the other woman caught her in her arms. Mrs. Harper placed her on the couch, and, seated by her side, supported her head on her shoulder. Her hands seemed to caress the young woman with every touch.

"Tell me, oh, tell me all!" Clara demanded, when the first wave of emotion had subsided. "Who were my father and my mother, and who am I?"

The elder woman restrained her emotion with an effort, and answered as composedly as she could,—

"There were several hundred passengers on the Pride of St. Louis when she left Cincinnati on that fateful day, on her regular trip to New Orleans. Your father and mother were on the boat—and I was on the boat. We were going down the river, to take ship at New Orleans for France, a country which your father loved."

"Who was my father?" asked Clara. The woman's words fell upon her ear like water on a thirsty soil.

"Your father was a Virginia gentleman, and belonged to one of the first families, the Staffords, of Melton County."

Clara drew herself up unconsciously, and into her face there came a frank expression of pride which became it wonderfully, setting off a beauty that needed only this to make it all but perfect of its type.

"I knew it must be so," she murmured. "I have often felt it. Blood will always tell. And my mother?"

"Your mother—also belonged to one of the first families of Virginia, and in her veins flowed some of the best blood of the Old Dominion."

"What was her maiden name?"

"Mary Fairfax. As I was saying, your father was a Virginia gentleman. He was as handsome a man as ever lived, and proud, oh, so proud!—and good, and kind. He was a graduate of the University and had studied abroad."

"My mother—was she beautiful?"

"She was much admired, and your father loved her from the moment he first saw her. Your father came back from Europe, upon his father's sudden death, and entered upon his inheritance. But he had been away from Virginia so long, and had read so many books, that he had outgrown his home. He did not believe that slavery was right, and one of the first things he did was to free his slaves. His views were not popular, and he sold out his lands a year before the war, with the intention of moving to Europe."

"In the mean time he had met and loved and married my mother?"

"In the mean time he had met and loved your mother."

"My mother was a Virginia belle, was she not?"

"The Fairfaxes," answered Mrs. Harper, "were the first of the first families, the bluest of the blue-bloods. The Miss Fairfaxes were all beautiful and all social favorites."

"What did my father do then, when he had sold out in Virginia?"

"He went with your mother and you—you were then just a year old—to Cincinnati, to settle up some business connected with his estate. When he had completed his business, he embarked on the Pride of St. Louis with you and your mother and a colored nurse."

"And how did you know about them?" asked Clara.

"I was one of the party. I was"—

"You were the colored nurse?—my 'mammy,' they would have called you in my old Virginia home?"

"Yes, child, I was—your mammy. Upon my bosom you have rested; my breasts once gave you nourishment; my hands once ministered to you; my arms sheltered you, and my heart loved you and mourned you like a mother loves and mourns her firstborn."

"Oh, how strange, how delightful!" exclaimed Clara. "Now I understand why you clasped me so tightly, and were so agitated when I told you my story. It is too good for me to believe. I am of good blood, of an old and aristocratic family. My presentiment has come true. I can marry my lover, and I shall owe all my happiness to you. How can I ever repay you?"

"You can kiss me, child, kiss your mammy."

Their lips met, and they were clasped in each other's arms. One put into the embrace all of her new-found joy, the other all the suppressed feeling of the last half hour, which in turn embodied the unsatisfied yearning of many years.

The music had ceased and the pupils had left the hall. Mrs. Harper's charges had supposed her gone, and had left for home without her. But the two women, sitting in Clara's chamber, hand in hand, were oblivious to external things and noticed neither the hour nor the cessation of the music.

"Why, dear mammy," said the young woman musingly, "did you not find me, and restore me to my people?"

"Alas, child! I was not white, and when I was picked up from the water, after floating miles down the river, the man who found me kept me prisoner for a time, and, there being no inquiry for me, pretended not to believe that I was free, and took me down to New Orleans and sold me as a slave. A few years later the war set me free. I went to St. Louis but could find no trace of you. I had hardly dared to hope that a child had been saved, when so many grown men and women had lost their lives. I made such inquiries as I could, but all in vain."

"Did you go to the orphan asylum?"

"The orphan asylum had been burned and with it all the records. The war had scattered the people so that I could find no one who knew about a lost child saved from a river wreck.

There were many orphans in those days, and one more or less was not likely to dwell in the public mind."

"Did you tell my people in Virginia?"

"They, too, were scattered by the war. Your uncles lost their lives on the battlefield. The family mansion was burned to the ground. Your father's remaining relatives were reduced to poverty, and moved away from Virginia."

"What of my mother's people?"

"They are all dead. God punished them. They did not love your father, and did not wish him to marry your mother. They helped to drive him to his death."

"I am alone in the world, then, without kith or kin," murmured Clara, "and yet, strange to say, I am happy. If I had known my people and lost them, I should be sad. They are gone, but they have left me their name and their blood. I would weep for my poor father and mother if I were not so glad."

Just then some one struck a chord upon the piano in the hall, and the sudden breaking of the stillness recalled Clara's attention to the lateness of the hour.

"I had forgotten about the class," she exclaimed. "I must go and attend to them."

They walked along the corridor and entered the hall. Dr. Winthrop was seated at the piano, drumming idly on the keys.

"I did not know where you had gone," he said. "I knew you would be around, of course, since the lights were not out, and so I came in here to wait for you."

"Listen, John, I have a wonderful story to tell you."

Then she told him Mrs. Harper's story. He listened attentively and sympathetically, at certain points taking his eyes from Clara's face and glancing keenly at Mrs. Harper, who was listening intently. As he looked from one to the other he noticed the resemblance between them, and something in his expression caused Mrs. Harper's eyes to fall, and then glance up appealingly.

"And now," said Clara, "I am happy. I know my name. I am a Virginia Stafford. I belong to one, yes, to two of what were the first families of Virginia. John, my family is as good as yours. If I remember my history correctly, the Cavaliers looked down upon the Roundheads."

"I admit my inferiority," he replied. "If you are happy I am glad."

"Clara Stafford," mused the girl. "It is a pretty name."

"You will never have to use it," her lover declared, "for now you will take mine."

"Then I shall have nothing left of all that I have found"—

"Except your husband," asserted Dr. Winthrop, putting his arm around her, with an air of assured possession.

Mrs. Harper was looking at them with moistened eyes in which joy and sorrow, love and gratitude, were strangely blended. Clara put out her hand to her impulsively.

"And my mammy," she cried, "my dear Virginia mammy."

The Sheriff's Children

BRANSON COUNTY, North Carolina, is in a sequestered district of one of the staidest and most conservative States of the Union. Society in Branson County is almost primitive in its simplicity. Most of the white people own the farms they till, and even before the war there were no very wealthy families to force their neighbors, by comparison, into the category of "poor whites."

To Branson County, as to most rural communities in the South, the war is the one historical event that overshadows all others. It is the era from which all local chronicles are dated,—births, deaths, marriages, storms, freshets. No description of the life of any Southern community would be perfect that failed to emphasize the all pervading influence of the great conflict.

Yet the fierce tide of war that had rushed through the cities and along the great highways of the country had comparatively speaking but slightly disturbed the sluggish current of life in this region, remote from railroads and navigable streams. To the north in Virginia, to the west in Tennessee, and all along the seaboard the war had raged; but the thunder of its cannon had not disturbed the echoes of Branson County, where the loudest sounds heard were the crack of some hunter's rifle, the baying of some deep-mouthed hound, or the yodel of some tuneful negro on his way through the pine forest. To the east, Sherman's army had passed on its march to the sea; but no straggling band of "bummers" had penetrated the confines of Branson County. The war, it is true, had robbed the county of the flower of its young manhood; but the burden of taxation, the doubt and uncertainty of the conflict, and the sting of ultimate defeat, had been borne by the people with an apathy that robbed misfortune of half its sharpness.

The nearest approach to town life afforded by Branson County is found in the little village of Troy, the county seat, a hamlet with a population of four or five hundred.

Ten years make little difference in the appearance of these remote Southern towns. If a railroad is built through one of them, it infuses some enterprise; the social corpse is galvanized by the fresh blood of civilization that pulses along the farthest ramifications of our great system of commercial highways. At the period of which I write, no railroad had come to Troy. If a traveler, accustomed to the bustling life of cities, could have ridden through Troy on a summer day, he might easily have fancied himself in a deserted village. Around him he would have seen weather-beaten houses, innocent of paint, the shingled roofs in many instances covered with a rich growth of moss. Here and there he would have met a razor-backed hog lazily rooting his way along the principal thoroughfare; and more than once he would probably have had to disturb the slumbers of some yellow dog, dozing away the hours in the ardent sunshine, and reluctantly yielding up his place in the middle of the dusty road.

On Saturdays the village presented a somewhat livelier appearance, and the shade trees around the court house square and along Front Street served as hitching-posts for a goodly number of horses and mules and stunted oxen, belonging to the farmer-folk who had come in to trade at the two or three local stores.

A murder was a rare event in Branson County. Every well-informed citizen could tell the number of homicides committed in the county for fifty years back, and whether the slayer, in any given instance, had escaped, either by flight or acquittal, or had suffered the penalty of the law. So, when it became known in Troy early one Friday morning in summer, about ten years after the war, that old Captain Walker, who had served in Mexico under Scott, and had left an arm on the field of Gettysburg, had been foully murdered during the night, there was intense excitement in the village. Business was practically suspended, and the citizens gathered in little groups to discuss the murder, and speculate upon the identity of the murderer. It transpired from testimony at the coroner's inquest, held during the morning, that a strange mulatto had been seen going in the direction of Captain Walker's house the night before, and had been met going away from Troy early Friday morning, by a farmer on his way to town. Other circumstances seemed to connect the stranger with the crime. The sheriff organized a posse to search for him, and early in the evening, when most of the citizens of Troy were at supper, the suspected man was brought in and lodged in the county jail.

By the following morning the news of the capture had spread to the farthest limits of the county. A much larger number of people than usual came to town that Saturday,—bearded men in straw hats and blue homespun shirts, and butternut trousers of great amplitude of material and vagueness of outline; women in homespun frocks and slat-bonnets, with faces as expressionless as the dreary sandhills which gave them a meagre sustenance.

The murder was almost the sole topic of conversation. A steady stream of curious observers visited the house of mourning, and gazed upon the rugged face of the old veteran, now stiff and cold in death; and more than one eye dropped a tear at the remembrance of the cheery smile, and the joke—sometimes superannuated, generally feeble, but always good-natured—with which the captain had been wont to greet his acquaintances. There was a growing sentiment of anger among these stern men, toward the murderer who had thus cut down their friend, and a strong feeling that ordinary justice was too slight a punishment for such a crime.

Toward noon there was an informal gathering of citizens in Dan Tyson's store.

"I hear it 'lowed that Square Kyahtah's too sick ter hol' co'te this evenin'," said one, "an' that the purlim'nary hearin' 'll haf ter go over 'tel nex' week."

A look of disappointment went round the crowd.

"Hit 's the durndes', meanes' murder ever committed in this caounty," said another, with moody emphasis.

"I s'pose the nigger 'lowed the Cap'n had some greenbacks," observed a third speaker.

"The Cap'n," said another, with an air of superior information, "has left two bairls of Confedrit money, which he 'spected 'ud be good some day er nuther."

This statement gave rise to a discussion of the speculative value of Confederate money; but in a little while the conversation returned to the murder.

"Hangin' air too good fer the murderer," said one; "he oughter be burnt, stidier bein' hung."

There was an impressive pause at this point, during which a jug of moonlight whiskey went the round of the crowd.

"Well," said a round-shouldered farmer, who, in spite of his peaceable expression and faded gray eye, was known to have been one of the most daring followers of a rebel guerrilla chieftain, "what air yer gwine ter do about it? Ef you fellers air gwine ter set down an' let a wuthless nigger kill the bes' white man in Branson, an' not say nuthin' ner do nuthin', *I'll* move outen the caounty."

This speech gave tone and direction to the rest of the conversation. Whether the fear of losing the round-shouldered farmer operated to bring about the result or not is immaterial to this narrative; but, at all events, the crowd decided to lynch the negro. They agreed that this was the least that could be done to avenge the death of their murdered friend, and that it was a becoming way in which to honor his memory. They had some vague notions of the majesty of the law and the rights of the citizen, but in the passion of the moment these sunk into oblivion; a white man had been killed by a negro.

"The Cap'n was an ole sodger," said one of his friends solemnly. "He 'll sleep better when he knows that a co'te-martial has be'n hilt an' jestice done."

By agreement the lynchers were to meet at Tyson's store at five o'clock in the afternoon, and proceed thence to the jail, which was situated down the Lumberton Dirt Road (as the old turnpike antedating the plank-road was called), about half a mile south of the court-house. When the preliminaries of the lynching had been arranged, and a committee appointed to manage the affair, the crowd dispersed, some to go to their dinners, and some to secure recruits for the lynching party.

It was twenty minutes to five o'clock, when an excited negro, panting and perspiring, rushed up to the back door of Sheriff Campbell's dwelling, which stood at a little distance from the jail and somewhat farther than the latter building from the court-house. A turbaned colored woman came to the door in response to the negro's knock.

"Hoddy, Sis' Nance."

"Hoddy, Brer Sam."

"Is de shurff in," inquired the negro.

"Yas, Brer Sam, he 's eatin' his dinner," was the answer.

"Will yer ax 'im ter step ter de do' a minute, Sis' Nance?"

The woman went into the dining-room, and a moment later the sheriff came to the door. He was a tall, muscular man, of a ruddier complexion than is usual among Southerners. A pair of keen, deep-set gray eyes looked out from under bushy eyebrows, and about his mouth was a masterful expression, which a full beard, once sandy in color, but now profusely sprinkled with gray, could not entirely conceal. The day was hot; the sheriff had discarded his coat and vest, and had his white shirt open at the throat.

"What do you want, Sam?" he inquired of the negro, who stood hat in hand, wiping the moisture from his face with a ragged shirt-sleeve.

"Shurff, dey gwine ter hang de pris'ner w'at 's lock' up in de jail. Dey 're comin' dis a-way now. I wuz layin' down on a sack er corn down at de sto', behine a pile er flour-bairls, w'en I hearn Doc' Cain en Kunnel Wright talkin' erbout it. I slip' outen de back do', en run here as fas' as I could. I hearn you say down ter de sto' once't dat you would n't let nobody take a pris'ner 'way fum you widout walkin' over yo' dead body, en I thought I 'd let you know 'fo' dey come, so yer could pertec' de pris'ner."

The sheriff listened calmly, but his face grew firmer, and a determined gleam lit up his gray eyes. His frame grew more erect, and he unconsciously assumed the attitude of a soldier who momentarily expects to meet the enemy face to face.

"Much obliged, Sam," he answered. "I 'll protect the prisoner. Who 's coming?"

"I dunno who-all *is* comin'," replied the negro. "Dere 's Mistah McSwayne, en Doc' Cain, en Maje' McDonal', en Kunnel Wright, en a heap er yuthers. I wuz so skeered I done furgot mo' d'n half un em. I spec' dey mus' be mos' here by dis time, so I 'll git outen de way, fer I don' want nobody fer ter think I wuz mix' up in dis business." The negro glanced nervously down the road toward the town, and made a movement as if to go away.

"Won't you have some dinner first?" asked the sheriff.

The negro looked longingly in at the open door, and sniffed the appetizing odor of boiled pork and collards.

"I ain't got no time fer ter tarry, Shurff," he said, "but Sis'

Nance mought gin me sump'n I could kyar in my han' en eat on de way."

A moment later Nancy brought him a huge sandwich of split corn-pone, with a thick slice of fat bacon inserted between the halves, and a couple of baked yams. The negro hastily replaced his ragged hat on his head, dropped the yams in the pocket of his capacious trousers, and, taking the sandwich in his hand, hurried across the road and disappeared in the woods beyond.

The sheriff reëntered the house, and put on his coat and hat. He then took down a double-barreled shotgun and loaded it with buckshot. Filling the chambers of a revolver with fresh cartridges, he slipped it into the pocket of the sack-coat which he wore.

A comely young woman in a calico dress watched these proceedings with anxious surprise.

"Where are you going, father?" she asked. She had not heard the conversation with the negro.

"I am goin' over to the jail," responded the sheriff. "There 's a mob comin' this way to lynch the nigger we 've got locked up. But they won't do it," he added, with emphasis.

"Oh, father! don't go!" pleaded the girl, clinging to his arm; "they 'll shoot you if you don't give him up."

"You never mind me, Polly," said her father reassuringly, as he gently unclasped her hands from his arm. "I 'll take care of myself and the prisoner, too. There ain't a man in Branson County that would shoot me. Besides, I have faced fire too often to be scared away from my duty. You keep close in the house," he continued, "and if any one disturbs you just use the old horse-pistol in the top bureau drawer. It 's a little old-fashioned, but it did good work a few years ago."

The young girl shuddered at this sanguinary allusion, but made no further objection to her father's departure.

The sheriff of Branson was a man far above the average of the community in wealth, education, and social position. His had been one of the few families in the county that before the war had owned large estates and numerous slaves. He had graduated at the State University at Chapel Hill, and had kept up some acquaintance with current literature and advanced thought. He had traveled some in his youth, and was looked up to in the county as an authority on all subjects connected with the outer world. At first an ardent supporter of the Union, he had opposed the secession movement in his native State as long as opposition availed to stem the tide of public opinion. Yielding at last to the force of circumstances, he had entered the Confederate service rather late in the war, and served with distinction through several campaigns, rising in time to the rank of colonel. After the war he had taken the oath of allegiance, and had been chosen by the people as the most available candidate for the office of sheriff, to which he had been elected without opposition. He had filled the office for several terms, and was universally popular with his constituents.

Colonel or Sheriff Campbell, as he was indifferently called, as the military or civil title happened to be most important in the opinion of the person addressing him, had a high sense of the responsibility attaching to his office. He had sworn to do his duty faithfully, and he knew what his duty was, as sheriff, perhaps more clearly than he had apprehended it in other passages of his life. It was, therefore, with no uncertainty in regard to his course that he prepared his weapons and went over to the jail. He had no fears for Polly's safety.

The sheriff had just locked the heavy front door of the jail behind him when a half dozen horsemen, followed by a crowd of men on foot, came round a bend in the road and drew near the jail. They halted in front of the picket fence that surrounded the building, while several of the committee of arrangements rode on a few rods farther to the sheriff's house. One of them dismounted and rapped on the door with his riding-whip.

"Is the sheriff at home?" he inquired.

"No, he has just gone out," replied Polly, who had come to the door.

"We want the jail keys," he continued.

"They are not here," said Polly. "The sheriff has them himself." Then she added, with assumed indifference, "He is at the jail now."

The man turned away, and Polly went into the front room, from which she peered anxiously between the slats of the green blinds of a window that looked toward the jail. Meanwhile the messenger returned to his companions and announced his discovery. It looked as though the sheriff had learned of their design and was preparing to resist it.

One of them stepped forward and rapped on the jail door.

"Well, what is it?" said the sheriff, from within.

"We want to talk to you, Sheriff," replied the spokesman.

There was a little wicket in the door; this the sheriff opened, and answered through it.

"All right, boys, talk away. You are all strangers to me, and I don't know what business you can have." The sheriff did not think it necessary to recognize anybody in particular on such an occasion; the question of identity sometimes comes up in the investigation of these extra-judicial executions.

"We 're a committee of citizens and we want to get into the jail."

"What for? It ain't much trouble to get into jail. Most people want to keep out."

The mob was in no humor to appreciate a joke, and the sheriff's witticism fell dead upon an unresponsive audience.

"We want to have a talk with the nigger that killed Cap'n Walker."

"You can talk to that nigger in the court-house, when he 's brought out for trial. Court will be in session here next week. I know what you fellows want, but you can't get my prisoner to-day. Do you want to take the bread out of a poor man's mouth? I get seventy-five cents a day for keeping this prisoner, and he 's the only one in jail. I can't have my family suffer just to please you fellows."

One or two young men in the crowd laughed at the idea of Sheriff Campbell's suffering for want of seventy-five cents a day; but they were frowned into silence by those who stood near them.

"Ef yer don't let us in," cried a voice, "we 'll bu's' the do' open."

"Bust away," answered the sheriff, raising his voice so that all could hear. "But I give you fair warning. The first man that tries it will be filled with buckshot. I 'm sheriff of this county; I know my duty, and I mean to do it."

"What 's the use of kicking, Sheriff?" argued one of the

leaders of the mob. "The nigger is sure to hang anyhow; he richly deserves it; and we 've got to do something to teach the niggers their places, or white people won't be able to live in the county."

"There 's no use talking, boys," responded the sheriff. "I 'm a white man outside, but in this jail I 'm sheriff; and if this nigger 's to be hung in this county, I propose to do the hanging. So you fellows might as well right-about-face, and march back to Troy. You 've had a pleasant trip, and the exercise will be good for you. You know *me.* I 've got powder and ball, and I 've faced fire before now, with nothing between me and the enemy, and I don't mean to surrender this jail while I 'm able to shoot." Having thus announced his determination, the sheriff closed and fastened the wicket, and looked around for the best position from which to defend the building.

The crowd drew off a little, and the leaders conversed together in low tones.

The Branson County jail was a small, two-story brick building, strongly constructed, with no attempt at architectural ornamentation. Each story was divided into two large cells by a passage running from front to rear. A grated iron door gave entrance from the passage to each of the four cells. The jail seldom had many prisoners in it, and the lower windows had been boarded up. When the sheriff had closed the wicket, he ascended the steep wooden stairs to the upper floor. There was no window at the front of the upper passage, and the most available position from which to watch the movements of the crowd below was the front window of the cell occupied by the solitary prisoner.

The sheriff unlocked the door and entered the cell. The prisoner was crouched in a corner, his yellow face, blanched with terror, looking ghastly in the semi-darkness of the room. A cold perspiration had gathered on his forehead, and his teeth were chattering with affright.

"For God's sake, Sheriff," he murmured hoarsely, "don't let 'em lynch me; I did n't kill the old man."

The sheriff glanced at the cowering wretch with a look of mingled contempt and loathing.

"Get up," he said sharply. "You will probably be hung

sooner or later, but it shall not be to-day, if I can help it. I 'll unlock your fetters, and if I can't hold the jail, you 'll have to make the best fight you can. If I 'm shot, I 'll consider my responsibility at an end."

There were iron fetters on the prisoner's ankles, and handcuffs on his wrists. These the sheriff unlocked, and they fell clanking to the floor.

"Keep back from the window," said the sheriff. "They might shoot if they saw you."

The sheriff drew toward the window a pine bench which formed a part of the scanty furniture of the cell, and laid his revolver upon it. Then he took his gun in hand, and took his stand at the side of the window where he could with least exposure of himself watch the movements of the crowd below.

The lynchers had not anticipated any determined resistance. Of course they had looked for a formal protest, and perhaps a sufficient show of opposition to excuse the sheriff in the eye of any stickler for legal formalities. They had not however come prepared to fight a battle, and no one of them seemed willing to lead an attack upon the jail. The leaders of the party conferred together with a good deal of animated gesticulation, which was visible to the sheriff from his outlook, though the distance was too great for him to hear what was said. At length one of them broke away from the group, and rode back to the main body of the lynchers, who were restlessly awaiting orders.

"Well, boys," said the messenger, "we 'll have to let it go for the present. The sheriff says he 'll shoot, and he 's got the drop on us this time. There ain't any of us that want to follow Cap'n Walker jest yet. Besides, the sheriff is a good fellow, and we don't want to hurt 'im. But," he added, as if to reassure the crowd, which began to show signs of disappointment, "the nigger might as well say his prayers, for he ain't got long to live."

There was a murmur of dissent from the mob, and several voices insisted that an attack be made on the jail. But pacific counsels finally prevailed, and the mob sullenly withdrew.

The sheriff stood at the window until they had disappeared around the bend in the road. He did not relax his watchfulness when the last one was out of sight. Their withdrawal might be a mere feint, to be followed by a further attempt. So closely, indeed, was his attention drawn to the outside, that he neither saw nor heard the prisoner creep stealthily across the floor, reach out his hand and secure the revolver which lay on the bench behind the sheriff, and creep as noiselessly back to his place in the corner of the room.

A moment after the last of the lynching party had disappeared there was a shot fired from the woods across the road; a bullet whistled by the window and buried itself in the wooden casing a few inches from where the sheriff was standing. Quick as thought, with the instinct born of a semi-guerrilla army experience, he raised his gun and fired twice at the point from which a faint puff of smoke showed the hostile bullet to have been sent. He stood a moment watching, and then rested his gun against the window, and reached behind him mechanically for the other weapon. It was not on the bench. As the sheriff realized this fact, he turned his head and looked into the muzzle of the revolver.

"Stay where you are, Sheriff," said the prisoner, his eyes glistening, his face almost ruddy with excitement.

The sheriff mentally cursed his own carelessness for allowing him to be caught in such a predicament. He had not expected anything of the kind. He had relied on the negro's cowardice and subordination in the presence of an armed white man as a matter of course. The sheriff was a brave man, but realized that the prisoner had him at an immense disadvantage. The two men stood thus for a moment, fighting a harmless duel with their eyes.

"Well, what do you mean to do?" asked the sheriff with apparent calmness.

"To get away, of course," said the prisoner, in a tone which caused the sheriff to look at him more closely, and with an involuntary feeling of apprehension; if the man was not mad, he was in a state of mind akin to madness, and quite as dangerous. The sheriff felt that he must speak the prisoner fair, and watch for a chance to turn the tables on him. The keen-eyed, desperate man before him was a different being altogether from the groveling wretch who had begged so piteously for life a few minutes before.

At length the sheriff spoke:—

"Is this your gratitude to me for saving your life at the risk of my own? If I had not done so, you would now be swinging from the limb of some neighboring tree."

"True," said the prisoner, "you saved my life, but for how long? When you came in, you said Court would sit next week. When the crowd went away they said I had not long to live. It is merely a choice of two ropes."

"While there 's life there 's hope," replied the sheriff. He uttered this commonplace mechanically, while his brain was busy in trying to think out some way of escape. "If you are innocent you can prove it."

The mulatto kept his eye upon the sheriff. "I did n't kill the old man," he replied; "but I shall never be able to clear myself. I was at his house at nine o'clock. I stole from it the coat that was on my back when I was taken. I would be convicted, even with a fair trial, unless the real murderer were discovered beforehand."

The sheriff knew this only too well. While he was thinking what argument next to use, the prisoner continued:—

"Throw me the keys—no, unlock the door."

The sheriff stood a moment irresolute. The mulatto's eye glittered ominously. The sheriff crossed the room and unlocked the door leading into the passage.

"Now go down and unlock the outside door."

The heart of the sheriff leaped within him. Perhaps he might make a dash for liberty, and gain the outside. He descended the narrow stairs, the prisoner keeping close behind him.

The sheriff inserted the huge iron key into the lock. The rusty bolt yielded slowly. It still remained for him to pull the door open.

"Stop!" thundered the mulatto, who seemed to divine the sheriff's purpose. "Move a muscle, and I 'll blow your brains out."

The sheriff obeyed; he realized that his chance had not yet come.

"Now keep on that side of the passage, and go back upstairs."

Keeping the sheriff under cover of the revolver, the mulatto followed him up the stairs. The sheriff expected the prisoner to lock him into the cell and make his own escape. He had about come to the conclusion that the best thing he could do under the circumstances was to submit quietly, and take his chances of recapturing the prisoner after the alarm had been given. The sheriff had faced death more than once upon the battlefield. A few minutes before, well armed, and with a brick wall between him and them he had dared a hundred men to fight; but he felt instinctively that the desperate man confronting him was not to be trifled with, and he was too prudent a man to risk his life against such heavy odds. He had Polly to look after, and there was a limit beyond which devotion to duty would be quixotic and even foolish.

"I want to get away," said the prisoner, "and I don't want to be captured; for if I am I know I will be hung on the spot. I am afraid," he added somewhat reflectively, "that in order to save myself I shall have to kill you."

"Good God!" exclaimed the sheriff in involuntary terror; "you would not kill the man to whom you owe your own life."

"You speak more truly than you know," replied the mulatto. "I indeed owe my life to you."

The sheriff started. he was capable of surprise, even in that moment of extreme peril. "Who are you?" he asked in amazement.

"Tom, Cicely's son," returned the other. He had closed the door and stood talking to the sheriff through the grated opening. "Don't you remember Cicely—Cicely whom you sold, with her child, to the speculator on his way to Alabama?"

The sheriff did remember. He had been sorry for it many a time since. It had been the old story of debts, mortgages, and bad crops. He had quarreled with the mother. The price offered for her and her child had been unusually large, and he had yielded to the combination of anger and pecuniary stress.

"Good God!" he gasped, "you would not murder your own father?"

"My father?" replied the mulatto. "It were well enough for me to claim the relationship, but it comes with poor grace from you to ask anything by reason of it. What father's duty have you ever performed for me? Did you give me your name, or even your protection? Other white men gave their colored sons freedom and money, and sent them to the free States. *You* sold *me* to the rice swamps."

"I at least gave you the life you cling to," murmured the sheriff.

"Life?" said the prisoner, with a sarcastic laugh. "What kind of a life? You gave me your own blood, your own features,—no man need look at us together twice to see that,—and you gave me a black mother. Poor wretch! She died under the lash, because she had enough womanhood to call her soul her own. You gave me a white man's spirit, and you made me a slave, and crushed it out."

"But you are free now," said the sheriff. He had not doubted, could not doubt, the mulatto's word. He knew whose passions coursed beneath that swarthy skin and burned in the black eyes opposite his own. He saw in this mulatto what he himself might have become had not the safeguards of parental restraint and public opinion been thrown around him.

"Free to do what?" replied the mulatto. "Free in name, but despised and scorned and set aside by the people to whose race I belong far more than to my mother's."

"There are schools," said the sheriff. "You have been to school." He had noticed that the mulatto spoke more eloquently and used better language than most Branson County people.

"I have been to school, and dreamed when I went that it would work some marvelous change in my condition. But what did I learn? I learned to feel that no degree of learning or wisdom will change the color of my skin and that I shall always wear what in my own country is a badge of degradation. When I think about it seriously I do not care particularly for such a life. It is the animal in me, not the man, that flees the gallows. I owe you nothing," he went on, "and expect nothing of you; and it would be no more than justice if I should avenge upon you my mother's wrongs and my own. But still I hate to shoot you; I have never yet taken human life—for I did *not* kill the old captain. Will you promise to give no alarm and make no attempt to capture me until morning, if I do not shoot?"

So absorbed were the two men in their colloquy and their own tumultuous thoughts that neither of them had heard the door below move upon its hinges. Neither of them had heard a light step come stealthily up the stairs, nor seen a slender form creep along the darkening passage toward the mulatto.

The sheriff hesitated. The struggle between his love of life and his sense of duty was a terrific one. It may seem strange that a man who could sell his own child into slavery should hesitate at such a moment, when his life was trembling in the balance. But the baleful influence of human slavery poisoned the very fountains of life, and created new standards of right. The sheriff was conscientious; his conscience had merely been warped by his environment. Let no one ask what his answer would have been; he was spared the necessity of a decision.

"Stop," said the mulatto, "you need not promise. I could not trust you if you did. It is your life for mine; there is but one safe way for me; you must die."

He raised his arm to fire, when there was a flash—a report from the passage behind him. His arm fell heavily at his side, and the pistol dropped at his feet.

The sheriff recovered first from his surprise, and throwing open the door secured the fallen weapon. Then seizing the prisoner he thrust him into the cell and locked the door upon him; after which he turned to Polly, who leaned half-fainting against the wall, her hands clasped over her heart.

"Oh, father, I was just in time!" she cried hysterically, and, wildly sobbing, threw herself into her father's arms.

"I watched until they all went away," she said. "I heard the shot from the woods and I saw you shoot. Then when you did not come out I feared something had happened, that perhaps you had been wounded. I got out the other pistol and ran over here. When I found the door open, I knew something was wrong, and when I heard voices I crept upstairs, and reached the top just in time to hear him say he would kill you. Oh, it was a narrow escape!"

When she had grown somewhat calmer, the sheriff left her standing there and went back into the cell. The prisoner's arm was bleeding from a flesh wound. His bravado had given place to a stony apathy. There was no sign in his face of fear or disappointment or feeling of any kind. The sheriff sent

Polly to the house for cloth, and bound up the prisoner's wound with a rude skill acquired during his army life.

"I 'll have a doctor come and dress the wound in the morning," he said to the prisoner. "It will do very well until then, if you will keep quiet. If the doctor asks you how the wound was caused, you can say that you were struck by the bullet fired from the woods. It would do you no good to have it known that you were shot while attempting to escape."

The prisoner uttered no word of thanks or apology, but sat in sullen silence. When the wounded arm had been bandaged, Polly and her father returned to the house.

The sheriff was in an unusually thoughtful mood that evening. He put salt in his coffee at supper, and poured vinegar over his pancakes. To many of Polly's questions he returned random answers. When he had gone to bed he lay awake for several hours.

In the silent watches of the night, when he was alone with God, there came into his mind a flood of unaccustomed thoughts. An hour or two before, standing face to face with death, he had experienced a sensation similar to that which drowning men are said to feel—a kind of clarifying of the moral faculty, in which the veil of the flesh, with its obscuring passions and prejudices, is pushed aside for a moment, and all the acts of one's life stand out, in the clear light of truth, in their correct proportions and relations,—a state of mind in which one sees himself as God may be supposed to see him. In the reaction following his rescue, this feeling had given place for a time to far different emotions. But now, in the silence of midnight, something of this clearness of spirit returned to the sheriff. He saw that he had owed some duty to this son of his,—that neither law nor custom could destroy a responsibility inherent in the nature of mankind. He could not thus, in the eyes of God at least, shake off the consequences of his sin. Had he never sinned, this wayward spirit would never have come back from the vanished past to haunt him. As these thoughts came, his anger against the mulatto died away, and in its place there sprang up a great pity. The hand of parental authority might have restrained the passions he had seen burning in the prisoner's eyes when the desperate man spoke the words which had seemed to doom his father to death. The sheriff felt that he might have saved this fiery spirit from the slough of slavery; that he might have sent him to the free North, and given him there, or in some other land, an opportunity to turn to usefulness and honorable pursuits the talents that had run to crime, perhaps to madness; he might, still less, have given this son of his the poor simulacrum of liberty which men of his caste could possess in a slave-holding community; or least of all, but still something, he might have kept the boy on the plantation, where the burdens of slavery would have fallen lightly upon him.

The sheriff recalled his own youth. He had inherited an honored name to keep untarnished; he had had a future to make; the picture of a fair young bride had beckoned him on to happiness. The poor wretch now stretched upon a pallet of straw between the brick walls of the jail had had none of these things,—no name, no father, no mother—in the true meaning of motherhood,—and until the past few years no possible future, and then one vague and shadowy in its outline, and dependent for form and substance upon the slow solution of a problem in which there were many unknown quantities.

From what he might have done to what he might yet do was an easy transition for the awakened conscience of the sheriff. It occurred to him, purely as a hypothesis, that he might permit his prisoner to escape; but his oath of office, his duty as sheriff, stood in the way of such a course, and the sheriff dismissed the idea from his mind. He could, however, investigate the circumstances of the murder, and move Heaven and earth to discover the real criminal, for he no longer doubted the prisoner's innocence; he could employ counsel for the accused, and perhaps influence public opinion in his favor. An acquittal once secured, some plan could be devised by which the sheriff might in some degree atone for his crime against this son of his—against society—against God.

When the sheriff had reached this conclusion he fell into an unquiet slumber, from which he awoke late the next morning.

He went over to the jail before breakfast and found the prisoner lying on his pallet, his face turned to the wall; he did not move when the sheriff rattled the door.

"Good-morning," said the latter, in a tone intended to waken the prisoner.

There was no response. The sheriff looked more keenly at the recumbent figure; there was an unnatural rigidity about its attitude.

He hastily unlocked the door and, entering the cell, bent over the prostrate form. There was no sound of breathing; he turned the body over—it was cold and stiff. The prisoner had torn the bandage from his wound and bled to death during the night. He had evidently been dead several hours.

A Matter of Principle

I

"WHAT our country needs most in its treatment of the race problem," observed Mr. Cicero Clayton at one of the monthly meetings of the Blue Vein Society, of which he was a prominent member, "is a clearer conception of the brotherhood of man."

The same sentiment in much the same words had often fallen from Mr. Clayton's lips,—so often, in fact, that the younger members of the society sometimes spoke of him—among themselves of course—as "Brotherhood Clayton." The sobriquet derived its point from the application he made of the principle involved in this oft-repeated proposition.

The fundamental article of Mr. Clayton's social creed was that he himself was not a negro.

"I know," he would say, "that the white people lump us all together as negroes, and condemn us all to the same social ostracism. But I don't accept this classification, for my part, and I imagine that, as the chief party in interest, I have a right to my opinion. People who belong by half or more of their blood to the most virile and progressive race of modern times have as much right to call themselves white as others have to call them negroes."

Mr. Clayton spoke warmly, for he was well informed, and had thought much upon the subject; too much, indeed, for he had not been able to escape entirely the tendency of too much concentration upon one subject to make even the clearest minds morbid.

"Of course we can't enforce our claims, or protect ourselves from being robbed of our birthright; but we can at least have principles, and try to live up to them the best we can. If we are not accepted as white, we can at any rate make it clear that we object to being called black. Our protest cannot fail in time to impress itself upon the better class of white people; for the Anglo-Saxon race loves justice, and will eventually do it, where it does not conflict with their own interests."

Whether or not the fact that Mr. Clayton meant no sarcasm, and was conscious of no inconsistency in this eulogy, tended to establish the racial identity he claimed may safely be left to the discerning reader.

In living up to his creed Mr. Clayton declined to associate to any considerable extent with black people. This was sometimes a little inconvenient, and occasionally involved a sacrifice of some pleasure for himself and his family, because they would not attend entertainments where many black people were likely to be present. But they had a social refuge in a little society of people like themselves; they attended, too, a church, of which nearly all the members were white, and they were connected with a number of the religious and benevolent associations open to all good citizens, where they came into contact with the better class of white people, and were treated, in their capacity of members, with a courtesy and consideration scarcely different from that accorded to other citizens.

Mr. Clayton's racial theory was not only logical enough, but was in his own case backed up by substantial arguments. He had begun life with a small patrimony, and had invested his money in a restaurant, which by careful and judicious attention had grown from a cheap eating-house into the most popular and successful confectionery and catering establishment in Groveland. His business occupied a double store on Oakwood Avenue. He owned houses and lots, and stocks and bonds, had good credit at the banks, and lived in a style befitting his income and business standing. In person he was of olive complexion, with slightly curly hair. His features approached the Cuban or Latin-American type rather than the familiar broad characteristics of the mulatto, this suggestion of something foreign being heightened by a Vandyke beard and a carefully waxed and pointed mustache. When he walked to church on Sunday mornings with his daughter Alice, they were a couple of such striking appearance as surely to attract attention.

Miss Alice Clayton was queen of her social set. She was young, she was handsome. She was nearly white; she frankly confessed her sorrow that she was not entirely so. She was accomplished and amiable, dressed in good taste, and had for her father by all odds the richest colored man—the term is used with apologies to Mr. Clayton, explaining that it does not necessarily mean a negro—in Groveland. So pronounced was her superiority that really she had but one social rival worthy of the name,—Miss Lura Watkins, whose father kept a prosperous livery stable and lived in almost as good style as the Claytons. Miss Watkins, while good-looking enough, was not so young nor quite so white as Miss Clayton. She was popular, however, among their mutual acquaintances, and there was a good-natured race between the two as to which should make the first and best marriage.

Marriages among Miss Clayton's set were serious affairs. Of course marriage is always a serious matter, whether it be a success or a failure, and there are those who believe that any marriage is better than no marriage. But among Miss Clayton's friends and associates matrimony took on an added seriousness because of the very narrow limits within which it could take place. Miss Clayton and her friends, by reason of their assumed superiority to black people, or perhaps as much by reason of a somewhat morbid shrinking from the curiosity manifested toward married people of strongly contrasting colors, would not marry black men, and except in rare instances white men would not marry them. They were therefore restricted for a choice to the young men of their own complexion. But these, unfortunately for the girls, had a wider choice. In any State where the laws permit freedom of the marriage contract, a man, by virtue of his sex, can find a wife of whatever complexion he prefers; of course he must not always ask too much in other respects, for most women like to better their social position when they marry. To the number thus lost by "going on the other side," as the phrase went, add the worthless contingent whom no self-respecting woman would marry, and the choice was still further restricted; so that it had become fashionable, when the supply of eligible men ran short, for those of Miss Clayton's set who could afford it to go traveling, ostensibly for pleasure, but with the serious hope that they might meet their fate away from home.

Miss Clayton had perhaps a larger option than any of her associates. Among such men as there were she could have taken her choice. Her beauty, her position, her accomplishments, her father's wealth, all made her eminently desirable. But, on the other hand, the same things rendered her more difficult to reach, and harder to please. To get access to her heart, too, it was necessary to run the gauntlet of her parents, which, until she had reached the age of twenty-three, no one had succeeded in doing safely. Many had called, but none had been chosen.

There was, however, one spot left unguarded, and through it Cupid, a veteran sharpshooter, sent a dart. Mr. Clayton had taken into his service and into his household a poor relation, a sort of cousin several times removed. This boy—his name was Jack—had gone into Mr. Clayton's service at a very youthful age,—twelve or thirteen. He had helped about the housework, washed the dishes, swept the floors, taken care of the lawn and the stable for three or four years, while he attended school. His cousin had then taken him into the store, where he had swept the floor, washed the windows, and done a class of work that kept fully impressed upon him the fact that he was a poor dependent. Nevertheless he was a cheerful lad, who took what he could get and was properly grateful, but always meant to get more. By sheer force of industry and affability and shrewdness, he forced his employer to promote him in time to a position of recognized authority in the establishment. Any one outside of the family would have perceived in him a very suitable husband for Miss Clayton; he was of about the same age, or a year or two older, was as fair of complexion as she, when she was not powdered, and was passably good-looking, with a bearing of which the natural manliness had been no more warped than his training and racial status had rendered inevitable; for he had early learned the law of growth, that to bend is better than to break. He was sometimes sent to accompany Miss Clayton to places in the evening, when she had no other escort, and it is quite likely that she discovered his good points before her parents did. That they should in time perceive them was inevitable. But even then, so accustomed were they to looking down upon the object of their former bounty, that they only spoke of the matter jocularly.

"Well, Alice," her father would say in his bluff way, "you 'll not be absolutely obliged to die an old maid. If we can't find anything better for you, there 's always Jack. As long as he does n't take to some other girl, you can fall back on him as a last chance. He 'd be glad to take you to get into the business."

Miss Alice had considered the joke a very poor one when first made, but by occasional repetition she became somewhat familiar with it. In time it got around to Jack himself, to whom it seemed no joke at all. He had long considered it a consummation devoutly to be wished, and when he became aware that the possibility of such a match had occurred to the other parties in interest, he made up his mind that the idea should in due course of time become an accomplished fact. He had even suggested as much to Alice, in a casual way, to feel his ground; and while she had treated the matter lightly, he was not without hope that she had been impressed by the suggestion. Before he had had time, however, to follow up this lead, Miss Clayton, in the spring of 187–, went away on a visit to Washington.

The occasion of her visit was a presidential inauguration. The new President owed his nomination mainly to the votes of the Southern delegates in the convention, and was believed to be correspondingly well disposed to the race from which the Southern delegates were for the most part recruited. Friends of rival and unsuccessful candidates for the nomination had more than hinted that the Southern delegates were very substantially rewarded for their support at the time when it was given; whether this was true or not the parties concerned know best. At any rate the colored politicians did not see it in that light, for they were gathered from near and far to press their claims for recognition and patronage. On the evening following the White House inaugural ball, the colored people of Washington gave an "inaugural" ball at a large public hall. It was under the management of their leading citizens, among them several high officials holding over from the last administration, and a number of professional and business men. This ball was the most noteworthy social event that colored circles up to that time had ever known. There were many visitors from various parts of the country. Miss

Clayton attended the ball, the honors of which she carried away easily. She danced with several partners, and was introduced to innumerable people whom she had never seen before, and whom she hardly expected ever to meet again. She went away from the ball, at four o'clock in the morning, in a glow of triumph, and with a confused impression of senators and representatives and lawyers and doctors of all shades, who had sought an introduction, led her through the dance, and overwhelmed her with compliments. She returned home the next day but one, after the most delightful week of her life.

II

One afternoon, about three weeks after her return from Washington, Alice received a letter through the mail. The envelope bore the words "House of Representatives" printed in one corner, and in the opposite corner, in a bold running hand, a Congressman's frank, "Hamilton M. Brown, M. C." The letter read as follows:—

HOUSE OF REPRESENTATIVES,
WASHINGTON, D. C., March 30, 187–.

MISS ALICE CLAYTON, GROVELAND.

DEAR FRIEND (if I may be permitted to call you so after so brief an acquaintance),—I remember with sincerest pleasure our recent meeting at the inaugural ball, and the sensation created by your beauty, your amiable manners, and your graceful dancing. Time has so strengthened the impression I then received, that I should have felt inconsolable had I thought it impossible ever to again behold the charms which had brightened the occasion of our meeting and eclipsed by their brilliancy the leading belles of the capital. I had hoped, however, to have the pleasure of meeting you again, and circumstances have fortunately placed it in my power to do so at an early date. You have doubtless learned that the contest over the election in the Sixth Congressional District of South Carolina has been decided in my favor, and that I now have the honor of representing my native State at the national capital. I have just been appointed a member of a special committee to visit and inspect the Sault River and the Straits of Mackinac, with reference to the needs of lake navigation. I have made arrangements to start a week ahead of the other members of the committee, whom I am to meet in Detroit on the 20th. I shall leave here on the 2d, and will arrive in Groveland on the 3d, by the 7.30 evening express. I shall remain in Groveland several days, in the course of which I shall be pleased to call, and renew the acquaintance so auspiciously begun in Washington, which it is my fondest hope may ripen into a warmer friendship.

If you do not regard my visit as presumptuous, and do not write me in the mean while forbidding it, I shall do myself the pleasure of waiting on you the morning after my arrival in Groveland.

With renewed expressions of my sincere admiration and profound esteem, I remain,

Sincerely yours,
HAMILTON M. BROWN, M. C.

To Alice, and especially to her mother, this bold and flowery letter had very nearly the force of a formal declaration. They read it over again and again, and spent most of the afternoon discussing it. There were few young men in Groveland eligible as husbands for so superior a person as Alice Clayton, and an addition to the number would be very acceptable. But the mere fact of his being a Congressman was not sufficient to qualify him; there were other considerations.

"I 've never heard of this Honorable Hamilton M. Brown," said Mr. Clayton. The letter had been laid before him at the supper-table. "It 's strange, Alice, that you have n't said anything about him before. You must have met lots of swell folks not to recollect a Congressman."

"But he was n't a Congressman then," answered Alice; "he was only a claimant. I remember Senator Bruce, and Mr. Douglass; but there were so many doctors and lawyers and politicians that I could n't keep track of them all. Still I have a faint impression of a Mr. Brown who danced with me."

She went into the parlor and brought out the dancing programme she had used at the Washington ball. She had decorated it with a bow of blue ribbon and preserved it as a souvenir of her visit.

"Yes," she said, after examining it, "I must have danced with him. Here are the initials—'H. M. B.' "

"What color is he?" asked Mr. Clayton, as he plied his knife and fork.

"I have a notion that he was rather dark—darker than any one I had ever danced with before."

"Why did you dance with him?" asked her father. "You were n't obliged to go back on your principles because you were away from home."

"Well, father, 'when you 're in Rome'—you know the rest. Mrs. Clearweather introduced me to several dark men, to him among others. They were her friends, and common decency required me to be courteous."

"If this man is black, we don't want to encourage him. If he 's the right sort, we 'll invite him to the house."

"And make him feel at home," added Mrs. Clayton, on hospitable thoughts intent.

"We must ask Sadler about him to-morrow," said Mr. Clayton, when he had drunk his coffee and lighted his cigar. "If he 's the right man he shall have cause to remember his visit to Groveland. We 'll show him that Washington is not the only town on earth."

The uncertainty of the family with regard to Mr. Brown was soon removed. Mr. Solomon Sadler, who was supposed to know everything worth knowing concerning the colored race, and everybody of importance connected with it, dropped in after supper to make an evening call. Sadler was familiar with the history of every man of negro ancestry who had distinguished himself in any walk of life. He could give the pedigree of Alexander Pushkin, the titles of scores of Dumas's novels (even Sadler had not time to learn them all), and could recite the whole of Wendell Phillips's lecture on Toussaint l'Ouverture. He claimed a personal acquaintance with Mr. Frederick Douglass, and had been often in Washington, where he was well known and well received in good colored society.

"Let me see," he said reflectively, when asked for information about the Honorable Hamilton M. Brown. "Yes, I think I know him. He studied at Oberlin just after the war. He was about leaving there when I entered. There were two H. M. Browns there—a Hamilton M. Brown and a Henry M. Brown. One was stout and dark and the other was slim and quite light; you could scarcely tell him from a dark white man. They used to call them 'light Brown' and 'dark Brown.' I did n't know either of them except by sight, for they were there only a few weeks after I went in. As I remember them, Hamilton was the fair one—a very good-looking, gentlemanly fellow, and, as I heard, a good student and a fine speaker."

"Do you remember what kind of hair he had?" asked Mr. Clayton.

"Very good indeed; straight, as I remember it. He looked something like a Spaniard or a Portuguese."

"Now that you describe him," said Alice, "I remember quite well dancing with such a gentleman; and I 'm wrong about my 'H. M. B.' The dark man must have been some one else; there are two others on my card that I can't remember distinctly, and he was probably one of those."

"I guess he 's all right, Alice," said her father when Sadler had gone away. "He evidently means business, and we must treat him white. Of course he must stay with us; there are no hotels in Groveland while he is here. Let 's see—he 'll be here in three days. That is n't very long, but I guess we can get ready. I 'll write a letter this afternoon—or you write it, and invite him to the house, and say I 'll meet him at the depot. And you may have *carte blanche* for making the preparations."

"We must have some people to meet him."

"Certainly; a reception is the proper thing. Sit down immediately and write the letter and I 'll mail it first thing in the morning, so he 'll get it before he has time to make other arrangements. And you and your mother put your heads together and make out a list of guests, and I 'll have the invitations printed to-morrow. We will show the darkeys of Groveland how to entertain a Congressman."

It will be noted that in moments of abstraction or excitement Mr. Clayton sometimes relapsed into forms of speech not entirely consistent with his principles. But some allowance must be made for his atmosphere; he could no more escape from it than the leopard can change his spots, or the— In deference to Mr. Clayton's feelings the quotation will be left incomplete.

Alice wrote the letter on the spot and it was duly mailed, and sped on its winged way to Washington.

The preparations for the reception were made as thoroughly and elaborately as possible on so short a notice. The invitations were issued; the house was cleaned from attic to cellar; an orchestra was engaged for the evening; elaborate floral decorations were planned and the flowers ordered. Even the refreshments, which ordinarily, in the household of a caterer, would be mere matter of familiar detail, became a subject of serious consultation and study.

The approaching event was a matter of very much interest to the fortunate ones who were honored with invitations, and this for several reasons. They were anxious to meet this sole representative of their race in the —th Congress, and as he was not one of the old-line colored leaders, but a new star risen on the political horizon, there was a special curiosity to see who he was and what he looked like. Moreover, the Claytons did not often entertain a large company, but when they did, it was on a scale commensurate with their means and position, and to be present on such an occasion was a thing to remember and to talk about. And, most important consideration of all, some remarks dropped by members of the Clayton family had given rise to the rumor that the Congressman was seeking a wife. This invested his visit with a romantic interest, and gave the reception a practical value; for there were other marriageable girls besides Miss Clayton, and if one was left another might be taken.

III

On the evening of April 3d, at fifteen minutes of six o'clock, Mr. Clayton, accompanied by Jack, entered the livery carriage waiting at his gate and ordered the coachman to drive to the Union Depot. He had taken Jack along, partly for company, and partly that Jack might relieve the Congressman of any trouble about his baggage, and make himself useful in case of emergency. Jack was willing enough to go, for he had foreseen in the visitor a rival for Alice's hand,—indeed he had heard more or less of the subject for several days,—and was glad to make a reconnaissance before the enemy arrived upon the field of battle. He had made—at least he had thought so—considerable progress with Alice during the three weeks since her return from Washington, and once or twice Alice had been perilously near the tender stage. This visit had disturbed the situation and threatened to ruin his chances; but he did not mean to give up without a struggle.

Arrived at the main entrance, Mr. Clayton directed the carriage to wait, and entered the station with Jack. The Union Depot at Groveland was an immense oblong structure, covering a dozen parallel tracks and furnishing terminal passenger facilities for half a dozen railroads. The tracks ran east and west, and the depot was entered from the south, at about the middle of the building. On either side of the entrance, the waiting-rooms, refreshment rooms, baggage and express departments, and other administrative offices, extended in a row for the entire length of the building; and beyond them and parallel with them stretched a long open space, separated from the tracks by an iron fence or *grille*. There were two entrance gates in the fence, at which tickets must be shown before access could be had to trains, and two other gates, by which arriving passengers came out.

Mr. Clayton looked at the blackboard on the wall underneath the station clock, and observed that the 7.30 train from Washington was five minutes late. Accompanied by Jack he walked up and down the platform until the train, with the usual accompaniment of panting steam and clanging bell and rumbling trucks, pulled into the station, and drew up on the third or fourth track from the iron railing. Mr. Clayton stationed himself at the gate nearest the rear end of the train, reasoning that the Congressman would ride in a parlor car, and would naturally come out by the gate nearest the point at which he left the train.

"You 'd better go and stand by the other gate, Jack," he said to his companion, "and stop him if he goes out that way."

The train was well filled and a stream of passengers poured

through. Mr. Clayton scanned the crowd carefully as they approached the gate, and scrutinized each passenger as he came through, without seeing any one that met the description of Congressman Brown, as given by Sadler, or any one that could in his opinion be the gentleman for whom he was looking. When the last one had passed through he was left to the conclusion that his expected guest had gone out by the other gate. Mr. Clayton hastened thither.

"Did n't he come out this way, Jack?" he asked.

"No, sir," replied the young man, "I have n't seen him."

"That 's strange," mused Mr. Clayton, somewhat anxiously. "He would hardly fail to come without giving us notice. Surely we must have missed him. We 'd better look around a little. You go that way and I 'll go this."

Mr. Clayton turned and walked several rods along the platform to the men's waiting-room, and standing near the door glanced around to see if he could find the object of his search. The only colored person in the room was a stout and very black man, wearing a broadcloth suit and a silk hat, and seated a short distance from the door. On the seat by his side stood a couple of valises. On one of them, the one nearest him, on which his arm rested, was written, in white letters, plainly legible,—

"H. M. Brown, M. C.
"Washington, D. C."

Mr. Clayton's feelings at this discovery can better be imagined than described. He hastily left the waiting-room, before the black gentleman, who was looking the other way, was even aware of his presence, and, walking rapidly up and down the platform, communed with himself upon what course of action the situation demanded. He had invited to his house, had come down to meet, had made elaborate preparations to entertain on the following evening, a light-colored man,—a white man by his theory, an acceptable guest, a possible husband for his daughter, an avowed suitor for her hand. If the Congressman had turned out to be brown, even dark brown, with fairly good hair, though he might not have desired him as a son-in-law, yet he could have welcomed him as a guest.

But even this softening of the blow was denied him, for the man in the waiting-room was palpably, aggressively black, with pronounced African features and woolly hair, without apparently a single drop of redeeming white blood. Could he, in the face of his well-known principles, his lifelong rule of conduct, take this negro into his home and introduce him to his friends? Could he subject his wife and daughter to the rude shock of such a disappointment? It would be bad enough for them to learn of the ghastly mistake, but to have him in the house would be twisting the arrow in the wound.

Mr. Clayton had the instincts of a gentleman, and realized the delicacy of the situation. But to get out of his difficulty without wounding the feelings of the Congressman required not only diplomacy but dispatch. Whatever he did must be done promptly; for if he waited many minutes the Congressman would probably take a carriage and be driven to Mr. Clayton's residence.

A ray of hope came for a moment to illumine the gloom of the situation. Perhaps the black man was merely sitting there, and not the owner of the valise! For there were two valises, one on each side of the supposed Congressman. For obvious reasons he did not care to make the inquiry himself, so he looked around for his companion, who came up a moment later.

"Jack," he exclaimed excitedly, "I 'm afraid we 're in the worst kind of a hole, unless there 's some mistake! Run down to the men's waiting-room and you 'll see a man and a valise, and you 'll understand what I mean. Ask that darkey if he is the Honorable Mr. Brown, Congressman from South Carolina. If he says yes, come back right away and let me know, without giving him time to ask any questions, and put your wits to work to help me out of the scrape."

"I wonder what 's the matter?" said Jack to himself, but did as he was told. In a moment he came running back.

"Yes, sir," he announced; "he says he 's the man."

"Jack," said Mr. Clayton desperately, "if you want to show your appreciation of what I 've done for you, you must suggest some way out of this. I 'd never dare to take that negro to my house, and yet I 'm obliged to treat him like a gentleman."

Jack's eyes had worn a somewhat reflective look since he had gone to make the inquiry. Suddenly his face brightened with intelligence, and then, as a newsboy ran into the station calling his wares, hardened into determination.

"Clarion, special extry 'dition! All about de epidemic er dipt'eria!" clamored the newsboy with shrill childish treble, as he made his way toward the waiting-room. Jack darted after him, and saw the man to whom he had spoken buy a paper. He ran back to his employer, and dragged him over toward the ticket-seller's window.

"I have it, sir!" he exclaimed, seizing a telegraph blank and writing rapidly, and reading aloud as he wrote. "How's this for a way out?"—

"DEAR SIR,—I write you this note here in the depot to inform you of an unfortunate event which has interfered with my plans and those of my family for your entertainment while in Groveland. Yesterday my daughter Alice complained of a sore throat, which by this afternoon had developed into a case of malignant diphtheria. In consequence our house has been quarantined; and while I have felt myself obliged to come down to the depot, I do not feel that I ought to expose you to the possibility of infection, and I therefore send you this by another hand. The bearer will conduct you to a carriage which I have ordered placed at your service, and unless you should prefer some other hotel, you will be driven to the Forest Hill House, where I beg you will consider yourself my guest during your stay in the city, and make the fullest use of every convenience it may offer. From present indications I fear no one of our family will be able to see you, which we shall regret beyond expression, as we have made elaborate arrangements for your entertainment. I still hope, however, that you may enjoy your visit, as there are many places of interest in the city, and many friends will doubtless be glad to make your acquaintance.

"With assurances of my profound regret, I am

"Sincerely yours,

"CICERO CLAYTON."

"Splendid!" cried Mr. Clayton. "You 've helped me out of a horrible scrape. Now, go and take him to the hotel and see him comfortably located, and tell them to charge the bill to me."

"I suspect, sir," suggested Jack, "that I 'd better not go up to the house, and you 'll have to stay in yourself for a day or two, to keep up appearances. I 'll sleep on the lounge at the store, and we can talk business over the telephone."

"All right, Jack, we 'll arrange the details later. But for Heaven's sake get him started, or he 'll be calling a hack to drive up to the house. I 'll go home on a street car."

"So far so good," sighed Mr. Clayton to himself as he escaped from the station. "Jack is a deuced clever fellow, and I 'll have to do something more for him. But the tug-of-war is yet to come. I 've got to bribe a doctor, shut up the house for a day or two, and have all the ill-humor of two disappointed women to endure until this negro leaves town. Well, I 'm sure my wife and Alice will back me up at any cost. No sacrifice is too great to escape having to entertain him; of course I have no prejudice against his color,—he can't help that,—but it is the *principle* of the thing. If we received him it would be a concession fatal to all my views and theories. And I am really doing him a kindness, for I 'm sure that all the world could not make Alice and her mother treat him with anything but cold politeness. It 'll be a great mortification to Alice, but I don't see how else I could have got out of it."

He boarded the first car that left the depot, and soon reached home. The house was lighted up, and through the lace curtains of the parlor windows he could see his wife and daughter, elegantly dressed, waiting to receive their distinguished visitor. He rang the bell impatiently, and a servant opened the door.

"The gentleman did n't come?" asked the maid.

"No," he said as he hung up his hat. This brought the ladies to the door.

"He did n't come?" they exclaimed. "What 's the matter?"

"I 'll tell you," he said. "Mary," this to the servant, a white girl, who stood in open-eyed curiosity, "we shan't need you any more to-night."

Then he went into the parlor, and, closing the door, told

his story. When he reached the point where he had discovered the color of the honorable Mr. Brown, Miss Clayton caught her breath, and was on the verge of collapse.

"That nigger," said Mrs. Clayton indignantly, "can never set foot in this house. But what did you do with him?"

Mr. Clayton quickly unfolded his plan, and described the disposition he had made of the Congressman.

"It 's an awful shame," said Mrs. Clayton. "Just think of the trouble and expense we have gone to! And poor Alice 'll never get over it, for everybody knows he came to see her and that he 's smitten with her. But you 've done just right; we never would have been able to hold up our heads again if we had introduced a black man, even a Congressman, to the people that are invited here to-morrow night, as a sweetheart of Alice. Why, she would n't marry him if he was President of the United States and plated with gold an inch thick. The very idea!"

"Well," said Mr. Clayton, "then we 've got to act quick. Alice must wrap up her throat—by the way, Alice, how *is* your throat?"

"It 's sore," sobbed Alice, who had been in tears almost from her father's return, "and I don't care if I do have diphtheria and die, no, I don't!" and she wept on.

"Wrap up your throat and go to bed, and I 'll go over to Doctor Pillsbury's and get a diphtheria card to nail up on the house. In the morning, first thing, we 'll have to write notes recalling the invitations for to-morrow evening, and have them delivered by messenger boys. We were fools for not finding out all about this man from some one who knew, before we invited him here. Sadler don't know more than half he thinks he does, anyway. And we 'll have to do this thing thoroughly, or our motives will be misconstrued, and people will say we are prejudiced and all that, when it is only a matter of principle with us."

The programme outlined above was carried out to the letter. The invitations were recalled, to the great disappointment of the invited guests. The family physician called several times during the day. Alice remained in bed, and the maid left without notice, in such a hurry that she forgot to take her best clothes.

Mr. Clayton himself remained at home. He had a telephone in the house, and was therefore in easy communication with his office, so that the business did not suffer materially by reason of his absence from the store. About ten o'clock in the morning a note came up from the hotel, expressing Mr. Brown's regrets and sympathy. Toward noon Mr. Clayton picked up the morning paper, which he had not theretofore had time to read, and was glancing over it casually, when his eye fell upon a column headed "A Colored Congressman." He read the article with astonishment that rapidly turned to chagrin and dismay. It was an interview describing the Congressman as a tall and shapely man, about thirty-five years old, with an olive complexion not noticeably darker than many a white man's, straight hair, and eyes as black as sloes.

"The bearing of this son of South Carolina reveals the polished manners of the Southern gentleman, and neither from his appearance nor his conversation would one suspect that the white blood which flows in his veins in such preponderating measure had ever been crossed by that of a darker race," wrote the reporter, who had received instructions at the office that for urgent business considerations the lake shipping interest wanted Representative Brown treated with marked consideration.

There was more of the article, but the introductory portion left Mr. Clayton in such a state of bewilderment that the paper fell from his hand. What was the meaning of it? Had he been mistaken? Obviously so, or else the reporter was wrong, which was manifestly improbable. When he had recovered himself somewhat, he picked up the newspaper and began reading where he had left off.

"Representative Brown traveled to Groveland in company with Bishop Jones of the African Methodist Jerusalem Church, who is *en route* to attend the general conference of his denomination at Detroit next week. The bishop, who came in while the writer was interviewing Mr. Brown, is a splendid type of the pure negro. He is said to be a man of great power among his people, which may easily be believed after one has looked upon his expressive countenance and heard him discuss the questions which affect the welfare of his church and his race."

Mr. Clayton stared at the paper. " 'The bishop,' " he repeated, " 'is a splendid type of the pure negro.' I must have mistaken the bishop for the Congressman! But how in the world did Jack get the thing balled up? I 'll call up the store and demand an explanation of him.

"Jack," he asked, "what kind of a looking man was the fellow you gave the note to at the depot?"

"He was a very wicked-looking fellow, sir," came back the answer. "He had a bad eye, looked like a gambler, sir. I am not surprised that you did n't want to entertain him, even if he was a Congressman."

"What color was he—that 's what I want to know—and what kind of hair did he have?"

"Why, he was about my complexion, sir, and had straight black hair."

The rules of the telephone company did not permit swearing over the line. Mr. Clayton broke the rules.

"Was there any one else with him?" he asked when he had relieved his mind.

"Yes, sir, Bishop Jones of the African Methodist Jerusalem Church was sitting there with him; they had traveled from Washington together. I drove the bishop to his stopping-place after I had left Mr. Brown at the hotel. I did n't suppose you 'd mind."

Mr. Clayton fell into a chair, and indulged in thoughts unutterable.

He folded up the paper and slipped it under the family Bible, where it was least likely to be soon discovered.

"I 'll hide the paper, anyway," he groaned. "I 'll never hear the last of this till my dying day, so I may as well have a few hours' respite. It 's too late to go back, and we 've got to play the farce out. Alice is really sick with disappointment, and to let her know this now would only make her worse. Maybe he 'll leave town in a day or two, and then she 'll be in condition to stand it. Such luck is enough to disgust a man with trying to do right and live up to his principles."

Time hung a little heavy on Mr. Clayton's hands during the day. His wife was busy with the housework. He answered several telephone calls about Alice's health, and called up the store occasionally to ask how the business was getting on.

After lunch he lay down on a sofa and took a nap, from which he was aroused by the sound of the door-bell. He went to the door. The evening paper was lying on the porch, and the newsboy, who had not observed the diphtheria sign until after he had rung, was hurrying away as fast as his legs would carry him.

Mr. Clayton opened the paper and looked it through to see if there was any reference to the visiting Congressman. He found what he sought and more. An article on the local page contained a résumé of the information given in the morning paper, with the following additional paragraph:—

"A reporter, who called at the Forest Hill this morning to interview Representative Brown, was informed that the Congressman had been invited to spend the remainder of his time in Groveland as the guest of Mr. William Watkins, the proprietor of the popular livery establishment on Main Street. Mr. Brown will remain in the city several days, and a reception will be tendered him at Mr. Watkins's on Wednesday evening."

"That ends it," sighed Mr. Clayton. "The dove of peace will never again rest on my roof-tree."

But why dwell longer on the sufferings of Mr. Clayton, or attempt to describe the feelings or chronicle the remarks of his wife and daughter when they learned the facts in the case?

As to Representative Brown, he was made welcome in the hospitable home of Mr. William Watkins. There was a large and brilliant assemblage at the party on Wednesday evening, at which were displayed the costumes prepared for the Clayton reception. Mr. Brown took a fancy to Miss Lura Watkins, to whom, before the week was over, he became engaged to be married. Meantime poor Alice, the innocent victim of circumstances and principles, lay sick abed with a supposititious case of malignant diphtheria, and a real case of acute disappointment and chagrin.

"Oh, Jack!" exclaimed Alice, a few weeks later, on the way home from evening church in company with the young man, "what a dreadful thing it all was! And to think of that hateful Lura Watkins marrying the Congressman!"

The street was shaded by trees at the point where they were passing, and there was no one in sight. Jack put his arm around her waist, and, leaning over, kissed her.

"Never mind, dear," he said soothingly, "you still have your 'last chance' left, and I 'll prove myself a better man than the Congressman."

Occasionally, at social meetings, when the vexed question of the future of the colored race comes up, as it often does, for discussion, Mr. Clayton may still be heard to remark sententiously:—

"What the white people of the United States need most, in dealing with this problem, is a higher conception of the brotherhood of man. For of one blood God made all the nations of the earth."

Cicely's Dream

I

THE OLD WOMAN stood at the back door of the cabin, shading her eyes with her hand, and looking across the vegetable garden that ran up to the very door. Beyond the garden she saw, bathed in the sunlight, a field of corn, just in the ear, stretching for half a mile, its yellow, pollen-laden tassels overtopping the dark green mass of broad glistening blades; and in the distance, through the faint morning haze of evaporating dew, the line of the woods, of a still darker green, meeting the clear blue of the summer sky. Old Dinah saw, going down the path, a tall, brown girl, in a homespun frock, swinging a slat-bonnet in one hand and a splint basket in the other.

"Oh, Cicely!" she called.

The girl turned and answered in a resonant voice, vibrating with youth and life,—

"Yes, granny!"

"Be sho' and pick a good mess er peas, chile, fer yo' gran'-daddy 's gwine ter be home ter dinner ter-day."

The old woman stood a moment longer and then turned to go into the house. What she had not seen was that the girl was not only young, but lithe and shapely as a sculptor's model; that her bare feet seemed to spurn the earth as they struck it; that though brown, she was not so brown but that her cheek was darkly red with the blood of another race than that which gave her her name and station in life; and the old woman did not see that Cicely's face was as comely as her figure was superb, and that her eyes were dreamy with vague yearnings.

Cicely climbed the low fence between the garden and the cornfield, and started down one of the long rows leading directly away from the house. Old Needham was a good ploughman, and straight as an arrow ran the furrow between the rows of corn, until it vanished in the distant perspective. The peas were planted beside alternate hills of corn, the corn-stalks serving as supports for the climbing pea-vines. The vines nearest the house had been picked more or less clear of the long green pods, and Cicely walked down the row for a quarter of a mile, to where the peas were more plentiful. And as she walked she thought of her dream of the night before.

She had dreamed a beautiful dream. The fact that it was a beautiful dream, a delightful dream, her memory retained very vividly. She was troubled because she could not remember just what her dream had been about. Of one other fact she was certain, that in her dream she had found something, and that her happiness had been bound up with the thing she had found. As she walked down the corn-row she ran over in her mind the various things with which she had always associated happiness. Had she found a gold ring? No, it was not a gold ring—of that she felt sure. Was it a soft, curly plume for her hat? She had seen town people with them, and had indulged in day-dreams on the subject; but it was not a feather. Was it a bright-colored silk dress? No; as much as she had always wanted one, it was not a silk dress. For an instant, in a dream, she had tasted some great and novel happiness, and when she awoke it was dashed from her lips, and she could not even enjoy the memory of it, except in a vague, indefinite, and tantalizing way.

Cicely was troubled, too, because dreams were serious things. Dreams had certain meanings, most of them, and some dreams went by contraries. If her dream had been a prophecy of some good thing, she had by forgetting it lost the pleasure of anticipation. If her dream had been one of those that go by contraries, the warning would be in vain, because she would not know against what evil to provide. So, with a sigh, Cicely said to herself that it was a troubled world, more or less; and having come to a promising point, began to pick the tenderest pea-pods and throw them into her basket.

By the time she had reached the end of the line the basket was nearly full. Glancing toward the pine woods beyond the rail fence, she saw a brier bush loaded with large, luscious blackberries. Cicely was fond of blackberries, so she set her basket down, climbed the fence, and was soon busily engaged in gathering the fruit, delicious even in its wild state.

She had soon eaten all she cared for. But the berries were still numerous, and it occurred to her that her granddaddy would like a blackberry pudding for dinner. Catching up her apron, and using it as a receptacle for the berries, she had gathered scarcely more than a handful when she heard a groan.

Cicely was not timid, and her curiosity being aroused by the sound, she stood erect, and remained in a listening attitude. In a moment the sound was repeated, and, gauging the point from which it came, she plunged resolutely into the thick underbrush of the forest. She had gone but a few yards when she stopped short with an exclamation of surprise and concern.

Upon the ground, under the shadow of the towering pines, a man lay at full length,—a young man, several years under thirty, apparently, so far as his age could be guessed from a face that wore a short soft beard, and was so begrimed with dust and incrusted with blood that little could be seen of the underlying integument. What was visible showed a skin browned by nature or by exposure. His hands were of even a darker brown, almost as dark as Cicely's own. A tangled mass of very curly black hair, matted with burs, dank with dew, and clotted with blood, fell partly over his forehead, on the edge of which, extending back into the hair, an ugly scalp wound was gaping, and, though apparently not just inflicted, was still bleeding slowly, as though reluctant to stop, in spite of the coagulation that had almost closed it.

Cicely with a glance took in all this and more. But, first of all, she saw the man was wounded and bleeding, and the nurse latent in all womankind awoke in her to the requirements of the situation. She knew there was a spring a few rods away, and ran swiftly to it. There was usually a gourd at the spring, but now it was gone. Pouring out the blackberries in a little heap where they could be found again, she took off her apron, dipped one end of it into the spring, and ran back to the wounded man. The apron was clean, and she squeezed a little stream of water from it into the man's mouth. He swallowed it with avidity. Cicely then knelt by his side, and with the wet end of her apron washed the blood from the wound lightly, and the dust from the man's face. Then she looked at her apron a moment, debating whether she should tear it or not.

"I 'm feared granny 'll be mad," she said to herself. "I reckon I 'll jes' use de whole apron."

So she bound the apron around his head as well as she could, and then sat down a moment on a fallen tree trunk, to think what she should do next. The man already seemed more comfortable; he had ceased moaning, and lay quiet, though breathing heavily.

"What shall I do with that man?" she reflected. "I don' know whether he 's a w'ite man or a black man. Ef he 's a w'ite man, I oughter go an' tell de w'ite folks up at de big house, an' dey 'd take keer of 'im. If he 's a black man, I oughter go tell granny. He don' look lack a black man somehow er nuther, an' yet he don' look lack a w'ite man; he 's too dahk, an' his hair 's too curly. But I mus' do somethin' wid 'im. He can't be lef' here ter die in de woods all by hisse'f. Reckon I 'll go an' tell granny."

She scaled the fence, caught up the basket of peas from where she had left it, and ran, lightly and swiftly as a deer, toward the house. Her short skirt did not impede her progress, and in a few minutes she had covered the half mile and was at the cabin door, a slight heaving of her full and yet youthful breast being the only sign of any unusual exertion.

Her story was told in a moment. The old woman took down a black bottle from a high shelf, and set out with Cicely across the cornfield, toward the wounded man.

As they went through the corn Cicely recalled part of her dream. She had dreamed that under some strange circumstances—what they had been was still obscure—she had met a young man—a young man whiter than she and yet not all white—and that he had loved her and courted her and married her. Her dream had been all the sweeter because in it she had first tasted the sweetness of love, and she had not recalled it before because only in her dream had she known or thought of love as something supremely desirable.

With the memory of her dream, however, her fears revived. Dreams were solemn things. To Cicely the fabric of a vision was by no means baseless. Her trouble arose from her not being able to recall, though she was well versed in dreamlore, just what event was foreshadowed by a dream of finding a wounded man. If the wounded man were of her own race, her dream would thus far have been realized, and having met the young man, the other joys might be expected to follow. If he should turn out to be a white man, then her dream was clearly one of the kind that go by contraries, and she could expect only sorrow and trouble and pain as the proper sequences of this fateful discovery.

II

The two women reached the fence that separated the cornfield from the pine woods.

"How is I gwine ter git ovuh dat fence, chile?" asked the old woman.

"Wait a minute, granny," said Cicely; "I 'll take it down."

It was only an eight-rail fence, and it was a matter of but a few minutes for the girl to lift down and lay to either side the ends of the rails that formed one of the angles. This done, the old woman easily stepped across the remaining two or three rails. It was only a moment before they stood by the wounded man. He was lying still, breathing regularly, and seemingly asleep.

"What is he, granny," asked the girl anxiously, "a w'ite man, or not?"

Old Dinah pushed back the matted hair from the wounded man's brow, and looked at the skin beneath. It was fairer there, but yet of a decided brown. She raised his hand, pushed back the tattered sleeve from his wrist, and then she laid his hand down gently.

"Mos' lackly he 's a mulatter man f'om up de country somewhar. He don' look lack dese yer niggers roun' yere, ner yet lack a w'ite man. But de po' boy 's in a bad fix, w'ateber he is, an' I 'spec's we bettah do w'at we kin fer 'im, an' w'en he comes to he 'll tell us w'at he is—er w'at he calls hisse'f. Hol' 'is head up, chile, an' I 'll po' a drop er dis yer liquor down his th'oat; dat 'll bring 'im to quicker 'n anything e'se I knows."

Cicely lifted the sick man's head, and Dinah poured a few drops of the whiskey between his teeth. He swallowed it readily enough. In a few minutes he opened his eyes and stared blankly at the two women. Cicely saw that his eyes were large and black, and glistening with fever.

"How you feelin', suh?" asked the old woman.

There was no answer.

"Is you feelin' bettah now?"

The wounded man kept on staring blankly. Suddenly he essayed to put his hand to his head, gave a deep groan, and fell back again unconscious.

"He 's gone ag'in," said Dinah. "I reckon we 'll hafter tote 'im up ter de house and take keer er 'im dere. W'ite folks would n't want ter fool wid a nigger man, an' we doan know who his folks is. He 's outer his head an' will be fer some time yet, an' we can't tell nuthin' 'bout 'im tel he comes ter his senses."

Cicely lifted the wounded man by the arms and shoulders. She was strong, with the strength of youth and a sturdy race. The man was pitifully emaciated; how much, the two women had not suspected until they raised him. They had no difficulty whatever, except for the awkwardness of such a burden, in lifting him over the fence and carrying him through the cornfield to the cabin.

They laid him on Cicely's bed in the little lean-to shed that formed a room separate from the main apartment of the cabin. The old woman sent Cicely to cook the dinner, while she gave her own attention exclusively to the still unconscious man. She brought water and washed him as though he were a child.

"Po' boy," she said, "he doan feel lack he 's be'n eatin' nuff to feed a sparrer. He 'pears ter be mos' starved ter def."

She washed his wound more carefully, made some lint,—the art was well known in the sixties,—and dressed his wound with a fair degree of skill.

"Somebody must 'a' be'n tryin' ter put yo' light out, chile," she muttered to herself as she adjusted the bandage around his head. "A little higher er a little lower, an' you would n' 'a' be'n yere ter tell de tale. Dem clo's," she argued, lifting the tattered garments she had removed from her patient, "don' b'long 'roun' yere. Dat kinder weavin' come f'om down to'ds Souf Ca'lina. I wish Needham 'u'd come erlong. He kin tell who dis man is, an' all erbout 'im."

She made a bowl of gruel, and fed it, drop by drop, to the sick man. This roused him somewhat from his stupor, but when Dinah thought he had enough of the gruel, and stopped feeding him, he closed his eyes again and relapsed into a heavy sleep that was so closely akin to unconsciousness as to be scarcely distinguishable from it.

When old Needham came home at noon, his wife, who had been anxiously awaiting his return, told him in a few words the story of Cicely's discovery and of the subsequent events.

Needham inspected the stranger with a professional eye. He had been something of a plantation doctor in his day, and was known far and wide for his knowledge of simple remedies. The negroes all around, as well as many of the poorer white people, came to him for the treatment of common ailments.

"He 's got a fevuh," he said, after feeling the patient's pulse and laying his hand on his brow, "an' we 'll hafter gib 'im some yarb tea an' nuss 'im tel de fevuh w'ars off. I 'spec'," he added, "dat I knows whar dis boy come f'om. He 's mos' lackly one er dem bright mulatters, f'om Robeson County—some of 'em call deyse'ves Croatan Injins—w'at's been conscripted an' sent ter wu'k on de fo'tifications down at Wimbleton er some'er's er nuther, an' done 'scaped, and got mos' killed gittin' erway, an' wuz n' none too well fed befo', an' nigh 'bout starved ter def sence. We 'll hafter hide dis man, er e'se we is lackly ter git inter trouble ou'se'ves by harb'rin' 'im. Ef dey ketch 'im yere, dey 's liable ter take 'im out an' shoot 'im—an' des ez lackly us too."

Cicely was listening with bated breath.

"Oh, gran'daddy," she cried with trembling voice, "don' let 'em ketch 'im! Hide 'im somewhar."

"I reckon we 'll leave 'im yere fer a day er so. Ef he had come f'om roun' yere I 'd be skeered ter keep 'im, fer de w'ite folks 'u'd prob'ly be lookin' fer 'im. But I knows ev'ybody w'at's be'n conscripted fer ten miles 'roun', an' dis yere boy don' b'long in dis neighborhood. W'en 'e gits so 'e kin he'p 'isse'f we 'll put 'im up in de lof' an' hide 'im till de Yankees come. Fer dey 're comin', sho'. I dremp' las' night dey wuz close ter han', and I hears de w'ite folks talkin' ter deyse'ves 'bout it. An' de time is comin' w'en de good Lawd gwine ter set his people free, an' it ain' gwine ter be long, nuther."

Needham's prophecy proved true. In less than a week the Confederate garrison evacuated the arsenal in the neighboring town of Patesville, blew up the buildings, destroyed the ordnance and stores, and retreated across the Cape Fear River, burning the river bridge behind them,—two acts of war afterwards unjustly attributed to General Sherman's army, which followed close upon the heels of the retreating Confederates.

When there was no longer any fear for the stranger's safety, no more pains were taken to conceal him. His wound had healed rapidly, and in a week he had been able with some help to climb up the ladder into the loft. In all this time, however, though apparently conscious, he had said no word to any one, nor had he seemed to comprehend a word that was spoken to him.

Cicely had been his constant attendant. After the first day, during which her granny had nursed him, she had sat by his bedside, had fanned his fevered brow, had held food and water and medicine to his lips. When it was safe for him to come down from the loft and sit in a chair under a spreading oak, Cicely supported him until he was strong enough to walk about the yard. When his strength had increased sufficiently to permit of greater exertion, she accompanied him on long rambles in the fields and woods.

In spite of his gain in physical strength, the newcomer changed very little in other respects. For a long time he neither spoke nor smiled. To questions put to him he simply gave no reply, but looked at his questioner with the blank unconsciousness of an infant. By and by he began to recognize Cicely, and to smile at her approach. The next step in returning consciousness was but another manifestation of the same sentiment. When Cicely would leave him he would look his regret, and be restless and uneasy until she returned.

The family were at a loss what to call him. To any inquiry as to his name he answered no more than to other questions.

"He come jes' befo' Sherman," said Needham, after a few weeks, "lack John de Baptis' befo' de Lawd. I reckon we bettah call 'im John."

So they called him John. He soon learned the name. As time went on Cicely found that he was quick at learning things. She taught him to speak her own negro English, which he pronounced with absolute fidelity to her intonations;

so that barring the quality of his voice, his speech was an echo of Cicely's own.

The summer wore away and the autumn came. John and Cicely wandered in the woods together and gathered walnuts, and chinquapins and wild grapes. When harvest time came, they worked in the fields side by side,—plucked the corn, pulled the fodder, and gathered the dried peas from the yellow pea-vines. Cicely was a phenomenal cotton-picker, and John accompanied her to the fields and stayed by her hours at a time, though occasionally he would complain of his head, and sit under a tree and rest part of the day while Cicely worked, the two keeping one another always in sight.

They did not have a great deal of intercourse with other people. Young men came to the cabin sometimes to see Cicely, but when they found her entirely absorbed in the stranger they ceased their visits. For a time Cicely kept him away, as much as possible, from others, because she did not wish them to see that there was anything wrong about him. This was her motive at first, but after a while she kept him to herself simply because she was happier so. He was hers—hers alone. She had found him, as Pharaoh's daughter had found Moses in the bulrushes; she had taught him to speak, to think, to love. She had not taught him to remember; she would not have wished him to; she would have been jealous of any past to which he might have proved bound by other ties. Her dream so far had come true. She had found him; he loved her. The rest of it would as surely follow, and that before long. For dreams were serious things, and time had proved hers to have been not a presage of misfortune, but one of the beneficent visions that are sent, that we may enjoy by anticipation the good things that are in store for us.

III

But a short interval of time elapsed after the passage of the warlike host that swept through North Carolina, until there appeared upon the scene the vanguard of a second army, which came to bring light and the fruits of liberty to a land which slavery and the havoc of war had brought to ruin. It is fashionable to assume that those who undertook the political rehabilitation of the Southern States merely rounded out the ruin that the war had wrought—merely ploughed up the desolate land and sowed it with salt. Perhaps the gentler judgments of the future may recognize that their task was a difficult one, and that wiser and honester men might have failed as egregiously. It may even, in time, be conceded that some good came out of the carpet-bag governments, as, for instance, the establishment of a system of popular education in the former slave States. Where it had been a crime to teach people to read or write, a schoolhouse dotted every hillside, and the State provided education for rich and poor, for white and black alike. Let us lay at least this token upon the grave of the carpet-baggers. The evil they did lives after them, and the statute of limitations does not seem to run against it. It is but just that we should not forget the good.

Long, however, before the work of political reconstruction had begun, a brigade of Yankee schoolmasters and school-ma'ams had invaded Dixie, and one of the latter had opened a Freedman's Bureau School in the town of Patesville, about four miles from Needham Green's cabin on the neighboring sandhills.

It had been quite a surprise to Miss Chandler's Boston friends when she had announced her intention of going South to teach the freedmen. Rich, accomplished, beautiful, and a social favorite, she was giving up the comforts and luxuries of Northern life to go among hostile strangers, where her associates would be mostly ignorant negroes. Perhaps she might meet occasionally an officer of some Federal garrison, or a traveler from the North; but to all intents and purposes her friends considered her as going into voluntary exile. But heroism was not rare in those days, and Martha Chandler was only one of the great multitude whose hearts went out toward an oppressed race, and who freely poured out their talents, their money, their lives,—whatever God had given them,—in the sublime and not unfruitful effort to transform three millions of slaves into intelligent freemen. Miss Chandler's friends knew, too, that she had met a great sorrow, and more than suspected that out of it had grown her determination to go South.

When Cicely Green heard that a school for colored people had been opened at Patesville she combed her hair, put on her Sunday frock and such bits of finery as she possessed, and set out for town early the next Monday morning.

There were many who came to learn the new gospel of education, which was to be the cure for all the freedmen's ills. The old and gray-haired, the full-grown man and woman, the toddling infant,—they came to acquire the new and wonderful learning that was to make them the equals of the white people. It was the teacher's task, by no means an easy one, to select from this incongruous mass the most promising material, and to distribute among them the second-hand books and clothing that were sent, largely by her Boston friends, to aid her in her work; to find out what they knew, to classify them by their intelligence rather than by their knowledge, for they were all lamentably ignorant. Some among them were the children of parents who had been free before the war, and of these some few could read and one or two could write. One paragon, who could repeat the multiplication table, was immediately promoted to the position of pupil teacher.

Miss Chandler took a liking to the tall girl who had come so far to sit under her instruction. There was a fine, free air in her bearing, a lightness in her step, a sparkle in her eye, that spoke of good blood,—whether fused by nature in its own alembic, out of material despised and spurned of men, or whether some obscure ancestral strain, the teacher could not tell. The girl proved intelligent and learned rapidly, indeed seemed almost feverishly anxious to learn. She was quiet, and was, though utterly untrained, instinctively polite, and profited from the first day by the example of her teacher's quiet elegance. The teacher dressed in simple black. When Cicely came back to school the second day, she had left off her glass beads and her red ribbon, and had arranged her hair as nearly like the teacher's as her skill and its quality would permit.

The teacher was touched by these efforts at imitation, and by the intense devotion Cicely soon manifested toward her. It was not a sycophantic, troublesome devotion, that made itself a burden to its object. It found expression in little things done rather than in any words the girl said. To the degree that the attraction was mutual, Martha recognized in it a sort of freemasonry of temperament that drew them together in spite of the differences between them. Martha felt sometimes, in the vague way that one speculates about the impossible, that if she were brown, and had been brought up in North Carolina, she would be like Cicely; and that if Cicely's ancestors had come over in the Mayflower, and Cicely had been reared on Beacon Street, in the shadow of the State House dome, Cicely would have been very much like herself.

Miss Chandler was lonely sometimes. Her duties kept her occupied all day. On Sundays she taught a Bible class in the schoolroom. Correspondence with bureau officials and friends at home furnished her with additional occupation. At times, nevertheless, she felt a longing for the company of women of her own race; but the white ladies of the town did not call, even in the most formal way, upon the Yankee school-teacher. Miss Chandler was therefore fain to do the best she could with such companionship as was available. She took Cicely to her home occasionally, and asked her once to stay all night. Thinking, however, that she detected a reluctance on the girl's part to remain away from home, she did not repeat her invitation.

Cicely, indeed, was filling a double rôle. The learning acquired from Miss Chandler she imparted to John at home. Every evening, by the light of the pine-knots blazing on Needham's ample hearth, she taught John to read the simple words she had learned during the day. Why she did not take him to school she had never asked herself; there were several other pupils as old as he seemed to be. Perhaps she still thought it necessary to protect him from curious remark. He worked with Needham by day, and she could see him at night, and all of Saturdays and Sundays. Perhaps it was the jealous selfishness of love. She had found him; he was hers. In the spring, when school was over, her granny had said that she might marry him. Till then her dream would not yet have come true, and she must keep him to herself. And yet she did not wish him to lose this golden key to the avenues of opportunity. She would not take him to school, but she would teach him each day all that she herself had learned. He was not difficult to teach, but learned, indeed, with what seemed to Cicely marvelous ease,—always, however, by her lead, and never of his own initiative. For while he could do a man's work, he was in most things but a child, without a child's curiosity. His love for Cicely appeared the only thing for which he needed no suggestion; and even that possessed an element of childish dependence that would have seemed, to minds trained to thoughtful observation, infinitely pathetic.

The spring came and cotton-planting time. The children began to drop out of Miss Chandler's school one by one, as their services were required at home. Cicely was among those who intended to remain in school until the term closed with the "exhibition," in which she was assigned a leading part. She had selected her recitation, or "speech," from among half a dozen poems that her teacher had suggested, and to memorizing it she devoted considerable time and study. The exhibition, as the first of its kind, was sure to be a notable event. The parents and friends of the children were invited to attend, and a colored church, recently erected,—the largest available building,—was secured as the place where the exercises should take place.

On the morning of the eventful day, uncle Needham, assisted by John, harnessed the mule to the two-wheeled cart, on which a couple of splint-bottomed chairs were fastened to accommodate Dinah and Cicely. John put on his best clothes,—an ill-fitting suit of blue jeans,—a round wool hat, a pair of coarse brogans, a homespun shirt, and a bright blue necktie. Cicely wore her best frock, a red ribbon at her throat, another in her hair, and carried a bunch of flowers in her hand. Uncle Needham and aunt Dinah were also in holiday array. Needham and John took their seats on opposite sides of the cart-frame, with their feet dangling down, and thus the equipage set out leisurely for the town.

Cicely had long looked forward impatiently to this day. She was going to marry John the next week, and then her dream would have come entirely true. But even this anticipated happiness did not overshadow the importance of the present occasion, which would be an epoch in her life, a day of joy and triumph. She knew her speech perfectly, and timidity was not one of her weaknesses. She knew that the red ribbons set off her dark beauty effectively, and that her dress fitted neatly the curves of her shapely figure. She confidently expected to win the first prize, a large morocco-covered Bible, offered by Miss Chandler for the best exercise.

Cicely and her companions soon arrived at Patesville. Their entrance into the church made quite a sensation, for Cicely was not only an acknowledged belle, but a general favorite, and to John there attached a tinge of mystery which inspired a respect not bestowed upon those who had grown up in the neighborhood. Cicely secured a seat in the front part of the church, next to the aisle, in the place reserved for the pupils. As the house was already partly filled by townspeople when the party from the country arrived, Needham and his wife and John were forced to content themselves with places somewhat in the rear of the room, from which they could see and hear what took place on the platform, but where they were not at all conspicuously visible to those at the front of the church.

The schoolmistress had not yet arrived, and order was preserved in the audience by two of the elder pupils, adorned with large rosettes of red, white, and blue, who ushered the most important visitors to the seats reserved for them. A national flag was gracefully draped over the platform, and under it hung a lithograph of the Great Emancipator, for it was thus these people thought of him. He had saved the Union, but the Union had never meant anything good to them. He had proclaimed liberty to the captive, which meant all to them; and to them he was and would ever be the Great Emancipator.

The schoolmistress came in at a rear door and took her seat upon the platform. Martha was dressed in white; for once she had laid aside the sombre garb in which alone she had been seen since her arrival at Patesville. She wore a yellow rose at her throat, a bunch of jasmine in her belt. A sense of responsibility for the success of the exhibition had deepened the habitual seriousness of her face, yet she greeted the audience with a smile.

"Don' Miss Chan'ler look sweet," whispered the little girls to one another, devouring her beauty with sparkling eyes, their lips parted over a wealth of ivory.

"De Lawd will bress dat chile," said one old woman, in soliloquy. "I t'ank de good Marster I 's libbed ter see dis day."

Even envy could not hide its noisome head: a pretty quadroon whispered to her neighbor:—

"I don't b'liebe she 's natch'ly ez white ez dat. I 'spec' she 's be'n powd'rin'! An' I know all dat hair can't be her'n; she 's got on a switch, sho 's you bawn."

"You knows dat ain' so, Ma'y 'Liza Smif," rejoined the other, with a look of stern disapproval; "you *knows* dat ain' so. You 'd gib yo' everlastin' soul 'f you wuz ez white ez Miss Chan'ler, en yo' ha'r wuz ez long ez her'n."

"By Jove, Maxwell!" exclaimed a young officer, who belonged to the Federal garrison stationed in the town, "but that girl is a beauty." The speaker and a companion were in fatigue uniform, and had merely dropped in for an hour between garrison duty. The ushers had wished to give them seats on the platform, but they had declined, thinking that perhaps their presence there might embarrass the teacher. They sought rather to avoid observation by sitting behind a pillar in the rear of the room, around which they could see without attracting undue attention.

"To think," the lieutenant went on, "of that Junonian figure, those lustrous orbs, that golden coronal, that flower of Northern civilization, being wasted on these barbarians!" The speaker uttered an exaggerated but suppressed groan.

His companion, a young man of clean-shaven face and serious aspect, nodded assent, but whispered reprovingly,—

"'Sh! some one will hear you. The exercises are going to begin."

When Miss Chandler stepped forward to announce the hymn to be sung by the school as the first exercise, every eye in the room was fixed upon her, except John's, which saw only Cicely. When the teacher had uttered a few words, he looked up to her, and from that moment did not take his eyes off Martha's face.

After the singing, a little girl, dressed in white, crossed by ribbons of red and blue, recited with much spirit a patriotic poem.

When Martha announced the third exercise, John's face took on a more than usually animated expression, and there was a perceptible deepening of the troubled look in his eyes, never entirely absent since Cicely had found him in the woods.

A little yellow boy, with long curls, and a frightened air, next ascended the platform.

"Now, Jimmie, be a man, and speak right out," whispered his teacher, tapping his arm reassuringly with her fan as he passed her.

Jimmie essayed to recite the lines so familiar to a past generation of schoolchildren:—

"I knew a widow very poor,
 Who four small children had;
The eldest was but six years old,
 A gentle, modest lad."

He ducked his head hurriedly in a futile attempt at a bow; then, following instructions previously given him, fixed his eyes upon a large cardboard motto hanging on the rear wall of the room, which admonished him in bright red letters to

"ALWAYS SPEAK THE TRUTH,"

and started off with assumed confidence—

"I knew a widow very poor,
 Who"—

At this point, drawn by an irresistible impulse, his eyes sought the level of the audience. Ah, fatal blunder! He stammered, but with an effort raised his eyes and began again:

"I knew a widow very poor,
 Who four"—

Again his treacherous eyes fell, and his little remaining self-possession utterly forsook him. He made one more despairing effort:—

"I knew a widow very poor,
 Who four small"—

and then, bursting into tears, turned and fled amid a murmur of sympathy.

Jimmie's inglorious retreat was covered by the singing in chorus of "The Star-spangled Banner," after which Cicely Green came forward to recite her poem.

"By Jove, Maxwell!" whispered the young officer, who was evidently a connoisseur of female beauty, "that is n't bad for a bronze Venus. I 'll tell you"—

"'Sh!" said the other. "Keep still."

When Cicely finished her recitation, the young officers began to applaud, but stopped suddenly in some confusion as they realized that they were the only ones in the audience so engaged. The colored people had either not learned how to express their approval in orthodox fashion, or else their respect for the sacred character of the edifice forbade any such demonstration. Their enthusiasm found vent, however, in a subdued murmur, emphasized by numerous nods and winks and suppressed exclamations. During the singing that followed Cicely's recitation the two officers quietly withdrew, their duties calling them away at this hour.

At the close of the exercises, a committee on prizes met in the vestibule, and unanimously decided that Cicely Green was entitled to the first prize. Proudly erect, with sparkling eyes and cheeks flushed with victory, Cicely advanced to the platform to receive the coveted reward. As she turned away, her eyes, shining with gratified vanity, sought those of her lover.

John sat bent slightly forward in an attitude of strained attention; and Cicely's triumph lost half its value when she saw that it was not at her, but at Miss Chandler, that his look was directed. Though she watched him thenceforward, not one glance did he vouchsafe to his jealous sweetheart, and never for an instant withdrew his eyes from Martha, or relaxed the unnatural intentness of his gaze. The imprisoned mind, stirred to unwonted effort, was struggling for liberty; and from Martha had come the first ray of outer light that had penetrated its dungeon.

Before the audience was dismissed, the teacher rose to bid her school farewell. Her intention was to take a vacation of three months; but what might happen in that time she did not know, and there were duties at home of such apparent urgency as to render her return to North Carolina at least doubtful; so that in her own heart her *au revoir* sounded very much like a farewell.

She spoke to them of the hopeful progress they had made, and praised them for their eager desire to learn. She told them of the serious duties of life, and of the use they should make of their acquirements. With prophetic finger she pointed them to the upward way which they must climb with patient feet to raise themselves out of the depths.

Then, an unusual thing with her, she spoke of herself. Her heart was full; it was with difficulty that she maintained her composure; for the faces that confronted her were kindly faces, and not critical, and some of them she had learned to love right well.

"I am going away from you, my children," she said; "but before I go I want to tell you how I came to be in North Carolina; so that if I have been able to do anything here among you for which you might feel inclined, in your good nature, to thank me, you may thank not me alone, but another who came before me, and whose work I have but taken up where *he* laid it down. I had a friend,—a dear friend,—why should I be ashamed to say it?—a lover, to whom I was to be married,—as I hope all you girls may some day be happily married. His country needed him, and I gave him up. He came to fight for the Union and for Freedom, for he believed that all men are brothers. He did not come back again—he gave up his life for you. Could I do less than he? I came to the land that he sanctified by his death, and I have tried in my weak way to tend the plant he watered with his blood, and which, in the fullness of time, will blossom forth into the perfect flower of liberty."

She could say no more, and as the whole audience thrilled in sympathy with her emotion, there was a hoarse cry from the men's side of the room, and John forced his way to the aisle and rushed forward to the platform.

"Martha! Martha!"

"Arthur! O Arthur!"

Pent-up love burst the flood-gates of despair and oblivion, and caught these two young hearts in its torrent. Captain Arthur Carey, of the 1st Massachusetts, long since reported missing, and mourned as dead, was restored to reason and to his world.

It seemed to him but yesterday that he had escaped from the Confederate prison at Salisbury; that in an encounter with a guard he had received a wound in the head; that he had wandered on in the woods, keeping himself alive by means of wild berries, with now and then a piece of bread or a potato from a friendly negro. It seemed but the night before that he had laid himself down, tortured with fever, weak from loss of blood, and with no hope that he would ever rise again. From that moment his memory of the past was a blank until he recognized Martha on the platform and took up again the thread of his former existence where it had been broken off.

And Cicely? Well, there is often another woman, and Cicely, all unwittingly to Carey or to Martha, had been the other woman. For, after all, her beautiful dream had been one of the kind that go by contraries.

The Passing of Grandison

I

WHEN it is said that it was done to please a woman, there ought perhaps to be enough said to explain anything; for what a man will not do to please a woman is yet to be discovered. Nevertheless, it might be well to state a few preliminary facts to make it clear why young Dick Owens tried to run one of his father's negro men off to Canada.

In the early fifties, when the growth of anti-slavery sentiment and the constant drain of fugitive slaves into the North had so alarmed the slaveholders of the border States as to lead to the passage of the Fugitive Slave Law, a young white man from Ohio, moved by compassion for the sufferings of a certain bondman who happened to have a "hard master," essayed to help the slave to freedom. The attempt was discovered and frustrated; the abductor was tried and convicted for slave-stealing, and sentenced to a term of imprisonment in the penitentiary. His death, after the expiration of only a small part of the sentence, from cholera contracted while nursing stricken fellow prisoners, lent to the case a melancholy interest that made it famous in anti-slavery annals.

Dick Owens had attended the trial. He was a youth of about twenty-two, intelligent, handsome, and amiable, but extremely indolent, in a graceful and gentlemanly way; or, as old Judge Fenderson put it more than once, he was lazy as the Devil,—a mere figure of speech, of course, and not one that did justice to the Enemy of Mankind. When asked why he never did anything serious, Dick would good-naturedly reply, with a well-modulated drawl, that he did n't have to. His father was rich; there was but one other child, an unmarried daughter, who because of poor health would probably never marry, and Dick was therefore heir presumptive to a large estate. Wealth or social position he did not need to seek, for he was born to both. Charity Lomax had shamed him into studying law, but notwithstanding an hour or so a day spent at old Judge Fenderson's office, he did not make remarkable headway in his legal studies.

"What Dick needs," said the judge, who was fond of tropes, as became a scholar, and of horses, as was befitting a Kentuckian, "is the whip of necessity, or the spur of ambition. If he had either, he would soon need the snaffle to hold him back."

But all Dick required, in fact, to prompt him to the most remarkable thing he accomplished before he was twenty-five, was a mere suggestion from Charity Lomax. The story was never really known to but two persons until after the war, when it came out because it was a good story and there was no particular reason for its concealment.

Young Owens had attended the trial of this slave-stealer, or martyr,—either or both,—and, when it was over, had gone to call on Charity Lomax, and, while they sat on the veranda after sundown, had told her all about the trial. He was a good talker, as his career in later years disclosed, and described the proceedings very graphically.

"I confess," he admitted, "that while my principles were against the prisoner, my sympathies were on his side. It appeared that he was of good family, and that he had an old father and mother, respectable people, dependent upon him for support and comfort in their declining years. He had been led into the matter by pity for a negro whose master ought to have been run out of the county long ago for abusing his slaves. If it had been merely a question of old Sam Briggs's negro, nobody would have cared anything about it. But father and the rest of them stood on the principle of the thing, and told the judge so, and the fellow was sentenced to three years in the penitentiary."

Miss Lomax had listened with lively interest.

"I 've always hated old Sam Briggs," she said emphatically, "ever since the time he broke a negro's leg with a piece of cordwood. When I hear of a cruel deed it makes the Quaker blood that came from my grandmother assert itself. Personally I wish that all Sam Briggs's negroes would run away. As for the young man, I regard him as a hero. He dared something for humanity. I could love a man who would take such chances for the sake of others."

"Could you love me, Charity, if I did something heroic?"

"You never will, Dick. You 're too lazy for any use. You 'll never do anything harder than playing cards or fox-hunting."

"Oh, come now, sweetheart! I 've been courting you for a year, and it 's the hardest work imaginable. Are you never going to love me?" he pleaded.

His hand sought hers, but she drew it back beyond his reach.

"I 'll never love you, Dick Owens, until you have done something. When that time comes, I 'll think about it."

"But it takes so long to do anything worth mentioning, and I don't want to wait. One must read two years to become a lawyer, and work five more to make a reputation. We shall both be gray by then."

"Oh, I don't know," she rejoined. "It does n't require a lifetime for a man to prove that he is a man. This one did something, or at least tried to."

"Well, I 'm willing to attempt as much as any other man. What do you want me to do, sweetheart? Give me a test."

"Oh, dear me!" said Charity, "I don't care what you *do*, so you do *something*. Really, come to think of it, why should I care whether you do anything or not?"

"I 'm sure I don't know why you should, Charity," rejoined Dick humbly, "for I 'm aware that I 'm not worthy of it."

"Except that I do hate," she added, relenting slightly, "to see a really clever man so utterly lazy and good for nothing."

"Thank you, my dear; a word of praise from you has sharpened my wits already. I have an idea! Will you love me if *I* run a negro off to Canada?"

"What nonsense!" said Charity scornfully. "You must be losing your wits. Steal another man's slave, indeed, while your father owns a hundred!"

"Oh, there 'll be no trouble about that," responded Dick lightly; "I 'll run off one of the old man's; we 've got too many anyway. It may not be quite as difficult as the other man found it, but it will be just as unlawful, and will demonstrate what I am capable of."

"Seeing 's believing," replied Charity. "Of course, what you are talking about now is merely absurd. I 'm going away for three weeks, to visit my aunt in Tennessee. If you 're able to tell me, when I return, that you 've done something to prove your quality, I 'll—well, you may come and tell me about it."

II

Young Owens got up about nine o'clock next morning, and while making his toilet put some questions to his personal attendant, a rather bright looking young mulatto of about his own age.

"Tom," said Dick.

"Yas, Mars Dick," responded the servant.

"I 'm going on a trip North. Would you like to go with me?"

Now, if there was anything that Tom would have liked to make, it was a trip North. It was something he had long contemplated in the abstract, but had never been able to muster up sufficient courage to attempt in the concrete. He was prudent enough, however, to dissemble his feelings.

"I would n't min' it, Mars Dick, ez long ez you 'd take keer er me an' fetch me home all right."

Tom's eyes belied his words, however, and his young master felt well assured that Tom needed only a good opportunity to make him run away. Having a comfortable home, and a dismal prospect in case of failure, Tom was not likely to take any desperate chances; but young Owens was satisfied that in a free State but little persuasion would be required to lead Tom astray. With a very logical and characteristic desire to gain his end with the least necessary expenditure of effort, he decided to take Tom with him, if his father did not object.

Colonel Owens had left the house when Dick went to breakfast, so Dick did not see his father till luncheon.

"Father," he remarked casually to the colonel, over the fried chicken, "I 'm feeling a trifle run down. I imagine my health would be improved somewhat by a little travel and change of scene."

"Why don't you take a trip North?" suggested his father. The colonel added to paternal affection a considerable respect for his son as the heir of a large estate. He himself had been "raised" in comparative poverty, and had laid the foundations of his fortune by hard work; and while he despised the ladder by which he had climbed, he could not entirely forget it, and unconsciously manifested, in his intercourse with his son, some of the poor man's deference toward the wealthy and well-born.

"I think I 'll adopt your suggestion, sir," replied the son, "and run up to New York; and after I 've been there awhile I may go on to Boston for a week or so. I 've never been there, you know."

"There are some matters you can talk over with my factor in New York," rejoined the colonel, "and while you are up there among the Yankees, I hope you 'll keep your eyes and ears open to find out what the rascally abolitionists are saying and doing. They 're becoming altogether too active for our comfort, and entirely too many ungrateful niggers are running away. I hope the conviction of that fellow yesterday may discourage the rest of the breed. I 'd just like to catch any one trying to run off one of my darkeys. He 'd get short shrift; I don't think any Court would have a chance to try him."

"They are a pestiferous lot," assented Dick, "and dangerous to our institutions. But say, father, if I go North I shall want to take Tom with me."

Now, the colonel, while a very indulgent father, had pronounced views on the subject of negroes, having studied them, as he often said, for a great many years, and, as he asserted oftener still, understanding them perfectly. It is scarcely worth while to say, either, that he valued more highly than if he had inherited them the slaves he had toiled and schemed for.

"I don't think it safe to take Tom up North," he declared, with promptness and decision. "He 's a good enough boy, but too smart to trust among those low-down abolitionists. I strongly suspect him of having learned to read, though I can't imagine how. I saw him with a newspaper the other day, and while he pretended to be looking at a woodcut, I 'm almost sure he was reading the paper. I think it by no means safe to take him."

Dick did not insist, because he knew it was useless. The colonel would have obliged his son in any other matter, but his negroes were the outward and visible sign of his wealth and station, and therefore sacred to him.

"Whom do you think it safe to take?" asked Dick. "I suppose I 'll have to have a body-servant."

"What 's the matter with Grandison?" suggested the colonel. "He 's handy enough, and I reckon we can trust him. He 's too fond of good eating, to risk losing his regular meals; besides, he 's sweet on your mother's maid, Betty, and I 've promised to let 'em get married before long. I 'll have Grandison up, and we 'll talk to him. Here, you boy Jack," called the colonel to a yellow youth in the next room who was catching flies and pulling their wings off to pass the time, "go down to the barn and tell Grandison to come here.

"Grandison," said the colonel, when the negro stood before him, hat in hand.

"Yas, marster."

"Have n't I always treated you right?"

"Yas, marster."

"Have n't you always got all you wanted to eat?"

"Yas, marster."

"And as much whiskey and tobacco as was good for you, Grandison?"

"Y-a-s, marster."

"I should just like to know, Grandison, whether you don't think yourself a great deal better off than those poor free negroes down by the plank road, with no kind master to look after them and no mistress to give them medicine when they 're sick and—and"—

"Well, I sh'd jes' reckon I is better off, suh, dan dem low-down free niggers, suh! Ef anybody ax 'em who dey b'long ter, dey has ter say nobody, er e'se lie erbout it. Anybody ax me who I b'longs ter, I ain' got no 'casion ter be shame' ter tell 'em, no, suh, 'deed I ain', suh!"

The colonel was beaming. This was true gratitude, and his feudal heart thrilled at such appreciative homage. What cold-blooded, heartless monsters they were who would break up this blissful relationship of kindly protection on the one hand, of wise subordination and loyal dependence on the other! The colonel always became indignant at the mere thought of such wickedness.

"Grandison," the colonel continued, "your young master Dick is going North for a few weeks, and I am thinking of letting him take you along. I shall send you on this trip, Grandison, in order that you may take care of your young master. He will need some one to wait on him, and no one can ever do it so well as one of the boys brought up with him on the old plantation. I am going to trust him in your hands, and I 'm sure you 'll do your duty faithfully, and bring him back home safe and sound—to old Kentucky."

Grandison grinned. "Oh yas, marster, I 'll take keer er young Mars Dick."

"I want to warn you, though, Grandison," continued the colonel impressively, "against these cussed abolitionists, who try to entice servants from their comfortable homes and their indulgent masters, from the blue skies, the green fields, and the warm sunlight of their southern home, and send them away off yonder to Canada, a dreary country, where the woods are full of wildcats and wolves and bears, where the snow lies up to the eaves of the houses for six months of the year, and the cold is so severe that it freezes your breath and curdles your blood; and where, when runaway niggers get sick and can't work, they are turned out to starve and die, unloved and uncared for. I reckon, Grandison, that you have too much sense to permit yourself to be led astray by any such foolish and wicked people."

"'Deed, suh, I would n' low none er dem cussed, low-down abolitioners ter come nigh me, suh. I 'd—I 'd—would I be 'lowed ter hit 'em, suh?"

"Certainly, Grandison," replied the colonel, chuckling, "hit 'em as hard as you can. I reckon they 'd rather like it. Begad, I believe they would! It would serve 'em right to be hit by a nigger!"

"Er ef I did n't hit 'em, suh," continued Grandison reflectively, "I 'd tell Mars Dick, en *he 'd* fix 'em. He 'd smash de face off'n 'em, suh, I jes' knows he would."

"Oh yes, Grandison, your young master will protect you. You need fear no harm while he is near."

"Dey won't try ter steal me, will dey, marster?" asked the negro, with sudden alarm.

"I don't know, Grandison," replied the colonel, lighting a fresh cigar. "They 're a desperate set of lunatics, and there 's no telling what they may resort to. But if you stick close to your young master, and remember always that he is your best friend, and understands your real needs, and has your true interests at heart, and if you will be careful to avoid strangers who try to talk to you, you 'll stand a fair chance of getting back to your home and your friends. And if you please your master Dick, he 'll buy you a present, and a string of beads for Betty to wear when you and she get married in the fall."

"Thanky, marster, thanky, suh," replied Grandison, oozing gratitude at every pore; "you is a good marster, to be sho', suh; yas, 'deed you is. You kin jes' bet me and Mars Dick gwine git 'long jes' lack I wuz own boy ter Mars Dick. En it won't be my fault ef he don' want me fer his boy all de time, w'en we come back home ag'in."

"All right, Grandison, you may go now. You need n't work any more to-day, and here 's a piece of tobacco for you off my own plug."

"Thanky, marster, thanky, marster! You is de bes' marster any nigger ever had in dis worl'." And Grandison bowed and scraped and disappeared round the corner, his jaws closing around a large section of the colonel's best tobacco.

"You may take Grandison," said the colonel to his son. "I allow he 's abolitionist-proof."

III

Richard Owens, Esq., and servant, from Kentucky, registered at the fashionable New York hostelry for Southerners in those days, a hotel where an atmosphere congenial to Southern institutions was sedulously maintained. But there were negro waiters in the dining-room, and mulatto bell-boys, and Dick had no doubt that Grandison, with the native gregariousness and garrulousness of his race, would foregather and palaver with them sooner or later, and Dick hoped that they would speedily inoculate him with the virus of freedom. For it was not Dick's intention to say anything to his servant about his plan to free him, for obvious reasons. To mention one of them, if Grandison should go away, and by legal process be recaptured, his young master's part in the matter would doubtless become known, which would be embarrassing to Dick, to say the least. If, on the other hand, he should merely give Grandison sufficient latitude, he had no doubt he would eventually lose him. For while not exactly skeptical about Grandison's perfervid loyalty, Dick had been a somewhat keen observer of human nature, in his own indolent way, and based his expectations upon the force of the example and argument that his servant could scarcely fail to encounter. Grandison should have a fair chance to become free by his own initiative; if it should become necessary to adopt other measures to get rid of him, it would be time enough to act when the necessity arose; and Dick Owens was not the youth to take needless trouble.

The young master renewed some acquaintances and made others, and spent a week or two very pleasantly in the best society of the metropolis, easily accessible to a wealthy, well-bred young Southerner, with proper introductions. Young women smiled on him, and young men of convivial habits pressed their hospitalities; but the memory of Charity's sweet, strong face and clear blue eyes made him proof against the blandishments of the one sex and the persuasions of the other. Meanwhile he kept Grandison supplied with pocket-money, and left him mainly to his own devices. Every night when Dick came in he hoped he might have to wait upon himself, and every morning he looked forward with pleasure to the prospect of making his toilet unaided. His hopes, however, were doomed to disappointment, for every night when he came in Grandison was on hand with a bootjack, and a nightcap mixed for his young master as the colonel had taught him to mix it, and every morning Grandison appeared with his master's boots blacked and his clothes brushed, and laid his linen out for the day.

"Grandison," said Dick one morning, after finishing his toilet, "this is the chance of your life to go around among your own people and see how they live. Have you met any of them?"

"Yas, suh, I 's seen some of 'em. But I don' keer nuffin fer 'em, suh. Dey 're diffe'nt f'm de niggers down ou' way. Dey 'lows dey 're free, but dey ain' got sense 'nuff ter know dey ain' half as well off as dey would be down Souf, whar dey 'd be 'preciated."

When two weeks had passed without any apparent effect of evil example upon Grandison, Dick resolved to go on to Boston, where he thought the atmosphere might prove more favorable to his ends. After he had been at the Revere House for a day or two without losing Grandison, he decided upon slightly different tactics.

Having ascertained from a city directory the addresses of several well-known abolitionists, he wrote them each a letter something like this:—

DEAR FRIEND AND BROTHER:—
A wicked slaveholder from Kentucky, stopping at the Revere House, has dared to insult the liberty-loving people of Boston by bringing his slave into their midst. Shall this be tolerated? Or shall steps be taken in the name of liberty to rescue a fellow-man from bondage? For obvious reasons I can only sign myself,

A FRIEND OF HUMANITY.

That his letter might have an opportunity to prove effective, Dick made it a point to send Grandison away from the hotel on various errands. On one of these occasions Dick watched him for quite a distance down the street. Grandison had scarcely left the hotel when a long-haired, sharp-featured man came out behind him, followed him, soon overtook him, and kept along beside him until they turned the next corner. Dick's hopes were roused by this spectacle, but sank correspondingly when Grandison returned to the hotel. As Grandison said nothing about the encounter, Dick hoped there might be some self-consciousness behind this unexpected reticence, the results of which might develop later on.

But Grandison was on hand again when his master came back to the hotel at night, and was in attendance again in the morning, with hot water, to assist at his master's toilet. Dick sent him on further errands from day to day, and upon one occasion came squarely up to him—inadvertently of course—while Grandison was engaged in conversation with a young white man in clerical garb. When Grandison saw Dick approaching, he edged away from the preacher and hastened toward his master, with a very evident expression of relief upon his countenance.

"Mars Dick," he said, "dese yer abolitioners is jes' pesterin' de life out er me tryin' ter git me ter run away. I don' pay no 'tention ter 'em, but dey riles me so sometimes dat I 'm feared I 'll hit some of 'em some er dese days, an' dat mought git me inter trouble. I ain' said nuffin' ter you 'bout it, Mars

Dick, fer I did n' wanter 'sturb yo' min'; but I don' like it, suh; no, suh, I don'! Is we gwine back home 'fo' long, Mars Dick?"

"We 'll be going back soon enough," replied Dick somewhat shortly, while he inwardly cursed the stupidity of a slave who could be free and would not, and registered a secret vow that if he were unable to get rid of Grandison without assassinating him, and were therefore compelled to take him back to Kentucky, he would see that Grandison got a taste of an article of slavery that would make him regret his wasted opportunities. Meanwhile he determined to tempt his servant yet more strongly.

"Grandison," he said next morning, "I 'm going away for a day or two, but I shall leave you here. I shall lock up a hundred dollars in this drawer and give you the key. If you need any of it, use it and enjoy yourself,—spend it all if you like,—for this is probably the last chance you 'll have for some time to be in a free State, and you 'd better enjoy your liberty while you may."

When he came back a couple of days later and found the faithful Grandison at his post, and the hundred dollars intact, Dick felt seriously annoyed. His vexation was increased by the fact that he could not express his feelings adequately. He did not even scold Grandison; how could he, indeed, find fault with one who so sensibly recognized his true place in the economy of civilization, and kept it with such touching fidelity?

"I can't say a thing to him," groaned Dick. "He deserves a leather medal, made out of his own hide tanned. I reckon I 'll write to father and let him know what a model servant he has given me."

He wrote his father a letter which made the colonel swell with pride and pleasure. "I really think," the colonel observed to one of his friends, "that Dick ought to have the nigger interviewed by the Boston papers, so that they may see how contented and happy our darkeys really are."

Dick also wrote a long letter to Charity Lomax, in which he said, among many other things, that if she knew how hard he was working, and under what difficulties, to accomplish something serious for her sake, she would no longer keep him in suspense, but overwhelm him with love and admiration.

Having thus exhausted without result the more obvious methods of getting rid of Grandison, and diplomacy having also proved a failure, Dick was forced to consider more radical measures. Of course he might run away himself, and abandon Grandison, but this would be merely to leave him in the United States, where he was still a slave, and where, with his notions of loyalty, he would speedily be reclaimed. It was necessary, in order to accomplish the purpose of his trip to the North, to leave Grandison permanently in Canada, where he would be legally free.

"I might extend my trip to Canada," he reflected, "but that would be too palpable. I have it! I 'll visit Niagara Falls on the way home, and lose him on the Canada side. When he once realizes that he is actually free, I 'll warrant that he 'll stay."

So the next day saw them westward bound, and in due course of time, by the somewhat slow conveyances of the period, they found themselves at Niagara. Dick walked and drove about the Falls for several days, taking Grandison along with him on most occasions. One morning they stood on the Canadian side, watching the wild whirl of the waters below them.

"Grandison," said Dick, raising his voice above the roar of the cataract, "do you know where you are now?"

"I 's wid you, Mars Dick; dat 's all I keers."

"You are now in Canada, Grandison, where your people go when they run away from their masters. If you wished, Grandison, you might walk away from me this very minute, and I could not lay my hand upon you to take you back."

Grandison looked around uneasily.

"Let 's go back ober de ribber, Mars Dick. I 's feared I 'll lose you ovuh heah, an' den I won' hab no marster, an' won't nebber be able to git back home no mo'."

Discouraged, but not yet hopeless, Dick said, a few minutes later,—

"Grandison, I 'm going up the road a bit, to the inn over yonder. You stay here until I return. I 'll not be gone a great while."

Grandison's eyes opened wide and he looked somewhat fearful.

"Is dey any er dem dadblasted abolitioners roun' heah, Mars Dick?"

"I don't imagine that there are," replied his master, hoping there might be. "But I 'm not afraid of *your* running away, Grandison. I only wish I were," he added to himself.

Dick walked leisurely down the road to where the white-washed inn, built of stone, with true British solidity, loomed up through the trees by the roadside. Arrived there he ordered a glass of ale and a sandwich, and took a seat at a table by a window, from which he could see Grandison in the distance. For a while he hoped that the seed he had sown might have fallen on fertile ground, and that Grandison, relieved from the restraining power of a master's eye, and finding himself in a free country, might get up and walk away; but the hope was vain, for Grandison remained faithfully at his post, awaiting his master's return. He had seated himself on a broad flat stone, and, turning his eyes away from the grand and awe-inspiring spectacle that lay close at hand, was looking anxiously toward the inn where his master sat cursing his ill-timed fidelity.

By and by a girl came into the room to serve his order, and Dick very naturally glanced at her; and as she was young and pretty and remained in attendance, it was some minutes before he looked for Grandison. When he did so his faithful servant had disappeared.

To pay his reckoning and go away without the change was a matter quickly accomplished. Retracing his footsteps toward the Falls, he saw, to his great disgust, as he approached the spot where he had left Grandison, the familiar form of his servant stretched out on the ground, his face to the sun, his mouth open, sleeping the time away, oblivious alike to the grandeur of the scenery, the thunderous roar of the cataract, or the insidious voice of sentiment.

"Grandison," soliloquized his master, as he stood gazing down at his ebony encumbrance, "I do not deserve to be an American citizen; I ought not to have the advantages I possess over you; and I certainly am not worthy of Charity Lomax, if I am not smart enough to get rid of you. I have an idea! You shall yet be free, and I will be the instrument of your deliverance. Sleep on, faithful and affectionate servitor, and dream of the blue grass and the bright skies of old Kentucky, for it is only in your dreams that you will ever see them again!"

Dick retraced his footsteps towards the inn. The young woman chanced to look out of the window and saw the handsome young gentleman she had waited on a few minutes before, standing in the road a short distance away, apparently engaged in earnest conversation with a colored man employed as hostler for the inn. She thought she saw something pass from the white man to the other, but at that moment her duties called her away from the window, and when she looked out again the young gentleman had disappeared, and the hostler, with two other young men of the neighborhood, one white and one colored, were walking rapidly towards the Falls.

IV

Dick made the journey homeward alone, and as rapidly as the conveyances of the day would permit. As he drew near home his conduct in going back without Grandison took on a more serious aspect than it had borne at any previous time, and although he had prepared the colonel by a letter sent several days ahead, there was still the prospect of a bad quarter of an hour with him; not, indeed, that his father would upbraid him, but he was likely to make searching inquiries. And notwithstanding the vein of quiet recklessness that had carried Dick through his preposterous scheme, he was a very poor liar, having rarely had occasion or inclination to tell anything but the truth. Any reluctance to meet his father was more than offset, however, by a stronger force drawing him homeward, for Charity Lomax must long since have returned from her visit to her aunt in Tennessee.

Dick got off easier than he had expected. He told a straight story, and a truthful one, so far as it went.

The colonel raged at first, but rage soon subsided into anger, and anger moderated into annoyance, and annoyance into a sort of garrulous sense of injury. The colonel thought he had been hardly used; he had trusted this negro, and he had broken faith. Yet, after all, he did not blame Grandison so much as he did the abolitionists, who were undoubtedly at the bottom of it.

As for Charity Lomax, Dick told her, privately of course,

that he had run his father's man, Grandison, off to Canada, and left him there.

"Oh, Dick," she had said with shuddering alarm, "what have you done? If they knew it they 'd send you to the penitentiary, like they did that Yankee."

"But they don't know it," he had replied seriously; adding, with an injured tone, "you don't seem to appreciate my heroism like you did that of the Yankee; perhaps it 's because I was n't caught and sent to the penitentiary. I thought you wanted me to do it."

"Why, Dick Owens!" she exclaimed. "You know I never dreamed of any such outrageous proceeding.

"But I presume I 'll have to marry you," she concluded, after some insistence on Dick's part, "if only to take care of you. You are too reckless for anything; and a man who goes chasing all over the North, being entertained by New York and Boston society and having negroes to throw away, needs some one to look after him."

"It 's a most remarkable thing," replied Dick fervently, "that your views correspond exactly with my profoundest convictions. It proves beyond question that we were made for one another."

They were married three weeks later. As each of them had just returned from a journey, they spent their honeymoon at home.

A week after the wedding they were seated, one afternoon, on the piazza of the colonel's house, where Dick had taken his bride, when a negro from the yard ran down the lane and threw open the big gate for the colonel's buggy to enter. The colonel was not alone. Beside him, ragged and travel-stained, bowed with weariness, and upon his face a haggard look that told of hardship and privation, sat the lost Gran dison.

The colonel alighted at the steps.

"Take the lines, Tom," he said to the man who had opened the gate, "and drive round to the barn. Help Grandison down,—poor devil, he 's so stiff he can hardly move!—and get a tub of water and wash him and rub him down, and feed him, and give him a big drink of whiskey, and then let him come round and see his young master and his new mistress."

The colonel's face wore an expression compounded of joy and indignation,—joy at the restoration of a valuable piece of property; indignation for reasons he proceeded to state.

"It 's astounding, the depths of depravity the human heart is capable of! I was coming along the road three miles away, when I heard some one call me from the roadside. I pulled up the mare, and who should come out of the woods but Grandison. The poor nigger could hardly crawl along, with the help of a broken limb. I was never more astonished in my life. You could have knocked me down with a feather. He seemed pretty far gone,—he could hardly talk above a whisper,—and I had to give him a mouthful of whiskey to brace him up so he could tell his story. It 's just as I thought from the beginning, Dick; Grandison had no notion of running away; he knew when he was well off, and where his friends were. All the persuasions of abolition liars and runaway niggers did not move him. But the desperation of those fanatics knew no bounds; their guilty consciences gave them no rest. They got the notion somehow that Grandison belonged to a nigger-catcher, and had been brought North as a spy to help capture ungrateful runaway servants. They actually kidnaped him—just think of it!—and gagged him and bound him and threw him rudely into a wagon, and carried him into the gloomy depths of a Canadian forest, and locked him in a lonely hut, and fed him on bread and water for three weeks. One of the scoundrels wanted to kill him, and persuaded the others that it ought to be done; but they got to quarreling about how they should do it, and before they had their minds made up Grandison escaped, and, keeping his back steadily to the North Star, made his way, after suffering incredible hardships, back to the old plantation, back to his master, his friends, and his home. Why, it 's as good as one of Scott's novels! Mr. Simms or some other one of our Southern authors ought to write it up."

"Don't you think, sir," suggested Dick, who had calmly smoked his cigar throughout the colonel's animated recital, "that that kidnaping yarn sounds a little improbable? Is n't there some more likely explanation?"

"Nonsense, Dick; it 's the gospel truth! Those infernal abolitionists are capable of anything—everything! Just think of their locking the poor, faithful nigger up, beating him, kicking him, depriving him of his liberty, keeping him on bread and water for three long, lonesome weeks, and he all the time pining for the old plantation!"

There were almost tears in the colonel's eyes at the picture of Grandison's sufferings that he conjured up. Dick still professed to be slightly skeptical, and met Charity's severely questioning eye with bland unconsciousness.

The colonel killed the fatted calf for Grandison, and for two or three weeks the returned wanderer's life was a slave's dream of pleasure. His fame spread throughout the county, and the colonel gave him a permanent place among the house servants, where he could always have him conveniently at hand to relate his adventures to admiring visitors.

About three weeks after Grandison's return the colonel's faith in sable humanity was rudely shaken, and its foundations almost broken up. He came near losing his belief in the fidelity of the negro to his master,—the servile virtue most highly prized and most sedulously cultivated by the colonel and his kind. One Monday morning Grandison was missing. And not only Grandison, but his wife, Betty the maid; his mother, aunt Eunice; his father, uncle Ike; his brothers, Tom and John, and his little sister Elsie, were likewise absent from the plantation; and a hurried search and inquiry in the neighborhood resulted in no information as to their whereabouts. So much valuable property could not be lost without an effort to recover it, and the wholesale nature of the transaction carried consternation to the hearts of those whose ledgers were chiefly bound in black. Extremely energetic measures were taken by the colonel and his friends. The fugitives were traced, and followed from point to point, on their northward run through Ohio. Several times the hunters were close upon their heels, but the magnitude of the escaping party begot unusual vigilance on the part of those who sympathized with the fugitives, and strangely enough, the underground railroad seemed to have had its tracks cleared and signals set for this particular train. Once, twice, the colonel thought he had them, but they slipped through his fingers.

One last glimpse he caught of his vanishing property, as he stood, accompanied by a United States marshal, on a wharf at a port on the south shore of Lake Erie. On the stern of a small steamboat which was receding rapidly from the wharf, with her nose pointing toward Canada, there stood a group of familiar dark faces, and the look they cast backward was not one of longing for the fleshpots of Egypt. The colonel saw Grandison point him out to one of the crew of the vessel, who waved his hand derisively toward the colonel. The latter shook his fist impotently—and the incident was closed.

Uncle Wellington's Wives

I

UNCLE WELLINGTON BRABOY was so deeply absorbed in thought as he walked slowly homeward from the weekly meeting of the Union League, that he let his pipe go out, a fact of which he remained oblivious until he had reached the little frame house in the suburbs of Patesville, where he lived with aunt Milly, his wife. On this particular occasion the club had been addressed by a visiting brother from the North, Professor Patterson, a tall, well-formed mulatto, who wore a perfectly fitting suit of broadcloth, a shiny silk hat, and linen of dazzling whiteness,—in short, a gentleman of such distinguished appearance that the doors and windows of the offices and stores on Front Street were filled with curious observers as he passed through that thoroughfare in the early part of the day. This polished stranger was a traveling organizer of Masonic lodges, but he also claimed to be a high officer in the Union League, and had been invited to lecture before the local chapter of that organization at Patesville.

The lecture had been largely attended, and uncle Wellington Braboy had occupied a seat just in front of the platform. The subject of the lecture was "The Mental, Moral, Physical, Political, Social, and Financial Improvement of the Negro Race in America," a theme much dwelt upon, with slight variations, by colored orators. For to this struggling people, then as now, the problem of their uncertain present and their doubtful future was the chief concern of life. The period was the hopeful one. The Federal Government retained some vestige of authority in the South, and the newly emancipated race cherished the delusion that under the Constitution, that enduring rock on which our liberties are founded, and under the equal laws it purported to guarantee, they would enter upon the era of freedom and opportunity which their Northern friends had inaugurated with such solemn sanctions. The speaker pictured in eloquent language the state of ideal equality and happiness enjoyed by colored people at the North: how they sent their children to school with the white children; how they sat by white people in the churches and theatres, ate with them in the public restaurants, and buried their dead in the same cemeteries. The professor waxed eloquent with the development of his theme, and, as a finishing touch to an alluring picture, assured the excited audience that the intermarriage of the races was common, and that he himself had espoused a white woman.

Uncle Wellington Braboy was a deeply interested listener. He had heard something of these facts before, but his information had always come in such vague and questionable shape that he had paid little attention to it. He knew that the Yankees had freed the slaves, and that runaway negroes had always gone to the North to seek liberty; any such equality, however, as the visiting brother had depicted, was more than uncle Wellington had ever conceived as actually existing anywhere in the world. At first he felt inclined to doubt the truth of the speaker's statements; but the cut of his clothes, the eloquence of his language, and the flowing length of his whiskers, were so far superior to anything uncle Wellington had ever met among the colored people of his native State, that he felt irresistibly impelled to the conviction that nothing less than the advantages claimed for the North by the visiting brother could have produced such an exquisite flower of civilization. Any lingering doubts uncle Wellington may have felt were entirely dispelled by the courtly bow and cordial grasp of the hand with which the visiting brother acknowledged the congratulations showered upon him by the audience at the close of his address.

The more uncle Wellington's mind dwelt upon the professor's speech, the more attractive seemed the picture of Northern life presented. Uncle Wellington possessed in large measure the imaginative faculty so freely bestowed by nature upon the race from which the darker half of his blood was drawn. He had indulged in occasional day-dreams of an ideal state of social equality, but his wildest flights of fancy had never located it nearer than heaven, and he had felt some misgivings about its practical working even there. Its desirability he had never doubted, and the speech of the evening before had given a local habitation and a name to the forms his imagination had bodied forth. Giving full rein to his fancy, he saw in the North a land flowing with milk and honey,—a land peopled by noble men and beautiful women, among whom colored men and women moved with the ease and grace of acknowledged right. Then he placed himself in the foreground of the picture. What a fine figure he would have made in the world if he had been born at the free North! He imagined himself dressed like the professor, and passing the contribution-box in a white church; and most pleasant of his dreams, and the hardest to realize as possible, was that of the gracious white lady he might have called wife. Uncle Wellington was a mulatto, and his features were those of his white father, though tinged with the hue of his mother's race; and as he lifted the kerosene lamp at evening, and took a long look at his image in the little mirror over the mantelpiece, he said to himself that he was a very good-looking man, and could have adorned a much higher sphere in life than that in which the accident of birth had placed him. He fell asleep and dreamed that he lived in a two-story brick house, with a spacious flower garden in front, the whole inclosed by a high iron fence; that he kept a carriage and servants, and never did a stroke of work. This was the highest style of living in Patesville, and he could conceive of nothing finer.

Uncle Wellington slept later than usual the next morning, and the sunlight was pouring in at the open window of the bedroom, when his dreams were interrupted by the voice of his wife, in tones meant to be harsh, but which no ordinary degree of passion could rob of their native unctuousness.

"Git up f'm dere, you lazy, good-fuh-nuffin' nigger! Is you gwine ter sleep all de mawnin'? I 's ti'ed er dis yer runnin' 'roun' all night an' den sleepin' all day. You won't git dat tater patch hoed ovuh ter-day 'less'n you git up f'm dere an' git at it."

Uncle Wellington rolled over, yawned cavernously, stretched himself, and with a muttered protest got out of bed and put on his clothes. Aunt Milly had prepared a smoking breakfast of hominy and fried bacon, the odor of which was very grateful to his nostrils.

"Is breakfus' done ready?" he inquired, tentatively, as he came into the kitchen and glanced at the table.

"No, it ain't ready, an' 't ain't gwine ter be ready 'tel you tote dat wood an' water in," replied aunt Milly severely, as she poured two teacups of boiling water on two tablespoonfuls of ground coffee.

Uncle Wellington went down to the spring and got a pail of water, after which he brought in some oak logs for the fireplace and some lightwood for kindling. Then he drew a chair towards the table and started to sit down.

"Wonduh what 's de matter wid you dis mawnin' anyhow," remarked aunt Milly. "You must 'a' be'n up ter some devilment las' night, fer yo' recommemb'ance is so po' dat you fus' fergit ter git up, an' den fergit ter wash yo' face an' hands fo' you set down ter de table. I don' 'low nobody ter eat at my table dat a-way."

"I don' see no use 'n washin' 'em so much," replied Wellington wearily. "Dey gits dirty ag'in right off, an' den you got ter wash 'em ovuh ag'in; it 's jes' pilin' up wuk what don' fetch in nuffin'. De dirt don' show nohow, 'n' I don' see no advantage in bein' black, ef you got to keep on washin' yo' face 'n' han's jes' lack w'ite folks." He nevertheless performed his ablutions in a perfunctory way, and resumed his seat at the breakfast-table.

"Ole 'oman," he asked, after the edge of his appetite had been taken off, "how would you lack ter live at de Norf?"

"I dunno nuffin' 'bout de Norf," replied aunt Milly. "It 's hard 'nuff ter git erlong heah, whar we knows all erbout it."

"De brother what 'dressed de meetin' las' night say dat de wages at de Norf is twicet ez big ez dey is heah."

"You could make a sight mo' wages heah ef you 'd 'ten' ter yo' wuk better," replied aunt Milly.

Uncle Wellington ignored this personality, and continued, "An' he say de cullud folks got all de privileges er de w'ite folks,—dat dey chillen goes ter school tergedder, dat dey sets on same seats in chu'ch, an' sarves on jury, 'n' rides on de kyars an' steamboats wid de w'ite folks, an' eats at de fus' table."

"Dat 'u'd suit you," chuckled aunt Milly, "an' you 'd stay dere fer de secon' table, too. How dis man know 'bout all dis yer foolis'ness?" she asked incredulously.

"He come f'm de Norf," said uncle Wellington, "an' he 'speunced it all hisse'f."

"Well, he can't make me b'lieve it," she rejoined, with a shake of her head.

"An' you would n' lack ter go up dere an' 'joy all dese privileges?" asked uncle Wellington, with some degree of earnestness.

The old woman laughed until her sides shook. "Who gwine ter take me up dere?" she inquired.

"You got de money yo'se'f."

"I ain' got no money fer ter was'e," she replied shortly, becoming serious at once; and with that the subject was dropped.

Uncle Wellington pulled a hoe from under the house, and took his way wearily to the potato patch. He did not feel like working, but aunt Milly was the undisputed head of the establishment, and he did not dare to openly neglect his work. In fact, he regarded work at any time as a disagreeable necessity to be avoided as much as possible.

His wife was cast in a different mould. Externally she would have impressed the casual observer as a neat, well-preserved, and good-looking black woman, of middle age, every curve of whose ample figure—and her figure was all curves—was suggestive of repose. So far from being indolent, or even deliberate in her movements, she was the most active and energetic woman in the town. She went through the physical exercises of a prayer-meeting with astonishing vigor. It was exhilarating to see her wash a shirt, and a study to watch her do it up. A quick jerk shook out the dampened garment; one pass of her ample palm spread it over the ironing-board, and a few well-directed strokes with the iron accomplished what would have occupied the ordinary laundress for half an hour.

To this uncommon, and in uncle Wellington's opinion unnecessary and unnatural activity, his own habits were a steady protest. If aunt Milly had been willing to support him in idleness, he would have acquiesced without a murmur in her habits of industry. This she would not do, and, moreover, insisted on his working at least half the time. If she had invested the proceeds of her labor in rich food and fine clothing, he might have endured it better; but to her passion for work was added a most detestable thrift. She absolutely refused to pay for Wellington's clothes, and required him to furnish a certain proportion of the family supplies. Her savings were carefully put by, and with them she had bought and paid for the modest cottage which she and her husband occupied. Under her careful hand it was always neat and clean; in summer the little yard was gay with bright-colored flowers, and woe to the heedless pickaninny who should stray into her yard and pluck a rose or a verbena! In a stout oaken chest under her bed she kept a capacious stocking, into which flowed a steady stream of fractional currency. She carried the key to this chest in her pocket, a proceeding regarded by uncle Wellington with no little disfavor. He was of the opinion—an opinion he would not have dared to assert in her presence—that his wife's earnings were his own property; and he looked upon this stocking as a drunkard's wife might regard the saloon which absorbed her husband's wages.

Uncle Wellington hurried over the potato patch on the morning of the conversation above recorded, and as soon as he saw aunt Milly go away with a basket of clothes on her head, returned to the house, put on his coat, and went uptown.

He directed his steps to a small frame building fronting on the main street of the village, at a point where the street was intersected by one of the several creeks meandering through the town, cooling the air, providing numerous swimming-holes for the amphibious small boy, and furnishing water-power for grist-mills and saw-mills. The rear of the building rested on long brick pillars, built up from the bottom of the steep bank of the creek, while the front was level with the street. This was the office of Mr. Matthew Wright, the sole representative of the colored race at the bar of Chinquapin County. Mr. Wright came of an "old issue" free colored family, in which, though the negro blood was present in an attenuated strain, a line of free ancestry could be traced beyond the Revolutionary War. He had enjoyed exceptional opportunities, and enjoyed the distinction of being the first, and for a long time the only colored lawyer in North Carolina. His services were frequently called into requisition by impecunious people of his own race; when they had money they went to white lawyers, who, they shrewdly conjectured, would have more influence with judge or jury than a colored lawyer, however able.

Uncle Wellington found Mr. Wright in his office. Having

inquired after the health of the lawyer's family and all his relations in detail, uncle Wellington asked for a professional opinion.

"Mistah Wright, ef a man's wife got money, whose money is dat befo' de law—his'n er her'n?"

The lawyer put on his professional air, and replied:—

"Under the common law, which in default of special legislative enactment is the law of North Carolina, the personal property of the wife belongs to her husband."

"But dat don' jes' tech de p'int, suh. I wuz axin' 'bout money."

"You see, uncle Wellington, your education has not rendered you familiar with legal phraseology. The term 'personal property' or 'estate' embraces, according to Blackstone, all property other than land, and therefore includes money. Any money a man's wife has is his, constructively, and will be recognized as his actually, as soon as he can secure possession of it."

"Dat is ter say, suh—my eddication don' quite 'low me ter understan' dat—dat is ter say"—

"That is to say, it 's yours when you get it. It is n't yours so that the law will help you get it; but on the other hand, when you once lay your hands on it, it is yours so that the law won't take it away from you."

Uncle Wellington nodded to express his full comprehension of the law as expounded by Mr. Wright, but scratched his head in a way that expressed some disappointment. The law seemed to wobble. Instead of enabling him to stand up fearlessly and demand his own, it threw him back upon his own efforts; and the prospect of his being able to overpower or outwit aunt Milly by any ordinary means was very poor.

He did not leave the office, but hung around awhile as though there were something further he wished to speak about. Finally, after some discursive remarks about the crops and politics, he asked, in an offhand, disinterested manner, as though the thought had just occurred to him:—

"Mistah Wright, w'ile's we 're talkin' 'bout law matters, what do it cos' ter git a defoce?"

"That depends upon circumstances. It is n't altogether a matter of expense. Have you and aunt Milly been having trouble?"

"Oh no, suh; I was jes' a-wond'rin'."

"You see," continued the lawyer, who was fond of talking, and had nothing else to do for the moment, "a divorce is not an easy thing to get in this State under any circumstances. It used to be the law that divorce could be granted only by special act of the legislature; and it is but recently that the subject has been relegated to the jurisdiction of the courts."

Uncle Wellington understood a part of this, but the answer had not been exactly to the point in his mind.

"S'pos'n', den, jes' fer de argyment, me an' my ole 'oman sh'd fall out en wanter separate, how could I git a defoce?"

"That would depend on what you quarreled about. It 's pretty hard work to answer general questions in a particular way. If you merely wished to separate, it would n't be necessary to get a divorce; but if you should want to marry again, you would have to be divorced, or else you would be guilty of bigamy, and could be sent to the penitentiary. But, by the way, uncle Wellington, when were you married?"

"I got married 'fo' de wah, when I was livin' down on Rockfish Creek."

"When you were in slavery?"

"Yas, suh."

"Did you have your marriage registered after the surrender?"

"No, suh; never knowed nuffin' 'bout dat."

After the war, in North Carolina and other States, the freed people who had sustained to each other the relation of husband and wife as it existed among slaves, were required by law to register their consent to continue in the marriage relation. By this simple expedient their former marriages of convenience received the sanction of law, and their children the seal of legitimacy. In many cases, however, where the parties lived in districts remote from the larger towns, the ceremony was neglected, or never heard of by the freedmen.

"Well," said the lawyer, "if that is the case, and you and aunt Milly should disagree, it would n't be necessary for you to get a divorce, even if you should want to marry again. You were never legally married."

"So Milly ain't my lawful wife, den?"

"She may be your wife in one sense of the word, but not in such a sense as to render you liable to punishment for bigamy if you should marry another woman. But I hope you will never want to do anything of the kind, for you have a very good wife now."

Uncle Wellington went away thoughtfully, but with a feeling of unaccustomed lightness and freedom. He had not felt so free since the memorable day when he had first heard of the Emancipation Proclamation. On leaving the lawyer's office, he called at the workshop of one of his friends, Peter Williams, a shoemaker by trade, who had a brother living in Ohio.

"Is you hearn f'm Sam lately?" uncle Wellington inquired, after the conversation had drifted through the usual generalities.

"His mammy got er letter f'm 'im las' week; he 's livin' in de town er Groveland now."

"How 's he gittin' on?"

"He says he gittin' on monst'us well. He 'low ez how he make five dollars a day w'ite-washin', an' have all he kin do."

The shoemaker related various details of his brother's prosperity, and uncle Wellington returned home in a very thoughtful mood, revolving in his mind a plan of future action. This plan had been vaguely assuming form ever since the professor's lecture, and the events of the morning had brought out the detail in bold relief.

Two days after the conversation with the shoemaker, aunt Milly went, in the afternoon, to visit a sister of hers who lived several miles out in the country. During her absence, which lasted until nightfall, uncle Wellington went uptown and purchased a cheap oilcloth valise from a shrewd son of Israel, who had penetrated to this locality with a stock of notions and cheap clothing. Uncle Wellington had his purchase done up in brown paper, and took the parcel under his arm. Arrived at home he unwrapped the valise, and thrust into its capacious jaws his best suit of clothes, some underwear, and a few other small articles for personal use and adornment. Then he carried the valise out into the yard, and, first looking cautiously around to see if there was any one in sight, concealed it in a clump of bushes in a corner of the yard.

It may be inferred from this proceeding that uncle Wellington was preparing for a step of some consequence. In fact, he had fully made up his mind to go to the North; but he still lacked the most important requisite for traveling with comfort, namely, the money to pay his expenses. The idea of tramping the distance which separated him from the promised land of liberty and equality had never occurred to him. When a slave, he had several times been importuned by fellow servants to join them in the attempt to escape from bondage, but he had never wanted his freedom badly enough to walk a thousand miles for it; if he could have gone to Canada by stage-coach, or by rail, or on horseback, with stops for regular meals, he would probably have undertaken the trip. The funds he now needed for his journey were in aunt Milly's chest. He had thought a great deal about his right to this money. It was his wife's savings, and he had never dared to dispute, openly, her right to exercise exclusive control over what she earned; but the lawyer had assured him of his right to the money, of which he was already constructively in possession, and he had therefore determined to possess himself actually of the coveted stocking. It was impracticable for him to get the key of the chest. Aunt Milly kept it in her pocket by day and under her pillow at night. She was a light sleeper, and, if not awakened by the abstraction of the key, would certainly have been disturbed by the unlocking of the chest. But one alternative remained, and that was to break open the chest in her absence.

There was a revival in progress at the colored Methodist church. Aunt Milly was as energetic in her religion as in other respects, and had not missed a single one of the meetings. She returned at nightfall from her visit to the country and prepared a frugal supper. Uncle Wellington did not eat as heartily as usual. Aunt Milly perceived his want of appetite, and spoke of it. He explained it by saying that he did not feel very well.

"Is you gwine ter chu'ch ter-night?" inquired his wife.

"I reckon I 'll stay home an' go ter bed," he replied. "I ain't be'n feelin' well dis evenin', an' I 'spec' I better git a good night's res'."

"Well, you kin stay ef you mineter. Good preachin' 'u'd make you feel better, but ef you ain't gwine, don' fergit ter tote in some wood an' lighterd 'fo' you go ter bed. De moon is shinin' bright, an' you can't have no 'scuse 'bout not bein' able ter see."

Uncle Wellington followed her out to the gate, and watched her receding form until it disappeared in the distance. Then he re-entered the house with a quick step, and taking a hatchet from a corner of the room, drew the chest from under the bed. As he applied the hatchet to the fastenings, a thought struck him, and by the flickering light of the pine-knot blazing on the hearth, a look of hesitation might have been seen to take the place of the determined expression his face had worn up to that time. He had argued himself into the belief that his present action was lawful and justifiable. Though this conviction had not prevented him from trembling in every limb, as though he were committing a mere vulgar theft, it had still nerved him to the deed. Now even his moral courage began to weaken. The lawyer had told him that his wife's property was his own; in taking it he was therefore only exercising his lawful right. But at the point of breaking open the chest, it occurred to him that he was taking this money in order to get away from aunt Milly, and that he justified his desertion of her by the lawyer's opinion that she was not his lawful wife. If she was not his wife, then he had no right to take the money; if she was his wife, he had no right to desert her, and would certainly have no right to marry another woman. His scheme was about to go to shipwreck on this rock, when another idea occurred to him.

"De lawyer say dat in one sense er de word de ole 'oman is my wife, an' in anudder sense er de word she ain't my wife. Ef I goes ter de Norf an' marry a w'ite 'oman, I ain't commit no brigamy, 'caze in dat sense er de word she ain't my wife; but ef I takes dis money, I ain't stealin' it, 'caze in dat sense er de word she is my wife. Dat 'splains all de trouble away."

Having reached this ingenious conclusion, uncle Wellington applied the hatchet vigorously, soon loosened the fastenings of the chest, and with trembling hands extracted from its depths a capacious blue cotton stocking. He emptied the stocking on the table. His first impulse was to take the whole, but again there arose in his mind a doubt—a very obtrusive, unreasonable doubt, but a doubt, nevertheless—of the absolute rectitude of his conduct; and after a moment's hesitation he hurriedly counted the money—it was in bills of small denominations—and found it to be about two hundred and fifty dollars. He then divided it into two piles of one hundred and twenty-five dollars each. He put one pile into his pocket, returned the remainder to the stocking, and replaced it where he had found it. He then closed the chest and shoved it under the bed. After having arranged the fire so that it could safely be left burning, he took a last look around the room, and went out into the moonlight, locking the door behind him, and hanging the key on a nail in the wall, where his wife would be likely to look for it. He then secured his valise from behind the bushes, and left the yard. As he passed by the wood-pile, he said to himself:—

"Well, I declar' ef I ain't done fergot ter tote in dat lighterd; I reckon de ole 'oman 'll ha' ter fetch it in herse'f dis time."

He hastened through the quiet streets, avoiding the few people who were abroad at that hour, and soon reached the railroad station, from which a North-bound train left at nine o'clock. He went around to the dark side of the train, and climbed into a second-class car, where he shrank into the darkest corner and turned his face away from the dim light of the single dirty lamp. There were no passengers in the car except one or two sleepy negroes, who had got on at some other station, and a white man who had gone into the car to smoke, accompanied by a gigantic bloodhound.

Finally the train crept out of the station. From the window uncle Wellington looked out upon the familiar cabins and turpentine stills, the new barrel factory, the brickyard where he had once worked for some time; and as the train rattled through the outskirts of the town, he saw gleaming in the moonlight the white headstones of the colored cemetery where his only daughter had been buried several years before.

Presently the conductor came around. Uncle Wellington had not bought a ticket, and the conductor collected a cash fare. He was not acquainted with uncle Wellington, but had just had a drink at the saloon near the depot, and felt at peace with all mankind.

"Where are you going, uncle?" he inquired carelessly.

Uncle Wellington's face assumed the ashen hue which

does duty for pallor in dusky countenances, and his knees began to tremble. Controlling his voice as well as he could, he replied that he was going up to Jonesboro, the terminus of the railroad, to work for a gentleman at that place. He felt immensely relieved when the conductor pocketed the fare, picked up his lantern, and moved away. It was very unphilosophical and very absurd that a man who was only doing right should feel like a thief, shrink from the sight of other people, and lie instinctively. Fine distinctions were not in uncle Wellington's line, but he was struck by the unreasonableness of his feelings, and still more by the discomfort they caused him. By and by, however, the motion of the train made him drowsy; his thoughts all ran together in confusion; and he fell asleep with his head on his valise, and one hand in his pocket, clasped tightly around the roll of money.

II

The train from Pittsburg drew into the Union Depot at Groveland, Ohio, one morning in the spring of 187–, with bell ringing and engine puffing; and from a smoking-car emerged the form of uncle Wellington Braboy, a little dusty and travel-stained, and with a sleepy look about his eyes. He mingled in the crowd, and, valise in hand, moved toward the main exit from the depot. There were several tracks to be crossed, and more than once a watchman snatched him out of the way of a baggage-truck, or a train backing into the depot. He at length reached the door, beyond which, and as near as the regulations would permit, stood a number of hackmen, vociferously soliciting patronage. One of them, a colored man, soon secured several passengers. As he closed the door after the last one he turned to uncle Wellington, who stood near him on the sidewalk, looking about irresolutely.

"Is you goin' uptown?" asked the hackman, as he prepared to mount the box.

"Yas, suh."

"I 'll take you up fo' a quahtah, ef you want ter git up here an' ride on de box wid me."

Uncle Wellington accepted the offer and mounted the box.

The hackman whipped up his horses, the carriage climbed the steep hill leading up to the town, and the passengers inside were soon deposited at their hotels.

"Whereabouts do you want to go?" asked the hackman of uncle Wellington, when the carriage was emptied of its last passengers.

"I want ter go ter Brer Sam Williams's," said Wellington.

"What 's his street an' number?"

Uncle Wellington did not know the street and number, and the hackman had to explain to him the mystery of numbered houses, to which he was a total stranger.

"Where is he from?" asked the hackman, "and what is his business?"

"He is f'm Norf Ca'lina," replied uncle Wellington, "an' makes his livin' w'itewashin'."

"I reckon I knows de man," said the hackman. "I 'spec' he 's changed his name. De man I knows is name' Johnson. He b'longs ter my chu'ch. I 'm gwine out dat way ter git a passenger fer de ten o'clock train, an I 'll take you by dere."

They followed one of the least handsome streets of the city for more than a mile, turned into a cross street, and drew up before a small frame house, from the front of which a sign, painted in white upon a black background, announced to the reading public, in letters inclined to each other at various angles, that whitewashing and kalsomining were "dun" there. A knock at the door brought out a slatternly looking colored woman. She had evidently been disturbed at her toilet, for she held a comb in one hand, and the hair on one side of her head stood out loosely, while on the other side it was braided close to her head. She called her husband, who proved to be the Patesville shoemaker's brother. The hackman introduced the traveler, whose name he had learned on the way out, collected his quarter, and drove away.

Mr. Johnson, the shoemaker's brother, welcomed uncle Wellington to Groveland, and listened with eager delight to the news of the old town, from which he himself had run away many years before, and followed the North Star to Groveland. He had changed his name from "Williams" to "Johnson," on account of the Fugitive Slave Law, which, at the time of his escape from bondage, had rendered it advisable for runaway slaves to court obscurity. After the war he had retained the adopted name. Mrs. Johnson prepared breakfast for her guest, who ate it with an appetite sharpened by his journey. After breakfast he went to bed, and slept until late in the afternoon.

After supper Mr. Johnson took uncle Wellington to visit some of the neighbors who had come from North Carolina before the war. They all expressed much pleasure at meeting "Mr. Braboy," a title which at first sounded a little odd to uncle Wellington. At home he had been "Wellin'ton," "Brer Wellin'ton," or "uncle Wellin'ton;" it was a novel experience to be called "Mister," and he set it down, with secret satisfaction, as one of the first fruits of Northern liberty.

"Would you lack ter look 'roun' de town a little?" asked Mr. Johnson at breakfast next morning. "I ain' got no job dis mawnin', an' I kin show you some er de sights."

Uncle Wellington acquiesced in this arrangement, and they walked up to the corner to the street-car line. In a few moments a car passed. Mr. Johnson jumped on the moving car, and uncle Wellington followed his example, at the risk of life or limb, as it was his first experience of street cars.

There was only one vacant seat in the car and that was between two white women in the forward end. Mr. Johnson motioned to the seat, but Wellington shrank from walking between those two rows of white people, to say nothing of sitting between the two women, so he remained standing in the rear part of the car. A moment later, as the car rounded a short curve, he was pitched sidewise into the lap of a stout woman magnificently attired in a ruffled blue calico gown. The lady colored up, and uncle Wellington, as he struggled to his feet amid the laughter of the passengers, was absolutely helpless with embarrassment, until the conductor came up behind him and pushed him toward the vacant place.

"Sit down, will you," he said; and before uncle Wellington could collect himself, he was seated between the two white women. Everybody in the car seemed to be looking at him. But he came to the conclusion, after he had pulled himself together and reflected a few moments, that he would find this method of locomotion pleasanter when he got used to it, and then he could score one more glorious privilege gained by his change of residence.

They got off at the public square, in the heart of the city, where there were flowers and statues, and fountains playing. Mr. Johnson pointed out the court-house, the post-office, the jail, and other public buildings fronting on the square. They visited the market near by, and from an elevated point, looked down upon the extensive lumber yards and factories that were the chief sources of the city's prosperity. Beyond these they could see the fleet of ships that lined the coal and iron ore docks of the harbor. Mr. Johnson, who was quite a fluent talker, enlarged upon the wealth and prosperity of the city; and Wellington, who had never before been in a town of more than three thousand inhabitants, manifested sufficient interest and wonder to satisfy the most exacting *cicerone.* They called at the office of a colored lawyer and member of the legislature, formerly from North Carolina, who, scenting a new constituent and a possible client, greeted the stranger warmly, and in flowing speech pointed out the superior advantages of life at the North, citing himself as an illustration of the possibilities of life in a country really free. As they wended their way homeward to dinner uncle Wellington, with quickened pulse and rising hopes, felt that this was indeed the promised land, and that it must be flowing with milk and honey.

Uncle Wellington remained at the residence of Mr. Johnson for several weeks before making any effort to find employment. He spent this period in looking about the city. The most commonplace things possessed for him the charm of novelty, and he had come prepared to admire. Shortly after his arrival, he had offered to pay for his board, intimating at the same time that he had plenty of money. Mr. Johnson declined to accept anything from him for board, and expressed himself as being only too proud to have Mr. Braboy remain in the house on the footing of an honored guest, until he had settled himself. He lightened in some degree, however, the burden of obligation under which a prolonged stay on these terms would have placed his guest, by soliciting from the latter occasional small loans, until uncle Wellington's roll of money began to lose its plumpness, and with an empty pocket staring him in the face, he felt the necessity of finding something to do.

During his residence in the city he had met several times his first acquaintance, Mr. Peterson, the hackman, who from time to time inquired how he was getting along. On one of these occasions Wellington mentioned his willingness to accept employment. As good luck would have it, Mr. Peterson knew of a vacant situation. He had formerly been coachman for a wealthy gentleman residing on Oakwood Avenue, but had resigned the situation to go into business for himself. His place had been filled by an Irishman, who had just been discharged for drunkenness, and the gentleman that very day had sent word to Mr. Peterson, asking him if he could recommend a competent and trustworthy coachman.

"Does you know anything erbout hosses?" asked Mr. Peterson.

"Yas, indeed, I does," said Wellington. "I wuz raise' 'mongs' hosses."

"I tol' my ole boss I 'd look out fer a man, an' ef you reckon you kin fill de 'quirements er de situation, I 'll take yo' roun' dere ter-morrer mornin'. You wants ter put on yo' bes' clothes an' slick up, fer dey 're partic'lar people. Ef you git de place I 'll expec' you ter pay me fer de time I lose in 'tendin' ter yo' business, fer time is money in dis country, an' folks don't do much fer nuthin'."

Next morning Wellington blacked his shoes carefully, put on a clean collar, and with the aid of Mrs. Johnson tied his cravat in a jaunty bow which gave him quite a sprightly air and a much younger look than his years warranted. Mr. Peterson called for him at eight o'clock. After traversing several cross streets they turned into Oakwood Avenue and walked along the finest part of it for about half a mile. The handsome houses of this famous avenue, the stately trees, the widespreading lawns, dotted with flower beds, fountains and statuary, made up a picture so far surpassing anything in Wellington's experience as to fill him with an almost oppressive sense of its beauty.

"Hit looks lack hebben," he said softly.

"It 's a pootty fine street," rejoined his companion, with a judicial air, "but I don't like dem big lawns. It 's too much trouble ter keep de grass down. One er dem lawns is big enough to pasture a couple er cows."

They went down a street running at right angles to the avenue, and turned into the rear of the corner lot. A large building of pressed brick, trimmed with stone, loomed up before them.

"Do de gemman lib in dis house?" asked Wellington, gazing with awe at the front of the building.

"No, dat 's de barn," said Mr. Peterson with good-natured contempt; and leading the way past a clump of shrubbery to the dwelling-house, he went up the back steps and rang the door-bell.

The ring was answered by a buxom Irishwoman, of a natural freshness of complexion deepened to a fiery red by the heat of a kitchen range. Wellington thought he had seen her before, but his mind had received so many new impressions lately that it was a minute or two before he recognized in her the lady whose lap he had involuntarily occupied for a moment on his first day in Groveland.

"Faith," she exclaimed as she admitted them, "an' it 's mighty glad I am to see ye ag'in, Misther Payterson! An' how hev ye be'n, Misther Payterson, sence I see ye lahst?"

"Middlin' well, Mis' Flannigan, middlin' well, 'ceptin' a tech er de rheumatiz. S'pose you be'n doin' well as usual?"

"Oh yis, as well as a dacent woman could do wid a drunken baste about the place like the lahst coachman. O Misther Payterson, it would make yer heart bleed to see the way the spalpeen cut up a-Saturday! But Misther Todd discharged 'im the same avenin', widout a characther, bad 'cess to 'im, an' we 've had no coachman sence at all, at all. An' it 's sorry I am"—

The lady's flow of eloquence was interrupted at this point by the appearance of Mr. Todd himself, who had been informed of the men's arrival. He asked some questions in regard to Wellington's qualifications and former experience, and in view of his recent arrival in the city was willing to accept Mr. Peterson's recommendation instead of a reference. He said a few words about the nature of the work, and stated his willingness to pay Wellington the wages formerly allowed Mr. Peterson, thirty dollars a month and board and lodging.

This handsome offer was eagerly accepted, and it was agreed that Wellington's term of service should begin immediately. Mr. Peterson, being familiar with the work, and financially interested, conducted the new coachman through the stables and showed him what he would have to do. The silver-mounted harness, the variety of carriages, the names of which he learned for the first time, the arrangements for feeding and watering the horses,—these appointments of a rich man's stable impressed Wellington very much, and he wondered that so much luxury should be wasted on mere horses. The room assigned to him, in the second story of the barn, was a finer apartment than he had ever slept in; and the salary attached to the situation was greater than the combined monthly earnings of himself and aunt Milly in their Southern home. Surely, he thought, his lines had fallen in pleasant places.

Under the stimulus of new surroundings Wellington applied himself diligently to work, and, with the occasional advice of Mr. Peterson, soon mastered the details of his employment. He found the female servants, with whom he took his meals, very amiable ladies. The cook, Mrs. Katie Flannigan, was a widow. Her husband, a sailor, had been lost at sea. She was a woman of many words, and when she was not lamenting the late Flannigan's loss,—according to her story he had been a model of all the virtues,—she would turn the batteries of her tongue against the former coachman. This gentleman, as Wellington gathered from frequent remarks dropped by Mrs. Flannigan, had paid her attentions clearly susceptible of a serious construction. These attentions had not borne their legitimate fruit, and she was still a widow unconsoled,—hence Mrs. Flannigan's tears. The housemaid was a plump, good-natured German girl, with a pronounced German accent. The presence on washdays of a Bohemian laundress, of recent importation, added another to the variety of ways in which the English tongue was mutilated in Mr. Todd's kitchen. Association with the white women drew out all the native gallantry of the mulatto, and Wellington developed quite a helpful turn. His politeness, his willingness to lend a hand in kitchen or laundry, and the fact that he was the only male servant on the place, combined to make him a prime favorite in the servants' quarters.

It was the general opinion among Wellington's acquaintances that he was a single man. He had come to the city alone, had never been heard to speak of a wife, and to personal questions bearing upon the subject of matrimony had always returned evasive answers. Though he had never questioned the correctness of the lawyer's opinion in regard to his slave marriage, his conscience had never been entirely at ease since his departure from the South, and any positive denial of his married condition would have stuck in his throat. The inference naturally drawn from his reticence in regard to the past, coupled with his expressed intention of settling permanently in Groveland, was that he belonged in the ranks of the unmarried, and was therefore legitimate game for any widow or old maid who could bring him down. As such game is bagged easiest at short range, he received numerous invitations to tea-parties, where he feasted on unlimited chicken and pound cake. He used to compare these viands with the plain fare often served by aunt Milly, and the result of the comparison was another item to the credit of the North upon his mental ledger. Several of the colored ladies who smiled upon him were blessed with good looks, and uncle Wellington, naturally of a susceptible temperament, as people of lively imagination are apt to be, would probably have fallen a victim to the charms of some woman of his own race, had it not been for a strong counter-attraction in the person of Mrs. Flannigan. The attentions of the lately discharged coachman had lighted anew the smouldering fires of her widowed heart, and awakened longings which still remained unsatisfied. She was thirty-five years old, and felt the need of some one else to love. She was not a woman of lofty ideals; with her a man was a man—

"For a' that an' a' that;"

and, aside from the accident of color, uncle Wellington was as personable a man as any of her acquaintance. Some people might have objected to his complexion; but then, Mrs. Flannigan argued, he was at least half white; and, this being the case, there was no good reason why he should be regarded as black.

Uncle Wellington was not slow to perceive Mrs. Flannigan's charms of person, and appreciated to the full the skill that prepared the choice tidbits reserved for his plate at dinner. The prospect of securing a white wife had been one of the principal inducements offered by a life at the North; but the awe of white people in which he had been reared was still too strong to permit his taking any active steps toward the object of his secret desire, had not the lady herself come to his assistance with a little of the native coquetry of her race.

"Ah, Misther Braboy," she said one evening when they sat at the supper table alone,—it was the second girl's afternoon off, and she had not come home to supper,—"it must be an awful lonesome life ye 've been afther l'adin', as a single man, wid no one to cook fer ye, or look afther ye."

"It are a kind er lonesome life, Mis' Flannigan, an' dat 's a fac'. But sence I had de privilege er eatin' yo' cookin' an' 'joyin' yo' society, I ain' felt a bit lonesome."

"Yer flatthrin' me, Misther Braboy. An' even if ye mane it"—

"I means eve'y word of it, Mis' Flannigan."

"An' even if ye mane it, Misther Braboy, the time is liable to come when things 'll be different; for service is uncertain, Misther Braboy. An' then you 'll wish you had some nice, clean woman, 'at knowed how to cook an' wash an' iron, ter look afther ye, an' make yer life comfortable."

Uncle Wellington sighed, and looked at her languishingly.

"It 'u'd all be well ernuff, Mis' Flannigan, ef I had n' met you; but I don' know whar I 's ter fin' a colored lady w'at 'll begin ter suit me after habbin' libbed in de same house wid you."

"Colored lady, indade! Why, Misther Braboy, ye don't nade ter demane yerself by marryin' a colored lady—not but they 're as good as anybody else, so long as they behave themselves. There 's many a white woman 'u'd be glad ter git as fine a lookin' man as ye are."

"Now *you 're* flattrin' *me*, Mis' Flannigan," said Wellington. But he felt a sudden and substantial increase in courage when she had spoken, and it was with astonishing ease that he found himself saying:—

"Dey ain' but one lady, Mis' Flannigan, dat could injuce me ter want ter change de lonesomeness er my singleness fer de 'sponsibilities er matermony, an' I 'm feared she 'd say no ef I 'd ax her."

"Ye 'd better ax her, Misther Braboy, an' not be wastin' time a-wond'rin'. Do I know the lady?"

"You knows 'er better 'n anybody else, Mis' Flannigan. *You* is de only lady I 'd be satisfied ter marry after knowin' you. Ef you casts me off I 'll spen' de rest er my days in lonesomeness an' mis'ry."

Mrs. Flannigan affected much surprise and embarrassment at this bold declaration.

"Oh, Misther Braboy," she said, covering him with a coy glance, "an' it 's rale 'shamed I am to hev b'en talkin' ter ye ez I hev. It looks as though I 'd b'en doin' the coortin'. I did n't drame that I 'd b'en able ter draw yer affections to mesilf."

"I 's loved you ever sence I fell in yo' lap on de street car de fus' day I wuz in Groveland," he said, as he moved his chair up closer to hers.

One evening in the following week they went out after supper to the residence of Rev. Cæsar Williams, pastor of the colored Baptist church, and, after the usual preliminaries, were pronounced man and wife.

III

According to all his preconceived notions, this marriage ought to have been the acme of uncle Wellington's felicity. But he soon found that it was not without its drawbacks. On the following morning Mr. Todd was informed of the marriage. He had no special objection to it, or interest in it, except that he was opposed on principle to having husband and wife in his employment at the same time. As a consequence, Mrs. Braboy, whose place could be more easily filled than that of her husband, received notice that her services would not be required after the end of the month. Her husband was retained in his place as coachman.

Upon the loss of her situation Mrs. Braboy decided to exercise the married woman's prerogative of letting her husband support her. She rented the upper floor of a small house in an Irish neighborhood. The newly wedded pair furnished their rooms on the installment plan and began housekeeping.

There was one little circumstance, however, that interfered

slightly with their enjoyment of that perfect freedom from care which ought to characterize a honeymoon. The people who owned the house and occupied the lower floor had rented the upper part to Mrs. Braboy in person, it never occurring to them that her husband could be other than a white man. When it became known that he was colored, the landlord, Mr. Dennis O'Flaherty, felt that he had been imposed upon, and, at the end of the first month, served notice upon his tenants to leave the premises. When Mrs. Braboy, with characteristic impetuosity, inquired the meaning of this proceeding, she was informed by Mr. O'Flaherty that he did not care to live in the same house "wid naygurs." Mrs. Braboy resented the epithet with more warmth than dignity, and for a brief space of time the air was green with choice specimens of brogue, the altercation barely ceasing before it had reached the point of blows.

It was quite clear that the Braboys could not longer live comfortably in Mr. O'Flaherty's house, and they soon vacated the premises, first letting the rent get a couple of weeks in arrears as a punishment to the too fastidious landlord. They moved to a small house on Hackman Street, a favorite locality with colored people.

For a while, affairs ran smoothly in the new home. The colored people seemed, at first, well enough disposed toward Mrs. Braboy, and she made quite a large acquaintance among them. It was difficult, however, for Mrs. Braboy to divest herself of the consciousness that she was white, and therefore superior to her neighbors. Occasional words and acts by which she manifested this feeling were noticed and resented by her keen-eyed and sensitive colored neighbors. The result was a slight coolness between them. That her few white neighbors did not visit her, she naturally and no doubt correctly imputed to disapproval of her matrimonial relations.

Under these circumstances, Mrs. Braboy was left a good deal to her own company. Owing to lack of opportunity in early life, she was not a woman of many resources, either mental or moral. It is therefore not strange that, in order to relieve her loneliness, she should occasionally have recourse to a glass of beer, and, as the habit grew upon her, to still stronger stimulants. Uncle Wellington himself was no teetotaler, and did not interpose any objection so long as she kept her potations within reasonable limits, and was apparently none the worse for them; indeed, he sometimes joined her in a glass. On one of these occasions he drank a little too much, and, while driving the ladies of Mr. Todd's family to the opera, ran against a lamp-post and overturned the carriage, to the serious discomposure of the ladies' nerves, and at the cost of his situation.

A coachman discharged under such circumstances is not in the best position for procuring employment at his calling, and uncle Wellington, under the pressure of need, was obliged to seek some other means of livelihood. At the suggestion of his friend Mr. Johnson, he bought a whitewash brush, a peck of lime, a couple of pails, and a hand-cart, and began work as a whitewasher. His first efforts were very crude, and for a while he lost a customer in every person he worked for. He nevertheless managed to pick up a living during the spring and summer months, and to support his wife and himself in comparative comfort.

The approach of winter put an end to the whitewashing season, and left uncle Wellington dependent for support upon occasional jobs of unskilled labor. The income derived from these was very uncertain, and Mrs. Braboy was at length driven, by stress of circumstances, to the washtub, that last refuge of honest, able-bodied poverty, in all countries where the use of clothing is conventional.

The last state of uncle Wellington was now worse than the first. Under the soft firmness of aunt Milly's rule, he had not been required to do a great deal of work, prompt and cheerful obedience being chiefly what was expected of him. But matters were very different here. He had not only to bring in the coal and water, but to rub the clothes and turn the wringer, and to humiliate himself before the public by emptying the tubs and hanging out the wash in full view of the neighbors; and he had to deliver the clothes when laundered.

At times Wellington found himself wondering if his second marriage had been a wise one. Other circumstances combined to change in some degree his once rose-colored conception of life at the North. He had believed that all men were equal in this favored locality, but he discovered more degrees of inequality than he had ever perceived at the South. A colored man might be as good as a white man in theory, but neither of them was of any special consequence without money, or talent, or position. Uncle Wellington found a great many privileges open to him at the North, but he had not been educated to the point where he could appreciate them or take advantage of them; and the enjoyment of many of them was expensive, and, for that reason alone, as far beyond his reach as they had ever been. When he once began to admit even the possibility of a mistake on his part, these considerations presented themselves to his mind with increasing force. On occasions when Mrs. Braboy would require of him some unusual physical exertion, or when too frequent applications to the bottle had loosened her tongue, uncle Wellington's mind would revert, with a remorseful twinge of conscience, to the *dolce far niente* of his Southern home; a film would come over his eyes and brain, and, instead of the red-faced Irishwoman opposite him, he could see the black but comely disk of aunt Milly's countenance bending over the washtub; the elegant brogue of Mrs. Braboy would deliquesce into the soft dialect of North Carolina; and he would only be aroused from this blissful reverie by a wet shirt or a handful of suds thrown into his face, with which gentle reminder his wife would recall his attention to the duties of the moment.

There came a time, one day in spring, when there was no longer any question about it: uncle Wellington was desperately homesick.

Liberty, equality, privileges,—all were but as dust in the balance when weighed against his longing for old scenes and faces. It was the natural reaction in the mind of a middle-aged man who had tried to force the current of a sluggish existence into a new and radically different channel. An active, industrious man, making the change in early life, while there was time to spare for the waste of adaptation, might have found in the new place more favorable conditions than in the old. In Wellington age and temperament combined to prevent the success of the experiment; the spirit of enterprise and ambition into which he had been temporarily galvanized could no longer prevail against the inertia of old habits of life and thought.

One day when he had been sent to deliver clothes he performed his errand quickly, and boarding a passing street car, paid one of his very few five-cent pieces to ride down to the office of the Hon. Mr. Brown, the colored lawyer whom he had visited when he first came to the city, and who was well known to him by sight and reputation.

"Mr. Brown," he said, "I ain' gitt'n' 'long very well wid my ole 'oman."

"What 's the trouble?" asked the lawyer, with business-like curtness, for he did not scent much of a fee.

"Well, de main trouble is she doan treat me right. An' den she gits drunk, an' wuss'n dat, she lays vi'lent han's on me. I kyars de marks er dat 'oman on my face now."

He showed the lawyer a long scratch on the neck.

"Why don't you defend yourself?"

"You don' know Mis' Braboy, suh; you don' know dat 'oman," he replied, with a shake of the head. "Some er dese yer w'ite women is monst'us strong in de wris'."

"Well, Mr. Braboy, it 's what you might have expected when you turned your back on your own people and married a white woman. You were n't content with being a slave to the white folks once, but you must try it again. Some people never know when they 've got enough. I don't see that there 's any help for you; unless," he added suggestively, "you had a good deal of money."

"'Pears ter me I heared somebody say sence I be'n up heah, dat it wuz 'gin de law fer w'ite folks an' colored folks ter marry."

"That was once the law, though it has always been a dead letter in Groveland. In fact, it was the law when you got married, and until I introduced a bill in the legislature last fall to repeal it. But even that law did n't hit cases like yours. It was unlawful to make such a marriage, but it was a good marriage when once made."

"I don' jes' git dat th'oo my head," said Wellington, scratching that member as though to make a hole for the idea to enter.

"It 's quite plain, Mr. Braboy. It 's unlawful to kill a man, but when he 's killed he 's just as dead as though the law permitted it. I 'm afraid you have n't much of a case, but if you 'll go to work and get twenty-five dollars together, I 'll see what I can do for you. We may be able to pull a case through on the ground of extreme cruelty. I might even start the case if you brought in ten dollars."

Wellington went away sorrowfully. The laws of Ohio were very little more satisfactory than those of North Carolina. And as for the ten dollars,—the lawyer might as well have told him to bring in the moon, or a deed for the Public Square. He felt very, very low as he hurried back home to supper, which he would have to go without if he were not on hand at the usual supper-time.

But just when his spirits were lowest, and his outlook for the future most hopeless, a measure of relief was at hand. He noticed, when he reached home, that Mrs. Braboy was a little preoccupied, and did not abuse him as vigorously as he expected after so long an absence. He also perceived the smell of strange tobacco in the house, of a better grade than he could afford to use. He thought perhaps some one had come in to see about the washing; but he was too glad of a respite from Mrs. Braboy's rhetoric to imperil it by indiscreet questions.

Next morning she gave him fifty cents.

"Braboy," she said, "ye 've be'n helpin' me nicely wid the washin', an' I 'm going ter give ye a holiday. Ye can take yer hook an' line an' go fishin' on the breakwater. I 'll fix ye a lunch, an' ye need n't come back till night. An' there 's half a dollar; ye can buy yerself a pipe er terbacky. But be careful an' don't waste it," she added, for fear she was overdoing the thing.

Uncle Wellington was overjoyed at this change of front on the part of Mrs. Braboy; if she would make it permanent he did not see why they might not live together very comfortably.

The day passed pleasantly down on the breakwater. The weather was agreeable, and the fish bit freely. Towards evening Wellington started home with a bunch of fish that no angler need have been ashamed of. He looked forward to a good warm supper; for even if something should have happened during the day to alter his wife's mood for the worse, any ordinary variation would be more than balanced by the substantial addition of food to their larder. His mouth watered at the thought of the finny beauties sputtering in the frying-pan.

He noted, as he approached the house, that there was no smoke coming from the chimney. This only disturbed him in connection with the matter of supper. When he entered the gate he observed further that the window-shades had been taken down.

"'Spec' de ole 'oman's been house-cleanin'," he said to himself. "I wonder she did n' make me stay an' he'p 'er."

He went round to the rear of the house and tried the kitchen door. It was locked. This was somewhat of a surprise, and disturbed still further his expectations in regard to supper. When he had found the key and opened the door, the gravity of his next discovery drove away for the time being all thoughts of eating.

The kitchen was empty. Stove, table, chairs, wash-tubs, pots and pans, had vanished as if into thin air.

"Fo' de Lawd's sake!" he murmured in open-mouthed astonishment.

He passed into the other room,—they had only two,—which had served as bedroom and sitting-room. It was as bare as the first, except that in the middle of the floor were piled uncle Wellington's clothes. It was not a large pile, and on the top of it lay a folded piece of yellow wrapping-paper.

Wellington stood for a moment as if petrified. Then he rubbed his eyes and looked around him.

"W'at do dis mean?" he said. "Is I er-dreamin', er does I see w'at I 'pears ter see?" He glanced down at the bunch of fish which he still held. "Heah 's de fish; heah 's de house; heah I is; but whar 's de ole 'oman, an' whar 's de fu'niture? *I* can't figure out w'at dis yer all means."

He picked up the piece of paper and unfolded it. It was written on one side. Here was the obvious solution of the mystery,—that is, it would have been obvious if he could have read it; but he could not, and so his fancy continued to play upon the subject. Perhaps the house had been robbed, or the furniture taken back by the seller, for it had not been entirely paid for.

Finally he went across the street and called to a boy in a neighbor's yard.

"Does you read writin', Johnnie?"

"Yes, sir, I 'm in the seventh grade."

"Read dis yer paper fuh me."

The youngster took the note, and with much labor read the following:—

"Mr. Braboy:

"In lavin' ye so suddint I have ter say that my first husban' has turned up unixpected, having been saved onbeknownst ter me from a wathry grave an' all the money wasted I spint fer masses fer ter rist his sole an' I wish I had it back I feel it my dooty ter go an' live wid 'im again. I take the furnacher because I bought it yer close is yors I leave them and wishin' yer the best of luck I remane oncet yer wife but now agin

"Mrs. Katie Flannigan.

"N. B. I 'm lavin town terday so it won't be no use lookin' fer me."

On inquiry uncle Wellington learned from the boy that shortly after his departure in the morning a white man had appeared on the scene, followed a little later by a moving-van, into which the furniture had been loaded and carried away. Mrs. Braboy, clad in her best clothes, had locked the door, and gone away with the strange white man.

The news was soon noised about the street. Wellington swapped his fish for supper and a bed at a neighbor's, and during the evening learned from several sources that the strange white man had been at his house the afternoon of the day before. His neighbors intimated that they thought Mrs. Braboy's departure a good riddance of bad rubbish, and Wellington did not dispute the proposition.

Thus ended the second chapter of Wellington's matrimonial experiences. His wife's departure had been the one thing needful to convince him, beyond a doubt, that he had been a great fool. Remorse and homesickness forced him to the further conclusion that he had been knave as well as fool, and had treated aunt Milly shamefully. He was not altogether a bad old man, though very weak and erring, and his better nature now gained the ascendency. Of course his disappointment had a great deal to do with his remorse; most people do not perceive the hideousness of sin until they begin to reap its consequences. Instead of the beautiful Northern life he had dreamed of, he found himself stranded, penniless, in a strange land, among people whose sympathy he had forfeited, with no one to lean upon, and no refuge from the storms of life. His outlook was very dark, and there sprang up within him a wild longing to get back to North Carolina,—back to the little whitewashed cabin, shaded with china and mulberry trees; back to the wood-pile and the garden; back to the old cronies with whom he had swapped lies and tobacco for so many years. He longed to kiss the rod of aunt Milly's domination. He had purchased his liberty at too great a price.

The next day he disappeared from Groveland. He had announced his departure only to Mr. Johnson, who sent his love to his relations in Patesville.

It would be painful to record in detail the return journey of uncle Wellington—Mr. Braboy no longer—to his native town; how many weary miles he walked; how many times he risked his life on railroad tracks and between freight cars; how he depended for sustenance on the grudging hand of back-door charity. Nor would it be profitable or delicate to mention any slight deviations from the path of rectitude, as judged by conventional standards, to which he may occasionally have been driven by a too insistent hunger; or to refer in the remotest degree to a compulsory sojourn of thirty days in a city where he had no references, and could show no visible means of support. True charity will let these purely personal matters remain locked in the bosom of him who suffered them.

IV

Just fifteen months after the date when uncle Wellington had left North Carolina, a weather-beaten figure entered the town of Patesville after nightfall, following the railroad track from the north. Few would have recognized in the hungry-looking old brown tramp, clad in dusty rags and limping along with bare feet, the trim-looking middle-aged mulatto who so few months before had taken the train from Patesville for the distant North; so, if he had but known it, there was no necessity for him to avoid the main streets and sneak around by unfrequented paths to reach the old place on the other side of the town. He encountered nobody that he knew, and soon the familiar shape of the little cabin rose before him. It stood distinctly outlined against the sky, and the light streaming from the half-opened shutters showed it to be occupied. As he drew nearer, every familiar detail of the place appealed to his memory and to his affections, and his heart went out to the old home and the old wife. As he came nearer still, the odor of fried chicken floated out upon the air and set his mouth to watering, and awakened unspeakable longings in his half-starved stomach.

At this moment, however, a fearful thought struck him; suppose the old woman had taken legal advice and married again during his absence? Turn about would have been only fair play. He opened the gate softly, and with his heart in his mouth approached the window on tiptoe and looked in.

A cheerful fire was blazing on the hearth, in front of which sat the familiar form of aunt Milly—and another, at the sight of whom uncle Wellington's heart sank within him. He knew the other person very well; he had sat there more than once before uncle Wellington went away. It was the minister of the church to which his wife belonged. The preacher's former visits, however, had signified nothing more than pastoral courtesy, or appreciation of good eating. His presence now was of serious portent; for Wellington recalled, with acute alarm, that the elder's wife had died only a few weeks before his own departure for the North. What was the occasion of his presence this evening? Was it merely a pastoral call? or was he courting? or had aunt Milly taken legal advice and married the elder?

Wellington remembered a crack in the wall, at the back of the house, through which he could see and hear, and quietly stationed himself there.

"Dat chicken smells mighty good, Sis' Milly," the elder was saying; "I can't fer de life er me see why dat low-down husban' er yo'n could ever run away f'm a cook like you. It 's one er de beatenis' things I ever heared. How he could lib wid you an' not 'preciate you *I* can't understan', no indeed I can't."

Aunt Milly sighed. "De trouble wid Wellin'ton wuz," she

replied, "dat he did n' know when he wuz well off. He wuz alluz wishin' fer change, er studyin' 'bout somethin' new."

"Ez fer me," responded the elder earnestly, "I likes things what has be'n prove' an' tried an' has stood de tes', an' I can't 'magine how anybody could spec' ter fin' a better housekeeper er cook dan you is, Sis' Milly. I 'm a gittin' mighty lonesome sence my wife died. De Good Book say it is not good fer man ter lib alone, en it 'pears ter me dat you an' me mought git erlong tergether monst'us well."

Wellington's heart stood still, while he listened with strained attention. Aunt Milly sighed.

"I ain't denyin', elder, but what I 've be'n kinder lonesome myse'f fer quite a w'ile, an' I doan doubt dat w'at de Good Book say 'plies ter women as well as ter men."

"You kin be sho' it do," averred the elder, with professional authoritativeness; "yas 'm, you kin be cert'n sho'."

"But, of co'se," aunt Milly went on, "havin' los' my ole man de way I did, it has tuk me some time fer ter git my feelin's straighten' out like dey oughter be."

"I kin 'magine yo' feelin's, Sis' Milly," chimed in the elder sympathetically, "w'en you come home dat night an' foun' yo' chist broke open, an' yo' money gone dat you had wukked an' slaved fuh f'm mawnin' 'tel night, year in an' year out, an' w'en you foun' dat no-'count nigger gone wid his clo's an' you lef' all alone in de worl' ter scuffle 'long by yo'-self."

"Yas, elder," responded aunt Milly, "I wa'n't used right. An' den w'en I heared 'bout his goin' ter de lawyer ter fin' out 'bout a defoce, an' w'en I heared w'at de lawyer said 'bout my not bein' his wife 'less he wanted me, it made me so mad, I made up my min' dat ef he ever put his foot on my do'sill ag'in, I 'd shet de do' in his face an' tell 'im ter go back whar he come f'm."

To Wellington, on the outside, the cabin had never seemed so comfortable, aunt Milly never so desirable, chicken never so appetizing, as at this moment when they seemed slipping away from his grasp forever.

"Yo' feelin's does you credit, Sis' Milly," said the elder, taking her hand, which for a moment she did not withdraw. "An' de way fer you ter close yo' do' tightes' ag'inst 'im is ter take me in his place. He ain' got no claim on you no mo'. He tuk his ch'ice 'cordin' ter w'at de lawyer tol' 'im, an' 'termine' dat he wa'n't yo' husban'. Ef he wa'n't yo' husban', he had no right ter take yo' money, an' ef he comes back here ag'in you kin hab 'im tuck up an' sent ter de penitenchy fer stealin' it."

Uncle Wellington's knees, already weak from fasting, trembled violently beneath him. The worst that he had feared was now likely to happen. His only hope of safety lay in flight, and yet the scene within so fascinated him that he could not move a step.

"It 'u'd serve him right," exclaimed aunt Milly indignantly, "ef he wuz sent ter de penitenchy fer life! Dey ain't nuthin' too mean ter be done ter 'im. What did I ever do dat he should use me like he did?"

The recital of her wrongs had wrought upon aunt Milly's feelings so that her voice broke, and she wiped her eyes with her apron.

The elder looked serenely confident, and moved his chair nearer hers in order the better to play the rôle of comforter. Wellington, on the outside, felt so mean that the darkness of the night was scarcely sufficient to hide him; it would be no more than right if the earth were to open and swallow him up.

"An' yet aftuh all, elder," said Milly with a sob, "though I knows you is a better man, an' would treat me right, I wuz so use' ter dat ole nigger, an' libbed wid 'im so long, dat ef he 'd open dat do' dis minute an' walk in, I 'm feared I 'd be foolish ernuff an' weak ernuff to forgive 'im an' take 'im back ag'in."

With a bound, uncle Wellington was away from the crack in the wall. As he ran round the house he passed the wood-pile and snatched up an armful of pieces. A moment later he threw open the door.

"Ole 'oman," he exclaimed, "here 's dat wood you tol' me ter fetch in! Why, elder," he said to the preacher, who had started from his seat with surprise, "w'at 's yo' hurry? Won't you stay an' hab some supper wid us?"

The Bouquet

MARY MYROVER'S friends were somewhat surprised when she began to teach a colored school. Miss Myrover's friends are mentioned here, because nowhere more than in a Southern town is public opinion a force which cannot be lightly contravened. Public opinion, however, did not oppose Miss Myrover's teaching colored children; in fact, all the colored public schools in town—and there were several—were taught by white teachers, and had been so taught since the State had undertaken to provide free public instruction for all children within its boundaries. Previous to that time, there had been a Freedman's Bureau school and a Presbyterian missionary school, but these had been withdrawn when the need for them became less pressing. The colored people of the town had been for some time agitating their right to teach their own schools, but as yet the claim had not been conceded.

The reason Miss Myrover's course created some surprise was not, therefore, the fact that a Southern white woman should teach a colored school; it lay in the fact that up to this time no woman of just her quality had taken up such work. Most of the teachers of colored schools were not of those who had constituted the aristocracy of the old régime; they might be said rather to represent the new order of things, in which labor was in time to become honorable, and men were, after a somewhat longer time, to depend, for their place in society, upon themselves rather than upon their ancestors. Mary Myrover belonged to one of the proudest of the old families. Her ancestors had been people of distinction in Virginia before a collateral branch of the main stock had settled in North Carolina. Before the war, they had been able to live up to their pedigree; but the war brought sad changes. Miss Myrover's father—the Colonel Myrover who led a gallant but desperate charge at Vicksburg—had fallen on the battlefield, and his tomb in the white cemetery was a shrine for the family. On the Confederate Memorial Day, no other grave was so profusely decorated with flowers, and, in the oration pronounced, the name of Colonel Myrover was always used to illustrate the highest type of patriotic devotion and self-sacrifice. Miss Myrover's brother, too, had fallen in the conflict; but his bones lay in some unknown trench, with those of a thousand others who had fallen on the same field. Ay, more, her lover, who had hoped to come home in the full tide of victory and claim his bride as a reward for gallantry, had shared the fate of her father and brother. When the war was over, the remnant of the family found itself involved in the common ruin,—more deeply involved, indeed, than some others; for Colonel Myrover had believed in the ultimate triumph of his cause, and had invested most of his wealth in Confederate bonds, which were now only so much waste paper.

There had been a little left. Mrs. Myrover was thrifty, and had laid by a few hundred dollars, which she kept in the house to meet unforeseen contingencies. There remained, too, their home, with an ample garden and a well-stocked orchard, besides a considerable tract of country land, partly cleared, but productive of very little revenue.

With their shrunken resources, Miss Myrover and her mother were able to hold up their heads without embarrassment for some years after the close of the war. But when things were adjusted to the changed conditions, and the stream of life began to flow more vigorously in the new channels, they saw themselves in danger of dropping behind, unless in some way they could add to their meagre income. Miss Myrover looked over the field of employment, never very wide for women in the South, and found it occupied. The only available position she could be supposed prepared to fill, and which she could take without distinct loss of caste, was that of a teacher, and there was no vacancy except in one of the colored schools. Even teaching was a doubtful experiment; it was not what she would have preferred, but it was the best that could be done.

"I don't like it, Mary," said her mother. "It 's a long step from owning such people to teaching them. What do they need with education? It will only make them unfit for work."

"They 're free now, mother, and perhaps they 'll work better if they 're taught something. Besides, it 's only a business arrangement, and does n't involve any closer contact than we have with our servants."

"Well, I should say not!" sniffed the old lady. "Not one of them will ever dare to presume on your position to take any liberties with us. *I*'ll see to that."

Miss Myrover began her work as a teacher in the autumn, at the opening of the school year. It was a novel experience at first. Though there had always been negro servants in the house, and though on the streets colored people were more numerous than those of her own race, and though she was so familiar with their dialect that she might almost be said to speak it, barring certain characteristic grammatical inaccuracies, she had never been brought in personal contact with so many of them at once as when she confronted the fifty or sixty faces—of colors ranging from a white almost as clear as her own to the darkest livery of the sun—which were gathered in the schoolroom on the morning when she began her duties. Some of the inherited prejudice of her caste, too, made itself felt, though she tried to repress any outward sign of it; and she could perceive that the children were not altogether responsive; they, likewise, were not entirely free from antagonism. The work was unfamiliar to her. She was not physically very strong, and at the close of the first day went home with a splitting headache. If she could have resigned then and there without causing comment or annoyance to others, she would have felt it a privilege to do so. But a night's rest banished her headache and improved her spirits, and the next morning she went to her work with renewed vigor, fortified by the experience of the first day.

Miss Myrover's second day was more satisfactory. She had some natural talent for organization, though hitherto unaware of it, and in the course of the day she got her classes formed and lessons under way. In a week or two she began to classify her pupils in her own mind, as bright or stupid, mischievous or well behaved, lazy or industrious, as the case might be, and to regulate her discipline accordingly. That she had come of a long line of ancestors who had exercised authority and mastership was perhaps not without its effect upon her character, and enabled her more readily to maintain good order in the school. When she was fairly broken in, she found the work rather to her liking, and derived much pleasure from such success as she achieved as a teacher.

It was natural that she should be more attracted to some of her pupils than to others. Perhaps her favorite—or, rather, the one she liked best, for she was too fair and just for conscious favoritism—was Sophy Tucker. Just the ground for the teacher's liking for Sophy might not at first be apparent. The girl was far from the whitest of Miss Myrover's pupils; in fact, she was one of the darker ones. She was not the brightest in intellect, though she always tried to learn her lessons. She was not the best dressed, for her mother was a poor widow, who went out washing and scrubbing for a living. Perhaps the real tie between them was Sophy's intense devotion to the teacher. It had manifested itself almost from the first day of the school, in the rapt look of admiration Miss Myrover always saw on the little black face turned toward her. In it there was nothing of envy, nothing of regret; nothing but worship for the beautiful white lady—she was not especially handsome, but to Sophy her beauty was almost divine—who had come to teach her. If Miss Myrover dropped a book, Sophy was the first to spring and pick it up; if she wished a chair moved, Sophy seemed to anticipate her wish; and so of all the numberless little services that can be rendered in a schoolroom.

Miss Myrover was fond of flowers, and liked to have them about her. The children soon learned of this taste of hers, and kept the vases on her desk filled with blossoms during their season. Sophy was perhaps the most active in providing them. If she could not get garden flowers, she would make excursions to the woods in the early morning, and bring in great dew-laden bunches of bay, or jasmine, or some other fragrant forest flower which she knew the teacher loved.

"When I die, Sophy," Miss Myrover said to the child one day, "I want to be covered with roses. And when they bury me, I 'm sure I shall rest better if my grave is banked with flowers, and roses are planted at my head and at my feet."

Miss Myrover was at first amused at Sophy's devotion; but when she grew more accustomed to it, she found it rather to her liking. It had a sort of flavor of the old régime, and she felt, when she bestowed her kindly notice upon her little black attendant, some of the feudal condescension of the mistress toward the slave. She was kind to Sophy, and permitted her to play the rôle she had assumed, which caused sometimes a little jealousy among the other girls. Once she gave Sophy a yellow ribbon which she took from her own hair. The child carried it home, and cherished it as a priceless treasure, to be worn only on the greatest occasions.

Sophy had a rival in her attachment to the teacher, but the rivalry was altogether friendly. Miss Myrover had a little dog, a white spaniel, answering to the name of Prince. Prince was a dog of high degree, and would have very little to do with the children of the school; he made an exception, however, in the case of Sophy, whose devotion for his mistress he seemed to comprehend. He was a clever dog, and could fetch and carry, sit up on his haunches, extend his paw to shake hands, and possessed several other canine accomplishments. He was very fond of his mistress, and always, unless shut up at home, accompanied her to school, where he spent most of his time lying under the teacher's desk, or, in cold weather, by the stove, except when he would go out now and then and chase an imaginary rabbit round the yard, presumably for exercise.

At school Sophy and Prince vied with each other in their attentions to Miss Myrover. But when school was over, Prince went away with her, and Sophy stayed behind; for Miss Myrover was white and Sophy was black, which they both understood perfectly well. Miss Myrover taught the colored children, but she could not be seen with them in public. If they occasionally met her on the street, they did not expect her to speak to them, unless she happened to be alone and no other white person was in sight. If any of the children felt slighted, she was not aware of it, for she intended no slight; she had not been brought up to speak to negroes on the street, and she could not act differently from other people. And though she was a woman of sentiment and capable of deep feeling, her training had been such that she hardly expected to find in those of darker hue than herself the same susceptibility—varying in degree, perhaps, but yet the same in kind—that gave to her own life the alternations of feeling that made it most worth living.

Once Miss Myrover wished to carry home a parcel of books. She had the bundle in her hand when Sophy came up.

"Lemme tote yo' bundle fer yer, Miss Ma'y?" she asked eagerly. "I 'm gwine yo' way."

"Thank you, Sophy," was the reply. "I 'll be glad if you will."

Sophy followed the teacher at a respectful distance. When they reached Miss Myrover's home, Sophy carried the bundle to the doorstep, where Miss Myrover took it and thanked her.

Mrs. Myrover came out on the piazza as Sophy was moving away. She said, in the child's hearing, and perhaps with the intention that she should hear: "Mary, I wish you would n't let those little darkeys follow you to the house. I don't want them in the yard. I should think you 'd have enough of them all day."

"Very well, mother," replied her daughter. "I won't bring any more of them. The child was only doing me a favor."

Mrs. Myrover was an invalid, and opposition or irritation of any kind brought on nervous paroxysms that made her miserable, and made life a burden to the rest of the household, so that Mary seldom crossed her whims. She did not bring Sophy to the house again, nor did Sophy again offer her services as porter.

One day in spring Sophy brought her teacher a bouquet of yellow roses.

"Dey come off'n my own bush, Miss Ma'y," she said proudly, "an' I did n' let nobody e'se pull 'em, but saved 'em all fer you, 'cause I know you likes roses so much. I 'm gwine bring 'em all ter you as long as dey las'."

"Thank you, Sophy," said the teacher; "you are a very good girl."

For another year Mary Myrover taught the colored school, and did excellent service. The children made rapid progress under her tuition, and learned to love her well; for they saw and appreciated, as well as children could, her fidelity to a trust that she might have slighted, as some others did, without much fear of criticism. Toward the end of her second year she sickened, and after a brief illness died.

Old Mrs. Myrover was inconsolable. She ascribed her daughter's death to her labors as teacher of negro children. Just how the color of the pupils had produced the fatal effects she did not stop to explain. But she was too old, and had suffered too deeply from the war, in body and mind and estate, ever to reconcile herself to the changed order of things following the return of peace; and, with an unsound yet perfectly explainable logic, she visited some of her displeasure upon those who had profited most, though passively, by her losses.

"I always feared something would happen to Mary," she said. "It seemed unnatural for her to be wearing herself out teaching little negroes who ought to have been working for her. But the world has hardly been a fit place to live in since the war, and when I follow her, as I must before long, I shall not be sorry to go."

She gave strict orders that no colored people should be admitted to the house. Some of her friends heard of this, and remonstrated. They knew the teacher was loved by the pupils, and felt that sincere respect from the humble would be a worthy tribute to the proudest. But Mrs. Myrover was obdurate.

"They had my daughter when she was alive," she said, "and they 've killed her. But she 's mine now, and I won't have them come near her. I don't want one of them at the funeral or anywhere around."

For a month before Miss Myrover's death Sophy had been watching her rosebush—the one that bore the yellow roses—for the first buds of spring, and, when these appeared, had awaited impatiently their gradual unfolding. But not until her teacher's death had they become full-blown roses. When Miss Myrover died, Sophy determined to pluck the roses and lay them on her coffin. Perhaps, she thought, they might even put them in her hand or on her breast. For Sophy remembered Miss Myrover's thanks and praise when she had brought her the yellow roses the spring before.

On the morning of the day set for the funeral, Sophy washed her face until it shone, combed and brushed her hair with painful conscientiousness, put on her best frock, plucked her yellow roses, and, tying them with the treasured ribbon her teacher had given her, set out for Miss Myrover's home.

She went round to the side gate—the house stood on a corner—and stole up the path to the kitchen. A colored woman, whom she did not know, came to the door.

"W'at yer want, chile?" she inquired.

"Kin I see Miss Ma'y?" asked Sophy timidly.

"I don't know, honey. Ole Miss Myrover say she don't want no cullud folks roun' de house endyoin' dis fun'al. I 'll look an' see if she 's roun' de front room, whar de co'pse is. You sed down heah an' keep still, an' ef she 's upstairs maybe I kin git yer in dere a minute. Ef I can't, I kin put yo' bokay 'mongs' de res', whar she won't know nuthin' erbout it."

A moment after she had gone, there was a step in the hall, and old Mrs. Myrover came into the kitchen.

"Dinah!" she said in a peevish tone; "Dinah!"

Receiving no answer, Mrs. Myrover peered around the kitchen, and caught sight of Sophy.

"What are you doing here?" she demanded.

"I—I 'm-m waitin' ter see de cook, ma'am," stammered Sophy.

"The cook is n't here now. I don't know where she is. Besides, my daughter is to be buried to-day, and I won't have any one visiting the servants until the funeral is over. Come back some other day, or see the cook at her own home in the evening."

She stood waiting for the child to go, and under the keen glance of her eyes Sophy, feeling as though she had been caught in some disgraceful act, hurried down the walk and out of the gate, with her bouquet in her hand.

"Dinah," said Mrs. Myrover, when the cook came back, "I don't want any strange people admitted here to-day. The house will be full of our friends, and we have no room for others."

"Yas 'm," said the cook. She understood perfectly what her mistress meant; and what the cook thought about her mistress was a matter of no consequence.

The funeral services were held at St. Paul's Episcopal Church, where the Myrovers had always worshiped. Quite a number of Miss Myrover's pupils went to the church to attend the services. The building was not a large one. There was a small gallery at the rear, to which colored people were admitted, if they chose to come, at ordinary services; and those who wished to be present at the funeral supposed that the usual custom would prevail. They were therefore surprised, when they went to the side entrance, by which colored people gained access to the gallery stairs, to be met by an usher who barred their passage.

"I 'm sorry," he said, "but I have had orders to admit no one until the friends of the family have all been seated. If you wish to wait until the white people have all gone in, and there 's any room left, you may be able to get into the back part of the gallery. Of course I can't tell yet whether there 'll be any room or not."

Now the statement of the usher was a very reasonable one; but, strange to say, none of the colored people chose to remain except Sophy. She still hoped to use her floral offering for its destined end, in some way, though she did not know just how. She waited in the yard until the church was filled with white people, and a number who could not gain admittance were standing about the doors. Then she went round to the side of the church, and, depositing her bouquet carefully on an old mossy gravestone, climbed up on the projecting sill of a window near the chancel. The window was of stained glass, of somewhat ancient make. The church was old, had indeed been built in colonial times, and the stained glass had been brought from England. The design of the window showed Jesus blessing little children. Time had dealt gently with the window, but just at the feet of the figure of Jesus a small triangular piece of glass had been broken out. To this aperture Sophy applied her eyes, and through it saw and heard what she could of the services within.

Before the chancel, on trestles draped in black, stood the sombre casket in which lay all that was mortal of her dear teacher. The top of the casket was covered with flowers; and lying stretched out underneath it she saw Miss Myrover's little white dog, Prince. He had followed the body to the church, and, slipping in unnoticed among the mourners, had taken his place, from which no one had the heart to remove him.

The white-robed rector read the solemn service for the dead, and then delivered a brief address, in which he dwelt upon the uncertainty of life, and, to the believer, the certain blessedness of eternity. He spoke of Miss Myrover's kindly spirit, and, as an illustration of her love and self-sacrifice for others, referred to her labors as a teacher of the poor ignorant negroes who had been placed in their midst by an all-wise Providence, and whom it was their duty to guide and direct in the station in which God had put them. Then the organ pealed, a prayer was said, and the long cortège moved from the church to the cemetery, about half a mile away, where the body was to be interred.

When the services were over, Sophy sprang down from her perch, and, taking her flowers, followed the procession. She did not walk with the rest, but at a proper and respectful distance from the last mourner. No one noticed the little black girl with the bunch of yellow flowers, or thought of her as interested in the funeral.

The cortège reached the cemetery and filed slowly through the gate; but Sophy stood outside, looking at a small sign in white letters on a black background:—

"*Notice.* This cemetery is for white people only. Others please keep out."

Sophy, thanks to Miss Myrover's painstaking instruction, could read this sign very distinctly. In fact, she had often read it before. For Sophy was a child who loved beauty, in a blind, groping sort of way, and had sometimes stood by the fence of the cemetery and looked through at the green mounds and shaded walks and blooming flowers within, and wished that she might walk among them. She knew, too, that the little sign on the gate, though so courteously worded, was no mere formality; for she had heard how a colored man, who had wandered into the cemetery on a hot night and fallen asleep on the flat top of a tomb, had been arrested as a vagrant and fined five dollars, which he had worked out on the streets, with a ball-and-chain attachment, at twenty-five cents a day. Since that time the cemetery gate had been locked at night.

So Sophy stayed outside, and looked through the fence. Her poor bouquet had begun to droop by this time, and the yellow ribbon had lost some of its freshness. Sophy could see the rector standing by the grave, the mourners gathered round; she could faintly distinguish the solemn words with which ashes were committed to ashes, and dust to dust. She heard the hollow thud of the earth falling on the coffin; and she leaned against the iron fence, sobbing softly, until the grave was filled and rounded off, and the wreaths and other floral pieces were disposed upon it. When the mourners began to move toward the gate, Sophy walked slowly down the street, in a direction opposite to that taken by most of the people who came out.

When they had all gone away, and the sexton had come out and locked the gate behind him, Sophy crept back. Her roses were faded now, and from some of them the petals had fallen. She stood there irresolute, loath to leave with her heart's desire unsatisfied, when, as her eyes sought again the teacher's last resting-place, she saw lying beside the new-made grave what looked like a small bundle of white wool. Sophy's eyes lighted up with a sudden glow.

"Prince! Here, Prince!" she called.

The little dog rose, and trotted down to the gate. Sophy pushed the poor bouquet between the iron bars. "Take that ter Miss Ma'y, Prince," she said, "that 's a good doggie."

The dog wagged his tail intelligently, took the bouquet carefully in his mouth, carried it to his mistress's grave, and laid it among the other flowers. The bunch of roses was so small that from where she stood Sophy could see only a dash of yellow against the white background of the mass of flowers.

When Prince had performed his mission he turned his eyes toward Sophy inquiringly, and when she gave him a nod of approval lay down and resumed his watch by the graveside. Sophy looked at him a moment with a feeling very much like envy, and then turned and moved slowly away.

The Web of Circumstance

I

WITHIN a low clapboarded hut, with an open front, a forge was glowing. In front a blacksmith was shoeing a horse, a sleek, well-kept animal with the signs of good blood and breeding. A young mulatto stood by and handed the blacksmith such tools as he needed from time to time. A group of negroes were sitting around, some in the shadow of the shop, one in the full glare of the sunlight. A gentleman was seated in a buggy a few yards away, in the shade of a spreading elm. The horse had loosened a shoe, and Colonel Thornton, who was a lover of fine horseflesh, and careful of it, had stopped at Ben Davis's blacksmith shop, as soon as he discovered the loose shoe, to have it fastened on.

"All right, Kunnel," the blacksmith called out. "Tom," he said, addressing the young man, "he'p me hitch up."

Colonel Thornton alighted from the buggy, looked at the shoe, signified his approval of the job, and stood looking on while the blacksmith and his assistant harnessed the horse to the buggy.

"Dat 's a mighty fine whip yer got dere, Kunnel," said Ben, while the young man was tightening the straps of the harness on the opposite side of the horse. "I wush I had one like it. Where kin yer git dem whips?"

"My brother brought me this from New York," said the Colonel. "You can't buy them down here."

The whip in question was a handsome one. The handle was wrapped with interlacing threads of variegated colors, forming an elaborate pattern, the lash being dark green. An octagonal ornament of glass was set in the end of the handle. "It cert'n'y is fine," said Ben; "I wish I had one like it." He looked at the whip longingly as Colonel Thornton drove away.

"'Pears ter me Ben gittin' mighty blooded," said one of the bystanders, "drivin' a hoss an' buggy, an' wantin' a whip like Colonel Thornton's."

"What 's de reason I can't hab a hoss an' buggy an' a whip

like Kunnel Tho'nton's, ef I pay fer 'em?" asked Ben. "We colored folks never had no chance ter git nothin' befo' de wah, but ef eve'y nigger in dis town had a tuck keer er his money sence de wah, like I has, an' bought as much lan' as I has, de niggers might 'a' got half de lan' by dis time," he went on, giving a finishing blow to a horseshoe, and throwing it on the ground to cool.

Carried away by his own eloquence, he did not notice the approach of two white men who came up the street from behind him.

"An' ef you niggers," he continued, raking the coals together over a fresh bar of iron, "would stop wastin' yo' money on 'scursions to put money in w'ite folks' pockets, an' stop buildin' fine chu'ches, an' buil' houses fer yo'se'ves, you 'd git along much faster."

"You 're talkin' sense, Ben," said one of the white men. "Yo'r people will never be respected till they 've got property."

The conversation took another turn. The white men transacted their business and went away. The whistle of a neighboring steam sawmill blew a raucous blast for the hour of noon, and the loafers shuffled away in different directions.

"You kin go ter dinner, Tom," said the blacksmith. "An' stop at de gate w'en yer go by my house, and tell Nancy I 'll be dere in 'bout twenty minutes. I got ter finish dis yer plough p'int fus'."

The young man walked away. One would have supposed, from the rapidity with which he walked, that he was very hungry. A quarter of an hour later the blacksmith dropped his hammer, pulled off his leather apron, shut the front door of the shop, and went home to dinner. He came into the house out of the fervent heat, and, throwing off his straw hat, wiped his brow vigorously with a red cotton handkerchief.

"Dem collards smells good," he said, sniffing the odor that came in through the kitchen door, as his good-looking yellow wife opened it to enter the room where he was. "I 've got a monst'us good appetite ter-day. I feels good, too. I paid Majah Ransom de intrus' on de mortgage dis mawnin' an' a hund'ed dollahs besides, an' I spec's ter hab de balance ready by de fust of nex' Jiniwary; an' den we won't owe nobody a cent. I tell yer dere ain' nothin' like propputy ter make a pusson feel like a man. But w'at 's de matter wid yer, Nancy? Is sump'n' skeered yer?"

The woman did seem excited and ill at ease. There was a heaving of the full bust, a quickened breathing, that betokened suppressed excitement.

"I—I—jes' seen a rattlesnake out in de gyahden," she stammered.

The blacksmith ran to the door. "Which way? Whar wuz he?" he cried.

He heard a rustling in the bushes at one side of the garden, and the sound of a breaking twig, and, seizing a hoe which stood by the door, he sprang toward the point from which the sound came.

"No, no," said the woman hurriedly, "it wuz over here," and she directed her husband's attention to the other side of the garden.

The blacksmith, with the uplifted hoe, its sharp blade gleaming in the sunlight, peered cautiously among the collards and tomato plants, listening all the while for the ominous rattle, but found nothing.

"I reckon he 's got away," he said, as he set the hoe up again by the door. "Whar 's de chillen?" he asked with some anxiety. "Is dey playin' in de woods?"

"No," answered his wife, "dey 've gone ter de spring."

The spring was on the opposite side of the garden from that on which the snake was said to have been seen, so the blacksmith sat down and fanned himself with a palm-leaf fan until the dinner was served.

"Yer ain't quite on time ter-day, Nancy," he said, glancing up at the clock on the mantel, after the edge of his appetite had been taken off. "Got ter make time ef yer wanter make money. Did n't Tom tell yer I 'd be heah in twenty minutes?"

"No," she said; "I seen him goin' pas'; he did n' say nothin'."

"I dunno w'at 's de matter wid dat boy," mused the blacksmith over his apple dumpling. "He 's gittin' mighty keerless heah lately; mus' hab sump'n' on 'is min',—some gal, I reckon."

The children had come in while he was speaking,—a slender, shapely boy, yellow like his mother, a girl several years younger, dark like her father: both bright-looking children and neatly dressed.

"I seen cousin Tom down by de spring," said the little girl, as she lifted off the pail of water that had been balanced on her head. "He come out er de woods jest ez we wuz fillin' our buckets."

"Yas," insisted the blacksmith, "he 's got some gal on his min'."

II

The case of the State of North Carolina *vs.* Ben Davis was called. The accused was led into court, and took his seat in the prisoner's dock.

"Prisoner at the bar, stand up."

The prisoner, pale and anxious, stood up. The clerk read the indictment, in which it was charged that the defendant by force and arms had entered the barn of one G. W. Thornton, and feloniously taken therefrom one whip, of the value of fifteen dollars.

"Are you guilty or not guilty?" asked the judge.

"Not guilty, yo' Honah; not guilty, Jedge. I never tuck de whip."

The State's attorney opened the case. He was young and zealous. Recently elected to the office, this was his first batch of cases, and he was anxious to make as good a record as possible. He had no doubt of the prisoner's guilt. There had been a great deal of petty thieving in the county, and several gentlemen had suggested to him the necessity for greater severity in punishing it. The jury were all white men. The prosecuting attorney stated the case.

"We expect to show, gentlemen of the jury, the facts set out in the indictment,—not altogether by direct proof, but by a chain of circumstantial evidence which is stronger even than the testimony of eyewitnesses. Men might lie, but circumstances cannot. We expect to show that the defendant is a man of dangerous character, a surly, impudent fellow; a man whose views of property are prejudicial to the welfare of society, and who has been heard to assert that half the property which is owned in this county has been stolen, and that, if justice were done, the white people ought to divide up the land with the negroes; in other words, a negro nihilist, a communist, a secret devotee of Tom Paine and Voltaire, a pupil of the anarchist propaganda, which, if not checked by the stern hand of the law, will fasten its insidious fangs on our social system, and drag it down to ruin."

"We object, may it please your Honor," said the defendant's attorney. "The prosecutor should defer his argument until the testimony is in."

"Confine yourself to the facts, Major," said the court mildly.

The prisoner sat with half-open mouth, overwhelmed by this flood of eloquence. He had never heard of Tom Paine or Voltaire. He had no conception of what a nihilist or an anarchist might be, and could not have told the difference between a propaganda and a potato.

"We expect to show, may it please the court, that the prisoner had been employed by Colonel Thornton to shoe a horse; that the horse was taken to the prisoner's blacksmith shop by a servant of Colonel Thornton's; that, this servant expressing a desire to go somewhere on an errand before the horse had been shod, the prisoner volunteered to return the horse to Colonel Thornton's stable; that he did so, and the following morning the whip in question was missing; that, from circumstances, suspicion naturally fell upon the prisoner, and a search was made of his shop, where the whip was found secreted; that the prisoner denied that the whip was there, but when confronted with the evidence of his crime, showed by his confusion that he was guilty beyond a peradventure."

The prisoner looked more anxious; so much eloquence could not but be effective with the jury.

The attorney for the defendant answered briefly, denying the defendant's guilt, dwelling upon his previous good character for honesty, and begging the jury not to pre-judge the case, but to remember that the law is merciful, and that the benefit of the doubt should be given to the prisoner.

The prisoner glanced nervously at the jury. There was nothing in their faces to indicate the effect upon them of the opening statements. It seemed to the disinterested listeners as if the defendant's attorney had little confidence in his client's cause.

Colonel Thornton took the stand and testified to his ownership of the whip, the place where it was kept, its value, and the fact that it had disappeared. The whip was produced in court and identified by the witness. He also testified to the conversation at the blacksmith shop in the course of which the prisoner had expressed a desire to possess a similar whip. The cross-examination was brief, and no attempt was made to shake the Colonel's testimony.

The next witness was the constable who had gone with a warrant to search Ben's shop. He testified to the circumstances under which the whip was found.

"He wuz brazen as a mule at fust, an' wanted ter git mad about it. But when we begun ter turn over that pile er truck in the cawner, he kinder begun ter trimble; when the whip-handle stuck out, his eyes commenced ter grow big, an' when we hauled the whip out he turned pale ez ashes, an' begun to swear he did n' take the whip an' did n' know how it got thar."

"You may cross-examine," said the prosecuting attorney triumphantly.

The prisoner felt the weight of the testimony, and glanced furtively at the jury, and then appealingly at his lawyer.

"You say that Ben denied that he had stolen the whip," said the prisoner's attorney, on cross-examination. "Did it not occur to you that what you took for brazen impudence might have been but the evidence of conscious innocence?"

The witness grinned incredulously, revealing thereby a few blackened fragments of teeth.

"I 've tuck up more 'n a hundred niggers fer stealin', Kurnel, an' I never seed one yit that did n' 'ny it ter the las'."

"Answer my question. Might not the witness's indignation have been a manifestation of conscious innocence? Yes or no?"

"Yes, it mought, an' the moon mought fall—but it don't."

Further cross-examination did not weaken the witness's testimony, which was very damaging, and every one in the court room felt instinctively that a strong defense would be required to break down the State's case.

"The State rests," said the prosecuting attorney, with a ring in his voice which spoke of certain victory.

There was a temporary lull in the proceedings, during which a bailiff passed a pitcher of water and a glass along the line of jury-men. The defense was then begun.

The law in its wisdom did not permit the defendant to testify in his own behalf. There were no witnesses to the facts, but several were called to testify to Ben's good character. The colored witnesses made him out possessed of all the virtues. One or two white men testified that they had never known anything against his reputation for honesty.

The defendant rested his case, and the State called its witnesses in rebuttal. They were entirely on the point of character. One testified that he had heard the prisoner say that, if the negroes had their rights, they would own at least half the property. Another testified that he had heard the defendant say that the negroes spent too much money on churches, and that they cared a good deal more for God than God had ever seemed to care for them.

Ben Davis listened to this testimony with half-open mouth and staring eyes. Now and then he would lean forward and speak perhaps a word, when his attorney would shake a warning finger at him, and he would fall back helplessly, as if abandoning himself to fate; but for a moment only, when he would resume his puzzled look.

The arguments followed. The prosecuting attorney briefly summed up the evidence, and characterized it as almost a mathematical proof of the prisoner's guilt. He reserved his eloquence for the closing argument.

The defendant's attorney had a headache, and secretly believed his client guilty. His address sounded more like an appeal for mercy than a demand for justice. Then the State's attorney delivered the maiden argument of his office, the speech that made his reputation as an orator, and opened up to him a successful political career.

The judge's charge to the jury was a plain, simple statement of the law as applied to circumstantial evidence, and the mere statement of the law foreshadowed the verdict.

The eyes of the prisoner were glued to the jury-box, and he looked more and more like a hunted animal. In the rear of the crowd of blacks who filled the back part of the room, partly concealed by the projecting angle of the fireplace, stood Tom, the blacksmith's assistant. If the face is the mirror of the soul, then this man's soul, taken off its guard in this moment of excitement, was full of lust and envy and all evil passions.

The jury filed out of their box, and into the jury room behind the judge's stand. There was a moment of relaxation in the court room. The lawyers fell into conversation across the table. The judge beckoned to Colonel Thornton, who stepped forward, and they conversed together a few moments. The prisoner was all eyes and ears in this moment of waiting, and from an involuntary gesture on the part of the judge he divined that they were speaking of him. It is a pity he could not hear what was said.

"How do you feel about the case, Colonel?" asked the judge.

"Let him off easy," replied Colonel Thornton. "He 's the best blacksmith in the county."

The business of the court seemed to have halted by tacit consent, in anticipation of a quick verdict. The suspense did not last long. Scarcely ten minutes had elapsed when there was a rap on the door, the officer opened it, and the jury came out.

The prisoner, his soul in his eyes, sought their faces, but met no reassuring glance; they were all looking away from him.

"Gentlemen of the jury, have you agreed upon a verdict?"

"We have," responded the foreman. The clerk of the court stepped forward and took the fateful slip from the foreman's hand.

The clerk read the verdict: "We, the jury impaneled and sworn to try the issues in this cause, do find the prisoner guilty as charged in the indictment."

There was a moment of breathless silence. Then a wild burst of grief from the prisoner's wife, to which his two children, not understanding it all, but vaguely conscious of some calamity, added their voices in two long, discordant wails, which would have been ludicrous had they not been heartrending.

The face of the young man in the back of the room expressed relief and badly concealed satisfaction. The prisoner fell back upon the seat from which he had half risen in his anxiety, and his dark face assumed an ashen hue. What he thought could only be surmised. Perhaps, knowing his innocence, he had not believed conviction possible; perhaps, conscious of guilt, he dreaded the punishment, the extent of which was optional with the judge, within very wide limits. Only one other person present knew whether or not he was guilty, and that other had slunk furtively from the court room.

Some of the spectators wondered why there should be so much ado about convicting a negro of stealing a buggy-whip. They had forgotten their own interest of the moment before. They did not realize out of what trifles grow the tragedies of life.

It was four o'clock in the afternoon, the hour for adjournment, when the verdict was returned. The judge nodded to the bailiff.

"Oyez, oyez! this court is now adjourned until ten o'clock to-morrow morning," cried the bailiff in a singsong voice. The judge left the bench, the jury filed out of the box, and a buzz of conversation filled the court room.

"Brace up, Ben, brace up, my boy," said the defendant's lawyer, half apologetically. "I did what I could for you, but you can never tell what a jury will do. You won't be sentenced till to-morrow morning. In the meantime I 'll speak to the judge and try to get him to be easy with you. He may let you off with a light fine."

The negro pulled himself together, and by an effort listened.

"Thanky, Majah," was all he said. He seemed to be thinking of something far away.

He barely spoke to his wife when she frantically threw herself on him, and clung to his neck, as he passed through the side room on his way to jail. He kissed his children mechanically, and did not reply to the soothing remarks made by the jailer.

III

There was a good deal of excitement in town the next morning. Two white men stood by the post office talking.

"Did yer hear the news?"

"No, what wuz it?"

"Ben Davis tried ter break jail las' night."

"You don't say so! What a fool! He ain't be'n sentenced yit."

"Well, now," said the other, "I 've knowed Ben a long time, an' he wuz a right good nigger. I kinder found it hard ter b'lieve he did steal that whip. But what 's a man's feelin's ag'in' the proof?"

They spoke on awhile, using the past tense as if they were speaking of a dead man.

"Ef I know Jedge Hart, Ben 'll wish he had slep' las' night, 'stidder tryin' ter break out'n jail."

At ten o'clock the prisoner was brought into court. He walked with shambling gait, bent at the shoulders, hopelessly, with downcast eyes, and took his seat with several other prisoners who had been brought in for sentence. His wife, accompanied by the children, waited behind him, and a number of his friends were gathered in the court room.

The first prisoner sentenced was a young white man, convicted several days before of manslaughter. The deed was done in the heat of passion, under circumstances of great provocation, during a quarrel about a woman. The prisoner was admonished of the sanctity of human life, and sentenced to one year in the penitentiary.

The next case was that of a young clerk, eighteen or nineteen years of age, who had committed a forgery in order to procure the means to buy lottery tickets. He was well connected, and the case would not have been prosecuted if the judge had not refused to allow it to be nolled, and, once brought to trial, a conviction could not have been avoided.

"You are a young man," said the judge gravely, yet not unkindly, "and your life is yet before you. I regret that you should have been led into evil courses by the lust for speculation, so dangerous in its tendencies, so fruitful of crime and misery. I am led to believe that you are sincerely penitent, and that, after such punishment as the law cannot remit without bringing itself into contempt, you will see the error of your ways and follow the strict path of rectitude. Your fault has entailed distress not only upon yourself, but upon your relatives, people of good name and good family, who suffer as keenly from your disgrace as you yourself. Partly out of consideration for their feelings, and partly because I feel that, under the circumstances, the law will be satisfied by the penalty I shall inflict, I sentence you to imprisonment in the county jail for six months, and a fine of one hundred dollars and the costs of this action."

"The jedge talks well, don't he?" whispered one spectator to another.

"Yes, and kinder likes ter hear hisse'f talk," answered the other.

"Ben Davis, stand up," ordered the judge.

He might have said "Ben Davis, wake up," for the jailer had to touch the prisoner on the shoulder to rouse him from his stupor. He stood up, and something of the hunted look came again into his eyes, which shifted under the stern glance of the judge.

"Ben Davis, you have been convicted of larceny, after a fair trial before twelve good men of this county. Under the testimony, there can be no doubt of your guilt. The case is an aggravated one. You are not an ignorant, shiftless fellow, but a man of more than ordinary intelligence among your people, and one who ought to know better. You have not even the poor excuse of having stolen to satisfy hunger or a physical appetite. Your conduct is wholly without excuse, and I can only regard your crime as the result of a tendency to offenses of this nature, a tendency which is only too common among your people; a tendency which is a menace to civilization, a menace to society itself, for society rests upon the sacred right of property. Your opinions, too, have been given a wrong turn; you have been heard to utter sentiments which, if disseminated among an ignorant people, would breed discontent, and give rise to strained relations between them and their best friends, their old masters, who understand their real nature and their real needs, and to whose justice and enlightened guidance they can safely trust. Have you anything to say why sentence should not be passed upon you?"

"Nothin', suh, cep'n dat I did n' take de whip."

"The law, largely, I think, in view of the peculiar circumstances of your unfortunate race, has vested a large discretion in courts as to the extent of the punishment for offenses of this kind. Taking your case as a whole, I am convinced that it is one which, for the sake of the example, deserves a severe punishment. Nevertheless, I do not feel disposed to give you the full extent of the law, which would be twenty years in the penitentiary,* but, considering the fact that you have a family, and have heretofore borne a good reputation in the community, I will impose upon you the light sentence of imprisonment for five years in the penitentiary at hard labor. And I hope that this will be a warning to you and others who may be similarly disposed, and that after your sentence has expired you may lead the life of a law-abiding citizen."

"O Ben! O my husband! O God!" moaned the poor wife, and tried to press forward to her husband's side.

"Keep back, Nancy, keep back," said the jailer. "You can see him in jail."

Several people were looking at Ben's face. There was one flash of despair, and then nothing but a stony blank, behind which he masked his real feelings, whatever they were.

Human character is a compound of tendencies inherited and habits acquired. In the anxiety, the fear of disgrace, spoke the nineteenth century civilization with which Ben Davis had been more or less closely in touch during twenty years of slavery and fifteen years of freedom. In the stolidity with which he received this sentence for a crime which he had not committed, spoke who knows what trait of inherited savagery? For stoicism is a savage virtue.

IV

One morning in June, five years later, a black man limped slowly along the old Lumberton plank road; a tall man, whose bowed shoulders made him seem shorter than he was, and a face from which it was difficult to guess his years, for in it the wrinkles and flabbiness of age were found side by side with firm white teeth, and eyes not sunken,—eyes bloodshot, and burning with something, either fever or passion. Though he

*There are no degrees of larceny in North Carolina, and the penalty for any offense lies in the discretion of the judge, to the limit of twenty years.

limped painfully with one foot, the other hit the ground impatiently, like the good horse in a poorly matched team. As he walked along, he was talking to himself:—

"I wonder what dey 'll do w'en I git back? I wonder how Nancy 's s'ported the fambly all dese years? Tuck in washin', I s'ppose,—she was a monst'us good washer an' ironer. I wonder ef de chillun 'll be too proud ter reco'nize deir daddy come back f'um de penetenchy? I 'spec' Billy must be a big boy by dis time. He won' b'lieve his daddy ever stole anything. I 'm gwine ter slip roun' an' s'prise 'em."

Five minutes later a face peered cautiously into the window of what had once been Ben Davis's cabin,—at first an eager face, its coarseness lit up with the fire of hope; a moment later a puzzled face; then an anxious, fearful face as the man stepped away from the window and rapped at the door.

"Is Mis' Davis home?" he asked of the woman who opened the door.

"Mis' Davis don' live here. You er mistook in de house."

"Whose house is dis?"

"It b'longs ter my husban', Mr. Smith,—Primus Smith."

"'Scuse me, but I knowed de house some years ago w'en I wuz here oncet on a visit, an' it b'longed ter a man name' Ben Davis."

"Ben Davis—Ben Davis?—oh yes, I 'member now. Dat wuz de gen'man w'at wuz sent ter de penitenchy fer sump'n er nuther,—sheep-stealin', I b'lieve. Primus," she called, "w'at wuz Ben Davis, w'at useter own dis yer house, sent ter de penitenchy fer?"

"Hoss-stealin'," came back the reply in sleepy accents, from the man seated by the fireplace.

The traveler went on to the next house. A neat-looking yellow woman came to the door when he rattled the gate, and stood looking suspiciously at him.

"W'at you want?" she asked.

"Please, ma'am, will you tell me whether a man name' Ben Davis useter live in dis neighborhood?"

"Useter live in de nex' house; wuz sent ter de penitenchy fer killin' a man."

"Kin yer tell me w'at went wid Mis' Davis?"

"Umph! I 's a 'spectable 'oman, I is, en don' mix wid dem

kind er people. She wuz 'n' no better 'n her husban'. She tuk up wid a man dat useter wuk fer Ben, an' dey 're livin' down by de ole wagon-ya'd, where no 'spectable 'oman ever puts her foot."

"An' de chillen?"

"De gal 's dead. Wuz 'n' no better 'n she oughter be'n. She fell in de crick an' got drown'; some folks say she wuz 'n' sober w'en it happen'. De boy tuck atter his pappy. He wuz 'rested las' week fer shootin' a w'ite man, an' wuz lynch' de same night. Dey wa'n't none of 'em no 'count after deir pappy went ter de penitenchy."

"What went wid de proputty?"

"Hit wuz sol' fer de mortgage, er de taxes, er de lawyer, er sump'n,—I don' know w'at. A w'ite man got it."

The man with the bundle went on until he came to a creek that crossed the road. He descended the sloping bank, and, sitting on a stone in the shade of a water-oak, took off his coarse brogans, unwound the rags that served him in lieu of stockings, and laved in the cool water the feet that were chafed with many a weary mile of travel.

After five years of unrequited toil, and unspeakable hardship in convict camps,—five years of slaving by the side of human brutes, and of nightly herding with them in vermin-haunted huts,—Ben Davis had become like them. For a while he had received occasional letters from home, but in the shifting life of the convict camp they had long since ceased to reach him, if indeed they had been written. For a year or two, the consciousness of his innocence had helped to make him resist the debasing influences that surrounded him. The hope of shortening his sentence by good behavior, too, had worked a similar end. But the transfer from one contractor to another, each interested in keeping as long as possible a good worker, had speedily dissipated any such hope. When hope took flight, its place was not long vacant. Despair followed, and black hatred of all mankind, hatred especially of the man to whom he attributed all his misfortunes. One who is suffering unjustly is not apt to indulge in fine abstractions, nor to balance probabilities. By long brooding over his wrongs, his mind became, if not unsettled, at least warped, and he imagined that Colonel Thornton had deliberately set a trap into which he had fallen. The Colonel, he convinced himself, had disapproved of his prosperity, and had schemed to destroy it. He reasoned himself into the belief that he represented in his person the accumulated wrongs of a whole race, and Colonel Thornton the race who had oppressed them. A burning desire for revenge sprang up in him, and he nursed it until his sentence expired and he was set at liberty. What he had learned since reaching home had changed his desire into a deadly purpose.

When he had again bandaged his feet and slipped them into his shoes, he looked around him, and selected a stout sapling from among the undergrowth that covered the bank of the stream. Taking from his pocket a huge clasp-knife, he cut off the length of an ordinary walking stick and trimmed it. The result was an ugly-looking bludgeon, a dangerous weapon when in the grasp of a strong man.

With the stick in his hand, he went on down the road until he approached a large white house standing some distance back from the street. The grounds were filled with a profusion of shrubbery. The negro entered the gate and secreted himself in the bushes, at a point where he could hear any one that might approach.

It was near midday, and he had not eaten. He had walked all night, and had not slept. The hope of meeting his loved ones had been meat and drink and rest for him. But as he sat waiting, outraged nature asserted itself, and he fell asleep, with his head on the rising root of a tree, and his face upturned.

And as he slept, he dreamed of his childhood; of an old black mammy taking care of him in the daytime, and of a younger face, with soft eyes, which bent over him sometimes at night, and a pair of arms which clasped him closely. He dreamed of his past,—of his young wife, of his bright children. Somehow his dreams all ran to pleasant themes for a while.

Then they changed again. He dreamed that he was in the convict camp, and, by an easy transition, that he was in hell, consumed with hunger, burning with thirst. Suddenly the grinning devil who stood over him with a barbed whip faded away, and a little white angel came and handed him a drink of water. As he raised it to his lips the glass slipped, and he struggled back to consciousness.

"Poo' man! Poo' man sick, an' sleepy. Dolly b'ing f'owers to cover poo' man up. Poo' man mus' be hungry. W'en Dolly get him covered up, she go b'ing poo' man some cake."

A sweet little child, as beautiful as a cherub escaped from Paradise, was standing over him. At first he scarcely comprehended the words the baby babbled out. But as they became clear to him, a novel feeling crept slowly over his heart. It had been so long since he had heard anything but curses and stern words of command, or the ribald songs of obscene merriment, that the clear tones of this voice from heaven cooled his calloused heart as the water of the brook had soothed his blistered feet. It was so strange, so unwonted a thing, that he lay there with half-closed eyes while the child brought leaves and flowers and laid them on his face and on his breast, and arranged them with little caressing taps.

She moved away, and plucked a flower. And then she spied another farther on, and then another, and, as she gathered them, kept increasing the distance between herself and the man lying there, until she was several rods away.

Ben Davis watched her through eyes over which had come an unfamiliar softness. Under the lingering spell of his dream, her golden hair, which fell in rippling curls, seemed like a halo of purity and innocence and peace, irradiating the atmosphere around her. It is true the thought occurred to Ben, vaguely, that through harm to her he might inflict the greatest punishment upon her father; but the idea came like a dark shape that faded away and vanished into nothingness as soon as it came within the nimbus that surrounded the child's person.

The child was moving on to pluck still another flower, when there came a sound of hoof-beats, and Ben was aware that a horseman, visible through the shrubbery, was coming along the curved path that led from the gate to the house. It must be the man he was waiting for, and now was the time to wreak his vengeance. He sprang to his feet, grasped his club, and stood for a moment irresolute. But either the instinct of the convict, beaten, driven, and debased, or the influence of the child, which was still strong upon him, impelled him, after the first momentary pause, to flee as though seeking safety.

His flight led him toward the little girl, whom he must pass in order to make his escape, and as Colonel Thornton turned the corner of the path he saw a desperate-looking negro, clad in filthy rags, and carrying in his hand a murderous bludgeon, running toward the child, who, startled by the sound of footsteps, had turned and was looking toward the approaching man with wondering eyes. A sickening fear came over the father's heart, and drawing the ever-ready revolver, which according to the Southern custom he carried always upon his person, he fired with unerring aim. Ben Davis ran a few yards farther, faltered, threw out his hands, and fell dead at the child's feet.

Some time, we are told, when the cycle of years has rolled around, there is to be another golden age, when all men will dwell together in love and harmony, and when peace and righteousness shall prevail for a thousand years. God speed the day, and let not the shining thread of hope become so enmeshed in the web of circumstance that we lose sight of it; but give us here and there, and now and then, some little foretaste of this golden age, that we may the more patiently and hopefully await its coming!

THE HOUSE
BEHIND THE CEDARS

(1900)

I

A STRANGER FROM SOUTH CAROLINA

TIME touches all things with destroying hand; and if he seem now and then to bestow the bloom of youth, the sap of spring, it is but a brief mockery, to be surely and swiftly followed by the wrinkles of old age, the dry leaves and bare branches of winter. And yet there are places where Time seems to linger lovingly long after youth has departed, and to which he seems loath to bring the evil day. Who has not known some even-tempered old man or woman who seemed to have drunk of the fountain of youth? Who has not seen somewhere an old town that, having long since ceased to grow, yet held its own without perceptible decline?

Some such trite reflection—as apposite to the subject as most random reflections are—passed through the mind of a young man who came out of the front door of the Patesville Hotel about nine o'clock one fine morning in spring, a few years after the Civil War, and started down Front Street toward the market-house. Arriving at the town late the previous evening, he had been driven up from the steamboat in a carriage, from which he had been able to distinguish only the shadowy outlines of the houses along the street; so that this morning walk was his first opportunity to see the town by daylight. He was dressed in a suit of linen duck—the day was warm—a panama straw hat, and patent leather shoes. In appearance he was tall, dark, with straight, black, lustrous hair, and very clean-cut, high-bred features. When he paused by the clerk's desk on his way out, to light his cigar, the day clerk, who had just come on duty, glanced at the register and read the last entry:—

" 'JOHN WARWICK, CLARENCE, SOUTH CAROLINA.'

"One of the South Ca'lina bigbugs, I reckon—probably in cotton, or turpentine." The gentleman from South Carolina, walking down the street, glanced about him with an eager look, in which curiosity and affection were mingled with a touch of bitterness. He saw little that was not familiar, or that he had not seen in his dreams a hundred times during the past ten years. There had been some changes, it is true, some melancholy changes, but scarcely anything by way of addition or improvement to counterbalance them. Here and there blackened and dismantled walls marked the place where handsome buildings once had stood, for Sherman's march to the sea had left its mark upon the town. The stores were mostly of brick, two stories high, joining one another after the manner of cities. Some of the names on the signs were familiar; others, including a number of Jewish names, were quite unknown to him.

A two minutes' walk brought Warwick—the name he had registered under, and as we shall call him—to the market-house, the central feature of Patesville, from both the commercial and the picturesque points of view. Standing foursquare in the heart of the town, at the intersection of the two main streets, a "jog" at each street corner left around the market-house a little public square, which at this hour was well occupied by carts and wagons from the country and empty drays awaiting hire. Warwick was unable to perceive much change in the market-house. Perhaps the surface of the red brick, long unpainted, had scaled off a little more here and there. There might have been a slight accretion of the moss and lichen on the shingled roof. But the tall tower, with its four-faced clock, rose as majestically and uncompromisingly as though the land had never been subjugated. Was it so irreconcilable, Warwick wondered, as still to peal out the curfew bell, which at nine o'clock at night had clamorously warned all negroes, slave or free, that it was unlawful for them to be abroad after that hour, under penalty of imprisonment or whipping? Was the old constable, whose chief business it had been to ring the bell, still alive and exercising the functions of his office, and had age lessened or increased the number of times that obliging citizens performed this duty for him during his temporary absences in the company of convivial spirits? A few moments later, Warwick saw a colored policeman in the old constable's place—a stronger reminder than even the burned buildings that war had left its mark upon the old town, with which Time had dealt so tenderly.

The lower story of the market-house was open on all four of its sides to the public square. Warwick passed through one of the wide brick arches and traversed the building with a leisurely step. He looked in vain into the stalls for the butcher who had sold fresh meat twice a week, on market days, and he felt a genuine thrill of pleasure when he recognized the red bandana turban of old Aunt Lyddy, the ancient negro woman who had sold him gingerbread and fried fish, and told him weird tales of witchcraft and conjuration, in the old days when, as an idle boy, he had loafed about the market-house. He did not speak to her, however, or give her any sign of recognition. He threw a glance toward a certain corner where steps led to the town hall above. On this stairway he had once seen a manacled free negro shot while being taken upstairs for examination under a criminal charge. Warwick recalled vividly how the shot had rung out. He could see again the livid look of terror on the victim's face, the gathering crowd, the resulting confusion. The murderer, he recalled, had been tried and sentenced to imprisonment for life, but was pardoned by a merciful governor after serving a year of his sentence. As Warwick was neither a prophet nor the son of a prophet, he could not foresee that, thirty years later, even this would seem an excessive punishment for so slight a misdemeanor.

Leaving the market-house, Warwick turned to the left, and kept on his course until he reached the next corner. After another turn to the right, a dozen paces brought him in front of a small weather-beaten frame building, from which projected a wooden sign-board bearing the inscription:—

ARCHIBALD STRAIGHT,
LAWYER.

He turned the knob, but the door was locked. Retracing his steps past a vacant lot, the young man entered a shop where a colored man was employed in varnishing a coffin, which stood on two trestles in the middle of the floor. Not at all impressed by the melancholy suggestiveness of his task, he was whistling a lively air with great gusto. Upon Warwick's entrance this effusion came to a sudden end, and the coffin-maker assumed an air of professional gravity.

"Good-mawnin', suh," he said, lifting his cap politely.

"Good-morning," answered Warwick. "Can you tell me anything about Judge Straight's office hours?"

"De ole jedge has be'n a little onreg'lar sence de wah, suh; but he gin'ally gits roun' 'bout ten o'clock er so. He 's be'n kin' er feeble fer de las' few yeahs. An' I reckon," continued the undertaker solemnly, his glance unconsciously seeking a row of fine caskets standing against the wall,—"I reckon he 'll soon be goin' de way er all de earth. 'Man dat is bawn er 'oman hath but a sho't time ter lib, an' is full er mis'ry. He cometh up an' is cut down lack as a flower.' 'De days er his life is three-sco' an' ten'—an' de ole jedge is libbed mo' d'n dat, suh, by five yeahs, ter say de leas'."

" 'Death,' " quoted Warwick, with whose mood the undertaker's remarks were in tune, " 'is the penalty that all must pay for the crime of living.' "

"Dat 's a fac', suh, dat 's a fac'; so dey mus'—so dey mus'. An' den all de dead has ter be buried. An' we does ou' sheer of it, suh, we does ou' sheer. We conduc's de obs'quies er all de bes' w'ite folks er de town, suh."

Warwick left the undertaker's shop and retraced his steps until he had passed the lawyer's office, toward which he threw an affectionate glance. A few rods farther led him past the old brick Presbyterian church, with its square tower, embowered in a stately grove; past the Catholic church, with its many crosses, and a painted wooden figure of St. James in a recess beneath the gable; and past the old Jefferson House, once the leading hotel of the town, in front of which political meetings had been held, and political speeches made, and political hard cider drunk, in the days of "Tippecanoe and Tyler too."

The street down which Warwick had come intersected Front Street at a sharp angle in front of the old hotel, forming a sort of flatiron block at the junction, known as Liberty Point,—perhaps because slave auctions were sometimes held there in the good old days. Just before Warwick reached Liberty Point, a young woman came down Front Street from the direction of the market-house. When their paths converged, Warwick kept on down Front Street behind her, it having been already his intention to walk in this direction.

Warwick's first glance had revealed the fact that the young woman was strikingly handsome, with a stately beauty seldom encountered. As he walked along behind her at a measured distance, he could not help noting the details that made up this pleasing impression, for his mind was singularly alive to beauty, in whatever embodiment. The girl's figure, he perceived, was admirably proportioned; she was evidently at the period when the angles of childhood were rounding into the promising curves of adolescence. Her abundant hair, of a dark and glossy brown, was neatly plaited and coiled above an ivory column that rose straight from a pair of gently sloping shoulders, clearly outlined beneath the light muslin frock that covered them. He could see that she was tastefully, though not richly, dressed, and that she walked with an elastic step that revealed a light heart and the vigor of perfect health. Her face, of course, he could not analyze, since he had caught only the one brief but convincing glimpse of it.

The young woman kept on down Front Street, Warwick maintaining his distance a few rods behind her. They passed a factory, a warehouse or two, and then, leaving the brick pavement, walked along on mother earth, under a leafy arcade of spreading oaks and elms. Their way led now through a residential portion of the town, which, as they advanced, gradually declined from staid respectability to poverty, open and unabashed. Warwick observed, as they passed through the respectable quarter, that few people who met the girl greeted her, and that some others whom she passed at gates or doorways gave her no sign of recognition; from which he inferred that she was possibly a visitor in the town and not well acquainted.

Their walk had continued not more than ten minutes when they crossed a creek by a wooden bridge and came to a row of mean houses standing flush with the street. At the door of one, an old black woman had stooped to lift a large basket, piled high with laundered clothes. The girl, as she passed, seized one end of the basket and helped the old woman to raise it to her head, where it rested solidly on the cushion of her head-kerchief. During this interlude, Warwick, though he had slackened his pace measurably, had so nearly closed the gap between himself and them as to hear the old woman say, with the dulcet negro intonation:—

"T'ank y', honey; de Lawd gwine bless you sho'. You wuz

alluz a good gal, and de Lawd love eve'ybody w'at he'p de po' ole nigger. You gwine ter hab good luck all yo' bawn days."

"I hope you 're a true prophet, Aunt Zilphy," laughed the girl in response.

The sound of her voice gave Warwick a thrill. It was soft and sweet and clear—quite in harmony with her appearance. That it had a faint suggestiveness of the old woman's accent he hardly noticed, for the current Southern speech, including his own, was rarely without a touch of it. The corruption of the white people's speech was one element—only one—of the negro's unconscious revenge for his own debasement.

The houses they passed now grew scattering, and the quarter of the town more neglected. Warwick felt himself wondering where the girl might be going in a neighborhood so uninviting. When she stopped to pull a half-naked negro child out of a mudhole and set him upon his feet, he thought she might be some young lady from the upper part of the town, bound on some errand of mercy, or going, perhaps, to visit an old servant or look for a new one. Once she threw a backward glance at Warwick, thus enabling him to catch a second glimpse of a singularly pretty face. Perhaps the young woman found his presence in the neighborhood as unaccountable as he had deemed hers; for, finding his glance fixed upon her, she quickened her pace with an air of startled timidity.

"A woman with such a figure," thought Warwick, "ought to be able to face the world with the confidence of Phryne confronting her judges."

By this time Warwick was conscious that something more than mere grace or beauty had attracted him with increasing force toward this young woman. A suggestion, at first faint and elusive, of something familiar, had grown stronger when he heard her voice, and became more and more pronounced with each rod of their advance; and when she stopped finally before a gate, and, opening it, went into a yard shut off from the street by a row of dwarf cedars, Warwick had already discounted in some measure the surprise he would have felt at seeing her enter there had he not walked down Front Street behind her. There was still sufficient unexpectedness about the act, however, to give him a decided thrill of pleasure.

"It must be Rena," he murmured. "Who could have dreamed that she would blossom out like that? It must surely be Rena!"

He walked slowly past the gate and peered through a narrow gap in the cedar hedge. The girl was moving along a sanded walk, toward a gray, unpainted house, with a steep roof, broken by dormer windows. The trace of timidity he had observed in her had given place to the more assured bearing of one who is upon his own ground. The garden walks were bordered by long rows of jonquils, pinks, and carnations, inclosing clumps of fragrant shrubs, lilies, and roses already in bloom. Toward the middle of the garden stood two fine magnolia-trees, with heavy, dark green, glistening leaves, while nearer the house two mighty elms shaded a wide piazza, at one end of which a honeysuckle vine, and at the other a Virginia creeper, running over a wooden lattice, furnished additional shade and seclusion. On dark or wintry days, the aspect of this garden must have been extremely sombre and depressing, and it might well have seemed a fit place to hide some guilty or disgraceful secret. But on the bright morning when Warwick stood looking through the cedars, it seemed, with its green frame and canopy and its bright carpet of flowers, an ideal retreat from the fierce sunshine and the sultry heat of the approaching summer.

The girl stooped to pluck a rose, and as she bent over it, her profile was clearly outlined. She held the flower to her face with a long-drawn inhalation, then went up the steps, crossed the piazza, opened the door without knocking, and entered the house with the air of one thoroughly at home.

"Yes," said the young man to himself, "it 's Rena, sure enough."

The house stood on a corner, around which the cedar hedge turned, continuing along the side of the garden until it reached the line of the front of the house. The piazza to a rear wing, at right angles to the front of the house, was open to inspection from the side street, which, to judge from its deserted look, seemed to be but little used. Turning into this street and walking leisurely past the back yard, which was only slightly screened from the street by a china-tree, Warwick perceived the young woman standing on the piazza, facing an elderly woman, who sat in a large rocking-chair, plying a pair of knitting-needles on a half-finished stocking. Warwick's walk led him within three feet of the side gate, which he felt an almost irresistible impulse to enter. Every detail of the house and garden was familiar; a thousand cords of memory and affection drew him thither; but a stronger counter-motive prevailed. With a great effort he restrained himself, and after a momentary pause, walked slowly on past the house, with a backward glance, which he turned away when he saw that it was observed.

Warwick's attention had been so fully absorbed by the house behind the cedars and the women there, that he had scarcely noticed, on the other side of the neglected by-street, two men working by a large open window, in a low, rude building with a clapboarded roof, directly opposite the back piazza occupied by the two women. Both the men were busily engaged in shaping barrel-staves, each wielding a sharp-edged drawing-knife on a piece of seasoned oak clasped tightly in a wooden vise.

"I jes' wonder who dat man is, an' w'at he 's doin' on dis street," observed the younger of the two, with a suspicious air. He had noticed the gentleman's involuntary pause and his interest in the opposite house, and had stopped work for a moment to watch the stranger as he went on down the street.

"Nev' min' 'bout dat man," said the elder one. "You 'ten' ter yo' wuk an' finish dat bairl-stave. You spen's enti'ely too much er yo' time stretchin' yo' neck atter other people. An' you need n' 'sturb yo'se'f 'bout dem folks 'cross de street, fer dey ain't yo' kin', an' you 're wastin' yo' time both'in' yo' min' wid 'em, er wid folks w'at comes on de street on account of 'em. Look sha'p now, boy, er you 'll git dat stave trim' too much."

The younger man resumed his work, but still found time to throw a slanting glance out of the window. The gentleman, he perceived, stood for a moment on the rotting bridge across the old canal, and then walked slowly ahead until he turned to the right into Back Street, a few rods farther on.

II

AN EVENING VISIT

TOWARD evening of the same day, Warwick took his way down Front Street in the gathering dusk. By the time night had spread its mantle over the earth, he had reached the gate by which he had seen the girl of his morning walk enter the cedar-bordered garden. He stopped at the gate and glanced toward the house, which seemed dark and silent and deserted.

"It 's more than likely," he thought, "that they are in the kitchen. I reckon I 'd better try the back door."

But as he drew cautiously near the corner, he saw a man's figure outlined in the yellow light streaming from the open door of a small house between Front Street and the cooper shop. Wishing, for reasons of his own, to avoid observation, Warwick did not turn the corner, but walked on down Front Street until he reached a point from which he could see, at a long angle, a ray of light proceeding from the kitchen window of the house behind the cedars.

"They are there," he muttered with a sigh of relief, for he had feared they might be away. "I suspect I 'll have to go to the front door, after all. No one can see me through the trees."

He retraced his steps to the front gate, which he essayed to open. There was apparently some defect in the latch, for it refused to work. Warwick remembered the trick, and with a slight sense of amusement, pushed his foot under the gate and gave it a hitch to the left, after which it opened readily enough. He walked softly up the sanded path, tiptoed up the steps and across the piazza, and rapped at the front door, not too loudly, lest this too might attract the attention of the man across the street. There was no response to his rap. He put his ear to the door and heard voices within, and the muffled sound of footsteps. After a moment he rapped again, a little louder than before.

There was an instant cessation of the sounds within. He

rapped a third time, to satisfy any lingering doubt in the minds of those who he felt sure were listening in some trepidation. A moment later a ray of light streamed through the keyhole.

"Who 's there?" a woman's voice inquired somewhat sharply.

"A gentleman," answered Warwick, not holding it yet time to reveal himself. "Does Mis' Molly Walden live here?"

"Yes," was the guarded answer. "I 'm Mis' Walden. What 's yo'r business?"

"I have a message to you from your son John."

A key clicked in the lock. The door opened, and the elder of the two women Warwick had seen upon the piazza stood in the doorway, peering curiously and with signs of great excitement into the face of the stranger.

"You 've got a message from my son, you say?" she asked with tremulous agitation. "Is he sick, or in trouble?"

"No. He 's well and doing well, and sends his love to you, and hopes you 've not forgotten him."

"Fergot him? No, God knows I ain't fergot him! But come in, sir, an' tell me somethin' mo' about him."

Warwick went in, and as the woman closed the door after him, he threw a glance round the room. On the wall, over the mantelpiece, hung a steel engraving of General Jackson at the battle of New Orleans, and, on the opposite wall, a framed fashion-plate from "Godey's Lady's Book." In the middle of the room an octagonal centre-table with a single leg, terminating in three sprawling feet, held a collection of curiously shaped sea-shells. There was a great haircloth sofa, somewhat the worse for wear, and a well-filled bookcase. The screen standing before the fireplace was covered with Confederate bank-notes of various denominations and designs, in which the heads of Jefferson Davis and other Confederate leaders were conspicuous.

"Imperious Cæsar, dead, and turned to clay,
Might stop a hole to keep the wind away,"

murmured the young man, as his eye fell upon this specimen of decorative art.

The woman showed her visitor to a seat. She then sat down

facing him and looked at him closely. "When did you last see my son?" she asked.

"I 've never met your son," he replied.

Her face fell. "Then the message comes through you from somebody else?"

"No, directly from your son."

She scanned his face with a puzzled look. This bearded young gentleman, who spoke so politely and was dressed so well, surely—no, it could not be! and yet—

Warwick was smiling at her through a mist of tears. An electric spark of sympathy flashed between them. They rose as if moved by one impulse, and were clasped in each other's arms.

"John, my John! It *is* John!"

"Mother—my dear old mother!"

"I did n't think," she sobbed, "that I 'd ever see you again."

He smoothed her hair and kissed her. "And are you glad to see me, mother?"

"Am I glad to see you? It 's like the dead comin' to life. I thought I 'd lost you forever, John, my son, my darlin' boy!" she answered, hugging him strenuously.

"I could n't live without seeing you, mother," he said. He meant it, too, or thought he did, although he had not seen her for ten years.

"You 've grown so tall, John, and are such a fine gentleman! And you *are* a gentleman now, John, ain't you—sure enough? Nobody knows the old story?"

"Well, mother, I 've taken a man's chance in life, and have tried to make the most of it; and I have n't felt under any obligation to spoil it by raking up old stories that are best forgotten. There are the dear old books: have they been read since I went away?"

"No, honey, there 's be'n nobody to read 'em, excep' Rena, an' she don't take to books quite like you did. But I 've kep' 'em dusted clean, an' kep' the moths an' the bugs out; for I hoped you 'd come back some day, an' knowed you 'd like to find 'em all in their places, jus' like you left 'em."

"That 's mighty nice of you, mother. You could have done no more if you had loved them for themselves. But where is

Rena? I saw her on the street to-day, but she did n't know me from Adam; nor did I guess it was she until she opened the gate and came into the yard."

"I 've be'n so glad to see you that I 'd fergot about her," answered the mother. "Rena, oh, Rena!"

The girl was not far away; she had been standing in the next room, listening intently to every word of the conversation, and only kept from coming in by a certain constraint that made a brother whom she had not met for so many years seem almost as much a stranger as if he had not been connected with her by any tie.

"Yes, mamma," she answered, coming forward.

"Rena, child, here 's yo'r brother John, who 's come back to see us. Tell 'im howdy."

As she came forward, Warwick rose, put his arm around her waist, drew her toward him, and kissed her affectionately, to her evident embarrassment. She was a tall girl, but he towered above her in quite a protecting fashion; and she thought with a thrill how fine it would be to have such a brother as this in the town all the time. How proud she would be, if she could but walk up the street with such a brother by her side! She could then hold up her head before all the world, oblivious to the glance of pity or contempt. She felt a very pronounced respect for this tall gentleman who held her blushing face between his hands and looked steadily into her eyes.

"You 're the little sister I used to read stories to, and whom I promised to come and see some day. Do you remember how you cried when I went away?"

"It seems but yesterday," she answered. "I 've still got the dime you gave me."

He kissed her again, and then drew her down beside him on the sofa, where he sat enthroned between the two loving and excited women. No king could have received more sincere or delighted homage. He was a man, come into a household of women,—a man of whom they were proud, and to whom they looked up with fond reverence. For he was not only a son,—a brother—but he represented to them the world from which circumstances had shut them out, and to which distance lent even more than its usual enchantment;

and they felt nearer to this far-off world because of the glory which Warwick reflected from it.

"You 're a very pretty girl," said Warwick, regarding his sister thoughtfully. "I followed you down Front Street this morning, and scarcely took my eyes off you all the way; and yet I did n't know you, and scarcely saw your face. You improve on acquaintance; to-night, I find you handsomer still."

"Now, John," said his mother, expostulating mildly, "you 'll spile her, if you don't min'."

The girl was beaming with gratified vanity. What woman would not find such praise sweet from almost any source, and how much more so from this great man, who, from his exalted station in the world, must surely know the things whereof he spoke! She believed every word of it; she knew it very well indeed, but wished to hear it repeated and itemized and emphasized.

"No, he won't, mamma," she asserted, "for he 's flattering me. He talks as if I was some rich young lady, who lives on the Hill,"—the Hill was the aristocratic portion of the town,—"instead of a poor"—

"Instead of a poor young girl, who has the hill to climb," replied her brother, smoothing her hair with his hand. Her hair was long and smooth and glossy, with a wave like the ripple of a summer breeze upon the surface of still water. It was the girl's great pride, and had been sedulously cared for. "What lovely hair! It has just the wave that yours lacks, mother."

"Yes," was the regretful reply, "I 've never be'n able to git that wave out. But her hair 's be'n took good care of, an' there ain't nary gal in town that 's got any finer."

"Don't worry about the wave, mother. It 's just the fashionable ripple, and becomes her immensely. I think my little Albert favors his Aunt Rena somewhat."

"Your little Albert!" they cried. "You 've got a child?"

"Oh, yes," he replied calmly, "a very fine baby boy."

They began to purr in proud contentment at this information, and made minute inquiries about the age and weight and eyes and nose and other important details of this precious infant. They inquired more coldly about the child's mother, of whom they spoke with greater warmth when they learned that she was dead. They hung breathless on Warwick's words as he related briefly the story of his life since he had left, years before, the house behind the cedars—how with a stout heart and an abounding hope he had gone out into a seemingly hostile world, and made fortune stand and deliver. His story had for the women the charm of an escape from captivity, with all the thrill of a pirate's tale. With the whole world before him, he had remained in the South, the land of his fathers, where, he conceived, he had an inalienable birthright. By some good chance he had escaped military service in the Confederate army, and, in default of older and more experienced men, had undertaken, during the rebellion, the management of a large estate, which had been left in the hands of women and slaves. He had filled the place so acceptably, and employed his leisure to such advantage, that at the close of the war he found himself—he was modest enough to think, too, in default of a better man—the husband of the orphan daughter of the gentleman who had owned the plantation, and who had lost his life upon the battlefield. Warwick's wife was of good family, and in a more settled condition of society it would not have been easy for a young man of no visible antecedents to win her hand. A year or two later, he had taken the oath of allegiance, and had been admitted to the South Carolina bar. Rich in his wife's right, he had been able to practice his profession upon a high plane, without the worry of sordid cares, and with marked success for one of his age.

"I suppose," he concluded, "that I have got along at the bar, as elsewhere, owing to the lack of better men. Many of the good lawyers were killed in the war, and most of the remainder were disqualified; while I had the advantage of being alive, and of never having been in arms against the government. People had to have lawyers, and they gave me their business in preference to the carpet-baggers. Fortune, you know, favors the available man."

His mother drank in with parted lips and glistening eyes the story of his adventures and the record of his successes. As Rena listened, the narrow walls that hemmed her in seemed to draw closer and closer, as though they must crush her. Her brother watched her keenly. He had been talking not only to inform the women, but with a deeper purpose, conceived since his morning walk, and deepened as he had followed, during his narrative, the changing expression of Rena's face and noted her intense interest in his story, her pride in his successes, and the occasional wistful look that indexed her self-pity so completely.

"An' I s'pose you 're happy, John?" asked his mother.

"Well, mother, happiness is a relative term, and depends, I imagine, upon how nearly we think we get what we think we want. I have had my chance and have n't thrown it away, and I suppose I ought to be happy. But then, I have lost my wife, whom I loved very dearly, and who loved me just as much, and I 'm troubled about my child."

"Why?" they demanded. "Is there anything the matter with him?"

"No, not exactly. He 's well enough, as babies go, and has a good enough nurse, as nurses go. But the nurse is ignorant, and not always careful. A child needs some woman of its own blood to love it and look after it intelligently."

Mis' Molly's eyes were filled with tearful yearning. She would have given all the world to warm her son's child upon her bosom; but she knew this could not be.

"Did your wife leave any kin?" she asked with an effort.

"No near kin; she was an only child."

"You 'll be gettin' married again," suggested his mother.

"No," he replied; "I think not."

Warwick was still reading his sister's face, and saw the spark of hope that gleamed in her expressive eye.

"If I had some relation of my own that I could take into the house with me," he said reflectively, "the child might be healthier and happier, and I should be much more at ease about him."

The mother looked from son to daughter with a dawning apprehension and a sudden pallor. When she saw the yearning in Rena's eyes, she threw herself at her son's feet.

"Oh, John," she cried despairingly, "don't take her away from me! Don't take her, John, darlin', for it 'd break my heart to lose her!"

Rena's arms were round her mother's neck, and Rena's voice was sounding in her ears. "There, there, mamma! Never mind! I won't leave you, mamma—dear old mamma! Your Rena 'll stay with you always, and never, never leave you."

John smoothed his mother's hair with a comforting touch, patted her withered cheek soothingly, lifted her tenderly to her place by his side, and put his arm about her.

"You love your children, mother?"

"They 're all I 've got," she sobbed, "an' they cos' me all I had. When the las' one 's gone, I 'll want to go too, for I 'll be all alone in the world. Don't take Rena, John; for if you do, I 'll never see her again, an' I can't bear to think of it. How would you like to lose yo'r one child?"

"Well, well, mother, we 'll say no more about it. And now tell me all about yourself, and about the neighbors, and how you got through the war, and who 's dead and who 's married—and everything."

The change of subject restored in some degree Mis' Molly's equanimity, and with returning calmness came a sense of other responsibilities.

"Good gracious, Rena!" she exclaimed. "John 's be'n in the house an hour, and ain't had nothin' to eat yet! Go in the kitchen an' spread a clean tablecloth, an' git out that 'tater pone, an' a pitcher o' that las' kag o' persimmon beer, an' let John take a bite an' a sip."

Warwick smiled at the mention of these homely dainties. "I thought of your sweet-potato pone at the hotel to-day, when I was at dinner, and wondered if you 'd have some in the house. There was never any like yours; and I 've forgotten the taste of persimmon beer entirely."

Rena left the room to carry out her hospitable commission. Warwick, taking advantage of her absence, returned after a while to the former subject.

"Of course, mother," he said calmly, "I would n't think of taking Rena away against your wishes. A mother's claim upon her child is a high and holy one. Of course she will have no chance here, where our story is known. The war has wrought great changes, has put the bottom rail on top, and all that—but it has n't wiped *that* out. Nothing but death can remove that stain, if it does not follow us even beyond the grave. Here she must forever be—nobody! With me she might have got out into the world; with her beauty she might have made a good marriage; and, if I mistake not, she has sense as well as beauty."

"Yes," sighed the mother, "she 's got good sense. She ain't as quick as you was, an' don't read as many books, but she 's keerful an' painstakin', an' always tries to do what 's right. She 's be'n thinkin' about goin' away somewhere an' tryin' to git a school to teach, er somethin', sence the Yankees have started 'em everywhere for po' white folks an' niggers too. But I don't like fer her to go too fur."

"With such beauty and brains," continued Warwick, "she could leave this town and make a place for herself. The place is already made. She has only to step into my carriage—after perhaps a little preparation—and ride up the hill which I have had to climb so painfully. It would be a great pleasure to me to see her at the top. But of course it is impossible—a mere idle dream. *Your* claim comes first; her duty chains her here."

"It would be so lonely without her," murmured the mother weakly, "an' I love her so—my las' one!"

"No doubt—no doubt," returned Warwick, with a sympathetic sign; "of course you love her. It 's not to be thought of for a moment. It 's a pity that she could n't have a chance here—but how could she? I had thought she might marry a gentleman; but I dare say she 'll do as well as the rest of her friends—as well as Mary B., for instance, who married—Homer Pettifoot, did you say? Or maybe Billy Oxendine might do for her. As long as she has never known any better, she 'll probably be as well satisfied as though she married a rich man, and lived in a fine house, and kept a carriage and servants, and moved with the best in the land."

The tortured mother could endure no more. The one thing she desired above all others was her daughter's happiness. Her own life had not been governed by the highest standards, but about her love for her beautiful daughter there was no taint of selfishness. The life her son had described had been to her always the ideal but unattainable life. Circumstances, some beyond her control, and others for which she was herself in a measure responsible, had put it forever and inconceivably beyond her reach. It had been conquered by her son. It beckoned to her daughter. The comparison of this free and noble life with the sordid existence of those around her broke down the last barrier of opposition.

"O Lord!" she moaned, "what shall I do without her? It 'll be lonely, John—so lonely!"

"You 'll have your home, mother," said Warwick tenderly, accepting the implied surrender. "You 'll have your friends and relatives, and the knowledge that your children are happy. I 'll let you hear from us often, and no doubt you can see Rena now and then. But you must let her go, mother,—it would be a sin against her to refuse."

"She may go," replied the mother brokenly. "I 'll not stand in her way—I 've got sins enough to answer for already."

Warwick watched her pityingly. He had stirred her feelings to unwonted depths, and his sympathy went out to her. If she had sinned, she had been more sinned against than sinning, and it was not his part to judge her. He had yielded to a sentimental weakness in deciding upon this trip to Patesville. A matter of business had brought him within a day's journey of the town, and an overmastering impulse had compelled him to seek the mother who had given him birth and the old town where he had spent the earlier years of his life. No one would have acknowledged sooner than he the folly of this visit. Men who have elected to govern their lives by principles of abstract right and reason, which happen, perhaps, to be at variance with what society considers equally right and reasonable, should, for fear of complications, be careful about descending from the lofty heights of logic to the common level of impulse and affection. Many years before, Warwick, when a lad of eighteen, had shaken the dust of the town from his feet, and with it, he fondly thought, the blight of his inheritance, and had achieved elsewhere a worthy career. But during all these years of absence he had cherished a tender feeling for his mother, and now again found himself in her house, amid the familiar surroundings of his childhood. His visit had brought joy to his mother's heart, and was now to bring its shrouded companion, sorrow. His mother had lived her life, for good or ill. A wider door was open to his sister—her mother must not bar the entrance.

"She may go," the mother repeated sadly, drying her tears. "I 'll give her up for her good."

"The table 's ready, mamma," said Rena, coming to the door.

The lunch was spread in the kitchen, a large unplastered room at the rear, with a wide fireplace at one end. Only yesterday, it seemed to Warwick, he had sprawled upon the hearth, turning sweet potatoes before the fire, or roasting groundpeas in the ashes; or, more often, reading, by the light of a blazing pine-knot or lump of resin, some volume from the bookcase in the hall. From Bulwer's novel, he had read the story of Warwick the Kingmaker, and upon leaving home had chosen it for his own. He was a new man, but he had the blood of an old race, and he would select for his own one of its worthy names. Overhead loomed the same smoky beams, decorated with what might have been, from all appearances, the same bunches of dried herbs, the same strings of onions and red peppers. Over in the same corner stood the same spinning-wheel, and through the open door of an adjoining room he saw the old loom, where in childhood he had more than once thrown the shuttle. The kitchen was different from the stately dining-room of the old colonial mansion where he now lived; but it was homelike, and it was familiar. The sight of it moved his heart, and he felt for the moment a sort of a blind anger against the fate which made it necessary that he should visit the home of his childhood, if at all, like a thief in the night. But he realized, after a moment, that the thought was pure sentiment, and that one who had gained so much ought not to complain if he must give up a little. He who would climb the heights of life must leave even the pleasantest valleys behind.

"Rena," asked her mother, "how 'd you like to go an' pay yo'r brother John a visit? I guess I might spare you for a little while."

The girl's eyes lighted up. She would not have gone if her mother had wished her to stay, but she would always have regarded this as the lost opportunity of her life.

"Are you sure you don't care, mamma?" she asked, hoping and yet doubting.

"Oh, I 'll manage to git along somehow or other. You can go an' stay till you git homesick, an' then John 'll let you come back home."

But Mis' Molly believed that she would never come back, except, like her brother, under cover of the night. She must lose her daughter as well as her son, and this should be the penance for her sin. That her children must expiate as well the sins of their fathers, who had sinned so lightly, after the manner of men, neither she nor they could foresee, since they could not read the future.

The next boat by which Warwick could take his sister away left early in the morning of the next day but one. He went back to his hotel with the understanding that the morrow should be devoted to getting Rena ready for her departure, and that Warwick would visit the household again the following evening; for, as has been intimated, there were several reasons why there should be no open relations between the fine gentleman at the hotel and the women in the house behind the cedars, who, while superior in blood and breeding to the people of the neighborhood in which they lived, were yet under the shadow of some cloud which clearly shut them out from the better society of the town. Almost any resident could have given one or more of these reasons, of which any one would have been sufficient to most of them; and to some of them Warwick's mere presence in the town would have seemed a bold and daring thing.

III

THE OLD JUDGE

On the morning following the visit to his mother, Warwick visited the old judge's office. The judge was not in, but the door stood open, and Warwick entered to await his return. There had been fewer changes in the office, where he had spent many, many hours, than in the town itself. The dust was a little thicker, the papers in the pigeon-holes of the walnut desk were a little yellower, the cobwebs in the corners a little more aggressive. The flies droned as drowsily and the murmur of the brook below was just as audible. Warwick stood at the rear window and looked out over a familiar view. Directly across the creek, on the low ground beyond, might be seen the dilapidated stone foundation of the house where once had lived Flora Macdonald, the Jacobite refugee, the most romantic character of North Carolina history. Old Judge Straight had had a tree cut away from the creek-side opposite his window, so that this historic ruin might be visible from his office; for the judge could trace the ties of blood that connected him collaterally with this famous personage. His pamphlet on Flora Macdonald, printed for private circulation, was highly prized by those of his friends who were fortunate enough to obtain a copy. To the left of the window a placid mill-pond spread its wide expanse, and to the right the creek disappeared under a canopy of overhanging trees.

A footstep sounded in the doorway, and Warwick, turning, faced the old judge. Time had left greater marks upon the lawyer than upon his office. His hair was whiter, his stoop more pronounced; when he spoke to Warwick, his voice had some of the shrillness of old age; and in his hand, upon which the veins stood out prominently, a decided tremor was perceptible.

"Good-morning, Judge Straight," said the young man, removing his hat with the graceful Southern deference of the young for the old.

"Good-morning, sir," replied the judge with equal courtesy.

"You don't remember me, I imagine," suggested Warwick.

"Your face seems familiar," returned the judge cautiously, "but I cannot for the moment recall your name. I shall be glad to have you refresh my memory."

"I was John Walden, sir, when you knew me."

The judge's face still gave no answering light of recognition.

"Your old office-boy," continued the younger man.

"Ah, indeed, so you were!" rejoined the judge warmly, extending his hand with great cordiality, and inspecting Warwick more closely through his spectacles. "Let me see—you went away a few years before the war, was n't it?"

"Yes, sir, to South Carolina."

"Yes, yes, I remember now! I had been thinking it was to the North. So many things have happened since then, that it taxes an old man's memory to keep track of them all. Well, well! and how have you been getting along?"

Warwick told his story in outline, much as he had given it to his mother and sister, and the judge seemed very much interested.

"And you married into a good family?" he asked.

"Yes, sir."

"And have children?"

"One."

"And you are visiting your mother?"

"Not exactly. I have seen her, but I am stopping at a hotel."

"H'm! Are you staying long?"

"I leave to-morrow."

"It 's well enough. I would n't stay too long. The people of a small town are inquisitive about strangers, and some of them have long memories. I remember we went over the law, which was in your favor; but custom is stronger than law—in these matters custom *is* law. It was a great pity that your father did not make a will. Well, my boy, I wish you continued good luck; I imagined you would make your way."

Warwick went away, and the old judge sat for a moment absorbed in reflection. "Right and wrong," he mused, "must be eternal verities, but our standards for measuring them vary with our latitude and our epoch. We make our customs lightly; once made, like our sins, they grip us in bands of steel; we become the creatures of our creations. By one standard my old office-boy should never have been born. Yet he is a son of Adam, and came into existence in the way ordained by God from the beginning of the world. In equity he would seem to be entitled to his chance in life; it might have been wiser, though, for him to seek it farther afield than South Carolina. It was too near home, even though the laws were with him."

IV

DOWN THE RIVER

NEITHER mother nor daughter slept a great deal during the night of Warwick's first visit. Mis' Molly anointed her sacrifice with tears and cried herself to sleep. Rena's emotions were more conflicting; she was sorry to leave her mother, but glad to go with her brother. The mere journey she was about to make was a great event for the two women to contemplate, to say nothing of the golden vision that lay beyond, for neither of them had ever been out of the town or its vicinity.

The next day was devoted to preparations for the journey. Rena's slender wardrobe was made ready and packed in a large valise. Towards sunset, Mis' Molly took off her apron, put on her slat-bonnet,—she was ever the pink of neatness,—picked her way across the street, which was muddy from a rain during the day, traversed the foot-bridge that spanned the ditch in front of the cooper shop, and spoke first to the elder of the two men working there.

"Good-evenin', Peter."

"Good-evenin', ma'm," responded the man briefly, and not relaxing at all the energy with which he was trimming a barrel-stave.

Mis' Molly then accosted the younger workman, a dark-brown young man, small in stature, but with a well-shaped head, an expressive forehead, and features indicative of kindness, intelligence, humor, and imagination. "Frank," she asked, "can I git you to do somethin' fer me soon in the mo'nin'?"

"Yas 'm, I reckon so," replied the young man, resting his hatchet on the chopping-block. "W'at is it, Mis' Molly?"

"My daughter 's goin' away on the boat, an' I 'lowed you would n' min' totin' her kyarpet-bag down to the w'arf, onless you 'd ruther haul it down on yo'r kyart. It ain't very heavy. Of co'se I 'll pay you fer yo'r trouble."

"Thank y', ma'm," he replied. He knew that she would not pay him, for the simple reason that he would not accept pay for such a service. "Is she gwine fur?" he asked, with a sorrowful look, which he could not entirely disguise.

"As fur as Wilmin'ton an' beyon'. She 'll be visitin' her brother John, who lives in—another State, an' wants her to come an' see him."

"Yas 'm, I 'll come. I won' need de kyart—I 'll tote de bag. 'Bout w'at time shill I come over?"

"Well, 'long 'bout seven o'clock or half pas'. She 's goin' on the Old North State, an' it leaves at eight."

Frank stood looking after Mis' Molly as she picked her way across the street, until he was recalled to his duty by a sharp word from his father.

"'Ten' ter yo' wuk, boy, 'ten' ter yo' wuk. You 're wastin' yo' time—wastin' yo' time!"

Yes, he was wasting his time. The beautiful young girl across the street could never be anything to him. But he had saved her life once, and had dreamed that he might render her again some signal service that might win her friendship, and convince her of his humble devotion. For Frank was not proud. A smile, which Peter would have regarded as condescending to a free man, who, since the war, was as good as anybody else; a kind word, which Peter would have considered offensively patronizing; a piece of Mis' Molly's famous potato pone from Rena's hands,—a bone to a dog, Peter called it once;—were ample rewards for the thousand and one small services Frank had rendered the two women who lived in the house behind the cedars.

Frank went over in the morning a little ahead of the appointed time, and waited on the back piazza until his services were required.

"You ain't gwine ter be gone long, is you, Miss Rena?" he inquired, when Rena came out dressed for the journey in her best frock, with broad white collar and cuffs.

Rena did not know. She had been asking herself the same question. All sorts of vague dreams had floated through her mind during the last few hours, as to what the future might bring forth. But she detected the anxious note in Frank's voice, and had no wish to give this faithful friend of the family unnecessary pain.

"Oh, no, Frank, I reckon not. I 'm supposed to be just going on a short visit. My brother has lost his wife, and wishes me to come and stay with him awhile, and look after his little boy."

"I 'm feared you 'll lack it better dere, Miss Rena," replied Frank sorrowfully, dropping his mask of unconcern, "an' den you won't come back, an' none er yo' frien's won't never see you no mo'."

"You don't think, Frank," asked Rena severely, "that I would leave my mother and my home and all my friends, and *never* come back again?"

"Why, no 'ndeed," interposed Mis' Molly wistfully, as she hovered around her daughter, giving her hair or her gown a touch here and there; "she 'll be so homesick in a month that she 'll be willin' to walk home."

"You would n' never hafter do dat, Miss Rena," returned Frank, with a disconsolate smile. "Ef you ever wanter come home, an' can't git back no other way, jes' let *me* know, an' I 'll take my mule an' my kyart an' fetch you back, ef it 's from de een' er de worl'."

"Thank you, Frank, I believe you would," said the girl kindly. "You 're a true friend, Frank, and I 'll not forget you while I'm gone."

The idea of her beautiful daughter riding home from the end of the world with Frank, in a cart, behind a one-eyed mule, struck Mis' Molly as the height of the ridiculous—she was in a state of excitement where tears or laughter would have come with equal ease—and she turned away to hide her merriment. Her daughter was going to live in a fine house, and marry a rich man, and ride in her carriage. Of course a negro would drive the carriage, but that was different from riding with one in a cart.

When it was time to go, Mis' Molly and Rena set out on foot for the river, which was only a short distance away. Frank followed with the valise. There was no gathering of friends to see Rena off, as might have been the case under different circumstances. Her departure had some of the characteristics of a secret flight; it was as important that her destination should not be known, as it had been that her brother should conceal his presence in the town.

Mis' Molly and Rena remained on the bank until the steamer announced, with a raucous whistle, its readiness to depart. Warwick was seen for a moment on the upper deck, from which he greeted them with a smile and a slight nod. He had bidden his mother an affectionate farewell the evening before. Rena gave her hand to Frank.

"Good-by, Frank," she said, with a kind smile; "I hope you and mamma will be good friends while I 'm gone."

The whistle blew a second warning blast, and the deck hands prepared to draw in the gangplank. Rena flew into her mother's arms, and then, breaking away, hurried on board and retired to her state-room, from which she did not emerge during the journey. The window-blinds were closed, darkening the room, and the stewardess who came to ask if she should bring her some dinner could not see her face distinctly, but perceived enough to make her surmise that the young lady had been weeping.

"Po' chile," murmured the sympathetic colored woman, "I reckon some er her folks is dead, er her sweetheart 's gone back on her, er e'se she 's had some kin' er bad luck er 'nuther. W'ite folks has deir troubles jes' ez well ez black folks, an' sometimes feels 'em mo', 'cause dey ain't ez use' ter 'em."

Mis' Molly went back in sadness to the lonely house behind the cedars, henceforth to be peopled for her with only the memory of those she had loved. She had paid with her heart's blood another installment on the Shylock's bond exacted by society for her own happiness of the past and her children's prospects for the future.

The journey down the sluggish river to the seaboard in the flat-bottomed, stern-wheel steamer lasted all day and most of the night. During the first half-day, the boat grounded now and then upon a sand-bank, and the half-naked negro deck-hands toiled with ropes and poles to release it. Several times before Rena fell asleep that night, the steamer would tie up at a landing, and by the light of huge pine torches she watched the boat hands send the yellow turpentine barrels down the steep bank in a long string, or pass cord-wood on board from hand to hand. The excited negroes, their white teeth and eyeballs glistening in the surrounding darkness to which their faces formed no relief; the white officers in brown linen, shouting, swearing, and gesticulating; the yellow, flickering torchlight over all,—made up a scene of which the weird interest would have appealed to a more *blasé* traveler than this girl upon her first journey.

During the day, Warwick had taken his meals in the dining-room, with the captain and the other cabin passengers. It was learned that he was a South Carolina lawyer, and not a carpet-bagger. Such credentials were unimpeachable, and the passengers found him a very agreeable traveling companion. Apparently sound on the subject of negroes, Yankees, and the righteousness of the lost cause, he yet discussed these themes in a lofty and impersonal manner that gave his words greater weight than if he had seemed warped by a personal grievance. His attitude, in fact, piqued the curiosity of one or two of the passengers.

"Did your people lose any niggers?" asked one of them.

"My father owned a hundred," he replied grandly.

Their respect for his views was doubled. It is easy to moralize about the misfortunes of others, and to find good in the evil that they suffer;—only a true philosopher could speak thus lightly of his own losses.

When the steamer tied up at the wharf at Wilmington, in the early morning, the young lawyer and a veiled lady passenger drove in the same carriage to a hotel. After they had breakfasted in a private room, Warwick explained to his sister the plan he had formed for her future. Henceforth she must be known as Miss Warwick, dropping the old name with the old life. He would place her for a year in a boarding-school at Charleston, after which she would take her place as the mistress of his house. Having imparted this information, he took his sister for a drive through the town. There for the first time Rena saw great ships, which, her brother told her, sailed across the mighty ocean to distant lands, whose flags he pointed out drooping lazily at the mastheads. The business portion of the town had "an ancient and fishlike smell," and most of the trade seemed to be in cotton and naval stores and products of the sea. The wharves were piled high with cotton bales, and there were acres of barrels of resin and pitch and tar and spirits of turpentine. The market, a long, low, wooden structure, in the middle of the principal street, was filled with a mass of people of all shades, from blue-black to Saxon blonde, gabbling and gesticulating over piles of oysters and clams and freshly caught fish of varied hue. By ten o'clock the sun was beating down so fiercely that the glitter of the white, sandy streets dazzled and pained the eyes unaccustomed to it, and Rena was glad to be driven back to the hotel. The travelers left together on an early afternoon train.

Thus for the time being was severed the last tie that bound Rena to her narrow past, and for some time to come the places and the people who had known her once were to know her no more.

Some few weeks later, Mis' Molly called upon old Judge Straight with reference to the taxes on her property.

"Your son came in to see me the other day," he remarked. "He seems to have got along."

"Oh, yes, judge, he 's done fine, John has; an' he 's took his sister away with him."

"Ah!" exclaimed the judge. Then after a pause he added, "I hope she may do as well."

"Thank you, sir," she said, with a curtsy, as she rose to go. "We 've always knowed that you were our friend and wished us well."

The judge looked after her as she walked away. Her bearing had a touch of timidity, a shade of affectation, and yet a certain pathetic dignity.

"It is a pity," he murmured, with a sigh, "that men cannot select their mothers. My young friend John has builded, whether wisely or not, very well; but he has come back into the old life and carried away a part of it, and I fear that this addition will weaken the structure."

V

THE TOURNAMENT

THE ANNUAL tournament of the Clarence Social Club was about to begin. The county fair-ground, where all was in readiness, sparkled with the youth and beauty of the town, standing here and there under the trees in animated groups, or moving toward the seats from which the pageant might be witnessed. A quarter of a mile of the race track, to right and left of the judges' stand, had been laid off for the lists. Opposite the grand stand, which occupied a considerable part of this distance, a dozen uprights had been erected at measured intervals. Projecting several feet over the track from each of these uprights was an iron crossbar, from which an iron hook depended. Between the uprights stout posts were planted, of such a height that their tops could be easily reached by a swinging sword-cut from a mounted rider passing upon the track. The influence of Walter Scott was strong upon the old South. The South before the war was essentially feudal, and Scott's novels of chivalry appealed forcefully to the feudal heart. During the month preceding the Clarence tournament, the local bookseller had closed out his entire stock of "Ivanhoe," consisting of five copies, and had taken orders for seven copies more. The tournament scene in this popular novel furnished the model after which these bloodless imitations of the ancient passages-at-arms were conducted, with such variations as were required to adapt them to a different age and civilization.

The best people gradually filled the grand stand, while the poorer white and colored folks found seats outside, upon what would now be known as the "bleachers," or stood alongside the lists. The knights, masquerading in fanciful costumes, in which bright-colored garments, gilt paper, and cardboard took the place of knightly harness, were mounted on spirited horses. Most of them were gathered at one end of the lists, while others practiced their steeds upon the unoccupied portion of the race track.

The judges entered the grand stand, and one of them, after

looking at his watch, gave a signal. Immediately a herald, wearing a bright yellow sash, blew a loud blast upon a bugle, and, big with the importance of his office, galloped wildly down the lists. An attendant on horseback busied himself hanging upon each of the pendent hooks an iron ring, of some two inches in diameter, while another, on foot, placed on top of each of the shorter posts a wooden ball some four inches through.

"It 's my first tournament," observed a lady near the front of the grand stand, leaning over and addressing John Warwick, who was seated in the second row, in company with a very handsome girl. "It is somewhat different from Ashby-de-la-Zouch."

"It is the renaissance of chivalry, Mrs. Newberry," replied the young lawyer, "and, like any other renaissance, it must adapt itself to new times and circumstances. For instance, when we build a Greek portico, having no Pentelic marble near at hand, we use a pine-tree, one of nature's columns, which Grecian art at its best could only copy and idealize. Our knights are not weighted down with heavy armor, but much more appropriately attired, for a day like this, in costumes that recall the picturesqueness, without the discomfort, of the old knightly harness. For an iron-headed lance we use a wooden substitute, with which we transfix rings instead of hearts; while our trusty blades hew their way through wooden blocks instead of through flesh and blood. It is a South Carolina renaissance which has points of advantage over the tournaments of the olden time."

"I 'm afraid, Mr. Warwick," said the lady, "that you 're the least bit heretical about our chivalry—or else you 're a little too deep for me."

"The last would be impossible, Mrs. Newberry; and I 'm sure our chivalry has proved its valor on many a hard-fought field. The spirit of a thing, after all, is what counts; and what is lacking here? We have the lists, the knights, the prancing steeds, the trial of strength and skill. If our knights do not run the physical risks of Ashby-de-la-Zouch, they have all the mental stimulus. Wounded vanity will take the place of wounded limbs, and there will be broken hopes in lieu of broken heads. How many hearts in yonder group of gallant horsemen beat high with hope! How many possible Queens of Love and Beauty are in this group of fair faces that surround us!"

The lady was about to reply, when the bugle sounded again, and the herald dashed swiftly back upon his prancing steed to the waiting group of riders. The horsemen formed three abreast, and rode down the lists in orderly array. As they passed the grand stand, each was conscious of the battery of bright eyes turned upon him, and each gave by his bearing some idea of his ability to stand fire from such weapons. One horse pranced proudly, another caracoled with grace. One rider fidgeted nervously, another trembled and looked the other way. Each horseman carried in his hand a long wooden lance and wore at his side a cavalry sabre, of which there were plenty to be had since the war, at small expense. Several left the ranks and drew up momentarily beside the grand stand, where they took from fair hands a glove or a flower, which was pinned upon the rider's breast or fastened upon his hat—a ribbon or a veil, which was tied about the lance like a pennon, but far enough from the point not to interfere with the usefulness of the weapon.

As the troop passed the lower end of the grand stand, a horse, excited by the crowd, became somewhat unmanageable, and in the effort to curb him, the rider dropped his lance. The prancing animal reared, brought one of his hoofs down upon the fallen lance with considerable force, and sent a broken piece of it flying over the railing opposite the grand stand, into the middle of a group of spectators standing there. The flying fragment was dodged by those who saw it coming, but brought up with a resounding thwack against the head of a colored man in the second row, who stood watching the grand stand with an eager and curious gaze. He rubbed his head ruefully, and made a good-natured response to the chaffing of his neighbors, who, seeing no great harm done, made witty and original remarks about the advantage of being black upon occasions where one's skull was exposed to danger. Finding that the blow had drawn blood, the young man took out a red bandana handkerchief and tied it around his head, meantime letting his eye roam over the faces in the grand stand, as though in search of some one that he expected or hoped to find there.

The knights, having reached the end of the lists, now turned and rode back in open order, with such skillful horsemanship as to evoke a storm of applause from the spectators. The ladies in the grand stand waved their handkerchiefs vigorously, and the men clapped their hands. The beautiful girl seated by Warwick's side accidentally let a little square of white lace-trimmed linen slip from her hand. It fluttered lightly over the railing, and, buoyed up by the air, settled slowly toward the lists. A young rider in the approaching rear rank saw the handkerchief fall, and darting swiftly forward, caught it on the point of his lance ere it touched the ground. He drew up his horse and made a movement as though to extend the handkerchief toward the lady, who was blushing profusely at the attention she had attracted by her carelessness. The rider hesitated a moment, glanced interrogatively at Warwick, and receiving a smile in return, tied the handkerchief around the middle of his lance and quickly rejoined his comrades at the head of the lists.

The young man with the bandage round his head, on the benches across the lists, had forced his way to the front row and was leaning against the railing. His restless eye was attracted by the falling handkerchief, and his face, hitherto anxious, suddenly lit up with animation.

"Yas, suh, yas, suh, it 's her!" he muttered softly. "It 's Miss Rena, sho 's you bawn. She looked lack a' angel befo', but now, up dere 'mongs' all dem rich, fine folks, she looks lack a whole flock er angels. Dey ain' one er dem ladies w'at could hol' a candle ter her. I wonder w'at dat man 's gwine ter do wid her handkercher? I s'pose he 's her gent'eman now. I wonder ef she 'd know me er speak ter me ef she seed me? I reckon she would, spite er her gittin' up so in de worl'; fer she wuz alluz good ter ev'ybody, an' dat let even *me* in," he concluded with a sigh.

"Who is the lady, Tryon?" asked one of the young men, addressing the knight who had taken the handkerchief.

"A Miss Warwick," replied the knight pleasantly, "Miss Rowena Warwick, the lawyer's sister."

"I did n't know he had a sister," rejoined the first speaker.

"I envy you your lady. There are six Rebeccas and eight Rowenas of my own acquaintance in the grand stand, but she throws them all into the shade. She has n't been here long, surely; I have n't seen her before."

"She has been away at school; she came only last night," returned the knight of the crimson sash, briefly. He was already beginning to feel a proprietary interest in the lady whose token he wore, and did not care to discuss her with a casual acquaintance.

The herald sounded the charge. A rider darted out from the group and galloped over the course. As he passed under each ring, he tried to catch it on the point of his lance,—a feat which made the management of the horse with the left hand necessary, and required a true eye and a steady arm. The rider captured three of the twelve rings, knocked three others off the hooks, and left six undisturbed. Turning at the end of the lists, he took the lance with the reins in the left hand and drew his sword with the right. He then rode back over the course, cutting at the wooden balls upon the posts. Of these he clove one in twain, to use the parlance of chivalry, and knocked two others off their supports. His performance was greeted with a liberal measure of applause, for which he bowed in smiling acknowledgment as he took his place among the riders.

Again the herald's call sounded, and the tourney went forward. Rider after rider, with varying skill, essayed his fortune with lance and sword. Some took a liberal proportion of the rings; others merely knocked them over the boundaries, where they were collected by agile little negro boys and handed back to the attendants. A balking horse caused the spectators much amusement and his rider no little chagrin.

The lady who had dropped the handkerchief kept her eye upon the knight who had bound it round his lance. "Who is he, John?" she asked the gentleman beside her.

"That, my dear Rowena, is my good friend and client, George Tryon, of North Carolina. If he had been a stranger, I should have said that he took a liberty; but as things stand, we ought to regard it as a compliment. The incident is quite in accord with the customs of chivalry. If George were but masked and you were veiled, we should have a romantic situation,—you the mysterious damsel in distress, he the unknown champion. The parallel, my dear, might not be so hard to draw, even as things are. But look, it is his turn now; I 'll wager that he makes a good run."

"I 'll take you up on that, Mr. Warwick," said Mrs. Newberry from behind, who seemed to have a very keen ear for whatever Warwick said.

Rena's eyes were fastened on her knight, so that she might lose no single one of his movements. As he rode down the lists, more than one woman found him pleasant to look upon. He was a tall, fair young man, with gray eyes, and a frank, open face. He wore a slight mustache, and when he smiled, showed a set of white and even teeth. He was mounted on a very handsome and spirited bay mare, was clad in a picturesque costume, of which velvet knee-breeches and a crimson scarf were the most conspicuous features, and displayed a marked skill in horsemanship. At the blast of the bugle his horse started forward, and, after the first few rods, settled into an even gallop. Tryon's lance, held truly and at the right angle, captured the first ring, then the second and third. His coolness and steadiness seemed not at all disturbed by the applause which followed, and one by one the remaining rings slipped over the point of his lance, until at the end he had taken every one of the twelve. Holding the lance with its booty of captured rings in his left hand, together with the bridle rein, he drew his sabre with the right and rode back over the course. His horse moved like clockwork, his eye was true and his hand steady. Three of the wooden balls fell from the posts, split fairly in the middle, while from the fourth he sliced off a goodly piece and left the remainder standing in its place.

This performance, by far the best up to this point, and barely escaping perfection, elicited a storm of applause. The rider was not so well known to the townspeople as some of the other participants, and his name passed from mouth to mouth in answer to numerous inquiries. The girl whose token he had worn also became an object of renewed interest, because of the result to her in case the knight should prove victor in the contest, of which there could now scarcely be a doubt; for but three riders remained, and it was very improbable that any one of them would excel the last. Wagers for the remainder of the tourney stood anywhere from five, and even from ten to one, in favor of the knight of the crimson sash, and when the last course had been run, his backers were jubilant. No one of those following him had displayed anything like equal skill.

The herald now blew his bugle and declared the tournament closed. The judges put their heads together for a moment. The bugle sounded again, and the herald announced in a loud voice that Sir George Tryon, having taken the greatest number of rings and split the largest number of balls, was proclaimed victor in the tournament and entitled to the flowery chaplet of victory.

Tryon, having bowed repeatedly in response to the liberal applause, advanced to the judges' stand and received the trophy from the hands of the chief judge, who exhorted him to wear the garland worthily, and to yield it only to a better man.

"It will be your privilege, Sir George," announced the judge, "as the chief reward of your valor, to select from the assembled beauty of Clarence the lady whom you wish to honor, to whom we will all do homage as the Queen of Love and Beauty."

Tryon took the wreath and bowed his thanks. Then placing the trophy on the point of his lance, he spoke earnestly for a moment to the herald, and rode past the grand stand, from which there was another outburst of applause. Returning upon his tracks, the knight of the crimson sash paused before the group where Warwick and his sister sat, and lowered the wreath thrice before the lady whose token he had won.

"Oyez! Oyez!" cried the herald; "Sir George Tryon, the victor in the tournament, has chosen Miss Rowena Warwick as the Queen of Love and Beauty, and she will be crowned at the feast to-night and receive the devoirs of all true knights."

The fair-ground was soon covered with scattered groups of the spectators of the tournament. In one group a vanquished knight explained in elaborate detail why it was that he had failed to win the wreath. More than one young woman wondered why some one of the home young men could not have taken the honors, or, if the stranger must win them, why he could not have selected some belle of the town as Queen of

Love and Beauty instead of this upstart girl who had blown into the town over night, as one might say.

Warwick and his sister, standing under a spreading elm, held a little court of their own. A dozen gentlemen and several ladies had sought an introduction before Tryon came up.

"I suppose John would have a right to call me out, Miss Warwick," said Tryon, when he had been formally introduced and had shaken hands with Warwick's sister, "for taking liberties with the property and name of a lady to whom I had not had an introduction; but I know John so well that you seemed like an old acquaintance; and when I saw you, and recalled your name, which your brother had mentioned more than once, I felt instinctively that you ought to be the queen. I entered my name only yesterday, merely to swell the number and make the occasion more interesting. These fellows have been practicing for a month, and I had no hope of winning. I should have been satisfied, indeed, if I had n't made myself ridiculous; but when you dropped your handkerchief, I felt a sudden inspiration; and as soon as I had tied it upon my lance, victory perched upon my saddle-bow, guided my lance and sword, and rings and balls went down before me like chaff before the wind. Oh, it was a great inspiration, Miss Warwick!"

Rena, for it was our Patesville acquaintance fresh from boarding-school, colored deeply at this frank and fervid flattery, and could only murmur an inarticulate reply. Her year of instruction, while distinctly improving her mind and manners, had scarcely prepared her for so sudden an elevation into a grade of society to which she had hitherto been a stranger. She was not without a certain courage, however, and her brother, who remained at her side, helped her over the most difficult situations.

"We 'll forgive you, George," replied Warwick, "if you 'll come home to luncheon with us."

"I 'm mighty sorry—awfully sorry," returned Tryon, with evident regret, "but I have another engagement, which I can scarcely break, even by the command of royalty. At what time shall I call for Miss Warwick this evening? I believe that privilege is mine, along with the other honors and rewards of victory,—unless she is bound to some one else."

"She is entirely free," replied Warwick. "Come as early as you like, and I 'll talk to you until she 's ready."

Tryon bowed himself away, and after a number of gentlemen and a few ladies had paid their respects to the Queen of Love and Beauty, and received an introduction to her, Warwick signaled to the servant who had his carriage in charge, and was soon driving homeward with his sister. No one of the party noticed a young negro, with a handkerchief bound around his head, who followed them until the carriage turned into the gate and swept up the wide drive that led to Warwick's doorstep.

"Well, Rena," said Warwick, when they found themselves alone, "you have arrived. Your début into society is a little more spectacular than I should have wished, but we must rise to the occasion and make the most of it. You are winning the first fruits of your opportunity. You are the most envied woman in Clarence at this particular moment, and, unless I am mistaken, will be the most admired at the ball to-night."

VI

THE QUEEN OF LOVE AND BEAUTY

SHORTLY after luncheon, Rena had a visitor in the person of Mrs. Newberry, a vivacious young widow of the town, who proffered her services to instruct Rena in the etiquette of the annual ball.

"Now, my dear," said Mrs. Newberry, "the first thing to do is to get your coronation robe ready. It simply means a gown with a long train. You have a lovely white waist. Get right into my buggy, and we 'll go down town to get the cloth, take it over to Mrs. Marshall's, and have her run you up a skirt this afternoon."

Rena placed herself unreservedly in the hands of Mrs. Newberry, who introduced her to the best dressmaker of the town, a woman of much experience in such affairs, who improvised during the afternoon a gown suited to the occasion. Mrs. Marshall had made more than a dozen ball dresses during the preceding month; being a wise woman and understanding her business thoroughly, she had made each one of them so that with a few additional touches it might serve for the Queen of Love and Beauty. This was her first direct order for the specific garment.

Tryon escorted Rena to the ball, which was held in the principal public hall of the town, and attended by all the best people. The champion still wore the costume of the morning, in place of evening dress, save that long stockings and dancing-pumps had taken the place of riding-boots.

Rena went through the ordeal very creditably. Her shyness was palpable, but it was saved from awkwardness by her native grace and good sense. She made up in modesty what she lacked in aplomb. Her months in school had not eradicated a certain self-consciousness born of her secret. The brain-cells never lose the impressions of youth, and Rena's Patesville life was not far enough removed to have lost its distinctness of outline. Of the two, the present was more of a dream, the past was the more vivid reality. At school she had learned something from books and not a little from observation. She had been able to compare herself with other girls, and to see wherein she excelled or fell short of them. With a sincere desire for improvement, and a wish to please her brother and do him credit, she had sought to make the most of her opportunities. Building upon a foundation of innate taste and intelligence, she had acquired much of the self-possession which comes from a knowledge of correct standards of deportment. She had moreover learned without difficulty, for it suited her disposition, to keep silence when she could not speak to advantage. A certain necessary reticence about the past added strength to a natural reserve. Thus equipped, she held her own very well in the somewhat trying ordeal of the ball, at which the fiction of queenship and the attendant ceremonies, which were pretty and graceful, made her the most conspicuous figure. Few of those who watched her move with easy grace through the measures of the dance could have guessed how nearly her heart was in her mouth during much of the time.

"You 're doing splendidly, my dear," said Mrs. Newberry, who had constituted herself Rena's chaperone.

"I trust your Gracious Majesty is pleased with the homage of your devoted subjects," said Tryon, who spent much of his time by her side and kept up the character of knight in his speech and manner.

"Very much," replied the Queen of Love and Beauty, with a somewhat tired smile. It *was* pleasant, but she would be glad, she thought, when it was all over.

"Keep up your courage," whispered her brother. "You are not only queen, but the belle of the ball. I am proud of you. A dozen women here would give a year off the latter end of life to be in your shoes to-night."

Rena felt immensely relieved when the hour arrived at which she could take her departure, which was to be the signal for the breaking-up of the ball. She was driven home in Tryon's carriage, her brother accompanying them. The night was warm, and the drive homeward under the starlight, in the open carriage, had a soothing effect upon Rena's excited nerves. The calm restfulness of the night, the cool blue depths of the unclouded sky, the solemn croaking of the frogs in a distant swamp, were much more in harmony with her nature than the crowded brilliancy of the ball-room. She closed her eyes, and, leaning back in the carriage, thought of her mother, who she wished might have seen her daughter this night. A momentary pang of homesickness pierced her tender heart, and she furtively wiped away the tears that came into her eyes.

"Good-night, fair Queen!" exclaimed Tryon, breaking into her reverie as the carriage rolled up to the doorstep, "and let your loyal subject kiss your hand in token of his fealty. May your Majesty never abdicate her throne, and may she ever count me her humble servant and devoted knight."

"And now, sister," said Warwick, when Tryon had been driven away, "now that the masquerade is over, let us to sleep, and to-morrow take up the serious business of life. Your day has been a glorious success!"

He put his arm around her and gave her a kiss and a brotherly hug.

"It is a dream," she murmured sleepily, "only a dream. I am Cinderella before the clock has struck. Good-night, dear John."

"Good-night, Rowena."

VII

'MID NEW SURROUNDINGS

WARWICK'S residence was situated in the outskirts of the town. It was a fine old plantation house, built in colonial times, with a stately colonnade, wide verandas, and long windows with Venetian blinds. It was painted white, and stood back several rods from the street, in a charming setting of palmettoes, magnolias, and flowering shrubs. Rena had always thought her mother's house large, but now it seemed cramped and narrow, in comparison with this roomy mansion. The furniture was old-fashioned and massive. The great brass andirons on the wide hearth stood like sentinels proclaiming and guarding the dignity of the family. The spreading antlers on the wall testified to a mighty hunter in some past generation. The portraits of Warwick's wife's ancestors—high-featured, proud men and women, dressed in the fashions of a bygone age—looked down from tarnished gilt frames. It was all very novel to her, and very impressive. When she ate off china, with silver knives and forks that had come down as heirlooms, escaping somehow the ravages and exigencies of the war time,—Warwick told her afterwards how he had buried them out of reach of friend or foe,—she thought that her brother must be wealthy, and she felt very proud of him and of her opportunity. The servants, of whom there were several in the house, treated her with a deference to which her eight months in school had only partly accustomed her. At school she had been one of many to be served, and had herself been held to obedience. Here, for the first time in her life, she was mistress, and tasted the sweets of power.

The household consisted of her brother and herself, a cook, a coachman, a nurse, and her brother's little son Albert. The child, with a fine instinct, had put out his puny arms to Rena at first sight, and she had clasped the little man to her bosom with a motherly caress. She had always loved weak creatures. Kittens and puppies had ever found a welcome and a meal at Rena's hands, only to be chased away by Mis' Molly, who had

had a wider experience. No shiftless poor white, no half-witted or hungry negro, had ever gone unfed from Mis' Molly's kitchen door if Rena were there to hear his plaint. Little Albert was pale and sickly when she came, but soon bloomed again in the sunshine of her care, and was happy only in her presence. Warwick found pleasure in their growing love for each other, and was glad to perceive that the child formed a living link to connect her with his home.

"Dat chile sutt'nly do lub Miss Rena, an' dat 's a fac', sho 's you bawn," remarked 'Lissa the cook to Mimy the nurse one day. "You 'll get yo' nose put out er j'int, ef you don't min'."

"I ain't frettin', honey," laughed the nurse good-naturedly. She was not at all jealous. She had the same wages as before, and her labors were materially lightened by the aunt's attention to the child. This gave Mimy much more time to flirt with Tom the coachman.

It was a source of much gratification to Warwick that his sister seemed to adapt herself so easily to the new conditions. Her graceful movements, the quiet elegance with which she wore even the simplest gown, the easy authoritativeness with which she directed the servants, were to him proofs of superior quality, and he felt correspondingly proud of her. His feeling for her was something more than brotherly love,—he was quite conscious that there were degrees in brotherly love, and that if she had been homely or stupid, he would never have disturbed her in the stagnant life of the house behind the cedars. There had come to him from some source, down the stream of time, a rill of the Greek sense of proportion, of fitness, of beauty, which is indeed but proportion embodied, the perfect adaptation of means to ends. He had perceived, more clearly than she could have appreciated it at that time, the undeveloped elements of discord between Rena and her former life. He had imagined her lending grace and charm to his own household. Still another motive, a purely psychological one, had more or less consciously influenced him. He had no fear that the family secret would ever be discovered,—he had taken his precautions too thoroughly, he thought, for that; and yet he could not but feel, at times, that if peradventure—it was a conceivable hypothesis—it should become known, his fine social position would collapse like a house of cards. Because of this knowledge, which the world around him did not possess, he had felt now and then a certain sense of loneliness; and there was a measure of relief in having about him one who knew his past, and yet whose knowledge, because of their common interest, would not interfere with his present or jeopardize his future. For he had always been, in a figurative sense, a naturalized foreigner in the world of wide opportunity, and Rena was one of his old compatriots, whom he was glad to welcome into the populous loneliness of his adopted country.

VIII

THE COURTSHIP

IN A FEW WEEKS the echoes of the tournament died away, and Rena's life settled down into a pleasant routine, which she found much more comfortable than her recent spectacular prominence. Her queenship, while not entirely forgiven by the ladies of the town, had gained for her a temporary social prominence. Among her own sex, Mrs. Newberry proved a warm and enthusiastic friend. Rumor whispered that the lively young widow would not be unwilling to console Warwick in the loneliness of the old colonial mansion, to which his sister was a most excellent medium of approach. Whether this was true or not it is unnecessary to inquire, for it is no part of this story, except as perhaps indicating why Mrs. Newberry played the part of the female friend, without whom no woman is ever launched successfully in a small and conservative society. Her brother's standing gave her the right of social entry; the tournament opened wide the door, and Mrs. Newberry performed the ceremony of introduction. Rena had many visitors during the month following the tournament, and might have made her choice from among a dozen suitors; but among them all, her knight of the handkerchief found most favor.

George Tryon had come to Clarence a few months before upon business connected with the settlement of his grandfather's estate. A rather complicated litigation had grown up around the affair, various phases of which had kept Tryon almost constantly in the town. He had placed matters in Warwick's hands, and had formed a decided friendship for his attorney, for whom he felt a frank admiration. Tryon was only twenty-three, and his friend's additional five years, supplemented by a certain professional gravity, commanded a great deal of respect from the younger man. When Tryon had known Warwick for a week, he had been ready to swear by him. Indeed, Warwick was a man for whom most people formed a liking at first sight. To this power of attraction he owed most of his success—first with Judge Straight, of Patesville, then with the lawyer whose office he had entered at Clarence, with the woman who became his wife, and with the clients for whom he transacted business. Tryon would have maintained against all comers that Warwick was the finest fellow in the world. When he met Warwick's sister, the foundation for admiration had already been laid. If Rena had proved to be a maiden lady of uncertain age and doubtful personal attractiveness, Tryon would probably have found in her a most excellent lady, worthy of all respect and esteem, and would have treated her with profound deference and sedulous courtesy. When she proved to be a young and handsome woman, of the type that he admired most, he was capable of any degree of infatuation. His mother had for a long time wanted him to marry the orphan daughter of an old friend, a vivacious blonde, who worshiped him. He had felt friendly towards her, but had shrunk from matrimony. He did not want her badly enough to give up his freedom. The war had interfered with his education, and though fairly well instructed, he had never attended college. In his own opinion, he ought to see something of the world, and have his youthful fling. Later on, when he got ready to settle down, if Blanche were still in the humor, they might marry, and sink to the humdrum level of other old married people. The fact that Blanche Leary was visiting his mother during his unexpectedly long absence had not operated at all to hasten his return to North Carolina. He had been having a very good time at Clarence, and, at the distance of several hundred miles, was safe for the time being from any immediate danger of marriage.

With Rena's advent, however, he had seen life through different glasses. His heart had thrilled at first sight of this tall girl, with the ivory complexion, the rippling brown hair, and the inscrutable eyes. When he became better acquainted with her, he liked to think that her thoughts centred mainly in himself; and in this he was not far wrong. He discovered that she had a short upper lip, and what seemed to him an eminently kissable mouth. After he had dined twice at Warwick's, subsequently to the tournament,—his lucky choice of Rena had put him at once upon a household footing with the family,—his views of marriage changed entirely. It now seemed to him the duty, as well as the high and holy privilege of a young man, to marry and manfully to pay his debt to society. When in Rena's presence, he could not imagine how he had ever contemplated the possibility of marriage with Blanche Leary,—she was utterly, entirely, and hopelessly unsuited to him. For a fair man of vivacious temperament, this stately dark girl was the ideal mate. Even his mother would admit this, if she could only see Rena. To win this beautiful girl for his wife would be a worthy task. He had crowned her Queen of Love and Beauty; since then she had ascended the throne of his heart. He would make her queen of his home and mistress of his life.

To Rena this brief month's courtship came as a new education. Not only had this fair young man crowned her queen, and honored her above all the ladies in town; but since then he had waited assiduously upon her, had spoken softly to her, had looked at her with shining eyes, and had sought to be alone with her. The time soon came when to touch his hand in greeting sent a thrill through her frame,—a time when she listened for his footstep and was happy in his presence. He had been bold enough at the tournament; he had since become somewhat bashful and constrained. He must be in love, she thought, and wondered how soon he would speak. If it were so sweet to walk with him in the garden, or along the shaded streets, to sit with him, to feel the touch of his hand, what happiness would it not be to hear him say that he loved her—to bear his name, to live with him always. To be thus loved and honored by this handsome young man,—she could hardly believe it possible. He would never speak—he would discover her secret and withdraw. She turned pale at the thought,—ah, God! something would happen,—it was too good to be true. The Prince would never try on the glass slipper.

Tryon first told his love for Rena one summer evening on their way home from church. They were walking in the moonlight along the quiet street, which, but for their presence, seemed quite deserted.

"Miss Warwick—Rowena," he said, clasping with his right hand the hand that rested on his left arm, "I love you! Do you—love me?"

To Rena this simple avowal came with much greater force than a more formal declaration could have had. It appealed to her own simple nature. Indeed, few women at such a moment criticise the form in which the most fateful words of life—but one—are spoken. Words, while pleasant, are really superfluous. Her whispered "Yes" spoke volumes.

They walked on past the house, along the country road into which the street soon merged. When they returned, an hour later, they found Warwick seated on the piazza, in a rocking-chair, smoking a fragrant cigar.

"Well, children," he observed with mock severity, "you are late in getting home from church. The sermon must have been extremely long."

"We have been attending an after-meeting," replied Tryon joyfully, "and have been discussing an old text, 'Little children, love one another,' and its corollary, 'It is not good for man to live alone.' John, I am the happiest man alive. Your sister has promised to marry me. I should like to shake my brother's hand."

Never does one feel so strongly the universal brotherhood of man as when one loves some other fellow's sister. Warwick sprang from his chair and clasped Tryon's extended hand with real emotion. He knew of no man whom he would have preferred to Tryon as a husband for his sister.

"My dear George—my dear sister," he exclaimed, "I am very, very glad. I wish you every happiness. My sister is the most fortunate of women."

"And I am the luckiest of men," cried Tryon.

"I wish you every happiness," repeated Warwick; adding, with a touch of solemnity, as a certain thought, never far distant, occurred to him, "I hope that neither of you may ever regret your choice."

Thus placed upon the footing of an accepted lover, Tryon's visits to the house became more frequent. He wished to fix a time for the marriage, but at this point Rena developed a strange reluctance.

"Can we not love each other for a while?" she asked. "To be engaged is a pleasure that comes but once; it would be a pity to cut it too short."

"It is a pleasure that I would cheerfully dispense with," he replied, "for the certainty of possession. I want you all to myself, and all the time. Things might happen. If I should die, for instance, before I married you"—

"Oh, don't suppose such awful things," she cried, putting her hand over his mouth.

He held it there and kissed it until she pulled it away.

"I should consider," he resumed, completing the sentence, "that my life had been a failure."

"If I should die," she murmured, "I should die happy in the knowledge that you had loved me."

"In three weeks," he went on, "I shall have finished my business in Clarence, and there will be but one thing to keep me here. When shall it be? I must take you home with me."

"I will let you know," she replied, with a troubled sigh, "in a week from to-day."

"I 'll call your attention to the subject every day in the mean time," he asserted. "I should n't like you to forget it."

Rena's shrinking from the irrevocable step of marriage was due to a simple and yet complex cause. Stated baldly, it was the consciousness of her secret; the complexity arose out of the various ways in which it seemed to bear upon her future. Our lives are so bound up with those of our fellow men that the slightest departure from the beaten path involves a multiplicity of small adjustments. It had not been difficult for Rena to conform her speech, her manners, and in a measure her modes of thought, to those of the people around her; but when this readjustment went beyond mere externals and concerned the vital issues of life, the secret that oppressed her took on a more serious aspect, with tragic possibilities. A discursive imagination was not one of her characteristics, or the danger of a marriage of which perfect frankness was not a condition might well have presented itself before her heart had become involved. Under the influence of doubt and fear acting upon love, the invisible bar to happiness glowed with a lambent flame that threatened dire disaster.

"Would he have loved me at all," she asked herself, "if he had known the story of my past? Or, having loved me, could he blame me now for what I cannot help?"

There were two shoals in the channel of her life, upon either of which her happiness might go to shipwreck. Since leaving the house behind the cedars, where she had been brought into the world without her own knowledge or consent, and had first drawn the breath of life by the involuntary contraction of certain muscles, Rena had learned, in a short time, many things; but she was yet to learn that the innocent suffer with the guilty, and feel the punishment the more keenly because unmerited. She had yet to learn that the old Mosaic formula, "The sins of the fathers shall be visited upon the children," was graven more indelibly upon the heart of the race than upon the tables of Sinai.

But would her lover still love her, if he knew all? She had read some of the novels in the bookcase in her mother's hall, and others at boarding-school. She had read that love was a conqueror, that neither life nor death, nor creed nor caste, could stay his triumphant course. Her secret was no legal bar to their union. If Rena could forget the secret, and Tryon should never know it, it would be no obstacle to their happiness. But Rena felt, with a sinking of the heart, that happiness was not a matter of law or of fact, but lay entirely within the domain of sentiment. We are happy when we think ourselves happy, and with a strange perversity we often differ from others with regard to what should constitute our happiness. Rena's secret was the worm in the bud, the skeleton in the closet.

"He says that he loves me. He *does* love me. Would he love me, if he knew?" She stood before an oval mirror brought from France by one of Warwick's wife's ancestors, and regarded her image with a coldly critical eye. She was as little vain as any of her sex who are endowed with beauty. She tried to place herself, in thus passing upon her own claims to consideration, in the hostile attitude of society toward her hidden disability. There was no mark upon her brow to brand her as less pure, less innocent, less desirable, less worthy to be loved, than these proud women of the past who had admired themselves in this old mirror.

"I think a man might love me for myself," she murmured pathetically, "and if he loved me truly, that he would marry me. If he would not marry me, then it would be because he did n't love me. I 'll tell George my secret. If he leaves me, then he does not love me."

But this resolution vanished into thin air before it was fully formulated. The secret was not hers alone; it involved her brother's position, to whom she owed everything, and in less degree the future of her little nephew, whom she had learned to love so well. She had the choice of but two courses of action, to marry Tryon or to dismiss him. The thought that she might lose him made him seem only more dear; to think that he might leave her made her sick at heart. In one week she was bound to give him an answer; he was more likely to ask for it at their next meeting.

IX

DOUBTS AND FEARS

RENA'S heart was too heavy with these misgivings for her to keep them to herself. On the morning after the conversation with Tryon in which she had promised him an answer within a week, she went into her brother's study, where he usually spent an hour after breakfast before going to his office. He looked up amiably from the book before him and read trouble in her face.

"Well, Rena, dear," he asked with a smile, "what 's the matter? Is there anything you want—money, or what? I should like to have Aladdin's lamp—though I 'd hardly need it—that you might have no wish unsatisfied."

He had found her very backward in asking for things that she needed. Generous with his means, he thought nothing too good for her. Her success had gratified his pride, and justified his course in taking her under his protection.

"Thank you, John. You give me already more than I need. It is something else, John. George wants me to say when I will marry him. I am afraid to marry him, without telling him. If he should find out afterwards, he might cast me off, or cease to love me. If he did not know it, I should be forever thinking of what he would do if he *should* find it out; or, if I should die without his having learned it, I should not rest easy in my grave for thinking of what he would have done if he *had* found it out."

Warwick's smile gave place to a grave expression at this somewhat comprehensive statement. He rose and closed the door carefully, lest some one of the servants might overhear the conversation. More liberally endowed than Rena with imagination, and not without a vein of sentiment, he had nevertheless a practical side that outweighed them both. With him, the problem that oppressed his sister had been in the main a matter of argument, of self-conviction. Once persuaded that he had certain rights, or ought to have them, by virtue of the laws of nature, in defiance of the customs of mankind, he had promptly sought to enjoy them. This he had been able to do by simply concealing his antecedents and making the most of his opportunities, with no troublesome qualms of conscience whatever. But he had already perceived, in their brief intercourse, that Rena's emotions, while less easily stirred, touched a deeper note than his, and dwelt upon it with greater intensity than if they had been spread over the larger field to which a more ready sympathy would have supplied so many points of access;—hers was a deep and silent current flowing between the narrow walls of a self-contained life, his the spreading river that ran through a pleasant landscape. Warwick's imagination, however, enabled him to put himself in touch with her mood and recognize its bearings upon her conduct. He would have preferred her taking the practical point of view, to bring her round to which he perceived would be a matter of diplomacy.

"How long have these weighty thoughts been troubling your small head?" he asked with assumed lightness.

"Since he asked me last night to name our wedding day."

"My dear child," continued Warwick, "you take too tragic a view of life. Marriage is a reciprocal arrangement, by which the contracting parties give love for love, care for keeping, faith for faith. It is a matter of the future, not of the past. What a poor soul it is that has not some secret chamber, sacred to itself; where one can file away the things others have no right to know, as well as things that one himself would fain forget! We are under no moral obligation to inflict upon others the history of our past mistakes, our wayward thoughts, our secret sins, our desperate hopes, or our heart-breaking disappointments. Still less are we bound to bring out from this secret chamber the dusty record of our ancestry.

'Let the dead past bury its dead.'

George Tryon loves you for yourself alone; it is not your ancestors that he seeks to marry."

"But would he marry me if he knew?" she persisted.

Warwick paused for reflection. He would have preferred to argue the question in a general way, but felt the necessity of satisfying her scruples, as far as might be. He had liked Tryon from the very beginning of their acquaintance. In all their intercourse, which had been very close for several months, he had been impressed by the young man's sunny temper, his straightforwardness, his intellectual honesty. Tryon's deference to Warwick as the elder man had very naturally proved an attraction. Whether this friendship would have stood the test of utter frankness about his own past was a merely academic speculation with which Warwick did not trouble himself. With his sister the question had evidently become a matter of conscience,—a difficult subject with which to deal in a person of Rena's temperament.

"My dear sister," he replied, "why should he know? We have n't asked him for his pedigree; we don't care to know it. If he cares for ours, he should ask for it, and it would then be time enough to raise the question. You love him, I imagine, and wish to make him happy?"

It is the highest wish of the woman who loves. The enamored man seeks his own happiness; the loving woman finds no sacrifice too great for the loved one. The fiction of chivalry made man serve woman; the fact of human nature makes woman happiest when serving where she loves.

"Yes, oh, yes," Rena exclaimed with fervor, clasping her hands unconsciously. "I 'm afraid he 'd be unhappy if he knew, and it would make me miserable to think him unhappy."

"Well, then," said Warwick, "suppose we should tell him our secret and put ourselves in his power, and that he should then conclude that he could n't marry you? Do you imagine he would be any happier than he is now, or than if he should never know?"

Ah, no! she could not think so. One could not tear love out of one's heart without pain and suffering.

There was a knock at the door. Warwick opened it to the nurse, who stood with little Albert in her arms.

"Please, suh," said the girl, with a curtsy, "de baby 's be'n cryin' an' frettin' fer Miss Rena, an' I 'lowed she mought want me ter fetch 'im, ef it would n't 'sturb her."

"Give me the darling," exclaimed Rena, coming forward and taking the child from the nurse. "It wants its auntie. Come to its auntie, bless its little heart!"

Little Albert crowed with pleasure and put up his pretty

mouth for a kiss. Warwick found the sight a pleasant one. If he could but quiet his sister's troublesome scruples, he might erelong see her fondling beautiful children of her own. Even if Rena were willing to risk her happiness, and he to endanger his position, by a quixotic frankness, the future of his child must not be compromised.

"You would n't want to make George unhappy," Warwick resumed when the nurse retired. "Very well; would you not be willing, for his sake, to keep a secret—your secret and mine, and that of the innocent child in your arms? Would you involve all of us in difficulties merely to secure your own peace of mind? Does n't such a course seem just the least bit selfish? Think the matter over from that point of view, and we 'll speak of it later in the day. I shall be with George all the morning, and I may be able, by a little management, to find out his views on the subject of birth and family, and all that. Some men are very liberal, and love is a great leveler. I 'll sound him, at any rate."

He kissed the baby and left Rena to her own reflections, to which his presentation of the case had given a new turn. It had never before occurred to her to regard silence in the light of self-sacrifice. It had seemed a sort of sin; her brother's argument made of it a virtue. It was not the first time, nor the last, that right and wrong had been a matter of view-point.

Tryon himself furnished the opening for Warwick's proposed examination. The younger man could not long remain silent upon the subject uppermost in his mind. "I am anxious, John," he said, "to have Rowena name the happiest day of my life—our wedding day. When the trial in Edgecombe County is finished, I shall have no further business here, and shall be ready to leave for home. I should like to take my bride with me, and surprise my mother."

Mothers, thought Warwick, are likely to prove inquisitive about their sons' wives, especially when taken unawares in matters of such importance. This seemed a good time to test the liberality of Tryon's views, and to put forward a shield for his sister's protection.

"Are you sure, George, that your mother will find the surprise agreeable when you bring home a bride of whom you know so little and your mother nothing at all?"

Tryon had felt that it would be best to surprise his mother. She would need only to see Rena to approve of her, but she was so far prejudiced in favor of Blanche Leary that it would be wisest to present the argument after having announced the irrevocable conclusion. Rena herself would be a complete justification for the accomplished deed.

"I think you ought to know, George," continued Warwick, without waiting for a reply to his question, "that my sister and I are not of an old family, or a rich family, or a distinguished family; that she can bring you nothing but herself; that we have no connections of which you could boast, and no relatives to whom we should be glad to introduce you. You must take us for ourselves alone—we are new people."

"My dear John," replied the young man warmly, "there is a great deal of nonsense about families. If a man is noble and brave and strong, if a woman is beautiful and good and true, what matters it about his or her ancestry? If an old family can give them these things, then it is valuable; if they possess them without it, then of what use is it, except as a source of empty pride, which they would be better without? If all new families were like yours, there would be no advantage in belonging to an old one. All I care to know of Rowena's family is that she is your sister; and you 'll pardon me, old fellow, if I add that she hardly needs even you,—she carries the stamp of her descent upon her face and in her heart."

"It makes me glad to hear you speak in that way," returned Warwick, delighted by the young man's breadth and earnestness.

"Oh, I mean every word of it," replied Tryon. "Ancestors, indeed, for Rowena! I will tell you a family secret, John, to prove how little I care for ancestors. My maternal great-great-grandfather, a hundred and fifty years ago, was hanged, drawn, and quartered for stealing cattle across the Scottish border. How is that for a pedigree? Behold in me the lineal descendant of a felon!"

Warwick felt much relieved at this avowal. His own statement had not touched the vital point involved; it had been at the best but a half-truth; but Tryon's magnanimity would doubtless protect Rena from any close inquiry concerning her past. It even occurred to Warwick for a moment that he might safely disclose the secret to Tryon; but an appreciation of certain facts of history and certain traits of human nature constrained him to put the momentary thought aside. It was a great relief, however, to imagine that Tryon might think lightly of this thing that he need never know.

"Well, Rena," he said to his sister when he went home at noon: "I 've sounded George."

"What did he say?" she asked eagerly.

"I told him we were people of no family, and that we had no relatives that we were proud of. He said he loved you for yourself, and would never ask you about your ancestry."

"Oh, I am so glad!" exclaimed Rena joyfully. This report left her very happy for about three hours, or until she began to analyze carefully her brother's account of what had been said. Warwick's statement had not been specific,—he had not told Tryon *the* thing. George's reply, in turn, had been a mere generality. The concrete fact that oppressed her remained unrevealed, and her doubt was still unsatisfied.

Rena was occupied with this thought when her lover next came to see her. Tryon came up the sanded walk from the gate and spoke pleasantly to the nurse, a good-looking yellow girl who was seated on the front steps, playing with little Albert. He took the boy from her arms, and she went to call Miss Warwick.

Rena came out, followed by the nurse, who offered to take the child.

"Never mind, Mimy, leave him with me," said Tryon.

The nurse walked discreetly over into the garden, remaining within call, but beyond the hearing of conversation in an ordinary tone.

"Rena, darling," said her lover, "when shall it be? Surely you won't ask me to wait a week. Why, that 's a lifetime!"

Rena was struck by a brilliant idea. She would test her lover. Love was a very powerful force; she had found it the greatest, grandest, sweetest thing in the world. Tryon had said that he loved her; he had said scarcely anything else for several weeks, surely nothing else worth remembering. She would test his love by a hypothetical question.

"You say you love me," she said, glancing at him with a sad thoughtfulness in her large dark eyes. "How much do you love me?"

"I love you all one can love. True love has no degrees; it is all or nothing!"

"Would you love me," she asked, with an air of coquetry that masked her concern, pointing toward the girl in the shrubbery, "if I were Albert's nurse yonder?"

"If you were Albert's nurse," he replied, with a joyous laugh, "he would have to find another within a week, for within a week we should be married."

The answer seemed to fit the question, but in fact, Tryon's mind and Rena's did not meet. That two intelligent persons should each attach a different meaning to so simple a form of words as Rena's question was the best ground for her misgiving with regard to the marriage. But love blinded her. She was anxious to be convinced. She interpreted the meaning of his speech by her own thought and by the ardor of his glance, and was satisfied with the answer.

"And now, darling," pleaded Tryon, "will you not fix the day that shall make me happy? I shall be ready to go away in three weeks. Will you go with me?"

"Yes," she answered, in a tumult of joy. She would never need to tell him her secret now. It would make no difference with him, so far as she was concerned; and she had no right to reveal her brother's secret. She was willing to bury the past in forgetfulness, now that she knew it would have no interest for her lover.

X

THE DREAM

THE MARRIAGE was fixed for the thirtieth of the month, immediately after which Tryon and his bride were to set out for North Carolina. Warwick would have liked it much if Tryon had lived in South Carolina; but the location of his North Carolina home was at some distance from Patesville, with which it had no connection by steam or rail, and indeed lay altogether out of the line of travel to Patesville. Rena had no acquaintance with people of social standing in North Carolina; and with the added maturity and charm due to her improved opportunities, it was unlikely that any former resident of Patesville who might casually meet her would see in the elegant young matron from South Carolina more than a passing resemblance to a poor girl who had once lived in an obscure part of the old town. It would of course be necessary for Rena to keep away from Patesville; save for her mother's sake, she would hardly be tempted to go back.

On the twentieth of the month, Warwick set out with Tryon for the county seat of the adjoining county, to try one of the lawsuits which had required Tryon's presence in South Carolina for so long a time. Their destination was a day's drive from Clarence, behind a good horse, and the trial was expected to last a week.

"This week will seem like a year," said Tryon ruefully, the evening before their departure, "but I 'll write every day, and shall expect a letter as often."

"The mail goes only twice a week, George," replied Rena.

"Then I shall have three letters in each mail."

Warwick and Tryon were to set out in the cool of the morning, after an early breakfast. Rena was up at daybreak that she might preside at the breakfast-table and bid the travelers good-by.

"John," said Rena to her brother in the morning, "I dreamed last night that mother was ill."

"Dreams, you know, Rena," answered Warwick lightly, "go by contraries. Yours undoubtedly signifies that our mother, God bless her simple soul! is at the present moment enjoying her usual perfect health. She was never sick in her life."

For a few months after leaving Patesville with her brother, Rena had suffered tortures of homesickness; those who have felt it know the pang. The severance of old ties had been abrupt and complete. At the school where her brother had taken her, there had been nothing to relieve the strangeness of her surroundings—no schoolmate from her own town, no relative or friend of the family near by. Even the compensation of human sympathy was in a measure denied her, for Rena was too fresh from her prison-house to doubt that sympathy would fail before the revelation of the secret the consciousness of which oppressed her at that time like a nightmare. It was not strange that Rena, thus isolated, should have been prostrated by homesickness for several weeks after leaving Patesville. When the paroxysm had passed, there followed a dull pain, which gradually subsided into a resignation as profound, in its way, as had been her longing for home. She loved, she suffered, with a quiet intensity of which her outward demeanor gave no adequate expression. From some ancestral source she had derived a strain of the passive fatalism by which alone one can submit uncomplainingly to the inevitable. By the same token, when once a thing had been decided, it became with her a finality, which only some extraordinary stress of emotion could disturb. She had acquiesced in her brother's plan; for her there was no withdrawing; her homesickness was an incidental thing which must be endured, as patiently as might be, until time should have brought a measure of relief.

Warwick had made provision for an occasional letter from Patesville, by leaving with his mother a number of envelopes directed to his address. She could have her letters written, inclose them in these envelopes, and deposit them in the post-office with her own hand. Thus the place of Warwick's residence would remain within her own knowledge, and his secret would not be placed at the mercy of any wandering Patesvillian who might perchance go to that part of South Carolina. By this simple means Rena had kept as closely in touch with her mother as Warwick had considered prudent;

any closer intercourse was not consistent with their present station in life.

The night after Warwick and Tryon had ridden away, Rena dreamed again that her mother was ill. Better taught people than she, in regions more enlightened than the South Carolina of that epoch, are disturbed at times by dreams. Mis' Molly had a profound faith in them. If God, in ancient times, had spoken to men in visions of the night, what easier way could there be for Him to convey his meaning to people of all ages? Science, which has shattered many an idol and destroyed many a delusion, has made but slight inroads upon the shadowy realm of dreams. For Mis' Molly, to whom science would have meant nothing and psychology would have been a meaningless term, the land of dreams was carefully mapped and bounded. Each dream had some special significance, or was at least susceptible of classification under some significant head. Dreams, as a general rule, went by contraries; but a dream three times repeated was a certain portent of the thing defined. Rena's few years of schooling at Patesville and her months at Charleston had scarcely disturbed these hoary superstitions which lurk in the dim corners of the brain. No lady in Clarence, perhaps, would have remained undisturbed by a vivid dream, three times repeated, of some event bearing materially upon her own life.

The first repetition of a dream was decisive of nothing, for two dreams meant no more than one. The power of the second lay in the suspense, the uncertainty, to which it gave rise. Two doubled the chance of a third. The day following this second dream was an anxious one for Rena. She could not for an instant dismiss her mother from her thoughts, which were filled too with a certain self-reproach. She had left her mother alone; if her mother were really ill, there was no one at home to tend her with loving care. This feeling grew in force, until by nightfall Rena had become very unhappy, and went to bed with the most dismal forebodings. In this state of mind, it is not surprising that she now dreamed that her mother was lying at the point of death, and that she cried out with heart-rending pathos:—

"Rena, my darlin', why did you forsake yo'r pore old mother? Come back to me, honey; I'll die ef I don't see you soon."

The stress of subconscious emotion engendered by the dream was powerful enough to wake Rena, and her mother's utterance seemed to come to her with the force of a fateful warning and a great reproach. Her mother was sick and needed her, and would die if she did not come. She felt that she must see her mother,—it would be almost like murder to remain away from her under such circumstances.

After breakfast she went into the business part of the town and inquired at what time a train would leave that would take her toward Patesville. Since she had come away from the town, a railroad had been opened by which the long river voyage might be avoided, and, making allowance for slow trains and irregular connections, the town of Patesville could be reached by an all-rail route in about twelve hours. Calling at the post-office for the family mail, she found there a letter from her mother, which she tore open in great excitement. It was written in an unpracticed hand and badly spelled, and was in effect as follows:—

> MY DEAR DAUGHTER,—I take my pen in hand to let you know that I am not very well. I have had a kind of misery in my side for two weeks, with palpitations of the heart, and I have been in bed for three days. I 'm feeling mighty poorly, but Dr. Green says that I 'll get over it in a few days. Old Aunt Zilphy is staying with me, and looking after things tolerably well. I hope this will find you and John enjoying good health. Give my love to John, and I hope the Lord will bless him and you too. Cousin Billy Oxendine has had a rising on his neck, and has had to have it lanced. Mary B. has another young one, a boy this time. Old man Tom Johnson was killed last week while trying to whip black Jim Brown, who lived down on the Wilmington Road. Jim has run away. There has been a big freshet in the river, and it looked at one time as if the new bridge would be washed away.
>
> Frank comes over every day or two and asks about you. He says to tell you that he don't believe you are coming back any more, but you are to remember him, and that foolishness he said about bringing you back from the end of the world with his mule and cart. He 's

very good to me, and brings over shavings and kindling-wood, and made me a new well-bucket for nothing. It 's a comfort to talk to him about you, though I have n't told him where you are living.

I hope this will find you and John both well, and doing well. I should like to see you, but if it 's the Lord's will that I should n't, I shall be thankful anyway that you have done what was the best for yourselves and your children, and that I have given you up for your own good.

Your affectionate mother,

MARY WALDEN.

Rena shed tears over this simple letter, which, to her excited imagination, merely confirmed the warning of her dream. At the date of its writing her mother had been sick in bed, with the symptoms of a serious illness. She had no nurse but a purblind old woman. Three days of progressive illness had evidently been quite sufficient to reduce her parent to the condition indicated by the third dream. The thought that her mother might die without the presence of any one who loved her pierced Rena's heart like a knife and lent wings to her feet. She wished for the enchanted horse of which her brother had read to her so many years before on the front piazza of the house behind the cedars, that she might fly through the air to her dying mother's side. She determined to go at once to Patesville.

Returning home, she wrote a letter to Warwick inclosing their mother's letter, and stating that she had dreamed an alarming dream for three nights in succession; that she had left the house in charge of the servants and gone to Patesville; and that she would return as soon as her mother was out of danger.

To her lover she wrote that she had been called away to visit a sick-bed, and would return very soon, perhaps by the time he got back to Clarence. These letters Rena posted on her way to the train, which she took at five o'clock in the afternoon. This would bring her to Patesville early in the morning of the following day.

XI

A LETTER AND A JOURNEY

WAR has been called the court of last resort. A lawsuit may with equal aptness be compared to a battle—the parallel might be drawn very closely all along the line. First we have the *casus belli*, the cause of action; then the various protocols and proclamations and general orders, by way of pleas, demurrers, and motions; then the preliminary skirmishes at the trial table; and then the final struggle, in which might is quite as likely to prevail as right, victory most often resting with the strongest battalions, and truth and justice not seldom overborne by the weight of odds upon the other side.

The lawsuit which Warwick and Tryon had gone to try did not, however, reach this ultimate stage, but, after a three days' engagement, resulted in a treaty of peace. The case was compromised and settled, and Tryon and Warwick set out on their homeward drive. They stopped at a farmhouse at noon, and while at table saw the stagecoach from the town they had just left, bound for their own destination. In the mail-bag under the driver's seat were Rena's two letters; they had been delivered at the town in the morning, and immediately remailed to Clarence, in accordance with orders left at the post-office the evening before. Tryon and Warwick drove leisurely homeward through the pines, all unconscious of the fateful squares of white paper moving along the road a few miles before them, which a mother's yearning and a daughter's love had thrown, like the apple of discord, into the narrow circle of their happiness.

They reached Clarence at four o'clock. Warwick got down from the buggy at his office. Tryon drove on to his hotel, to make a hasty toilet before visiting his sweetheart.

Warwick glanced at his mail, tore open the envelope addressed in his sister's handwriting, and read the contents with something like dismay. She had gone away on the eve of her wedding, her lover knew not where, to be gone no one knew how long, on a mission which could not be frankly disclosed.

A dim foreboding of disaster flashed across his mind. He thrust the letter into his pocket, with others yet unopened, and started toward his home. Reaching the gate, he paused a moment and then walked on past the house. Tryon would probably be there in a few minutes, and he did not care to meet him without first having had the opportunity for some moments of reflection. He must fix upon some line of action in this emergency.

Meanwhile Tryon had reached his hotel and opened his mail. The letter from Rena was read first, with profound disappointment. He had really made concessions in the settlement of that lawsuit—had yielded several hundred dollars of his just dues, in order that he might get back to Rena three days earlier. Now he must cool his heels in idleness for at least three days before she would return. It was annoying, to say the least. He wished to know where she had gone, that he might follow her and stay near her until she should be ready to come back. He might ask Warwick—no, she might have had some good reason for not having mentioned her destination. She had probably gone to visit some of the poor relations of whom her brother had spoken so frankly, and she would doubtless prefer that he should not see her amid any surroundings but the best. Indeed, he did not know that he would himself care to endanger, by suggestive comparisons, the fine aureole of superiority that surrounded her. She represented in her adorable person and her pure heart the finest flower of the finest race that God had ever made—the supreme effort of creative power, than which there could be no finer. The flower would soon be his; why should he care to dig up the soil in which it grew?

Tryon went on opening his letters. There were several bills and circulars, and then a letter from his mother, of which he broke the seal:—

> My dearest George,—This leaves us well. Blanche is still with me, and we are impatiently awaiting your return. In your absence she seems almost like a daughter to me. She joins me in the hope that your lawsuits are progressing favorably, and that you will be with us soon. . . .
>
> On your way home, if it does not keep you away from us too long, would it not be well for you to come by

way of Patesville, and find out whether there is any prospect of our being able to collect our claim against old Mr. Duncan McSwayne's estate? You must have taken the papers with you, along with the rest, for I do not find them here. Things ought to be settled enough now for people to realize on some of their securities. Your grandfather always believed the note was good, and meant to try to collect it, but the war interfered. He said to me, before he died, that if the note was ever collected, he would use the money to buy a wedding present for your wife. Poor father! he is dead and gone to heaven; but I am sure that even there he would be happier if he knew the note was paid and the money used as he intended.

If you go to Patesville, call on my cousin, Dr. Ed. Green, and tell him who you are. Give him my love. I have n't seen him for twenty years. He used to be very fond of the ladies, a very gallant man. He can direct you to a good lawyer, no doubt. Hoping to see you soon,

Your loving mother,
ELIZABETH TRYON.

P. S. Blanche joins me in love to you.

This affectionate and motherly letter did not give Tryon unalloyed satisfaction. He was glad to hear that his mother was well, but he had hoped that Blanche Leary might have finished her visit by this time. The reasonable inference from the letter was that Blanche meant to await his return. Her presence would spoil the fine romantic flavor of the surprise he had planned for his mother; it would never do to expose his bride to an unannounced meeting with the woman whom he had tacitly rejected. There would be one advantage in such a meeting: the comparison of the two women would be so much in Rena's favor that his mother could not hesitate for a moment between them. The situation, however, would have elements of constraint, and he did not care to expose either Rena or Blanche to any disagreeable contingency. It would be better to take his wife on a wedding trip, and notify his mother, before he returned home, of his marriage. In the extremely improbable case that she should disapprove his choice after having seen his wife, the ice would at least have been broken before his arrival at home.

"By Jove!" he exclaimed suddenly, striking his knee with his hand, "why should n't I run up to Patesville while Rena 's gone? I can leave here at five o'clock, and get there some time to-morrow morning. I can transact my business during the day, and get back the day after to-morrow; for Rena might return ahead of time, just as we did, and I shall want to be here when she comes; I 'd rather wait a year for a legal opinion on a doubtful old note than to lose one day with my love. The train goes in twenty minutes. My bag is already packed. I 'll just drop a line to George and tell him where I 've gone."

He put Rena's letter into his breast pocket, and turning to his trunk, took from it a handful of papers relating to the claim in reference to which he was going to Patesville. These he thrust into the same pocket with Rena's letter; he wished to read both letter and papers while on the train. It would be a pleasure merely to hold the letter before his eyes and look at the lines traced by her hand. The papers he wished to study, for the more practical purpose of examining into the merits of his claim against the estate of Duncan McSwayne.

When Warwick reached home, he inquired if Mr. Tryon had called.

"No, suh," answered the nurse, to whom he had put the question; "he ain't be'n here yet, suh."

Warwick was surprised and much disturbed.

"De baby 's be'n cryin' for Miss Rena," suggested the nurse, "an' I s'pec' he 'd like to see you, suh. Shall I fetch 'im?"

"Yes, bring him to me."

He took the child in his arms and went out upon the piazza. Several porch pillows lay invitingly near. He pushed them toward the steps with his foot, sat down upon one, and placed little Albert upon another. He was scarcely seated when a messenger from the hotel came up the walk from the gate and handed him a note. At the same moment he heard the long shriek of the afternoon train leaving the station on the opposite side of the town.

He tore the envelope open anxiously, read the note, smiled a sickly smile, and clenched the paper in his hand unconsciously. There was nothing he could do. The train had gone;

there was no telegraph to Patesville, and no letter could leave Clarence for twenty-four hours. The best laid schemes go wrong at times—the stanchest ships are sometimes wrecked, or skirt the breakers perilously. Life is a sea, full of strange currents and uncharted reefs—whoever leaves the traveled path must run the danger of destruction. Warwick was a lawyer, however, and accustomed to balance probabilities.

"He may easily be in Patesville a day or two without meeting her. She will spend most of her time at mother's bedside, and he will be occupied with his own affairs."

If Tryon should meet her—well, he was very much in love, and he had spoken very nobly of birth and blood. Warwick would have preferred, nevertheless, that Tryon's theories should not be put to this particular test. Rena's scruples had so far been successfully combated; the question would be opened again, and the situation unnecessarily complicated, if Tryon should meet Rena in Patesville.

"Will he or will he not?" he asked himself. He took a coin from his pocket and spun it upon the floor. "Heads, he sees her; tails, he does not."

The coin spun swiftly and steadily, leaving upon the eye the impression of a revolving sphere. Little Albert, left for a moment to his own devices, had crept behind his father and was watching the whirling disk with great pleasure. He felt that he would like to possess this interesting object. The coin began to move more slowly, and was wabbling to its fall, when the child stretched forth his chubby fist and caught it ere it touched the floor.

XII

TRYON GOES TO PATESVILLE

TRYON arrived in the early morning and put up at the Patesville Hotel, a very comfortable inn. After a bath, breakfast, and a visit to the barber-shop, he inquired of the hotel clerk the way to the office of Dr. Green, his mother's cousin.

"On the corner, sir," answered the clerk, "by the market-house, just over the drugstore. The doctor drove past here only half an hour ago. You 'll probably catch him in his office."

Tryon found the office without difficulty. He climbed the stair, but found no one in except a young colored man seated in the outer office, who rose promptly as Tryon entered.

"No, suh," replied the man to Tryon's question, "he ain't hyuh now. He 's gone out to see a patient, suh, but he 'll be back soon. Won't you set down in de private office an' wait fer 'im, suh?"

Tryon had not slept well during his journey, and felt somewhat fatigued. Through the open door of the next room he saw an inviting armchair, with a window at one side, and upon the other a table strewn with papers and magazines.

"Yes," he answered, "I 'll wait."

He entered the private office, sank into the armchair, and looked out of the window upon the square below. The view was mildly interesting. The old brick market-house with the tower was quite picturesque. On a wagon-scale at one end the public weighmaster was weighing a load of hay. In the booths under the wide arches several old negro women were frying fish on little charcoal stoves—the odor would have been appetizing to one who had not breakfasted. On the shady side stood half a dozen two-wheeled carts, loaded with lightwood and drawn by diminutive steers, or superannuated army mules branded on the flank with the cabalistic letters "C.S.A.," which represented a vanished dream, or "U.S.A.," which, as any negro about the market-house would have borne witness, signified a very concrete fact. Now and then a lady or gentleman passed with leisurely step—no one ever hurried in Patesville—or some poor white sandhiller slouched listlessly along toward store or bar-room.

Tryon mechanically counted the slabs of gingerbread on the nearest market-stall, and calculated the cubical contents of several of the meagre loads of wood. Having exhausted the view, he turned to the table at his elbow and picked up a medical journal, in which he read first an account of a marvelous surgical operation. Turning the leaves idly, he came upon an article by a Southern writer, upon the perennial race problem that has vexed the country for a century. The writer maintained that owing to a special tendency of the negro blood, however diluted, to revert to the African type, any future amalgamation of the white and black races, which foolish and wicked Northern negrophiles predicted as the ultimate result of the new conditions confronting the South, would therefore be an ethnological impossibility; for the smallest trace of negro blood would inevitably drag down the superior race to the level of the inferior, and reduce the fair Southland, already devastated by the hand of the invader, to the frightful level of Hayti, the awful example of negro incapacity. To forefend their beloved land, now doubly sanctified by the blood of her devoted sons who had fallen in the struggle to maintain her liberties and preserve her property, it behooved every true Southron to stand firm against the abhorrent tide of radicalism, to maintain the supremacy and purity of his all-pervading, all-conquering race, and to resist by every available means the threatened domination of an inferior and degraded people, who were set to rule hereditary freemen ere they had themselves scarce ceased to be slaves.

When Tryon had finished the article, which seemed to him a well-considered argument, albeit a trifle bombastic, he threw the book upon the table. Finding the armchair wonderfully comfortable, and feeling the fatigue of his journey, he yielded to a drowsy impulse, leaned his head on the cushioned back of the chair, and fell asleep. According to the habit of youth, he dreamed, and pursuant to his own individual habit, he dreamed of Rena. They were walking in the moonlight, along the quiet road in front of her brother's house. The air was redolent with the perfume of flowers. His arm was around her waist. He had asked her if she loved him, and was awaiting her answer in tremulous but confident expectation. She opened her lips to speak. The sound that came from them seemed to be:—

"Is Dr. Green in? No? Ask him, when he comes back, please, to call at our house as soon as he can."

Tryon was in that state of somnolence in which one may dream and yet be aware that one is dreaming,—the state where one, during a dream, dreams that one pinches one's self to be sure that one is not dreaming. He was therefore aware of a ringing quality about the words he had just heard that did not comport with the shadowy converse of a dream—an incongruity in the remark, too, which marred the harmony of the vision. The shock was sufficient to disturb Tryon's slumber, and he struggled slowly back to consciousness. When fully awake, he thought he heard a light footfall descending the stairs.

"Was there some one here?" he inquired of the attendant in the outer office, who was visible through the open door.

"Yas, suh," replied the boy, "a young cullud 'oman wuz in jes' now, axin' fer de doctuh."

Tryon felt a momentary touch of annoyance that a negro woman should have intruded herself into his dream at its most interesting point. Nevertheless, the voice had been so real, his imagination had reproduced with such exactness the dulcet tones so dear to him, that he turned his head involuntarily and looked out of the window. He could just see the flutter of a woman's skirt disappearing around the corner.

A moment later the doctor came bustling in,—a plump, rosy man of fifty or more, with a frank, open countenance and an air of genial good nature. Such a doctor, Tryon fancied, ought to enjoy a wide popularity. His mere presence would suggest life and hope and healthfulness.

"My dear boy," exclaimed the doctor cordially, after Tryon had introduced himself, "I 'm delighted to meet you—or any one of the old blood. Your mother and I were sweethearts, long ago, when we both wore pinafores, and went to see our grandfather at Christmas; and I met her more than once, and paid her more than one compliment, after she had grown to be a fine young woman. You 're like her, too, but not quite so handsome—you 've more of what I suppose to be the Tryon favor, though I never met your father. So one of old Duncan McSwayne's notes went so far as that? Well, well, I don't know where you won't find them. One of them turned up here the other day from New York.

"The man you want to see," he added later in the conversation, "is old Judge Straight. He 's getting somewhat stiff in the joints, but he knows more law, and more about the McSwayne estate, than any other two lawyers in town. If anybody can collect your claim, Judge Straight can. I 'll send my boy Dave over to his office. Dave," he called to his attendant, "run over to Judge Straight's office and see if he 's there.

"There was a freshet here a few weeks ago," he went on, when the colored man had departed, "and they had to open the flood-gates and let the water out of the mill pond, for if the dam had broken, as it did twenty years ago, it would have washed the pillars from under the judge's office and let it down in the creek, and"—

"Jedge Straight ain't in de office jes' now, suh," reported the doctor's man Dave, from the head of the stairs.

"Did you ask when he 'd be back?"

"No, suh, you did n't tell me ter, suh."

"Well, now, go back and inquire.

"The niggers," he explained to Tryon, "are getting mighty trifling since they 've been freed. Before the war, that boy would have been around there and back before you could say Jack Robinson; now, the lazy rascal takes his time just like a white man."

Dave returned more promptly than from his first trip. "Jedge Straight 's dere now, suh," he said. "He 's done come in."

"I 'll take you right around and introduce you," said the doctor, running on pleasantly, like a babbling brook. "I don't know whether the judge ever met your mother or not, but he knows a gentleman when he sees one, and will be glad to meet you and look after your affair. See to the patients, Dave, and say I 'll be back shortly, and don't forget any messages left for me. Look sharp, now! You know your failing!"

They found Judge Straight in his office. He was seated by the rear window, and had fallen into a gentle doze—the air of

Patesville was conducive to slumber. A visitor from some bustling city might have rubbed his eyes, on any but a market-day, and imagined the whole town asleep—that the people were somnambulists and did not know it. The judge, an old hand, roused himself so skillfully, at the sound of approaching footsteps, that his visitors could not guess but that he had been wide awake. He shook hands with the doctor, and acknowledged the introduction to Tryon with a rare old-fashioned courtesy, which the young man thought a very charming survival of the manners of a past and happier age.

"No," replied the judge, in answer to a question by Dr. Green, "I never met his mother; I was a generation ahead of her. I was at school with her father, however, fifty years ago—fifty years ago! No doubt that seems to you a long time, young gentleman?"

"It is a long time, sir," replied Tryon. "I must live more than twice as long as I have in order to cover it."

"A long time, and a troubled time," sighed the judge. "I could wish that I might see this unhappy land at peace with itself before I die. Things are in a sad tangle; I can't see the way out. But the worst enemy has been slain, in spite of us. We are well rid of slavery."

"But the negro we still have with us," remarked the doctor, "for here comes my man Dave. What is it, Dave?" he asked sharply, as the negro stuck his head in at the door.

"Doctuh Green," he said, "I fuhgot ter tell you, suh, dat dat young 'oman wuz at de office agin jes' befo' you come in, an' said fer you to go right down an' see her mammy ez soon ez you could."

"Ah, yes, and you 've just remembered it! I 'm afraid you 're entirely too forgetful for a doctor's office. You forgot about old Mrs. Latimer, the other day, and when I got there she had almost choked to death. Now get back to the office, and remember, the next time you forget anything, I 'll hire another boy; remember that! That boy's head," he remarked to his companions, after Dave had gone, "reminds me of nothing so much as a dried gourd, with a handful of cowpeas rattling around it, in lieu of gray matter. An old woman out in Redbank got a fishbone in her throat, the other day, and nearly choked to death before I got there. A white woman, sir, came very near losing her life because of a lazy, trifling negro!"

"I should think you would discharge him, sir," suggested Tryon.

"What would be the use?" rejoined the doctor. "All negroes are alike, except that now and then there 's a pretty woman along the border-line. Take this patient of mine, for instance,—I 'll call on her after dinner, her case is not serious,—thirty years ago she would have made any man turn his head to look at her. You know who I mean, don't you, judge?"

"Yes. I think so," said the judge promptly. "I 've transacted a little business for her now and then."

"I don't know whether you 've seen the daughter or not—I 'm sure you have n't for the past year or so, for she 's been away. But she 's in town now, and, by Jove, the girl is really beautiful. And I 'm a judge of beauty. Do you remember my wife thirty years ago, judge?"

"She was a very handsome woman, Ed," replied the other judicially. "If I had been twenty years younger, I should have cut you out."

"You mean you would have tried. But as I was saying, this girl is a beauty; I reckon we might guess where she got some of it, eh, Judge? Human nature is human nature, but it 's a d—d shame that a man should beget a child like that and leave it to live the life open for a negro. If she had been born white, the young fellows would be tumbling over one another to get her. Her mother would have to look after her pretty closely as things are, if she stayed here; but she disappeared mysteriously a year or two ago, and has been at the North, I 'm told, passing for white. She 'll probably marry a Yankee; he won't know any better, and it will serve him right—she 's only too white for them. She has a very striking figure, something on the Greek order, stately and slow-moving. She has the manners of a lady, too—a beautiful woman, if she is a nigger!"

"I quite agree with you, Ed," remarked the judge dryly, "that the mother had better look closely after the daughter."

"Ah, no, judge," replied the other, with a flattered smile, "my admiration for beauty is purely abstract. Twenty-five years ago, when I was younger"—

"When you were young," corrected the judge.

"When you and I were younger," continued the doctor ingeniously,—"twenty-five years ago, I could not have answered for myself. But I would advise the girl to stay at the North, if she can. She 's certainly out of place around here."

Tryon found the subject a little tiresome, and the doctor's enthusiasm not at all contagious. He could not possibly have been interested in a colored girl, under any circumstances, and he was engaged to be married to the most beautiful white woman on earth. To mention a negro woman in the same room where he was thinking of Rena seemed little short of profanation. His friend the doctor was a jovial fellow, but it was surely doubtful taste to refer to his wife in such a conversation. He was very glad when the doctor dropped the subject and permitted him to go more into detail about the matter which formed his business in Patesville. He took out of his pocket the papers concerning the McSwayne claim and laid them on the judge's desk.

"You 'll find everything there, sir,—the note, the contract, and some correspondence that will give you the hang of the thing. Will you be able to look over them to-day? I should like," he added a little nervously, "to go back to-morrow."

"What!" exclaimed Dr. Green vivaciously, "insult our town by staying only one day? It won't be long enough to get acquainted with our young ladies. Patesville girls are famous for their beauty. But perhaps there 's a loadstone in South Carolina to draw you back? Ah, you change color! To my mind there 's nothing finer than the ingenuous blush of youth. But we 'll spare you if you 'll answer one question—is it serious?"

"I 'm to be married in two weeks, sir," answered Tryon. The statement sounded very pleasant, in spite of the slight embarrassment caused by the inquiry.

"Good boy!" rejoined the doctor, taking his arm familiarly—they were both standing now. "You ought to have married a Patesville girl, but you people down towards the eastern counties seldom come this way, and we are evidently too late to catch you."

"I 'll look your papers over this morning," said the judge, "and when I come from dinner will stop at the court house and examine the records and see whether there 's anything we can get hold of. If you 'll drop in around three or four o'clock, I may be able to give you an opinion."

"Now, George," exclaimed the doctor, "we 'll go back to the office for a spell, and then I 'll take you home with me to luncheon."

Tryon hesitated.

"Oh, you must come! Mrs. Green would never forgive me if I did n't bring you. Strangers are rare birds in our society, and when they come we make them welcome. Our enemies may overturn our institutions, and try to put the bottom rail on top, but they cannot destroy our Southern hospitality. There are so many carpet-baggers and other social vermin creeping into the South, with the Yankees trying to force the niggers on us, that it 's a genuine pleasure to get acquainted with another real Southern gentleman, whom one can invite into one's house without fear of contamination, and before whom one can express his feelings freely and be sure of perfect sympathy."

XIII

AN INJUDICIOUS PAYMENT

When Judge Straight's visitors had departed, he took up the papers which had been laid loosely on the table as they were taken out of Tryon's breast-pocket, and commenced their perusal. There was a note for five hundred dollars, many years overdue, but not yet outlawed by lapse of time; a contract covering the transaction out of which the note had grown; and several letters and copies of letters modifying the terms of the contract. The judge had glanced over most of the papers, and was getting well into the merits of the case, when he unfolded a letter which read as follows:—

> My dearest George,—I am going away for about a week, to visit the bedside of an old friend, who is very ill, and may not live. Do not be alarmed about me, for I shall very likely be back by the time you are.
>
> Yours lovingly,
> Rowena Warwick.

The judge was unable to connect this letter with the transaction which formed the subject of his examination. Age had dimmed his perceptions somewhat, and it was not until he had finished the letter, and read it over again, and noted the signature at the bottom a second time, that he perceived that the writing was in a woman's hand, that the ink was comparatively fresh, and that the letter was dated only a couple of days before. While he still held the sheet in his hand, it dawned upon him slowly that he held also one of the links in a chain of possible tragedy which he himself, he became uncomfortably aware, had had a hand in forging.

"It is the Walden woman's daughter, as sure as fate! Her name is Rena. Her brother goes by the name of Warwick. She has come to visit her sick mother. My young client, Green's relation, is her lover—is engaged to marry her—is in town, and is likely to meet her!"

The judge was so absorbed in the situation thus suggested that he laid the papers down and pondered for a moment the curious problem involved. He was quite aware that two races had not dwelt together, side by side, for nearly three hundred years, without mingling their blood in greater or less degree; he was old enough, and had seen curious things enough, to know that in this mingling the current had not always flowed in one direction. Certain old decisions with which he was familiar; old scandals that had crept along obscure channels; old facts that had come to the knowledge of an old practitioner, who held in the hollow of his hand the honor of more than one family, made him know that there was dark blood among the white people—not a great deal, and that very much diluted, and, so long as it was sedulously concealed or vigorously denied, or lost in the mists of tradition, or ascribed to a foreign or an aboriginal strain, having no perceptible effect upon the racial type.

Such people were, for the most part, merely on the ragged edge of the white world, seldom rising above the level of overseers, or slave-catchers, or sheriff's officers, who could usually be relied upon to resent the drop of black blood that tainted them, and with the zeal of the proselyte to visit their hatred of it upon the unfortunate blacks that fell into their hands. One curse of negro slavery was, and one part of its baleful heritage is, that it poisoned the fountains of human sympathy. Under a system where men might sell their own children without social reprobation or loss of prestige, it was not surprising that some of them should hate their distant cousins. There were not in Patesville half a dozen persons capable of thinking Judge Straight's thoughts upon the question before him, and perhaps not another who would have adopted the course he now pursued toward this anomalous family in the house behind the cedars.

"Well, here we are again, as the clown in the circus remarks," murmured the judge. "Ten years ago, in a moment of sentimental weakness and of quixotic loyalty to the memory of an old friend,—who, by the way, had not cared enough for his own children to take them away from the South, as he might have done, or to provide for them handsomely, as he perhaps meant to do,—I violated the traditions of my class and stepped from the beaten path to help the misbegotten son of my old friend out of the slough of despond, in which he had learned, in some strange way, that he was floundering. Ten years later, the ghost of my good deed returns to haunt me, and makes me doubt whether I have wrought more evil than good. I wonder," he mused, "if he will find her out?"

The judge was a man of imagination; he had read many books and had personally outlived some prejudices. He let his mind run on the various phases of the situation.

"If he found her out, would he by any possibility marry her?"

"It is not likely," he answered himself. "If he made the discovery here, the facts would probably leak out in the town. It is something that a man might do in secret, but only a hero or a fool would do openly."

The judge sighed as he contemplated another possibility. He had lived for seventy years under the old régime. The young man was a gentleman—so had been the girl's father. Conditions were changed, but human nature was the same. Would the young man's love turn to disgust and repulsion, or would it merely sink from the level of worship to that of desire? Would the girl, denied marriage, accept anything less? Her mother had,—but conditions were changed. Yes, conditions were changed, so far as the girl was concerned; there was a possible future for her under the new order of things; but white people had not changed their opinion of the negroes, except for the worse. The general belief was that they were just as inferior as before, and had, moreover, been spoiled by a disgusting assumption of equality, driven into their thick skulls by Yankee malignity bent upon humiliating a proud though vanquished foe.

If the judge had had sons and daughters of his own, he might not have done what he now proceeded to do. But the old man's attitude toward society was chiefly that of an observer, and the narrow stream of sentiment left in his heart chose to flow toward the weaker party in this unequal conflict,—a young woman fighting for love and opportunity against the ranked forces of society, against immemorial tradition, against pride of family and of race.

"It may be the unwisest thing I ever did," he said to himself, turning to his desk and taking up a quill pen, "and may result in more harm than good; but I was always from childhood in sympathy with the under dog. There is certainly as much reason in my helping the girl as the boy, for being a woman, she is less able to help herself."

He dipped his pen into the ink and wrote the following lines:—

> MADAM,—If you value your daughter's happiness, keep her at home for the next day or two.

This note he dried by sprinkling it with sand from a box near at hand, signed with his own name, and, with a fine courtesy, addressed to "Mrs. Molly Walden." Having first carefully sealed it in an envelope, he stepped to the open door, and spied, playing marbles on the street near by, a group of negro boys, one of whom the judge called by name.

"Here, Billy," he said, handing the boy the note, "take this to Mis' Molly Walden. Do you know where she lives—down on Front Street, in the house behind the cedars?"

"Yas, suh, I knows de place."

"Make haste, now. When you come back and tell me what she says, I 'll give you ten cents. On second thoughts, I shall be gone to lunch, so here 's your money," he added, handing the lad the bit of soiled paper by which the United States government acknowledged its indebtedness to the bearer in the sum of ten cents.

Just here, however, the judge made his mistake. Very few mortals can spare the spring of hope, the motive force of expectation. The boy kept the note in his hand, winked at his companions, who had gathered as near as their awe of the judge would permit, and started down the street. As soon as the judge had disappeared, Billy beckoned to his friends, who speedily overtook him. When the party turned the corner of Front Street and were safely out of sight of Judge Straight's office, the capitalist entered the grocery store and invested his unearned increment in gingerbread. When the ensuing saturnalia was over, Billy finished the game of marbles which the judge had interrupted, and then set out to execute his commission. He had nearly reached his objective point when he met upon the street a young white lady, whom he did not know, and for whom, the path being narrow at that point, he stepped out into the gutter. He reached the house behind the cedars, went round to the back door, and handed the envelope to Mis' Molly, who was seated on the rear piazza, propped up by pillows in a comfortable rocking-chair.

"Laws-a-massy!" she exclaimed weakly, "what is it?"

"It 's a lettuh, ma'm," answered the boy, whose expanding nostrils had caught a pleasant odor from the kitchen, and who was therefore in no hurry to go away.

"Who 's it fur?" she asked.

"It 's fuh you, ma'm," replied the lad.

"An' who 's it from?" she inquired, turning the envelope over and over, and examining it with the impotent curiosity of one who cannot read.

"F'm ole Jedge Straight, ma'm. He tole me ter fetch it ter you. Is you got a roasted 'tater you could gimme, ma'm?"

"Shorely, chile. I 'll have Aunt Zilphy fetch you a piece of 'tater pone, if you 'll hol' on a minute."

She called to Aunt Zilphy, who soon came hobbling out of the kitchen with a large square of the delicacy,—a flat cake made of mashed sweet potatoes, mixed with beaten eggs, sweetened and flavored to suit the taste, and baked in a Dutch oven upon the open hearth.

The boy took the gratuity, thanked her, and turned to go. Mis' Molly was still scanning the superscription of the letter. "I wonder," she murmured, "what old Judge Straight can be writin' to me about. Oh, boy!"

"Yas 'm," answered the messenger, looking back.

"Can you read writin'?"

"No 'm."

"All right. Never mind."

She laid the letter carefully on the chimney-piece of the kitchen. "I reckon it 's somethin' mo' 'bout the taxes," she thought, "or maybe somebody wants to buy one er my lots. Rena 'll be back terreckly, an' she kin read it an' find out. I 'm glad my child'en have be'n to school. They never could have got where they are now if they had n't."

XIV

A LOYAL FRIEND

MENTION has been made of certain addressed envelopes which John Warwick, on the occasion of his visit to Patesville, had left with his illiterate mother, by the use of which she might communicate with her children from time to time. On one occasion, Mis' Molly, having had a letter written, took one of these envelopes from the chest where she kept her most valued possessions, and was about to inclose the letter when some one knocked at the back door. She laid the envelope and letter on a table in her bedroom, and went to answer the knock. The wind, blowing across the room through the open windows, picked up the envelope and bore it into the street. Mis' Molly, on her return, missed it, looked for it, and being unable to find it, took another envelope. An hour or two later another gust of wind lifted the bit of paper from the ground and carried it into the open door of the cooper shop. Frank picked it up, and observing that it was clean and unused, read the superscription. In his conversations with Mis' Molly, which were often about Rena,—the subject uppermost in both their minds,—he had noted the mystery maintained by Mis' Molly about her daughter's whereabouts, and had often wondered where she might be. Frank was an intelligent fellow, and could put this and that together. The envelope was addressed to a place in South Carolina. He was aware, from some casual remark of Mis' Molly's, that Rena had gone to live in South Carolina. Her son's name was John—that he had changed his last name was more than likely. Frank was not long in reaching the conclusion that Rena was to be found near the town named on the envelope, which he carefully preserved for future reference.

For a whole year Frank had yearned for a smile or a kind word from the only woman in the world. Peter, his father, had rallied him somewhat upon his moodiness after Rena's departure.

"Now 's de time, boy, fer you ter be lookin' roun' fer some

nice gal er yo' own color, w'at 'll 'preciate you, an' won't be 'shamed er you. You 're wastin' time, boy, wastin' time, shootin' at a mark outer yo' range."

But Frank said nothing in reply, and afterwards the old man, who was not without discernment, respected his son's mood and was silent in turn; while Frank fed his memory with his imagination, and by their joint aid kept hope alive.

Later an opportunity to see her presented itself. Business in the cooper shop was dull. A barrel factory had been opened in the town, and had well-nigh paralyzed the cooper's trade. The best mechanic could hardly compete with a machine. One man could now easily do the work of Peter's shop. An agent appeared in town seeking laborers for one of the railroads which the newly organized carpet-bag governments were promoting. Upon inquiry Frank learned that their destination was near the town of Clarence, South Carolina. He promptly engaged himself for the service, and was soon at work in the neighborhood of Warwick's home. There he was employed steadily until a certain holiday, upon which a grand tournament was advertised to take place in a neighboring town. Work was suspended, and foremen and laborers attended the festivities.

Frank had surmised that Rena would be present on such an occasion. He had more than guessed, too, that she must be looked for among the white people rather than among the black. Hence the interest with which he had scanned the grand stand. The result has already been recounted. He had recognized her sweet face; he had seen her enthroned among the proudest and best. He had witnessed and gloried in her triumph. He had seen her cheek flushed with pleasure, her eyes lit up with smiles. He had followed her carriage, had made the acquaintance of Mimy the nurse, and had learned all about the family. When finally he left the neighborhood to return to Patesville, he had learned of Tryon's attentions, and had heard the servants' gossip with reference to the marriage, of which they knew the details long before the principals had approached the main fact. Frank went away without having received one smile or heard one word from Rena; but he had seen her: she was happy; he was content in the knowledge of her happiness. She was doubtless secure in the belief that her secret was unknown. Why should he, by revealing his presence, sow the seeds of doubt or distrust in the garden of her happiness? He sacrificed the deepest longing of a faithful heart, and went back to the cooper shop lest perchance she might accidentally come upon him some day and suffer the shock which he had sedulously spared her.

"I would n' want ter skeer her," he mused, "er make her feel bad, an' dat 's w'at I 'd mos' lackly do ef she seed me. She 'll be better off wid me out'n de road. She 'll marry dat rich w'ite gent'eman,—he won't never know de diffe'nce,—an' be a w'ite lady, ez she would 'a' be'n, ef some ole witch had n' changed her in her cradle. But maybe some time she 'll 'member de little nigger w'at use' ter nuss her w'en she wuz a chile, an' fished her out'n de ole canal, an' would 'a' died fer her ef it would 'a' done any good."

Very generously too, and with a fine delicacy, he said nothing to Mis' Molly of his having seen her daughter, lest she might be disquieted by the knowledge that he shared the family secret,—no great mystery now, this pitiful secret, but more far-reaching in its consequences than any blood-curdling crime. The taint of black blood was the unpardonable sin, from the unmerited penalty of which there was no escape except by concealment. If there be a dainty reader of this tale who scorns a lie, and who writes the story of his life upon his sleeve for all the world to read, let him uncurl his scornful lip and come down from the pedestal of superior morality, to which assured position and wide opportunity have lifted him, and put himself in the place of Rena and her brother, upon whom God had lavished his best gifts, and from whom society would have withheld all that made these gifts valuable. To undertake what they tried to do required great courage. Had they possessed the sneaking, cringing, treacherous character traditionally ascribed to people of mixed blood—the character which the blessed institutions of a free slave-holding republic had been well adapted to foster among them; had they been selfish enough to sacrifice to their ambition the mother who gave them birth, society would have been placated or humbugged, and the voyage of their life might have been one of unbroken smoothness.

When Rena came back unexpectedly at the behest of her

dream, Frank heard again the music of her voice, felt the joy of her presence and the benison of her smile. There was, however, a subtle difference in her bearing. Her words were not less kind, but they seemed to come from a remoter source. She was kind, as the sun is warm or the rain refreshing; she was especially kind to Frank, because he had been good to her mother. If Frank felt the difference in her attitude, he ascribed it to the fact that she had been white, and had taken on something of the white attitude toward the negro; and Frank, with an equal unconsciousness, clothed her with the attributes of the superior race. Only her drop of black blood, he conceived, gave him the right to feel toward her as he would never have felt without it; and if Rena guessed her faithful devotee's secret, the same reason saved his worship from presumption. A smile and a kind word were little enough to pay for a life's devotion.

On the third day of Rena's presence in Patesville, Frank was driving up Front Street in the early afternoon, when he nearly fell off his cart in astonishment as he saw seated in Dr. Green's buggy, which was standing in front of the Patesville Hotel, the young gentleman who had won the prize at the tournament, and who, as he had learned, was to marry Rena. Frank was quite certain that she did not know of Tryon's presence in the town. Frank had been over to Mis' Molly's in the morning, and had offered his services to the sick woman, who had rapidly become convalescent upon her daughter's return. Mis' Molly had spoken of some camphor that she needed. Frank had volunteered to get it. Rena had thanked him, and had spoken of going to the drugstore during the afternoon. It was her intention to leave Patesville on the following day.

"Ef dat man sees her in dis town," said Frank to himself, "dere 'll be trouble. She don't know *he 's* here, an' I 'll bet he don't know *she 's* here."

Then Frank was assailed by a very strong temptation. If, as he surmised, the joint presence of the two lovers in Patesville was a mere coincidence, a meeting between them would probably result in the discovery of Rena's secret.

"If she 's found out," argued the tempter, "she 'll come back to her mother, and you can see her every day."

But Frank's love was not of the selfish kind. He put temptation aside, and applied the whip to the back of his mule with a vigor that astonished the animal and moved him to unwonted activity. In an unusually short space of time he drew up before Mis' Molly's back gate, sprang from the cart, and ran up to Mis' Molly on the porch.

"Is Miss Rena here?" he demanded breathlessly.

"No, Frank; she went up town 'bout an hour ago to see the doctor an' git me some camphor gum."

Frank uttered a groan, rushed from the house, sprang into the cart, and goaded the terrified mule into a gallop that carried him back to the market-house in half the time it had taken him to reach Mis' Molly's.

"I wonder what in the worl' 's the matter with Frank," mused Mis' Molly, in vague alarm. "Ef he had n't be'n in such a hurry, I 'd 'a' axed him to read Judge Straight's letter. But Rena 'll be home soon."

When Frank reached the doctor's office, he saw Tryon seated in the doctor's buggy, which was standing by the window of the drugstore. Frank ran upstairs and asked the doctor's man if Miss Walden had been there.

"Yas," replied Dave, "she wuz here a little w'ile ago, an' said she wuz gwine downstairs ter de drugsto'. I would n' be s'prise' ef you 'd fin' her dere now."

XV

MINE OWN PEOPLE

THE DRIVE by which Dr. Green took Tryon to his own house led up Front Street about a mile, to the most aristocratic portion of the town, situated on the hill known as Haymount, or, more briefly, "The Hill." The Hill had lost some of its former glory, however, for the blight of a four years' war was everywhere. After reaching the top of this wooded eminence, the road skirted for some little distance the brow of the hill. Below them lay the picturesque old town, a mass of vivid green, dotted here and there with gray roofs that rose above the tree-tops. Two long ribbons of streets stretched away from the Hill to the faint red line that marked the high bluff beyond the river at the farther side of the town. The market-house tower and the slender spires of half a dozen churches were sharply outlined against the green background. The face of the clock was visible, but the hours could have been read only by eyes of phenomenal sharpness. Around them stretched ruined walls, dismantled towers, and crumbling earthworks—footprints of the god of war, one of whose temples had crowned this height. For many years before the rebellion a Federal arsenal had been located at Patesville. Seized by the state troops upon the secession of North Carolina, it had been held by the Confederates until the approach of Sherman's victorious army, whereupon it was evacuated and partially destroyed. The work of destruction begun by the retreating garrison was completed by the conquerors, and now only ruined walls and broken cannon remained of what had once been the chief ornament and pride of Patesville.

The front of Dr. Green's spacious brick house, which occupied an ideally picturesque site, was overgrown by a network of clinging vines, contrasting most agreeably with the mellow red background. A low brick wall, also overrun with creepers, separated the premises from the street and shut in a well-kept flower garden, in which Tryon, who knew something of plants, noticed many rare and beautiful specimens.

Mrs. Green greeted Tryon cordially. He did not have the doctor's memory with which to fill out the lady's cheeks or restore the lustre of her hair or the sparkle of her eyes, and thereby justify her husband's claim to be a judge of beauty; but her kind-hearted hospitality was obvious, and might have made even a plain woman seem handsome. She and her two fair daughters, to whom Tryon was duly presented, looked with much favor upon their handsome young kinsman; for among the people of Patesville, perhaps by virtue of the prevalence of Scottish blood, the ties of blood were cherished as things of value, and never forgotten except in case of the unworthy—an exception, by the way, which one need hardly go so far to seek.

The Patesville people were not exceptional in the weaknesses and meannesses which are common to all mankind, but for some of the finer social qualities they were conspicuously above the average. Kindness, hospitality, loyalty, a chivalrous deference to women,—all these things might be found in large measure by those who saw Patesville with the eyes of its best citizens, and accepted their standards of politics, religion, manners, and morals.

The doctor, after the introductions, excused himself for a moment. Mrs. Green soon left Tryon with the young ladies and went to look after luncheon. Her first errand, however, was to find the doctor.

"Is he well off, Ed?" she asked her husband.

"Lots of land, and plenty of money, if he is ever able to collect it. He has inherited two estates."

"He 's a good-looking fellow," she mused. "Is he married?"

"There you go again," replied her husband, shaking his forefinger at her in mock reproach. "To a woman with marriageable daughters all roads lead to matrimony, the centre of a woman's universe. All men must be sized up by their matrimonial availability. No, he is n't married."

"That 's nice," she rejoined reflectively. "I think we ought to ask him to stay with us while he is in town, don't you?"

"He 's not married," rejoined the doctor slyly, "but the next best thing—he 's engaged."

"Come to think of it," said the lady, "I 'm afraid we would n't have the room to spare, and the girls would hardly have time to entertain him. But we 'll have him up several times. I like his looks. I wish you had sent me word he was coming; I 'd have had a better luncheon."

"Make him a salad," rejoined the doctor, "and get out a bottle of the best claret. Thank God, the Yankees did n't get into my wine cellar! The young man must be treated with genuine Southern hospitality,—even if he were a Mormon and married ten times over."

"Indeed, he would not, Ed,—the idea! I 'm ashamed of you. Hurry back to the parlor and talk to him. The girls may want to primp a little before luncheon; we don't have a young man every day."

"Beauty unadorned," replied the doctor, "is adorned the most. My profession qualifies me to speak upon the subject. They are the two handsomest young women in Patesville, and the daughters of the most beautiful"—

"Don't you dare to say the word," interrupted Mrs. Green, with placid good nature. "I shall never grow old while I am living with a big boy like you. But I must go and make the salad."

At dinner the conversation ran on the family connections and their varying fortunes in the late war. Some had died upon the battlefield, and slept in unknown graves; some had been financially ruined by their faith in the "lost cause," having invested their all in the securities of the Confederate Government. Few had anything left but land, and land without slaves to work it was a drug in the market.

"I was offered a thousand acres, the other day, at twenty-five cents an acre," remarked the doctor. "The owner is so land-poor that he can't pay the taxes. They have taken our negroes and our liberties. It may be better for our grandchildren that the negroes are free, but it 's confoundedly hard on us to take them without paying for them. They may exalt our slaves over us temporarily, but they have not broken our spirit, and cannot take away our superiority of blood and breeding. In time we shall regain control. The negro is an inferior creature; God has marked him with the badge of servitude, and has adjusted his intellect to a servile condition. We will not long submit to his domination. I give you a toast, sir: The Anglo-Saxon race: may it remain forever, as now, the head and front of creation, never yielding its rights, and ready always to die, if need be, in defense of its liberties!"

"With all my heart, sir," replied Tryon, who felt in this company a thrill of that pleasure which accompanies conscious superiority,—"with all my heart, sir, if the ladies will permit me."

"We will join you," they replied. The toast was drunk with great enthusiasm.

"And now, my dear George," exclaimed the doctor, "to change one good subject for another, tell us who is the favored lady?"

"A Miss Rowena Warwick, sir," replied Tryon, vividly conscious of four pairs of eyes fixed upon him, but, apart from the momentary embarrassment, welcoming the subject as the one he would most like to speak upon.

"A good, strong old English name," observed the doctor.

"The heroine of 'Ivanhoe'!" exclaimed Miss Harriet.

"Warwick the Kingmaker!" said Miss Mary. "Is she tall and fair, and dignified and stately?"

"She is tall, dark rather than fair, and full of tender grace and sweet humility."

"She should have been named Rebecca instead of Rowena," rejoined Miss Mary, who was well up in her Scott.

"Tell us something about her people," asked Mrs. Green,—to which inquiry the young ladies looked assent.

In this meeting of the elect of his own class and kin Tryon felt a certain strong illumination upon the value of birth and blood. Finding Rena among people of the best social standing, the subsequent intimation that she was a girl of no family had seemed a small matter to one so much in love. Nevertheless, in his present company he felt a decided satisfaction in being able to present for his future wife a clean bill of social health.

"Her brother is the most prominent lawyer of Clarence. They live in a fine old family mansion, and are among the best people of the town."

"Quite right, my boy," assented the doctor. "None but the best are good enough for the best. You must bring her to Patesville some day. But bless my life!" he exclaimed, looking at his watch, "I must be going. Will you stay with the ladies awhile, or go back down town with me?"

"I think I had better go with you, sir. I shall have to see Judge Straight."

"Very well. But you must come back to supper, and we 'll have a few friends in to meet you. You must see some of the best people."

The doctor's buggy was waiting at the gate. As they were passing the hotel on their drive down town, the clerk came out to the curbstone and called to the doctor.

"There 's a man here, doctor, who 's been taken suddenly ill. Can you come in a minute?"

"I suppose I 'll have to. Will you wait for me here, George, or will you drive down to the office? I can walk the rest of the way."

"I think I 'll wait here, doctor," answered Tryon. "I 'll step up to my room a moment. I 'll be back by the time you 're ready."

It was while they were standing before the hotel, before alighting from the buggy, that Frank Fowler, passing on his cart, saw Tryon and set out as fast as he could to warn Mis' Molly and her daughter of his presence in the town.

Tryon went up to his room, returned after a while, and resumed his seat in the buggy, where he waited fifteen minutes longer before the doctor was ready. When they drew up in front of the office, the doctor's man Dave was standing in the doorway, looking up the street with an anxious expression, as though struggling hard to keep something upon his mind.

"Anything wanted, Dave?" asked the doctor.

"Dat young 'oman 's be'n heah ag'in, suh, an' wants ter see you bad. She 's in de drugstore dere now, suh. Bless Gawd!" he added to himself fervently, "I 'membered dat. Dis yer recommemb'ance er mine is gwine ter git me inter trouble ef I don' look out, an' dat 's a fac', sho'."

The doctor sprang from the buggy with an agility remarkable in a man of sixty. "Just keep your seat, George," he said to Tryon, "until I have spoken to the young woman, and then we 'll go across to Straight's. Or, if you 'll drive along a little farther, you can see the girl through the window. She 's worth the trouble, if you like a pretty face."

Tryon liked one pretty face; moreover, tinted beauty had never appealed to him. More to show a proper regard for what interested the doctor than from any curiosity of his own, he drove forward a few feet, until the side of the buggy was opposite the drugstore window, and then looked in.

Between the colored glass bottles in the window he could see a young woman, a tall and slender girl, like a lily on its stem. She stood talking with the doctor, who held his hat in his hand with as much deference as though she were the proudest dame in town. Her face was partly turned away from the window, but as Tryon's eye fell upon her, he gave a great start. Surely, no two women could be so much alike. The height, the graceful droop of the shoulders, the swan-like poise of the head, the well-turned little ear,—surely, no two women could have them all identical! But, pshaw! the notion was absurd, it was merely the reflex influence of his morning's dream.

She moved slightly; it was Rena's movement. Surely he knew the gown, and the style of hair-dressing! She rested her hand lightly on the back of a chair. The ring that glittered on her finger could be none other than his own.

The doctor bowed. The girl nodded in response, and, turning, left the store. Tryon leaned forward from the buggy-seat and kept his eye fixed on the figure that moved across the floor of the drugstore. As she came out, she turned her face casually toward the buggy, and there could no longer be any doubt as to her identity.

When Rena's eyes fell upon the young man in the buggy, she saw a face as pale as death, with starting eyes, in which love, which once had reigned there, had now given place to astonishment and horror. She stood a moment as if turned to stone. One appealing glance she gave,—a look that might have softened adamant. When she saw that it brought no answering sign of love or sorrow or regret, the color faded from her cheek, the light from her eye, and she fell fainting to the ground.

XVI

THE BOTTOM FALLS OUT

THE FIRST EFFECT of Tryon's discovery was, figuratively speaking, to knock the bottom out of things for him. It was much as if a boat on which he had been floating smoothly down the stream of pleasure had sunk suddenly and left him struggling in deep waters. The full realization of the truth, which followed speedily, had for the moment reversed his mental attitude toward her, and love and yearning had given place to anger and disgust. His agitation could hardly have escaped notice had not the doctor's attention, and that of the crowd that quickly gathered, been absorbed by the young woman who had fallen. During the time occupied in carrying her into the drugstore, restoring her to consciousness, and sending her home in a carriage, Tryon had time to recover in some degree his self-possession. When Rena had been taken home, he slipped away for a long walk, after which he called at Judge Straight's office and received the judge's report upon the matter presented. Judge Straight had found the claim, in his opinion, a good one; he had discovered property from which, in case the claim were allowed, the amount might be realized. The judge, who had already been informed of the incident at the drugstore, observed Tryon's preoccupation and guessed shrewdly at its cause, but gave no sign. Tryon left the matter of the note unreservedly in the lawyer's hands, with instructions to communicate to him any further developments.

Returning to the doctor's office, Tryon listened to that genial gentleman's comments on the accident, his own concern in which he, by a great effort, was able to conceal. The doctor insisted upon his returning to the Hill for supper. Tryon pleaded illness. The doctor was solicitous, felt his pulse, examined his tongue, pronounced him feverish, and prescribed a sedative. Tryon sought refuge in his room at the hotel, from which he did not emerge again until morning.

His emotions were varied and stormy. At first he could see

nothing but the fraud of which he had been made the victim. A negro girl had been foisted upon him for a white woman, and he had almost committed the unpardonable sin against his race of marrying her. Such a step, he felt, would have been criminal at any time; it would have been the most odious treachery at this epoch, when his people had been subjugated and humiliated by the Northern invaders, who had preached negro equality and abolished the wholesome laws decreeing the separation of the races. But no Southerner who loved his poor, downtrodden country, or his race, the proud Anglo-Saxon race which traced the clear stream of its blood to the cavaliers of England, could tolerate the idea that even in distant generations that unsullied current could be polluted by the blood of slaves. The very thought was an insult to the white people of the South. For Tryon's liberality, of which he had spoken so nobly and so sincerely, had been confined unconsciously, and as a matter of course, within the boundaries of his own race. The Southern mind, in discussing abstract questions relative to humanity, makes always, consciously or unconsciously, the mental reservation that the conclusions reached do not apply to the negro, unless they can be made to harmonize with the customs of the country.

But reasoning thus was not without effect upon a mind by nature reasonable above the average. Tryon's race impulse and social prejudice had carried him too far, and the swing of the mental pendulum brought his thoughts rapidly back in the opposite direction. Tossing uneasily on the bed, where he had thrown himself down without undressing, the air of the room oppressed him, and he threw open the window. The cool night air calmed his throbbing pulses. The moonlight, streaming through the window, flooded the room with a soft light, in which he seemed to see Rena standing before him, as she had appeared that afternoon, gazing at him with eyes that implored charity and forgiveness. He burst into tears,—bitter tears, that strained his heartstrings. He was only a youth. She was his first love, and he had lost her forever. She was worse than dead to him; for if he had seen her lying in her shroud before him, he could at least have cherished her memory; now, even this consolation was denied him.

The town clock—which so long as it was wound up regularly recked nothing of love or hate, joy or sorrow—solemnly tolled out the hour of midnight and sounded the knell of his lost love. Lost she was, as though she had never been, as she had indeed had no right to be. He resolutely determined to banish her image from his mind. See her again he could not; it would be painful to them both; it could be productive of no good to either. He had felt the power and charm of love, and no ordinary shock could have loosened its hold; but this catastrophe, which had so rudely swept away the groundwork of his passion, had stirred into new life all the slumbering pride of race and ancestry which characterized his caste. How much of this sensitive superiority was essential and how much accidental; how much of it was due to the ever-suggested comparison with a servile race; how much of it was ignorance and self-conceit; to what extent the boasted purity of his race would have been contaminated by the fair woman whose image filled his memory,—of these things he never thought. He was not influenced by sordid considerations; he would have denied that his course was controlled by any narrow prudence. If Rena had been white, pure white (for in his creed there was no compromise), he would have braved any danger for her sake. Had she been merely of illegitimate birth, he would have overlooked the bar sinister. Had her people been simply poor and of low estate, he would have brushed aside mere worldly considerations, and would have bravely sacrificed convention for love; for his liberality was not a mere form of words. But the one objection which he could not overlook was, unhappily, the one that applied to the only woman who had as yet moved his heart. He tried to be angry with her, but after the first hour he found it impossible. He was a man of too much imagination not to be able to put himself, in some measure at least, in her place,—to perceive that for her the step which had placed her in Tryon's world was the working out of nature's great law of self-preservation, for which he could not blame her. But for the sheerest accident,—no, rather, but for a providential interference,—he would have married her, and might have gone to the grave unconscious that she was other than she seemed.

The clock struck the hour of two. With a shiver he closed the window, undressed by the moonlight, drew down the shade, and went to bed. He fell into an unquiet slumber, and dreamed again of Rena. He must learn to control his waking thoughts; his dreams could not be curbed. In that realm Rena's image was for many a day to remain supreme. He dreamed of her sweet smile, her soft touch, her gentle voice. In all her fair young beauty she stood before him, and then by some hellish magic she was slowly transformed into a hideous black hag. With agonized eyes he watched her beautiful tresses become mere wisps of coarse wool, wrapped round with dingy cotton strings; he saw her clear eyes grow bloodshot, her ivory teeth turn to unwholesome fangs. With a shudder he awoke, to find the cold gray dawn of a rainy day stealing through the window.

He rose, dressed himself, went down to breakfast, then entered the writing-room and penned a letter which, after reading it over, he tore into small pieces and threw into the waste-basket. A second shared the same fate. Giving up the task, he left the hotel and walked down to Dr. Green's office.

"Is the doctor in?" he asked of the colored attendant.

"No, suh," replied the man; "he 's gone ter see de young cullud gal w'at fainted w'en de doctuh was wid you yistiddy."

Tryon sat down at the doctor's desk and hastily scrawled a note, stating that business compelled his immediate departure. He thanked the doctor for courtesies extended, and left his regards for the ladies. Returning to the hotel, he paid his bill and took a hack for the wharf, from which a boat was due to leave at nine o'clock.

As the hack drove down Front Street, Tryon noted idly the houses that lined the street. When he reached the sordid district in the lower part of the town, there was nothing to attract his attention until the carriage came abreast of a row of cedar-trees, beyond which could be seen the upper part of a large house with dormer windows. Before the gate stood a horse and buggy, which Tryon thought he recognized as Dr. Green's. He leaned forward and addressed the driver.

"Can you tell me who lives there?" Tryon asked, pointing to the house.

"A cullud 'oman, suh," the man replied, touching his hat. "Mis' Molly Walden an' her daughter Rena."

The vivid impression he received of this house, and the

spectre that rose before him of a pale, broken-hearted girl within its gray walls, weeping for a lost lover and a vanished dream of happiness, did not argue well for Tryon's future peace of mind. Rena's image was not to be easily expelled from his heart; for the laws of nature are higher and more potent than merely human institutions, and upon anything like a fair field are likely to win in the long run.

XVII

TWO LETTERS

WARWICK awaited events with some calmness and some philosophy,—he could hardly have had the one without the other; and it required much philosophy to make him wait a week in patience for information upon a subject in which he was so vitally interested. The delay pointed to disaster. Bad news being expected, delay at least put off the evil day. At the end of the week he received two letters,—one addressed in his own handwriting and postmarked Patesville, N. C.; the other in the handwriting of George Tryon. He opened the Patesville letter, which ran as follows:—

MY DEAR SON,—Frank is writing this letter for me. I am not well, but, thank the Lord, I am better than I was.

Rena has had a heap of trouble on account of me and my sickness. If I could of dreamt that I was going to do so much harm, I would of died and gone to meet my God without writing one word to spoil my girl's chances in life; but I did n't know what was going to happen, and I hope the Lord will forgive me.

Frank knows all about it, and so I am having him write this letter for me, as Rena is not well enough yet. Frank has been very good to me and to Rena. He was down to your place and saw Rena there, and never said a word about it to nobody, not even to me, because he did n't want to do Rena no harm. Frank is the best friend I have got in town, because he does so much for me and don't want nothing in return. (He tells me not to put this in about him, but I want you to know it.)

And now about Rena. She come to see me, and I got better right away, for it was longing for her as much as anything else that made me sick, and I was mighty mizzable. When she had been here three days and was going back next day, she went up town to see the doctor for me, and while she was up there she fainted and fell down in the street, and Dr. Green sent her home in his buggy and come down to see her. He could n't tell what was the matter with her, but she has been sick ever since and out of her head some of the time, and keeps on calling on somebody by the name of George, which was the young white man she told me she was going to marry. It seems he was in town the day Rena was took sick, for Frank saw him up street and run all the way down here to tell me, so that she could keep out of his way, while she was still up town waiting for the doctor and getting me some camphor gum for my camphor bottle. Old Judge Straight must have knowed something about it, for he sent me a note to keep Rena in the house, but the little boy he sent it by did n't bring it till Rena was already gone up town, and, as I could n't read, of course I did n't know what it said. Dr. Green heard Rena running on while she was out of her head, and I reckon he must have suspicioned something, for he looked kind of queer and went away without saying nothing. Frank says she met this man on the street, and when he found out she was n't white, he said or done something that broke her heart and she fainted and fell down.

I am writing you this letter because I know you will be worrying about Rena not coming back. If it was n't for Frank, I hardly know how I could write to you. Frank is not going to say nothing about Rena's passing for white and meeting this man, and neither am I; and I don't suppose Judge Straight will say nothing, because he is our good friend; and Dr. Green won't say nothing about it, because Frank says Dr. Green's cook Nancy says this young man named George stopped with him and was some cousin or relation to the family, and they would n't want people to know that any of their kin was thinking about marrying a colored girl, and the white folks have all been mad since J. B. Thompson married his black housekeeper when she got religion and would n't live with him no more.

All the rest of the connection are well. I have just been in to see how Rena is. She is feeling some better, I think, and says give you her love and she will write you a letter in a few days, as soon as she is well enough. She bust out crying while she was talking, but I reckon that is better than being out of her head. I hope this may find you well, and that this man of Rena's won't say nor do nothing down there to hurt you. He has not wrote to Rena nor sent her no word. I reckon he is very mad.

Your affectionate mother,

MARY WALDEN.

This letter, while confirming Warwick's fears, relieved his suspense. He at least knew the worst, unless there should be something still more disturbing in Tryon's letter, which he now proceeded to open, and which ran as follows:—

JOHN WARWICK, ESQ.

Dear Sir,—When I inform you, as you are doubtless informed ere the receipt of this, that I saw your sister in Patesville last week and learned the nature of those antecedents of yours and hers at which you hinted so obscurely in a recent conversation, you will not be surprised to learn that I take this opportunity of renouncing any pretensions to Miss Warwick's hand, and request you to convey this message to her, since it was through you that I formed her acquaintance. I think perhaps that few white men would deem it necessary to make an explanation under the circumstances, and I do not know that I need say more than that no one, considering where and how I met your sister, would have dreamed of even the possibility of what I have learned. I might with justice reproach you for trifling with the most sacred feelings of a man's heart; but I realize the hardship of your position and hers, and can make allowances. I would never have sought to know this thing; I would doubtless have been happier had I gone through life without finding it out; but having the knowledge, I cannot ignore it, as you must understand perfectly well. I regret that she should be distressed or disappointed,—she has not suffered alone.

I need scarcely assure you that I shall say nothing about this affair, and that I shall keep your secret as though it were my own. Personally, I shall never be able to think of you as other than a white man, as you may gather from the tone of this letter; and while I cannot marry your sister, I wish her every happiness, and remain,

Yours very truly,

GEORGE TRYON.

Warwick could not know that this formal epistle was the last of a dozen that Tryon had written and destroyed during the week since the meeting in Patesville,—hot, blistering letters, cold, cutting letters, scornful, crushing letters. Though none of them was sent, except this last, they had furnished a safety-valve for his emotions, and had left him in a state of mind that permitted him to write the foregoing.

And now, while Rena is recovering from her illness, and Tryon from his love, and while Fate is shuffling the cards for another deal, a few words may be said about the past life of the people who lived in the rear of the flower garden, in the quaint old house beyond the cedars, and how their lives were mingled with those of the men and women around them and others that were gone. For connected with our kind we must be; if not by our virtues, then by our vices,—if not by our services, at least by our needs.

XVIII

UNDER THE OLD RÉGIME

FOR MANY YEARS before the civil war there had lived, in the old house behind the cedars, a free colored woman who went by the name of Molly Walden—her rightful name, for her parents were free-born and legally married. She was a tall woman, straight as an arrow. Her complexion in youth was of an old ivory tint, which at the period of this story, time had darkened measurably. Her black eyes, now faded, had once sparkled with the fire of youth. High cheek-bones, straight black hair, and a certain dignified reposefulness of manner pointed to an aboriginal descent. Tradition gave her to the negro race. Doubtless she had a strain of each, with white blood very visibly predominating over both. In Louisiana or the West Indies she would have been called a quadroon, or more loosely, a creole; in North Carolina, where fine distinctions were not the rule in matters of color, she was sufficiently differentiated when described as a bright mulatto.

Molly's free birth carried with it certain advantages, even in the South before the war. Though degraded from its high estate, and shorn of its choicest attributes, the word "freedom" had nevertheless a cheerful sound, and described a condition that left even to colored people who could claim it some liberty of movement and some control of their own persons. They were not citizens, yet they were not slaves. No negro, save in books, ever refused freedom; many of them ran frightful risks to achieve it. Molly's parents were of the class, more numerous in North Carolina than elsewhere, known as "old issue free negroes," which took its rise in the misty colonial period, when race lines were not so closely drawn, and the population of North Carolina comprised many Indians, runaway negroes, and indentured white servants from the seaboard plantations, who mingled their blood with great freedom and small formality. Free colored people in North Carolina exercised the right of suffrage as late as 1835, and some of them, in spite of galling restrictions, attained to a considerable degree of prosperity, and dreamed of a still brighter future, when the growing tyranny of the slave power crushed their hopes and crowded the free people back upon the black mass just beneath them. Mis' Molly's father had been at one time a man of some means. In an evil hour, with an overweening confidence in his fellow men, he indorsed a note for a white man who, in a moment of financial hardship, clapped his colored neighbor on the back and called him brother. Not poverty, but wealth, is the most potent leveler. In due time the indorser was called upon to meet the maturing obligation. This was the beginning of a series of financial difficulties which speedily involved him in ruin. He died prematurely, a disappointed and disheartened man, leaving his family in dire poverty.

His widow and surviving children lived on for a little while at the house he had owned, just outside of the town, on one of the main traveled roads. By the wayside, near the house, there was a famous deep well. The slim, barefoot girl, with sparkling eyes and voluminous hair, who played about the yard and sometimes handed water in a gourd to travelers, did not long escape critical observation. A gentleman drove by one day, stopped at the well, smiled upon the girl, and said kind words. He came again, more than once, and soon, while scarcely more than a child in years, Molly was living in her own house, hers by deed of gift, for her protector was rich and liberal. Her mother nevermore knew want. Her poor relations could always find a meal in Molly's kitchen. She did not flaunt her prosperity in the world's face; she hid it discreetly behind the cedar screen. Those who wished could know of it, for there were few secrets in Patesville; those who chose could as easily ignore it. There were few to trouble themselves about the secluded life of an obscure woman of a class which had no recognized place in the social economy. She worshiped the ground upon which her lord walked, was humbly grateful for his protection, and quite as faithful as the forbidden marriage vow could possibly have made her. She led her life in material peace and comfort, and with a certain amount of dignity. Of her false relation to society she was not without some vague conception; but the moral point involved was so confused with other questions growing out of slavery and caste as to cause her, as a rule, but little uneasiness; and only now and then, in the moments of deeper feeling that come sometimes to all who live and love, did there break through the mists of ignorance and prejudice surrounding her a flash of light by which she saw, so far as she was capable of seeing, her true position, which in the clear light of truth no special pleading could entirely justify. For she was free, she had not the slave's excuse. With every inducement to do evil and few incentives to do well, and hence entitled to charitable judgment, she yet had freedom of choice, and therefore could not wholly escape blame. Let it be said, in further extenuation, that no other woman lived in neglect or sorrow because of her. She robbed no one else. For what life gave her she returned an equivalent; and what she did not pay, her children settled to the last farthing.

Several years before the war, when Mis' Molly's daughter Rena was a few years old, death had suddenly removed the source of their prosperity.

The household was not left entirely destitute. Mis' Molly owned her home, and had a store of gold pieces in the chest beneath her bed. A small piece of real estate stood in the name of each of the children, the income from which contributed to their maintenance. Larger expectations were dependent upon the discovery of a promised will, which never came to light. Mis' Molly wore black for several years after this bereavement, until the teacher and the preacher, following close upon the heels of military occupation, suggested to the colored people new standards of life and character, in the light of which Mis' Molly laid her mourning sadly and shamefacedly aside. She had eaten of the fruit of the Tree of Knowledge. After the war she formed the habit of church-going, and might have been seen now and then, with her daughter, in a retired corner of the gallery of the white Episcopal church. Upon the ground floor was a certain pew which could be seen from her seat, where once had sat a gentleman whose pleasures had not interfered with the practice of his religion. She might have had a better seat in a church where a Northern missionary would have preached a sermon better suited to her comprehension and her moral needs, but she preferred the other. She was not white, alas! she was shut out from this seeming paradise; but she liked to see the distant glow of the celestial city, and to recall the days when she had basked in its radiance. She did not sympathize greatly with the new era opened up for the emancipated slaves; she had no ideal love of liberty; she was no broader and no more altruistic than the white people around her, to whom she had always looked up; and she sighed for the old days, because to her they had been the good days. Now, not only was her king dead, but the shield of his memory protected her no longer.

Molly had lost one child, and his grave was visible from the kitchen window, under a small clump of cedars in the rear of the two-acre lot. For even in the towns many a household had its private cemetery in those old days when the living were close to the dead, and ghosts were not the mere chimeras of a sick imagination, but real though unsubstantial entities, of which it was almost disgraceful not to have seen one or two. Had not the Witch of Endor called up the shade of Samuel the prophet? Had not the spirit of Mis' Molly's dead son appeared to her, as well as the ghostly presence of another she had loved?

In 1855, Mis' Molly's remaining son had grown into a tall, slender lad of fifteen, with his father's patrician features and his mother's Indian hair, and no external sign to mark him off from the white boys on the street. He soon came to know, however, that there was a difference. He was informed one day that he was black. He denied the proposition and thrashed the child who made it. The scene was repeated the next day, with a variation,—he was himself thrashed by a larger boy. When he had been beaten five or six times, he ceased to argue the point, though to himself he never admitted the charge. His playmates might call him black; the mirror proved that God, the Father of all, had made him white; and God, he had been taught, made no mistakes,—having made him white, He must have meant him to be white.

In the "hall" or parlor of his mother's house stood a quaintly carved black walnut bookcase, containing a small but remarkable collection of books, which had at one time been used, in his hours of retreat and relaxation from business and politics, by the distinguished gentleman who did not give his name to Mis' Molly's children,—to whom it would have been a valuable heritage, could they have had the right to bear it. Among the books were a volume of Fielding's complete works, in fine print, set in double columns; a set of Bulwer's novels; a collection of everything that Walter Scott—the literary idol of the South—had ever written; Beaumont and Fletcher's plays, cheek by jowl with the history of the virtuous Clarissa Harlowe; the Spectator and Tristram Shandy, Robinson Crusoe and the Arabian Nights. On these secluded shelves Roderick Random, Don Quixote, and Gil Blas for a long time ceased their wanderings, the Pilgrim's Progress was suspended, Milton's mighty harmonies were dumb, and Shakespeare reigned over a silent kingdom. An illustrated Bible, with a wonderful Apocrypha, was flanked on one side by Volney's Ruins of Empire and on the other by Paine's Age of Reason, for the collector of the books had been a man of catholic taste as well as of inquiring mind, and no one who could have criticised his reading ever penetrated behind the cedar hedge. A history of the French Revolution consorted amiably with a homespun chronicle of North Carolina, rich in biographical notices of distinguished citizens and inscriptions from their tombstones, upon reading which one might well wonder why North Carolina had not long ago eclipsed the rest of the world in wealth, wisdom, glory, and renown. On almost every page of this monumental work could be found the most ardent panegyrics of liberty, side by side with the slavery statistics of the State,—an incongruity of which the learned author was deliciously unconscious.

When John Walden was yet a small boy, he had learned all that could be taught by the faded mulatto teacher in the long, shiny black frock coat, whom local public opinion permitted to teach a handful of free colored children for a pittance barely enough to keep soul and body together. When the boy had learned to read, he discovered the library, which for several years had been without a reader, and found in it the portal of a new world, peopled with strange and marvelous beings. Lying prone upon the floor of the shaded front piazza, behind the fragrant garden, he followed the fortunes of Tom Jones and Sophia; he wept over the fate of Eugene Aram; he penetrated with Richard the Lion-heart into Saladin's tent, with Gil Blas into the robbers' cave; he flew through the air on the magic carpet or the enchanted horse, or tied with Sindbad to the roc's leg. Sometimes he read or repeated the simpler stories to his little sister, sitting wide-eyed by his side. When he had read all the books,—indeed, long before he had read them all,—he too had tasted of the fruit of the Tree of Knowledge: contentment took its flight, and happiness lay far beyond the sphere where he was born. The blood of his white fathers, the heirs of the ages, cried out for its own, and after the manner of that blood set about getting the object of its desire.

Near the corner of Mackenzie Street, just one block north of the Patesville market-house, there had stood for many years before the war, on the verge of the steep banks of Beaver Creek, a small frame office building, the front of which was level with the street, while the rear rested on long brick pillars founded on the solid rock at the edge of the brawling stream below. Here, for nearly half a century, Archibald Straight had transacted legal business for the best people of Northumberland County. Full many a lawsuit had he won, lost, or settled; many a spendthrift had he saved from ruin, and not a few families from disgrace. Several times honored by election to the bench, he had so dispensed justice tempered with mercy as to win the hearts of all good citizens, and especially those of the poor, the oppressed, and the socially disinherited. The rights of the humblest negro, few as they might be, were as sacred to him as those of the proudest aristocrat, and he had sentenced a man to be hanged for the murder of his own slave. An old-fashioned man, tall and spare of figure and bowed somewhat with age, he was always correctly clad in a long frock coat of broadcloth, with a high collar and a black stock. Courtly in address to his social equals (superiors he had none), he was kind and considerate to those beneath him. He owned a few domestic servants, no one of whom had ever felt the weight of his hand, and for whose ultimate freedom he had provided in his will. In the long-drawn-out slavery agitation he had taken a keen interest, rather as observer than as participant. As the heat of controversy increased, his lack of zeal for the peculiar institution led to his defeat for the bench by a more active partisan. His was too just a mind not to perceive the arguments on both sides; but, on the whole, he had stood by the ancient landmarks, content to let events drift to a conclusion he did not expect to see; the institutions of his fathers would probably last his lifetime.

One day Judge Straight was sitting in his office reading a recently published pamphlet,—presenting an elaborate proslavery argument, based upon the hopeless intellectual inferiority of the negro, and the physical and moral degeneration of mulattoes, who combined the worst qualities of their two ancestral races,—when a barefooted boy walked into the office, straw hat in hand, came boldly up to the desk at which the old judge was sitting, and said as the judge looked up through his gold-rimmed glasses,—

"Sir, I want to be a lawyer!"

"God bless me!" exclaimed the judge. "It is a singular desire, from a singular source, and expressed in a singular way. Who the devil are you, sir, that wish so strange a thing as to become a lawyer—everybody's servant?"

"And everybody's master, sir," replied the lad stoutly.

"That is a matter of opinion, and open to argument," rejoined the judge, amused and secretly flattered by this tribute to his profession, "though there may be a grain of truth in what you say. But what is your name, Mr. Would-be-lawyer?"

"John Walden, sir," answered the lad.

"John Walden?—Walden?" mused the judge. "What Walden can that be? Do you belong in town?"

"Yes, sir."

"Humph! I can't imagine who you are. It 's plain that you are a lad of good blood, and yet I don't know whose son you can be. What is your father's name?"

The lad hesitated, and flushed crimson.

The old gentleman noted his hesitation. "It is a wise son," he thought, "that knows his own father. He is a bright lad, and will have this question put to him more than once. I 'll see how he will answer it."

The boy maintained an awkward silence, while the old judge eyed him keenly.

"My father 's dead," he said at length, in a low voice. "I 'm Mis' Molly Walden's son." He had expected, of course, to tell who he was, if asked, but had not foreseen just the form of the inquiry; and while he had thought more of his race than of his illegitimate birth, he realized at this moment as never before that this question too would be always with him. As put now by Judge Straight, it made him wince. He had not read his father's books for nothing.

"God bless my soul!" exclaimed the judge in genuine surprise at this answer; "and you want to be a lawyer!" The situation was so much worse than he had suspected that even an old practitioner, case-hardened by years of life at the trial table and on the bench, was startled for a moment into a comical sort of consternation, so apparent that a lad less stout-hearted would have weakened and fled at the sight of it.

"Yes, sir. Why not?" responded the boy, trembling a little at the knees, but stoutly holding his ground.

"He wants to be a lawyer, and he asks me why not!" muttered the judge, speaking apparently to himself. He rose from his chair, walked across the room, and threw open a window. The cool morning air brought with it the babbling of the stream below and the murmur of the mill near by. He glanced across the creek to the ruined foundation of an old house on the low ground beyond the creek. Turning from the window, he looked back at the boy, who had remained standing between him and the door. At that moment another lad came along the street and stopped opposite the open doorway. The presence of the two boys in connection with the book he had been reading suggested a comparison. The judge knew the lad outside as the son of a leading merchant of the town. The merchant and his wife were both of old families which had lived in the community for several generations, and whose blood was presumably of the purest strain; yet the boy was sallow, with amorphous features, thin shanks, and stooping shoulders. The youth standing in the judge's office, on the contrary, was straight, shapely, and well-grown. His eye was clear, and he kept it fixed on the old gentleman with a look in which there was nothing of cringing. He was no darker than many a white boy bronzed by the Southern sun; his hair and eyes were black, and his features of the high-bred, clean-cut order that marks the patrician type the world over. What struck the judge most forcibly, however, was the lad's resemblance to an old friend and companion and client. He recalled a certain conversation with this old friend, who had said to him one day:

"Archie, I 'm coming in to have you draw my will. There are some children for whom I would like to make ample provision. I can't give them anything else, but money will make them free of the world."

The judge's friend had died suddenly before carrying out this good intention. The judge had taken occasion to suggest the existence of these children, and their father's intentions concerning them, to the distant relatives who had inherited his friend's large estate. They had chosen to take offense at the suggestion. One had thought it in shocking bad taste; another considered any mention of such a subject an insult to his cousin's memory. A third had said, with flashing eyes, that the woman and her children had already robbed the estate of enough; that it was a pity the little niggers were not slaves—that they would have added measurably to the value of the property. Judge Straight's manner indicated some disapproval of their attitude, and the settlement of the estate was placed in other hands than his. Now, this son, with his father's face and his father's voice, stood before his father's friend, demanding entrance to the golden gate of opportunity, which society barred to all who bore the blood of the despised race.

As he kept on looking at the boy, who began at length to grow somewhat embarrassed under this keen scrutiny, the judge's mind reverted to certain laws and judicial decisions that he had looked up once or twice in his lifetime. Even the law, the instrument by which tyranny riveted the chains upon its victims, had revolted now and then against the senseless and unnatural prejudice by which a race ascribing its superiority to right of blood permitted a mere suspicion of servile blood to outweigh a vast preponderance of its own.

"Why, indeed, should he not be a lawyer, or anything else that a man might be, if it be in him?" asked the judge, speaking rather to himself than to the boy. "Sit down," he ordered, pointing to a chair on the other side of the room. That he should ask a colored lad to be seated in his presence was of itself enough to stamp the judge as eccentric. "You want to be a lawyer," he went on, adjusting his spectacles. "You are aware, of course, that you are a negro?"

"I am white," replied the lad, turning back his sleeve and holding out his arm, "and I am free, as all my people were before me."

The old lawyer shook his head, and fixed his eyes upon the lad with a slightly quizzical smile. "You are black," he said, "and you are not free. You cannot travel without your papers; you cannot secure accommodations at an inn; you could not vote, if you were of age; you cannot be out after nine o'clock without a permit. If a white man struck you, you could not return the blow, and you could not testify against him in a court of justice. You are black, my lad, and you are not free. Did you ever hear of the Dred Scott decision, delivered by the great, wise, and learned Judge Taney?"

"No, sir," answered the boy.

"It is too long to read," rejoined the judge, taking up the pamphlet he had laid down upon the lad's entrance, "but it says in substance, as quoted by this author, that negroes are beings 'of an inferior order, and altogether unfit to associate with the white race, either in social or political relations; in fact, so inferior that they have no rights which the white man is bound to respect, and that the negro may justly and lawfully be reduced to slavery for his benefit.' That is the law of this nation, and that is the reason why you cannot be a lawyer."

"It may all be true," replied the boy, "but it don't apply to me. It says 'the negro.' A negro is black; I am white, and not black."

"Black as ink, my lad," returned the lawyer, shaking his head. " 'One touch of nature makes the whole world kin,' says the poet. Somewhere, sometime, you had a black ancestor. One drop of black blood makes the whole man black."

"Why should n't it be the other way, if the white blood is so much superior?" inquired the lad.

"Because it is more convenient as it is—and more profitable."

"It is not right," maintained the lad.

"God bless me!" exclaimed the old gentleman, "he is invading the field of ethics! He will be questioning the righteousness of slavery next! I 'm afraid you would n't make a good lawyer, in any event. Lawyers go by the laws—they abide by the accomplished fact; to them, whatever is, is right. The laws do not permit men of color to practice law, and public sentiment would not allow one of them to study it."

"I had thought," said the lad, "that I might pass for white. There are white people darker than I am."

"Ah, well, that is another matter; but"—

The judge stopped for a moment, struck by the absurdity of his arguing such a question with a mulatto boy. He really must be falling into premature dotage. The proper thing would be to rebuke the lad for his presumption and advise him to learn to take care of horses, or make boots, or lay bricks. But again he saw his old friend in the lad's face, and again he looked in vain for any sign of negro blood. The least earmark would have turned the scale, but he could not find it.

"That is another matter," he repeated. "Here you have started as black, and must remain so. But if you wish to move away, and sink your past into oblivion, the case might be different. Let us see what the law is; you might not need it if you went far enough, but it is well enough to be within it—liberty is sweeter when founded securely on the law."

He took down a volume bound in legal calf and glanced through it. "The color line is drawn in North Carolina at four generations removed from the negro; there have been judicial decisions to that effect. I imagine that would cover your case. But let us see what South Carolina may say about it," he continued, taking another book. "I think the law is even more liberal there. Ah, this is the place:—

" 'The term mulatto,' " he read, " 'is not invariably applicable to every admixture of African blood with the European, nor is one having all the features of a white to be ranked with the degraded class designated by the laws of this State as persons of color, because of some remote taint of the negro race. Juries would probably be justified in holding a person to be white in whom the admixture of African blood did not exceed one eighth. And even where color or feature are doubtful, it is a question for the jury to decide by reputation, by reception into society, and by their exercise of the privileges of the white man, as well as by admixture of blood.' "

"Then I need not be black?" the boy cried, with sparkling eyes.

"No," replied the lawyer, "you need not be black, away from Patesville. You have the somewhat unusual privilege, it seems, of choosing between two races, and if you are a lad of spirit, as I think you are, it will not take you long to make your choice. As you have all the features of a white man, you would, at least in South Carolina, have simply to assume the place and exercise the privileges of a white man. You might, of course, do the same thing anywhere, as long as no one knew your origin. But the matter has been adjudicated there in several cases, and on the whole I think South Carolina is the place for you. They 're more liberal there, perhaps because they have many more blacks than whites, and would like to lessen the disproportion."

"From this time on," said the boy, "I am white."

"Softly, softly, my Caucasian fellow citizen," returned the judge, chuckling with quiet amusement. "You are white in the abstract, before the law. You may cherish the fact in secret, but I would not advise you to proclaim it openly just yet. You must wait until you go away—to South Carolina."

"And can I learn to be a lawyer, sir?" asked the lad.

"It seems to me that you ought to be reasonably content for one day with what you have learned already. You cannot be a lawyer until you are white, in position as well as in theory, nor until you are twenty-one years old. I need an office boy. If you are willing to come into my office, sweep it, keep my books dusted, and stay here when I am out, I do not care. To the rest of the town you will be my servant, and still a negro. If you choose to read my books when no one is about and be white in your own private opinion, I have no objection. When you have made up your mind to go away, perhaps what you have read may help you. But mum 's the word! If I hear a whisper of this from any other source, out you go, neck and crop! I am willing to help you make a man of yourself, but it can only be done under the rose."

For two years John Walden openly swept the office and surreptitiously read the law books of old Judge Straight. When he was eighteen, he asked his mother for a sum of money, kissed her good-by, and went out into the world. When his sister, then a pretty child of seven, cried because her big brother was going away, he took her up in his arms, gave her a silver dime with a hole in it for a keepsake, hugged her close, and kissed her.

"Nev' min', sis," he said soothingly. "Be a good little gal, an' some o' these days I 'll come back to see you and bring you somethin' fine."

In after years, when Mis' Molly was asked what had become of her son, she would reply with sad complacency,—

"He 's gone over on the other side."

As we have seen, he came back ten years later.

Many years before, when Mis' Molly, then a very young woman, had taken up her residence in the house behind the cedars, the gentleman heretofore referred to had built a cabin on the opposite corner, in which he had installed a trusted slave by the name of Peter Fowler and his wife Nancy. Peter was a good mechanic, and hired his time from his master with the provision that Peter and his wife should do certain work for Mis' Molly and serve as a sort of protection for her. In course of time Peter, who was industrious and thrifty, saved enough money to purchase his freedom and that of his wife and their one child, and to buy the little house across the street, with the cooper shop behind it. After they had acquired their freedom, Peter and Nancy did no work for Mis' Molly save as they were paid for it, and as a rule preferred not to work at all for the woman who had been practically their mistress; it made them seem less free. Nevertheless, the two households had remained upon good terms, even after the death of the man whose will had brought them together, and who had remained Peter's patron after he had ceased to be his master. There was no intimate association between the two families. Mis' Molly felt herself infinitely superior to Peter and his wife,—scarcely less superior than her poor white neighbors felt themselves to Mis' Molly. Mis' Molly always meant to be kind, and treated Peter and Nancy with a certain good-natured condescension. They resented this, never openly or offensively, but always in a subconscious sort of way, even when they did not speak of it among themselves—much as they had resented her mistress-ship in the old days. For after all, they argued, in spite of her airs and graces, her white face and her fine clothes, was she not a negro, even as themselves? and since the slaves had been freed, was not one negro as good as another?

Peter's son Frank had grown up with little Rena. He was several years older than she, and when Rena was a small child Mis' Molly had often confided her to his care, and he had watched over her and kept her from harm. When Frank became old enough to go to work in the cooper shop, Rena, then six or seven, had often gone across to play among the clean white shavings. Once Frank, while learning the trade, had let slip a sharp steel tool, which flying toward Rena had grazed her arm and sent the red blood coursing along the white flesh and soaking the muslin sleeve. He had rolled up the sleeve and stanched the blood and dried her tears. For a long time thereafter her mother kept her away from the shop and was very cold to Frank. One day the little girl wandered down to the bank of the old canal. It had been raining for several days, and the water was quite deep in the channel. The child slipped and fell into the stream. From the open window of the cooper shop Frank heard a scream. He ran down to the canal and pulled her out, and carried her all wet and dripping to the house. From that time he had been restored to favor. He had watched the girl grow up to womanhood in the years following the war, and had been sorry when she became too old to play about the shop.

He never spoke to her of love,—indeed, he never thought of his passion in such a light. There would have been no legal barrier to their union; there would have been no frightful menace to white supremacy in the marriage of the negro and the octoroon: the drop of dark blood bridged the chasm. But Frank knew that she did not love him, and had not hoped that she might. His was one of those rare souls that can give with small hope of return. When he had made the scar upon her arm, by the same token she had branded him her slave forever; when he had saved her from a watery grave, he had given his life to her. There are depths of fidelity and devotion in the negro heart that have never been fathomed or fully appreciated. Now and then in the kindlier phases of slavery these qualities were brightly conspicuous, and in them, if wisely appealed to, lies the strongest hope of amity between the two races whose destiny seems bound up together in the

Western world. Even a dumb brute can be won by kindness. Surely it were worth while to try some other weapon than scorn and contumely and hard words upon people of our common race,—the human race, which is bigger and broader than Celt or Saxon, barbarian or Greek, Jew or Gentile, black or white; for we are all children of a common Father, forget it as we may, and each one of us is in some measure his brother's keeper.

XIX

GOD MADE US ALL

RENA was convalescent from a two-weeks' illness when her brother came to see her. He arrived at Patesville by an early morning train before the town was awake, and walked unnoticed from the station to his mother's house. His meeting with his sister was not without emotion: he embraced her tenderly, and Rena became for a few minutes a very Niobe of grief.

"Oh, it was cruel, cruel!" she sobbed. "I shall never get over it."

"I know it, my dear," replied Warwick soothingly,—"I know it, and I 'm to blame for it. If I had never taken you away from here, you would have escaped this painful experience. But do not despair; all is not lost. Tryon will not marry you, as I hoped he might, while I feared the contrary; but he is a gentleman, and will be silent. Come back and try again."

"No, John. I could n't go through it a second time. I managed very well before, when I thought our secret was unknown; but now I could never be sure. It would be borne on every wind, for aught I knew, and every rustling leaf might whisper it. The law, you said, made us white; but not the law, nor even love, can conquer prejudice. *He* spoke of my beauty, my grace, my sweetness! I looked into his eyes and believed him. And yet he left me without a word! What would I do in Clarence now? I came away engaged to be married, with even the day set; I should go back forsaken and discredited; even the servants would pity me."

"Little Albert is pining for you," suggested Warwick. "We could make some explanation that would spare your feelings."

"Ah, do not tempt me, John! I love the child, and am grieved to leave him. I 'm grateful, too, John, for what you have done for me. I am not sorry that I tried it. It opened my eyes, and I would rather die of knowledge than live in ignorance. But I could not go through it again, John; I am not strong enough. I could do you no good; I have made you trouble enough already. Get a mother for Albert—Mrs. Newberry would marry you, secret and all, and would be good to the child. Forget me, John, and take care of yourself. Your friend has found you out through me—he may have told a dozen people. You think he will be silent;—I thought he loved me, and he left me without a word, and with a look that told me how he hated and despised me. I would not have believed it—even of a white man."

"You do him an injustice," said her brother, producing Tryon's letter. "He did not get off unscathed. He sent you a message."

She turned her face away, but listened while he read the letter. "He did not love me," she cried angrily, when he had finished, "or he would not have cast me off—he would not have looked at me so. The law would have let him marry me. I seemed as white as he did. He might have gone anywhere with me, and no one would have stared at us curiously; no one need have known. The world is wide—there must be some place where a man could live happily with the woman he loved."

"Yes, Rena, there is; and the world is wide enough for you to get along without Tryon."

"For a day or two," she went on, "I hoped he might come back. But his expression in that awful moment grew upon me, haunted me day and night, until I shuddered at the thought that I might ever see him again. He looked at me as though I were not even a human being. I do not love him any longer, John; I would not marry him if I were white, or he were as I am. He did not love me—or he would have acted differently. He might have loved me and have left me—he could not have loved me and have looked at me so!"

She was weeping hysterically. There was little he could say to comfort her. Presently she dried her tears. Warwick was reluctant to leave her in Patesville. Her childish happiness had been that of ignorance; she could never be happy there again. She had flowered in the sunlight; she must not pine away in the shade.

"If you won't come back with me, Rena, I'll send you to some school at the North, where you can acquire a liberal education, and prepare yourself for some career of usefulness. You may marry a better man than even Tryon."

"No," she replied firmly, "I shall never marry any man, and I 'll not leave mother again. God is against it; I 'll stay with my own people."

"God has nothing to do with it," retorted Warwick. "God is too often a convenient stalking-horse for human selfishness. If there is anything to be done, so unjust, so despicable, so wicked that human reason revolts at it, there is always some smug hypocrite to exclaim, 'It is the will of God.' "

"God made us all," continued Rena dreamily, "and for some good purpose, though we may not always see it. He made some people white, and strong, and masterful, and—heartless. He made others black and homely, and poor and weak"—

"And a lot of others 'poor white' and shiftless," smiled Warwick.

"He made us, too," continued Rena, intent upon her own thought, "and He must have had a reason for it. Perhaps He meant us to bring the others together in his own good time. A man may make a new place for himself—a woman is born and bound to hers. God must have meant me to stay here, or He would not have sent me back. I shall accept things as they are. Why should I seek the society of people whose friendship—and love—one little word can turn to scorn? I was right, John; I ought to have told him. Suppose he had married me and then had found it out?"

To Rena's argument of divine foreordination Warwick attached no weight whatever. He had seen God's heel planted for four long years upon the land which had nourished slavery. Had God ordained the crime that the punishment might follow? It would have been easier for Omnipotence to prevent the crime. The experience of his sister had stirred up a certain bitterness against white people—a feeling which he had put aside years ago, with his dark blood, but which sprang anew into life when the fact of his own origin was brought home to him so forcibly through his sister's misfortune. His sworn friend and promised brother-in-law had thrown him over promptly, upon the discovery of the hidden drop of dark blood. How many others of his friends would do the same, if they but knew of it? He had begun to feel a little of the spiritual estrangement from his associates that he had noticed in

Rena during her life at Clarence. The fact that several persons knew his secret had spoiled the fine flavor of perfect security hitherto marking his position. George Tryon was a man of honor among white men, and had deigned to extend the protection of his honor to Warwick as a man, though no longer as a friend; to Rena as a woman, but not as a wife. Tryon, however, was only human, and who could tell when their paths in life might cross again, or what future temptation Tryon might feel to use a damaging secret to their disadvantage? Warwick had cherished certain ambitions, but these he must now put behind him. In the obscurity of private life, his past would be of little moment; in the glare of a political career, one's antecedents are public property, and too great a reserve in regard to one's past is regarded as a confession of something discreditable. Frank, too, knew the secret—a good, faithful fellow, even where there was no obligation of fidelity; he ought to do something for Frank to show their appreciation of his conduct. But what assurance was there that Frank would always be discreet about the affairs of others? Judge Straight knew the whole story, and old men are sometimes garrulous. Dr. Green suspected the secret; he had a wife and daughters. If old Judge Straight could have known Warwick's thoughts, he would have realized the fulfillment of his prophecy. Warwick, who had builded so well for himself, had weakened the structure of his own life by trying to share his good fortune with his sister.

"Listen, Rena," he said, with a sudden impulse, "we 'll go to the North or West—I 'll go with you—far away from the South and the Southern people, and start life over again. It will be easier for you, it will not be hard for me—I am young, and have means. There are no strong ties to bind me to the South. I would have a larger outlook elsewhere."

"And what about our mother?" asked Rena.

It would be necessary to leave her behind, they both perceived clearly enough, unless they were prepared to surrender the advantage of their whiteness and drop back to the lower rank. The mother bore the mark of the Ethiopian—not pronouncedly, but distinctly; neither would Mis' Molly, in all probability, care to leave home and friends and the graves of her loved ones. She had no mental resources to supply the place of these; she was, moreover, too old to be transplanted; she would not fit into Warwick's scheme for a new life.

"I left her once," said Rena, "and it brought pain and sorrow to all three of us. She is not strong, and I will not leave her here to die alone. This shall be my home while she lives, and if I leave it again, it shall be for only a short time, to go where I can write to her freely, and hear from her often. Don't worry about me, John,—I shall do very well."

Warwick sighed. He was sincerely sorry to leave his sister, and yet he saw that for the time being her resolution was not to be shaken. He must bide his time. Perhaps, in a few months, she would tire of the old life. His door would be always open to her, and he would charge himself with her future.

"Well, then," he said, concluding the argument, "we 'll say no more about it for the present. I 'll write to you later. I was afraid that you might not care to go back just now, and so I brought your trunk along with me."

He gave his mother the baggage-check. She took it across to Frank, who, during the day, brought the trunk from the depot. Mis' Molly offered to pay him for the service, but he would accept nothing.

"Lawd, no, Mis' Molly; I did n' hafter go out'n my way ter git dat trunk. I had a load er sperrit-bairls ter haul ter de still, an' de depot wuz right on my way back. It 'd be robbin' you ter take pay fer a little thing lack dat."

"My son John 's here," said Mis' Molly, "an' he wants to see you. Come into the settin'-room. We don't want folks to know he 's in town; but you know all our secrets, an' we can trust you like one er the family."

"I 'm glad to see you again, Frank," said Warwick, extending his hand and clasping Frank's warmly. "You 've grown up since I saw you last, but it seems you are still our good friend."

"Our very good friend," interjected Rena.

Frank threw her a grateful glance. "Yas, suh," he said, looking Warwick over with a friendly eye, "an' you is growed some, too. I seed you, you know, down dere where you live; but I did n' let on, fer you an' Mis' Rena wuz w'ite as anybody; an' eve'ybody said you wuz good ter cullud folks, an' he'ped 'em in deir lawsuits an' one way er 'nuther, an' I wuz jes' plum' glad ter see you gettin' 'long so fine, dat I wuz, certain sho', an' no mistake about it."

"Thank you, Frank, and I want you to understand how much I appreciate"—

"How much we all appreciate," corrected Rena.

"Yes, how much we all appreciate, and how grateful we all are for your kindness to mother for so many years. I know from her and from my sister how good you 've been to them."

"Lawd, suh!" returned Frank deprecatingly, "you 're makin' a mountain out'n a molehill. I ain't done nuthin' ter speak of—not half ez much ez I would 'a' done. I wuz glad ter do w'at little I could, fer frien'ship's sake."

"We value your friendship, Frank, and we 'll not forget it."

"No, Frank," added Rena, "we will never forget it, and you shall always be our good friend."

Frank left the room and crossed the street with swelling heart. He would have given his life for Rena. A kind word was doubly sweet from her lips; no service would be too great to pay for her friendship.

When Frank went out to the stable next morning to feed his mule, his eyes opened wide with astonishment. In place of the decrepit, one-eyed army mule he had put up the night before, a fat, sleek specimen of vigorous mulehood greeted his arrival with the sonorous hehaw of lusty youth. Hanging on a peg near by was a set of fine new harness, and standing under the adjoining shed, as he perceived, a handsome new cart.

"Well, well!" exclaimed Frank; "ef I did n' mos' know whar dis mule, an' dis kyart, an' dis harness come from, I 'd 'low dere 'd be'n witchcraf' er cunjin' wukkin' here. But, oh my, dat is a fine mule!—I mos' wush I could keep 'im."

He crossed the road to the house behind the cedars, and found Mis' Molly in the kitchen. "Mis' Molly," he protested, "I ain't done nuthin' ter deserve dat mule. W'at little I done fer you wa'n't done fer pay. I 'd ruther not keep dem things."

"Fer goodness' sake, Frank!" exclaimed his neighbor, with a well-simulated air of mystification, "what are you talkin' about?"

"You knows w'at I 'm talkin' about, Mis' Molly; you knows well ernuff I 'm talkin' about dat fine mule an' kyart an' harness over dere in my stable."

"How should I know anything about 'em?" she asked.

"Now, Mis' Molly! You folks is jes' tryin' ter fool me, an' make me take somethin' fer nuthin'. I lef' my ole mule an' kyart an' harness in de stable las' night, an' dis mawnin' dey 're gone, an' new ones in deir place. Co'se you knows whar dey come from!"

"Well, now, Frank, sence you mention it, I did see a witch flyin' roun' here las' night on a broomstick, an' it 'peared ter me she lit on yo'r barn, an' I s'pose she turned yo'r old things into new ones. I would n't bother my mind about it if I was you, for she may turn 'em back any night, you know; an' you might as well have the use of 'em in the mean while."

"Dat 's all foolishness, Mis' Molly, an' I 'm gwine ter fetch dat mule right over here an' tell yo' son ter gimme my ole one back."

"My son 's gone," she replied, "an' I don't know nothin' about yo'r old mule. And what would I do with a mule, anyhow? I ain't got no barn to put him in."

"I suspect you don't care much for us after all, Frank," said Rena reproachfully—she had come in while they were talking. "You meet with a piece of good luck, and you 're afraid of it, lest it might have come from us."

"Now, Miss Rena, you ought n't ter say dat," expostulated Frank, his reluctance yielding immediately. "I 'll keep de mule an' de kyart an' de harness—fac', I 'll have ter keep 'em, 'cause I ain't got no others. But dey 're gwine ter be yo'n ez much ez mine. W'enever you wants anything hauled, er wants yo' lot ploughed, er anything—dat 's yo' mule, an' I 'm yo' man an' yo' mammy's."

So Frank went back to the stable, where he feasted his eyes on his new possessions, fed and watered the mule, and curried and brushed his coat until it shone like a looking-glass.

"Now dat," remarked Peter, at the breakfast-table, when informed of the transaction, "is somethin' lack rale w'ite folks."

No real white person had ever given Peter a mule or a cart.

He had rendered one of them unpaid service for half a lifetime, and had paid for the other half; and some of them owed him substantial sums for work performed. But "to him that hath shall be given"—Warwick paid for the mule, and the real white folks got most of the credit.

XX

DIGGING UP ROOTS

When the first great shock of his discovery wore off, the fact of Rena's origin lost to Tryon some of its initial repugnance—indeed, the repugnance was not to the woman at all, as their past relations were evidence, but merely to the thought of her as a wife. It could hardly have failed to occur to so reasonable a man as Tryon that Rena's case could scarcely be unique. Surely in the past centuries of free manners and easy morals that had prevailed in remote parts of the South, there must have been many white persons whose origin would not have borne too microscopic an investigation. Family trees not seldom have a crooked branch; or, to use a more apposite figure, many a flock has its black sheep. Being a man of lively imagination, Tryon soon found himself putting all sorts of hypothetical questions about a matter which he had already definitely determined. If he had married Rena in ignorance of her secret, and had learned it afterwards, would he have put her aside? If, knowing her history, he had nevertheless married her, and she had subsequently displayed some trait of character that would suggest the negro, could he have forgotten or forgiven the taint? Could he still have held her in love and honor? If not, could he have given her the outward seeming of affection, or could he have been more than coldly tolerant? He was glad that he had been spared this ordeal. With an effort he put the whole matter definitely and conclusively aside, as he had done a hundred times already.

Returning to his home, after an absence of several months in South Carolina, it was quite apparent to his mother's watchful eye that he was in serious trouble. He was absent-minded, monosyllabic, sighed deeply and often, and could not always conceal the traces of secret tears. For Tryon was young, and possessed of a sensitive soul—a source of happiness or misery, as the Fates decree. To those thus dowered, the heights of rapture are accessible, the abysses of despair yawn threateningly; only the dull monotony of contentment is denied.

Mrs. Tryon vainly sought by every gentle art a woman knows to win her son's confidence. "What is the matter, George, dear?" she would ask, stroking his hot brow with her small, cool hand as he sat moodily nursing his grief. "Tell your mother, George. Who else could comfort you so well as she?"

"Oh, it 's nothing, mother,—nothing at all," he would reply, with a forced attempt at lightness. "It 's only your fond imagination, you best of mothers."

It was Mrs. Tryon's turn to sigh and shed a clandestine tear. Until her son had gone away on this trip to South Carolina, he had kept no secrets from her: his heart had been an open book, of which she knew every page; now, some painful story was inscribed therein which he meant she should not read. If she could have abdicated her empire to Blanche Leary or have shared it with her, she would have yielded gracefully; but very palpably some other influence than Blanche's had driven joy from her son's countenance and lightness from his heart.

Miss Blanche Leary, whom Tryon found in the house upon his return, was a demure, pretty little blonde, with an amiable disposition, a talent for society, and a pronounced fondness for George Tryon. A poor girl, of an excellent family impoverished by the war, she was distantly related to Mrs. Tryon, had for a long time enjoyed that lady's favor, and was her choice for George's wife when he should be old enough to marry. A woman less interested than Miss Leary would have perceived that there was something wrong with Tryon. Miss Leary had no doubt that there was a woman at the bottom of it,—for about what else should youth worry but love? or if one's love affairs run smoothly, why should one worry about anything at all? Miss Leary, in the nineteen years of her mundane existence, had not been without mild experiences of the heart, and had hovered for some time on the verge of disappointment with respect to Tryon himself. A sensitive pride would have driven more than one woman away at the sight of the man of her preference sighing like a furnace for some absent fair one. But Mrs. Tryon was so cordial, and insisted so strenuously upon her remaining, that Blanche's love, which was strong, conquered her pride, which was no more than a reasonable young woman ought to have who sets success above mere sentiment. She remained in the house and bided her opportunity. If George practically ignored her for a time, she did not throw herself at all in his way. She went on a visit to some girls in the neighborhood and remained away a week, hoping that she might be missed. Tryon expressed no regret at her departure and no particular satisfaction upon her return. If the house was duller in her absence, he was but dimly conscious of the difference. He was still fighting a battle in which a susceptible heart and a reasonable mind had locked horns in a well-nigh hopeless conflict. Reason, common-sense, the instinctive ready-made judgments of his training and environment,—the deep-seated prejudices of race and caste,—commanded him to dismiss Rena from his thoughts. His stubborn heart simply would not let go.

XXI

A GILDED OPPORTUNITY

ALTHOUGH the whole fabric of Rena's new life toppled and fell with her lover's defection, her sympathies, broadened by culture and still more by her recent emotional experience, did not shrink, as would have been the case with a more selfish soul, to the mere limits of her personal sorrow, great as this seemed at the moment. She had learned to love, and when the love of one man failed her, she turned to humanity, as a stream obstructed in its course overflows the adjacent country. Her early training had not directed her thoughts to the darker people with whose fate her own was bound up so closely, but rather away from them. She had been taught to despise them because they were not so white as she was, and had been slaves while she was free. Her life in her brother's home, by removing her from immediate contact with them, had given her a different point of view,—one which emphasized their shortcomings, and thereby made vastly clearer to her the gulf that separated them from the new world in which she lived; so that when misfortune threw her back upon them, the reaction brought her nearer than before. Where once she had seemed able to escape from them, they were now, it appeared, her inalienable race. Thus doubly equipped, she was able to view them at once with the mental eye of an outsider and the sympathy of a sister: she could see their faults, and judge them charitably; she knew and appreciated their good qualities. With her quickened intelligence she could perceive how great was their need and how small their opportunity; and with this illumination came the desire to contribute to their help. She had not the breadth or culture to see in all its ramifications the great problem which still puzzles statesmen and philosophers; but she was conscious of the wish, and of the power, in a small way, to do something for the advancement of those who had just set their feet upon the ladder of progress.

This new-born desire to be of service to her rediscovered

people was not long without an opportunity for expression. Yet the Fates willed that her future should be but another link in a connected chain: she was to be as powerless to put aside her recent past as she had been to escape from the influence of her earlier life. There are sordid souls that eat and drink and breed and die, and imagine they have lived. But Rena's life since her great awakening had been that of the emotions, and her temperament made of it a continuous life. Her successive states of consciousness were not detachable, but united to form a single if not an entirely harmonious whole. To her sensitive spirit to-day was born of yesterday, to-morrow would be but the offspring of to-day.

One day, along toward noon, her mother received a visit from Mary B. Pettifoot, a second cousin, who lived on Back Street, only a short distance from the house behind the cedars. Rena had gone out, so that the visitor found Mis' Molly alone.

"I heared you say, Cousin Molly," said Mary B. (no one ever knew what the B. in Mary's name stood for,—it was a mere ornamental flourish), "that Rena was talkin' 'bout teachin' school. I 've got a good chance fer her, ef she keers ter take it. My cousin Jeff Wain 'rived in town this mo'nin', f'm 'way down in Sampson County, ter git a teacher fer the nigger school in his deestric'. I s'pose he mought 'a' got one f'm 'roun' Newbern, er Goldsboro, er some er them places eas', but he 'lowed he 'd like to visit some er his kin an' ole frien's, an' so kill two birds with one stone."

"I seed a strange mulatter man, with a bay hoss an' a new buggy, drivin' by here this mo'nin' early, from down to'ds the river," rejoined Mis' Molly. "I wonder if that wuz him?"

"Did he have on a linen duster?" asked Mary B.

"Yas, an' 'peared to be a very well sot up man," replied Mis' Molly, "'bout thirty-five years old, I should reckon."

"That wuz him," assented Mary B. "He 's got a fine hoss an' buggy, an' a gol' watch an' chain, an' a big plantation, an' lots er hosses an' mules an' cows an' hawgs. He raise' fifty bales er cotton las' year, an' he 's be'n ter the legislatur'."

"My gracious!" exclaimed Mis' Molly, struck with awe at this catalogue of the stranger's possessions—he was evidently worth more than a great many "rich" white people,—all white people in North Carolina in those days were either "rich" or "poor," the distinction being one of caste rather than of wealth. "Is he married?" she inquired with interest.

"No,—single. You mought 'low it was quare that he should n' be married at his age; but he was crossed in love oncet,"—Mary B. heaved a self-conscious sigh,—"an' has stayed single ever sence. That wuz ten years ago, but as some husban's is long-lived, an' there ain' no mo' chance fer 'im now than there wuz then, I reckon some nice gal mought stan' a good show er ketchin' 'im, ef she 'd play her kyards right."

To Mis' Molly this was news of considerable importance. She had not thought a great deal of Rena's plan to teach; she considered it lowering for Rena, after having been white, to go among the negroes any more than was unavoidable. This opportunity, however, meant more than mere employment for her daughter. She had felt Rena's disappointment keenly, from the practical point of view, and, blaming herself for it, held herself all the more bound to retrieve the misfortune in any possible way. If she had not been sick, Rena would not have dreamed the fateful dream that had brought her to Patesville; for the connection between the vision and the reality was even closer in Mis' Molly's eyes than in Rena's. If the mother had not sent the letter announcing her illness and confirming the dream, Rena would not have ruined her promising future by coming to Patesville. But the harm had been done, and she was responsible, ignorantly of course, but none the less truly, and it only remained for her to make amends, as far as possible. Her highest ambition, since Rena had grown up, had been to see her married and comfortably settled in life. She had no hope that Tryon would come back. Rena had declared that she would make no further effort to get away from her people; and, furthermore, that she would never marry. To this latter statement Mis' Molly secretly attached but little importance. That a woman should go single from the cradle to the grave did not accord with her experience in life of the customs of North Carolina. She respected a grief she could not entirely fathom, yet did not for a moment believe that Rena would remain unmarried.

"You 'd better fetch him roun' to see me, Ma'y B.," she

said, "an' let 's see what he looks like. I 'm pertic'lar 'bout my gal. She says she ain't goin' to marry nobody; but of co'se we know that 's all foolishness."

"I 'll fetch him roun' this evenin' 'bout three o'clock," said the visitor, rising. "I mus' hurry back now an' keep him comp'ny. Tell Rena ter put on her bes' bib an' tucker; for Mr. Wain is pertic'lar too, an' I 've already be'n braggin' 'bout her looks."

When Mary B., at the appointed hour, knocked at Mis' Molly's front door,—the visit being one of ceremony, she had taken her cousin round to the Front Street entrance and through the flower garden,—Mis' Molly was prepared to receive them. After a decent interval, long enough to suggest that she had not been watching their approach and was not over-eager about the visit, she answered the knock and admitted them into the parlor. Mr. Wain was formally introduced, and seated himself on the ancient haircloth sofa, under the framed fashion-plate, while Mary B. sat by the open door and fanned herself with a palm-leaf fan.

Mis' Molly's impression of Wain was favorable. His complexion was of a light brown—not quite so fair as Mis' Molly would have preferred; but any deficiency in this regard, or in the matter of the stranger's features, which, while not unpleasing, leaned toward the broad mulatto type, was more than compensated in her eyes by very straight black hair, and, as soon appeared, a great facility of complimentary speech. On his introduction Mr. Wain bowed low, assumed an air of great admiration, and expressed his extreme delight in making the acquaintance of so distinguished-looking a lady.

"You 're flatt'rin' me, Mr. Wain," returned Mis' Molly, with a gratified smile. "But you want to meet my daughter befo' you commence th'owin' bokays. Excuse my leavin' you—I 'll go an' fetch her."

She returned in a moment, followed by Rena. "Mr. Wain, 'low me to int'oduce you to my daughter Rena. Rena, this is Ma'y B.'s cousin on her pappy's side, who 's come up from Sampson to git a school-teacher."

Rena bowed gracefully. Wain stared a moment in genuine astonishment, and then bent himself nearly double, keeping his eyes fixed meanwhile upon Rena's face. He had expected to see a pretty yellow girl, but had been prepared for no such radiant vision of beauty as this which now confronted him.

"Does—does you mean ter say, Mis' Walden, dat—dat dis young lady is yo' own daughter?" he stammered, rallying his forces for action.

"Why not, Mr. Wain?" asked Mis' Molly, bridling with mock resentment. "Do you mean ter 'low that she wuz changed in her cradle, er is she too good-lookin' to be my daughter?"

"My deah Mis' Walden! it 'ud be wastin' wo'ds fer me ter say dat dey ain' no young lady too good-lookin' ter be yo' daughter; but you 're lookin' so young yo'sef dat I 'd ruther take her fer yo' sister."

"Yas," rejoined Mis' Molly, with animation, "they ain't many years between us. I wuz ruther young myself when she wuz bo'n."

"An', mo'over," Wain went on, "it takes me a minute er so ter git my min' use' ter thinkin' er Mis' Rena as a cullud young lady. I mought 'a' seed her a hund'ed times, an' I 'd 'a' never dreamt but w'at she wuz a w'ite young lady, f'm one er de bes' families."

"Yas, Mr. Wain," replied Mis' Molly complacently, "all three er my child'en wuz white, an' one of 'em has be'n on the other side fer many long years. Rena has be'n to school, an' has traveled, an' has had chances—better chances than anybody roun' here knows."

"She 's jes' de lady I 'm lookin' fer, ter teach ou' school," rejoined Wain, with emphasis. "Wid her schoolin' an' my riccommen', she kin git a fus'-class ce'tifikit an' draw fo'ty dollars a month; an' a lady er her color kin keep a lot er little niggers straighter 'n a darker lady could. We jus' got ter have her ter teach ou' school—ef we kin git her."

Rena's interest in the prospect of employment at her chosen work was so great that she paid little attention to Wain's compliments. Mis' Molly led Mary B. away to the kitchen on some pretext, and left Rena to entertain the gentleman. She questioned him eagerly about the school, and he gave the most glowing accounts of the elegant schoolhouse, the bright pupils, and the congenial society of the neighborhood. He spoke almost entirely in superlatives, and, after making due allowance for what Rena perceived to be a temperamental tendency to exaggeration, she concluded that she would find in the school a worthy field of usefulness, and in this polite and good-natured though somewhat wordy man a coadjutor upon whom she could rely in her first efforts; for she was not over-confident of her powers, which seemed to grow less as the way opened for their exercise.

"Do you think I 'm competent to teach the school?" she asked of the visitor, after stating some of her qualifications.

"Oh, dere 's no doubt about it, Miss Rena," replied Wain, who had listened with an air of great wisdom, though secretly aware that he was too ignorant of letters to form a judgment; "you kin teach de school all right, an' could ef you did n't know half ez much. You won't have no trouble managin' de child'en, nuther. Ef any of 'em gits onruly, jes' call on me fer he'p, an' I 'll make 'em walk Spanish. I 'm chuhman er de school committee, an' I 'll lam de hide off'n any scholar dat don' behave. You kin trus' me fer dat, sho' ez I 'm a-settin' here."

"Then," said Rena, "I 'll undertake it, and do my best. I 'm sure you 'll not be too exacting."

"Yo' bes', Miss Rena, 'll be de bes' dey is. Don' you worry ner fret. Dem niggers won't have no other teacher after dey 've once laid eyes on you: I 'll guarantee dat. Dere won't be no trouble, not a bit."

"Well, Cousin Molly," said Mary B. to Mis' Molly in the kitchen, "how does the plan strike you?"

"Ef Rena 's satisfied, I am," replied Mis' Molly. "But you 'd better say nothin' about ketchin' a beau, or any such foolishness, er else she 'd be just as likely not to go nigh Sampson County."

"Befo' Cousin Jeff goes back," confided Mary B., "I 'd like ter give 'im a party, but my house is too small. I wuz wonderin'," she added tentatively, "ef I could n' borry yo' house."

"Shorely, Ma'y B. I 'm int'rested in Mr. Wain on Rena's account, an' it 's as little as I kin do to let you use my house an' help you git things ready."

The date of the party was set for Thursday night, as Wain was to leave Patesville on Friday morning, taking with him the new teacher. The party would serve the double purpose of a compliment to the guest and a farewell to Rena, and it might prove the precursor, the mother secretly hoped, of other festivities to follow at some later date.

XXII

IMPERATIVE BUSINESS

ONE Wednesday morning, about six weeks after his return home, Tryon received a letter from Judge Straight with reference to the note left with him at Patesville for collection. This communication properly required an answer, which might have been made in writing within the compass of ten lines. No sooner, however, had Tryon read the letter than he began to perceive reasons why it should be answered in person. He had left Patesville under extremely painful circumstances, vowing that he would never return; and yet now the barest pretext, by which no one could have been deceived except willingly, was sufficient to turn his footsteps thither again. He explained to his mother—with a vagueness which she found somewhat puzzling, but ascribed to her own feminine obtuseness in matters of business—the reasons that imperatively demanded his presence in Patesville. With an early start he could drive there in one day,—he had an excellent roadster, a light buggy, and a recent rain had left the road in good condition,—a day would suffice for the transaction of his business, and the third day would bring him home again. He set out on his journey on Thursday morning, with this programme very clearly outlined.

Tryon would not at first have admitted even to himself that Rena's presence in Patesville had any bearing whatever upon his projected visit. The matter about which Judge Straight had written might, it was clear, be viewed in several aspects. The judge had written him concerning the one of immediate importance. It would be much easier to discuss the subject in all its bearings, and clean up the whole matter, in one comprehensive personal interview.

The importance of this business, then, seemed very urgent for the first few hours of Tryon's journey. Ordinarily a careful driver and merciful to his beast, his eagerness to reach Patesville increased gradually until it became necessary to exercise some self-restraint in order not to urge his faithful mare beyond her powers; and soon he could no longer pretend obliviousness of the fact that some attraction stronger than the whole amount of Duncan McSwayne's note was urging him irresistibly toward his destination. The old town beyond the distant river, his heart told him clamorously, held the object in all the world to him most dear. Memory brought up in vivid detail every moment of his brief and joyous courtship,—each tender word, each enchanting smile, every fond caress. He lived his past happiness over again down to the moment of that fatal discovery. What horrible fate was it that had involved him—nay, that had caught this sweet delicate girl in such a blind alley? A wild hope flashed across his mind: perhaps the ghastly story might not be true; perhaps, after all, the girl was no more a negro than she seemed. He had heard sad stories of white children, born out of wedlock, abandoned by sinful parents to the care or adoption of colored women, who had reared them as their own, the children's future basely sacrificed to hide the parents' shame. He would confront this reputed mother of his darling and wring the truth from her. He was in a state of mind where any sort of a fairy tale would have seemed reasonable. He would almost have bribed some one to tell him that the woman he had loved, the woman he still loved (he felt a thrill of lawless pleasure in the confession), was not the descendant of slaves,—that he might marry her, and not have before his eyes the gruesome fear that some one of their children might show even the faintest mark of the despised race.

At noon he halted at a convenient hamlet, fed and watered his mare, and resumed his journey after an hour's rest. By this time he had well-nigh forgotten about the legal business that formed the ostensible occasion for his journey, and was conscious only of a wild desire to see the woman whose image was beckoning him on to Patesville as fast as his horse could take him.

At sundown he stopped again, about ten miles from the town, and cared for his now tired beast. He knew her capacity, however, and calculated that she could stand the additional ten miles without injury. The mare set out with reluctance, but soon settled resignedly down into a steady jog.

Memory had hitherto assailed Tryon with the vision of past

joys. As he neared the town, imagination attacked him with still more moving images. He had left her, this sweet flower of womankind—white or not, God had never made a fairer!—he had seen her fall to the hard pavement, with he knew not what resulting injury. He had left her tender frame—the touch of her finger-tips had made him thrill with happiness—to be lifted by strange hands, while he with heartless pride had driven deliberately away, without a word of sorrow or regret. He had ignored her as completely as though she had never existed. That he had been deceived was true. But had he not aided in his own deception? Had not Warwick told him distinctly that they were of no family, and was it not his own fault that he had not followed up the clue thus given him? Had not Rena compared herself to the child's nurse, and had he not assured her that if she were the nurse, he would marry her next day? The deception had been due more to his own blindness than to any lack of honesty on the part of Rena and her brother. In the light of his present feelings they seemed to have been absurdly outspoken. He was glad that he had kept his discovery to himself. He had considered himself very magnanimous not to have exposed the fraud that was being perpetrated upon society: it was with a very comfortable feeling that he now realized that the matter was as profound a secret as before.

"She ought to have been born white," he muttered, adding weakly, "I would to God that I had never found her out!"

Drawing near the bridge that crossed the river to the town, he pictured to himself a pale girl, with sorrowful, tear-stained eyes, pining away in the old gray house behind the cedars for love of him, dying, perhaps, of a broken heart. He would hasten to her; he would dry her tears with kisses; he would express sorrow for his cruelty.

The tired mare had crossed the bridge and was slowly toiling up Front Street; she was near the limit of her endurance, and Tryon did not urge her.

They might talk the matter over, and if they must part, part at least they would in peace and friendship. If he could not marry her, he would never marry any one else; it would be cruel for him to seek happiness while she was denied it, for, having once given her heart to him, she could never, he was sure,—so instinctively fine was her nature,—she could never love any one less worthy than himself, and would therefore probably never marry. He knew from a Clarence acquaintance, who had written him a letter, that Rena had not reappeared in that town.

If he should discover—the chance was one in a thousand—that she was white; or if he should find it too hard to leave her—ah, well! he was a white man, one of a race born to command. He would make her white; no one beyond the old town would ever know the difference. If, perchance, their secret should be disclosed, the world was wide; a man of courage and ambition, inspired by love, might make a career anywhere. Circumstances made weak men; strong men mould circumstances to do their bidding. He would not let his darling die of grief, whatever the price must be paid for her salvation. She was only a few rods away from him now. In a moment he would see her; he would take her tenderly in his arms, and heart to heart they would mutually forgive and forget, and, strengthened by their love, would face the future boldly and bid the world do its worst.

XXIII

THE GUEST OF HONOR

THE EVENING of the party arrived. The house had been thoroughly cleaned in preparation for the event, and decorated with the choicest treasures of the garden. By eight o'clock the guests had gathered. They were all mulattoes,—all people of mixed blood were called "mulattoes" in North Carolina. There were dark mulattoes and bright mulattoes. Mis' Molly's guests were mostly of the bright class, most of them more than half white, and few of them less. In Mis' Molly's small circle, straight hair was the only palliative of a dark complexion. Many of the guests would not have been casually distinguishable from white people of the poorer class. Others bore unmistakable traces of Indian ancestry,—for Cherokee and Tuscarora blood was quite widely diffused among the free negroes of North Carolina, though well-nigh lost sight of by the curious custom of the white people to ignore anything but the negro blood in those who were touched by its potent current. Very few of those present had been slaves. The free colored people of Patesville were numerous enough before the war to have their own "society," and human enough to despise those who did not possess advantages equal to their own; and at this time they still looked down upon those who had once been held in bondage. The only black man present occupied a chair which stood on a broad chest in one corner, and extracted melody from a fiddle to which a whole generation of the best people of Patesville had danced and made merry. Uncle Needham seldom played for colored gatherings, but made an exception in Mis' Molly's case; she was not white, but he knew her past; if she was not the rose, she had at least been near the rose. When the company had gathered, Mary B., as mistress of ceremonies, whispered to Uncle Needham, who tapped his violin sharply with the bow.

"Ladies an' gent'emens, take yo' pa'dners fer a Fuhginny reel!"

Mr. Wain, as the guest of honor, opened the ball with his

hostess. He wore a broadcloth coat and trousers, a heavy glittering chain across the spacious front of his white waistcoat, and a large red rose in his buttonhole. If his boots were slightly run down at the heel, so trivial a detail passed unnoticed in the general splendor of his attire. Upon a close or hostile inspection there would have been some features of his ostensibly good-natured face—the shifty eye, the full and slightly drooping lower lip—which might have given a student of physiognomy food for reflection. But whatever the latent defects of Wain's character, he proved himself this evening a model of geniality, presuming not at all upon his reputed wealth, but winning golden opinions from those who came to criticise, of whom, of course, there were a few, the company being composed of human beings.

When the dance began, Wain extended his large, soft hand to Mary B., yellow, buxom, thirty, with white and even teeth glistening behind her full red lips. A younger sister of Mary B.'s was paired with Billy Oxendine, a funny little tailor, a great gossip, and therefore a favorite among the women. Mis' Molly graciously consented, after many protestations of lack of skill and want of practice, to stand up opposite Homer Pettifoot, Mary B.'s husband, a tall man, with a slight stoop, a bald crown, and full, dreamy eyes,—a man of much imagination and a large fund of anecdote. Two other couples completed the set; others were restrained by bashfulness or religious scruples, which did not yield until later in the evening.

The perfumed air from the garden without and the cut roses within mingled incongruously with the alien odors of musk and hair oil, of which several young barbers in the company were especially redolent. There was a play of sparkling eyes and glancing feet. Mary B. danced with the languorous grace of an Eastern odalisque, Mis' Molly with the mincing, hesitating step of one long out of practice. Wain performed saltatory prodigies. This was a golden opportunity for the display in which his soul found delight. He introduced variations hitherto unknown to the dance. His skill and suppleness brought a glow of admiration into the eyes of the women, and spread a cloud of jealousy over the faces of several of the younger men, who saw themselves eclipsed.

Rena had announced in advance her intention to take no active part in the festivities. "I don't feel like dancing, mamma—I shall never dance again."

"Well, now, Rena," answered her mother, "of co'se you 're too dignified, sence you 've be'n 'sociatin' with white folks, to be hoppin' roun' an' kickin' up like Ma'y B. an' these other yaller gals; but of co'se, too, you can't slight the comp'ny entirely, even ef it ain't jest exac'ly our party,—you 'll have to pay 'em some little attention, 'specially Mr. Wain, sence you 're goin' down yonder with 'im."

Rena conscientiously did what she thought politeness required. She went the round of the guests in the early part of the evening and exchanged greetings with them. To several requests for dances she replied that she was not dancing. She did not hold herself aloof because of pride; any instinctive shrinking she might have felt by reason of her recent association with persons of greater refinement was offset by her still more newly awakened zeal for humanity; they were her people, she must not despise them. But the occasion suggested painful memories of other and different scenes in which she had lately participated. Once or twice these memories were so vivid as almost to over-power her. She slipped away from the company, and kept in the background as much as possible without seeming to slight any one.

The guests as well were dimly conscious of a slight barrier between Mis' Molly's daughter and themselves. The time she had spent apart from these friends of her youth had rendered it impossible for her ever to meet them again upon the plane of common interests and common thoughts. It was much as though one, having acquired the vernacular of his native country, had lived in a foreign land long enough to lose the language of his childhood without acquiring fully that of his adopted country. Miss Rowena Warwick could never again become quite the Rena Walden who had left the house behind the cedars no more than a year and a half before. Upon this very difference were based her noble aspirations for usefulness,—one must stoop in order that one may lift others. Any other young woman present would have been importuned beyond her powers of resistance. Rena's reserve was respected.

When supper was announced, somewhat early in the evening, the dancers found seats in the hall or on the front piazza. Aunt Zilphy, assisted by Mis' Molly and Mary B., passed around the refreshments, which consisted of fried chicken, buttered biscuits, pound-cake, and eggnog. When the first edge of appetite was taken off, the conversation waxed animated. Homer Pettifoot related, with minute detail, an old, threadbare hunting lie, dating, in slightly differing forms, from the age of Nimrod, about finding twenty-five partridges sitting in a row on a rail, and killing them all with a single buckshot, which passed through twenty-four and lodged in the body of the twenty-fifth, from which it was extracted and returned to the shot-pouch for future service.

This story was followed by a murmur of incredulity—of course, the thing was possible, but Homer's faculty for exaggeration was so well known that any statement of his was viewed with suspicion. Homer seemed hurt at this lack of faith, and was disposed to argue the point; but the sonorous voice of Mr. Wain on the other side of the room cut short his protestations, in much the same way that the rising sun extinguishes the light of lesser luminaries.

"I wuz a member er de fus' legislatur' after de wah," Wain was saying. "When I went up f'm Sampson in de fall, I had to pass th'ough Smithfiel'. I got in town in de afternoon, an' put up at de bes' hotel. De lan'lo'd did n' have no s'picion but what I wuz a white man, an' he gimme a room, an' I had supper an' breakfas', an' went on ter Rolly nex' mornin'. W'en de session wuz over, I come along back, an' w'en I got ter Smithfiel', I driv' up ter de same hotel. I noticed, as soon as I got dere, dat de place had run down consid'able—dere wuz weeds growin' in de yard, de winders wuz dirty, an' ev'ything roun' dere looked kinder lonesome an' shif'less. De lan'lo'd met me at de do'; he looked mighty down in de mouth, an' sezee:—

" 'Look a-here, w'at made you come an' stop at my place widout tellin' me you wuz a black man? Befo' you come th'ough dis town I had a fus'-class business. But w'en folks found out dat a nigger had put up here, business drapped right off, an' I 've had ter shet up my hotel. You oughter be 'shamed er yo'se'f fer ruinin' a po' man w'at had n' never done no harm ter you. You 've done a mean, low-lived thing, an' a jes' God 'll punish you fer it.'

"De po' man acshully bust inter tears," continued Mr. Wain magnanimously, "an' I felt so sorry fer 'im—he wuz a po' white man tryin' ter git up in de worl'—dat I hauled out my purse an' gin 'im ten dollars, an' he 'peared monst'ous glad ter git it."

"How good-hearted! How kin'!" murmured the ladies. "It done credit to yo' feelin's."

"Don't b'lieve a word er dem lies," muttered one young man to another sarcastically. "He could n' pass fer white, 'less'n it wuz a mighty dark night."

Upon this glorious evening of his life, Mr. Jefferson Wain had one distinctly hostile critic, of whose presence he was blissfully unconscious. Frank Fowler had not been invited to the party,—his family did not go with Mary B.'s set. Rena had suggested to her mother that he be invited, but Mis' Molly had demurred on the ground that it was not her party, and that she had no right to issue invitations. It is quite likely that she would have sought an invitation for Frank from Mary B.; but Frank was black, and would not harmonize with the rest of the company, who would not have Mis' Molly's reasons for treating him well. She had compromised the matter by stepping across the way in the afternoon and suggesting that Frank might come over and sit on the back porch and look at the dancing and share in the supper.

Frank was not without a certain honest pride. He was sensitive enough, too, not to care to go where he was not wanted. He would have curtly refused any such maimed invitation to any other place. But would he not see Rena in her best attire, and might she not perhaps, in passing, speak a word to him?

"Thank y', Mis' Molly," he replied, "I 'll prob'ly come over."

"You 're a big fool, boy," observed his father after Mis' Molly had gone back across the street, "ter be stickin' roun' dem yaller niggers 'cross de street, an' slobb'rin' an' slav'rin' over 'em, an' hangin' roun' deir back do' wuss 'n ef dey wuz w'ite folks. I 'd see 'em dead fus'!"

Frank himself resisted the temptation for half an hour after the music began, but at length he made his way across the street and stationed himself at the window opening upon the back piazza. When Rena was in the room, he had eyes for her only, but when she was absent, he fixed his attention mainly upon Wain. With jealous clairvoyance he observed that Wain's eyes followed Rena when she left the room, and lit up when she returned. Frank had heard that Rena was going away with this man, and he watched Wain closely, liking him less the longer he looked at him. To his fancy, Wain's style and skill were affectation, his good-nature mere hypocrisy, and his glance at Rena the eye of the hawk upon his quarry. He had heard that Wain was unmarried, and he could not see how, this being so, he could help wishing Rena for a wife. Frank would have been content to see her marry a white man, who would have raised her to a plane worthy of her merits. In this man's shifty eye he read the liar—his wealth and standing were probably as false as his seeming good-humor.

"Is that you, Frank?" said a soft voice near at hand.

He looked up with a joyful thrill. Rena was peering intently at him, as if trying to distinguish his features in the darkness. It was a bright moonlight night, but Frank stood in the shadow of the piazza.

"Yas 'm, it 's me, Miss Rena. Yo' mammy said I could come over an' see you-all dance. You ain' be'n out on de flo' at all, ter-night."

"No, Frank, I don't care for dancing. I shall not dance to-night."

This answer was pleasing to Frank. If he could not hope to dance with her, at least the men inside—at least this snake in the grass from down the country—should not have that privilege.

"But you must have some supper, Frank," said Rena. "I 'll bring it myself."

"No, Miss Rena, I don' keer fer nothin'—I did n' come over ter eat—r'al'y I did n't."

"Nonsense, Frank, there 's plenty of it. I have no appetite, and you shall have my portion."

She brought him a slice of cake and a glass of eggnog. When Mis' Molly, a minute later, came out upon the piazza, Frank left the yard and walked down the street toward the old canal. Rena had spoken softly to him; she had fed him with her own dainty hands. He might never hope that she would see in him anything but a friend; but he loved her, and he would watch over her and protect her, wherever she might be. He did not believe that she would ever marry the grinning hypocrite masquerading back there in Mis' Molly's parlor; but the man would bear watching.

Mis' Molly had come to call her daughter into the house. "Rena," she said, "Mr. Wain wants ter know if you won't dance just one dance with him."

"Yas, Rena," pleaded Mary B., who followed Miss Molly out to the piazza, "jes' one dance. I don't think you 're treatin' my comp'ny jes' right, Cousin Rena."

"You 're goin' down there with 'im," added her mother, "an' it 'd be just as well to be on friendly terms with 'im."

Wain himself had followed the women. "Sho'ly, Miss Rena, you 're gwine ter honah me wid one dance? I 'd go 'way f'm dis pa'ty sad at hea't ef I had n' stood up oncet wid de young lady er de house."

As Rena, weakly persuaded, placed her hand on Wain's arm and entered the house, a buggy, coming up Front Street, paused a moment at the corner, and then turning slowly, drove quietly up the nameless by-street, concealed by the intervening cedars, until it reached a point from which the occupant could view, through the open front window, the interior of the parlor.

XXIV

SWING YOUR PARTNERS

MOVED by tenderness and thoughts of self-sacrifice, which had occupied his mind to the momentary exclusion of all else, Tryon had scarcely noticed, as he approached the house behind the cedars, a strain of lively music, to which was added, as he drew still nearer, the accompaniment of other festive sounds. He suddenly awoke, however, to the fact that these signs of merriment came from the house at which he had intended to stop;—he had not meant that Rena should pass another sleepless night of sorrow, or that he should himself endure another needless hour of suspense.

He drew rein at the corner. Shocked surprise, a nascent anger, a vague alarm, an insistent curiosity, urged him nearer. Turning the mare into the side street and keeping close to the fence, he drove ahead in the shadow of the cedars until he reached a gap through which he could see into the open door and windows of the brightly lighted hall.

There was evidently a ball in progress. The fiddle was squeaking merrily to a tune that he remembered well,—it was associated with one of the most delightful evenings of his life, that of the tournament ball. A mellow negro voice was calling with a rhyming accompaniment the figures of a quadrille. Tryon, with parted lips and slowly hardening heart, leaned forward from the buggy-seat, gripping the rein so tightly that his nails cut into the opposing palm. Above the clatter of noisy conversation rose the fiddler's voice:—

"Swing yo' pa'dners; doan be shy,
Look yo' lady in de eye!
Th'ow yo' ahm aroun' huh wais';
Take yo' time—dey ain' no has'e!"

To the middle of the floor, in full view through an open window, advanced the woman who all day long had been the burden of his thoughts—not pale with grief and hollow-eyed with weeping, but flushed with pleasure, around her waist the arm of a burly, grinning mulatto, whose face was offensively familiar to Tryon.

With a muttered curse of concentrated bitterness, Tryon struck the mare a sharp blow with the whip. The sensitive creature, spirited even in her great weariness, resented the lash and started off with the bit in her teeth. Perceiving that it would be difficult to turn in the narrow roadway without running into the ditch at the left, Tryon gave the mare rein and dashed down the street, scarcely missing, as the buggy crossed the bridge, a man standing abstractedly by the old canal, who sprang aside barely in time to avoid being run over.

Meantime Rena was passing through a trying ordeal. After the first few bars, the fiddler plunged into a well-known air, in which Rena, keenly susceptible to musical impressions, recognized the tune to which, as Queen of Love and Beauty, she had opened the dance at her entrance into the world of life and love, for it was there she had met George Tryon. The combination of music and movement brought up the scene with great distinctness. Tryon, peering angrily through the cedars, had not been more conscious than she of the external contrast between her partners on this and the former occasion. She perceived, too, as Tryon from the outside had not, the difference between Wain's wordy flattery (only saved by his cousin's warning from pointed and fulsome adulation), and the tenderly graceful compliment, couched in the romantic terms of chivalry, with which the knight of the handkerchief had charmed her ear. It was only by an immense effort that she was able to keep her emotions under control until the end of the dance, when she fled to her chamber and burst into tears. It was not the cruel Tryon who had blasted her love with his deadly look that she mourned, but the gallant young knight who had worn her favor on his lance and crowned her Queen of Love and Beauty.

Tryon's stay in Patesville was very brief. He drove to the hotel and put up for the night. During many sleepless hours his mind was in a turmoil with a very different set of thoughts from those which had occupied it on the way to town. Not the least of them was a profound self-contempt for his own lack of discernment. How had he been so blind as not to have read long ago the character of this wretched girl who had bewitched him? To-night his eyes had been opened—he had seen her with the mask thrown off, a true daughter of a race in which the sensuous enjoyment of the moment took precedence of taste or sentiment or any of the higher emotions. Her few months of boarding-school, her brief association with white people, had evidently been a mere veneer over the underlying negro, and their effects had slipped away as soon as the intercourse had ceased. With the monkey-like imitativeness of the negro she had copied the manners of white people while she lived among them, and had dropped them with equal facility when they ceased to serve a purpose. Who but a negro could have recovered so soon from what had seemed a terrible bereavement?—she herself must have felt it at the time, for otherwise she would not have swooned. A woman of sensibility, as this one had seemed to be, should naturally feel more keenly, and for a longer time than a man, an injury to the affections; but he, a son of the ruling race, had been miserable for six weeks about a girl who had so far forgotten him as already to plunge headlong into the childish amusements of her own ignorant and degraded people. What more, indeed, he asked himself savagely,—what more could be expected of the base-born child of the plaything of a gentleman's idle hour, who to this ignoble origin added the blood of a servile race? And he, George Tryon, had honored her with his love; he had very nearly linked his fate and joined his blood to hers by the solemn sanctions of church and state. Tryon was not a devout man, but he thanked God with religious fervor that he had been saved a second time from a mistake which would have wrecked his whole future. If he had yielded to the momentary weakness of the past night,—the outcome of a sickly sentimentality to which he recognized now, in the light of reflection, that he was entirely too prone,—he would have regretted it soon enough. The black streak would have been sure to come out in some form, sooner or later, if not in the wife, then in her children. He saw clearly enough, in this hour of revulsion, that with his temperament and training such a union could never have been happy. If all the world had been ignorant of the dark secret, it would always have been in his own thoughts, or at least never far away. Each fault of hers that the close daily association of husband and wife might reveal,—the most flawless of sweethearts do not pass scathless through the long test of matrimony,—every wayward impulse of his children, every defect of mind, morals, temper, or health, would have been ascribed to the dark ancestral strain. Happiness under such conditions would have been impossible.

When Tryon lay awake in the early morning, after a few brief hours of sleep, the business which had brought him to Patesville seemed, in the cold light of reason, so ridiculously inadequate that he felt almost ashamed to have set up such a pretext for his journey. The prospect, too, of meeting Dr. Green and his family, of having to explain his former sudden departure, and of running a gauntlet of inquiry concerning his marriage to the aristocratic Miss Warwick of South Carolina; the fear that some one at Patesville might have suspected a connection between Rena's swoon and his own flight,—these considerations so moved this impressionable and impulsive young man that he called a bell-boy, demanded an early breakfast, ordered his horse, paid his reckoning, and started upon his homeward journey forthwith. A certain distrust of his own sensibility, which he felt to be curiously inconsistent with his most positive convictions, led him to seek the river bridge by a roundabout route which did not take him past the house where, a few hours before, he had seen the last fragment of his idol shattered beyond the hope of repair.

The party broke up at an early hour, since most of the guests were working-people, and the travelers were to make an early start next day. About nine in the morning, Wain drove round to Mis' Molly's. Rena's trunk was strapped behind the buggy, and she set out, in the company of Wain, for her new field of labor. The school term was only two months in length, and she did not expect to return until its expiration. Just before taking her seat in the buggy, Rena felt a sudden sinking of the heart.

"Oh, mother," she whispered, as they stood wrapped in a close embrace, "I 'm afraid to leave you. I left you once, and it turned out so miserably."

"It 'll turn out better this time, honey," replied her mother soothingly. "Good-by, child. Take care of yo'self an' yo'r money, and write to yo'r mammy."

One kiss all round, and Rena was lifted into the buggy. Wain seized the reins, and under his skillful touch the pretty mare began to prance and curvet with restrained impatience. Wain could not resist the opportunity to show off before the party, which included Mary B.'s entire family and several other neighbors, who had gathered to see the travelers off.

"Good-by ter Patesville! Good-by, folkses all!" he cried, with a wave of his disengaged hand.

"Good-by, mother! Good-by, all!" cried Rena, as with tears in her heart and a brave smile on her face she left her home behind her for the second time.

When they had crossed the river bridge, the travelers came to a long stretch of rising ground, from the summit of which they could look back over the white sandy road for nearly a mile. Neither Rena nor her companion saw Frank Fowler behind the chinquapin bush at the foot of the hill, nor the gaze of mute love and longing with which he watched the buggy mount the long incline. He had not been able to trust himself to bid her farewell. He had seen her go away once before with every prospect of happiness, and come back, a dove with a wounded wing, to the old nest behind the cedars. She was going away again, with a man whom he disliked and distrusted. If she had met misfortune before, what were her prospects for happiness now?

The buggy paused at the top of the hill, and Frank, shading his eyes with his hand, thought he could see her turn and look behind. Look back, dear child, towards your home and those who love you! For who knows more than this faithful worshiper what threads of the past Fate is weaving into your future, or whether happiness or misery lies before you?

XXV

BALANCE ALL

THE ROAD to Sampson County lay for the most part over the pine-clad sandhills,—an alternation of gentle rises and gradual descents, with now and then a swamp of greater or less extent. Long stretches of the highway led through the virgin forest, for miles unbroken by a clearing or sign of human habitation.

They traveled slowly, with frequent pauses in shady places, for the weather was hot. The journey, made leisurely, required more than a day, and might with slight effort be prolonged into two. They stopped for the night at a small village, where Wain found lodging for Rena with an acquaintance of his, and for himself with another, while a third took charge of the horse, the accommodation for travelers being limited. Rena's appearance and manners were the subject of much comment. It was necessary to explain to several curious white people that Rena was a woman of color. A white woman might have driven with Wain without attracting remark,—most white ladies had negro coachmen. That a woman of Rena's complexion should eat at a negro's table, or sleep beneath a negro's roof, was a seeming breach of caste which only black blood could excuse. The explanation was never questioned. No white person of sound mind would ever claim to be a negro.

They resumed their journey somewhat late in the morning. Rena would willingly have hastened, for she was anxious to plunge into her new work; but Wain seemed disposed to prolong the pleasant drive, and beguiled the way for a time with stories of wonderful things he had done and strange experiences of a somewhat checkered career. He was shrewd enough to avoid any subject which would offend a modest young woman, but too obtuse to perceive that much of what he said would not commend him to a person of refinement. He made little reference to his possessions, concerning which so much had been said at Patesville; and this reticence was a point in his favor. If he had not been so much upon his guard and Rena so much absorbed by thoughts of her future work, such a drive would have furnished a person of her discernment a very fair measure of the man's character. To these distractions must be added the entire absence of any idea that Wain might have amorous designs upon her; and any shortcomings of manners or speech were excused by the broad mantle of charity which Rena in her new-found zeal for the welfare of her people was willing to throw over all their faults. They were the victims of oppression; they were not responsible for its results.

Toward the end of the second day, while nearing their destination, the travelers passed a large white house standing back from the road at the foot of a lane. Around it grew wide-spreading trees and well-kept shrubbery. The fences were in good repair. Behind the house and across the road stretched extensive fields of cotton and waving corn. They had passed no other place that showed such signs of thrift and prosperity.

"Oh, what a lovely place!" exclaimed Rena. "That is yours, is n't it?"

"No; we ain't got to my house yet," he answered. "Dat house b'longs ter de riches' people roun' here. Dat house is over in de nex' county. We 're right close to de line now."

Shortly afterwards they turned off from the main highway they had been pursuing, and struck into a narrower road to the left.

"De main road," explained Wain, "goes on to Clinton, 'bout five miles er mo' away. Dis one we 're turnin' inter now will take us to my place, which is 'bout three miles fu'ther on. We 'll git dere now in an hour er so."

Wain lived in an old plantation house, somewhat dilapidated, and surrounded by an air of neglect and shiftlessness, but still preserving a remnant of dignity in its outlines and comfort in its interior arrangements. Rena was assigned a large room on the second floor. She was somewhat surprised at the make-up of the household. Wain's mother—an old woman, much darker than her son—kept house for him. A sister with two children lived in the house. The element of surprise lay in the presence of two small children left by Wain's wife, of whom Rena now heard for the first time. He had lost his wife, he informed Rena sadly, a couple of years before.

"Yas, Miss Rena," he sighed, "de Lawd give her, an' de Lawd tuck her away. Blessed be de name er de Lawd." He accompanied this sententious quotation with a wicked look from under his half-closed eyelids that Rena did not see.

The following morning Wain drove her in his buggy over to the county town, where she took the teacher's examination. She was given a seat in a room with a number of other candidates for certificates, but the fact leaking out from some remark of Wain's that she was a colored girl, objection was quietly made by several of the would-be teachers to her presence in the room, and she was requested to retire until the white teachers should have been examined. An hour or two later she was given a separate examination, which she passed without difficulty. The examiner, a gentleman of local standing, was dimly conscious that she might not have found her exclusion pleasant, and was especially polite. It would have been strange, indeed, if he had not been impressed by her sweet face and air of modest dignity, which were all the more striking because of her social disability. He fell into conversation with her, became interested in her hopes and aims, and very cordially offered to be of service, if at any time he might, in connection with her school.

"You have the satisfaction," he said, "of receiving the only first-grade certificate issued to-day. You might teach a higher grade of pupils than you will find at Sandy Run, but let us hope that you may in time raise them to your own level."

"Which I doubt very much," he muttered to himself, as she went away with Wain. "What a pity that such a woman should be a nigger! If she were anything to me, though, I should hate to trust her anywhere near that saddle-colored scoundrel. He 's a thoroughly bad lot, and will bear watching."

Rena, however, was serenely ignorant of any danger from the accommodating Wain. Absorbed in her own thoughts and plans, she had not sought to look beneath the surface of his somewhat over-done politeness. In a few days she began her work as teacher, and sought to forget in the service of others the dull sorrow that still gnawed at her heart.

XXVI

THE SCHOOLHOUSE IN THE WOODS

BLANCHE LEARY, closely observant of Tryon's moods, marked a decided change in his manner after his return from his trip to Patesville. His former moroseness had given way to a certain defiant lightness, broken now and then by an involuntary sigh, but maintained so well, on the whole, that his mother detected no lapses whatever. The change was characterized by another feature agreeable to both the women: Tryon showed decidedly more interest than ever before in Miss Leary's society. Within a week he asked her several times to play a selection on the piano, displaying, as she noticed, a decided preference for gay and cheerful music, and several times suggesting a change when she chose pieces of a sentimental cast. More than once, during the second week after his return, he went out riding with her; she was a graceful horsewoman, perfectly at home in the saddle, and appearing to advantage in a riding-habit. She was aware that Tryon watched her now and then, with an eye rather critical than indulgent.

"He is comparing me with some other girl," she surmised. "I seem to stand the test very well. I wonder who the other is, and what was the trouble?"

Miss Leary exerted all her powers to interest and amuse the man she had set out to win, and who seemed nearer than ever before. Tryon, to his pleased surprise, discovered in her mind depths that he had never suspected. She displayed a singular affinity for the tastes that were his—he could not, of course, know how carefully she had studied them. The old wound, recently reopened, seemed to be healing rapidly, under conditions more conducive than before to perfect recovery. No longer, indeed, was he pursued by the picture of Rena discovered and unmasked—this he had definitely banished from the realm of sentiment to that of reason. The haunting image of Rena loving and beloved, amid the harmonious surroundings of her brother's home, was not so readily displaced. Nevertheless, he reached in several weeks a point from which he could consider her as one thinks of a dear one removed by the hand of death, or smitten by some incurable ailment of mind or body. Erelong, he fondly believed, the recovery would be so far complete that he could consign to the tomb of pleasant memories even the most thrilling episodes of his ill-starred courtship.

"George," said Mrs. Tryon one morning while her son was in this cheerful mood, "I 'm sending Blanche over to Major McLeod's to do an errand for me. Would you mind driving her over? The road may be rough after the storm last night, and Blanche has an idea that no one drives so well as you."

"Why, yes, mother, I 'll be glad to drive Blanche over. I want to see the major myself."

They were soon bowling along between the pines, behind the handsome mare that had carried Tryon so well at the Clarence tournament. Presently he drew up sharply.

"A tree has fallen squarely across the road," he exclaimed. "We shall have to turn back a little way and go around."

They drove back a quarter of a mile and turned into a by-road leading to the right through the woods. The solemn silence of the pine forest is soothing or oppressive, according to one's mood. Beneath the cool arcade of the tall, overarching trees a deep peace stole over Tryon's heart. He had put aside indefinitely and forever an unhappy and impossible love. The pretty and affectionate girl beside him would make an ideal wife. Of her family and blood he was sure. She was his mother's choice, and his mother had set her heart upon their marriage. Why not speak to her now, and thus give himself the best possible protection against stray flames of love?

"Blanche," he said, looking at her kindly.

"Yes, George?" Her voice was very gentle, and slightly tremulous. Could she have divined his thought? Love is a great clairvoyant.

"Blanche, dear, I"—

A clatter of voices broke upon the stillness of the forest and interrupted Tryon's speech. A sudden turn to the left brought the buggy to a little clearing, in the midst of which stood a small log schoolhouse. Out of the schoolhouse a swarm of colored children were emerging, the suppressed energy of the school hour finding vent in vocal exercise of various sorts. A group had already formed a ring, and were singing with great volume and vigor:—

"Miss Jane, she loves sugar an' tea,
Miss Jane, she loves candy.
Miss Jane, she can whirl all around
An' kiss her love quite handy.

"De oak grows tall,
De pine grows slim,
So rise you up, my true love,
An' let me come in."

"What a funny little darkey!" exclaimed Miss Leary, pointing to a diminutive lad who was walking on his hands, with his feet balanced in the air. At sight of the buggy and its occupants this sable acrobat, still retaining his inverted position, moved toward the newcomers, and, reversing himself with a sudden spring, brought up standing beside the buggy.

"Hoddy, Mars Geo'ge!" he exclaimed, bobbing his head and kicking his heel out behind in approved plantation style.

"Hello, Plato," replied the young man, "what are you doing here?"

"Gwine ter school, Mars Geo'ge," replied the lad; "larnin' ter read an' write, suh, lack de w'ite folks."

"Wat you callin' dat w'ite man marster fur?" whispered a tall yellow boy to the acrobat addressed as Plato. "You don' b'long ter him no mo'; you 're free, an' ain' got sense ernuff ter know it."

Tryon threw a small coin to Plato, and holding another in his hand suggestively, smiled toward the tall yellow boy, who looked regretfully at the coin, but stood his ground; he would call no man master, not even for a piece of money.

During this little colloquy, Miss Leary had kept her face turned toward the schoolhouse.

"What a pretty girl!" she exclaimed. "There," she added, as Tryon turned his head toward her, "you are too late. She has retired into her castle. Oh, Plato!"

"Yas, missis," replied Plato, who was prancing round the

buggy in great glee, on the strength of his acquaintance with the white folks.

"Is your teacher white?"

"No, ma'm, she ain't w'ite; she 's black. She looks lack she 's w'ite, but she 's black."

Tryon had not seen the teacher's face, but the incident had jarred the old wound; Miss Leary's description of the teacher, together with Plato's characterization, had stirred lightly sleeping memories. He was more or less abstracted during the remainder of the drive, and did not recur to the conversation that had been interrupted by coming upon the schoolhouse.

The teacher, glancing for a moment through the open door of the schoolhouse, had seen a handsome young lady staring at her,—Miss Leary had a curiously intent look when she was interested in anything, with no intention whatever to be rude,—and beyond the lady the back and shoulder of a man, whose face was turned the other way. There was a vague suggestion of something familiar about the equipage, but Rena shrank from this close scrutiny and withdrew out of sight before she had had an opportunity to identify the vague resemblance to something she had known.

Miss Leary had missed by a hair's-breadth the psychological moment, and felt some resentment toward the little negroes who had interrupted her lover's train of thought. Negroes have caused a great deal of trouble among white people. How deeply the shadow of the Ethiopian had fallen upon her own happiness, Miss Leary of course could not guess.

XXVII

AN INTERESTING ACQUAINTANCE

A FEW DAYS later, Rena looked out of the window near her desk and saw a low basket phaeton, drawn by a sorrel pony, driven sharply into the clearing and drawn up beside an oak sapling. The occupant of the phaeton, a tall, handsome, well-preserved lady in middle life, with slightly gray hair, alighted briskly from the phaeton, tied the pony to the sapling with a hitching-strap, and advanced to the schoolhouse door.

Rena wondered who the lady might be. She had a benevolent aspect, however, and came forward to the desk with a smile, not at all embarrassed by the wide-eyed inspection of the entire school.

"How do you do?" she said, extending her hand to the teacher. "I live in the neighborhood and am interested in the colored people—a good many of them once belonged to me. I heard something of your school, and thought I should like to make your acquaintance."

"It is very kind of you, indeed," murmured Rena respectfully.

"Yes," continued the lady, "I am not one of those who sit back and blame their former slaves because they were freed. They are free now,—it is all decided and settled,—and they ought to be taught enough to enable them to make good use of their freedom. But really, my dear,—you must n't feel offended if I make a mistake,—I am going to ask you something very personal." She looked suggestively at the gaping pupils.

"The school may take the morning recess now," announced the teacher. The pupils filed out in an orderly manner, most of them stationing themselves about the grounds in such places as would keep the teacher and the white lady in view. Very few white persons approved of the colored schools; no other white person had ever visited this one.

"Are you really colored?" asked the lady, when the children had withdrawn.

A year and a half earlier, Rena would have met the question by some display of self-consciousness. Now, she replied simply and directly.

"Yes, ma'am, I am colored."

The lady, who had been studying her as closely as good manners would permit, sighed regretfully.

"Well, it 's a shame. No one would ever think it. If you chose to conceal it, no one would ever be the wiser. What is your name, child, and where were you brought up? You must have a romantic history."

Rena gave her name and a few facts in regard to her past. The lady was so much interested, and put so many and such searching questions, that Rena really found it more difficult to suppress the fact that she had been white, than she had formerly had in hiding her African origin. There was about the girl an air of real refinement that pleased the lady,—the refinement not merely of a fine nature, but of contact with cultured people; a certain reserve of speech and manner quite inconsistent with Mrs. Tryon's experience of colored women. The lady was interested and slightly mystified. A generous, impulsive spirit,—her son's own mother,—she made minute inquiries about the school and the pupils, several of whom she knew by name. Rena stated that the two months' term was nearing its end, and that she was training the children in various declamations and dialogues for the exhibition at the close.

"I shall attend it," declared the lady positively. "I 'm sure you are doing a good work, and it 's very noble of you to undertake it when you might have a very different future. If I can serve you at any time, don't hesitate to call upon me. I live in the big white house just before you turn out of the Clinton road to come this way. I 'm only a widow, but my son George lives with me and has some influence in the neighborhood. He drove by here yesterday with the lady he is going to marry. It was she who told me about you."

Was it the name, or some subtle resemblance in speech or feature, that recalled Tryon's image to Rena's mind? It was not so far away—the image of the loving Tryon—that any powerful witchcraft was required to call it up. His mother was a widow; Rena had thought, in happier days, that she might be such a kind lady as this. But the cruel Tryon who had left her—his mother would be some hard, cold, proud woman, who would regard a negro as but little better than a dog, and who would not soil her lips by addressing a colored person upon any other terms than as a servant. She knew, too, that Tryon did not live in Sampson County, though the exact location of his home was not clear to her.

"And where are you staying, my dear?" asked the good lady.

"I 'm boarding at Mrs. Wain's," answered Rena.

"Mrs. Wain's?"

"Yes, they live in the old Campbell place."

"Oh, yes—Aunt Nancy. She 's a good enough woman, but we don't think much of her son Jeff. He married my Amanda after the war—she used to belong to me, and ought to have known better. He abused her most shamefully, and had to be threatened with the law. She left him a year or so ago and went away; I have n't seen her lately. Well, good-by, child; I 'm coming to your exhibition. If you ever pass my house, come in and see me."

The good lady had talked for half an hour, and had brought a ray of sunshine into the teacher's monotonous life, heretofore lighted only by the uncertain lamp of high resolve. She had satisfied a pardonable curiosity, and had gone away without mentioning her name.

Rena saw Plato untying the pony as the lady climbed into the phaeton.

"Who was the lady, Plato?" asked the teacher when the visitor had driven away.

"Dat 'uz my ole mist'iss, ma'm," returned Plato proudly,—"ole Mis' 'Liza."

"Mis' 'Liza who?" asked Rena.

"Mis' 'Liza Tryon. I use' ter b'long ter her. Dat 'uz her son, my young Mars Geo'ge, w'at driv pas' hyuh yistiddy wid 'is sweetheart."

XXVIII

THE LOST KNIFE

RENA had found her task not a difficult one so far as discipline was concerned. Her pupils were of a docile race, and school to them had all the charm of novelty. The teacher commanded some awe because she was a stranger, and some, perhaps, because she was white; for the theory of blackness as propounded by Plato could not quite counterbalance in the young African mind the evidence of their own senses. She combined gentleness with firmness; and if these had not been sufficient, she had reserves of character which would have given her the mastery over much less plastic material than these ignorant but eager young people. The work of instruction was simple enough, for most of the pupils began with the alphabet, which they acquired from Webster's blue-backed spelling-book, the palladium of Southern education at that epoch. The much abused carpet-baggers had put the spelling-book within reach of every child of school age in North Carolina,—a fact which is often overlooked when the carpet-baggers are held up to public odium. Even the devil should have his due, and is not so black as he is painted.

At the time when she learned that Tryon lived in the neighborhood, Rena had already been subjected for several weeks to a trying ordeal. Wain had begun to persecute her with marked attentions. She had at first gone to board at his house,—or, by courtesy, with his mother. For a week or two she had considered his attentions in no other light than those of a member of the school committee sharing her own zeal and interested in seeing the school successfully carried on. In this character Wain had driven her to the town for her examination; he had busied himself about putting the schoolhouse in order, and in various matters affecting the conduct of the school. He had jocularly offered to come and whip the children for her, and had found it convenient to drop in occasionally, ostensibly to see what progress the work was making.

"Dese child'en," he would observe sonorously, in the presence of the school, "oughter be monst'ous glad ter have de chance er settin' under yo' instruction, Miss Rena. I 'm sho' eve'body in dis neighbo'hood 'preciates de priv'lege er havin' you in ou' mids'."

Though slightly embarrassing to the teacher, these public demonstrations were endurable so long as they could be regarded as mere official appreciation of her work. Sincerely in earnest about her undertaking, she had plunged into it with all the intensity of a serious nature which love had stirred to activity. A pessimist might have sighed sadly or smiled cynically at the notion that a poor, weak girl, with a dangerous beauty and a sensitive soul, and troubles enough of her own, should hope to accomplish anything appreciable toward lifting the black mass still floundering in the mud where slavery had left it, and where emancipation had found it,—the mud in which, for aught that could be seen to the contrary, her little feet, too, were hopelessly entangled. It might have seemed like expecting a man to lift himself by his boot-straps.

But Rena was no philosopher, either sad or cheerful. She could not even have replied to this argument, that races must lift themselves, and the most that can be done by others is to give them opportunity and fair play. Hers was a simpler reasoning,—the logic by which the world is kept going onward and upward when philosophers are at odds and reformers are not forthcoming. She knew that for every child she taught to read and write she opened, if ever so little, the door of opportunity, and she was happy in the consciousness of performing a duty which seemed all the more imperative because newly discovered. Her zeal, indeed, for the time being was like that of an early Christian, who was more willing than not to die for his faith. Rena had fully and firmly made up her mind to sacrifice her life upon this altar. Her absorption in the work had not been without its reward, for thereby she had been able to keep at a distance the spectre of her lost love. Her dreams she could not control, but she banished Tryon as far as possible from her waking thoughts.

When Wain's attentions became obviously personal, Rena's new vestal instinct took alarm, and she began to apprehend his character more clearly. She had long ago learned that his pretensions to wealth were a sham. He was nominal owner of a large plantation, it is true; but the land was worn out, and mortgaged to the limit of its security value. His reputed droves of cattle and hogs had dwindled to a mere handful of lean and listless brutes.

Her clear eye, when once set to take Wain's measure, soon fathomed his shallow, selfish soul, and detected, or at least divined, behind his mask of good-nature a lurking brutality which filled her with vague distrust, needing only occasion to develop it into active apprehension,—occasion which was not long wanting. She avoided being alone with him at home by keeping carefully with the women of the house. If she were left alone,—and they soon showed a tendency to leave her on any pretext whenever Wain came near,—she would seek her own room and lock the door. She preferred not to offend Wain; she was far away from home and in a measure in his power, but she dreaded his compliments and sickened at his smile. She was also compelled to hear his relations sing his praises.

"My son Jeff," old Mrs. Wain would say, "is de bes' man you ever seed. His fus' wife had de easies' time an' de happies' time er ary woman in dis settlement. He 's grieve' fer her a long time, but I reckon he 's gittin' over it, an' de nex' 'oman w'at marries him 'll git a box er pyo' gol', ef I does say it as is his own mammy."

Rena had thought Wain rather harsh with his household, except in her immediate presence. His mother and sister seemed more or less afraid of him, and the children often anxious to avoid him.

One day, he timed his visit to the schoolhouse so as to walk home with Rena through the woods. When she became aware of his purpose, she called to one of the children who was loitering behind the others, "Wait a minute, Jenny. I 'm going your way, and you can walk along with me."

Wain with difficulty hid a scowl behind a smiling front. When they had gone a little distance along the road through the woods, he clapped his hand upon his pocket.

"I declare ter goodness," he exclaimed, "ef I ain't dropped my pocket-knife! I thought I felt somethin' slip th'ough dat hole in my pocket jes' by the big pine stump in the schoolhouse ya'd. Jinny, chile, run back an' hunt fer my knife, an'

I 'll give yer five cents ef yer find it. Me an' Miss Rena 'll walk on slow 'tel you ketches us."

Rena did not dare to object, though she was afraid to be alone with this man. If she could have had a moment to think, she would have volunteered to go back with Jenny and look for the knife, which, although a palpable subterfuge on her part, would have been one to which Wain could not object; but the child, dazzled by the prospect of reward, had darted back so quickly that this way of escape was cut off. She was evidently in for a declaration of love, which she had taken infinite pains to avoid. Just the form it would assume, she could not foresee. She was not long left in suspense. No sooner was the child well out of sight than Wain threw his arms suddenly about her waist and smilingly attempted to kiss her.

Speechless with fear and indignation, she tore herself from his grasp with totally unexpected force, and fled incontinently along the forest path. Wain—who, to do him justice, had merely meant to declare his passion in what he had hoped might prove a not unacceptable fashion—followed in some alarm, expostulating and apologizing as he went. But he was heavy and Rena was light, and fear lent wings to her feet. He followed her until he saw her enter the house of Elder Johnson, the father of several of her pupils, after which he sneaked uneasily homeward, somewhat apprehensive of the consequences of his abrupt wooing, which was evidently open to an unfavorable construction. When, an hour later, Rena sent one of the Johnson children for some of her things, with a message explaining that the teacher had been invited to spend a few days at Elder Johnson's, Wain felt a pronounced measure of relief. For an hour he had even thought it might be better to relinquish his pursuit. With a fatuousness born of vanity, however, no sooner had she sent her excuse than he began to look upon her visit to Johnson's as a mere exhibition of coyness, which, together with her conduct in the woods, was merely intended to lure him on.

Right upon the heels of the perturbation caused by Wain's conduct, Rena discovered that Tryon lived in the neighborhood; that not only might she meet him any day upon the highway, but that he had actually driven by the schoolhouse.

That he knew or would know of her proximity there could be no possible doubt, since she had freely told his mother her name and her home. A hot wave of shame swept over her at the thought that George Tryon might imagine she were following him, throwing herself in his way, and at the thought of the construction which he might place upon her actions. Caught thus between two emotional fires, at the very time when her school duties, owing to the approaching exhibition, demanded all her energies, Rena was subjected to a physical and mental strain that only youth and health could have resisted, and then only for a short time.

XXIX

PLATO EARNS HALF A DOLLAR

TRYON'S first feeling, when his mother at the dinner-table gave an account of her visit to the schoolhouse in the woods, was one of extreme annoyance. Why, of all created beings, should this particular woman be chosen to teach the colored school at Sandy Run? Had she learned that he lived in the neighborhood, and had she sought the place hoping that he might consent to renew, on different terms, relations which could never be resumed upon their former footing? Six weeks before, he would not have believed her capable of following him; but his last visit to Patesville had revealed her character in such a light that it was difficult to predict what she might do. It was, however, no affair of his. He was done with her; he had dismissed her from his own life, where she had never properly belonged, and he had filled her place, or would soon fill it, with another and worthier woman. Even his mother, a woman of keen discernment and delicate intuitions, had been deceived by this girl's specious exterior. She had brought away from her interview of the morning the impression that Rena was a fine, pure spirit, born out of place, through some freak of Fate, devoting herself with heroic self-sacrifice to a noble cause. Well, he had imagined her just as pure and fine, and she had deliberately, with a negro's low cunning, deceived him into believing that she was a white girl. The pretended confession of the brother, in which he had spoken of the humble origin of the family, had been, consciously or unconsciously, the most disingenuous feature of the whole miserable performance. They had tried by a show of frankness to satisfy their own consciences,—they doubtless had enough of white blood to give them a rudimentary trace of such a moral organ,—and by the same act to disarm him against future recriminations, in the event of possible discovery. How was he to imagine that persons of their appearance and pretensions were tainted with negro blood? The more he dwelt upon the subject, the more angry he became with those who had surprised his virgin heart and deflowered it by such low trickery. The man who brought the first negro into the British colonies had committed a crime against humanity and a worse crime against his own race. The father of this girl had been guilty of a sin against society for which others—for which he, George Tryon—must pay the penalty. As slaves, negroes were tolerable. As freemen, they were an excrescence, an alien element incapable of absorption into the body politic of white men. He would like to send them all back to the Africa from which their forefathers had come,—unwillingly enough, he would admit,—and he would like especially to banish this girl from his own neighborhood; not indeed that her presence would make any difference to him, except as a humiliating reminder of his own folly and weakness with which he could very well dispense.

Of this state of mind Tryon gave no visible manifestation beyond a certain taciturnity, so much at variance with his recent liveliness that the ladies could not fail to notice it. No effort upon the part of either was able to affect his mood, and they both resigned themselves to await his lordship's pleasure to be companionable.

For a day or two, Tryon sedulously kept away from the neighborhood of the schoolhouse at Sandy Run. He really had business which would have taken him in that direction, but made a détour of five miles rather than go near his abandoned and discredited sweetheart.

But George Tryon was wisely distrustful of his own impulses. Driving one day along the road to Clinton, he overhauled a diminutive black figure trudging along the road, occasionally turning a handspring by way of diversion.

"Hello, Plato," called Tryon, "do you want a lift?"

"Hoddy, Mars Geo'ge. Kin I ride wid you?"

"Jump up."

Plato mounted into the buggy with the agility to be expected from a lad of his acrobatic accomplishments. The two almost immediately fell into conversation upon perhaps the only subject of common interest between them. Before the town was reached, Tryon knew, so far as Plato could make it plain, the estimation in which the teacher was held by pupils and parents. He had learned the hours of opening and dismissal of the school, where the teacher lived, her habits of coming to and going from the schoolhouse, and the road she always followed.

"Does she go to church or anywhere else with Jeff Wain, Plato?" asked Tryon.

"No, suh, she don' go nowhar wid nobody excep'n' ole Elder Johnson er Mis' Johnson, an' de child'en. She use' ter stop at Mis' Wain's, but she 's stayin' wid Elder Johnson now. She alluz makes some er de child'en go home wid er f'm school," said Plato, proud to find in Mars Geo'ge an appreciative listener,—"sometimes one an' sometimes anudder. I 's be'n home wid 'er twice, an' it 'll be my tu'n ag'in befo' long."

"Plato," remarked Tryon impressively, as they drove into the town, "do you think you could keep a secret?"

"Yas, Mars Geo'ge, ef you says I shill."

"Do you see this fifty-cent piece?" Tryon displayed a small piece of paper money, crisp and green in its newness.

"Yas, Mars Geo'ge," replied Plato, fixing his eyes respectfully on the government's promise to pay. Fifty cents was a large sum of money. His acquaintance with Mars Geo'ge gave him the privilege of looking at money. When he grew up, he would be able, in good times, to earn fifty cents a day.

"I am going to give this to you, Plato."

Plato's eyes opened wide as saucers. "Me, Mars Geo'ge?" he asked in amazement.

"Yes, Plato. I 'm going to write a letter while I 'm in town, and want you to take it. Meet me here in half an hour, and I 'll give you the letter. Meantime, keep your mouth shut."

"Yas, Mars Geo'ge," replied Plato with a grin that distended that organ unduly. That he did not keep it shut may be inferred from the fact that within the next half hour he had eaten and drunk fifty cents' worth of candy, ginger-pop, and other available delicacies that appealed to the youthful palate. Having nothing more to spend, and the high prices prevailing for some time after the war having left him capable of locomotion, Plato was promptly on hand at the appointed time and place.

Tryon placed a letter in Plato's hand, still sticky with molasses candy,—he had inclosed it in a second cover by way of protection. "Give that letter," he said, "to your teacher; don't say a word about it to a living soul; bring me an answer, and give it into my own hand, and you shall have another half dollar."

Tryon was quite aware that by a surreptitious correspondence he ran some risk of compromising Rena. But he had felt, as soon as he had indulged his first opportunity to talk of her, an irresistible impulse to see her and speak to her again. He could scarcely call at her boarding-place,—what possible proper excuse could a young white man have for visiting a colored woman? At the schoolhouse she would be surrounded by her pupils, and a private interview would be as difficult, with more eyes to remark and more tongues to comment upon it. He might address her by mail, but did not know how often she sent to the nearest post-office. A letter mailed in the town must pass through the hands of a postmaster notoriously inquisitive and evil-minded, who was familiar with Tryon's handwriting and had ample time to attend to other people's business. To meet the teacher alone on the road seemed scarcely feasible, according to Plato's statement. A messenger, then, was not only the least of several evils, but really the only practicable way to communicate with Rena. He thought he could trust Plato, though miserably aware that he could not trust himself where this girl was concerned.

The letter handed by Tryon to Plato, and by the latter delivered with due secrecy and precaution, ran as follows:—

> DEAR MISS WARWICK,—You may think it strange that I should address you after what has passed between us; but learning from my mother of your presence in the neighborhood, I am constrained to believe that you do not find my proximity embarrassing, and I cannot resist the wish to meet you at least once more, and talk over the circumstances of our former friendship. From a practical point of view this may seem superfluous, as the matter has been definitely settled. I have no desire to find fault with you; on the contrary, I wish to set myself right with regard to my own actions, and to assure you of my good wishes. In other words, since we must part, I would rather we parted friends than enemies. If nature

and society—or Fate, to put it another way—have decreed that we cannot live together, it is nevertheless possible that we may carry into the future a pleasant though somewhat sad memory of a past friendship. Will you not grant me one interview? I appreciate the difficulty of arranging it; I have found it almost as hard to communicate with you by letter. I will suit myself to your convenience and meet you at any time and place you may designate. Please answer by bearer, who I think is trustworthy, and believe me, whatever your answer may be,

Respectfully yours,
G. T.

The next day but one Tryon received through the mail the following reply to his letter:—

GEORGE TRYON, ESQ.

Dear Sir,—I have requested your messenger to say that I will answer your letter by mail, which I shall now proceed to do. I assure you that I was entirely ignorant of your residence in this neighborhood, or it would have been the last place on earth in which I should have set foot.

As to our past relations, they were ended by your own act. I frankly confess that I deceived you; I have paid the penalty, and have no complaint to make. I appreciate the delicacy which has made you respect my brother's secret, and thank you for it. I remember the whole affair with shame and humiliation, and would willingly forget it.

As to a future interview, I do not see what good it would do either of us. You are white, and you have given me to understand that I am black. I accept the classification, however unfair, and the consequences, however unjust, one of which is that we cannot meet in the same parlor, in the same church, at the same table, or anywhere, in social intercourse; upon a steamboat we would not sit at the same table; we could not walk together on the street, or meet publicly anywhere and converse, without unkind remark. As a white man, this might not mean a great deal to you; as a woman, shut out already by my color from much that is desirable, my good name remains my most valuable possession. I beg of you to let me alone. The best possible proof you can give me of your good wishes is to relinquish any desire or attempt to see me. I shall have finished my work here in a few days. I have other troubles, of which you know nothing, and any meeting with you would only add to a burden which is already as much as I can bear. To speak of parting is superfluous—we have already parted. It were idle to dream of a future friendship between people so widely different in station. Such a friendship, if possible in itself, would never be tolerated by the lady whom you are to marry, with whom you drove by my schoolhouse the other day. A gentleman so loyal to his race and its traditions as you have shown yourself could not be less faithful to the lady to whom he has lost his heart and his memory in three short months.

No, Mr. Tryon, our romance is ended, and better so. We could never have been happy. I have found a work in which I may be of service to others who have fewer opportunities than mine have been. Leave me in peace, I beseech you, and I shall soon pass out of your neighborhood as I have passed out of your life, and hope to pass out of your memory.

Yours very truly,
ROWENA WALDEN.

XXX

AN UNUSUAL HONOR

To Rena's high-strung and sensitive nature, already under very great tension from her past experience, the ordeal of the next few days was a severe one. On the one hand, Jeff Wain's infatuation had rapidly increased, in view of her speedy departure. From Mrs. Tryon's remark about Wain's wife Amanda, and from things Rena had since learned, she had every reason to believe that this wife was living, and that Wain must be aware of the fact. In the light of this knowledge, Wain's former conduct took on a blacker significance than, upon reflection, she had charitably clothed it with after the first flush of indignation. That he had not given up his design to make love to her was quite apparent, and, with Amanda alive, his attentions, always offensive since she had gathered their import, became in her eyes the expression of a villainous purpose, of which she could not speak to others, and from which she felt safe only so long as she took proper precautions against it. In a week her school would be over, and then she would get Elder Johnson, or some one else than Wain, to take her back to Patesville. True, she might abandon her school and go at once; but her work would be incomplete, she would have violated her contract, she would lose her salary for the month, explanations would be necessary, and would not be forthcoming, She might feign sickness,—indeed, it would scarcely be feigning, for she felt far from well; she had never, since her illness, quite recovered her former vigor—but the inconvenience to others would be the same, and her self-sacrifice would have had, at its very first trial, a lame and impotent conclusion. She had as yet no fear of personal violence from Wain; but, under the circumstances, his attentions were an insult. He was evidently bent upon conquest, and vain enough to think he might achieve it by virtue of his personal attractions. If he could have understood how she loathed the sight of his narrow eyes, with their puffy lids, his thick, tobacco-stained lips, his doubtful teeth, and his unwieldy person, Wain, a monument of conceit that he was, might have shrunk, even in his own estimation, to something like his real proportions. Rena believed that, to defend herself from persecution at his hands, it was only necessary that she never let him find her alone. This, however, required constant watchfulness. Relying upon his own powers, and upon a woman's weakness and aversion to scandal, from which not even the purest may always escape unscathed, and convinced by her former silence that he had nothing serious to fear, Wain made it a point to be present at every public place where she might be. He assumed, in conversation with her which she could not avoid, and stated to others, that she had left his house because of a previous promise to divide the time of her stay between Elder Johnson's house and his own. He volunteered to teach a class in the Sunday-school which Rena conducted at the colored Methodist church, and when she remained to service, occupied a seat conspicuously near her own. In addition to these public demonstrations, which it was impossible to escape, or, it seemed, with so thick-skinned an individual as Wain, even to discourage, she was secretly and uncomfortably conscious that she could scarcely stir abroad without the risk of encountering one of two men, each of whom was on the lookout for an opportunity to find her alone.

The knowledge of Tryon's presence in the vicinity had been almost as much as Rena could bear. To it must be added the consciousness that he, too, was pursuing her, to what end she could not tell. After his letter to her brother, and the feeling therein displayed, she found it necessary to crush once or twice a wild hope that, her secret being still unknown save to a friendly few, he might return and claim her. Now, such an outcome would be impossible. He had become engaged to another woman,—this in itself would be enough to keep him from her, if it were not an index of a vastly more serious barrier, a proof that he had never loved her. If he had loved her truly, he would never have forgotten her in three short months,—three long months they had heretofore seemed to her, for in them she had lived a lifetime of experience. Another impassable barrier lay in the fact that his mother had met her, and that she was known in the neighborhood. Thus cut off from any hope that she might be anything to him, she had no wish to meet her former lover; no possible good could come of such a meeting; and yet her fluttering heart told her that if he should come, as his letter foreshadowed that he might,—if he should come, the loving George of old, with soft words and tender smiles and specious talk of friendship—ah! then, her heart would break! She must not meet him—at any cost she must avoid him.

But this heaping up of cares strained her endurance to the breaking-point. Toward the middle of the last week, she knew that she had almost reached the limit, and was haunted by a fear that she might break down before the week was over. Now her really fine nature rose to the emergency, though she mustered her forces with a great effort. If she could keep Wain at his distance and avoid Tryon for three days longer, her school labors would be ended and she might retire in peace and honor.

"Miss Rena," said Plato to her on Tuesday, "ain't it 'bout time I wuz gwine home wid you ag'in?"

"You may go with me to-morrow, Plato," answered the teacher.

After school Plato met an anxious-eyed young man in the woods a short distance from the schoolhouse.

"Well, Plato, what news?"

"I 's gwine ter see her home ter-morrer, Mars Geo'ge."

"To-morrow!" replied Tryon; "how very unfortunate! I wanted you to go to town to-morrow to take an important message for me. I 'm sorry, Plato—you might have earned another dollar."

To lie is a disgraceful thing, and yet there are times when, to a lover's mind, love dwarfs all ordinary laws. Plato scratched his head disconsolately, but suddenly a bright thought struck him.

"Can't I go ter town fer you atter I 've seed her home, Mars Geo'ge?"

"N-o, I 'm afraid it would be too late," returned Tryon doubtfully.

"Den I 'll haf ter ax 'er ter lemme go nex' day," said Plato, with resignation. The honor might be postponed or, if necessary, foregone; the opportunity to earn a dollar was the chance of a lifetime and must not be allowed to slip.

"No, Plato," rejoined Tryon, shaking his head, "I should n't want to deprive you of so great a pleasure." Tryon was entirely sincere in this characterization of Plato's chance; he would have given many a dollar to be sure of Plato's place and Plato's welcome. Rena's letter had re-inflamed his smouldering passion; only opposition was needed to fan it to a white heat. Wherein lay the great superiority of his position, if he was denied the right to speak to the one person in the world whom he most cared to address? He felt some dim realization of the tyranny of caste, when he found it not merely pressing upon an inferior people who had no right to expect anything better, but barring his own way to something that he desired. He meant her no harm—but he must see her. He could never marry her now—but he must see her. He was conscious of a certain relief at the thought that he had not asked Blanche Leary to be his wife. His hand was unpledged. He could not marry the other girl, of course, but they must meet again. The rest he would leave to Fate, which seemed reluctant to disentangle threads which it had woven so closely.

"I think, Plato, that I see an easier way out of the difficulty. Your teacher, I imagine, merely wants some one to see her safely home. Don't you think, if you should go part of the way, that I might take your place for the rest, while you did my errand?"

"Why, sho'ly, Mars Geo'ge, you could take keer er her better 'n I could—better 'n anybody could—co'se you could!"

Mars Geo'ge was white and rich, and could do anything. Plato was proud of the fact that he had once belonged to Mars Geo'ge. He could not conceive of any one so powerful as Mars Geo'ge, unless it might be God, of whom Plato had heard more or less, and even here the comparison might not be quite fair to Mars Geo'ge, for Mars Geo'ge was the younger of the two. It would undoubtedly be a great honor for the teacher to be escorted home by Mars Geo'ge. The teacher was a great woman, no doubt, and looked white; but Mars Geo'ge was the real article. Mars Geo'ge had never been known to go with a black woman before, and the teacher would doubtless thank Plato for arranging that so great an honor should fall upon her. Mars Ge'oge had given him fifty cents twice, and would now give him a dollar. Noble Mars Geo'ge! Fortunate teacher! Happy Plato!

"Very well, Plato. I think we can arrange it so that you can kill the two rabbits at one shot. Suppose that we go over the road that she will take to go home."

They soon arrived at the schoolhouse. School had been out an hour, and the clearing was deserted. Plato led the way by the road through the woods to a point where, amid somewhat thick underbrush, another path intersected the road they were following.

"Now, Plato," said Tryon, pausing here, "this would be a good spot for you to leave the teacher and for me to take your place. This path leads to the main road, and will take you to town very quickly. I should n't say anything to the teacher about it at all; but when you and she get here, drop behind and run along this path until you meet me,—I 'll be waiting a few yards down the road,—and then run to town as fast as your legs will carry you. As soon as you are gone, I 'll come out and tell the teacher that I 've sent you away on an errand, and will myself take your place. You shall have a dollar, and I 'll ask her to let you go home with her the next day. But you must n't say a word about it, Plato, or you won't get the dollar, and I 'll not ask the teacher to let you go home with her again."

"All right, Mars Geo'ge, I ain't gwine ter say no mo' d'n ef de cat had my tongue."

XXXI

IN DEEP WATERS

RENA was unusually fatigued at the close of her school on Wednesday afternoon. She had been troubled all day with a headache, which, beginning with a dull pain, had gradually increased in intensity until every nerve was throbbing like a trip-hammer. The pupils seemed unusually stupid. A discouraging sense of the insignificance of any part she could perform towards the education of three million people with a school term of two months a year hung over her spirit like a pall. As the object of Wain's attentions, she had begun to feel somewhat like a wild creature who hears the pursuers on its track, and has the fear of capture added to the fatigue of flight. But when this excitement had gone too far and had neared the limit of exhaustion came Tryon's letter, with the resulting surprise and consternation. Rena had keyed herself up to a heroic pitch to answer it; but when the inevitable reaction came, she was overwhelmed with a sickening sense of her own weakness. The things which in another sphere had constituted her strength and shield were now her undoing, and exposed her to dangers from which they lent her no protection. Not only was this her position in theory, but the pursuers were already at her heels. As the day wore on, these dark thoughts took on an added gloom, until, when the hour to dismiss school arrived, she felt as though she had not a friend in the world. This feeling was accentuated by a letter which she had that morning received from her mother, in which Mis' Molly spoke very highly of Wain, and plainly expressed the hope that her daughter might like him so well that she would prefer to remain in Sampson County.

Plato, bright-eyed and alert, was waiting in the school-yard until the teacher should be ready to start. Having warned away several smaller children who had hung around after school as though to share his prerogative of accompanying the teacher, Plato had swung himself into the low branches of an oak at the edge of the clearing, from which he was hanging by his legs, head downward. He dropped from this reposeful attitude when the teacher appeared at the door, and took his place at her side.

A premonition of impending trouble caused the teacher to hesitate. She wished that she had kept more of the pupils behind. Something whispered that danger lurked in the road she customarily followed. Plato seemed insignificantly small and weak, and she felt miserably unable to cope with any difficult or untoward situation.

"Plato," she suggested, "I think we 'll go round the other way to-night, if you don't mind."

Visions of Mars Geo'ge disappointed, of a dollar unearned and unspent, flitted through the narrow brain which some one, with the irony of ignorance or of knowledge, had mocked with the name of a great philosopher. Plato was not an untruthful lad, but he seldom had the opportunity to earn a dollar. His imagination, spurred on by the instinct of self-interest, rose to the emergency.

"I 's feared you mought git snake-bit gwine roun' dat way, Miss Rena. My brer Jim kill't a water-moccasin down dere yistiddy 'bout ten feet long."

Rena had a horror of snakes, with which the swamp by which the other road ran was infested. Snakes were a vivid reality; her presentiment was probably a mere depression of spirits due to her condition of nervous exhaustion. A cloud had come up and threatened rain, and the wind was rising ominously. The old way was the shorter; she wanted above all things to get to Elder Johnson's and go to bed. Perhaps sleep would rest her tired brain—she could not imagine herself feeling worse, unless she should break down altogether.

She plunged into the path and hastened forward so as to reach home before the approaching storm. So completely was she absorbed in her own thoughts that she scarcely noticed that Plato himself seemed preoccupied. Instead of capering along like a playful kitten or puppy, he walked by her side unusually silent. When they had gone a short distance and were approaching a path which intersected their road at something near a right angle, the teacher missed Plato. He had dropped behind a moment before; now he had disappeared entirely.

Her vague alarm of a few moments before returned with redoubled force.

"Plato!" she called; "Plato!"

There was no response, save the soughing of the wind through the swaying treetops. She stepped hastily forward, wondering if this were some childish prank. If so, it was badly timed, and she would let Plato feel the weight of her displeasure.

Her forward step had brought her to the junction of the two paths, where she paused doubtfully. The route she had been following was the most direct way home, but led for quite a distance through the forest, which she did not care to traverse alone. The intersecting path would soon take her to the main road, where she might find shelter or company, or both. Glancing around again in search of her missing escort, she became aware that a man was approaching her from each of the two paths. In one she recognized the eager and excited face of George Tryon, flushed with anticipation of their meeting, and yet grave with uncertainty of his reception. Advancing confidently along the other path she saw the face of Jeff Wain, drawn, as she imagined in her anguish, with evil passions which would stop at nothing.

What should she do? There was no sign of Plato—for aught she could see or hear of him, the earth might have swallowed him up. Some deadly serpent might have stung him. Some wandering rabbit might have tempted him aside. Another thought struck her. Plato had been very quiet—there had been something on his conscience—perhaps he had betrayed her! But to which of the two men, and to what end?

The problem was too much for her overwrought brain. She turned and fled. A wiser instinct might have led her forward. In the two conflicting dangers she might have found safety. The road after all was a public way. Any number of persons might meet there accidentally. But she saw only the darker side of the situation. To turn to Tryon for protection before Wain had by some overt act manifested the evil purpose which she as yet only suspected would be, she imagined, to acknowledge a previous secret acquaintance with Tryon, thus placing her reputation at Wain's mercy, and to charge herself with a burden of obligation toward a man whom she wished to avoid and had refused to meet. If, on the other hand, she should go forward to meet Wain, he would undoubtedly offer to accompany her homeward. Tryon would inevitably observe the meeting, and suppose it prearranged. Not for the world would she have him think so—why she should care for his opinion, she did not stop to argue. She turned and fled, and to avoid possible pursuit, struck into the underbrush at an angle which she calculated would bring her in a few rods to another path which would lead quickly into the main road. She had run only a few yards when she found herself in the midst of a clump of prickly shrubs and briars. Meantime the storm had burst; the rain fell in torrents. Extricating herself from the thorns, she pressed forward, but instead of coming out upon the road, found herself penetrating deeper and deeper into the forest.

The storm increased in violence. The air grew darker and darker. It was near evening, the clouds were dense, the thick woods increased the gloom. Suddenly a blinding flash of lightning pierced the darkness, followed by a sharp clap of thunder. There was a crash of falling timber. Terror-stricken, Rena flew forward through the forest, the underbrush growing closer and closer as she advanced. Suddenly the earth gave way beneath her feet and she sank into a concealed morass. By clasping the trunk of a neighboring sapling she extricated herself with an effort, and realized with a horrible certainty that she was lost in the swamp.

Turning, she tried to retrace her steps. A flash of lightning penetrated the gloom around her, and barring her path she saw a huge black snake,—harmless enough, in fact, but to her excited imagination frightful in appearance. With a wild shriek she turned again, staggered forward a few yards, stumbled over a projecting root, and fell heavily to the earth.

When Rena had disappeared in the underbrush, Tryon and Wain had each instinctively set out in pursuit of her, but owing to the gathering darkness, the noise of the storm, and the thickness of the underbrush, they missed not only Rena but each other, and neither was aware of the other's presence in the forest. Wain kept up the chase until the rain drove him to shelter. Tryon, after a few minutes, realized that she had fled to escape him, and that to pursue her would be to defeat rather than promote his purpose. He desisted, therefore, and returning to the main road, stationed himself at a point where he could watch Elder Johnson's house, and having waited for a while without any signs of Rena, concluded that she had taken refuge in some friendly cabin. Turning homeward disconsolately as night came on, he intercepted Plato on his way back from town, and pledged him to inviolable secrecy so effectually that Plato, when subsequently questioned, merely answered that he had stopped a moment to gather some chinquapins, and when he had looked around the teacher was gone.

Rena not appearing at supper-time nor for an hour later, the elder, somewhat anxious, made inquiries about the neighborhood, and finding his guest at no place where she might be expected to stop, became somewhat alarmed. Wain's house was the last to which he went. He had surmised that there was some mystery connected with her leaving Wain's, but had never been given any definite information about the matter. In response to his inquiries, Wain expressed surprise, but betrayed a certain self-consciousness which did not escape the elder's eye. Returning home, he organized a search-party from his own family and several near neighbors, and set out with dogs and torches to scour the woods for the missing teacher. A couple of hours later, they found her lying unconscious in the edge of the swamp, only a few rods from a well-defined path which would soon have led her to the open highway. Strong arms lifted her gently and bore her home. Mrs. Johnson undressed her and put her to bed, administering a homely remedy, of which whiskey was the principal ingredient, to counteract the effects of the exposure. There was a doctor within five miles, but no one thought of sending for him, nor was it at all likely that it would have been possible to get him for such a case at such an hour.

Rena's illness, however, was more deeply seated than her friends could imagine. A tired body, in sympathy with an overwrought brain, had left her peculiarly susceptible to the nervous shock of her forest experience. The exposure for several hours in her wet clothing to the damps and miasma of the swamp had brought on an attack of brain fever. The next morning, she was delirious. One of the children took word to the schoolhouse that the teacher was sick and there would be no school that day. A number of curious and sympathetic people came in from time to time and suggested various remedies, several of which old Mrs. Johnson, with catholic impartiality, administered to the helpless teacher, who from delirium gradually sunk into a heavy stupor scarcely distinguishable from sleep. It was predicted that she would probably be well in the morning; if not, it would then be time to consider seriously the question of sending for a doctor.

XXXII

THE POWER OF LOVE

After Tryon's failure to obtain an interview with Rena through Plato's connivance, he decided upon a different course of procedure. In a few days her school term would be finished. He was not less desirous to see her, was indeed as much more eager as opposition would be likely to make a very young man who was accustomed to having his own way, and whose heart, as he had discovered, was more deeply and permanently involved than he had imagined. His present plan was to wait until the end of the school; then, when Rena went to Clinton on the Saturday or Monday to draw her salary for the month, he would see her in the town, or, if necessary, would follow her to Patesville. No power on earth should keep him from her long, but he had no desire to interfere in any way with the duty which she owed to others. When the school was over and her work completed, then he would have his innings. Writing letters was too unsatisfactory a method of communication—he must see her face to face.

The first of his three days of waiting had passed, when, about ten o'clock on the morning of the second day, which seemed very long in prospect, while driving along the road toward Clinton, he met Plato, with a rabbit trap in his hand.

"Well, Plato," he asked, "why are you absent from the classic shades of the academy to-day?"

"Hoddy, Mars Geo'ge. W'at wuz dat you say?"

"Why are you not at school to-day?"

"Ain' got no teacher, Mars Geo'ge. Teacher 's gone!"

"Gone!" exclaimed Tryon, with a sudden leap of the heart. "Gone where? What do you mean?"

"Teacher got los' in de swamp, night befo' las', 'cause Plato wa'n't dere ter show her de way out'n de woods. Elder Johnson foun' 'er wid dawgs and tawches, an' fotch her home an' put her ter bed. No school yistiddy. She wuz out'n her haid las' night, an' dis mawnin' she wuz gone."

"Gone where?"

"Dey don' nobody know whar, suh."

Leaving Plato abruptly, Tryon hastened down the road toward Elder Johnson's cabin. This was no time to stand on punctilio. The girl had been lost in the woods in the storm, amid the thunder and lightning and the pouring rain. She was sick with fright and exposure, and he was the cause of it all. Bribery, corruption, and falsehood had brought punishment in their train, and the innocent had suffered while the guilty escaped. He must learn at once what had become of her. Reaching Elder Johnson's house, he drew up by the front fence and gave the customary halloa, which summoned a woman to the door.

"Good-morning," he said, nodding unconsciously, with the careless politeness of a gentleman to his inferiors. "I 'm Mr. Tryon. I have come to inquire about the sick teacher."

"Why, suh," the woman replied respectfully, "she got los' in de woods night befo' las', an' she wuz out'n her min' most er de time yistiddy. Las' night she must 'a' got out er bed an' run away w'en eve'ybody wuz soun' asleep, fer dis mawnin' she wuz gone, an' none er us knows whar she is."

"Has any search been made for her?"

"Yas, suh, my husban' an' de child'en has been huntin' roun' all de mawnin', an' he 's gone ter borry a hoss now ter go fu'ther. But Lawd knows dey ain' no tellin' whar she 'd go, 'less'n she got her min' back sence she lef'."

Tryon's mare was in good condition. He had money in his pocket and nothing to interfere with his movements. He set out immediately on the road to Patesville, keeping a lookout by the roadside, and stopping each person he met to inquire if a young woman, apparently ill, had been seen traveling along the road on foot. No one had met such a traveler. When he had gone two or three miles, he drove through a shallow branch that crossed the road. The splashing of his horse's hoofs in the water prevented him from hearing a low groan that came from the woods by the roadside.

He drove on, making inquiries at each farmhouse and of every person whom he encountered. Shortly after crossing the branch, he met a young negro with a cartload of tubs and buckets and piggins, and asked him if he had seen on the road a young white woman with dark eyes and hair, apparently sick or demented. The young man answered in the negative, and Tryon pushed forward anxiously.

At noon he stopped at a farmhouse and swallowed a hasty meal. His inquiries here elicited no information, and he was just leaving when a young man came in late to dinner and stated, in response to the usual question, that he had met, some two hours before, a young woman who answered Tryon's description, on the Lillington road, which crossed the main road to Patesville a short distance beyond the farmhouse. He had spoken to the woman. At first she had paid no heed to his question. When addressed a second time, she had answered in a rambling and disconnected way, which indicated to his mind that there was something wrong with her.

Tryon thanked his informant and hastened to the Lillington road. Stopping as before to inquire, he followed the woman for several hours, each mile of the distance taking him farther away from Patesville. From time to time he heard of the woman. Toward nightfall he found her. She was white enough, with the sallowness of the sandhill poor white. She was still young, perhaps, but poverty and a hard life made her look older than she ought. She was not fair, and she was not Rena. When Tryon came up to her, she was sitting on the doorsill of a miserable cabin, and held in her hand a bottle, the contents of which had never paid any revenue tax. She had walked twenty miles that day, and had beguiled the tedium of the journey by occasional potations, which probably accounted for the incoherency of speech which several of those who met her had observed. When Tryon drew near, she tendered him the bottle with tipsy cordiality. He turned in disgust and retraced his steps to the Patesville road, which he did not reach until nightfall. As it was too dark to prosecute the search with any chance of success, he secured lodging for the night, intending to resume his quest early in the morning.

XXXIII

A MULE AND A CART

FRANK FOWLER'S heart was filled with longing for a sight of Rena's face. When she had gone away first, on the ill-fated trip to South Carolina, her absence had left an aching void in his life; he had missed her cheerful smile, her pleasant words, her graceful figure moving about across the narrow street. His work had grown monotonous during her absence; the clatter of hammer and mallet, that had seemed so merry when punctuated now and then by the strains of her voice, became a mere humdrum rapping of wood upon wood and iron upon iron. He had sought work in South Carolina with the hope that he might see her. He had satisfied this hope, and had tried in vain to do her a service; but Fate had been against her; her castle of cards had come tumbling down. He felt that her sorrow had brought her nearer to him. The distance between them depended very much upon their way of looking at things. He knew that her experience had dragged her through the valley of humiliation. His unselfish devotion had reacted to refine and elevate his own spirit. When he heard the suggestion, after her second departure, that she might marry Wain, he could not but compare himself with this new aspirant. He, Frank, was a man, an honest man—a better man than the shifty scoundrel with whom she had ridden away. She was but a woman, the best and sweetest and loveliest of all women, but yet a woman. After a few short years of happiness or sorrow,—little of joy, perhaps, and much of sadness, which had begun already,—they would both be food for worms. White people, with a deeper wisdom perhaps than they used in their own case, regarded Rena and himself as very much alike. They were certainly both made by the same God, in much the same physical and mental mould; they breathed the same air, ate the same food, spoke the same speech, loved and hated, laughed and cried, lived and would die, the same. If God had meant to rear any impassable barrier between people of contrasting complexions, why did He not express the prohibition as He had done between other orders of creation?

When Rena had departed for Sampson County, Frank had reconciled himself to her absence by the hope of her speedy return. He often stepped across the street to talk to Mis' Molly about her. Several letters had passed between mother and daughter, and in response to Frank's inquiries his neighbor uniformly stated that Rena was well and doing well, and sent her love to all inquiring friends. But Frank observed that Mis' Molly, when pressed as to the date of Rena's return, grew more and more indefinite; and finally the mother, in a burst of confidential friendship, told Frank of all her hopes with reference to the stranger from down the country.

"Yas, Frank," she concluded, "it 'll be her own fault ef she don't become a lady of proputty, fer Mr. Wain is rich, an' owns a big plantation, an' hires a lot of hands, and is a big man in the county. He 's crazy to git her, an' it all lays in her own han's."

Frank did not find this news reassuring. He believed that Wain was a liar and a scoundrel. He had nothing more than his intuitions upon which to found this belief, but it was none the less firm. If his estimate of the man's character were correct, then his wealth might be a fiction, pure and simple. If so, the truth should be known to Mis' Molly, so that instead of encouraging a marriage with Wain, she would see him in his true light, and interpose to rescue her daughter from his importunities. A day or two after this conversation, Frank met in the town a negro from Sampson County, made his acquaintance, and inquired if he knew a man by the name of Jeff Wain.

"Oh, Jeff Wain!" returned the countryman slightingly; "yas, I knows 'im, an' don' know no good of 'im. One er dese yer biggity, braggin' niggers—talks lack he own de whole county, an' ain't wuth no mo' d'n I is—jes' a big bladder wid a handful er shot rattlin' roun' in it. Had a wife, when I wuz dere, an' beat her an' 'bused her so she had ter run away."

This was alarming information. Wain had passed in the town as a single man, and Frank had had no hint that he had ever been married. There was something wrong somewhere. Frank determined that he would find out the truth and, if possible, do something to protect Rena against the obviously evil designs of the man who had taken her away. The barrel factory had so affected the cooper's trade that Peter and Frank had turned their attention more or less to the manufacture of small woodenware for domestic use. Frank's mule was eating off its own head, as the saying goes. It required but little effort to persuade Peter that his son might take a load of buckets and tubs and piggins into the country and sell them or trade them for country produce at a profit.

In a few days Frank had his stock prepared, and set out on the road to Sampson County. He went about thirty miles the first day, and camped by the roadside for the night, resuming the journey at dawn. After driving for an hour through the tall pines that overhung the road like the stately arch of a cathedral aisle, weaving a carpet for the earth with their brown spines and cones, and soothing the ear with their ceaseless murmur, Frank stopped to water his mule at a point where the white, sandy road, widening as it went, sloped downward to a clear-running branch. On the right a bay-tree bending over the stream mingled the heavy odor of its flowers with the delicate perfume of a yellow jessamine vine that had overrun a clump of saplings on the left. From a neighboring tree a silver-throated mocking-bird poured out a flood of riotous melody. A group of minnows, startled by the splashing of the mule's feet, darted away into the shadow of the thicket, their quick passage leaving the amber water filled with laughing light.

The mule drank long and lazily, while over Frank stole thoughts in harmony with the peaceful scene,—thoughts of Rena, young and beautiful, her friendly smile, her pensive dark eyes. He would soon see her now, and if she had any cause for fear or unhappiness, he would place himself at her service—for a day, a week, a month, a year, a lifetime, if need be.

His reverie was broken by a slight noise from the thicket at his left. "I wonder who dat is?" he muttered. "It soun's mighty quare, ter say de leas'."

He listened intently for a moment, but heard nothing further. "It must 'a' be'n a rabbit er somethin' scamp'in' th'ough de woods. G'long dere, Cæsar!"

As the mule stepped forward, the sound was repeated. This time it was distinctly audible, the long, low moan of some one in sickness or distress.

"Dat ain't no rabbit," said Frank to himself. "Dere 's somethin' wrong dere. Stan' here, Cæsar, till I look inter dis matter."

Pulling out from the branch, Frank sprang from the saddle and pushed his way cautiously through the outer edge of the thicket.

"Good Lawd!" he exclaimed with a start, "it 's a woman—a w'ite woman!"

The slender form of a young woman lay stretched upon the ground in a small open space a few yards in extent. Her face was turned away, and Frank could see at first only a tangled mass of dark brown hair, matted with twigs and leaves and cockleburs, and hanging in wild profusion around her neck.

Frank stood for a moment irresolute, debating the serious question whether he should investigate further with a view to rendering assistance, or whether he should put as great a distance as possible between himself and this victim, as she might easily be, of some violent crime, lest he should himself be suspected of it—a not unlikely contingency, if he were found in the neighborhood and the woman should prove unable to describe her assailant. While he hesitated, the figure moved restlessly, and a voice murmured:—

"Mamma, oh, mamma!"

The voice thrilled Frank like an electric shock. Trembling in every limb, he sprang forward toward the prostrate figure. The woman turned her head, and he saw that it was Rena. Her gown was torn and dusty, and fringed with burs and briars. When she had wandered forth, half delirious, pursued by imaginary foes, she had not stopped to put on her shoes, and her little feet were blistered and swollen and bleeding. Frank knelt by her side and lifted her head on his arm. He put his hand upon her brow; it was burning with fever.

"Miss Rena! Rena! don't you know me?"

She turned her wild eyes on him suddenly. "Yes, I know you, Jeff Wain. Go away from me! Go away!"

Her voice rose to a scream; she struggled in his grasp and struck at him fiercely with her clenched fists. Her sleeve fell back and disclosed the white scar made by his own hand so many years before.

"You 're a wicked man," she panted. "Don't touch me! I hate you and despise you!"

Frank could only surmise how she had come here, in such a condition. When she spoke of Wain in this manner, he drew his own conclusions. Some deadly villainy of Wain's had brought her to this pass. Anger stirred his nature to the depths, and found vent in curses on the author of Rena's misfortunes.

"Damn him!" he groaned. "I 'll have his heart's blood fer dis, ter de las' drop!"

Rena now laughed and put up her arms appealingly. "George," she cried, in melting tones, "dear George, do you love me? How much do you love me? Ah, you don't love me!" she moaned; "I 'm black; you don't love me; you despise me!"

Her voice died away into a hopeless wail. Frank knelt by her side, his faithful heart breaking with pity, great tears rolling untouched down his dusky cheeks.

"Oh, my honey, my darlin'," he sobbed, "Frank loves you better 'n all de worl'."

Meantime the sun shone on as brightly as before, the mocking-bird sang yet more joyously. A gentle breeze sprang up and wafted the odor of bay and jessamine past them on its wings. The grand triumphal sweep of nature's onward march recked nothing of life's little tragedies.

When the first burst of his grief was over, Frank brought water from the branch, bathed Rena's face and hands and feet, and forced a few drops between her reluctant lips. He then pitched the cartload of tubs, buckets, and piggins out into the road, and gathering dried leaves and pine-straw, spread them in the bottom of the cart. He stooped, lifted her frail form in his arms, and laid it on the leafy bed. Cutting a couple of hickory withes, he arched them over the cart, and gathering an armful of jessamine quickly wove it into an awning to protect her from the sun. She was quieter now, and seemed to fall asleep.

"Go ter sleep, honey," he murmured caressingly,—"go ter sleep, an' Frank 'll take you home ter yo' mammy!"

Toward noon he was met by a young white man, who peered inquisitively into the canopied cart.

"Hello!" exclaimed the stranger, "who 've you got there?"

"A sick woman, suh."

"Why, she 's white, as I 'm a sinner!" he cried, after a closer inspection. "Look a-here, nigger, what are you doin' with this white woman?"

"She 's not w'ite, boss,—she's a bright mulatter."

"Yas, mighty bright," continued the stranger suspiciously. "Where are you goin' with her?"

"I 'm takin' her ter Patesville, ter her mammy."

The stranger passed on. Toward evening Frank heard hounds baying in the distance. A fox, weary with running, brush drooping, crossed the road ahead of the cart. Presently, the hounds straggled across the road, followed by two or three hunters on horseback, who stopped at sight of the strangely canopied cart. They stared at the sick girl and demanded who she was.

"I don't b'lieve she 's black at all," declared one, after Frank's brief explanation. "This nigger has a bad eye,—he 's up ter some sort of devilment. What ails the girl?"

"'Pears ter be some kind of a fever," replied Frank; adding diplomatically, "I don't know whether it 's ketchin' er no—she 's be'n out er her head most er de time."

They drew off a little at this. "I reckon it 's all right," said the chief spokesman. The hounds were baying clamorously in the distance. The hunters followed the sound and disappeared in the woods.

Frank drove all day and all night, stopping only for brief periods of rest and refreshment. At dawn, from the top of the long white hill, he sighted the river bridge below. At sunrise he rapped at Mis' Molly's door.

Upon rising at dawn, Tryon's first step, after a hasty breakfast, was to turn back toward Clinton. He had wasted half a day in following the false scent on the Lillington road. It seemed, after reflection, unlikely that a woman seriously ill should have been able to walk any considerable distance before her strength gave out. In her delirium, too, she might have wandered in a wrong direction, imagining any road to lead to Patesville. It would be a good plan to drive back home, continuing his inquiries meantime, and ascertain whether or not she had been found by those who were seeking her, including many whom Tryon's inquiries had placed upon the alert. If she should prove still missing, he would resume the journey to Patesville and continue the search in that direction. She had probably not wandered far from the highroad; even in delirium she would be likely to avoid the deep woods, with which her illness was associated.

He had retraced more than half the distance to Clinton when he overtook a covered wagon. The driver, when questioned, said that he had met a young negro with a mule, and a cart in which lay a young woman, white to all appearance, but claimed by the negro to be a colored girl who had been taken sick on the road, and whom he was conveying home to her mother at Patesville. From a further description of the cart Tryon recognized it as the one he had met the day before. The woman could be no other than Rena. He turned his mare and set out swiftly on the road to Patesville.

If anything could have taken more complete possession of George Tryon at twenty-three than love successful and triumphant, it was love thwarted and denied. Never in the few brief delirious weeks of his courtship had he felt so strongly drawn to the beautiful sister of the popular lawyer, as he was now driven by an aching heart toward the same woman stripped of every adventitious advantage and placed, by custom, beyond the pale of marriage with men of his own race. Custom was tyranny. Love was the only law. Would God have made hearts to so yearn for one another if He had meant them to stay forever apart? If this girl should die, it would be he who had killed her, by his cruelty, no less surely than if with his own hand he had struck her down. He had been so dazzled by his own superiority, so blinded by his own glory, that he had ruthlessly spurned and spoiled the image of God in this fair creature, whom he might have had for his own treasure,—whom, please God, he would yet have, at any cost, to love and cherish while they both should live. There were difficulties—they had seemed insuperable, but love would surmount them. Sacrifices must be made, but if the world without love would be nothing, then why not give up the world for love? He would hasten to Patesville. He would find her; he would tell her that he loved her, that she was all the world to him, that he had come to marry her, and take her away where they might be happy together. He pictured to himself the joy that would light up her face; he felt her soft arms around his neck, her tremulous kisses upon his lips. If she were ill, his love would woo her back to health,—if disappointment and sorrow had contributed to her illness, joy and gladness should lead to her recovery.

He urged the mare forward; if she would but keep up her present pace, he would reach Patesville by nightfall.

Dr. Green had just gone down the garden path to his buggy at the gate. Mis' Molly came out to the back piazza, where Frank, weary and haggard, sat on the steps with Homer Pettifoot and Billy Oxendine, who, hearing of Rena's return, had come around after their day's work.

"Rena wants to see you, Frank," said Mis' Molly, with a sob.

He walked in softly, reverently, and stood by her bedside. She turned her gentle eyes upon him and put out her slender hand, which he took in his own broad palm.

"Frank," she murmured, "my good friend—my best friend—you loved me best of them all."

The tears rolled untouched down his cheeks. "I 'd 'a' died, fer you, Miss Rena," he said brokenly.

Mary B. threw open a window to make way for the passing spirit, and the red and golden glory of the setting sun, triumphantly ending his daily course, flooded the narrow room with light.

Between sunset and dark a traveler, seated in a dusty buggy drawn by a tired horse, crossed the long river bridge and drove up Front Street. Just as the buggy reached the gate in front of the house behind the cedars, a woman was tying a piece of crape upon the door-knob. Pale with apprehension, Tryon sat as if petrified, until a tall, side-whiskered mulatto came down the garden walk to the front gate.

"Who 's dead?" demanded Tryon hoarsely, scarcely recognizing his own voice.

"A young cullud 'oman, suh," answered Homer Pettifoot, touching his hat, "Mis' Molly Walden's daughter Rena."

THE MARROW OF TRADITION

(1901)

I like you and your book, ingenious Hone!
In whose capacious all-embracing leaves
The very marrow of tradition 's shown.

CHARLES LAMB,
To the Editor of the Every-Day Book.

CONTENTS

I

AT BREAK OF DAY

"STAY HERE beside her, major. I shall not be needed for an hour yet. Meanwhile I 'll go downstairs and snatch a bit of sleep, or talk to old Jane."

The night was hot and sultry. Though the windows of the chamber were wide open, and the muslin curtains looped back, not a breath of air was stirring. Only the shrill chirp of the cicada and the muffled croaking of the frogs in some distant marsh broke the night silence. The heavy scent of magnolias, overpowering even the strong smell of drugs in the sick-room, suggested death and funeral wreaths, sorrow and tears, the long home, the last sleep. The major shivered with apprehension as the slender hand which he held in his own contracted nervously and in a spasm of pain clutched his fingers with a viselike grip.

Major Carteret, though dressed in brown linen, had thrown off his coat for greater comfort. The stifling heat, in spite of the palm-leaf fan which he plied mechanically, was scarcely less oppressive than his own thoughts. Long ago, while yet a mere boy in years, he had come back from Appomattox to find his family, one of the oldest and proudest in the state, hopelessly impoverished by the war,—even their ancestral home swallowed up in the common ruin. His elder brother had sacrificed his life on the bloody altar of the lost cause, and his father, broken and chagrined, died not many years later, leaving the major the last of his line. He had tried in various pursuits to gain a foothold in the new life, but with indifferent success until he won the hand of Olivia Merkell, whom he had seen grow from a small girl to glorious womanhood. With her money he had founded the Morning Chronicle, which he had made the leading organ of his party and the most influential paper in the State. The fine old house in which they lived was hers. In this very room she had first drawn the breath of life; it had been their nuptial chamber; and here, too, within a few hours, she might die, for it seemed impossible that one could long endure such frightful agony and live.

One cloud alone had marred the otherwise perfect serenity of their happiness. Olivia was childless. To have children to perpetuate the name of which he was so proud, to write it still higher on the roll of honor, had been his dearest hope. His disappointment had been proportionately keen. A few months ago this dead hope had revived, and altered the whole aspect of their lives. But as time went on, his wife's age had begun to tell upon her, until even Dr. Price, the most cheerful and optimistic of physicians, had warned him, while hoping for the best, to be prepared for the worst. To add to the danger, Mrs. Carteret had only this day suffered from a nervous shock, which, it was feared, had hastened by several weeks the expected event.

Dr. Price went downstairs to the library, where a dim light was burning. An old black woman, dressed in a gingham frock, with a red bandana handkerchief coiled around her head by way of turban, was seated by an open window. She rose and curtsied as the doctor entered and dropped into a willow rocking-chair near her own.

"How did this happen, Jane?" he asked in a subdued voice, adding, with assumed severity, "You ought to have taken better care of your mistress."

"Now look a-hyuh, Doctuh Price," returned the old woman in an unctuous whisper, "you don' wanter come talkin' none er yo' foolishness 'bout my not takin' keer er Mis' 'Livy. *She* never would 'a' said sech a thing! Seven er eight mont's ago, w'en she sent fer me, I says ter her, says I:—

" 'Lawd, Lawd, honey! You don' tell me dat after all dese long w'ary years er waitin' de good Lawd is done heared yo' prayer an' is gwine ter sen' you de chile you be'n wantin' so long an' so bad? Bless his holy name! Will I come an' nuss yo' baby? Why, honey, I nussed you, an' nussed yo' mammy thoo her las' sickness, an' laid her out w'en she died. I would n't *let* nobody e'se nuss yo' baby; an' mo'over, I 'm gwine ter come an' nuss you too. You 're young side er me, Mis' 'Livy, but you 're ove'ly ole ter be havin' yo' fus' baby, an' you 'll need somebody roun', honey, w'at knows all 'bout de fam'ly, an' deir ways an' deir weaknesses, an' I don' know who dat 'd be ef it wa'n't me.'

" ''Deed, Mammy Jane,' says she, 'dere ain' nobody e'se I 'd have but you. You kin come ez soon ez you wanter an' stay ez long ez you mineter.'

"An hyuh I is, an' hyuh I 'm gwine ter stay. Fer Mis' 'Livy is my ole mist'ess's daughter, an' my ole mist'ess wuz good ter me, an' dey ain' none er her folks gwine ter suffer ef ole Jane kin he'p it."

"Your loyalty does you credit, Jane," observed the doctor; "but you have n't told me yet what happened to Mrs. Carteret to-day. Did the horse run away, or did she see something that frightened her?"

"No, suh, de hoss did n' git skeered at nothin', but Mis' 'Livy did see somethin', er somebody; an' it wa'n't no fault er mine ner her'n neither,—it goes fu'ther back, suh, fu'ther dan dis day er dis year. Does you 'member de time w'en my ole mist'ess, Mis' 'Livy upstairs's mammy, died? No? Well, you wuz prob'ly 'way ter school den, studyin' ter be a doctuh. But I 'll tell you all erbout it.

"W'en my ole mist'ess, Mis' 'Liz'beth Merkell,—an' a good mist'ess she wuz,—tuck sick fer de las' time, her sister Polly—ole Mis' Polly Ochiltree w'at is now—come ter de house ter he'p nuss her. Mis' 'Livy upstairs yander wuz erbout six years ole den, de sweetes' little angel you ever laid eyes on; an' on her dyin' bed Mis' 'Liz'beth ax' Mis' Polly fer ter stay hyuh an' take keer er her chile, an' Mis' Polly she promise'. She wuz a widder fer de secon' time, an' did n' have no child'en, an' could jes' as well come as not.

"But dere wuz trouble after de fune'al, an' it happen' right hyuh in dis lib'ary. Mars Sam wuz settin' by de table, w'en Mis' Polly come downstairs, slow an' solemn, an' stood dere in de middle er de flo', all in black, till Mars Sam sot a cheer fer her.

" 'Well, Samuel,' says she, 'now dat we 've done all we can fer po' 'Liz'beth, it only 'mains fer us ter consider Olivia's future.'

"Mars Sam nodded his head, but did n' say nothin'.

" 'I don' need ter tell you,' says she, 'dat I am willin' ter carry out de wishes er my dead sister, an' sac'ifice my own comfo't, an' make myse'f yo' housekeeper an' yo' child's nuss, fer my dear sister's sake. It wuz her dyin' wish, an' on it I will ac', ef it is also yo'n.'

"Mars Sam did n' want Mis' Polly ter come, suh; fur he did n' like Mis' Polly. He wuz skeered er Miss Polly."

"I don't wonder," yawned the doctor, "if she was anything like she is now."

"Wuss, suh, fer she wuz younger, an' stronger. She always would have her say, no matter 'bout what, an' her own way, no matter who 'posed her. She had already be'n in de house fer a week, an' Mars Sam knowed ef she once come ter stay, she 'd be de mist'ess of eve'ybody in it an' him too. But w'at could he do but say yas?

" 'Den it is unde'stood, is it,' says Mis' Polly, w'en he had spoke, 'dat I am ter take cha'ge er de house?'

" 'All right, Polly,' says Mars Sam, wid a deep sigh.

"Mis' Polly 'lowed he wuz sighin' fer my po' dead mist'ess, fer she did n' have no idee er his feelin's to'ds her,—she alluz did 'low dat all de gent'emen wuz in love wid 'er.

" 'You won' fin' much ter do,' Mars Sam went on, 'fer Julia is a good housekeeper, an' kin ten' ter mos' eve'ything, under yo' d'rections.'

"Mis' Polly stiffen' up like a ramrod. 'It mus' be unde'stood, Samuel,' says she, 'dat w'en I 'sumes cha'ge er yo' house, dere ain' gwine ter be no 'vided 'sponsibility; an' as fer dis Julia, me an' her could n' git 'long tergether nohow. Ef I stays, Julia goes.'

"W'en Mars Sam heared dat, he felt better, an' 'mence' ter pick up his courage. Mis' Polly had showed her han' too plain. My mist'ess had n' got col' yit, an' Mis' Polly, who 'd be'n a widder fer two years dis las' time, wuz already fig'rin' on takin' her place fer good, an' she did n' want no other woman roun' de house dat Mars Sam might take a' intrus' in.

" 'My dear Polly,' says Mars Sam, quite determine', 'I could n' possibly sen' Julia 'way. Fac' is, I could n' git 'long widout Julia. She 'd be'n runnin' dis house like clockwo'k befo' you come, an' I likes her ways. My dear, dead 'Liz'beth sot a heap er sto' by Julia, an' I 'm gwine ter keep her here fer 'Liz'beth's sake.'

"Mis' Polly's eyes flash' fire.

" 'Ah,' says she, 'I see—I see! You perfers her housekeepin' ter mine, indeed! Dat is a fine way ter talk ter a lady! An' a heap er rispec' you is got fer de mem'ry er my po' dead sister!'

"Mars Sam knowed w'at she 'lowed she seed wa'n't so; but he did n' let on, fer it only made him de safer. He wuz willin' fer her ter 'magine w'at she please', jes' so long ez she kep' out er his house an' let him alone.

" 'No, Polly,' says he, gittin' bolder ez she got madder, 'dere ain' no use talkin'. Nothin' in de worl' would make me part wid Julia.'

"Mis' Polly she was r'ared an' she pitch', but Mars Sam helt on like grim death. Mis' Polly would n' give in neither, an' so she fin'lly went away. Dey made some kind er 'rangement afterwa'ds, an' Miss Polly tuck Mis' 'Livy ter her own house. Mars Sam paid her bo'd an' 'lowed Mis' Polly somethin' fer takin' keer er her."

"And Julia stayed?"

"Julia stayed, suh, an' a couple er years later her chile wuz bawn, right here in dis house."

"But you said," observed the doctor, "that Mrs. Ochiltree was in error about Julia."

"Yas, suh, so she wuz, w'en my ole mist'ess died. But dis wuz two years after,—an' w'at has ter be has ter be. Julia had a easy time; she had a black gal ter wait on her, a buggy to ride in, an' eve'ything she wanted. Eve'ybody s'posed Mars Sam would give her a house an' lot, er leave her somethin' in his will. But he died suddenly, and did n' leave no will, an' Mis' Polly got herse'f 'pinted gyardeen ter young Mis' 'Livy, an' driv Julia an' her young un out er de house, an' lived here in dis house wid Mis' 'Livy till Mis' 'Livy ma'ied Majah Carteret."

"And what became of Julia?" asked Dr. Price.

Such relations, the doctor knew very well, had been all too common in the old slavery days, and not a few of them had been projected into the new era. Sins, like snakes, die hard. The habits and customs of a people were not to be changed in a day, nor by the stroke of a pen. As family physician, and father confessor by brevet, Dr. Price had looked upon more than one hidden skeleton; and no one in town had had better opportunities than old Jane for learning the undercurrents in the lives of the old families.

"Well," resumed Jane, "eve'ybody s'posed, after w'at had happen', dat Julia 'd keep on livin' easy, fer she wuz young an' good-lookin'. But she did n'. She tried ter make a livin' sewin', but Mis' Polly would n' let de bes' w'ite folks hire her. Den she tuck up washin', but did n' do no better at dat; an' bimeby she got so discourage' dat she ma'ied a shif'less yaller man, an' died er consumption soon after,—an' wuz 'bout ez well off, fer dis man could n' hardly feed her nohow."

"And the child?"

"One er de No'the'n w'ite lady teachers at de mission school tuck a likin' ter little Janet, an' put her thoo school, an' den sent her off ter de No'th fer ter study ter be a school teacher. W'en she come back, 'stead er teachin' she ma'ied ole Adam Miller's son."

"The rich stevedore's son, Dr. Miller?"

"Yas, suh, dat 's de man,—you knows 'im. Dis yer boy wuz jes' gwine 'way fer ter study ter be a doctuh, an' he ma'ied dis Janet, an' tuck her 'way wid 'im. Dey went off ter Europe, er Irope, er Orope, er somewhere er 'nother, 'way off yander, an' come back here las' year an' sta'ted dis yer horspital an' school fer ter train de black gals fer nusses."

"He 's a very good doctor, Jane, and is doing a useful work. Your chapter of family history is quite interesting,—I knew part of it before, in a general way; but you have n't yet told me what brought on Mrs. Carteret's trouble."

"I 'm jes' comin' ter dat dis minute, suh,—w'at I be'n tellin' you is all a part of it. Dis yer Janet, w'at 's Mis' 'Livy's half-sister, is ez much like her ez ef dey wuz twins. Folks sometimes takes 'em fer one ernudder,—I s'pose it tickles Janet mos' ter death, but it do make Mis' 'Livy rippin'. An' den 'way back yander jes' after de wah, w'en de ole Carteret mansion had ter be sol', Adam Miller bought it, an' dis yer Janet an' her husban' is be'n livin' in it ever sence ole Adam died, 'bout a year ago; an' dat makes de majah mad, 'ca'se he don' wanter see cullud folks livin' in de ole fam'ly mansion w'at he wuz bawn in. An' mo'over, an' dat 's de wust of all, w'iles Mis' 'Livy ain' had no child'en befo', dis yer sister er her'n is got a fine-lookin' little yaller boy, w'at favors de fam'ly so dat ef Mis' 'Livy 'd see de chile anywhere, it 'd mos' break her heart fer ter think 'bout her not havin' no child'en herse'f. So ter-day, w'en Mis' 'Livy wuz out ridin' an' met dis yer Janet wid her boy, an' w'en Mis' 'Livy got ter studyin' 'bout her own chances, an' how she mought not come thoo safe, she jes' had a fit er hysterics right dere in de buggy. She wuz mos' home, an' William got her here, an' you knows de res'."

Major Carteret, from the head of the stairs, called the doctor anxiously.

"You had better come along up now, Jane," said the doctor.

For two long hours they fought back the grim spectre that stood by the bedside. The child was born at dawn. Both mother and child, the doctor said, would live.

"Bless its 'ittle hea't!" exclaimed Mammy Jane, as she held up the tiny mite, which bore as much resemblance to mature humanity as might be expected of an infant which had for only a few minutes drawn the breath of life. "Bless its 'ittle hea't! it 's de ve'y spit an' image er its pappy!"

The doctor smiled. The major laughed aloud. Jane's unconscious witticism, or conscious flattery, whichever it might be, was a welcome diversion from the tense strain of the last few hours.

"Be that as it may," said Dr. Price cheerfully, "and I 'll not dispute it, the child is a very fine boy,—a very fine boy, indeed! Take care of it, major," he added with a touch of solemnity, "for your wife can never bear another."

With the child's first cry a refreshing breeze from the distant ocean cooled the hot air of the chamber; the heavy odor of the magnolias, with its mortuary suggestiveness, gave place to the scent of rose and lilac and honeysuckle. The birds in the garden were singing lustily.

All these sweet and pleasant things found an echo in the major's heart. He stood by the window, and looking toward the rising sun, breathed a silent prayer of thanksgiving. All nature seemed to rejoice in sympathy with his happiness at the fruition of this long-deferred hope, and to predict for this wonderful child a bright and glorious future.

Old Mammy Jane, however, was not entirely at ease concerning the child. She had discovered, under its left ear, a small mole, which led her to fear that the child was born for bad luck. Had the baby been black, or yellow, or poor-white, Jane would unhesitatingly have named, as his ultimate fate, a not uncommon form of taking off, usually resultant upon the infraction of certain laws, or, in these swift modern days, upon too violent a departure from established social customs. It was manifestly impossible that a child of such high quality as the grandson of her old mistress should die by judicial strangulation; but nevertheless the warning was a serious thing, and not to be lightly disregarded.

Not wishing to be considered as a prophet of evil omen, Jane kept her own counsel in regard to this significant discovery. But later, after the child was several days old, she filled a small vial with water in which the infant had been washed, and took it to a certain wise old black woman, who lived on the farther edge of the town and was well known to be versed in witchcraft and conjuration. The conjure woman added to the contents of the bottle a bit of calamus root, and one of the cervical vertebræ from the skeleton of a black cat, with several other mysterious ingredients, the nature of which she did not disclose. Following instructions given her, Aunt Jane buried the bottle in Carteret's back yard, one night during the full moon, as a good-luck charm to ward off evil from the little grandson of her dear mistress, so long since dead and gone to heaven.

II

THE CHRISTENING PARTY

THEY named the Carteret baby Theodore Felix. Theodore was a family name, and had been borne by the eldest son for several generations, the major himself being a second son. Having thus given the child two beautiful names, replete with religious and sentimental significance, they called him—"Dodie."

The baby was christened some six weeks after its birth, by which time Mrs. Carteret was able to be out. Old Mammy Jane, who had been brought up in the church, but who, like some better informed people in all ages, found religion not inconsistent with a strong vein of superstition, felt her fears for the baby's future much relieved when the rector had made the sign of the cross and sprinkled little Dodie with the water from the carved marble font, which had come from England in the reign of King Charles the Martyr, as the ill-fated son of James I. was known to St. Andrew's. Upon this special occasion Mammy Jane had been provided with a seat downstairs among the white people, to her own intense satisfaction, and to the secret envy of a small colored attendance in the gallery, to whom she was ostentatiously pointed out by her grandson Jerry, porter at the Morning Chronicle office, who sat among them in the front row.

On the following Monday evening the major gave a christening party in honor of this important event. Owing to Mrs. Carteret's still delicate health, only a small number of intimate friends and family connections were invited to attend. These were the rector of St. Andrew's; old Mrs. Polly Ochiltree, the godmother; old Mr. Delamere, a distant relative and also one of the sponsors; and his grandson, Tom Delamere. The major had also invited Lee Ellis, his young city editor, for whom he had a great liking apart from his business value, and who was a frequent visitor at the house. These, with the family itself, which consisted of the major, his wife, and his half-sister, Clara Pemberton, a young woman of about eighteen, made up the eight persons for whom covers were laid.

Ellis was the first to arrive, a tall, loose-limbed young man, with a slightly freckled face, hair verging on auburn, a firm chin, and honest gray eyes. He had come half an hour early, and was left alone for a few minutes in the parlor, a spacious, high-ceilinged room, with large windows, and fitted up in excellent taste, with stately reminiscences of a past generation. The walls were hung with figured paper. The ceiling was whitewashed, and decorated in the middle with a plaster centre-piece, from which hung a massive chandelier sparkling with prismatic rays from a hundred crystal pendants. There was a handsome mantel, set with terra-cotta tiles, on which fauns and satyrs, nymphs and dryads, disported themselves in idyllic abandon. The furniture was old, and in keeping with the room.

At seven o'clock a carriage drove up, from which alighted an elderly gentleman, with white hair and mustache, and bowed somewhat with years. Short of breath and painfully weak in the legs, he was assisted from the carriage by a colored man, apparently about forty years old, to whom short side-whiskers and spectacles imparted an air of sobriety. This attendant gave his arm respectfully to the old gentleman, who leaned upon it heavily, but with as little appearance of dependence as possible. The servant, assuming a similar unconsciousness of the weight resting upon his arm, assisted the old gentleman carefully up the steps.

"I 'm all right now, Sandy," whispered the gentleman as soon as his feet were planted firmly on the piazza. "You may come back for me at nine o'clock."

Having taken his hand from his servant's arm, he advanced to meet a lady who stood in the door awaiting him, a tall, elderly woman, gaunt and angular of frame, with a mottled face, and high cheekbones partially covered by bands of hair entirely too black and abundant for a person of her age, if one might judge from the lines of her mouth, which are rarely deceptive in such matters.

"Perhaps you 'd better not send your man away, Mr. Delamere," observed the lady, in a high shrill voice, which grated upon the old gentleman's ears. He was slightly hard of hearing, but, like most deaf people, resented being screamed at. "You might need him before nine o'clock. One never knows what may happen after one has had the second stroke. And moreover, our butler has fallen down the back steps—negroes are so careless!—and sprained his ankle so that he can't stand. I 'd like to have Sandy stay and wait on the table in Peter's place, if you don't mind."

"I thank you, Mrs. Ochiltree, for your solicitude," replied Mr. Delamere, with a shade of annoyance in his voice, "but my health is very good just at present, and I do not anticipate any catastrophe which will require my servant's presence before I am ready to go home. But I have no doubt, madam," he continued, with a courteous inclination, "that Sandy will be pleased to serve you, if you desire it, to the best of his poor knowledge."

"I shill be honored, ma'am," assented Sandy, with a bow even deeper than his master's, "only I 'm 'feared I ain't rightly dressed fer ter wait on table. I wuz only goin' ter pra'r-meetin', an' so I didn' put on my bes' clo's. Ef Mis' Ochiltree ain' gwine ter need me fer de nex' fifteen minutes, I kin ride back home in de ca'ige an' dress myse'f suitable fer de occasion, suh."

"If you think you 'll wait on the table any better," said Mrs. Ochiltree, "you may go along and change your clothes; but hurry back, for it is seven now, and dinner will soon be served."

Sandy retired with a bow. While descending the steps to the carriage, which had waited for him, he came face to face with a young man just entering the house.

"Am I in time for dinner, Sandy?" asked the newcomer.

"Yas, Mistuh Tom, you 're in plenty er time. Dinner won't be ready till *I* git back, which won' be fer fifteen minutes er so yit."

Throwing away the cigarette which he held between his fingers, the young man crossed the piazza with a light step, and after a preliminary knock, for an answer to which he did not wait, entered the house with the air of one thoroughly at home. The lights in the parlor had been lit, and Ellis, who sat talking to Major Carteret when the newcomer entered, covered him with a jealous glance.

Slender and of medium height, with a small head of almost perfect contour, a symmetrical face, dark almost to swarthiness, black eyes, which moved somewhat restlessly, curly hair of raven tint, a slight mustache, small hands and feet, and fashionable attire, Tom Delamere, the grandson of the old gentleman who had already arrived, was easily the handsomest young man in Wellington. But no discriminating observer would have characterized his beauty as manly. It conveyed no impression of strength, but did possess a certain element, feline rather than feminine, which subtly negatived the idea of manliness.

He gave his hand to the major, nodded curtly to Ellis, saluted his grandfather respectfully, and inquired for the ladies.

"Olivia is dressing for dinner," replied the major; "Mrs. Ochiltree is in the kitchen, struggling with the servants. Clara— Ah, here she comes now!"

Ellis, whose senses were preternaturally acute where Clara was concerned, was already looking toward the hall and was the first to see her. Clad in an evening gown of simple white, to the close-fitting corsage of which she had fastened a bunch of pink roses, she was to Ellis a dazzling apparition. To him her erect and well-moulded form was the embodiment of symmetry, her voice sweet music, her movements the perfection of grace; and it scarcely needed a lover's imagination to read in her fair countenance a pure heart and a high spirit,—the truthfulness that scorns a lie, the pride which is not haughtiness. There were suggestive depths of tenderness, too, in the curl of her lip, the droop of her long lashes, the glance of her blue eyes,—depths that Ellis had long since divined, though he had never yet explored them. She gave Ellis a friendly nod as she came in, but for the smile with which she greeted Delamere, Ellis would have given all that he possessed,—not a great deal, it is true, but what could a man do more?

"You are the last one, Tom," she said reproachfully. "Mr. Ellis has been here half an hour."

Delamere threw a glance at Ellis which was not exactly friendly. Why should this fellow always be on hand to emphasize his own shortcomings?

"The rector is not here," answered Tom triumphantly. "You see I am not the last."

"The rector," replied Clara, "was called out of town at six o'clock this evening, to visit a dying man, and so cannot be here. You are the last, Tom, and Mr. Ellis was the first."

Ellis was ruefully aware that this comparison in his favor was the only visible advantage that he had gained from his early arrival. He had not seen Miss Pemberton a moment sooner by reason of it. There had been a certain satisfaction in being in the same house with her, but Delamere had arrived in time to share or, more correctly, to monopolize, the sunshine of her presence.

Delamere gave a plausible excuse which won Clara's pardon and another enchanting smile, which pierced Ellis like a dagger. He knew very well that Delamere's excuse was a lie. Ellis himself had been ready as early as six o'clock, but judging this to be too early, had stopped in at the Clarendon Club for half an hour, to look over the magazines. While coming out he had glanced into the card-room, where he had seen his rival deep in a game of cards, from which Delamere had evidently not been able to tear himself until the last moment. He had accounted for his lateness by a story quite inconsistent with these facts.

The two young people walked over to a window on the opposite side of the large room, where they stood talking to one another in low tones. The major had left the room for a moment. Old Mr. Delamere, who was watching his grandson and Clara with an indulgent smile, proceeded to rub salt into Ellis's wounds.

"They make a handsome couple," he observed. "I remember well when her mother, in her youth an ideally beautiful woman, of an excellent family, married Daniel Pemberton, who was not of so good a family, but had made money. The major, who was only a very young man then, disapproved of the match; he considered that his mother, although a widow and nearly forty, was marrying beneath her. But he has been a good brother to Clara, and a careful guardian of her estate. Ah, young gentleman, you cannot appreciate, except in imagination, what it means, to one standing on the brink of eternity, to feel sure that he will live on in his children and his children's children!"

Ellis was appreciating at that moment what it meant, in cold blood, with no effort of the imagination, to see the girl whom he loved absorbed completely in another man. She had looked at him only once since Tom Delamere had entered the room, and then merely to use him as a spur with which to prick his favored rival.

"Yes, sir," he returned mechanically, "Miss Clara is a beautiful young lady."

"And Tom is a good boy—a fine boy," returned the old gentleman. "I am very well pleased with Tom, and shall be entirely happy when I see them married."

Ellis could not echo this sentiment. The very thought of this marriage made him miserable. He had always understood that the engagement was merely tentative, a sort of family understanding, subject to confirmation after Delamere should have attained his majority, which was still a year off, and when the major should think Clara old enough to marry. Ellis saw Delamere with the eye of a jealous rival, and judged him mercilessly,—whether correctly or not the sequel will show. He did not at all believe that Tom Delamere would make a fit husband for Clara Pemberton; but his opinion would have had no weight,—he could hardly have expressed it without showing his own interest. Moreover, there was no element of the sneak in Lee Ellis's make-up. The very fact that he might profit by the other's discomfiture left Delamere secure, so far as he could be affected by anything that Ellis might say. But Ellis did not shrink from a fair fight, and though in this one the odds were heavily against him, yet so long as this engagement remained indefinite, so long, indeed, as the object of his love was still unwed, he would not cease to hope. Such a sacrifice as this marriage clearly belonged in the catalogue of impossibilities. Ellis had not lived long enough to learn that impossibilities are merely things of which we have not learned, or which we do not wish to happen.

Sandy returned at the end of a quarter of an hour, and dinner was announced. Mr. Delamere led the way to the dining-room with Mrs. Ochiltree. Tom followed with Clara. The major went to the head of the stairs and came down with Mrs. Carteret upon his arm, her beauty rendered more delicate by the pallor of her countenance and more complete by the happiness with which it glowed. Ellis went in alone. In the rector's absence it was practically a family party which sat down, with the exception of Ellis, who, as we have seen, would willingly have placed himself in the same category.

The table was tastefully decorated with flowers, which grew about the house in lavish profusion. In warm climates nature adorns herself with true feminine vanity.

"What a beautiful table!" exclaimed Tom, before they were seated.

"The decorations are mine," said Clara proudly. "I cut the flowers and arranged them all myself."

"Which accounts for the admirable effect," rejoined Tom with a bow, before Ellis, to whom the same thought had occurred, was able to express himself. He had always counted himself the least envious of men, but for this occasion he coveted Tom Delamere's readiness.

"The beauty of the flowers," observed old Mr. Delamere, with sententious gallantry, "is reflected upon all around them. It is a handsome company."

Mrs. Ochiltree beamed upon the table with a dry smile.

"I don't perceive any effect that it has upon you or me," she said. "And as for the young people, 'Handsome is as handsome does.' If Tom here, for instance, were as good as he looks"—

"You flatter me, Aunt Polly," Tom broke in hastily, anticipating the crack of the whip; he was familiar with his aunt's conversational idiosyncrasies.

"If you are as good as you look," continued the old lady, with a cunning but indulgent smile, "some one has been slandering you."

"Thanks, Aunt Polly! Now you don't flatter me."

"There is Mr. Ellis," Mrs. Ochiltree went on, "who is not half so good-looking, but is steady as a clock, I dare say."

"Now, Aunt Polly," interposed Mrs. Carteret, "let the gentlemen alone."

"She does n't mean half what she says," continued Mrs. Carteret apologetically, "and only talks that way to people whom she likes."

Tom threw Mrs. Carteret a grateful glance. He had been apprehensive, with the sensitiveness of youth, lest his old great-aunt should make a fool of him before Clara's family. Nor had he relished the comparison with Ellis, who was out of place, anyway, in this family party. He had never liked the fellow, who was too much of a plodder and a prig to make a suitable associate for a whole-souled, generous-hearted young gentleman. He tolerated him as a visitor at Carteret's and as a member of the Clarendon Club, but that was all.

"Mrs. Ochiltree has a characteristic way of disguising her feelings," observed old Mr. Delamere, with a touch of sarcasm.

Ellis had merely flushed and felt uncomfortable at the reference to himself. The compliment to his character hardly offset the reflection upon his looks. He knew he was not exactly handsome, but it was not pleasant to have the fact emphasized in the presence of the girl he loved; he would like at least fair play, and judgment upon the subject left to the young lady.

Mrs. Ochiltree was quietly enjoying herself. In early life she had been accustomed to impale fools on epigrams, like flies on pins, to see them wriggle. But with advancing years she had lost in some measure the faculty of nice discrimination,—it was pleasant to see her victims squirm, whether they were fools or friends. Even one's friends, she argued, were not always wise, and were sometimes the better for being told the truth. At her niece's table she felt at liberty to speak her mind, which she invariably did, with a frankness that sometimes bordered on brutality. She had long ago outgrown the period where ambition or passion, or its partners, envy and hatred, were springs of action in her life, and simply retained a mild enjoyment in the exercise of an old habit, with no active malice whatever. The ruling passion merely grew stronger as the restraining faculties decreased in vigor.

A diversion was created at this point by the appearance of old Mammy Jane, dressed in a calico frock, with clean white neckerchief and apron, carrying the wonderful baby in honor of whose naming this feast had been given. Though only six weeks old, the little Theodore had grown rapidly, and Mammy Jane declared was already quite large for his age, and displayed signs of an unusually precocious intelligence. He was passed around the table and duly admired. Clara thought his hair was fine. Ellis inquired about his teeth. Tom put his finger in the baby's fist to test his grip. Old Mr. Delamere was unable to decide as yet whether he favored most his father or his mother. The object of these attentions endured them patiently for several minutes, and then protested with a vocal vigor which led to his being taken promptly back upstairs. Whatever fate might be in store for him, he manifested no sign of weak lungs.

"Sandy," said Mrs. Carteret when the baby had retired, "pass that tray standing upon the side table, so that we may all see the presents."

Mr. Delamere had brought a silver spoon, and Tom a napkin ring. Ellis had sent a silver watch; it was a little premature, he admitted, but the boy would grow to it, and could use it to play with in the mean time. It had a glass back, so that he might see the wheels go round. Mrs. Ochiltree's present was an old and yellow ivory rattle, with a handle which the child could bite while teething, and a knob screwed on at the end to prevent the handle from slipping through the baby's hand.

"I saw that in your cedar chest, Aunt Polly," said Clara, "when I was a little girl, and you used to pull the chest out from under your bed to get me a dime."

"You kept the rattle in the right-hand corner of the chest," said Tom, "in the box with the red silk purse, from which you took the gold piece you gave me every Christmas."

A smile shone on Mrs. Ochiltree's severe features at this appreciation, like a ray of sunlight on a snow-bank.

"Aunt Polly's chest is like the widow's cruse," said Mrs. Carteret, "which was never empty."

"Or Fortunatus's purse, which was always full," added old Mr. Delamere, who read the Latin poets, and whose allusions were apt to be classical rather than scriptural.

"It will last me while I live," said Mrs. Ochiltree, adding cautiously, "but there 'll not be a great deal left. It won't take much to support an old woman for twenty years."

Mr. Delamere's man Sandy had been waiting upon the table with the decorum of a trained butler, and a gravity all his own. He had changed his suit of plain gray for a long blue coat with brass buttons, which dated back to the fashion of a former generation, with which he wore a pair of plaid trousers of strikingly modern cut and pattern. With his whiskers, his spectacles, and his solemn air of responsibility, he would have presented, to one unfamiliar with the negro type, an amusingly impressive appearance. But there was nothing incongruous about Sandy to this company, except perhaps to Tom Delamere, who possessed a keen eye for contrasts and always regarded Sandy, in that particular rig, as a very comical darkey.

"Is it quite prudent, Mrs. Ochiltree," suggested the major at a moment when Sandy, having set down the tray, had left the room for a little while, "to mention, in the presence of the servants, that you keep money in the house?"

"I beg your pardon, major," observed old Mr. Delamere, with a touch of stiffness. "The only servant in hearing of the conversation has been my own; and Sandy is as honest as any man in Wellington."

"You mean, sir," replied Carteret, with a smile, "as honest as any *negro* in Wellington."

"I make no exceptions, major," returned the old gentleman, with emphasis. "I would trust Sandy with my life,—he saved it once at the risk of his own."

"No doubt," mused the major, "the negro is capable of a certain doglike fidelity,—I make the comparison in a kindly sense,—a certain personal devotion which is admirable in itself, and fits him eminently for a servile career. I should imagine, however, that one could more safely trust his life with a negro than his portable property."

"Very clever, major! I read your paper, and know that your feeling is hostile toward the negro, but"—.

The major made a gesture of dissent, but remained courteously silent until Mr. Delamere had finished.

"For my part," the old gentleman went on, "I think they have done very well, considering what they started from, and their limited opportunities. There was Adam Miller, for instance, who left a comfortable estate. His son George carries on the business, and the younger boy, William, is a good doctor and stands well with his profession. His hospital is a good thing, and if my estate were clear, I should like to do something for it."

"You are mistaken, sir, in imagining me hostile to the negro," explained Carteret. "On the contrary, I am friendly to his best interests. I give him employment; I pay taxes for schools to educate him, and for court-houses and jails to keep him in order. I merely object to being governed by an inferior and servile race."

Mrs. Carteret's face wore a tired expression. This question was her husband's hobby, and therefore her own nightmare. Moreover, she had her personal grievance against the negro race, and the names mentioned by old Mr. Delamere had brought it vividly before her mind. She had no desire to mar the harmony of the occasion by the discussion of a distasteful subject.

Mr. Delamere, glancing at his hostess, read something of this thought, and refused the challenge to further argument.

"I do not believe, major," he said, "that Olivia relishes the topic. I merely wish to say that Sandy is an exception to any rule which you may formulate in derogation of the negro. Sandy is a gentleman in ebony!"

Tom could scarcely preserve his gravity at this characterization of old Sandy, with his ridiculous air of importance, his long blue coat, and his loud plaid trousers. That suit would make a great costume for a masquerade. He would borrow it some time,—there was nothing in the world like it.

"Well, Mr. Delamere," returned the major good-humoredly, "no doubt Sandy is an exceptionally good negro,—he might well be, for he has had the benefit of your example all his life,—and we know that he is a faithful servant. But nevertheless, if I were Mrs. Ochiltree, I should put my money in the bank. Not all negroes are as honest as Sandy, and an elderly lady might not prove a match for a burly black burglar."

"Thank you, major," retorted Mrs. Ochiltree, with spirit, "I 'm not yet too old to take care of myself. That cedar chest has been my bank for forty years, and I shall not change my habits at my age."

At this moment Sandy reentered the room. Carteret made a warning gesture, which Mrs. Ochiltree chose not to notice.

"I 've proved a match for two husbands, and am not afraid of any man that walks the earth, black or white, by day or night. I have a revolver, and know how to use it. Whoever attempts to rob me will do so at his peril."

After dinner Clara played the piano and sang duets with Tom Delamere. At nine o'clock Mr. Delamere's carriage came for him, and he went away accompanied by Sandy. Under cover of the darkness the old gentleman leaned on his servant's arm with frank dependence, and Sandy lifted him into the carriage with every mark of devotion.

Ellis had already excused himself to go to the office and look over the late proofs for the morning paper. Tom remained a few minutes longer than his grandfather, and upon taking his leave went round to the Clarendon Club, where he spent an hour or two in the card-room with a couple of congenial friends. Luck seemed to favor him, and he went home at midnight with a comfortable balance of winnings. He was fond of excitement, and found a great deal of it in cards. To lose was only less exciting than to win. Of late he had developed into a very successful player,—so successful, indeed, that several members of the club generally found excuses to avoid participating in a game where he made one.

III

THE EDITOR AT WORK

To go back a little, for several days after his child's birth Major Carteret's chief interest in life had been confined to the four walls of the chamber where his pale wife lay upon her bed of pain, and those of the adjoining room where an old black woman crooned lovingly over a little white infant. A new element had been added to the major's consciousness, broadening the scope and deepening the strength of his affections. He did not love Olivia the less, for maternity had crowned her wifehood with an added glory; but side by side with this old and tried attachment was a new passion, stirring up dormant hopes and kindling new desires. His regret had been more than personal at the thought that with himself an old name should be lost to the State; and now all the old pride of race, class, and family welled up anew, and swelled and quickened the current of his life.

Upon the major's first appearance at the office, which took place the second day after the child's birth, he opened a box of cigars in honor of the event. The word had been passed around by Ellis, and the whole office force, including reporters, compositors, and pressmen, came in to congratulate the major and smoke at his expense. Even Jerry, the colored porter,—Mammy Jane's grandson and therefore a protégé of the family,—presented himself among the rest, or rather, after the rest. The major shook hands with them all except Jerry, though he acknowledged the porter's congratulations with a kind nod and put a good cigar into his outstretched palm, for which Jerry thanked him without manifesting any consciousness of the omission. He was quite aware that under ordinary circumstances the major would not have shaken hands with white workingmen, to say nothing of negroes; and he had merely hoped that in the pleasurable distraction of the moment the major might also overlook the distinction of color. Jerry's hope had been shattered, though not rudely; for the major had spoken pleasantly and the cigar was a good one.

Mr. Ellis had once shaken hands with Jerry,—but Mr. Ellis was a young man, whose Quaker father had never owned any slaves, and he could not be expected to have as much pride as one of the best "quality," whose families had possessed land and negroes for time out of mind. On the whole, Jerry preferred the careless nod of the editor-in-chief to the more familiar greeting of the subaltern.

Having finished this pleasant ceremony, which left him with a comfortable sense of his new dignity, the major turned to his desk. It had been much neglected during the week, and more than one matter claimed his attention; but as typical of the new trend of his thoughts, the first subject he took up was one bearing upon the future of his son. Quite obviously the career of a Carteret must not be left to chance,—it must be planned and worked out with a due sense of the value of good blood.

There lay upon his desk a letter from a well-known promoter, offering the major an investment which promised large returns, though several years must elapse before the enterprise could be put upon a paying basis. The element of time, however, was not immediately important. The Morning Chronicle provided him an ample income. The money available for this investment was part of his wife's patrimony. It was invested in a local cotton mill, which was paying ten per cent., but this was a beggarly return compared with the immense profits promised by the offered investment,—profits which would enable his son, upon reaching manhood, to take a place in the world commensurate with the dignity of his ancestors, one of whom, only a few generations removed, had owned an estate of ninety thousand acres of land and six thousand slaves.

This letter having been disposed of by an answer accepting the offer, the major took up his pen to write an editorial. Public affairs in the state were not going to his satisfaction. At the last state election his own party, after an almost unbroken rule of twenty years, had been defeated by the so-called "Fusion" ticket, a combination of Republicans and Populists. A clean sweep had been made of the offices in the state, which were now filled by new men. Many of the smaller places had gone to colored men, their people having voted almost solidly for the Fusion ticket. In spite of the fact that the population of Wellington was two thirds colored, this state of things was gall and wormwood to the defeated party, of which the Morning Chronicle was the acknowledged organ. Major Carteret shared this feeling. Only this very morning, while passing the city hall, on his way to the office, he had seen the steps of that noble building disfigured by a fringe of job-hunting negroes, for all the world—to use a local simile—like a string of buzzards sitting on a rail, awaiting their opportunity to batten upon the helpless corpse of a moribund city.

Taking for his theme the unfitness of the negro to participate in government,—an unfitness due to his limited education, his lack of experience, his criminal tendencies, and more especially to his hopeless mental and physical inferiority to the white race,—the major had demonstrated, it seemed to him clearly enough, that the ballot in the hands of the negro was a menace to the commonwealth. He had argued, with entire conviction, that the white and black races could never attain social and political harmony by commingling their blood; he had proved by several historical parallels that no two unassimilable races could ever live together except in the relation of superior and inferior; and he was just dipping his gold pen into the ink to indite his conclusions from the premises thus established, when Jerry, the porter, announced two visitors.

"Gin'l Belmont an' Cap'n McBane would like ter see you, suh."

"Show them in, Jerry."

The man who entered first upon this invitation was a dapper little gentleman with light-blue eyes and a Vandyke beard. He wore a frock coat, patent leather shoes, and a Panama hat. There were crow's-feet about his eyes, which twinkled with a hard and, at times, humorous shrewdness. He had sloping shoulders, small hands and feet, and walked with the leisurely step characteristic of those who have been reared under hot suns.

Carteret gave his hand cordially to the gentleman thus described.

"How do you do, Captain McBane," he said, turning to the second visitor.

The individual thus addressed was strikingly different in appearance from his companion. His broad shoulders, burly form, square jaw, and heavy chin betokened strength, energy, and unscrupulousness. With the exception of a small, bristling mustache, his face was clean shaven, with here and there a speck of dried blood due to a carelessly or unskillfully handled razor. A single deep-set gray eye was shadowed by a beetling brow, over which a crop of coarse black hair, slightly streaked with gray, fell almost low enough to mingle with his black, bushy eyebrows. His coat had not been brushed for several days, if one might judge from the accumulation of dandruff upon the collar, and his shirt-front, in the middle of which blazed a showy diamond, was plentifully stained with tobacco juice. He wore a large slouch hat, which, upon entering the office, he removed and held in his hand.

Having greeted this person with an unconscious but quite perceptible diminution of the warmth with which he had welcomed the other, the major looked around the room for seats for his visitors, and perceiving only one chair, piled with exchanges, and a broken stool propped against the wall, pushed a button, which rang a bell in the hall, summoning the colored porter to his presence.

"Jerry," said the editor when his servant appeared, "bring a couple of chairs for these gentlemen."

While they stood waiting, the visitors congratulated the major on the birth of his child, which had been announced in the Morning Chronicle, and which the prominence of the family made in some degree a matter of public interest.

"And now that you have a son, major," remarked the gentleman first described, as he lit one of the major's cigars, "you 'll be all the more interested in doing something to make this town fit to live in, which is what we came up to talk about. Things are in an awful condition! A negro justice of the peace has opened an office on Market Street, and only yesterday summoned a white man to appear before him. Negro lawyers get most of the business in the criminal court. Last evening a group of young white ladies, going quietly along the street arm-in-arm, were forced off the sidewalk by a crowd of negro girls. Coming down the street just now, I saw a spectacle of social equality and negro domination that made my blood boil with indignation,—a white and a black convict, chained together, crossing the city in charge of a negro officer! We cannot stand that sort of thing, Carteret,—it is the last straw! Something must be done, and that quickly!"

The major thrilled with responsive emotion. There was something prophetic in this opportune visit. The matter was not only in his own thoughts, but in the air; it was the spontaneous revulsion of white men against the rule of an inferior race. These were the very men, above all others in the town, to join him in a movement to change these degrading conditions.

General Belmont, the smaller of the two, was a man of good family, a lawyer by profession, and took an active part in state and local politics. Aristocratic by birth and instinct, and a former owner of slaves, his conception of the obligations and rights of his caste was nevertheless somewhat lower than that of the narrower but more sincere Carteret. In serious affairs Carteret desired the approval of his conscience, even if he had to trick that docile organ into acquiescence. This was not difficult to do in politics, for he believed in the divine right of white men and gentlemen, as his ancestors had believed in and died for the divine right of kings. General Belmont was not without a gentleman's distaste for meanness, but he permitted no fine scruples to stand in the way of success. He had once been minister, under a Democratic administration, to a small Central American state. Political rivals had characterized him as a tricky demagogue, which may of course have been a libel. He had an amiable disposition, possessed the gift of eloquence, and was a prime social favorite.

Captain George McBane had sprung from the poor-white class, to which, even more than to the slaves, the abolition of slavery had opened the door of opportunity. No longer overshadowed by a slaveholding caste, some of this class had rapidly pushed themselves forward. Some had made honorable records. Others, foremost in negro-baiting and election frauds, had done the dirty work of politics, as their fathers had done that of slavery, seeking their reward at first in minor offices,—for which men of gentler breeding did not care,—until their ambition began to reach out for higher honors.

Of this class McBane—whose captaincy, by the way, was merely a polite fiction—had been one of the most successful. He had held, until recently, as the reward of questionable political services, a contract with the State for its convict labor, from which in a few years he had realized a fortune. But the methods which made his contract profitable had not commended themselves to humane people, and charges of cruelty and worse had been preferred against him. He was rich enough to escape serious consequences from the investigation which followed, but when the Fusion ticket carried the state he lost his contract, and the system of convict labor was abolished. Since then McBane had devoted himself to politics: he was ambitious for greater wealth, for office, and for social recognition. A man of few words and self-engrossed, he seldom spoke of his aspirations except where speech might favor them, preferring to seek his ends by secret "deals" and combinations rather than to challenge criticism and provoke rivalry by more open methods.

At sight, therefore, of these two men, with whose careers and characters he was entirely familiar, Carteret felt sweep over his mind the conviction that now was the time and these the instruments with which to undertake the redemption of the state from the evil fate which had befallen it.

Jerry, the porter, who had gone downstairs to the counting-room to find two whole chairs, now entered with one in each hand. He set a chair for the general, who gave him an amiable nod, to which Jerry responded with a bow and a scrape. Captain McBane made no acknowledgment, but fixed Jerry so fiercely with his single eye that upon placing the chair Jerry made his escape from the room as rapidly as possible.

"I don' like dat Cap'n McBane," he muttered, upon reaching the hall. "Dey says he got dat eye knock' out tryin' ter whip a cullud 'oman, when he wuz a boy, an' dat he ain' never had no use fer niggers sence,—'cep'n' fer what he could make outen 'em wid his convic' labor contrac's. His daddy wuz a' overseer befo' 'im, an' it come nachul fer him ter be a nigger-driver. I don' want dat one eye er his'n restin' on me no longer 'n I kin he'p, an' I don' know how I 'm gwine ter like dis job ef he 's gwine ter be comin' roun' here. He ain' nothin' but po' w'ite trash nohow; but Lawd! Lawd! look at de money he 's got,—livin' at de hotel, wearin' di'mon's, an' colloguin' wid de bes' quality er dis town! 'Pears ter me de bottom rail is gittin' mighty close ter de top. Well, I s'pose it all comes f'm bein' w'ite. I wush ter Gawd I wuz w'ite!"

After this fervent aspiration, having nothing else to do for the time being, except to remain within call, and having caught a few words of the conversation as he went in with the chairs, Jerry, who possessed a certain amount of curiosity, placed close to the wall the broken stool upon which he sat while waiting in the hall, and applied his ear to a hole in the plastering of the hallway. There was a similar defect in the inner wall, between the same two pieces of studding, and while this inner opening was not exactly opposite the outer, Jerry was enabled, through the two, to catch in a more or less fragmentary way what was going on within.

He could hear the major, now and then, use the word "negro," and McBane's deep voice was quite audible when he referred, it seemed to Jerry with alarming frequency, to "the damned niggers," while the general's suave tones now and then pronounced the word "niggro,"—a sort of compromise between ethnology and the vernacular. That the gentlemen were talking politics seemed quite likely, for gentlemen generally talked politics when they met at the Chronicle office. Jerry could hear the words "vote," "franchise," "eliminate," "constitution," and other expressions which marked the general tenor of the talk, though he could not follow it all,—partly because he could not hear everything distinctly, and partly because of certain limitations which nature had placed in the way of Jerry's understanding anything very difficult or abstruse.

He had gathered enough, however, to realize, in a vague way, that something serious was on foot, involving his own race, when a bell sounded over his head, at which he sprang up hastily and entered the room where the gentlemen were talking.

"Jerry," said the major, "wait on Captain McBane."

"Yas, suh," responded Jerry, turning toward the captain, whose eye he carefully avoided meeting directly.

"Take that half a dollar, boy," ordered McBane, "an' go 'cross the street to Mr. Sykes's, and tell him to send me three whiskies. Bring back the change, and make has'e."

The captain tossed the half dollar at Jerry, who, looking to one side, of course missed it. He picked the money up, however, and backed out of the room. Jerry did not like Captain

McBane, to begin with, and it was clear that the captain was no gentleman, or he would not have thrown the money at him. Considering the source, Jerry might have overlooked this discourtesy had it not been coupled with the remark about the change, which seemed to him in very poor taste.

Returning in a few minutes with three glasses on a tray, he passed them round, handed Captain McBane his change, and retired to the hall.

"Gentlemen," exclaimed the captain, lifting his glass, "I propose a toast: 'No nigger domination.' "

"Amen!" said the others, and three glasses were solemnly drained.

"Major," observed the general, smacking his lips, "*I* should like to use Jerry for a moment, if you will permit me."

Jerry appeared promptly at the sound of the bell. He had remained conveniently near,—calls of this sort were apt to come in sequence.

"Jerry," said the general, handing Jerry half a dollar, "go over to Mr. Brown's,—I get my liquor there,—and tell them to send me three glasses of my special mixture. And, Jerry,—you may keep the change!"

"Thank y', gin'l, thank y', marster," replied Jerry, with unctuous gratitude, bending almost double as he backed out of the room.

"Dat 's a gent'eman, a rale ole-time gent'eman," he said to himself when he had closed the door. "But dere 's somethin' gwine on in dere,—dere sho' is! 'No nigger damnation!' Dat soun's all right,—I 'm sho' dere ain' no nigger I knows w'at wants damnation, do' dere 's lots of 'em w'at deserves it; but ef dat one-eyed Cap'n McBane got anything ter do wid it, w'atever it is, it don' mean no good fer de niggers,—damnation 'd be better fer 'em dan dat Cap'n McBane! He looks at a nigger lack he could jes' eat 'im alive."

"This mixture, gentlemen," observed the general when Jerry had returned with the glasses, "was originally compounded by no less a person than the great John C. Calhoun himself, who confided the recipe to my father over the convivial board. In this nectar of the gods, gentlemen, I drink with you to 'White Supremacy!' "

"White Supremacy everywhere!" added McBane with fervor.

"Now and forever!" concluded Carteret solemnly.

When the visitors, half an hour later, had taken their departure, Carteret, inspired by the theme, and in less degree by the famous mixture of the immortal Calhoun, turned to his desk and finished, at a white heat, his famous editorial in which he sounded the tocsin of a new crusade.

At noon, when the editor, having laid down his pen, was leaving the office, he passed Jerry in the hall without a word or a nod. The major wore a rapt look, which Jerry observed with a vague uneasiness.

"He looks jes' lack he wuz walkin' in his sleep," muttered Jerry uneasily. "Dere 's somethin' up, sho 's you bawn! 'No nigger damnation!' Anybody 'd 'low dey wuz all gwine ter heaven; but I knows better! W'en a passel er w'ite folks gits ter talkin' 'bout de niggers lack dem in yander, it 's mo' lackly dey 're gwine ter ketch somethin' e'se dan heaven! I got ter keep my eyes open an' keep up wid w'at 's happenin'. Ef dere 's gwine ter be anudder flood 'roun' here, I wants ter git in de ark wid de w'ite folks,—I may haf ter be anudder Ham, an' sta't de cullud race all over ag'in."

IV

THEODORE FELIX

THE YOUNG HEIR of the Carterets had thriven apace, and at six months old was, according to Mammy Jane, whose experience qualified her to speak with authority, the largest, finest, smartest, and altogether most remarkable baby that had ever lived in Wellington. Mammy Jane had recently suffered from an attack of inflammatory rheumatism, as the result of which she had returned to her own home. She nevertheless came now and then to see Mrs. Carteret. A younger nurse had been procured to take her place, but it was understood that Jane would come whenever she might be needed.

"You really mean that about Dodie, do you, Mammy Jane?" asked the delighted mother, who never tired of hearing her own opinion confirmed concerning this wonderful child, which had come to her like an angel from heaven.

"Does I mean it!" exclaimed Mammy Jane, with a tone and an expression which spoke volumes of reproach. "Now, Mis' 'Livy, what is I ever uttered er said er spoke er done dat would make you s'pose I could tell you a lie 'bout yo' own chile?"

"No, Mammy Jane, I 'm sure you would n't."

"'Deed, ma'am, I 'm tellin' you de Lawd's truf. I don' haf ter tell no lies ner strain no p'ints 'bout my ole mist'ess's gran'chile. Dis yer boy is de ve'y spit an' image er yo' brother, young Mars Alick, w'at died w'en he wuz 'bout eight mont's ole, w'iles I wuz laid off havin' a baby er my own, an' could n' be roun' ter look after 'im. An' dis chile is a rale quality chile, he is,—I never seed a baby wid sech fine hair fer his age, ner sech blue eyes, ner sech a grip, ner sech a heft. W'y, dat chile mus' weigh 'bout twenty-fo' poun's, an' he not but six mont's ole. Does dat gal w'at does de nussin' w'iles I 'm gone ten' ter dis chile right, Mis' 'Livy?"

"She does fairly well, Mammy Jane, but I could hardly expect her to love the baby as you do. There 's no one like you, Mammy Jane."

"'Deed dere ain't, honey; you is talkin' de gospel truf now! None er dese yer young folks ain' got de trainin' my ole mis-t'ess give me. Dese yer new-fangle' schools don' l'arn 'em nothin' ter compare wid it. I 'm jes' gwine ter give dat gal a piece er my min', befo' I go, so she 'll ten' ter dis chile right."

The nurse came in shortly afterwards, a neat-looking brown girl, dressed in a clean calico gown, with a nurse's cap and apron.

"Look a-here, gal," said Mammy Jane sternly, "I wants you ter understan' dat you got ter take good keer er dis chile; fer I nussed his mammy dere, an' his gran'mammy befo' 'im, an' you is got a priv'lege dat mos' lackly you don' 'preciate. I wants you to 'member, in yo' incomin's an' outgoin's, dat I got my eye on you, an' am gwine ter see dat you does yo' wo'k right."

"Do you need me for anything, ma'am?" asked the young nurse, who had stood before Mrs. Carteret, giving Mammy Jane a mere passing glance, and listening impassively to her harangue. The nurse belonged to the younger generation of colored people. She had graduated from the mission school, and had received some instruction in Dr. Miller's class for nurses. Standing, like most young people of her race, on the border line between two irreconcilable states of life, she had neither the picturesqueness of the slave, nor the unconscious dignity of those of whom freedom has been the immemorial birthright; she was in what might be called the chip-on-the-shoulder stage, through which races as well as individuals must pass in climbing the ladder of life,—not an interesting, at least not an agreeable stage, but an inevitable one, and for that reason entitled to a paragraph in a story of Southern life, which, with its as yet imperfect blending of old with new, of race with race, of slavery with freedom, is like no other life under the sun.

Had this old woman, who had no authority over her, been a little more polite, or a little less offensive, the nurse might have returned her a pleasant answer. These old-time negroes, she said to herself, made her sick with their slavering over the white folks, who, she supposed, favored them and made much of them because they had once belonged to them,—much the same reason why they fondled their cats and dogs. For her own part, they gave her nothing but her wages, and small wages at that, and she owed them nothing more than equivalent service. It was purely a matter of business; she sold her time for their money. There was no question of love between them.

Receiving a negative answer from Mrs. Carteret, she left the room without a word, ignoring Mammy Jane completely, and leaving that venerable relic of ante-bellum times gasping in helpless astonishment.

"Well, I nevuh!" she ejaculated, as soon as she could get her breath, "ef dat ain' de beatinis' pe'fo'mance I ever seed er heared of! Dese yer young niggers ain' got de manners dey wuz bawned wid! I don' know w'at dey 're comin' to, w'en dey ain' got no mo' rispec' fer ole age—I don' know—I don' know!"

"Now what are you croaking about, Jane?" asked Major Carteret, who came into the room and took the child into his arms.

Mammy Jane hobbled to her feet and bobbed a curtsy. She was never lacking in respect to white people of proper quality; but Major Carteret, the quintessence of aristocracy, called out all her reserves of deference. The major was always kind and considerate to these old family retainers, brought up in the feudal atmosphere now so rapidly passing away. Mammy Jane loved Mrs. Carteret; toward the major she entertained a feeling bordering upon awe.

"Well, Jane," returned the major sadly, when the old nurse had related her grievance, "the old times have vanished, the old ties have been ruptured. The old relations of dependence and loyal obedience on the part of the colored people, the responsibility of protection and kindness upon that of the whites, have passed away forever. The young negroes are too self-assertive. Education is spoiling them, Jane; they have been badly taught. They are not content with their station in life. Some time they will overstep the mark. The white people are patient, but there is a limit to their endurance.

"Dat 's w'at I tells dese young niggers," groaned Mammy Jane, with a portentous shake of her turbaned head, "w'en I hears 'em gwine on wid deir foolishniss; but dey don' min' me. Dey 'lows dey knows mo' d'n I does, 'ca'se dey be'n l'arnt ter look in a book. But, pshuh! my ole mist'ess showed me mo' d'n dem niggers 'll l'arn in a thousan' years! I 's fetch' my gran'son' Jerry up ter be 'umble, an' keep in 'is place. An' I tells dese other niggers dat ef dey 'd do de same, an' not crowd de w'ite folks, dey 'd git ernuff ter eat, an' live out deir days in peace an' comfo't. But dey don' min' me—dey don' min' me!"

"If all the colored people were like you and Jerry, Jane," rejoined the major kindly, "there would never be any trouble. You have friends upon whom, in time of need, you can rely implicitly for protection and succor. You served your mistress faithfully before the war; you remained by her when the other negroes were running hither and thither like sheep without a shepherd; and you have transferred your allegiance to my wife and her child. We think a great deal of you, Jane."

"Yes, indeed, Mammy Jane," assented Mrs. Carteret, with sincere affection, glancing with moist eyes from the child in her husband's arms to the old nurse, whose dark face was glowing with happiness at these expressions of appreciation, "you shall never want so long as we have anything. We would share our last crust with you."

"Thank y', Mis' 'Livy," said Jane with reciprocal emotion, "I knows who my frien's is, an' I ain' gwine ter let nothin' worry me. But fer de Lawd's sake, Mars Philip, gimme dat chile, an' lemme pat 'im on de back, er he 'll choke hisse'f ter death!"

The old nurse had been the first to observe that little Dodie, for some reason, was gasping for breath. Catching the child from the major's arms, she patted it on the back, and shook it gently. After a moment of this treatment, the child ceased to gasp, but still breathed heavily, with a strange, whistling noise.

"Oh, my child!" exclaimed the mother, in great alarm, taking the baby in her own arms, "what can be the matter with him, Mammy Jane?"

"Fer de Lawd's sake, ma'am, I don' know, 'less he 's swallered somethin'; an' he ain' had nothin' in his han's but de rattle Mis' Polly give 'im."

Mrs. Carteret caught up the ivory rattle, which hung suspended by a ribbon from the baby's neck.

"He has swallowed the little piece off the end of the handle," she cried, turning pale with fear, "and it has lodged in his throat. Telephone Dr. Price to come immediately, Philip, before my baby chokes to death! Oh, my baby, my precious baby!"

An anxious half hour passed, during which the child lay quiet, except for its labored breathing. The suspense was relieved by the arrival of Dr. Price, who examined the child carefully.

"It 's a curious accident," he announced at the close of his inspection. "So far as I can discover, the piece of ivory has been drawn into the trachea, or windpipe, and has lodged in the mouth of the right bronchus. I 'll try to get it out without an operation, but I can't guarantee the result."

At the end of another half hour Dr. Price announced his inability to remove the obstruction without resorting to more serious measures.

"I do not see," he declared, "how an operation can be avoided."

"Will it be dangerous?" inquired the major anxiously, while Mrs. Carteret shivered at the thought.

"It will be necessary to cut into his throat from the outside. All such operations are more or less dangerous, especially on small children. If this were some other child, I might undertake the operation unassisted; but I know how you value this one, major, and I should prefer to share the responsibility with a specialist."

"Is there one in town?" asked the major.

"No, but we can get one from out of town."

"Send for the best one in the country," said the major, "who can be got here in time. Spare no expense, Dr. Price. We value this child above any earthly thing."

"The best is the safest," replied Dr. Price. "I will send for Dr. Burns, of Philadelphia, the best surgeon in that line in America. If he can start at once, he can reach here in sixteen or eighteen hours, and the case can wait even longer, if inflammation does not set in."

The message was dispatched forthwith. By rare good fortune the eminent specialist was able to start within an hour or two after the receipt of Dr. Price's telegram. Meanwhile the baby remained restless and uneasy, the doctor spending most of his time by its side. Mrs. Carteret, who had never been quite strong since the child's birth, was a prey to the most agonizing apprehensions.

Mammy Jane, while not presuming to question the opinion of Dr. Price, and not wishing to add to her mistress's distress, was secretly oppressed by forebodings which she was unable to shake off. The child was born for bad luck. The mole under its ear, just at the point where the hangman's knot would strike, had foreshadowed dire misfortune. She had already observed several little things which had rendered her vaguely anxious.

For instance, upon one occasion, on entering the room where the baby had been left alone, asleep in his crib, she had met a strange cat hurrying from the nursery, and, upon examining closely the pillow upon which the child lay, had found a depression which had undoubtedly been due to the weight of the cat's body. The child was restless and uneasy, and Jane had ever since believed that the cat had been sucking little Dodie's breath, with what might have been fatal results had she not appeared just in the nick of time.

This untimely accident of the rattle, a fatality for which no one could be held responsible, had confirmed the unlucky omen. Jane's duties in the nursery did not permit her to visit her friend the conjure woman; but she did find time to go out in the back yard at dusk, and to dig up the charm which she had planted there. It had protected the child so far; but perhaps its potency had become exhausted. She picked up the bottle, shook it vigorously, and then laid it back, with the other side up. Refilling the hole, she made a cross over the top with the thumb of her left hand, and walked three times around it.

What this strange symbolism meant, or whence it derived its origin, Aunt Jane did not know. The cross was there, and the Trinity, though Jane was scarcely conscious of these, at this moment, as religious emblems. But she hoped, on general principles, that this performance would strengthen the charm and restore little Dodie's luck. It certainly had its moral effect upon Jane's own mind, for she was able to sleep better, and contrived to impress Mrs. Carteret with her own hopefulness.

V

A JOURNEY SOUTHWARD

AS THE south-bound train was leaving the station at Philadelphia, a gentleman took his seat in the single sleeping-car attached to the train, and proceeded to make himself comfortable. He hung up his hat and opened his newspaper, in which he remained absorbed for a quarter of an hour. When the train had left the city behind, he threw the paper aside, and looked around at the other occupants of the car. One of these, who had been on the car since it had left New York, rose from his seat upon perceiving the other's glance, and came down the aisle.

"How do you do, Dr. Burns?" he said, stopping beside the seat of the Philadelphia passenger.

The gentleman looked up at the speaker with an air of surprise, which, after the first keen, incisive glance, gave place to an expression of cordial recognition.

"Why, it 's Miller!" he exclaimed, rising and giving the other his hand, "William Miller—Dr. Miller, of course. Sit down, Miller, and tell me all about yourself,—what you 're doing, where you 've been, and where you 're going. I 'm delighted to meet you, and to see you looking so well—and so prosperous."

"I deserve no credit for either, sir," returned the other, as he took the proffered seat, "for I inherited both health and prosperity. It is a fortunate chance that permits me to meet you."

The two acquaintances, thus opportunely thrown together so that they might while away in conversation the tedium of their journey, represented very different and yet very similar types of manhood. A celebrated traveler, after many years spent in barbarous or savage lands, has said that among all varieties of mankind the similarities are vastly more important and fundamental than the differences. Looking at these two men with the American eye, the differences would perhaps be the more striking, or at least the more immediately apparent, for the first was white and the second black, or, more correctly speaking, brown; it was even a light brown, but both his swarthy complexion and his curly hair revealed what has been described in the laws of some of our states as a "visible admixture" of African blood.

Having disposed of this difference, and having observed that the white man was perhaps fifty years of age and the other not more than thirty, it may be said that they were both tall and sturdy, both well dressed, the white man with perhaps a little more distinction; both seemed from their faces and their manners to be men of culture and accustomed to the society of cultivated people. They were both handsome men, the elder representing a fine type of Anglo-Saxon, as the term is used in speaking of our composite white population; while the mulatto's erect form, broad shoulders, clear eyes, fine teeth, and pleasingly moulded features showed nowhere any sign of that degeneration which the pessimist so sadly maintains is the inevitable heritage of mixed races.

As to their personal relations, it has already appeared that they were members of the same profession. In past years they had been teacher and pupil. Dr. Alvin Burns was professor in the famous medical college where Miller had attended lectures. The professor had taken an interest in his only colored pupil, to whom he had been attracted by his earnestness of purpose, his evident talent, and his excellent manners and fine physique. It was in part due to Dr. Burns's friendship that Miller had won a scholarship which had enabled him, without drawing too heavily upon his father's resources, to spend in Europe, studying in the hospitals of Paris and Vienna, the two most delightful years of his life. The same influence had strengthened his natural inclination toward operative surgery, in which Dr. Burns was a distinguished specialist of national reputation.

Miller's father, Adam Miller, had been a thrifty colored man, the son of a slave, who, in the olden time, had bought himself with money which he had earned and saved, over and above what he had paid his master for his time. Adam Miller had inherited his father's thrift, as well as his trade, which was that of a stevedore, or contractor for the loading and unloading of vessels at the port of Wellington. In the flush turpentine days following a few years after the civil war, he had made money. His savings, shrewdly invested, had by constant accessions become a competence. He had brought up his eldest son to the trade; the other he had given a professional education, in the proud hope that his children or his grandchildren might be gentlemen in the town where their ancestors had once been slaves.

Upon his father's death, shortly after Dr. Miller's return from Europe, and a year or two before the date at which this story opens, he had promptly spent part of his inheritance in founding a hospital, to which was to be added a training school for nurses, and in time perhaps a medical college and a school of pharmacy. He had been strongly tempted to leave the South, and seek a home for his family and a career for himself in the freer North, where race antagonism was less keen, or at least less oppressive, or in Europe, where he had never found his color work to his disadvantage. But his people had needed him, and he had wished to help them, and had sought by means of this institution to contribute to their uplifting. As he now informed Dr. Burns, he was returning from New York, where he had been in order to purchase equipment for his new hospital, which would soon be ready for the reception of patients.

"How much I can accomplish I do not know," said Miller, "but I 'll do what I can. There are eight or nine million of us, and it will take a great deal of learning of all kinds to leaven that lump."

"It is a great problem, Miller, the future of your race," returned the other, "a tremendously interesting problem. It is a serial story which we are all reading, and which grows in vital interest with each successive installment. It is not only your problem, but ours. Your race must come up or drag ours down."

"We shall come up," declared Miller; "slowly and painfully, perhaps, but we shall win our way. If our race had made as much progress everywhere as they have made in Wellington, the problem would be well on the way toward solution."

"Wellington?" exclaimed Dr. Burns. "That 's where I 'm going. A Dr. Price, of Wellington, has sent for me to perform an operation on a child's throat. Do you know Dr. Price?"

"Quite well," replied Miller, "he is a friend of mine."

"So much the better. I shall want you to assist me. I read in the Medical Gazette, the other day, an account of a very interesting operation of yours. I felt proud to number you among my pupils. It was a remarkable case—a rare case. I must certainly have you with me in this one."

"I shall be delighted, sir," returned Miller, "if it is agreeable to all concerned."

Several hours were passed in pleasant conversation while the train sped rapidly southward. They were already far down in Virginia, and had stopped at a station beyond Richmond, when the conductor entered the car.

"All passengers," he announced, "will please transfer to the day coaches ahead. The sleeper has a hot box, and must be switched off here."

Dr. Burns and Miller obeyed the order, the former leading the way into the coach immediately in front of the sleeping-car.

"Let 's sit here, Miller," he said, having selected a seat near the rear of the car and deposited his suitcase in a rack. "It 's on the shady side."

Miller stood a moment hesitatingly, but finally took the seat indicated, and a few minutes later the journey was again resumed.

When the train conductor made his round after leaving the station, he paused at the seat occupied by the two doctors, glanced interrogatively at Miller, and then spoke to Dr. Burns, who sat in the end of the seat nearest the aisle.

"This man is with you?" he asked, indicating Miller with a slight side movement of his head, and a keen glance in his direction.

"Certainly," replied Dr. Burns curtly, and with some surprise. "Don't you see that he is?"

The conductor passed on. Miller paid no apparent attention to this little interlude, though no syllable had escaped him. He resumed the conversation where it had been broken off, but nevertheless followed with his eyes the conductor, who stopped at a seat near the forward end of the car, and engaged in conversation with a man whom Miller had not hitherto noticed.

As this passenger turned his head and looked back toward

Miller, the latter saw a broad-shouldered, burly white man, and recognized in his square-cut jaw, his coarse, firm mouth, and the single gray eye with which he swept Miller for an instant with a scornful glance, a well-known character of Wellington, with whom the reader has already made acquaintance in these pages. Captain McBane wore a frock coat and a slouch hat; several buttons of his vest were unbuttoned, and his solitaire diamond blazed in his soiled shirt-front like the headlight of a locomotive.

The conductor in his turn looked back at Miller, and retraced his steps. Miller braced himself for what he feared was coming, though he had hoped, on account of his friend's presence, that it might be avoided.

"Excuse me, sir," said the conductor, addressing Dr. Burns, "but did I understand you to say that this man was your servant?"

"No, indeed!" replied Dr. Burns indignantly. "The gentleman is not my servant, nor anybody's servant, but is my friend. But, by the way, since we are on the subject, may I ask what affair it is of yours?"

"It 's very much my affair," returned the conductor, somewhat nettled at this questioning of his authority. "I 'm sorry to part *friends*, but the law of Virginia does not permit colored passengers to ride in the white cars. You 'll have to go forward to the next coach," he added, addressing Miller this time.

"I have paid my fare on the sleeping-car, where the separate-car law does not apply," remonstrated Miller.

"I can't help that. You can doubtless get your money back from the sleeping-car company. But this is a day coach, and is distinctly marked 'White,' as you must have seen before you sat down here. The sign is put there for that purpose."

He indicated a large card neatly framed and hung at the end of the car, containing the legend, "White," in letters about a foot long, painted in white upon a dark background, typical, one might suppose, of the distinction thereby indicated.

"You shall not stir a step, Miller," exclaimed Dr. Burns wrathfully. "This is an outrage upon a citizen of a free country. You shall stay right here."

"I 'm sorry to discommode you," returned the conductor, "but there 's no use kicking. It 's the law of Virginia, and I am bound by it as well as you. I have already come near losing my place because of not enforcing it, and I can take no more such chances, since I have a family to support."

"And my friend has his rights to maintain," returned Dr. Burns with determination. "There is a vital principle at stake in the matter."

"Really, sir," argued the conductor, who was a man of peace and not fond of controversy, "there 's no use talking—he absolutely cannot ride in this car."

"How can you prevent it?" asked Dr. Burns, lapsing into the argumentative stage.

"The law gives me the right to remove him by force. I can call on the train crew to assist me, or on the other passengers. If I should choose to put him off the train entirely, in the middle of a swamp, he would have no redress—the law so provides. If I did not wish to use force, I could simply switch this car off at the next siding, transfer the white passengers to another, and leave you and your friend in possession until you were arrested and fined or imprisoned."

"What he says is absolutely true, doctor," interposed Miller at this point. "It is the law, and we are powerless to resist it. If we made any trouble, it would merely delay your journey and imperil a life at the other end. I 'll go into the other car."

"You shall not go alone," said Dr. Burns stoutly, rising in his turn. "A place that is too good for you is not good enough for me. I will sit wherever you do."

"I 'm sorry again," said the conductor, who had quite recovered his equanimity, and calmly conscious of his power, could scarcely restrain an amused smile; "I dislike to interfere, but white passengers are not permitted to ride in the colored car."

"This is an outrage," declared Dr. Burns, "a d——d outrage! You are curtailing the rights, not only of colored people, but of white men as well. I shall sit where I please!"

"I warn you, sir," rejoined the conductor, hardening again, "that the law will be enforced. The beauty of the system lies in its strict impartiality—it applies to both races alike."

"And is equally infamous in both cases," declared Dr. Burns. "I shall immediately take steps"—

"Never mind, doctor," interrupted Miller, soothingly, "it 's only for a little while. I 'll reach my destination just as surely in the other car, and we can't help it, anyway. I 'll see you again at Wellington."

Dr. Burns, finding resistance futile, at length acquiesced and made way for Miller to pass him.

The colored doctor took up his valise and crossed the platform to the car ahead. It was an old car, with faded upholstery, from which the stuffing projected here and there through torn places. Apparently the floor had not been swept for several days. The dust lay thick upon the window sills, and the water-cooler, from which he essayed to get a drink, was filled with stale water which had made no recent acquaintance with ice. There was no other passenger in the car, and Miller occupied himself in making a rough calculation of what it would cost the Southern railroads to haul a whole car for every colored passenger. It was expensive, to say the least; it would be cheaper, and quite as considerate of their feelings, to make the negroes walk.

The car was conspicuously labeled at either end with large cards, similar to those in the other car, except that they bore the word "Colored" in black letters upon a white background. The author of this piece of legislation had contrived, with an ingenuity worthy of a better cause, that not merely should the passengers be separated by the color line, but that the reason for this division should be kept constantly in mind. Lest a white man should forget that he was white,—not a very likely contingency,—these cards would keep him constantly admonished of the fact; should a colored person endeavor, for a moment, to lose sight of his disability, these staring signs would remind him continually that between him and the rest of mankind not of his own color, there was by law a great gulf fixed.

Having composed himself, Miller had opened a newspaper, and was deep in an editorial which set forth in glowing language the inestimable advantages which would follow to certain recently acquired islands by the introduction of American liberty, when the rear door of the car opened to give entrance to Captain George McBane, who took a seat near the door and lit a cigar. Miller knew him quite well by sight and by reputation, and detested him as heartily. He represented the aggressive, offensive element among the white people of the New South, who made it hard for a negro to maintain his self-respect or to enjoy even the rights conceded to colored men by Southern laws. McBane had undoubtedly identified him to the conductor in the other car. Miller had no desire to thrust himself upon the society of white people, which, indeed, to one who had traveled so much and so far, was no novelty; but he very naturally resented being at this late day—the law had been in operation only a few months—branded and tagged and set apart from the rest of mankind upon the public highways, like an unclean thing. Nevertheless, he preferred even this to the exclusive society of Captain George McBane.

"Porter," he demanded of the colored train attaché who passed through the car a moment later, "is this a smoking car for white men?"

"No, suh," replied the porter, "but they comes in here sometimes, when they ain' no cullud ladies on the kyar."

"Well, I have paid first-class fare, and I object to that man's smoking in here. You tell him to go out."

"I 'll tell the conductor, suh," returned the porter in a low tone. "I 'd jus' as soon talk ter the devil as ter that man."

The white man had spread himself over two seats, and was smoking vigorously, from time to time spitting carelessly in the aisle, when the conductor entered the compartment.

"Captain," said Miller, "this car is plainly marked 'Colored.' I have paid first-class fare, and I object to riding in a smoking car."

"All right," returned the conductor, frowning irritably. "I 'll speak to him."

He walked over to the white passenger, with whom he was evidently acquainted, since he adressed him by name.

"Captain McBane," he said, "it 's against the law for you to ride in the nigger car."

"Who are you talkin' to?" returned the other. "I 'll ride where I damn please."

"Yes, sir, but the colored passenger objects. I 'm afraid I 'll have to ask you to go into the smoking-car."

"The hell you say!" rejoined McBane. "I 'll leave this car

when I get good and ready, and that won't be till I've finished this cigar. See?"

He was as good as his word. The conductor escaped from the car before Miller had time for further expostulation. Finally McBane, having thrown the stump of his cigar into the aisle and added to the floor a finishing touch in the way of expectoration, rose and went back into the white car.

Left alone in his questionable glory, Miller buried himself again in his newspaper, from which he did not look up until the engine stopped at a tank station to take water.

As the train came to a standstill, a huge negro, covered thickly with dust, crawled off one of the rear trucks unobserved, and ran round the rear end of the car to a watering-trough by a neighboring well. Moved either by extreme thirst or by the fear that his time might be too short to permit him to draw a bucket of water, he threw himself down by the trough, drank long and deep, and plunging his head into the water, shook himself like a wet dog, and crept furtively back to his dangerous perch.

Miller, who had seen this man from the car window, had noticed a very singular thing. As the dusty tramp passed the rear coach, he cast toward it a glance of intense ferocity. Up to that moment the man's face, which Miller had recognized under its grimy coating, had been that of an ordinarily good-natured, somewhat reckless, pleasure-loving negro, at present rather the worse for wear. The change that now came over it suggested a concentrated hatred almost uncanny in its murderousness. With awakened curiosity Miller followed the direction of the negro's glance, and saw that it rested upon a window where Captain McBane sat looking out. When Miller looked back, the negro had disappeared.

At the next station a Chinaman, of the ordinary laundry type, boarded the train, and took his seat in the white car without objection. At another point a colored nurse found a place with her mistress.

"White people," said Miller to himself, who had seen these passengers from the window, "do not object to the negro as a servant. As the traditional negro,—the servant,—he is welcomed; as an equal, he is repudiated."

Miller was something of a philosopher. He had long ago

had the conclusion forced upon him that an educated man of his race, in order to live comfortably in the United States, must be either a philosopher or a fool; and since he wished to be happy, and was not exactly a fool, he had cultivated philosophy. By and by he saw a white man, with a dog, enter the rear coach. Miller wondered whether the dog would be allowed to ride with his master, and if not, what disposition would be made of him. He was a handsome dog, and Miller, who was fond of animals, would not have objected to the company of a dog, as a dog. He was nevertheless conscious of a queer sensation when he saw the porter take the dog by the collar and start in his own direction, and felt consciously relieved when the canine passenger was taken on past him into the baggage-car ahead. Miller's hand was hanging over the arm of his seat, and the dog, an intelligent shepherd, licked it as he passed. Miller was not entirely sure that he would not have liked the porter to leave the dog there; he was a friendly dog, and seemed inclined to be sociable.

Toward evening the train drew up at a station where quite a party of farm laborers, fresh from their daily toil, swarmed out from the conspicuously labeled colored waiting-room, and into the car with Miller. They were a jolly, good-natured crowd, and, free from the embarrassing presence of white people, proceeded to enjoy themselves after their own fashion. Here an amorous fellow sat with his arm around a buxom girl's waist. A musically inclined individual—his talents did not go far beyond inclination—produced a mouth-organ and struck up a tune, to which a limber-legged boy danced in the aisle. They were noisy, loquacious, happy, dirty, and malodorous. For a while Miller was amused and pleased. They were his people, and he felt a certain expansive warmth toward them in spite of their obvious shortcomings. By and by, however, the air became too close, and he went out upon the platform. For the sake of the democratic ideal, which meant so much to his race, he might have endured the affliction. He could easily imagine that people of refinement, with the power in their hands, might be tempted to strain the democratic ideal in order to avoid such contact; but personally, and apart from the mere matter of racial sympathy, these people were just as offensive to him as to the whites in the other end of the train. Surely, if a classification of passengers on trains was at all desirable, it might be made upon some more logical and considerate basis than a mere arbitrary, tactless, and, by the very nature of things, brutal drawing of a color line. It was a veritable bed of Procrustes, this standard which the whites had set for the negroes. Those who grew above it must have their heads cut off, figuratively speaking,—must be forced back to the level assigned to their race; those who fell beneath the standard set had their necks stretched, literally enough, as the ghastly record in the daily papers gave conclusive evidence.

Miller breathed more freely when the lively crowd got off at the next station, after a short ride. Moreover, he had a light heart, a conscience void of offense, and was only thirty years old. His philosophy had become somewhat jaded on this journey, but he pulled it together for a final effort. Was it not, after all, a wise provision of nature that had given to a race, destined to a long servitude and a slow emergence therefrom, a cheerfulness of spirit which enabled them to catch pleasure on the wing, and endure with equanimity the ills that seemed inevitable? The ability to live and thrive under adverse circumstances is the surest guaranty of the future. The race which at the last shall inherit the earth—the residuary legatee of civilization—will be the race which remains longest upon it. The negro was here before the Anglo-Saxon was evolved, and his thick lips and heavy-lidded eyes looked out from the inscrutable face of the Sphinx across the sands of Egypt while yet the ancestors of those who now oppress him were living in caves, practicing human sacrifice, and painting themselves with woad—and the negro is here yet.

" 'Blessed are the meek,' " quoted Miller at the end of these consoling reflections, " 'for they shall inherit the earth.' If this be true, the negro may yet come into his estate, for meekness seems to be set apart as his portion."

The journey came to an end just as the sun had sunk into the west.

Simultaneously with Miller's exit from the train, a great black figure crawled off the trucks of the rear car, on the side opposite the station platform. Stretching and shaking himself with a free gesture, the black man, seeing himself unobserved, moved somewhat stiffly round the end of the car to the station platform.

"'Fo de Lawd!" he muttered, "ef I had n' had a cha'm' life, I 'd 'a' never got here on dat ticket, an' dat 's a fac'—it sho' am! I kind er 'lowed I wuz gone a dozen times, ez it wuz. But I got my job ter do in dis worl', an' I knows I ain' gwine ter die 'tel I 've 'complished it. I jes' want one mo' look at dat man, an' den I 'll haf ter git somethin' ter eat; fer two raw turnips in twelve hours is slim pickin's fer a man er my size!"

VI

JANET

As the train drew up at the station platform, Dr. Price came forward from the white waiting-room, and stood expectantly by the door of the white coach. Miller, having left his car, came down the platform in time to intercept Burns as he left the train, and to introduce him to Dr. Price.

"My carriage is in waiting," said Dr. Price. "I should have liked to have you at my own house, but my wife is out of town. We have a good hotel, however, and you will doubtless find it more convenient."

"You are very kind, Dr. Price. Miller, won't you come up and dine with me?"

"Thank you, no," said Miller, "I am expected at home. My wife and child are waiting for me in the buggy yonder by the platform."

"Oh, very well; of course you must go; but don't forget our appointment. Let 's see, Dr. Price, I can eat and get ready in half an hour—that will make it"—

"I have asked several of the local physicians to be present at eight o'clock," said Dr. Price. "The case can safely wait until then."

"Very well, Miller, be on hand at eight. I shall expect you without fail. Where shall he come, Dr. Price?"

"To the residence of Major Philip Carteret, on Vine Street."

"I have invited Dr. Miller to be present and assist in the operation," Dr. Burns continued, as they drove toward the hotel. "He was a favorite pupil of mine, and is a credit to the profession. I presume you saw his article in the Medical Gazette?"

"Yes, and I assisted him in the case," returned Dr. Price. "It was a colored lad, one of his patients, and he called me in to help him. He is a capable man, and very much liked by the white physicians."

Miller's wife and child were waiting for him in fluttering

anticipation. He kissed them both as he climbed into the buggy.

"We came at four o'clock," said Mrs. Miller, a handsome young woman, who might be anywhere between twenty-five and thirty, and whose complexion, in the twilight, was not distinguishable from that of a white person, "but the train was late two hours, they said. We came back at six, and have been waiting ever since."

"Yes, papa," piped the child, a little boy of six or seven, who sat between them, "and I am very hungry."

Miller felt very much elated as he drove homeward through the twilight. By his side sat the two persons whom he loved best in all the world. His affairs were prosperous. Upon opening his office in the city, he had been received by the members of his own profession with a cordiality generally frank, and in no case much reserved. The colored population of the city was large, but in the main poor, and the white physicians were not unwilling to share this unprofitable practice with a colored doctor worthy of confidence. In the intervals of the work upon his hospital, he had built up a considerable practice among his own people; but except in the case of some poor unfortunate whose pride had been lost in poverty or sin, no white patient had ever called upon him for treatment. He knew very well the measure of his powers,—a liberal education had given him opportunity to compare himself with other men,—and was secretly conscious that in point of skill and knowledge he did not suffer by comparison with any other physician in the town. He liked to believe that the race antagonism which hampered his progress and that of his people was a mere temporary thing, the outcome of former conditions, and bound to disappear in time, and that when a colored man should demonstrate to the community in which he lived that he possessed character and power, that community would find a way in which to enlist his services for the public good.

He had already made himself useful, and had received many kind words and other marks of appreciation. He was now offered a further confirmation of his theory: having recognized his skill, the white people were now ready to take advantage of it. Any lurking doubt he may have felt when first invited by

Dr. Burns to participate in the operation, had been dispelled by Dr. Price's prompt acquiescence.

On the way homeward Miller told his wife of this appointment. She was greatly interested; she was herself a mother, with an only child. Moreover, there was a stronger impulse than mere humanity to draw her toward the stricken mother. Janet had a tender heart, and could have loved this white sister, her sole living relative of whom she knew. All her life long she had yearned for a kind word, a nod, a smile, the least thing that imagination might have twisted into a recognition of the tie between them. But it had never come.

And yet Janet was not angry. She was of a forgiving temper; she could never bear malice. She was educated, had read many books, and appreciated to the full the social forces arrayed against any such recognition as she had dreamed of. Of the two barriers between them a man might have forgiven the one; a woman would not be likely to overlook either the bar sinister or the difference of race, even to the slight extent of a silent recognition. Blood is thicker than water, but, if it flow too far from conventional channels, may turn to gall and wormwood. Nevertheless, when the heart speaks, reason falls into the background, and Janet would have worshiped this sister, even afar off, had she received even the slightest encouragement. So strong was this weakness that she had been angry with herself for her lack of pride, or even of a decent self-respect. It was, she sometimes thought, the heritage of her mother's race, and she was ashamed of it as part of the taint of slavery. She had never acknowledged, even to her husband, from whom she concealed nothing else, her secret thoughts upon this lifelong sorrow. This silent grief was nature's penalty, or society's revenge, for whatever heritage of beauty or intellect or personal charm had come to her with her father's blood. For she had received no other inheritance. Her sister was rich by right of her birth; if Janet had been fortunate, her good fortune had not been due to any provision made for her by her white father.

She knew quite well how passionately, for many years, her proud sister had longed and prayed in vain for the child which had at length brought joy into her household, and she could feel, by sympathy, all the sickening suspense with which the child's parents must await the result of this dangerous operation.

"O Will," she adjured her husband anxiously, when he had told her of the engagement, "you must be very careful. Think of the child's poor mother! Think of our own dear child, and what it would mean to lose him!"

VII

THE OPERATION

DR. PRICE was not entirely at ease in his mind as the two doctors drove rapidly from the hotel to Major Carteret's. Himself a liberal man, from his point of view, he saw no reason why a colored doctor might not operate upon a white male child,—there are fine distinctions in the application of the color line,—but several other physicians had been invited, some of whom were men of old-fashioned notions, who might not relish such an innovation.

This, however, was but a small difficulty compared with what might be feared from Major Carteret himself. For he knew Carteret's unrelenting hostility to anything that savored of recognition of the negro as the equal of white men. It was traditional in Wellington that no colored person had ever entered the front door of the Carteret residence, and that the luckless individual who once presented himself there upon alleged business and resented being ordered to the back door had been unceremoniously thrown over the piazza railing into a rather thorny clump of rose-bushes below. If Miller were going as a servant, to hold a basin or a sponge, there would be no difficulty; but as a surgeon—well, he would n't borrow trouble. Under the circumstances the major might yield a point.

But as they neared the house the major's unyielding disposition loomed up formidably. Perhaps if the matter were properly presented to Dr. Burns, he might consent to withdraw the invitation. It was not yet too late to send Miller a note.

"By the way, Dr. Burns," he said, "I 'm very friendly to Dr. Miller, and should personally like to have him with us tonight. But—I ought to have told you this before, but I could n't very well do so, on such short notice, in Miller's presence—we are a conservative people, and our local customs are not very flexible. We jog along in much the same old way our fathers did. I 'm not at all sure that Major Carteret or the other gentlemen would consent to the presence of a negro doctor."

"I think you misjudge your own people," returned Dr. Burns, "they are broader than you think. We have our prejudices against the negro at the North, but we do not let them stand in the way of anything that *we* want. At any rate, it is too late now, and I will accept the responsibility. If the question is raised, I will attend to it. When I am performing an operation I must be *aut Cæsar, aut nullus.*"

Dr. Price was not reassured, but he had done his duty and felt the reward of virtue. If there should be trouble, he would not be responsible. Moreover, there was a large fee at stake, and Dr. Burns was not likely to prove too obdurate.

They were soon at Carteret's, where they found assembled the several physicians invited by Dr. Price. These were successively introduced as Drs. Dudley, Hooper, and Ashe, all of whom were gentlemen of good standing, socially and in their profession, and considered it a high privilege to witness so delicate an operation at the hands of so eminent a member of their profession.

Major Carteret entered the room and was duly presented to the famous specialist. Carteret's anxious look lightened somewhat at sight of the array of talent present. It suggested, of course, the gravity of the impending event, but gave assurance of all the skill and care which science could afford.

Dr. Burns was shown to the nursery, from which he returned in five minutes.

"The case is ready," he announced. "Are the gentlemen all present?"

"I believe so," answered Dr. Price quickly.

Miller had not yet arrived. Perhaps, thought Dr. Price, a happy accident, or some imperative call, had detained him. This would be fortunate indeed. Dr. Burns's square jaw had a very determined look. It would be a pity if any acrimonious discussion should arise on the eve of a delicate operation. If the clock on the mantel would only move faster, the question might never come up.

"I don't see Dr. Miller," observed Dr. Burns, looking around the room. "I asked him to come at eight. There are ten minutes yet."

Major Carteret looked up with a sudden frown.

"May I ask to whom you refer?" he inquired, in an ominous tone.

The other gentlemen showed signs of interest, not to say emotion. Dr. Price smiled quizzically.

"Dr. Miller, of your city. He was one of my favorite pupils. He is also a graduate of the Vienna hospitals, and a surgeon of unusual skill. I have asked him to assist in the operation."

Every eye was turned toward Carteret, whose crimsoned face had set in a look of grim determination.

"The person to whom you refer is a negro, I believe?" he said.

"He is a colored man, certainly," returned Dr. Burns, "though one would never think of his color after knowing him well."

"I do not know, sir," returned Carteret, with an effort at self-control, "what the customs of Philadelphia or Vienna may be; but in the South we do not call negro doctors to attend white patients. I could not permit a negro to enter my house upon such an errand."

"I am here, sir," replied Dr. Burns with spirit, "to perform a certain operation. Since I assume the responsibility, the case must be under my entire control. Otherwise I cannot operate."

"Gentlemen," interposed Dr. Price, smoothly, "I beg of you both—this is a matter for calm discussion, and any asperity is to be deplored. The life at stake here should not be imperiled by any consideration of minor importance."

"Your humanity does you credit, sir," retorted Dr. Burns. "But other matters, too, are important. I have invited this gentleman here. My professional honor is involved, and I merely invoke my rights to maintain it. It is a matter of principle, which ought not to give way to a mere prejudice."

"That also states the case for Major Carteret," rejoined Dr. Price, suavely. "He has certain principles,—call them prejudices, if you like,—certain inflexible rules of conduct by which he regulates his life. One of these, which he shares with us all in some degree, forbids the recognition of the negro as a social equal."

"I do not know what Miller's social value may be," replied Dr. Burns, stoutly, "or whether you gain or lose by your attitude toward him. I have invited him here in a strictly professional capacity, with which his color is not at all concerned."

"Dr. Burns does not quite appreciate Major Carteret's point of view," said Dr. Price. "This is not with him an unimportant matter, or a mere question of prejudice, or even of personal taste. It is a sacred principle, lying at the very root of our social order, involving the purity and prestige of our race. You Northern gentlemen do not quite appreciate our situation; if you lived here a year or two you would act as we do. Of course," he added, diplomatically, "if there were no alternative—if Dr. Burns were willing to put Dr. Miller's presence on the ground of imperative necessity"—

"I do nothing of the kind, sir," retorted Dr. Burns with some heat. "I have not come all the way from Philadelphia to undertake an operation which I cannot perform without the aid of some particular physician. I merely stand upon my professional rights."

Carteret was deeply agitated. The operation must not be deferred; his child's life might be endangered by delay. If the negro's presence were indispensable he would even submit to it, though in order to avoid so painful a necessity, he would rather humble himself to the Northern doctor. The latter course involved merely a personal sacrifice—the former a vital principle. Perhaps there was another way of escape. Miller's presence could not but be distasteful to Mrs. Carteret for other reasons. Miller's wife was the living evidence of a painful episode in Mrs. Carteret's family, which the doctor's presence would inevitably recall. Once before, Mrs. Carteret's life had been endangered by encountering, at a time of great nervous strain, this ill-born sister and her child. She was even now upon the verge of collapse at the prospect of her child's suffering, and should be protected from the intrusion of any idea which might add to her distress.

"Dr. Burns," he said, with the suave courtesy which was part of his inheritance, "I beg your pardon for my heat, and throw myself upon your magnanimity, as between white men"—

"I am a gentleman, sir, before I am a white man," interposed Dr. Burns, slightly mollified, however, by Carteret's change of manner.

"The terms should be synonymous," Carteret could not refrain from saying. "As between white men, and gentlemen, I say to you, frankly, that there are vital, personal reasons, apart from Dr. Miller's color, why his presence in this house would be distasteful. With this statement, sir, I throw myself upon your mercy. My child's life is worth more to me than any earthly thing, and I must be governed by your decision."

Dr. Burns was plainly wavering. The clock moved with provoking slowness. Miller would be there in five minutes.

"May I speak with you privately a moment, doctor?" asked Dr. Price.

They withdrew from the room and were engaged in conversation for a few moments. Dr. Burns finally yielded.

"I shall nevertheless feel humiliated when I meet Miller again," he said, "but of course if there is a personal question involved, that alters the situation. Had it been merely a matter of color, I should have maintained my position. As things stand, I wash my hands of the whole affair, so far as Miller is concerned, like Pontius Pilate—yes, indeed, sir, I feel very much like that individual."

"I 'll explain the matter to Miller," returned Dr. Price, amiably, "and make it all right with him. We Southern people understand the negroes better than you do, sir. Why should we not? They have been constantly under our interested observation for several hundred years. You feel this vastly more than Miller will. He knows the feeling of the white people, and is accustomed to it. He wishes to live and do business here, and is quite too shrewd to antagonize his neighbors or come where he is not wanted. He is in fact too much of a gentleman to do so."

"I shall leave the explanation to you entirely," rejoined Dr. Burns, as they reëntered the other room.

Carteret led the way to the nursery, where the operation was to take place. Dr. Price lingered for a moment. Miller was not likely to be behind the hour, if he came at all, and it would be well to head him off before the operation began.

Scarcely had the rest left the room when the doorbell sounded, and a servant announced Dr. Miller.

Dr. Price stepped into the hall and met Miller face to face.

He had meant to state the situation to Miller frankly, but

now that the moment had come he wavered. He was a fine physician, but he shrank from strenuous responsibilities. It had been easy to theorize about the negro; it was more difficult to look this man in the eyes—whom at this moment he felt to be as essentially a gentleman as himself—and tell him the humiliating truth.

As a physician his method was to ease pain—he would rather take the risk of losing a patient from the use of an anæsthetic than from the shock of an operation. He liked Miller, wished him well, and would not wittingly wound his feelings. He really thought him too much of a gentleman for the town, in view of the restrictions with which he must inevitably be hampered. There was something melancholy, to a cultivated mind, about a sensitive, educated man who happened to be off color. Such a person was a sort of social misfit, an odd quantity, educated out of his own class, with no possible hope of entrance into that above it. He felt quite sure that if he had been in Miller's place, he would never have settled in the South—he would have moved to Europe, or to the West Indies, or some Central or South American state where questions of color were not regarded as vitally important.

Dr. Price did not like to lie, even to a negro. To a man of his own caste, his word was his bond. If it were painful to lie, it would be humiliating to be found out. The principle of *noblesse oblige* was also involved in the matter. His claim of superiority to the colored doctor rested fundamentally upon the fact that he was white and Miller was not; and yet this superiority, for which he could claim no credit, since he had not made himself, was the very breath of his nostrils,—he would not have changed places with the other for wealth untold; and as a gentleman, he would not care to have another gentleman, even a colored man, catch him in a lie. Of this, however, there was scarcely any danger. A word to the other surgeons would insure their corroboration of whatever he might tell Miller. No one of them would willingly wound Dr. Miller or embarrass Dr. Price; indeed, they need not know that Miller had come in time for the operation.

"I 'm sorry, Miller," he said with apparent regret, "but we were here ahead of time, and the case took a turn which would admit of no delay, so the gentlemen went in. Dr. Burns is with the patient now, and asked me to explain why we did not wait for you."

"I 'm sorry too," returned Miller, regretfully, but nothing doubting. He was well aware that in such cases danger might attend upon delay. He had lost his chance, through no fault of his own or of any one else.

"I hope that all is well?" he said, hesitatingly, not sure whether he would be asked to remain.

"All is well, so far. Step round to my office in the morning, Miller, or come in when you 're passing, and I 'll tell you the details."

This was tantamount to a dismissal, so Miller took his leave. Descending the doorsteps, he stood for a moment, undecided whether to return home or to go to the hotel and await the return of Dr. Burns, when he heard his name called from the house in a low tone.

"Oh, doctuh!"

He stepped back toward the door, outside of which stood the colored servant who had just let him out.

"Dat 's all a lie, doctuh," he whispered, "'bout de operation bein' already pe'fo'med. Dey-all had jes' gone in de minute befo' you come—Doctuh Price had n' even got out 'n de room. Dey be'n quollin' 'bout you fer de las' ha'f hour. Majah Ca'te'et say he would n' have you, an' de No'then doctuh say he would n't do nothin' widout you, an' Doctuh Price he j'ined in on bofe sides, an' dey had it hot an' heavy, nip an' tuck, till bimeby Majah Ca'te'et up an' say it wa'n't altogether yo' color he objected to, an' wid dat de No'then doctuh give in. He 's a fine man, suh, but dey wuz too much fer 'im!"

"Thank you, Sam, I 'm much obliged," returned Miller mechanically. "One likes to know the truth."

Truth, it has been said, is mighty, and must prevail; but it sometimes leaves a bad taste in the mouth. In the ordinary course of events Miller would not have anticipated such an invitation, and for that reason had appreciated it all the more. The rebuff came with a corresponding shock. He had the heart of a man, the sensibilities of a cultivated gentleman; the one was sore, the other deeply wounded. He was not altogether sure, upon reflection, whether he blamed Dr. Price very much for the amiable lie, which had been meant to spare his feelings, or thanked Sam a great deal for the unpalatable truth.

Janet met him at the door. "How is the baby?" she asked excitedly.

"Dr. Price says he is doing well."

"What is the matter, Will, and why are you back so soon?"

He would have spared her the story, but she was a woman, and would have it. He was wounded, too, and wanted sympathy, of which Janet was an exhaustless fountain. So he told her what had happened. She comforted him after the manner of a loving woman, and felt righteously indignant toward her sister's husband, who had thus been instrumental in the humiliation of her own. Her anger did not embrace her sister, and yet she felt obscurely that their unacknowledged relationship had been the malignant force which had given her husband pain, and defeated his honorable ambition.

When Dr. Price entered the nursery, Dr. Burns was leaning attentively over the operating table. The implements needed for the operation were all in readiness—the knives, the basin, the sponge, the materials for dressing the wound—all the ghastly paraphernalia of vivisection.

Mrs. Carteret had been banished to another room, where Clara vainly attempted to soothe her. Old Mammy Jane, still burdened by her fears, fervently prayed the good Lord to spare the life of the sweet little grandson of her dear old mistress.

Dr. Burns had placed his ear to the child's chest, which had been bared for the incision. Dr. Price stood ready to administer the anæsthetic. Little Dodie looked up with a faint expression of wonder, as if dimly conscious of some unusual event. The major shivered at the thought of what the child must undergo.

"There 's a change in his breathing," said Dr. Burns, lifting his head. "The whistling noise is less pronounced, and he breathes easier. The obstruction seems to have shifted."

Applying his ear again to the child's throat, he listened for a moment intently, and then picking the baby up from the table, gave it a couple of sharp claps between the shoulders.

Simultaneously a small object shot out from the child's mouth, struck Dr. Price in the neighborhood of his waistband, and then rattled lightly against the floor. Whereupon the baby, as though conscious of his narrow escape, smiled and gurgled, and reaching upward clutched the doctor's whiskers with his little hand, which, according to old Jane, had a stronger grip than any other infant's in Wellington.

VIII

THE CAMPAIGN DRAGS

THE CAMPAIGN for white supremacy was dragging. Carteret had set out, in the columns of the Morning Chronicle, all the reasons why this movement, inaugurated by the three men who had met, six months before, at the office of the Chronicle, should be supported by the white public. Negro citizenship was a grotesque farce—Sambo and Dinah raised from the kitchen to the cabinet were a spectacle to make the gods laugh. The laws by which it had been sought to put the negroes on a level with the whites must be swept away in theory, as they had failed in fact. If it were impossible, without a further education of public opinion, to secure the repeal of the fifteenth amendment, it was at least the solemn duty of the state to endeavor, through its own constitution, to escape from the domination of a weak and incompetent electorate and confine the negro to that inferior condition for which nature had evidently designed him.

In spite of the force and intelligence with which Carteret had expressed these and similar views, they had not met the immediate response anticipated. There were thoughtful men, willing to let well enough alone, who saw no necessity for such a movement. They believed that peace, prosperity, and popular education offered a surer remedy for social ills than the reopening of issues supposed to have been settled. There were timid men who shrank from civic strife. There were busy men, who had something else to do. There were a few fair men, prepared to admit, privately, that a class constituting half to two thirds of the population were fairly entitled to some representation in the law-making bodies. Perhaps there might have been found, somewhere in the state, a single white man ready to concede that all men were entitled to equal rights before the law.

That there were some white men who had learned little and forgotten nothing goes without saying, for knowledge and wisdom are not impartially distributed among even the most favored race. There were ignorant and vicious negroes, and they had a monopoly of neither ignorance nor crime, for there were prosperous negroes and poverty-stricken whites. Until Carteret and his committee began their baleful campaign the people of the state were living in peace and harmony. The anti-negro legislation in more southern states, with large negro majorities, had awakened scarcely an echo in this state, with a population two thirds white. Even the triumph of the Fusion party had not been regarded as a race issue. It remained for Carteret and his friends to discover, with inspiration from whatever supernatural source the discriminating reader may elect, that the darker race, docile by instinct, humble by training, patiently waiting upon its as yet uncertain destiny, was an incubus, a corpse chained to the body politic, and that the negro vote was a source of danger to the state, no matter how cast or by whom directed.

To discuss means for counteracting this apathy, a meeting of the "Big Three," as they had begun to designate themselves jocularly, was held at the office of the "Morning Chronicle," on the next day but one after little Dodie's fortunate escape from the knife.

"It seems," said General Belmont, opening the discussion, "as though we had undertaken more than we can carry through. It is clear that we must reckon on opposition, both at home and abroad. If we are to hope for success, we must extend the lines of our campaign. The North, as well as our own people, must be convinced that we have right upon our side. We are conscious of the purity of our motives, but we should avoid even the appearance of evil."

McBane was tapping the floor impatiently with his foot during this harangue.

"I don't see the use," he interrupted, "of so much beating about the bush. We may as well be honest about this thing. We are going to put the niggers down because we want to, and think we can; so why waste our time in mere pretense? I 'm no hypocrite myself,—if I want a thing I take it, provided I 'm strong enough."

"My dear captain," resumed the general, with biting suavity, "your frankness does you credit,—'an honest man 's the noblest work of God,'—but we cannot carry on politics in these degenerate times without a certain amount of diplomacy. In the good old days when your father was alive, and perhaps nowadays in the discipline of convicts, direct and simple methods might be safely resorted to; but this is a modern age, and in dealing with so fundamental a right as the suffrage we must profess a decent regard for the opinions of even that misguided portion of mankind which may not agree with us. This is the age of crowds, and we must have the crowd with us."

The captain flushed at the allusion to his father's calling, at which he took more offense than at the mention of his own. He knew perfectly well that these old aristocrats, while reaping the profits of slavery, had despised the instruments by which they were attained—the poor-white overseer only less than the black slave. McBane was rich; he lived in Wellington, but he had never been invited to the home of either General Belmont or Major Carteret, nor asked to join the club of which they were members. His face, therefore, wore a distinct scowl, and his single eye glowed ominously. He would help these fellows carry the state for white supremacy, and then he would have his innings,—he would have more to say than they dreamed, as to who should fill the offices under the new deal. Men of no better birth or breeding than he had represented Southern states in Congress since the war. Why should he not run for governor, representative, whatever he chose? He had money enough to buy out half a dozen of these broken-down aristocrats, and money was all-powerful.

"You see, captain," the general went on, looking McBane smilingly and unflinchingly in the eye, "we need white immigration—we need Northern capital. 'A good name is better than great riches,' and we must prove our cause a righteous one."

"We must be armed at all points," added Carteret, "and prepared for defense as well as for attack,—we must make our campaign a national one."

"For instance," resumed the general, "you, Carteret, represent the Associated Press. Through your hands passes all the news of the state. What more powerful medium for the propagation of an idea? The man who would govern a nation by writing its songs was a blethering idiot beside the fellow who can edit its news dispatches. The negroes are playing into our hands,—every crime that one of them commits is reported by us. With the latitude they have had in this state they are growing more impudent and self-assertive every day. A yellow demagogue in New York made a speech only a few days ago, in which he deliberately, and in cold blood, advised negroes to defend themselves to the death when attacked by white people! I remember well the time when it was death for a negro to strike a white man."

"It 's death now, if he strikes the right one," interjected McBane, restored to better humor by this mention of a congenial subject.

The general smiled a fine smile. He had heard the story of how McBane had lost his other eye.

"The local negro paper is quite outspoken, too," continued the general, "if not impudent. We must keep track of that; it may furnish us some good campaign material."

"Yes," returned Carteret, "we must see to that. I threw a copy into the waste-basket this morning, without looking at it. Here it is now!"

IX

A WHITE MAN'S "NIGGER"

CARTERET fished from the depths of the waste-basket and handed to the general an eighteen by twenty-four sheet, poorly printed on cheap paper, with a "patent" inside, a number of advertisements of proprietary medicines, quack doctors, and fortune-tellers, and two or three columns of editorial and local news. Candor compels the admission that it was not an impressive sheet in any respect, except when regarded as the first local effort of a struggling people to make public expression of their life and aspirations. From this point of view it did not speak at all badly for a class to whom, a generation before, newspapers, books, and learning had been forbidden fruit.

"It 's an elegant specimen of journalism, is n't it?" laughed the general, airily. "Listen to this 'ad':—

" 'Kinky, curly hair made straight by one application of our specific. Our face bleach will turn the skin of a black or brown person four or five shades lighter, and of a mulatto perfectly white. When you get the color you wish, stop using the preparation.'

"Just look at those heads!—'Before using' and 'After using.' We 'd better hurry, or there 'll be no negroes to disfranchise! If they don't stop till they get the color they desire, and the stuff works according to contract, they 'll all be white. Ah! what have we here? This looks as though it might be serious."

Opening the sheet the general read aloud an editorial article, to which Carteret listened intently, his indignation increasing in strength from the first word to the last, while McBane's face grew darkly purple with anger.

The article was a frank and somewhat bold discussion of lynching and its causes. It denied that most lynchings were for the offense most generally charged as their justification, and declared that, even of those seemingly traced to this cause, many were not for crimes at all, but for voluntary acts which might naturally be expected to follow from the miscegenation laws by which it was sought, in all the Southern

States, to destroy liberty of contract, and, for the purpose of maintaining a fanciful purity of race, to make crimes of marriages to which neither nature nor religion nor the laws of other states interposed any insurmountable barrier. Such an article in a Northern newspaper would have attracted no special attention, and might merely have furnished food to an occasional reader for serious thought upon a subject not exactly agreeable; but coming from a colored man, in a Southern city, it was an indictment of the laws and social system of the South that could not fail of creating a profound sensation.

"Infamous—infamous!" exclaimed Carteret, his voice trembling with emotion. "The paper should be suppressed immediately."

"The impudent nigger ought to be horsewhipped and run out of town," growled McBane.

"Gentlemen," said the general soothingly, after the first burst of indignation had subsided, "I believe we can find a more effective use for this article, which, by the way, will not bear too close analysis,—there 's some truth in it, at least there 's an argument."

"That is not the point," interrupted Carteret.

"No," interjected McBane with an oath, "that ain't at all the point. Truth or not, no damn nigger has any right to say it."

"This article," said Carteret, "violates an unwritten law of the South. If we are to tolerate this race of weaklings among us, until they are eliminated by the stress of competition, it must be upon terms which we lay down. One of our conditions is violated by this article, in which our wisdom is assailed, and our women made the subject of offensive comment. We must make known our disapproval."

"I say lynch the nigger, break up the press, and burn down the newspaper office," McBane responded promptly.

"Gentlemen," interposed the general, "would you mind suspending the discussion for a moment, while I send Jerry across the street? I think I can then suggest a better plan."

Carteret rang the bell for Jerry, who answered promptly. He had been expecting such a call ever since the gentlemen had gone in.

"Jerry," said the general, "step across to Brown's and tell

him to send me three Calhoun cocktails. Wait for them,—here 's the money."

"Yas, suh," replied Jerry, taking the proffered coin.

"And make has'e, charcoal," added McBane, "for we 're gettin' damn dry."

A momentary cloud of annoyance darkened Carteret's brow. McBane had always grated upon his aristocratic susceptibilities. The captain was an upstart, a product of the democratic idea operating upon the poor white man, the descendant of the indentured bondservant and the socially unfit. He had wealth and energy, however, and it was necessary to make use of him; but the example of such men was a strong incentive to Carteret in his campaign against the negro. It was distasteful enough to rub elbows with an illiterate and vulgar white man of no ancestry,—the risk of similar contact with negroes was to be avoided at any cost. He could hardly expect McBane to be a gentleman, but when among men of that class he might at least try to imitate their manners. A gentleman did not order his own servants around offensively, to say nothing of another's.

The general had observed Carteret's annoyance, and remarked pleasantly while they waited for the servant's return:—

"Jerry, now, is a very good negro. He 's not one of your new negroes, who think themselves as good as white men, and want to run the government. Jerry knows his place,—he is respectful, humble, obedient, and content with the face and place assigned to him by nature."

"Yes, he 's one of the best of 'em," sneered McBane. "He 'll call any man 'master' for a quarter, or 'God' for half a dollar; for a dollar he 'll grovel at your feet, and for a cast-off coat you can buy an option on his immortal soul,—if he has one! I 've handled niggers for ten years, and I know 'em from the ground up. They 're all alike,—they 're a scrub race, an affliction to the country, and the quicker we 're rid of 'em all the better."

Carteret had nothing to say by way of dissent. McBane's sentiments, in their last analysis, were much the same as his, though he would have expressed them less brutally.

"The negro," observed the general, daintily flicking the ash from his cigar, "is all right in his place and very useful to the community. We lived on his labor for quite a long time, and lived very well. Nevertheless we are better off without slavery, for we can get more out of the free negro, and with less responsibility. I really do not see how we could get along without the negroes. If they were all like Jerry, we 'd have no trouble with them."

Having procured the drinks, Jerry, the momentary subject of the race discussion which goes on eternally in the South, was making his way back across the street, somewhat disturbed in mind.

"O Lawd!" he groaned, "I never troubles trouble till trouble troubles me; but w'en I got dem drinks befo', Gin'l Belmont gimme half a dollar an' tol' me ter keep de change. Dis time he did n' say nothin' 'bout de change. I s'pose he jes' fergot erbout it, but w'at is a po' nigger gwine ter do w'en he has ter conten' wid w'ite folks's fergitfulniss? I don' see no way but ter do some fergittin' myse'f. I 'll jes' stan' outside de do' here till dey gits so wrop' up in deir talk dat dey won' 'member nothin' e'se, an' den at de right minute I 'll han' de glasses 'roun, an' mos' lackly de gin'l 'll fergit all 'bout de change."

While Jerry stood outside, the conversation within was plainly audible, and some inkling of its purport filtered through his mind.

"Now, gentlemen," the general was saying, "here 's my plan. That editorial in the negro newspaper is good campaign matter, but we should reserve it until it will be most effective. Suppose we just stick it in a pigeon-hole, and let the editor,—what 's his name?"

"The nigger's name is Barber," replied McBane. "I 'd like to have him under me for a month or two; he 'd write no more editorials."

"Let Barber have all the rope he wants," resumed the general, "and he 'll be sure to hang himself. In the mean time we will continue to work up public opinion,—we can use this letter privately for that purpose,—and when the state campaign opens we 'll print the editorial, with suitable comment, scatter it broadcast throughout the state, fire the Southern heart, organize the white people on the color line, have a little demonstration with red shirts and shotguns, scare the negroes into fits, win the state for white supremacy, and teach our colored fellow citizens that we are tired of negro domination and have put an end to it forever. The Afro-American Banner will doubtless die about the same time."

"And so will the editor!" exclaimed McBane ferociously; "I 'll see to that. But I wonder where that nigger is with them cocktails? I 'm so thirsty I could swallow blue blazes."

"Here 's yo' drinks, gin'l," announced Jerry, entering with the glasses on a tray.

The gentlemen exchanged compliments and imbibed—McBane at a gulp, Carteret with more deliberation, leaving about half the contents of his glass.

The general drank slowly, with every sign of appreciation. "If the illustrious statesman," he observed, "whose name this mixture bears, had done nothing more than invent it, his fame would still deserve to go thundering down the endless ages."

"It ain't bad liquor," assented McBane, smacking his lips.

Jerry received the empty glasses on the tray and left the room. He had scarcely gained the hall when the general called him back.

"O Lawd!" groaned Jerry, "he 's gwine ter ax me fer de change. Yas, suh, yas, suh; comin', gin'l, comin', suh!"

"You may keep the change, Jerry," said the general.

Jerry's face grew radiant at this announcement. "Yas, suh, gin'l; thank y', suh; much obleedzed, suh. I wuz jus' gwine ter fetch it in, suh, w'en I had put de tray down. Thank y', suh, truly, suh!"

Jerry backed and bowed himself out into the hall.

"Dat wuz a close shave," he muttered, as he swallowed the remaining contents of Major Carteret's glass. "I 'lowed dem twenty cents wuz gone dat time,—an' whar I wuz gwine ter git de money ter take my gal ter de chu'ch festibal ter-night, de Lawd only knows!—'less'n I borried it off'n Mr. Ellis, an' I owes him sixty cents a'ready. But I wonduh w'at dem w'ite folks in dere is up ter? Dere 's one thing sho',—dey 're gwine ter git after de niggers some way er 'nuther, an' w'en dey does, whar is Jerry gwine ter be? Dat 's de mos' impo'tantes' question. I 'm gwine ter look at dat newspaper dey be'n talkin' 'bout, an' 'less'n my min' changes might'ly, I 'm gwine ter keep my mouf shet an' stan' in wid de Angry-Saxon race,—ez dey calls deyse'ves nowadays,—an' keep on de right side er my bread an' meat. W'at nigger ever give me twenty cents in all my bawn days?"

"By the way, major," said the general, who lingered behind McBane as they were leaving, "is Miss Clara's marriage definitely settled upon?"

"Well, general, not exactly; but it 's the understanding that they will marry when they are old enough."

"I was merely thinking," the general went on, "that if I were you I 'd speak to Tom about cards and liquor. He gives more time to both than a young man can afford. I 'm speaking in his interest and in Miss Clara's,—we of the old families ought to stand together."

"Thank you, general, for the hint. I 'll act upon it."

This political conference was fruitful in results. Acting upon the plans there laid out, McBane traveled extensively through the state, working up sentiment in favor of the new movement. He possessed a certain forceful eloquence; and white supremacy was so obviously the divine intention that he had merely to affirm the doctrine in order to secure adherents.

General Belmont, whose business required him to spend much of the winter in Washington and New York, lost no opportunity to get the ear of lawmakers, editors, and other leaders of national opinion, and to impress upon them, with persuasive eloquence, the impossibility of maintaining existing conditions, and the tremendous blunder which had been made in conferring the franchise upon the emancipated race.

Carteret conducted the press campaign, and held out to the Republicans of the North the glittering hope that, with the elimination of the negro vote, and a proper deference to Southern feeling, a strong white Republican party might be built up in the New South. How well the bait took is a matter of history,—but the promised result is still in the future. The disfranchisement of the negro has merely changed the form of the same old problem. The negro had no vote before the rebellion, and few other rights, and yet the negro question was, for a century, the pivot of American politics. It plunged the nation into a bloody war, and it will trouble the

American government and the American conscience until a sustained attempt is made to settle it upon principles of justice and equity.

The personal ambitions entertained by the leaders of this movement are but slightly involved in this story. McBane's aims have been touched upon elsewhere. The general would have accepted the nomination for governor of the state, with a vision of a senatorship in the future. Carteret hoped to vindicate the supremacy of his race, and make the state fit for his son to live in, and, incidentally, he would not refuse any office, worthy of his dignity, which a grateful people might thrust upon him.

So powerful a combination of bigot, self-seeking demagogue, and astute politician was fraught with grave menace to the peace of the state and the liberties of the people,—by which is meant the whole people, and not any one class, sought to be built up at the expense of another.

X

DELAMERE PLAYS A TRUMP

CARTERET did not forget what General Belmont had said in regard to Tom. The major himself had been young, not so very long ago, and was inclined toward indulgence for the foibles of youth. A young gentleman should have a certain knowledge of life,—but there were limits. Clara's future happiness must not be imperiled.

The opportunity to carry out this purpose was not long delayed. Old Mr. Delamere wished to sell some timber which had been cut at Belleview, and sent Tom down to the Chronicle office to leave an advertisement. The major saw him at the desk, invited him into his sanctum, and delivered him a mild lecture. The major was kind, and talked in a fatherly way about the danger of extremes, the beauty of moderation, and the value of discretion as a rule of conduct. He mentioned collaterally the unblemished honor of a fine old family, its contemplated alliance with his own, and dwelt upon the sweet simplicity of Clara's character. The major was a man of feeling and of tact, and could not have put the subject in a way less calculated to wound the *amour propre* of a very young man.

Delamere had turned red with anger while the major was speaking. He was impulsive, and an effort was required to keep back the retort that sprang once or twice to his lips; but his conscience was not clear, and he could not afford hard words with Clara's guardian and his grandfather's friend. Clara was rich, and the most beautiful girl in town; they were engaged; he loved her as well as he could love anything of which he seemed sure; and he did not mean that any one else should have her. The major's mild censure disturbed slightly his sense of security; and while the major's manner did not indicate that he knew anything definite against him, it would be best to let well enough alone.

"Thank you, major," he said, with well-simulated frankness. "I realize that I may have been a little careless, more from thoughtlessness than anything else; but my heart is all right, sir, and I am glad that my conduct has been brought to your attention, for what you have said enables me to see it in a different light. I will be more careful of my company hereafter; for I love Clara, and mean to try to be worthy of her. Do you know whether she will be at home this evening?"

"I have heard nothing to the contrary," replied the major warmly. "Call her up by telephone and ask—or come up and see. You 're always welcome, my boy."

Upon leaving the office, which was on the second floor, Tom met Ellis coming up the stairs. It had several times of late occurred to Tom that Ellis had a sneaking fondness for Clara. Panoplied in his own engagement, Tom had heretofore rather enjoyed the idea of a hopeless rival. Ellis was such a solemn prig, and took life so seriously, that it was a pleasure to see him sit around sighing for the unattainable. That he should be giving pain to Ellis added a certain zest to his own enjoyment.

But this interview with the major had so disquieted him that upon meeting Ellis upon the stairs he was struck by a sudden suspicion. He knew that Major Carteret seldom went to the Clarendon Club, and that he must have got his information from some one else. Ellis was a member of the club, and a frequent visitor. Who more likely than he to try to poison Clara's mind, or the minds of her friends, against her accepted lover? Tom did not think that the world was using him well of late; bad luck had pursued him, in cards and other things, and despite his assumption of humility, Carteret's lecture had left him in an ugly mood. He nodded curtly to Ellis without relaxing the scowl that disfigured his handsome features.

"That 's the damned sneak who 's been giving me away," he muttered. "I 'll get even with him yet for this."

Delamere's suspicions with regard to Ellis's feelings were not, as we have seen, entirely without foundation. Indeed, he had underestimated the strength of this rivalry and its chances of success. Ellis had been watching Delamere for a year. There had been nothing surreptitious about it, but his interest in Clara had led him to note things about his favored rival which might have escaped the attention of others less concerned.

Ellis was an excellent judge of character, and had formed a

very decided opinion of Tom Delamere. To Ellis, unbiased by ancestral traditions, biased perhaps by jealousy, Tom Delamere was a type of the degenerate aristocrat. If, as he had often heard, it took three or four generations to make a gentleman, and as many more to complete the curve and return to the base from which it started, Tom Delamere belonged somewhere on the downward slant, with large possibilities of further decline. Old Mr. Delamere, who might be taken as the apex of an ideal aristocratic development, had been distinguished, during his active life, as Ellis had learned, for courage and strength of will, courtliness of bearing, deference to his superiors, of whom there had been few, courtesy to his equals, kindness and consideration for those less highly favored, and above all, a scrupulous sense of honor; his grandson Tom was merely the shadow without the substance, the empty husk without the grain. Of grace he had plenty. In manners he could be perfect, when he so chose. Courage and strength he had none. Ellis had seen this fellow, who boasted of his descent from a line of cavaliers, turn pale with fright and spring from a buggy to which was harnessed a fractious horse, which a negro stable-boy drove fearlessly. A valiant carpet-knight, skilled in all parlor exercises, great at whist or euchre, a dream of a dancer, unexcelled in cakewalk or "coon" impersonations, for which he was in large social demand, Ellis had seen him kick an inoffensive negro out of his path and treat a poor-white man with scant courtesy. He suspected Delamere of cheating at cards, and knew that others entertained the same suspicion. For while regular in his own habits,—his poverty would not have permitted him any considerable extravagance,—Ellis's position as a newspaper man kept him in touch with what was going on about town. He was a member, proposed by Carteret, of the Clarendon Club, where cards were indulged in within reasonable limits, and a certain set were known to bet dollars in terms of dimes.

Delamere was careless, too, about money matters. He had a habit of borrowing, right and left, small sums which might be conveniently forgotten by the borrower, and for which the lender would dislike to ask. Ellis had a strain of thrift, derived from a Scotch ancestry, and a tenacious memory for financial details. Indeed, he had never had so much money that he could lose track of it. He never saw Delamere without being distinctly conscious that Delamere owed him four dollars, which he had lent at a time when he could ill afford to spare it. It was a prerogative of aristocracy, Ellis reflected, to live upon others, and the last privilege which aristocracy in decay would willingly relinquish. Neither did the aristocratic memory seem able to retain the sordid details of a small pecuniary transaction.

No doubt the knowledge that Delamere was the favored lover of Miss Pemberton lent a touch of bitterness to Ellis's reflections upon his rival. Ellis had no grievance against the "aristocracy" of Wellington. The "best people" had received him cordially, though his father had not been of their caste; but Ellis hated a hypocrite, and despised a coward, and he felt sure that Delamere was both. Otherwise he would have struggled against his love for Clara Pemberton. His passion for her had grown with his appreciation of Delamere's unworthiness. As a friend of the family, he knew the nature and terms of the engagement, and that if the marriage took place at all, it would not be for at least a year. This was a long time,—many things might happen in a year, especially to a man like Tom Delamere. If for any reason Delamere lost his chance, Ellis meant to be next in the field. He had not made love to Clara, but he had missed no opportunity of meeting her and making himself quietly and unobtrusively agreeable.

On the day after this encounter with Delamere on the stairs of the Chronicle office, Ellis, while walking down Vine Street, met old Mrs. Ochiltree. She was seated in her own buggy, which was of ancient build and pattern, driven by her colored coachman and man of all work.

"Mr. Ellis," she called in a shrill voice, having directed her coachman to draw up at the curb as she saw the young man approaching, "come here. I want to speak to you."

Ellis came up to the buggy and stood uncovered beside it.

"People are saying," said Mrs. Ochiltree, "that Tom Delamere is drinking hard, and has to be carried home intoxicated, two or three times a week, by old Mr. Delamere's man Sandy. Is there any truth in the story?"

"My dear Mrs. Ochiltree, I am not Tom Delamere's keeper. Sandy could tell you better than I."

"You are dodging my question, Mr. Ellis. Sandy would n't tell me the truth, and I know that you would n't lie,—you don't look like a liar. They say Tom is gambling scandalously. What do you know about that?"

"You must excuse me, Mrs. Ochiltree. A great deal of what we hear is mere idle gossip, and the truth is often grossly exaggerated. I 'm a member of the same club with Delamere, and gentlemen who belong to the same club are not in the habit of talking about one another. As long as a man retains his club membership, he 's presumed to be a gentleman. I would n't say anything against Delamere if I could."

"You don't need to," replied the old lady, shaking her finger at him with a cunning smile. "You are a very open young man, Mr. Ellis, and I can read you like a book. You are much smarter than you look, but you can't fool me. Good-morning."

Mrs. Ochiltree drove immediately to her niece's, where she found Mrs. Carteret and Clara at home. Clara was very fond of the baby, and was holding him in her arms. He was a fine baby, and bade fair to realize the bright hopes built upon him.

"You hold a baby very naturally, Clara," chuckled the old lady. "I suppose you are in training. But you ought to talk to Tom. I have just learned from Mr. Ellis that Tom is carried home drunk two or three times a week, and that he is gambling in the most reckless manner imaginable."

Clara's eyes flashed indignantly. Ere she could speak, Mrs. Carteret exclaimed:—

"Why, Aunt Polly! did Mr. Ellis say that?"

"I got it from Dinah," she replied, "who heard it from her husband, who learned it from a waiter at the club. And"—

"Pshaw!" said Mrs. Carteret, "mere servants' gossip."

"No, it is n't, Olivia. I met Mr. Ellis on the street, and asked him point blank, and he did n't deny it. He 's a member of the club, and ought to know."

"Well, Aunt Polly, it can't be true. Tom is here every other night, and how could he carry on so without showing the signs of it? and where would he get the money? You know he has only a moderate allowance."

"He may win it at cards,—it 's better to be born lucky than rich," returned Mrs. Ochiltree. "Then he has expectations, and can get credit. There 's no doubt that Tom is going on shamefully."

Clara's indignation had not yet found vent in speech; Olivia had said all that was necessary, but she had been thinking rapidly. Even if all this had been true, why should Mr. Ellis have said it? Or, if he had not stated it directly, he had left the inference to be drawn. It seemed a most unfair and ungentlemanly thing. What motive could Ellis have for such an act?

She was not long in reaching a conclusion which was not flattering to Ellis. Mr. Ellis came often to the house, and she had enjoyed his society in a friendly way. That he had found her pleasant company had been very evident. She had never taken his attentions seriously, however, or regarded his visits as made especially to her, nor had the rest of the family treated them from that point of view. Her engagement to Tom Delamere, though not yet formally ratified, was so well understood by the world of Wellington that Mr. Ellis would scarcely have presumed to think of her as anything more than a friend.

This revelation of her aunt's, however, put a different face upon his conduct. Certain looks and sighs and enigmatical remarks of Ellis, to which she had paid but casual attention and attached no particular significance, now recurred to her memory with a new meaning. He had now evidently tried, in a roundabout way, to besmirch Tom's character and undermine him in her regard. While loving Tom, she had liked Ellis well enough, as a friend; but he had abused the privileges of friendship, and she would teach him a needed lesson.

Nevertheless, Mrs. Ochiltree's story had given Clara food for thought. She was uneasily conscious, after all, that there might be a grain of truth in what had been said, enough, at least, to justify her in warning Tom to be careful, lest his enemies should distort some amiable weakness into a serious crime.

She put this view of the case to Tom at their next meeting, assuring him, at the same time, of her unbounded faith and confidence. She did not mention Ellis's name, lest Tom, in righteous indignation, might do something rash, which he might thereafter regret. If any subtler or more obscure motive kept her silent as to Ellis, she was not aware of it; for Clara's views of life were still in the objective stage, and she had not yet fathomed the deepest recesses of her own consciousness.

Delamere had the cunning of weakness. He knew, too, better than any one else could know, how much truth there was in the rumors concerning him, and whether or not they could be verified too easily for him to make an indignant denial. After a little rapid reflection, he decided upon a different course.

"Clara," he said with a sigh, taking the hand which she generously yielded to soften any suggestion of reproach which he may have read into her solicitude, "you are my guardian angel. I do not know, of course, who has told you this pack of lies,—for I can see that you have heard more than you have told me,—but I think I could guess the man they came from. I am not perfect, Clara, though I have done nothing of which a gentleman should be ashamed. There is one sure way to stop the tongue of calumny. My home life is not ideal,—grandfather is an old, weak man, and the house needs the refining and softening influence of a lady's presence. I do not love club life; its ideals are not elevating. With you by my side, dearest, I should be preserved from every influence except the purest and the best. Don't you think, dearest, that the major might be induced to shorten our weary term of waiting?"

"Oh, Tom," she demurred blushingly, "I shall be young enough at eighteen; and you are barely twenty-one."

But Tom proved an eloquent pleader, and love a still more persuasive advocate. Clara spoke to the major the same evening, who looked grave at the suggestion, and said he would think about it. They were both very young; but where both parties were of good family, in good health and good circumstances, an early marriage might not be undesirable. Tom was perhaps a little unsettled, but blood would tell in the long run, and marriage always exercised a steadying influence.

The only return, therefore, which Ellis received for his well-meant effort to ward off Mrs. Ochiltree's embarrassing inquiries was that he did not see Clara upon his next visit, which was made one afternoon while he was on night duty at the office. In conversation with Mrs. Carteret he learned that Clara's marriage had been definitely agreed upon, and the date fixed,—it was to take place in about six months. Meeting Miss Pemberton on the street the following day, he received the slightest of nods. When he called again at the house, after a week of misery, she treated him with a sarcastic coolness which chilled his heart.

"How have I offended you, Miss Clara?" he demanded desperately, when they were left alone for a moment.

"Offended me?" she replied, lifting her eyebrows with an air of puzzled surprise. "Why, Mr. Ellis! What could have put such a notion into your head? Oh dear, I think I hear Dodie,—I know you 'll excuse me, Mr. Ellis, won't you? Sister Olivia will be back in a moment; and we 're expecting Aunt Polly this afternoon,—if you 'll stay awhile she 'll be glad to talk to you! You can tell her all the interesting news about your friends!"

XI

THE BABY AND THE BIRD

WHEN Ellis, after this rebuff, had disconsolately taken his leave, Clara, much elated at the righteous punishment she had inflicted upon the slanderer, ran upstairs to the nursery, and, snatching Dodie from Mammy Jane's arms, began dancing gayly with him round the room.

"Look a-hyuh, honey," said Mammy Jane, "you better be keerful wid dat chile, an' don' drap 'im on de flo'. You might let him fall on his head an' break his neck. My, my! but you two does make a pretty pictur'! You 'll be wantin' ole Jane ter come an' nuss yo' child'en some er dese days," she chuckled unctuously.

Mammy Jane had been very much disturbed by the recent dangers through which little Dodie had passed; and his escape from strangulation, in the first place, and then from the knife had impressed her as little less than miraculous. She was not certain whether this result had been brought about by her manipulation of the buried charm, or by the prayers which had been offered for the child, but was inclined to believe that both had coöperated to avert the threatened calamity. The favorable outcome of this particular incident had not, however, altered the general situation. Prayers and charms, after all, were merely temporary things, which must be constantly renewed, and might be forgotten or overlooked; while the mole, on the contrary, neither faded nor went away. If its malign influence might for a time seem to disappear, it was merely lying dormant, like the germs of some deadly disease, awaiting its opportunity to strike at an unguarded spot.

Clara and the baby were laughing in great glee, when a mockingbird, perched on the topmost bough of a small tree opposite the nursery window, burst suddenly into song, with many a trill and quaver. Clara, with the child in her arms, sprang to the open window.

"Sister Olivia," she cried, turning her face toward Mrs.

Carteret, who at that moment entered the room, "come and look at Dodie."

The baby was listening intently to the music, meanwhile gurgling with delight, and reaching his chubby hands toward the source of this pleasing sound. It seemed as though the mockingbird were aware of his appreciative audience, for he ran through the songs of a dozen different birds, selecting, with the discrimination of a connoisseur and entire confidence in his own powers, those which were most difficult and most alluring.

Mrs. Carteret approached the window, followed by Mammy Jane, who waddled over to join the admiring party. So absorbed were the three women in the baby and the bird that neither one of them observed a neat top buggy, drawn by a sleek sorrel pony, passing slowly along the street before the house. In the buggy was seated a lady, and beside her a little boy, dressed in a child's sailor suit and a straw hat. The lady, with a wistful expression, was looking toward the party grouped in the open window.

Mrs. Carteret, chancing to lower her eyes for an instant, caught the other woman's look directed toward her and her child. With a glance of cold aversion she turned away from the window.

Old Mammy Jane had observed this movement, and had divined the reason for it. She stood beside Clara, watching the retreating buggy.

"Uhhuh!" she said to herself, "it 's huh sister Janet! She ma'ied a doctuh, an' all dat, an' she lives in a big house, an' she 's be'n roun' de worl' an de Lawd knows where e'se; but Mis' 'Livy don' like de sight er her, an' never will, ez long ez de sun rises an' sets. Dey ce't'nly does favor one anudder,—anybody mought 'low dey wuz twins, ef dey did n' know better. Well, well! Fo'ty yeahs ago who 'd 'a' ever expected ter see a nigger gal ridin' in her own buggy? My, my! but I don' know,—I don' know! It don' look right, an' it ain' gwine ter las'!—you can't make me b'lieve!"

Meantime Janet, stung by Mrs. Carteret's look,—the nearest approach she had ever made to a recognition of her sister's existence,—had turned away with hardening face. She had struck her pony sharply with the whip, much to the gentle creature's surprise, when the little boy, who was still looking back, caught his mother's sleeve and exclaimed excitedly:—

"Look, look, mamma! The baby,—the baby!"

Janet turned instantly, and with a mother's instinct gave an involuntary cry of alarm.

At the moment when Mrs. Carteret had turned away from the window, and while Mammy Jane was watching Janet, Clara had taken a step forward, and was leaning against the window-sill. The baby, convulsed with delight, had given a spasmodic spring and slipped from Clara's arms. Instinctively the young woman gripped the long skirt as it slipped through her hands, and held it tenaciously, though too frightened for an instant to do more. Mammy Jane, ashen with sudden dread, uttered an inarticulate scream, but retained self-possession enough to reach down and draw up the child, which hung dangerously suspended, head downward, over the brick pavement below.

"Oh, Clara, Clara, how could you!" exclaimed Mrs. Carteret reproachfully; "you might have killed my child!"

She had snatched the child from Jane's arms, and was holding him closely to her own breast. Struck by a sudden thought, she drew near the window and looked out. Twice within a few weeks her child had been in serious danger, and upon each occasion a member of the Miller family had been involved, for she had heard of Dr. Miller's presumption in trying to force himself where he must have known he would be unwelcome.

Janet was just turning her head away as the buggy moved slowly off. Olivia felt a violent wave of antipathy sweep over her toward this baseborn sister who had thus thrust herself beneath her eyes. If she had not cast her brazen glance toward the window, she herself would not have turned away and lost sight of her child. To this shameless intrusion, linked with Clara's carelessness, had been due the catastrophe, so narrowly averted, which might have darkened her own life forever. She took to her bed for several days, and for a long time was cold toward Clara, and did not permit her to touch the child.

Mammy Jane entertained a theory of her own about the accident, by which the blame was placed, in another way, exactly where Mrs. Carteret had laid it. Julia's daughter, Janet, had been looking intently toward the window just before little Dodie had sprung from Clara's arms. Might she not have cast the evil eye upon the baby, and sought thereby to draw him out of the window? One would not ordinarily expect so young a woman to possess such a power, but she might have acquired it, for this very purpose, from some more experienced person. By the same reasoning, the mockingbird might have been a familiar of the witch, and the two might have conspired to lure the infant to destruction. Whether this were so or not, the transaction at least wore a peculiar look. There was no use telling Mis' 'Livy about it, for she did n't believe, or pretended not to believe, in witchcraft and conjuration. But one could not be too careful. The child was certainly born to be exposed to great dangers,—the mole behind the left ear was an unfailing sign,—and no precaution should be omitted to counteract its baleful influence.

While adjusting the baby's crib, a few days later, Mrs. Carteret found fastened under one of the slats a small bag of cotton cloth, about half an inch long and tied with a black thread, upon opening which she found a few small roots or fibres and a pinch of dried and crumpled herbs. It was a good-luck charm which Mammy Jane had placed there to ward off the threatened evil from the grandchild of her dear old mistress. Mrs. Carteret's first impulse was to throw the bag into the fire, but on second thoughts she let it remain. To remove it would give unnecessary pain to the old nurse. Of course these old negro superstitions were absurd,—but if the charm did no good, it at least would do no harm.

XII

ANOTHER SOUTHERN PRODUCT

ONE MORNING shortly after the opening of the hospital, while Dr. Miller was making his early rounds, a new patient walked in with a smile on his face and a broken arm hanging limply by his side. Miller recognized in him a black giant by the name of Josh Green, who for many years had worked on the docks for Miller's father,—and simultaneously identified him as the dust-begrimed negro who had stolen a ride to Wellington on the trucks of a passenger car.

"Well, Josh," asked the doctor, as he examined the fracture, "how did you get this? Been fighting again?"

"No, suh, I don' s'pose you could ha'dly call it a fight. One er dem dagoes off'n a Souf American boat gimme some er his jaw, an' I give 'im a back answer, an' here I is wid a broken arm. He got holt er a belayin'-pin befo' I could hit 'im."

"What became of the other man?" demanded Miller suspiciously. He perceived, from the indifference with which Josh bore the manipulation of the fractured limb, that such an accident need not have interfered seriously with the use of the remaining arm, and he knew that Josh had a reputation for absolute fearlessness.

"Lemme see," said Josh reflectively, "ef I kin 'member w'at *did* become er him! Oh, yes, I 'member now! Dey tuck him ter de Marine Horspittle in de amberlance, 'cause his leg wuz broke, an' I reckon somethin' must 'a' accident'ly hit 'im in de jaw, fer he wuz scatt'rin' teeth all de way 'long de street. I did n' wan' ter kill de man, fer he might have somebody dependin' on 'im, an' I knows how dat 'd be ter dem. But no man kin call me a damn' low-down nigger and keep on enjoyin' good health right along."

"It was considerate of you to spare his life," said Miller dryly, "but you 'll hit the wrong man some day. These are bad times for bad negroes. You 'll get into a quarrel with a white man, and at the end of it there 'll be a lynching, or a funeral.

You 'd better be peaceable and endure a little injustice, rather than run the risk of a sudden and violent death."

"I expec's ter die a vi'lent death in a quarrel wid a w'ite man," replied Josh, in a matter-of-fact tone, "an' fu'thermo', he 's gwine ter die at the same time, er a little befo'. I be'n takin' my own time 'bout killin' 'im; I ain' be'n crowdin' de man, but I 'll be ready after a w'ile, an' den he kin look out!"

"And I suppose you 're merely keeping in practice on these other fellows who come your way. When I get your arm dressed, you 'd better leave town till that fellow's boat sails; it may save you the expense of a trial and three months in the chain-gang. But this talk about killing a man is all nonsense. What has any man in this town done to you, that you should thirst for his blood?"

"No, suh, it ain' nonsense,—it 's straight, solem' fac'. I 'm gwine ter kill dat man as sho' as I 'm settin' in dis cheer; an' dey ain' nobody kin say I ain' got a right ter kill 'im. Does you 'member de Ku-Klux?"

"Yes, but I was a child at the time, and recollect very little about them. It is a page of history which most people are glad to forget."

"Yas, suh; I was a chile, too, but I wuz right in it, an' so I 'members mo' erbout it 'n you does. My mammy an' daddy lived 'bout ten miles f'm here, up de river. One night a crowd er w'ite men come ter ou' house an' tuck my daddy out an' shot 'im ter death, an' skeered my mammy so she ain' be'n herse'f f'm dat day ter dis. I wa'n't mo' 'n ten years ole at de time, an' w'en my mammy seed de w'ite men comin', she tol' me ter run. I hid in de bushes an' seen de whole thing, an' it wuz branded on my mem'ry, suh, like a red-hot iron bran's de skin. De w'ite folks had masks on, but one of 'em fell off,—he wuz de boss, he wuz de head man, an' tol' de res' w'at ter do,—an' I seen his face. It wuz a easy face ter 'member; an' I swo' den, 'way down deep in my hea't, little ez I wuz, dat some day er 'nother I 'd kill dat man. I ain't never had no doubt erbout it; it 's jus' w'at I 'm livin' fer, an' I know I ain' gwine ter die till I 've done it. Some lives fer one thing an' some fer another, but dat 's my job. I ain' be'n in no has'e, fer I 'm not ole yit, an' dat man is in good health. I 'd like ter see a little er de worl' befo' I takes chances on leavin' it sudden; an', mo'over, somebody 's got ter take keer er de ole 'oman. But her time 'll come some er dese days, an den *his* time 'll be come—an' prob'ly mine. But I ain' keerin' 'bout myse'f: w'en I git thoo wid him, it won' make no dif-f'ence 'bout me."

Josh was evidently in dead earnest. Miller recalled, very vividly, the expression he had seen twice on his patient's face, during the journey to Wellington. He had often seen Josh's mother, old Aunt Milly,—"Silly Milly," the children called her,—wandering aimlessly about the street, muttering to herself incoherently. He had felt a certain childish awe at the sight of one of God's creatures who had lost the light of reason, and he had always vaguely understood that she was the victim of human cruelty, though he had dated it farther back into the past. This was his first knowledge of the real facts of the case.

He realized, too, for a moment, the continuity of life, how inseparably the present is woven with the past, how certainly the future will be but the outcome of the present. He had supposed this old wound healed. The negroes were not a vindictive people. If, swayed by passion or emotion, they sometimes gave way to gusts of rage, these were of brief duration. Absorbed in the contemplation of their doubtful present and their uncertain future, they gave little thought to the past,—it was a dark story, which they would willingly forget. He knew the timeworn explanation that the Ku-Klux movement, in the main, was merely an ebullition of boyish spirits, begun to amuse young white men by playing upon the fears and superstitions of ignorant negroes. Here, however, was its tragic side,—the old wound still bleeding, the fruit of one tragedy, the seed of another. He could not approve of Josh's application of the Mosaic law of revenge, and yet the incident was not without significance. Here was a negro who could remember an injury, who could shape his life to a definite purpose, if not a high or holy one. When his race reached the point where they would resent a wrong, there was hope that they might soon attain the stage where they would try, and, if need be, die, to defend a right. This man, too, had a purpose in life, and was willing to die that he might accomplish it. Miller was willing to give up his life to a cause. Would he be equally willing, he asked himself, to die for it? Miller had no prophetic instinct to tell him how soon he would have the opportunity to answer his own question. But he could not encourage Josh to carry out this dark and revengeful purpose. Every worthy consideration required him to dissuade his patient from such a desperate course.

"You had better put away these murderous fancies, Josh," he said seriously. "The Bible says that we should 'forgive our enemies, bless them that curse us, and do good to them that despitefully use us.' "

"Yas, suh, I 've l'arnt all dat in Sunday-school, an' I 've heared de preachers say it time an' time ag'in. But it 'pears ter me dat dis fergitfulniss an' fergivniss is mighty one-sided. De w'ite folks don' fergive nothin' de niggers does. Dey got up de Ku-Klux, dey said, on 'count er de kyarpit-baggers. Dey be'n talkin' 'bout de kyarpit-baggers ever sence, an' dey 'pears ter fergot all 'bout de Ku-Klux. But I ain' fergot. De niggers is be'n train' ter fergiveniss; an' fer fear dey might fergit how ter fergive, de w'ite folks gives 'em somethin' new ev'y now an' den, ter practice on. A w'ite man kin do w'at he wants ter a nigger, but de minute de nigger gits back at 'im, up goes de nigger, an' don' come down tell somebody cuts 'im down. If a nigger gits a' office, er de race 'pears ter be prosperin' too much, de w'ite folks up an' kills a few, so dat de res' kin keep on fergivin' an' bein' thankful dat dey 're lef' alive. Don' talk ter me 'bout dese w'ite folks,—I knows 'em, I does! Ef a nigger wants ter git down on his marrow-bones, an' eat dirt, an' call 'em 'marster,' *he 's* a good nigger, dere 's room fer *him*. But I ain' no w'ite folks' nigger, I ain'. I don' call no man 'marster.' I don' wan' nothin' but w'at I wo'k fer, but I wants all er dat. I never moles's no w'ite man, 'less 'n he moles's me fus'. But w'en de ole 'oman dies, doctuh, an' I gits a good chance at dat w'ite man,—dere ain' no use talkin', suh!—dere 's gwine ter be a mix-up, an' a fune'al, er two fune'als—er may be mo', ef anybody is keerliss enough to git in de way."

"Josh," said the doctor, laying a cool hand on the other's brow, "you 're feverish, and don't know what you 're talking about. I should n't let my mind dwell on such things, and you must keep quiet until this arm is well, or you may never be able to hit any one with it again."

Miller determined that when Josh got better he would talk to him seriously and dissuade him from this dangerous design. He had not asked the name of Josh's enemy, but the look of murderous hate which the dust-begrimed tramp of the railway journey had cast at Captain George McBane rendered any such question superfluous. McBane was probably deserving of any evil fate which might befall him; but such a revenge would do no good, would right no wrong; while every such crime, committed by a colored man, would be imputed to the race, which was already staggering under a load of obloquy because, in the eyes of a prejudiced and undiscriminating public, it must answer as a whole for the offenses of each separate individual. To die in defense of the right was heroic. To kill another for revenge was pitifully human and weak: "Vengeance is mine, I will repay," saith the Lord.

XIII

THE CAKEWALK

OLD Mr. Delamere's servant, Sandy Campbell, was in deep trouble.

A party of Northern visitors had been staying for several days at the St. James Hotel. The gentlemen of the party were concerned in a projected cotton mill, while the ladies were much interested in the study of social conditions, and especially in the negro problem. As soon as their desire for information became known, they were taken courteously under the wing of prominent citizens and their wives, who gave them, at elaborate luncheons, the Southern white man's views of the negro, sighing sentimentally over the disappearance of the good old negro of before the war, and gravely deploring the degeneracy of his descendants. They enlarged upon the amount of money the Southern whites had spent for the education of the negro, and shook their heads over the inadequate results accruing from this unexampled generosity. It was sad, they said, to witness this spectacle of a dying race, unable to withstand the competition of a superior type. The severe reprisals taken by white people for certain crimes committed by negroes were of course not the acts of the best people, who deplored them; but still a certain charity should be extended towards those who in the intense and righteous anger of the moment should take the law into their own hands and deal out rough but still substantial justice; for no negro was ever lynched without incontestable proof of his guilt. In order to be perfectly fair, and give their visitors an opportunity to see both sides of the question, they accompanied the Northern visitors to a colored church where they might hear a colored preacher, who had won a jocular popularity throughout the whole country by an oft-repeated sermon intended to demonstrate that the earth was flat like a pancake. This celebrated divine could always draw a white audience, except on the days when his no less distinguished white rival in the field of sensationalism preached his equally famous sermon to prove that hell was exactly one half mile, linear measure, from the city limits of Wellington. Whether accidentally or not, the Northern visitors had no opportunity to meet or talk alone with any colored person in the city except the servants at the hotel. When one of the party suggested a visit to the colored mission school, a Southern friend kindly volunteered to accompany them.

The visitors were naturally much impressed by what they learned from their courteous hosts, and felt inclined to sympathize with the Southern people, for the negro is not counted as a Southerner, except to fix the basis of congressional representation. There might of course be things to criticise here and there, certain customs for which they did not exactly see the necessity, and which seemed in conflict with the highest ideals of liberty; but surely these courteous, soft-spoken ladies and gentlemen, entirely familiar with local conditions, who descanted so earnestly and at times pathetically upon the grave problems confronting them, must know more about it than people in the distant North, without their means of information. The negroes who waited on them at the hotel seemed happy enough, and the teachers whom they had met at the mission school had been well-dressed, well-mannered, and apparently content with their position in life. Surely a people who made no complaints could not be very much oppressed.

In order to give the visitors, ere they left Wellington, a pleasing impression of Southern customs, and particularly of the joyous, happy-go-lucky disposition of the Southern darky and his entire contentment with existing conditions, it was decided by the hotel management to treat them, on the last night of their visit, to a little diversion, in the shape of a genuine negro cakewalk.

On the afternoon of this same day Tom Delamere strolled into the hotel, and soon gravitated to the bar, where he was a frequent visitor. Young men of leisure spent much of their time around the hotel, and no small part of it in the bar. Delamere had been to the club, but had avoided the card-room. Time hanging heavy on his hands, he had sought the hotel in the hope that some form of distraction might present itself.

"Have you heard the latest, Mr. Delamere?" asked the bartender, as he mixed a cocktail for his customer.

"No, Billy; what is it?"

"There 's to be a big cakewalk upstairs to-night. The No'the'n gentlemen an' ladies who are down here to see about the new cotton fact'ry want to study the nigger some more, and the boss has got up a cakewalk for 'em, 'mongst the waiters and chambermaids, with a little outside talent."

"Is it to be public?" asked Delamere.

"Oh, no, not generally, but friends of the house won't be barred out. The clerk 'll fix it for you. Ransom, the head waiter, will be floor manager."

Delamere was struck with a brilliant idea. The more he considered it, the brighter it seemed. Another cocktail imparted additional brilliancy to the conception. He had been trying, after a feeble fashion, to keep his promise to Clara, and was really suffering from lack of excitement.

He left the bar-room, found the head waiter, held with him a short conversation, and left in his intelligent and itching palm a piece of money.

The cakewalk was a great success. The most brilliant performer was a late arrival, who made his appearance just as the performance was about to commence. The newcomer was dressed strikingly, the conspicuous features of his attire being a long blue coat with brass buttons and a pair of plaid trousers. He was older, too, than the other participants, which made his agility the more remarkable. His partner was a new chambermaid, who had just come to town, and whom the head waiter introduced to the newcomer upon his arrival. The cake was awarded to this couple by a unanimous vote. The man presented it to his partner with a grandiloquent flourish, and returned thanks in a speech which sent the Northern visitors into spasms of delight at the quaintness of the darky dialect and the darky wit. To cap the climax, the winner danced a buck dance with a skill and agility that brought a shower of complimentary silver, which he gathered up and passed to the head waiter.

Ellis was off duty for the evening. Not having ventured to put in an appearance at Carteret's since his last rebuff, he found himself burdened with a superfluity of leisure, from which he essayed to find relief by dropping into the hotel office at about nine o'clock. He was invited up to see the cakewalk, which he rather enjoyed, for there was some graceful dancing and posturing. But the grotesque contortions of one participant had struck him as somewhat overdone, even for the comical type of negro. He recognized the fellow, after a few minutes' scrutiny, as the body-servant of old Mr. Delamere. The man's present occupation, or choice of diversion, seemed out of keeping with his employment as attendant upon an invalid old gentleman, and strangely inconsistent with the gravity and decorum which had been so noticeable when this agile cakewalker had served as butler at Major Carteret's table, upon the occasion of the christening dinner. There was a vague suggestion of unreality about this performance, too, which Ellis did not attempt to analyze, but which recurred vividly to his memory upon a subsequent occasion.

Ellis had never pretended to that intimate knowledge of negro thought and character by which some of his acquaintances claimed the ability to fathom every motive of a negro's conduct, and predict in advance what any one of the darker race would do under a given set of circumstances. He would not have believed that a white man could possess two so widely varying phases of character; but as to negroes, they were as yet a crude and undeveloped race, and it was not safe to make predictions concerning them. No one could tell at what moment the thin veneer of civilization might peel off and reveal the underlying savage.

The champion cakewalker, much to the surprise of his sable companions, who were about equally swayed by admiration and jealousy, disappeared immediately after the close of the performance. Any one watching him on his way home through the quiet streets to old Mr. Delamere's would have seen him now and then shaking with laughter. It had been excellent fun. Nevertheless, as he neared home, a certain aspect of the affair, hitherto unconsidered, occurred to him, and it was in a rather serious frame of mind that he cautiously entered the house and sought his own room.

The cakewalk had results which to Sandy were very serious. The following week he was summoned before the disciplinary committee of his church and charged with unchristian conduct, in the following particulars, to wit: dancing, and participating in a sinful diversion called a cakewalk, which was calculated to bring the church into disrepute and make it the mockery of sinners.

Sandy protested his innocence vehemently, but in vain. The proof was overwhelming. He was positively identified by Sister 'Manda Patterson, the hotel cook, who had watched the whole performance from the hotel corridor for the sole, single, solitary, and only purpose, she averred, of seeing how far human wickedness could be carried by a professing Christian. The whole thing had been shocking and offensive to her, and only a stern sense of duty had sustained her in looking on, that she might be qualified to bear witness against the offender. She had recognized his face, his clothes, his voice, his walk—there could be no shadow of doubt that it was Brother Sandy. This testimony was confirmed by one of the deacons, whose son, a waiter at the hotel, had also seen Sandy at the cakewalk.

Sandy stoutly insisted that he was at home the whole evening; that he had not been near the hotel for three months; that he had never in his life taken part in a cakewalk, and that he did not know how to dance. It was replied that wickedness, like everything else, must have a beginning; that dancing was an art that could be acquired in secret, and came natural to some people. In the face of positive proof, Sandy's protestations were of no avail; he was found guilty, and suspended from church fellowship until he should have repented and made full confession.

Sturdily refusing to confess a fault of which he claimed to be innocent, Sandy remained in contumacy, thereby falling somewhat into disrepute among the members of his church, the largest in the city. The effect of a bad reputation being subjective as well as objective, and poor human nature arguing that one may as well have the game as the name, Sandy insensibly glided into habits of which the church would not have approved, though he took care that they should not interfere with his duties to Mr. Delamere. The consolation thus afforded, however, followed as it was by remorse of conscience, did not compensate him for the loss of standing in the church, which to him was a social club as well as a religious temple. At times, in conversation with young Delamere, he would lament his hard fate.

Tom laughed until he cried at the comical idea which Sandy's plaint always brought up, of half-a-dozen negro preachers sitting in solemn judgment upon that cakewalk,—it had certainly been a good cakewalk!—and sending poor Sandy to spiritual Coventry.

"Cheer up, Sandy, cheer up!" he would say when Sandy seemed most depressed. "Go into my room and get yourself a good drink of liquor. The devil's church has a bigger congregation than theirs, and we have the consolation of knowing that when we die, we 'll meet all our friends on the other side. Brace up, Sandy, and be a man, or, if you can't be a man, be as near a man as you can!"

Hoping to revive his drooping spirits, Sandy too often accepted the proffered remedy.

XIV

THE MAUNDERINGS OF OLD MRS. OCHILTREE

When Mrs. Carteret had fully recovered from the shock attendant upon the accident at the window, where little Dodie had so narrowly escaped death or serious injury, she ordered her carriage one afternoon and directed the coachman to drive her to Mrs. Ochiltree's.

Mrs. Carteret had discharged her young nurse only the day before, and had sent for Mammy Jane, who was now recovered from her rheumatism, to stay until she could find another girl. The nurse had been ordered not to take the child to negroes' houses. Yesterday, in driving past the old homestead of her husband's family, now occupied by Dr. Miller and his family, Mrs. Carteret had seen her own baby's carriage standing in the yard.

When the nurse returned home, she was immediately discharged. She offered some sort of explanation, to the effect that her sister worked for Mrs. Miller, and that some family matter had rendered it necessary for her to see her sister. The explanation only aggravated the offense: if Mrs. Carteret could have overlooked the disobedience, she would by no means have retained in her employment a servant whose sister worked for the Miller woman.

Old Mrs. Ochiltree had within a few months begun to show signs of breaking up. She was over seventy years old, and had been of late, by various afflictions, confined to the house much of the time. More than once within the year, Mrs. Carteret had asked her aunt to come and live with her; but Mrs. Ochiltree, who would have regarded such a step as an acknowledgment of weakness, preferred her lonely independence. She resided in a small, old-fashioned house, standing back in the middle of a garden on a quiet street. Two old servants made up her modest household.

This refusal to live with her niece had been lightly borne, for Mrs. Ochiltree was a woman of strong individuality, whose comments upon her acquaintance, present or absent, were marked by a frankness at times no less than startling. This characteristic caused her to be more or less avoided. Mrs. Ochiltree was aware of this sentiment on the part of her acquaintance, and rather exulted in it. She hated fools. Only fools ran away from her, and that because they were afraid she would expose their folly. If most people were fools, it was no fault of hers, and she was not obliged to indulge them by pretending to believe that they knew anything. She had once owned considerable property, but was reticent about her affairs, and told no one how much she was worth, though it was supposed that she had considerable ready money, besides her house and some other real estate. Mrs. Carteret was her nearest living relative, though her grand-nephew Tom Delamere had been a great favorite with her. If she did not spare him her tongue-lashings, it was nevertheless expected in the family that she would leave him something handsome in her will.

Mrs. Ochiltree had shared in the general rejoicing upon the advent of the Carteret baby. She had been one of his godmothers, and had hinted at certain intentions held by her concerning him. During Mammy Jane's administration she had tried the old nurse's patience more or less by her dictatorial interference. Since her partial confinement to the house, she had gone, when her health and the weather would permit, to see the child, and at other times had insisted that it be sent to her in charge of the nurse at least every other day.

Mrs. Ochiltree's faculties had shared insensibly in the decline of her health. This weakness manifested itself by fits of absent-mindedness, in which she would seemingly lose connection with the present, and live over again, in imagination, the earlier years of her life. She had buried two husbands, had tried in vain to secure a third, and had never borne any children. Long ago she had petrified into a character which nothing under heaven could change, and which, if death is to take us as it finds us, and the future life to keep us as it takes us, promised anything but eternal felicity to those with whom she might associate after this life. Tom Delamere had been heard to say, profanely, that if his Aunt Polly went to heaven, he would let his mansion in the skies on a long lease, at a low figure.

When the carriage drove up with Mrs. Carteret, her aunt was seated on the little front piazza, with her wrinkled hands folded in her lap, dozing the afternoon away in fitful slumber.

"Tie the horse, William," said Mrs. Carteret, "and then go in and wake Aunt Polly, and tell her I want her to come and drive with me."

Mrs. Ochiltree had not observed her niece's approach, nor did she look up when William drew near. Her eyes were closed, and she would let her head sink slowly forward, recovering it now and then with a spasmodic jerk.

"Colonel Ochiltree," she muttered, "was shot at the battle of Culpepper Court House, and left me a widow for the second time. But I would not have married any man on earth after him."

"Mis' Ochiltree!" cried William, raising his voice, "oh, Mis' Ochiltree!"

"If I had found a man,—a real man,—I might have married again. I did not care for weaklings. I could have married John Delamere if I had wanted him. But pshaw! I could have wound him round"—

"Go round to the kitchen, William," interrupted Mrs. Carteret impatiently, "and tell Aunt Dinah to come and wake her up."

William returned in a few moments with a fat, comfortable looking black woman, who curtsied to Mrs. Carteret at the gate, and then going up to her mistress seized her by the shoulder and shook her vigorously.

"Wake up dere, Mis' Polly," she screamed, as harshly as her mellow voice would permit. "Mis' 'Livy wants you ter go drivin' wid 'er!"

"Dinah," exclaimed the old lady, sitting suddenly upright with a defiant assumption of wakefulness, "why do you take so long to come when I call? Bring me my bonnet and shawl. Don't you see my niece waiting for me at the gate?"

"Hyuh dey is, hyuh dey is!" returned Dinah, producing the bonnet and shawl, and assisting Mrs. Ochiltree to put them on.

Leaning on William's arm, the old lady went slowly down the walk, and was handed to the rear seat with Mrs. Carteret.

"How 's the baby to-day, Olivia, and why did n't you bring him?"

"He has a cold to-day, and is a little hoarse," replied Mrs. Carteret, "so I thought it best not to bring him out. Drive out the Weldon road, William, and back by Pine Street."

The drive led past an eminence crowned by a handsome brick building of modern construction, evidently an institution of some kind, surrounded on three sides by a grove of venerable oaks.

"Hugh Poindexter," Mrs. Ochiltree exclaimed explosively, after a considerable silence, "has been building a new house, in place of the old family mansion burned during the war."

"It is n't Mr. Poindexter's house, Aunt Polly. That is the new colored hospital built by the colored doctor."

"The new colored hospital, indeed, and the colored doctor! Before the war the negroes were all healthy, and when they got sick we took care of them ourselves! Hugh Poindexter has sold the graves of his ancestors to a negro,—I should have starved first!"

"He had his grandfather's grave opened, and there was nothing to remove, except a few bits of heart-pine from the coffin. All the rest had crumbled into dust."

"And he sold the dust to a negro! The world is upside down."

"He had the tombstone transferred to the white cemetery, Aunt Polly, and he has moved away."

"Esau sold his birthright for a mess of pottage. When I die, if you outlive me, Olivia, which is not likely, I shall leave my house and land to this child! He is a Carteret,—he would never sell them to a negro. I can't trust Tom Delamere, I 'm afraid."

The carriage had skirted the hill, passing to the rear of the new building.

"Turn to the right, William," ordered Mrs. Carteret, addressing the coachman, "and come back past the other side of the hospital."

A turn to the right into another road soon brought them to the front of the building, which stood slightly back from the street, with no intervening fence or inclosure. A sorrel pony in a light buggy was fastened to a hitching-post near the entrance. As they drove past, a lady came out of the front door and descended the steps, holding by the hand a very pretty child about six years old.

"Who is that woman, Olivia?" asked Mrs. Ochiltree abruptly, with signs of agitation.

The lady coming down the steps darted at the approaching carriage a look which lingered involuntarily.

Mrs. Carteret, perceiving this glance, turned away coldly.

With a sudden hardening of her own features the other woman lifted the little boy into the buggy and drove sharply away in the direction opposite to that taken by Mrs. Carteret's carriage.

"Who is that woman, Olivia?" repeated Mrs. Ochiltree, with marked emotion.

"I have not the honor of her acquaintance," returned Mrs. Carteret sharply. "Drive faster, William."

"I want to know who that woman is," persisted Mrs. Ochiltree querulously. "William," she cried shrilly, poking the coachman in the back with the end of her cane, "who is that woman?"

"Dat 's Mis' Miller, ma'am," returned the coachman, touching his hat; "Doctuh Miller's wife."

"What was her mother's name?"

"Her mother's name wuz Julia Brown. She 's be'n dead dese twenty years er mo'. Why, you knowed Julia, Mis' Polly!—she used ter b'long ter yo' own father befo' de wah; an' after de wah she kep' house fer"—

"Look to your horses, William!" exclaimed Mrs. Carteret sharply.

"It 's that hussy's child," said Mrs. Ochiltree, turning to her niece with great excitement. "When your father died, I turned the mother and the child out into the street. The mother died and went to—the place provided for such as she. If I had n't been just in time, Olivia, they would have turned you out. I saved the property for you and your son! You can thank me for it all!"

"Hush, Aunt Polly, for goodness' sake! William will hear you. Tell me about it when you get home."

Mrs. Ochiltree was silent, except for a few incoherent mumblings. What she might say, what distressing family secret she might repeat in William's hearing, should she take another talkative turn, was beyond conjecture.

Olivia looked anxiously around for something to distract her aunt's attention, and caught sight of a colored man, dressed in sober gray, who was coming toward the carriage.

"There 's Mr. Delamere's Sandy!" exclaimed Mrs. Carteret, touching her aunt on the arm. "I wonder how his master is? Sandy, oh, Sandy!"

Sandy approached the carriage, lifting his hat with a slight exaggeration of Chesterfieldian elegance. Sandy, no less than his master, was a survival of an interesting type. He had inherited the feudal deference for his superiors in position, joined to a certain self-respect which saved him from sycophancy. His manners had been formed upon those of old Mr. Delamere, and were not a bad imitation; for in the man, as in the master, they were the harmonious reflection of a mental state.

"How is Mr. Delamere, Sandy?" asked Mrs. Carteret, acknowledging Sandy's salutation with a nod and a smile.

"He ain't ez peart ez he has be'n, ma'am," replied Sandy, "but he 's doin' tol'able well. De doctuh say he 's good fer a dozen years yit, ef he 'll jes' take good keer of hisse'f an' keep f'm gittin' excited; fer sence dat secon' stroke, excitement is dange'ous fer 'im."

"I 'm sure you take the best care of him," returned Mrs. Carteret kindly.

"You can't do anything for him, Sandy," interposed old Mrs. Ochiltree, shaking her head slowly to emphasize her dissent. "All the doctors in creation could n't keep him alive another year. I shall outlive him by twenty years, though we are not far from the same age."

"Lawd, ma'am!" exclaimed Sandy, lifting his hands in affected amazement,—his study of gentle manners had been more than superficial,—"whoever would 'a' s'picion' dat you an' Mars John wuz nigh de same age? I 'd 'a' 'lowed you wuz ten years younger 'n him, easy, ef you wuz a day!"

"Give my compliments to the poor old gentleman," returned Mrs. Ochiltree, with a simper of senile vanity, though her back was weakening under the strain of the effort to sit erect that she might maintain this illusion of comparative youthfulness. "Bring him to see me some day when he is able to walk."

"Yas 'm, I will," rejoined Sandy. "He 's gwine out ter Belleview nex' week, fer ter stay a mont' er so, but I 'll fetch him 'roun' w'en he comes back. I 'll tell 'im dat you ladies 'quired fer 'im."

Sandy made another deep bow, and held his hat in his hand until the carriage had moved away. He had not condescended to notice the coachman at all, who was one of the young negroes of the new generation; while Sandy regarded himself as belonging to the quality, and seldom stooped to notice those beneath him. It would not have been becoming in him, either, while conversing with white ladies, to have noticed a colored servant. Moreover, the coachman was a Baptist, while Sandy was a Methodist, though under a cloud, and considered a Methodist in poor standing as better than a Baptist of any degree of sanctity.

"Lawd, Lawd!" chuckled Sandy, after the carriage had departed, "I never seed nothin' lack de way dat ole lady do keep up her temper! Wid one foot in de grave, an' de other hov-'rin' on de edge, she talks 'bout my ole marster lack he wuz in his secon' chil'hood. But I 'm jes' willin' ter bet dat he 'll outlas' her! She ain't half de woman she wuz dat night I waited on de table at de christenin' pa'ty, w'en she 'lowed she wuz n' feared er no man livin'."

XV

MRS. CARTERET SEEKS AN EXPLANATION

As a stone dropped into a pool of water sets in motion a series of concentric circles which disturb the whole mass in varying degree, so Mrs. Ochiltree's enigmatical remark had started in her niece's mind a disturbing train of thought. Had her words, Mrs. Carteret asked herself, any serious meaning, or were they the mere empty babblings of a clouded intellect?

"William," she said to the coachman when they reached Mrs. Ochiltree's house, "you may tie the horse and help us out. I shall be here a little while."

William helped the ladies down, assisted Mrs. Ochiltree into the house, and then went round to the kitchen. Dinah was an excellent hand at potato-pone and other culinary delicacies dear to the Southern heart, and William was a welcome visitor in her domain.

"Now, Aunt Polly," said Mrs. Carteret resolutely, as soon as they were alone, "I want to know what you meant by what you said about my father and Julia, and this—this child of hers?"

The old woman smiled cunningly, but her expression soon changed to one more grave.

"Why do you want to know?" she asked suspiciously. "You 've got the land, the houses, and the money. You 've nothing to complain of. Enjoy yourself, and be thankful!"

"I 'm thankful to God," returned Olivia, "for all his good gifts,—and He has blessed me abundantly,—but why should I be thankful to *you* for the property my father left me?"

"Why should you be thankful to me?" rejoined Mrs. Ochiltree with querulous indignation. "You 'd better ask why *should n't* you be thankful to me. What have I not done for you?"

"Yes, Aunt Polly, I know you 've done a great deal. You reared me in your own house when I had been cast out of my father's; you have been a second mother to me, and I am very grateful,—you can never say that I have not shown my gratitude. But if you have done anything else for me, I wish to know it. Why should I thank you for my inheritance?"

"Why should you thank me? Well, because I drove that woman and her brat away."

"But she had no right to stay, Aunt Polly, after father died. Of course she had no moral right before, but it was his house, and he could keep her there if he chose. But after his death she surely had no right."

"Perhaps not so surely as you think,—if she had not been a negro. Had she been white, there might have been a difference. When I told her to go, she said"—

"What did she say, Aunt Polly," demanded Olivia eagerly.

It seemed for a moment as though Mrs. Ochiltree would speak no further: but her once strong will, now weakened by her bodily infirmities, yielded to the influence of her niece's imperious demand.

"I 'll tell you the whole story," she said, "and then you 'll know what I did for you and yours."

Mrs. Ochiltree's eyes assumed an introspective expression, and her story, as it advanced, became as keenly dramatic as though memory had thrown aside the veil of intervening years and carried her back directly to the events which she now described.

"Your father," she said, "while living with that woman, left home one morning the picture of health. Five minutes later he tottered into the house groaning with pain, stricken unto death by the hand of a just God, as a punishment for his sins."

Olivia gave a start of indignation, but restrained herself.

"I was at once informed of what had happened, for I had means of knowing all that took place in the household. Old Jane—she was younger then—had come with you to my house; but her daughter remained, and through her I learned all that went on.

"I hastened immediately to the house, entered without knocking, and approached Mr. Merkell's bedroom, which was on the lower floor and opened into the hall. The door was ajar, and as I stood there for a moment I heard your father's voice.

" 'Listen, Julia,' he was saying. 'I shall not live until the doctor comes. But I wish you to know, *dear* Julia!'—he called her 'dear Julia!'—'before I die, that I have kept my promise. You did me one great service, Julia,—you saved me from Polly Ochiltree!' Yes, Olivia, that is what he said! 'You have served me faithfully and well, and I owe you a great deal, which I have tried to pay.'

" 'Oh, Mr. Merkell, dear Mr. Merkell,' cried the hypocritical hussy, falling to her knees by his bedside, and shedding her crocodile tears, 'you owe me nothing. You have done more for me than I could ever repay. You will not die and leave me,—no, no, it cannot be!'

" 'Yes, I am going to die,—I am dying now, Julia. But listen,—compose yourself and listen, for this is a more important matter. Take the keys from under my pillow, open the desk in the next room, look in the second drawer on the right, and you will find an envelope containing three papers: one of them is yours, one is the paper I promised to make, and the third is a letter which I wrote last night. As soon as the breath has left my body, deliver the envelope to the address indorsed upon it. Do not delay one moment, or you may live to regret it. Say nothing until you have delivered the package, and then be guided by the advice which you receive,—it will come from a friend of mine who will not see you wronged.'

"I slipped away from the door without making my presence known and entered, by a door from the hall, the room adjoining the one where Mr. Merkell lay. A moment later there was a loud scream. Returning quickly to the hall, I entered Mr. Merkell's room as though just arrived.

" 'How is Mr. Merkell?' I demanded, as I crossed the threshold.

" 'He is dead,' sobbed the woman, without lifting her head,—she had fallen on her knees by the bedside. She had good cause to weep, for my time had come.

" 'Get up,' I said. 'You have no right here. You pollute Mr. Merkell's dead body by your touch. Leave the house immediately,—your day is over!'

" 'I will not!' she cried, rising to her feet and facing me with brazen-faced impudence. 'I have a right to stay,—he has given me the right!'

" 'Ha, ha!' I laughed. 'Mr. Merkell is dead, and I am mistress here henceforth. Go, and go at once,—do you hear?'

" 'I hear, but I shall not heed. I can prove my rights! I shall not leave!'

" 'Very well,' I replied, 'we shall see. The law will decide.'

"I left the room, but did not leave the house. On the contrary, I concealed myself where I could see what took place in the room adjoining the death-chamber.

"She entered the room a moment later, with her child on one arm and the keys in the other hand. Placing the child on the floor, she put the key in the lock, and seemed surprised to find the desk already unfastened. She opened the desk, picked up a roll of money and a ladies' watch, which first caught her eye, and was reaching toward the drawer upon the right, when I interrupted her:—

" 'Well, thief, are you trying to strip the house before you leave it?'

"She gave an involuntary cry, clasped one hand to her bosom and with the other caught up her child, and stood like a wild beast at bay.

" 'I am not a thief,' she panted. 'The things are mine!'

" 'You lie,' I replied. 'You have no right to them,—no more right than you have to remain in this house!'

" 'I have a right,' she persisted, 'and I can prove it!'

"She turned toward the desk, seized the drawer, and drew it open. Never shall I forget her look,—never shall I forget that moment; it was the happiest of my life. The drawer was empty!

"Pale as death she turned and faced me.

" 'The papers!' she shrieked, 'the papers! *You* have stolen them!'

" 'Papers?' I laughed, 'what papers? Do you take me for a thief, like yourself?'

" 'There were papers here,' she cried, 'only a minute since. They are mine,—give them back to me!'

" 'Listen, woman,' I said sternly, 'you are lying—or dreaming. My brother-in-law's papers are doubtless in his safe at his office, where they ought to be. As for the rest,—you are a thief.'

" 'I am not,' she screamed; 'I am his wife. He married me, and the papers that were in the desk will prove it.'

" 'Listen,' I exclaimed, when she had finished,—'listen carefully, and take heed to what I say. You are a liar. You have no proofs,—there never were any proofs of what you say, because it never happened,—it is absurd upon the face of it. Not one person in Wellington would believe it. Why should he marry you? He did not need to! You are merely lying,—you are not even self-deceived. If he had really married you, you would have made it known long ago. That you did not is proof that your story is false.'

"She was hit so hard that she trembled and sank into a chair. But I had no mercy—she had saved your father from *me*—'dear Julia,' indeed!

" 'Stand up,' I ordered. 'Do not dare to sit down in my presence. I have you on the hip, my lady, and will teach you your place.'

"She struggled to her feet, and stood supporting herself with one hand on the chair. I could have killed her, Olivia! She had been my father's slave; if it had been before the war, I would have had her whipped to death.

" 'You are a thief,' I said, 'and of that there *are* proofs. I have caught you in the act. The watch in your bosom is my own, the money belongs to Mr. Merkell's estate, which belongs to my niece, his daughter Olivia. I saw you steal them. My word is worth yours a hundred times over, for I am a lady, and you are—what? And now hear me: if ever you breathe to a living soul one word of this preposterous story, I will charge you with the theft, and have you sent to the penitentiary. Your child will be taken from you, and you shall never see it again. I will give you now just ten minutes to take your brat and your rags out of this house forever. But before you go, put down your plunder there upon the desk!'

"She laid down the money and the watch, and a few minutes later left the house with the child in her arms.

"And now, Olivia, you know how I saved your estate, and why you should be grateful to me."

Olivia had listened to her aunt's story with intense interest. Having perceived the old woman's mood, and fearful lest any interruption might break the flow of her narrative, she had with an effort kept back the one question which had been hovering upon her lips, but which could now no longer be withheld.

"What became of the papers, Aunt Polly?"

"Ha, ha!" chuckled Mrs. Ochiltree with a cunning look, "did I not tell you that she found no papers?"

A change had come over Mrs. Ochiltree's face, marking the reaction from her burst of energy. Her eyes were half closed, and she was muttering incoherently. Olivia made some slight effort to arouse her, but in vain, and realizing the futility of any further attempt to extract information from her aunt at this time, she called William and drove homeward.

XVI

ELLIS TAKES A TRICK

LATE one afternoon a handsome trap, drawn by two spirited bays, drove up to Carteret's gate. Three places were taken by Mrs. Carteret, Clara, and the major, leaving the fourth seat vacant.

"I 've asked Ellis to drive out with us," said the major, as he took the lines from the colored man who had the trap in charge. "We 'll go by the office and pick him up."

Clara frowned, but perceiving Mrs. Carteret's eye fixed upon her, restrained any further expression of annoyance.

The major's liking for Ellis had increased within the year. The young man was not only a good journalist, but possessed sufficient cleverness and tact to make him excellent company. The major was fond of argument, but extremely tenacious of his own opinions. Ellis handled the foils of discussion with just the requisite skill to draw out the major, permitting himself to be vanquished, not too easily, but, as it were, inevitably, by the major's incontrovertible arguments.

Olivia had long suspected Ellis of feeling a more than friendly interest in Clara. Herself partial to Tom, she had more than once thought it hardly fair to Delamere, or even to Clara, who was young and impressionable, to have another young man constantly about the house. True, there had seemed to be no great danger, for Ellis had neither the family nor the means to make him a suitable match for the major's sister; nor had Clara made any secret of her dislike for Ellis, or of her resentment for his supposed depreciation of Delamere. Mrs. Carteret was inclined to a more just and reasonable view of Ellis's conduct in this matter, but nevertheless did not deem it wise to undeceive Clara. Dislike was a stout barrier, which remorse might have broken down. The major, absorbed in schemes of empire and dreams of his child's future, had not become cognizant of the affair. His wife, out of friendship for Tom, had refrained from mentioning it; while the major, with a delicate regard for Clara's feelings, had said nothing at home in regard to his interview with her lover.

At the Chronicle office Ellis took the front seat beside the major. After leaving the city pavements, they bowled along merrily over an excellent toll-road, built of oyster shells from the neighboring sound, stopping at intervals to pay toll to the gate-keepers, most of whom were white women with tallow complexions and snuff-stained lips,—the traditional "poor-white." For part of the way the road was bordered with a growth of scrub oak and pine, interspersed with stretches of cleared land, white with the opening cotton or yellow with ripening corn. To the right, along the distant river-bank, were visible here and there groups of turpentine pines, though most of this growth had for some years been exhausted. Twenty years before, Wellington had been the world's greatest shipping port for naval stores. But as the turpentine industry had moved southward, leaving a trail of devastated forests in its rear, the city had fallen to a poor fifth or sixth place in this trade, relying now almost entirely upon cotton for its export business.

Occasionally our party passed a person, or a group of persons,—mostly negroes approximating the pure type, for those of lighter color grew noticeably scarcer as the town was left behind. Now and then one of these would salute the party respectfully, while others glanced at them indifferently or turned away. There would have seemed, to a stranger, a lack of spontaneous friendliness between the people of these two races, as though each felt that it had no part or lot in the other's life. At one point the carriage drew near a party of colored folks who were laughing and jesting among themselves with great glee. Paying no attention to the white people, they continued to laugh and shout boisterously as the carriage swept by.

Major Carteret's countenance wore an angry look.

"The negroes around this town are becoming absolutely insufferable," he averred. "They are sadly in need of a lesson in manners."

Half an hour later they neared another group, who were also making merry. As the carriage approached, they became mute and silent as the grave until the major's party had passed.

"The negroes are a sullen race," remarked the major thoughtfully. "They will learn their lesson in a rude school, and perhaps much sooner than they dream. By the way," he added, turning to the ladies, "what was the arrangement with Tom? Was he to come out this evening?"

"He came out early in the afternoon," replied Clara, "to go a-fishing. He is to join us at the hotel."

After an hour's drive they reached the hotel, in front of which stretched the beach, white and inviting, along the shallow sound. Mrs. Carteret and Clara found seats on the veranda. Having turned the trap over to a hostler, the major joined a group of gentlemen, among whom was General Belmont, and was soon deep in the discussion of the standing problem of how best to keep the negroes down.

Ellis remained by the ladies. Clara seemed restless and ill at ease. Half an hour elapsed and Delamere had not appeared.

"I wonder where Tom is," said Mrs. Carteret.

"I guess he has n't come in yet from fishing," said Clara. "I wish he would come. It 's lonesome here. Mr. Ellis, would you mind looking about the hotel and seeing if there 's any one here that we know?"

For Ellis the party was already one too large. He had accepted this invitation eagerly, hoping to make friends with Clara during the evening. He had never been able to learn definitely the reason of her coldness, but had dated it from his meeting with old Mrs. Ochiltree, with which he felt it was obscurely connected. He had noticed Delamere's scowling look, too, at their last meeting. Clara's injustice, whatever its cause, he felt keenly. To Delamere's scowl he had paid little attention,—he despised Tom so much that, but for his engagement to Clara, he would have held his opinions in utter contempt.

He had even wished that Clara might make some charge against him,—he would have preferred that to her attitude of studied indifference, the only redeeming feature about which was that it *was* studied, showing that she, at least, had him in mind. The next best thing, he reasoned, to having a woman love you, is to have her dislike you violently,—the main point is that you should be kept in mind, and made the subject of strong emotions. He thought of the story of Hall Caine's, where the woman, after years of persecution at the hands of an unwelcome suitor, is on the point of yielding, out of sheer irresistible admiration for the man's strength and persistency, when the lover, unaware of his victory and despairing of success, seizes her in his arms and, springing into the sea, finds a watery grave for both. The analogy of this case with his own was, of course, not strong. He did not anticipate any tragedy in their relations; but he was glad to be thought of upon almost any terms. He would not have done a mean thing to make her think of him; but if she did so because of a misconception, which he was given no opportunity to clear up, while at the same time his conscience absolved him from evil and gave him the compensating glow of martyrdom, it was at least better than nothing.

He would, of course, have preferred to be upon a different footing. It had been a pleasure to have her speak to him during the drive,—they had exchanged a few trivial remarks in the general conversation. It was a greater pleasure to have her ask a favor of him,—a pleasure which, in this instance, was partly offset when he interpreted her request to mean that he was to look for Tom Delamere. He accepted the situation gracefully, however, and left the ladies alone.

Knowing Delamere's habits, he first went directly to the bar-room,—the atmosphere would be congenial, even if he were not drinking. Delamere was not there. Stepping next into the office, he asked the clerk if young Mr. Delamere had been at the hotel.

"Yes, sir," returned the man at the desk, "he was here at luncheon, and then went out fishing in a boat with several other gentlemen. I think they came back about three o'clock. I 'll find out for you."

He rang the bell, to which a colored boy responded.

"Front," said the clerk, "see if young Mr. Delamere's upstairs. Look in 255 or 256, and let me know at once."

The bell-boy returned in a moment.

"Yas, suh," he reported, with a suppressed grin, "he 's in 256, suh. De do' was open, an' I seed 'im from de hall, suh."

"I wish you 'd go up and tell him," said Ellis, "that— What are you grinning about?" he asked suddenly, noticing the waiter's expression.

"Nothin', suh, nothin' at all, suh," responded the negro, lapsing into the stolidity of a wooden Indian. "What shall I tell Mr. Delamere, suh?"

"Tell him," resumed Ellis, still watching the boy suspiciously,—"no, I 'll tell him myself."

He ascended the broad stair to the second floor. There was an upper balcony and a parlor, with a piano for the musically inclined. To reach these one had to pass along the hall upon which the room mentioned by the bell-boy opened. Ellis was quite familiar with the hotel. He could imagine circumstances under which he would not care to speak to Delamere; he would merely pass through the hall and glance into the room casually, as any one else might do, and see what the darky downstairs might have meant by his impudence.

It required but a moment to reach the room. The door was not wide open, but far enough ajar for him to see what was going on within.

Two young men, members of the fast set at the Clarendon Club, were playing cards at a small table, near which stood another, decorated with an array of empty bottles and glasses. Sprawling on a lounge, with flushed face and disheveled hair, his collar unfastened, his vest buttoned awry, lay Tom Delamere, breathing stertorously, in what seemed a drunken sleep. Lest there should be any doubt of the cause of his condition, the fingers of his right hand had remained clasped mechanically around the neck of a bottle which lay across his bosom.

Ellis turned away in disgust, and went slowly back to the ladies.

"There seems to be no one here yet," he reported. "We came a little early for the evening crowd. The clerk says Tom Delamere was here to luncheon, but he has n't seen him for several hours."

"He 's not a very gallant cavalier," said Mrs. Carteret severely. "He ought to have been waiting for us."

Clara was clearly disappointed, and made no effort to conceal her displeasure, leaving Ellis in doubt as to whether or not he were its object. Perhaps she suspected him of not having made a very thorough search. Her next remark might have borne such a construction.

"Sister Olivia," she said pettishly, "let 's go up to the parlor. I can play the piano anyway, if there 's no one to talk to."

"I find it very comfortable here, Clara," replied her sister placidly. "Mr. Ellis will go with you. You 'll probably find some one in the parlor, or they 'll come when you begin to play."

Clara's expression was not cordial, but she rose as if to go. Ellis was in a quandary. If she went through the hall, the chances were at least even that she would see Delamere. He did not care a rap for Delamere,—if he chose to make a public exhibition of himself, it was his own affair; but to see him would surely spoil Miss Pemberton's evening, and, in her frame of mind, might lead to the suspicion that Ellis had prearranged the exposure. Even if she should not harbor this unjust thought, she would not love the witness of her discomfiture. We had rather not meet the persons who have seen, even though they never mention, the skeletons in our closets. Delamere had disposed of himself for the evening. Ellis would have a fairer field with Delamere out of sight and unaccounted for, than with Delamere in evidence in his present condition.

"Would n't you rather take a stroll on the beach, Miss Clara?" he asked, in the hope of creating a diversion.

"No, I 'm going to the parlor. *You* need n't come, Mr. Ellis, if you 'd rather go down to the beach. I can quite as well go alone."

"I 'd rather go with you," he said meekly.

They were moving toward the door opening into the hall, from which the broad staircase ascended. Ellis, whose thoughts did not always respond quickly to a sudden emergency, was puzzling his brain as to how he should save her from any risk of seeing Delamere. Through the side door leading from the hall into the office, he saw the bell-boy to whom he had spoken seated on the bench provided for the servants.

"Won't you wait for me just a moment, Miss Clara, while I step into the office? I 'll be with you in an instant."

Clara hesitated.

"Oh, certainly," she replied nonchalantly.

Ellis went direct to the bell-boy. "Sit right where you are," he said, "and don't move a hair. What is the lady in the hall doing?"

"She 's got her back tu'ned this way, suh. I 'spec' she 's lookin' at the picture on the opposite wall, suh."

"All right," whispered Ellis, pressing a coin into the servant's hand. "I 'm going up to the parlor with the lady. You go up ahead of us, and keep in front of us along the hall. Don't dare to look back. I shall keep on talking to the lady, so that you can tell by my voice where we are. When you get to room 256, go in and shut the door behind you: pretend that you were called,—ask the gentlemen what they want,—tell any kind of a lie you like,—but keep the door shut until you 're sure we 've got by. Do you hear?"

"Yes, suh," replied the negro intelligently.

The plan worked without a hitch. Ellis talked steadily, about the hotel, the furnishings, all sorts of irrelevant subjects, to which Miss Pemberton paid little attention. She was angry with Delamere, and took no pains to conceal her feelings. The bell-boy entered room 256 just before they reached the door. Ellis had heard loud talking as they approached, and as they were passing there was a crash of broken glass, as though some object had been thrown at the door.

"What is the matter there?" exclaimed Clara, quickening her footsteps and instinctively drawing closer to Ellis.

"Some one dropped a glass, I presume," replied Ellis calmly.

Miss Pemberton glanced at him suspiciously. She was in a decidedly perverse mood. Seating herself at the piano, she played brilliantly for a quarter of an hour. Quite a number of couples strolled up to the parlor, but Delamere was not among them.

"Oh dear!" exclaimed Miss Pemberton, as she let her fingers fall upon the keys with a discordant crash, after the last note, "I don't see why we came out here to-night. Let 's go back downstairs."

Ellis felt despondent. He had done his utmost to serve and to please Miss Pemberton, but was not likely, he foresaw, to derive much benefit from his opportunity. Delamere was evidently as much or more in her thoughts by reason of his absence than if he had been present. If the door should have been opened, and she should see him from the hall upon their return, Ellis could not help it. He took the side next to the door, however, meaning to hurry past the room so that she might not recognize Delamere.

Fortunately the door was closed and all quiet within the room. On the stairway they met the bell-boy, rubbing his head with one hand and holding a bottle of seltzer upon a tray in the other. The boy was well enough trained to give no sign of recognition, though Ellis guessed the destination of the bottle.

Ellis hardly knew whether to feel pleased or disappointed at the success of his manœuvres. He had spared Miss Pemberton some mortification, but he had saved Tom Delamere from merited exposure. Clara ought to know the truth, for her own sake.

On the beach, a few rods away, fires were burning, around which several merry groups had gathered. The smoke went mostly to one side, but a slight whiff came now and then to where Mrs. Carteret sat awaiting them.

"They 're roasting oysters," said Mrs. Carteret. "I wish you 'd bring me some, Mr. Ellis."

Ellis strolled down to the beach. A large iron plate, with a turned-up rim like a great baking-pan, supported by legs which held it off the ground, was set over a fire built upon the sand. This primitive oven was heaped with small oysters in the shell, taken from the neighboring sound, and hauled up to the hotel by a negro whose pony cart stood near by. A wet coffee-sack of burlaps was spread over the oysters, which, when steamed sufficiently, were opened by a colored man and served gratis to all who cared for them.

Ellis secured a couple of plates of oysters, which he brought to Mrs. Carteret and Clara; they were small, but finely flavored.

Meanwhile Delamere, who possessed a remarkable faculty of recuperation from the effects of drink, had waked from his sleep, and remembering his engagement, had exerted himself to overcome the ravages of the afternoon's debauch. A dash of cold water braced him up somewhat. A bottle of seltzer and a big cup of strong coffee still further strengthened his nerves.

When Ellis returned to the veranda, after having taken away the plates, Delamere had joined the ladies and was explaining the cause of his absence.

He had been overcome by the heat, he said, while out fishing, and had been lying down ever since. Perhaps he ought to have sent for a doctor, but the fellows had looked after him. He had n't sent word to his friends because he had n't wished to spoil their evening.

"That was very considerate of you, Tom," said Mrs. Carteret dryly, "but you ought to have let us know. We have been worrying about you very much. Clara has found the evening dreadfully dull."

"Indeed, no, sister Olivia," said the young lady cheerfully, "I 've been having a lovely time. Mr. Ellis and I have been up in the parlor; I played the piano; and we 've been eating oysters and having a most delightful time. Won't you take me down there to the beach, Mr. Ellis? I want to see the fires. Come on."

"Can't I go?" asked Tom jealously.

"No, indeed, you must n't stir a foot! You must not overtax yourself so soon; it might do you serious injury. Stay here with sister Olivia."

She took Ellis's arm with exaggerated cordiality. Delamere glared after them angrily. Ellis did not stop to question her motives, but took the goods the gods provided. With no very great apparent effort, Miss Pemberton became quite friendly, and they strolled along the beach, in sight of the hotel, for nearly half an hour. As they were coming up she asked him abruptly,—

"Mr. Ellis, did you know Tom was in the hotel?"

Ellis was looking across the sound, at the lights of a distant steamer which was making her way toward the harbor.

"I wonder," he said musingly, as though he had not heard her question, "if that is the Ocean Belle?"

"And was he really sick?" she demanded.

"She 's later than usual this trip," continued Ellis, pursuing his thought. "She was due about five o'clock."

Miss Pemberton, under cover of the darkness, smiled a fine smile, which foreboded ill for some one. When they joined the party on the piazza, the major had come up and was

choose, may stem the flood long enough to give justice a chance. Keep track of the white people while I 'm gone, Watson; and you, Josh, learn what the colored folks are saying, and do nothing rash until I return. In the meantime, do all that you can to find out who did commit this most atrocious murder."

XXIII

BELLEVIEW

Miller did not reach his destination without interruption. At one point a considerable stretch of the road was under repair, which made it necessary for him to travel slowly. His horse cast a shoe, and threatened to go lame; but in the course of time he arrived at the entrance gate of Belleview, entering which he struck into a private road, bordered by massive oaks, whose multitudinous branches, hung with long streamers of trailing moss, formed for much of the way a thick canopy above his head. It took him only a few minutes to traverse the quarter of a mile that lay between the entrance gate and the house itself.

This old colonial plantation, rich in legendary lore and replete with historic distinction, had been in the Delamere family for nearly two hundred years. Along the bank of the river which skirted its domain the famous pirate Blackbeard had held high carnival, and was reputed to have buried much treasure, vague traditions of which still lingered among the negroes and poor-whites of the country roundabout. The beautiful residence, rising white and stately in a grove of ancient oaks, dated from 1750, and was built of brick which had been brought from England. Enlarged and improved from generation to generation, it stood, like a baronial castle, upon a slight eminence from which could be surveyed the large demesne still belonging to the estate, which had shrunk greatly from its colonial dimensions. While still embracing several thousand acres, part forest and part cleared land, it had not of late years been profitable; in spite of which Mr. Delamere, with the conservatism of his age and caste, had never been able to make up his mind to part with any considerable portion of it. His grandson, he imagined, could make the estate pay and yet preserve it in its integrity. Here, in pleasant weather, surrounded by the scenes which he loved, old Mr. Delamere spent much of the time during his declining years.

Dr. Miller had once passed a day at Belleview, upon Mr. Delamere's invitation. For this old-fashioned gentleman, whose ideals not even slavery had been able to spoil, regarded himself as a trustee for the great public, which ought, in his opinion, to take as much pride as he in the contemplation of this historic landmark. In earlier years Mr. Delamere had been a practicing lawyer, and had numbered Miller's father among his clients. He had always been regarded as friendly to the colored people, and, until age and ill health had driven him from active life, had taken a lively interest in their advancement since the abolition of slavery. Upon the public opening of Miller's new hospital, he had made an effort to be present, and had made a little speech of approval and encouragement which had manifested his kindliness and given Miller much pleasure.

It was with the consciousness, therefore, that he was approaching a friend, as well as Sandy's master, that Miller's mind was chiefly occupied as his tired horse, scenting the end of his efforts, bore him with a final burst of speed along the last few rods of the journey; for the urgency of Miller's errand, involving as it did the issues of life and death, did not permit him to enjoy the charm of mossy oak or forest reaches, or even to appreciate the noble front of Belleview House when it at last loomed up before him.

"Well, William," said Mr. Delamere, as he gave his hand to Miller from the armchair in which he was seated under the broad and stately portico, "I did n't expect to see you out here. You 'll excuse my not rising,—I 'm none too firm on my legs. Did you see anything of my man Sandy back there on the road? He ought to have been here by nine o'clock, and it 's now one. Sandy is punctuality itself, and I don't know how to account for his delay."

Clearly there need be no time wasted in preliminaries. Mr. Delamere had gone directly to the subject in hand.

"He will not be here to-day, sir," replied Miller. "I have come to you on his account."

In a few words Miller stated the situation.

"Preposterous!" exclaimed the old gentleman, with more vigor than Miller had supposed him to possess. "Sandy is absolutely incapable of such a crime as robbery, to say nothing of murder; and as for the rest, that is absurd upon the face of it! And so the poor old woman is dead! Well, well, well! she could not have lived much longer anyway; but Sandy did not kill her,—it 's simply impossible! Why, *I* raised that boy! He was born on my place. I 'd as soon believe such a thing of my own grandson as of Sandy! No negro raised by a Delamere would ever commit such a crime. I really believe, William, that Sandy has the family honor of the Delameres quite as much at heart as I have. Just tell them I say Sandy is innocent, and it will be all right."

"I 'm afraid, sir," rejoined Miller, who kept his voice up so that the old gentleman could understand without having it suggested that Miller knew he was hard of hearing, "that you don't quite appreciate the situation. *I* believe Sandy innocent; *you* believe him innocent; but there are suspicious circumstances which do not explain themselves, and the white people of the city believe him guilty, and are going to lynch him before he has a chance to clear himself."

"Why does n't he explain the suspicious circumstances?" asked Mr. Delamere. "Sandy is truthful and can be believed. I would take Sandy's word as quickly as another man's oath."

"He has no chance to explain," said Miller. "The case is prejudged. A crime has been committed. Sandy is charged with it. He is black, and therefore he is guilty. No colored lawyer would be allowed in the jail, if one should dare to go there. No white lawyer will intervene. He 'll be lynched to-night, without judge, jury, or preacher, unless we can stave the thing off for a day or two."

"Have you seen my grandson?" asked the old gentleman. "Is he not looking after Sandy?"

"No, sir. It seems he went down the river this morning to fish, before the murder was discovered; no one knows just where he has gone, or at what hour he will return."

"Well, then," said Mr. Delamere, rising from his chair with surprising vigor, "I shall have to go myself. No faithful servant of mine shall be hanged for a crime he did n't commit, so long as I have a voice to speak or a dollar to spend. There 'll be no trouble after I get there, William. The people are naturally wrought up at such a crime. A fine old woman,—she had some detestable traits, and I was always afraid she wanted to marry me, but she was of an excellent family and had many good points,—an old woman of one of the best families, struck down by the hand of a murderer! You must remember, William, that blood is thicker than water, and that the provocation is extreme, and that a few hotheads might easily lose sight of the great principles involved and seek immediate vengeance, without too much discrimination. But they are good people, William, and when I have spoken, and they have an opportunity for the sober second thought, they will do nothing rashly, but will wait for the operation of the law, which will, of course, clear Sandy."

"I 'm sure I hope so," returned Miller. "Shall I try to drive you back, sir, or will you order your own carriage?"

"My horses are fresher, William, and I 'll have them brought around. You can take the reins, if you will,—I 'm rather old to drive,—and my man will come behind with your buggy."

In a few minutes they set out along the sandy road. Having two fresh horses, they made better headway than Miller had made coming out, and reached Wellington easily by three o'clock.

"I think, William," said Mr. Delamere, as they drove into the town, "that I had first better talk with Sandy. He may be able to explain away the things that seem to connect him with this atrocious affair; and that will put me in a better position to talk to other people about it."

Miller drove directly to the county jail. Thirty or forty white men, who seemed to be casually gathered near the door, closed up when the carriage approached. The sheriff, who had seen them from the inside, came to the outer door and spoke to the visitor through a grated wicket.

"Mr. Wemyss," said Mr. Delamere, when he had made his way to the entrance with the aid of his cane, "I wish to see my servant, Sandy Campbell, who is said to be in your custody."

The sheriff hesitated. Meantime there was some parleying in low tones among the crowd outside. No one interfered, however, and in a moment the door opened sufficiently to give entrance to the old gentleman, after which it closed quickly and clangorously behind him.

Feeling no desire to linger in the locality, Miller, having

seen his companion enter the jail, drove the carriage round to Mr. Delamere's house, and leaving it in charge of a servant with instructions to return for his master in a quarter of an hour, hastened to his own home to meet Watson and Josh and report the result of his efforts.

XXIV

TWO SOUTHERN GENTLEMEN

THE IRON BOLT rattled in the lock, the door of a cell swung open, and when Mr. Delamere had entered was quickly closed again.

"Well, Sandy!"

"Oh, Mars John! Is you fell from hebben ter he'p me out er here? I prayed de Lawd ter sen' you, an' He answered my prayer, an' here you is, Mars John,—here you is! Oh, Mars John, git me out er dis place!"

"Tut, tut, Sandy!" answered his master; "of course I 'll get you out. That 's what I 've come for. How in the world did such a mistake ever happen? You would no more commit such a crime than I would!"

"No, suh, 'deed I would n', an' you know I would n'! I would n' want ter bring no disgrace on de fam'ly dat raise' me, ner ter make no trouble fer you, suh; but here I is, suh, lock' up in jail, an' folks talkin' 'bout hangin' me fer somethin' dat never entered my min', suh. I swea' ter God I never thought er sech a thing!"

"Of course you did n't, Sandy," returned Mr. Delamere soothingly; "and now the next thing, and the simplest thing, is to get you out of this. I 'll speak to the officers, and at the preliminary hearing to-morrow I 'll tell them all about you, and they will let you go. You won't mind spending one night in jail for your sins."

"No, suh, ef I wuz sho' I 'd be 'lowed ter spen' it here. But dey say dey 're gwine ter lynch me ter-night,—I kin hear 'em talkin' f'm de winders er de cell, suh."

"Well, *I* say, Sandy, that they shall do no such thing! Lynch a man brought up by a Delamere, for a crime of which he is innocent? Preposterous! I 'll speak to the authorities and see that you are properly protected until this mystery is unraveled. If Tom had been here, he would have had you out before now, Sandy. My grandson is a genuine Delamere, is he not, Sandy?"

"Yas, suh, yas, suh," returned Sandy, with a lack of enthusiasm which he tried to conceal from his master. "An' I s'pose ef he had n' gone fishin' so soon dis mawnin', he 'd 'a' be'n lookin' after me, suh."

"It has been my love for him and your care of me, Sandy," said the old gentleman tremulously, "that have kept me alive so long; but now explain to me everything concerning this distressing matter, and I shall then be able to state your case to better advantage."

"Well, suh," returned Sandy, "I mought 's well tell de whole tale an' not hol' nothin' back. I wuz kind er lonesome las' night, an' sence I be'n tu'ned outen de chu'ch on account er dat cakewalk I did n' go ter, so he'p me God! I did n' feel like gwine ter prayer-meetin', so I went roun' ter see Solomon Williams, an' he wa'n't home, an' den I walk' down street an' met Josh Green, an' he ax' me inter Sam Taylor's place, an' I sot roun' dere wid Josh till 'bout 'leven o'clock, w'en I sta'ted back home. I went straight ter de house, suh, an' went ter bed an' ter sleep widout sayin' a wo'd ter a single soul excep' Mistuh Tom, who wuz settin' up readin' a book w'en I come in. I wish I may drap dead in my tracks, suh, ef dat ain't de God's truf, suh, eve'y wo'd of it!"

"I believe every word of it, Sandy; now tell me about the clothes that you are said to have been found cleaning, and the suspicious articles that were found in your room?"

"Dat 's w'at beats me, Mars John," replied Sandy, shaking his head mournfully. "W'en I lef' home las' night after supper, my clo's wuz all put erway in de closet in my room, folded up on de she'f ter keep de moths out. Dey wuz my good clo's,—de blue coat dat you wo' ter de weddin' fo'ty years ago, an' dem dere plaid pants I gun Mistuh Cohen fo' dollars fer three years ago; an' w'en I looked in my closet dis mawnin', suh, befo' I got ready ter sta't fer Belleview, dere wuz my clo's layin' on de flo', all muddy an' crumple' up, des lack somebody had wo' 'em in a fight! Somebody e'se had wo' my clo's,—er e'se dere 'd be'n some witchcraf', er some sort er devilment gwine on dat I can't make out, suh, ter save my soul!"

"There was no witchcraft, Sandy, but that there was some

deviltry might well be. Now, what other negro, who might have been mistaken for you, could have taken your clothes? Surely no one about the house?"

"No, suh, no, suh. It could n't 'a' be'n Jeff, fer he wuz at Belleview wid you; an' it could n't 'a' be'n Billy, fer he wuz too little ter wear my clo's; an' it could n't 'a' be'n Sally, fer she 's a 'oman. It 's a myst'ry ter me, suh!"

"Have you no enemies? Is there any one in Wellington whom you imagine would like to do you an injury?"

"Not a livin' soul dat I knows of, suh. I 've be'n tu'ned out'n de chu'ch, but I don' know who my enemy is dere, er ef it wuz all a mistake, like dis yer jailin' is; but de Debbil is in dis somewhar, Mars John,—an' I got my reasons fer sayin' so."

"What do you mean, Sandy?"

Sandy related his experience of the preceding evening: how he had seen the apparition preceding him to the house, and how he had questioned Tom upon the subject.

"There 's some mystery here, Sandy," said Mr. Delamere reflectively. "Have you told me all, now, upon your honor? I am trying to save your life, Sandy, and I must be able to trust your word implicitly. You must tell me every circumstance; a very little and seemingly unimportant bit of evidence may sometimes determine the issue of a great lawsuit. There is one thing especially, Sandy: where did you get the gold which was found in your trunk?"

Sandy's face lit up with hopefulness.

"Why, Mars John, I kin 'splain dat part easy. Dat wuz money I had lent out, an' I got back f'm— But no, suh, I promise' not ter tell."

"Circumstances absolve you from your promise, Sandy. Your life is of more value to you than any other thing. If you will explain where you got the gold, and the silk purse that contained it, which is said to be Mrs. Ochiltree's, you will be back home before night."

Old Mr. Delamere's faculties, which had been waning somewhat in sympathy with his health, were stirred to unusual acuteness by his servant's danger. He was watching Sandy with all the awakened instincts of the trial lawyer. He could see clearly enough that, in beginning to account for the possession of the gold, Sandy had started off with his explanation in all sincerity. At the mention of the silk purse, however, his face had blanched to an ashen gray, and the words had frozen upon his lips.

A less discerning observer might have taken these things as signs of guilt, but not so Mr. Delamere.

"Well, Sandy," said his master encouragingly, "go on. You got the gold from"—

Sandy remained silent. He had had a great shock, and had taken a great resolution.

"Mars John," he asked dreamily, "you don' b'lieve dat I done dis thing?"

"Certainly not, Sandy, else why should I be here?"

"An' nothin' would n' make you b'lieve it, suh?"

"No, Sandy,—I could not believe it of you. I 've known you too long and too well."

"An' you would n' b'lieve it, not even ef I would n' say one wo'd mo' about it?"

"No, Sandy, I believe you no more capable of this crime than I would be,—or my grandson, Tom. I wish Tom were here, that he might help me overcome your stubbornness; but you 'll not be so foolish, so absurdly foolish, Sandy, as to keep silent and risk your life merely to shield some one else, when by speaking you might clear up this mystery and be restored at once to liberty. Just tell me where you got the gold," added the old gentleman persuasively. "Come, now, Sandy, that 's a good fellow!"

"Mars John," asked Sandy softly, "w'en my daddy, 'way back yander befo' de wah, wuz about ter be sol' away f'm his wife an' child'en, you bought him an' dem, an' kep' us all on yo' place tergether, did n't you, suh?"

"Yes, Sandy, and he was a faithful servant, and proved worthy of all I did for him."

"And w'en he had wo'ked fer you ten years, suh, you sot 'im free?"

"Yes, Sandy, he had earned his freedom."

"An' w'en de wah broke out, an' my folks wuz scattered, an' I did n' have nothin' ter do ner nowhar ter go, you kep' me on yo' place, and tuck me ter wait on you, suh, did n't you?"

"Yes, Sandy, and you have been a good servant and a good friend; but tell me now about this gold, and I 'll go and get you out of this, right away, for I need you, Sandy, and you 'll not be of any use to me shut up here!"

"Jes' hol' on a minute befo' you go, Mars John; fer ef dem people outside should git holt er me befo' you *does* git me out er here, I may never see you no mo', suh, in dis worl'. W'en Mars Billy McLean shot me by mistake, w'ile we wuz out huntin' dat day, who wuz it boun' up my woun's an' kep' me from bleedin' ter def, an' kyar'ed me two miles on his own shoulders ter a doctuh?"

"Yes, Sandy, and when black Sally ran away with your young mistress and Tom, when Tom was a baby, who stopped the runaway, and saved their lives at the risk of his own?"

"Dat wa'n't nothin', suh; anybody could 'a' done dat, w'at wuz strong ernuff an' swif' ernuff. You is be'n good ter me, suh, all dese years, an' I 've tried ter do my duty by you, suh, an' by Mistuh Tom, who wuz yo' own gran'son, an' de las' one er de fam'ly."

"Yes, you have, Sandy, and when I am gone, which will not be very long, Tom will take care of you, and see that you never want. But we are wasting valuable time, Sandy, in these old reminiscences. Let us get back to the present. Tell me about the gold, now, so that I may at once look after your safety. It may not even be necessary for you to remain here all night."

"Jes' one wo'd mo', Mars John, befo' you go! I know you're gwine ter do de bes' you kin fer me, an' I 'm sorry I can't he'p you no mo' wid it; but ef dere should be any accident, er ef you *can't* git me out er here, don' bother yo' min' 'bout it no mo', suh, an' don' git yo'se'f ixcited, fer you know de doctuh says, suh, dat you can't stan' ixcitement; but jes' leave me in de han's er de Lawd, suh,—*He 'll* look after me, here er hereafter. I know I 've fell f'm grace mo' d'n once, but I 've done made my peace wid Him in dis here jail-house, suh, an' I ain't 'feared ter die—ef I haf ter. I ain' got no wife ner child'n ter mo'n fer me, an' I 'll die knowin' dat I 've done my duty ter dem dat hi'ed me, an' trusted me, an' had claims on me. Fer I wuz raise' by a Delamere, suh, an' all de ole Delameres wuz gent'emen, an' deir principles spread ter de niggers 'round 'em, suh; an' ef I has ter die fer somethin' I did n' do,—I kin die, suh, like a gent'eman! But ez fer dat gol', suh, I ain' gwine ter say one wo'd mo' 'bout it ter nobody in dis worl'!"

Nothing could shake Sandy's determination. Mr. Delamere argued, expostulated, but all in vain. Sandy would not speak.

More and more confident of some mystery, which would come out in time, if properly investigated, Mr. Delamere, strangely beset by a vague sense of discomfort over and beyond that occasioned by his servant's danger, hurried away upon his errand of mercy. He felt less confident of the outcome than when he had entered the jail, but was quite as much resolved that no effort should be spared to secure protection for Sandy until there had been full opportunity for the truth to become known.

"Take good care of your prisoner, sheriff," he said sternly, as he was conducted to the door. "He will not be long in your custody, and I shall see that you are held strictly accountable for his safety."

"I 'll do what I can, sir," replied the sheriff in an even tone and seemingly not greatly impressed by this warning. "If the prisoner is taken from me, it will be because the force that comes for him is too strong for resistance."

"There should be no force too strong for an honest man in your position to resist,—whether successfully or not is beyond the question. The officer who is intimidated by threats, or by his own fears, is recreant to his duty, and no better than the mob which threatens him. But you will have no such test, Mr. Wemyss! I shall see to it myself that there is no violence!"

XXV

THE HONOR OF A FAMILY

MR. DELAMERE'S coachman, who, in accordance with instructions left by Miller, had brought the carriage around to the jail and was waiting anxiously at the nearest corner, drove up with some trepidation as he saw his master emerge from the prison. The old gentleman entered the carriage and gave the order to be driven to the office of the Morning Chronicle. According to Jerry, the porter, whom he encountered at the door, Carteret was in his office, and Mr. Delamere, with the aid of his servant, climbed the stairs painfully and found the editor at his desk.

"Carteret," exclaimed Mr. Delamere, "what is all this talk about lynching my man for murder and robbery and criminal assault? It 's perfectly absurd! The man was raised by me; he has lived in my house forty years. He has been honest, faithful, and trustworthy. He would no more be capable of this crime than you would, or my grandson Tom. Sandy has too much respect for the family to do anything that would reflect disgrace upon it."

"My dear Mr. Delamere," asked Carteret, with an indulgent smile, "how could a negro possibly reflect discredit upon a white family? I should really like to know."

"How, sir? A white family raised him. Like all the negroes, he has been clay in the hands of the white people. They are what we have made them, or permitted them to become."

"We are not God, Mr. Delamere! We do not claim to have created these—masterpieces."

"No; but we thought to overrule God's laws, and we enslaved these people for our greed, and sought to escape the manstealer's curse by laying to our souls the flattering unction that we were making of barbarous negroes civilized and Christian men. If we did not, if instead of making them Christians we have made some of them brutes, we have only ourselves to blame, and if these prey upon society, it is our just punishment! But my negroes, Carteret, were well raised and well behaved. This man is innocent of this offense, I solemnly affirm, and I want your aid to secure his safety until a fair trial can be had."

"On your bare word, sir?" asked Carteret, not at all moved by this outburst.

Old Mr. Delamere trembled with anger, and his withered cheek flushed darkly, but he restrained his feelings, and answered with an attempt at calmness:—

"Time was, sir, when the word of a Delamere was held as good as his bond, and those who questioned it were forced to maintain their skepticism upon the field of honor. Time was, sir, when the law was enforced in this state in a manner to command the respect of the world! Our lawyers, our judges, our courts, were a credit to humanity and civilization. I fear I have outlasted my epoch,—I have lived to hear of white men, the most favored of races, the heirs of civilization, the conservators of liberty, howling like red Indians around a human being slowly roasting at the stake."

"My dear sir," said Carteret soothingly, "you should undeceive yourself. This man is no longer your property. The negroes are no longer under our control, and with their emancipation ceased our responsibility. Their insolence and disregard for law have reached a point where they must be sternly rebuked."

"The law," retorted Mr. Delamere, "furnishes a sufficient penalty for any crime, however heinous, and our code is by no means lenient. To my old-fashioned notions, death would seem an adequate punishment for any crime, and torture has been abolished in civilized countries for a hundred years. It would be better to let a crime go entirely unpunished, than to use it as a pretext for turning the whole white population into a mob of primitive savages, dancing in hellish glee around the mangled body of a man who has never been tried for a crime. All this, however, is apart from my errand, which is to secure your assistance in heading off this mob until Sandy can have a fair hearing and an opportunity to prove his innocence."

"How can I do that, Mr. Delamere?"

"You are editor of the Morning Chronicle. The Chronicle is the leading newspaper of the city. This morning's issue practically suggested the mob; the same means will stop it. I will pay the expense of an extra edition, calling off the mob, on the ground that newly discovered evidence has shown the prisoner's innocence."

"But where is the evidence?" asked Carteret.

Again Mr. Delamere flushed and trembled. "*My* evidence, sir! I say the negro was morally incapable of the crime. A man of forty-five does not change his nature over-night. He is no more capable of a disgraceful deed than my grandson would be!"

Carteret smiled sadly.

"I am sorry, Mr. Delamere," he said, "that you should permit yourself to be so exercised about a worthless scoundrel who has forfeited his right to live. The proof against him is overwhelming. As to his capability of crime, we will apply your own test. You have been kept in the dark too long, Mr. Delamere,—indeed, we all have,—about others as well as this negro. Listen, sir: last night, at the Clarendon Club, Tom Delamere was caught cheating outrageously at cards. He had been suspected for some time; a trap was laid for him, and he fell into it. Out of regard for you and for my family, he has been permitted to resign quietly, with the understanding that he first pay off his debts, which are considerable."

Mr. Delamere's face, which had taken on some color in the excitement of the interview, had gradually paled to a chalky white while Carteret was speaking. His head sunk forward; already an old man, he seemed to have aged ten years in but little more than as many seconds.

"Can this be true?" he demanded in a hoarse whisper. "Is it—entirely authentic?"

"True as gospel; true as it is that Mrs. Ochiltree has been murdered, and that this negro killed her. Ellis was at the club a few minutes after the affair happened, and learned the facts from one of the participants. Tom made no attempt at denial. We have kept the matter out of the other papers, and I would have spared your feelings,—I surely would not wish to wound them,—but the temptation proved too strong for me, and it seemed the only way to convince you: it was your own test. If a gentleman of a distinguished name and an honorable ancestry, with all the restraining forces of social position surrounding him, to hold him in check, can stoop to dishonor, what is the improbability of an illiterate negro's being at least *capable* of crime?"

"Enough, sir," said the old gentleman. "You have proved enough. My grandson may be a scoundrel,—I can see, in the light of this revelation, how he might be; and he seems not to have denied it. I maintain, nevertheless, that my man Sandy is innocent of the charge against him. He *has* denied it, and it has not been proved. Carteret, I owe that negro my life; he, and his father before him, have served me and mine faithfully and well. I cannot see him killed like a dog, without judge or jury,—no, not even if he were guilty, which I do not believe!"

Carteret felt a twinge of remorse for the pain he had inflicted upon this fine old man, this ideal gentleman of the ideal past,—the past which he himself so much admired and regretted. He would like to spare his old friend any further agitation; he was in a state of health where too great excitement might prove fatal. But how could he? The negro was guilty, and sure to die sooner or later. He had not meant to interfere, and his intervention might be fruitless.

"Mr. Delamere," he said gently, "there is but one way to gain time. You say the negro is innocent. Appearances are against him. The only way to clear him is to produce the real criminal, or prove an alibi. If you, or some other white man of equal standing, could swear that the negro was in your presence last night at any hour when this crime could have taken place, it might be barely possible to prevent the lynching for the present; and when he is tried, which will probably be not later than next week, he will have every opportunity to defend himself, with you to see that he gets no less than justice. I think it can be managed, though there is still a doubt. I will do my best, for your sake, Mr. Delamere,—solely for your sake, be it understood, and not for that of the negro, in whom you are entirely deceived."

"I shall not examine your motives, Carteret," replied the other, "if you can bring about what I desire."

"Whatever is done," added Carteret, "must be done quickly. It is now four o'clock; no one can answer for what may happen after seven. If he can prove an alibi, there may yet be time to save him. White men might lynch a negro on

suspicion; they would not kill a man who was proven, by the word of white men, to be entirely innocent."

"I do not know," returned Mr. Delamere, shaking his head sadly. "After what you have told me, it is no longer safe to assume what white men will or will not do;—what I have learned here has shaken my faith in humanity. I am going away, but shall return in a short time. Shall I find you here?"

"I will await your return," said Carteret.

He watched Mr. Delamere pityingly as the old man moved away on the arm of the coachman waiting in the hall. He did not believe that Mr. Delamere could prove an alibi for his servant, and without some positive proof the negro would surely die,—as he well deserved to die.

XXVI

THE DISCOMFORT OF ELLIS

Mr. Ellis was vaguely uncomfortable. In the first excitement following the discovery of the crime, he had given his bit of evidence, and had shared the universal indignation against the murderer. When public feeling took definite shape in the intention to lynch the prisoner, Ellis felt a sudden sense of responsibility growing upon himself. When he learned, an hour later, that it was proposed to burn the negro, his part in the affair assumed a still graver aspect; for his had been the final word to fix the prisoner's guilt.

Ellis did not believe in lynch law. He had argued against it, more than once, in private conversation, and had written several editorials against the practice, while in charge of the Morning Chronicle during Major Carteret's absence. A young man, however, and merely representing another, he had not set up as a reformer, taking rather the view that this summary method of punishing crime, with all its possibilities of error, to say nothing of the resulting disrespect of the law and contempt for the time-honored methods of establishing guilt, was a mere temporary symptom of the unrest caused by the unsettled relations of the two races at the South. There had never before been any special need for any vigorous opposition to lynch law, so far as the community was concerned, for there had not been a lynching in Wellington since Ellis had come there, eight years before, from a smaller town, to seek a place for himself in the world of action. Twenty years before, indeed, there had been wild doings, during the brief Ku-Klux outbreak, but that was before Ellis's time,—or at least when he was but a child. He had come of a Quaker family,—the modified Quakers of the South,—and while sharing in a general way the Southern prejudice against the negro, his prejudices had been tempered by the peaceful tenets of his father's sect. His father had been a Whig, and a nonslaveholder; and while he had gone with the South in the civil war so far as a man of peace could go, he had not done so for love of slavery.

As the day wore on, Ellis's personal responsibility for the intended *auto-da-fé* bore more heavily upon him. Suppose he had been wrong? He had seen the accused negro; he had recognized him by his clothes, his whiskers, his spectacles, and his walk; but he had also seen another man, who resembled Sandy so closely that but for the difference in their clothes, he was forced to acknowledge, he could not have told them apart. Had he not seen the first man, he would have sworn with even greater confidence that the second was Sandy. There had been, he recalled, about one of the men—he had not been then nor was he now able to tell which—something vaguely familiar, and yet seemingly discordant to whichever of the two it was, or, as it seemed to him now, to any man of that race. His mind reverted to the place where he had last seen Sandy, and then a sudden wave of illumination swept over him, and filled him with a thrill of horror. The cakewalk,—the dancing,—the speech,—they were not Sandy's at all, nor any negro's! It was a white man who had stood in the light of the street lamp, so that the casual passer-by might see and recognize in him old Mr. Delamere's servant. The scheme was a dastardly one, and worthy of a heart that was something worse than weak and vicious.

Ellis resolved that the negro should not, if he could prevent it, die for another's crime; but what proof had he himself to offer in support of his theory? Then again, if he denounced Tom Delamere as the murderer, it would involve, in all probability, the destruction of his own hopes with regard to Clara. Of course she could not marry Delamere after the disclosure,—the disgraceful episode at the club would have been enough to make that reasonably certain; it had put a nail in Delamere's coffin, but this crime had driven it in to the head and clinched it. On the other hand, would Miss Pemberton ever speak again to the man who had been the instrument of bringing disgrace upon the family? Spies, detectives, police officers, may be useful citizens, but they are rarely pleasant company for other people. We fee the executioner, but we do not touch his bloody hand. We might feel a certain tragic admiration for Brutus condemning his sons to death, but we would scarcely invite Brutus to dinner after the event. It would harrow our feelings too much.

Perhaps, thought Ellis, there might be a way out of the dilemma. It might be possible to save this innocent negro without, for the time being, involving Delamere. He believed that murder will out, but it need not be through his initiative. He determined to go to the jail and interview the prisoner, who might give such an account of himself as would establish his innocence beyond a doubt. If so, Ellis would exert himself to stem the tide of popular fury. If, as a last resort, he could save Sandy only by denouncing Delamere, he would do his duty, let it cost him what it might.

The gravity of his errand was not lessened by what he saw and heard on the way to the jail. The anger of the people was at a white heat. A white woman had been assaulted and murdered by a brutal negro. Neither advanced age, nor high social standing, had been able to protect her from the ferocity of a black savage. Her sex, which should have been her shield and buckler, had made her an easy mark for the villainy of a black brute. To take the time to try him would be a criminal waste of public money. To hang him would be too slight a punishment for so dastardly a crime. An example must be made.

Already the preparations were under way for the impending execution. A T-rail from the railroad yard had been procured, and men were burying it in the square before the jail. Others were bringing chains, and a load of pine wood was piled in convenient proximity. Some enterprising individual had begun the erection of seats from which, for a pecuniary consideration, the spectacle might be the more easily and comfortably viewed.

Ellis was stopped once or twice by persons of his acquaintance. From one he learned that the railroads would run excursions from the neighboring towns in order to bring spectators to the scene; from another that the burning was to take place early in the evening, so that the children might not be kept up beyond their usual bedtime. In one group that he passed he heard several young men discussing the question of which portions of the negro's body they would prefer for souvenirs. Ellis shuddered and hastened forward. Whatever was to be done must be done quickly, or it would be too late. He saw that already it would require a strong case in favor of the accused to overcome the popular verdict.

Going up the steps of the jail, he met Mr. Delamere, who was just coming out, after a fruitless interview with Sandy.

"Mr. Ellis," said the old gentleman, who seemed greatly agitated, "this is monstrous!"

"It is indeed, sir!" returned the younger man. "I mean to stop it if I can. The negro did not kill Mrs. Ochiltree."

Mr. Delamere looked at Ellis keenly, and, as Ellis recalled afterwards, there was death in his eyes. Unable to draw a syllable from Sandy, he had found his servant's silence more eloquent than words. Ellis felt a presentiment that this affair, however it might terminate, would be fatal to this fine old man, whom the city could ill spare, in spite of his age and infirmities.

"Mr. Ellis," asked Mr. Delamere, in a voice which trembled with ill-suppressed emotion, "do you know who killed her?"

Ellis felt a surging pity for his old friend; but every step that he had taken toward the jail had confirmed and strengthened his own resolution that this contemplated crime, which he dimly felt to be far more atrocious than that of which Sandy was accused, in that it involved a whole community rather than one vicious man, should be stopped at any cost. Deplorable enough had the negro been guilty, it became, in view of his certain innocence, an unspeakable horror, which for all time would cover the city with infamy.

"Mr. Delamere," he replied, looking the elder man squarely in the eyes, "I think I do,—and I am very sorry."

"And who was it, Mr. Ellis?"

He put the question hopelessly, as though the answer were a foregone conclusion.

"I do not wish to say at present," replied Ellis, with a remorseful pang, "unless it becomes absolutely necessary, to save the negro's life. Accusations are dangerous,—as this case proves,—unless the proof be certain."

For a moment it seemed as though Mr. Delamere would collapse upon the spot. Rallying almost instantly, however, he took the arm which Ellis involuntarily offered, and said with an effort:—

"Mr. Ellis, you are a gentleman whom it is an honor to know. If you have time, I wish you would go with me to my house,—I can hardly trust myself alone,—and thence to the Chronicle office. This thing shall be stopped, and you will help me stop it."

It required but a few minutes to cover the half mile that lay between the prison and Mr. Delamere's residence.

XXVII

THE VAGARIES OF THE HIGHER LAW

Mr. Delamere went immediately to his grandson's room, which he entered alone, closing and locking the door behind him. He had requested Ellis to wait in the carriage.

The bed had been made, and the room was apparently in perfect order. There was a bureau in the room, through which Mr. Delamere proceeded to look thoroughly. Finding one of the drawers locked, he tried it with a key of his own, and being unable to unlock it, took a poker from beside the stove and broke it ruthlessly open.

The contents served to confirm what he had heard concerning his grandson's character. Thrown together in disorderly confusion were bottles of wine and whiskey; soiled packs of cards; a dice-box with dice; a box of poker chips, several revolvers, and a number of photographs and paper-covered books at which the old gentleman merely glanced to ascertain their nature.

So far, while his suspicion had been strengthened, he had found nothing to confirm it. He searched the room more carefully, and found, in the wood-box by the small heating-stove which stood in the room, a torn and crumpled bit of paper. Stooping to pick this up, his eye caught a gleam of something yellow beneath the bureau, which lay directly in his line of vision.

First he smoothed out the paper. It was apparently the lower half of a label, or part of the cover of a small box, torn diagonally from corner to corner. From the business card at the bottom, which gave the name of a firm of manufacturers of theatrical supplies in a Northern city, and from the letters remaining upon the upper and narrower half, the bit of paper had plainly formed part of the wrapper of a package of burnt cork.

Closing his fingers spasmodically over this damning piece of evidence, Mr. Delamere knelt painfully, and with the aid of his cane drew out from under the bureau the yellow object which had attracted his attention. It was a five-dollar gold piece of a date back toward the beginning of the century.

To make assurance doubly sure, Mr. Delamere summoned the cook from the kitchen in the back yard. In answer to her master's questions, Sally averred that Mr. Tom had got up very early, had knocked at her window,—she slept in a room off the kitchen in the yard,—and had told her that she need not bother about breakfast for him, as he had had a cold bite from the pantry; that he was going hunting and fishing, and would be gone all day. According to Sally, Mr. Tom had come in about ten o'clock the night before. He had forgotten his night-key, Sandy was out, and she had admitted him with her own key. He had said that he was very tired and was going immediately to bed.

Mr. Delamere seemed perplexed; the crime had been committed later in the evening than ten o'clock. The cook cleared up the mystery.

"I reckon he must 'a' be'n dead ti'ed, suh, fer I went back ter his room fifteen er twenty minutes after he come in fer ter fin' out w'at he wanted fer breakfus'; an' I knock' two or three times, rale ha'd, an' Mistuh Tom did n' wake up no mo' d'n de dead. He sho'ly had a good sleep, er he 'd never 'a' got up so ea'ly."

"Thank you, Sally," said Mr. Delamere, when the woman had finished, "that will do."

"Will you be home ter suppah, suh?" asked the cook.

"Yes."

It was a matter of the supremest indifference to Mr. Delamere whether he should ever eat again, but he would not betray his feelings to a servant. In a few minutes he was driving rapidly with Ellis toward the office of the Morning Chronicle. Ellis could see that Mr. Delamere had discovered something of tragic import. Neither spoke. Ellis gave all his attention to the horses, and Mr. Delamere remained wrapped in his own sombre reflections.

When they reached the office, they were informed by Jerry that Major Carteret was engaged with General Belmont and Captain McBane. Mr. Delamere knocked peremptorily at the door of the inner office, which was opened by Carteret in person.

"Oh, it is you, Mr. Delamere."

"Carteret," exclaimed Mr. Delamere, "I must speak to you immediately, and alone."

"Excuse me a moment, gentlemen," said Carteret, turning to those within the room. "I 'll be back in a moment—don't go away."

Ellis had left the room, closing the door behind him. Mr. Delamere and Carteret were quite alone.

"Carteret," declared the old gentleman, "this murder must not take place."

" 'Murder' is a hard word," replied the editor, frowning slightly.

"It is the right word," rejoined Mr. Delamere, decidedly. "It would be a foul and most unnatural murder, for Sandy did not kill Mrs. Ochiltree."

Carteret with difficulty restrained a smile of pity. His old friend was very much excited, as the tremor in his voice gave proof. The criminal was his trusted servant, who had proved unworthy of confidence. No one could question Mr. Delamere's motives; but he was old, his judgment was no longer to be relied upon. It was a great pity that he should so excite and over-strain himself about a worthless negro, who had forfeited his life for a dastardly crime. Mr. Delamere had had two paralytic strokes, and a third might prove fatal. He must be dealt with gently.

"Mr. Delamere," he said, with patient tolerance, "I think you are deceived. There is but one sure way to stop this execution. If your servant is innocent, you must produce the real criminal. If the negro, with such overwhelming proofs against him, is not guilty, who is?"

"I will tell you who is," replied Mr. Delamere. "The murderer is,"—the words came with a note of anguish, as though torn from his very heart,—"the murderer is Tom Delamere, my own grandson!"

"Impossible, sir!" exclaimed Carteret, starting back involuntarily. "That could not be! The man was seen leaving the house, and he was black!"

"All cats are gray in the dark, Carteret; and, moreover, nothing is easier than for a white man to black his face. God alone knows how many crimes have been done in this guise!

Tom Delamere, to get the money to pay his gambling debts, committed this foul murder, and then tried to fasten it upon as honest and faithful a soul as ever trod the earth."

Carteret, though at first overwhelmed by this announcement, perceived with quick intuition that it might easily be true. It was but a step from fraud to crime, and in Delamere's need of money there lay a palpable motive for robbery,—the murder may have been an afterthought. Delamere knew as much about the cedar chest as the negro could have known, and more.

But a white man must not be condemned without proof positive.

"What foundation is there, sir," he asked, "for this astounding charge?"

Mr. Delamere related all that had taken place since he had left Belleview a couple of hours before, and as he proceeded, step by step, every word carried conviction to Carteret. Tom Delamere's skill as a mimic and a negro impersonator was well known; he had himself laughed at more than one of his performances. There had been a powerful motive, and Mr. Delamere's discoveries had made clear the means. Tom's unusual departure, before breakfast, on a fishing expedition was a suspicious circumstance. There was a certain devilish ingenuity about the affair which he would hardly have expected of Tom Delamere, but for which the reason was clear enough. One might have thought that Tom would have been satisfied with merely blacking his face, and leaving to chance the identification of the negro who might be apprehended. He would hardly have implicated, out of pure malignity, his grandfather's old servant, who had been his own care-taker for many years. Here, however, Carteret could see where Tom's own desperate position operated to furnish a probable motive for the crime. The surest way to head off suspicion from himself was to direct it strongly toward some particular person, and this he had been able to do conclusively by his access to Sandy's clothes, his skill in making up to resemble him, and by the episode of the silk purse. By placing himself beyond reach during the next day, he would not be called upon to corroborate or deny any inculpating statements which Sandy might make, and in the very probable case that the crime should be summarily avenged, any such statements on Sandy's part would be regarded as mere desperate subterfuges of the murderer to save his own life. It was a bad affair.

"The case seems clear," said Carteret reluctantly but conclusively. "And now, what shall we do about it?"

"I want you to print a handbill," said Mr. Delamere, "and circulate it through the town, stating that Sandy Campbell is innocent and Tom Delamere guilty of this crime. If this is not done, I will go myself and declare it to all who will listen, and I will publicly disown the villain who is no more grandson of mine. There is no deeper sink of iniquity into which he could fall."

Carteret's thoughts were chasing one another tumultuously. There could be no doubt that the negro was innocent, from the present aspect of affairs, and he must not be lynched; but in what sort of position would the white people be placed, if Mr. Delamere carried out his Spartan purpose of making the true facts known? The white people of the city had raised the issue of their own superior morality, and had themselves made this crime a race question. The success of the impending "revolution," for which he and his *confrères* had labored so long, depended in large measure upon the maintenance of their race prestige, which would be injured in the eyes of the world by such a fiasco. While they might yet win by sheer force, their cause would suffer in the court of morals, where they might stand convicted as pirates, instead of being applauded as patriots. Even the negroes would have the laugh on them,—the people whom they hoped to make approve and justify their own despoilment. To be laughed at by the negroes was a calamity only less terrible than failure or death.

Such an outcome of an event which had already been heralded to the four corners of the earth would throw a cloud of suspicion upon the stories of outrage which had gone up from the South for so many years, and had done so much to win the sympathy of the North for the white South and to alienate it from the colored people. The reputation of the race was threatened. They must not lynch the negro, and yet, for the credit of the town, its aristocracy, and the race, the truth of this ghastly story must not see the light,—at least not yet.

"Mr. Delamere," he exclaimed, "I am shocked and humiliated. The negro must be saved, of course, but—consider the family honor."

"Tom is no longer a member of my family. I disown him. He has covered the family name—my name, sir—with infamy. We have no longer a family honor. I wish never to hear his name spoken again!"

For several minutes Carteret argued with his old friend. Then he went into the other room and consulted with General Belmont.

As a result of these conferences, and of certain urgent messages sent out, within half an hour thirty or forty of the leading citizens of Wellington were gathered in the Morning Chronicle office. Several other curious persons, observing that there was something in the wind, and supposing correctly that it referred to the projected event of the evening, crowded in with those who had been invited.

Carteret was in another room, still arguing with Mr. Delamere. "It 's a mere formality, sir," he was saying suavely, "accompanied by a mental reservation. We know the facts; but this must be done to justify us, in the eyes of the mob, in calling them off before they accomplish their purpose."

"Carteret," said the old man, in a voice eloquent of the struggle through which he had passed, "I would not perjure myself to prolong my own miserable existence another day, but God will forgive a sin committed to save another's life. Upon your head be it, Carteret, and not on mine!"

"Gentlemen," said Carteret, entering with Mr. Delamere the room where the men were gathered, and raising his hand for silence, "the people of Wellington were on the point of wreaking vengeance upon a negro who was supposed to have been guilty of a terrible crime. The white men of this city, impelled by the highest and holiest sentiments, were about to take steps to defend their hearthstones and maintain the purity and ascendency of their race. Your purpose sprung from hearts wounded in their tenderest susceptibilities."

"'Rah, 'rah!" shouted a tipsy sailor, who had edged in with the crowd.

"But this same sense of justice," continued Carteret oratorically, "which would lead you to visit swift and terrible punishment upon the guilty, would not permit you to slay an innocent man. Even a negro, as long as he behaves himself and keeps in his place, is entitled to the protection of the law. We may be stern and unbending in the punishment of crime, as befits our masterful race, but we hold the scales of justice with even and impartial hand."

"'Rah f' 'mpa'tial han'!" cried the tipsy sailor, who was immediately ejected with slight ceremony.

"We have discovered, beyond a doubt, that the negro Sandy Campbell, now in custody, did not commit this robbery and murder, but that it was perpetrated by some unknown man, who has fled from the city. Our venerable and distinguished fellow townsman, Mr. Delamere, in whose employment this Campbell has been for many years, will vouch for his character, and states, furthermore, that Campbell was with him all last night, covering any hour at which this crime could have been committed."

"If Mr. Delamere will swear to that," said some one in the crowd, "the negro should not be lynched."

There were murmurs of dissent. The preparations had all been made. There would be great disappointment if the lynching did not occur.

"Let Mr. Delamere swear, if he wants to save the nigger," came again from the crowd.

"Certainly," assented Carteret. "Mr. Delamere can have no possible objection to taking the oath. Is there a notary public present, or a justice of the peace?"

A man stepped forward. "I am a justice of the peace," he announced.

"Very well, Mr. Smith," said Carteret, recognizing the speaker. "With your permission, I will formulate the oath, and Mr. Delamere may repeat it after me, if he will. I solemnly swear,"—

"I solemnly swear,"—

Mr. Delamere's voice might have come from the tomb, so hollow and unnatural did it sound.

"So help me God,"—

"So help me God,"—

"That the negro Sandy Campbell, now in jail on the charge of murder, robbery, and assault, was in my presence last night between the hours of eight and two o'clock."

Mr. Delamere repeated this statement in a firm voice; but to Ellis, who was in the secret, his words fell upon the ear like clods dropping upon the coffin in an open grave.

"I wish to add," said General Belmont, stepping forward, "that it is not our intention to interfere, by anything which may be done at this meeting, with the orderly process of the law, or to advise the prisoner's immediate release. The prisoner will remain in custody, Mr. Delamere, Major Carteret, and I guaranteeing that he will be proved entirely innocent at the preliminary hearing to-morrow morning."

Several of those present looked relieved; others were plainly disappointed; but when the meeting ended, the news went out that the lynching had been given up. Carteret immediately wrote and had struck off a handbill giving a brief statement of the proceedings, and sent out a dozen boys to distribute copies among the people in the streets. That no precaution might be omitted, a call was issued to the Wellington Grays, the crack independent military company of the city, who in an incredibly short time were on guard at the jail.

Thus a slight change in the point of view had demonstrated the entire ability of the leading citizens to maintain the dignified and orderly processes of the law whenever they saw fit to do so.

The night passed without disorder, beyond the somewhat rough handling of two or three careless negroes that came in the way of small parties of the disappointed who had sought alcoholic consolation.

At ten o'clock the next morning, a preliminary hearing of the charge against Campbell was had before a magistrate. Mr. Delamere, perceptibly older and more wizened than he had seemed the day before, and leaning heavily on the arm of a servant, repeated his statement of the evening before. Only one or two witnesses were called, among whom was Mr. Ellis, who swore positively that in his opinion the prisoner was not the man whom he had seen and at first supposed to be Campbell. The most sensational piece of testimony was that of Dr. Price, who had examined the body, and who swore that the wound in the head was not necessarily fatal, and might have been due to a fall,—that she had more than likely died of shock attendant upon the robbery, she being of advanced age and feeble health. There was no evidence, he said, of any other personal violence.

Sandy was not even bound over to the grand jury, but was discharged upon the ground that there was not sufficient evidence upon which to hold him. Upon his release he received the congratulations of many present, some of whom would cheerfully have done him to death a few hours before. With the childish fickleness of a mob, they now experienced a satisfaction almost as great as, though less exciting than, that attendant upon taking life. We speak of the mysteries of inanimate nature. The workings of the human heart are the profoundest mystery of the universe. One moment they make us despair of our kind, and the next we see in them the reflection of the divine image. Sandy, having thus escaped from the Mr. Hyde of the mob, now received the benediction of its Dr. Jekyll. Being no cynical philosopher, and realizing how nearly the jaws of death had closed upon him, he was profoundly grateful for his escape, and felt not the slightest desire to investigate or criticise any man's motives.

With the testimony of Dr. Price, the worst feature of the affair came to an end. The murder eliminated or rendered doubtful, the crime became a mere vulgar robbery, the extent of which no one could estimate, since no living soul knew how much money Mrs. Ochiltree had had in the cedar chest. The absurdity of the remaining charge became more fully apparent in the light of the reaction from the excitement of the day before.

Nothing further was ever done about the case; but though the crime went unpunished, it carried evil in its train. As we have seen, the charge against Campbell had been made against the whole colored race. All over the United States the Associated Press had flashed the report of another dastardly outrage by a burly black brute,—all black brutes it seems are burly,—and of the impending lynching with its prospective horrors. This news, being highly sensational in its character, had been displayed in large black type on the front pages of the daily papers. The dispatch that followed, to the effect that the accused had been found innocent and the lynching frustrated, received slight attention, if any, in a fine-print paragraph on an inside page. The facts of the case never came out at all. The family honor of the Delameres was preserved, and the prestige of the white race in Wellington was not seriously impaired.

Upon leaving the preliminary hearing, old Mr. Delamere had requested General Belmont to call at his house during the day upon professional business. This the general did in the course of the afternoon.

"Belmont," said Mr. Delamere, "I wish to make my will. I should have drawn it with my own hand; but you know my motives, and can testify to my soundness of mind and memory."

He thereupon dictated a will, by the terms of which he left to his servant, Sandy Campbell, three thousand dollars, as a mark of the testator's appreciation of services rendered and sufferings endured by Sandy on behalf of his master. After some minor dispositions, the whole remainder of the estate was devised to Dr. William Miller, in trust for the uses of his hospital and training-school for nurses, on condition that the institution be incorporated and placed under the management of competent trustees. Tom Delamere was not mentioned in the will.

"There, Belmont," he said, "that load is off my mind. Now, if you will call in some witnesses,—most of my people can write,—I shall feel entirely at ease."

The will was signed by Mr. Delamere, and witnessed by Jeff and Billy, two servants in the house, neither of whom received any information as to its contents, beyond the statement that they were witnessing their master's will.

"I wish to leave that with you for safe keeping, Belmont," said Mr. Delamere, after the witnesses had retired. "Lock it up in your safe until I die, which will not be very long, since I have no further desire to live."

An hour later Mr. Delamere suffered a third paralytic stroke, from which he died two days afterwards, without having in the meantime recovered the power of speech.

The will was never produced. The servants stated, and General Belmont admitted, that Mr. Delamere had made a will a few days before his death; but since it was not discoverable, it seemed probable that the testator had destroyed it. This was all the more likely, the general was inclined to think, because the will had been of a most unusual character. What the contents of the will were, he of course did not state, it having been made under the seal of professional secrecy.

This suppression was justified by the usual race argument: Miller's hospital was already well established, and, like most negro institutions, could no doubt rely upon Northern philanthropy for any further support it might need. Mr. Delamere's property belonged of right to the white race, and by the higher law should remain in the possession of white people. Loyalty to one's race was a more sacred principle than deference to a weak old man's whims.

Having reached this conclusion, General Belmont's first impulse was to destroy the will; on second thoughts he locked it carefully away in his safe. He would hold it awhile. It might some time be advisable to talk the matter over with young Delamere, who was of a fickle disposition and might wish to change his legal adviser.

XXVIII

IN SEASON AND OUT

WELLINGTON soon resumed its wonted calm, and in a few weeks the intended lynching was only a memory. The robbery and assault, however, still remained a mystery to all but a chosen few. The affair had been dropped as absolutely as though it had never occurred. No colored man ever learned the reason of this sudden change of front, and Sandy Campbell's loyalty to his old employer's memory kept him silent. Tom Delamere did not offer to retain Sandy in his service, though he presented him with most of the old gentleman's wardrobe. It is only justice to Tom to state that up to this time he had not been informed of the contents of his grandfather's latest will. Major Carteret gave Sandy employment as butler, thus making a sort of vicarious atonement, on the part of the white race, of which the major felt himself in a way the embodiment, for the risk to which Sandy had been subjected.

Shortly after these events Sandy was restored to the bosom of the church, and, enfolded by its sheltering arms, was no longer tempted to stray from the path of rectitude, but became even a more rigid Methodist than before his recent troubles.

Tom Delamere did not call upon Clara again in the character of a lover. Of course they could not help meeting, from time to time, but he never dared presume upon their former relations. Indeed, the social atmosphere of Wellington remained so frigid toward Delamere that he left town, and did not return for several months.

Ellis was aware that Delamere had been thrown over, but a certain delicacy restrained him from following up immediately the advantage which the absence of his former rival gave him. It seemed to him, with the quixotry of a clean, pure mind, that Clara would pass through a period of mourning for her lost illusion, and that it would be indelicate, for the time being, to approach her with a lover's attentions. The work of the office had been unusually heavy of late. The major, deeply absorbed in politics, left the detail work of the paper to Ellis. Into the intimate counsels of the revolutionary committee Ellis had not been admitted, nor would he have desired to be. He knew, of course, in a general way, the results that it was sought to achieve; and while he did not see their necessity, he deferred to the views of older men, and was satisfied to remain in ignorance of anything which he might disapprove. Moreover, his own personal affairs occupied his mind to an extent that made politics or any other subject a matter of minor importance.

As for Dr. Miller, he never learned of Mr. Delamere's good intentions toward his institution, but regretted the old gentleman's death as the loss of a sincere friend and well-wisher of his race in their unequal struggle.

Despite the untiring zeal of Carteret and his associates, the campaign for the restriction of the suffrage, which was to form the basis of a permanent white supremacy, had seemed to languish for a while after the Ochiltree affair. The lull, however, was only temporary, and more apparent than real, for the forces adverse to the negro were merely gathering strength for a more vigorous assault. While little was said in Wellington, public sentiment all over the country became every day more favorable to the views of the conspirators. The nation was rushing forward with giant strides toward colossal wealth and world-dominion, before the exigencies of which mere abstract ethical theories must not be permitted to stand. The same argument that justified the conquest of an inferior nation could not be denied to those who sought the suppression of an inferior race. In the South, an obscure jealousy of the negro's progress, an obscure fear of the very equality so contemptuously denied, furnished a rich soil for successful agitation. Statistics of crime, ingeniously manipulated, were made to present a fearful showing against the negro. Vital statistics were made to prove that he had degenerated from an imaginary standard of physical excellence which had existed under the benign influence of slavery. Constant lynchings emphasized his impotence, and bred everywhere a growing contempt for his rights.

At the North, a new Pharaoh had risen, who knew not Israel,—a new generation, who knew little of the fierce passions which had played around the negro in a past epoch, and derived their opinions of him from the "coon song" and the police reports. Those of his old friends who survived were disappointed that he had not flown with clipped wings; that he had not in one generation of limited opportunity attained the level of the whites. The whole race question seemed to have reached a sort of *impasse*, a blind alley, of which no one could see the outlet. The negro had become a target at which any one might try a shot. Schoolboys gravely debated the question as to whether or not the negro should exercise the franchise. The pessimist gave him up in despair; while the optimist, smilingly confident that everything would come out all right in the end, also turned aside and went his buoyant way to more pleasing themes.

For a time there were white men in the state who opposed any reactionary step unless it were of general application. They were conscientious men, who had learned the ten commandments and wished to do right; but this class was a small minority, and their objections were soon silenced by the all-powerful race argument. Selfishness is the most constant of human motives. Patriotism, humanity, or the love of God may lead to sporadic outbursts which sweep away the heaped-up wrongs of centuries; but they languish at times, while the love of self works on ceaselessly, unwearyingly, burrowing always at the very roots of life, and heaping up fresh wrongs for other centuries to sweep away. The state was at the mercy of venal and self-seeking politicians, bent upon regaining their ascendency at any cost, stultifying their own minds by vague sophistries and high-sounding phrases, which deceived none but those who wished to be deceived, and these but imperfectly; and dulling the public conscience by a loud clamor in which the calm voice of truth was for the moment silenced. So the cause went on.

Carteret, as spokesman of the campaign, and sincerest of all its leaders, performed prodigies of labor. The Morning Chronicle proclaimed, in season and out, the doctrine of "White Supremacy." Leaving the paper in charge of Ellis, the major made a tour of the state, rousing the white people of the better class to an appreciation of the terrible danger which confronted them in the possibility that a few negroes might hold a few offices or dictate the terms upon which white men should fill them. Difficulties were explained away. The provisions of the Federal Constitution, it was maintained, must yield to the "higher law," and if the Constitution could neither be altered nor bent to this end, means must be found to circumvent it.

The device finally hit upon for disfranchising the colored people in this particular state was the notorious "grandfather clause." After providing various restrictions of the suffrage, based upon education, character, and property, which it was deemed would in effect disfranchise the colored race, an exception was made in favor of all citizens whose fathers or grandfathers had been entitled to vote prior to 1867. Since none but white men could vote prior to 1867, this exception obviously took in the poor and ignorant whites, while the same class of negroes were excluded.

It was ingenious, but it was not fair. In due time a constitutional convention was called, in which the above scheme was adopted and submitted to a vote of the people for ratification. The campaign was fought on the color line. Many white Republicans, deluded with the hope that by the elimination of the negro vote their party might receive accessions from the Democratic ranks, went over to the white party. By fraud in one place, by terrorism in another, and everywhere by the resistless moral force of the united whites, the negroes were reduced to the apathy of despair, their few white allies demoralized, and the amendment adopted by a large majority. The negroes were taught that this is a white man's country, and that the sooner they made up their minds to this fact, the better for all concerned. The white people would be good to them so long as they behaved themselves and kept their place. As theoretical equals,—practical equality being forever out of the question, either by nature or by law,—there could have been nothing but strife between them, in which the weaker party would invariably have suffered most.

Some colored men accepted the situation thus outlined, if not as desirable, at least as inevitable. Most of them, however, had little faith in this condescending friendliness which was to take the place of constitutional rights. They knew they had been treated unfairly; that their enemies had prevailed against them; that their whilom friends had stood passively by and seen them undone. Many of the most enterprising and progressive left the state, and those who remain still labor under a sense of wrong and outrage which renders them distinctly less valuable as citizens.

The great steal was made, but the thieves did not turn honest,—the scheme still shows the mark of the burglar's tools. Sins, like chickens, come home to roost. The South paid a fearful price for the wrong of negro slavery; in some form or other it will doubtless reap the fruits of this later iniquity.

Drastic as were these "reforms," the results of which we have anticipated somewhat, since the new Constitution was not to take effect immediately, they moved all too slowly for the little coterie of Wellington conspirators, whose ambitions and needs urged them to prompt action. Under the new Constitution it would be two full years before the "nigger amendment" became effective, and meanwhile the Wellington district would remain hopelessly Republican. The committee decided, about two months before the fall election, that an active local campaign must be carried on, with a view to discourage the negroes from attending the polls on election day.

The question came up for discussion one forenoon in a meeting at the office of the Morning Chronicle, at which all of the "Big Three" were present.

"Something must be done," declared McBane, "and that damn quick. Too many white people are saying that it will be better to wait until the amendment goes into effect. That would mean to leave the niggers in charge of this town for two years after the state has declared for white supremacy! I 'm opposed to leaving it in their hands one hour,—them 's my sentiments!"

This proved to be the general opinion, and the discussion turned to the subject of ways and means.

"What became of that editorial in the nigger paper?" inquired the general in his blandest tones, cleverly directing a smoke ring toward the ceiling. "It lost some of its point back there, when we came near lynching that nigger; but now that that has blown over, why would n't it be a good thing to bring into play at the present juncture? Let 's read it over again."

Carteret extracted the paper from the pigeon-hole where he had placed it some months before. The article was read aloud with emphasis and discussed phrase by phrase. Of its wording there could be little criticism,—it was temperately and even cautiously phrased. As suggested by the general, the Ochiltree affair had proved that it was not devoid of truth. Its great offensiveness lay in its boldness: that a negro should publish in a newspaper what white people would scarcely acknowledge to themselves in secret was much as though a Russian *moujik* or a German peasant should rush into print to question the divine right of the Lord's Anointed. The article was racial *lèse-majesté* in the most aggravated form. A peg was needed upon which to hang a *coup d'état*, and this editorial offered the requisite opportunity. It was unanimously decided to republish the obnoxious article, with comment adapted to fire the inflammable Southern heart and rouse it against any further self-assertion of the negroes in politics or elsewhere.

"The time is ripe!" exclaimed McBane. "In a month we can have the niggers so scared that they won't dare stick their heads out of doors on 'lection day."

"I wonder," observed the general thoughtfully, after this conclusion had been reached, "if we could n't have Jerry fetch us some liquor?"

Jerry appeared in response to the usual summons. The general gave him the money, and ordered three Calhoun cocktails. When Jerry returned with the glasses on a tray, the general observed him with pointed curiosity.

"What in h—ll is the matter with you, Jerry? Your black face is splotched with brown and yellow patches, and your hair shines as though you had fallen head-foremost into a firkin of butter. What 's the matter with you?"

Jerry seemed much embarrassed by this inquiry.

"Nothin', suh, nothin'," he stammered. "It 's—it 's jes' somethin' I be'n puttin' on my hair, suh, ter improve de quality, suh."

"Jerry," returned the general, bending a solemn look upon the porter, "you have been playing with edged tools, and your days are numbered. You have been reading the Afro-American Banner."

He shook open the paper, which he had retained in his hand, and read from one of the advertisements:—

" 'Kinky, curly hair made straight in two applications. Dark skins lightened two shades; mulattoes turned perfectly white.'

"This stuff is rank poison, Jerry," continued the general with a mock solemnity which did not impose upon Jerry, who nevertheless listened with an air of great alarm. He suspected that the general was making fun of him; but he also knew that the general would like to think that Jerry believed him in earnest; and to please the white folks was Jerry's consistent aim in life. "I can see the signs of decay in your face, and your hair will all fall out in a week or two at the latest,—mark my words!"

McBane had listened to this pleasantry with a sardonic sneer. It was a waste of valuable time. To Carteret it seemed in doubtful taste. These grotesque advertisements had their tragic side. They were proof that the negroes had read the handwriting on the wall. These pitiful attempts to change their physical characteristics were an acknowledgment, on their own part, that the negro was doomed, and that the white man was to inherit the earth and hold all other races under his heel. For, as the months had passed, Carteret's thoughts, centring more and more upon the negro, had led him farther and farther, until now he was firmly convinced that there was no permanent place for the negro in the United States, if indeed anywhere in the world, except under the ground. More pathetic even than Jerry's efforts to escape from the universal doom of his race was his ignorance that even if he could, by some strange alchemy, bleach his skin and straighten his hair, there would still remain, underneath it all, only the unbleached darky,—the ass in the lion's skin.

When the general had finished his facetious lecture, Jerry backed out of the room shamefacedly, though affecting a greater confusion than he really felt. Jerry had not reasoned so closely as Carteret, but he had realized that it was a distinct advantage to be white,—an advantage which white people had utilized to secure all the best things in the world; and he had entertained the vague hope that by changing his complexion he might share this prerogative. While he suspected the general's sincerity, he nevertheless felt a little apprehensive lest the general's prediction about the effects of the face-bleach and other preparations might prove true,—the general was a white gentleman and ought to know,—and decided to abandon their use.

This purpose was strengthened by his next interview with the major. When Carteret summoned him, an hour later, after the other gentlemen had taken their leave, Jerry had washed his head thoroughly and there remained no trace of the pomade. An attempt to darken the lighter spots in his cuticle by the application of printer's ink had not proved equally successful,—the retouching left the spots as much too dark as they had formerly been too light.

"Jerry," said Carteret sternly, "when I hired you to work for the Chronicle, you were black. The word 'negro' means 'black.' The best negro is a black negro, of the pure type, as it came from the hand of God. If you wish to get along well with the white people, the blacker you are the better,—white people do not like negroes who want to be white. A man should be content to remain as God made him and where God placed him. So no more of this nonsense. Are you going to vote at the next election?"

"What would you 'vise me ter do, suh?" asked Jerry cautiously.

"I do not advise you. You ought to have sense enough to see where your own interests lie. I put it to you whether you cannot trust yourself more safely in the hands of white gentlemen, who are your true friends, than in the hands of ignorant and purchasable negroes and unscrupulous white scoundrels?"

"Dere 's no doubt about it, suh," assented Jerry, with a vehemence proportioned to his desire to get back into favor. "I ain' gwine ter have nothin' ter do wid de 'lection, suh! Ef I don' vote, I kin keep my job, can't I, suh?"

The major eyed Jerry with an air of supreme disgust. What could be expected of a race so utterly devoid of tact? It seemed as though this negro thought a white gentleman might want to bribe him to remain away from the polls; and the negro's willingness to accept the imaginary bribe demonstrated the venal nature of the colored race,—its entire lack of moral principle!

"You will retain your place, Jerry," he said severely, "so long as you perform your duties to my satisfaction and behave yourself properly."

With this grandiloquent subterfuge Carteret turned to his next article on white supremacy. Jerry did not delude himself with any fine-spun sophistry. He knew perfectly well that he held his job upon the condition that he stayed away from the polls at the approaching election. Jerry was a fool—

"The world of fools hath such a store,
That he who would not see an ass,
Must stay at home and shut his door
And break his looking-glass."

But while no one may be entirely wise, there are degrees of folly, and Jerry was not all kinds of a fool.

XXIX

MUTTERINGS OF THE STORM

EVENTS moved rapidly during the next few days. The reproduction, in the Chronicle, of the article from the Afro-American Banner, with Carteret's inflammatory comment, took immediate effect. It touched the Southern white man in his most sensitive spot. To him such an article was an insult to white womanhood, and must be resented by some active steps,—mere words would be no answer at all. To meet words with words upon such a subject would be to acknowledge the equality of the negro and his right to discuss or criticise the conduct of the white people.

The colored people became alarmed at the murmurings of the whites, which seemed to presage a coming storm. A number of them sought to arm themselves, but ascertained, upon inquiring at the stores, that no white merchant would sell a negro firearms. Since all the dealers in this sort of merchandise were white men, the negroes had to be satisfied with oiling up the old army muskets which some of them possessed, and the few revolvers with which a small rowdy element generally managed to keep themselves supplied. Upon an effort being made to purchase firearms from a Northern city, the express company, controlled by local men, refused to accept the consignment. The white people, on the other hand, procured both arms and ammunition in large quantities, and the Wellington Grays drilled with great assiduity at their armory.

All this went on without any public disturbance of the town's tranquillity. A stranger would have seen nothing to excite his curiosity. The white people did their talking among themselves, and merely grew more distant in their manner toward the colored folks, who instinctively closed their ranks as the whites drew away. With each day that passed the feeling grew more tense. The editor of the Afro-American Banner, whose office had been quietly garrisoned for several nights by armed negroes, became frightened, and disappeared from the town between two suns.

The conspirators were jubilant at the complete success of their plans. It only remained for them to so direct this aroused public feeling that it might completely accomplish the desired end,—to change the political complexion of the city government and assure the ascendency of the whites until the amendment should go into effect. A revolution, and not a riot, was contemplated.

With this end in view, another meeting was called at Carteret's office.

"We are now ready," announced General Belmont, "for the final act of this drama. We must decide promptly, or events may run away from us."

"What do you suggest?" asked Carteret.

"Down in the American tropics," continued the general, "they have a way of doing things. I was in Nicaragua, ten years ago, when Paterno's revolution drove out Igorroto's government. It was as easy as falling off a log. Paterno had the arms and the best men. Igorroto was not looking for trouble, and the guns were at his breast before he knew it. We have the guns. The negroes are not expecting trouble, and are easy to manage compared with the fiery mixture that flourishes in the tropics."

"I should not advocate murder," returned Carteret. "We are animated by high and holy principles. We wish to right a wrong, to remedy an abuse, to save our state from anarchy and our race from humiliation. I don't object to frightening the negroes, but I am opposed to unnecessary bloodshed."

"I 'm not quite so particular," struck in McBane. "They need to be taught a lesson, and a nigger more or less would n't be missed. There 's too many of 'em now."

"Of course," continued Carteret, "if we should decide upon a certain mode of procedure, and the negroes should resist, a different reasoning might apply; but I will have no premeditated murder."

"In Central and South America," observed the general reflectively, "none are hurt except those who get in the way."

"There 'll be no niggers hurt," said McBane contemptuously, "unless they strain themselves running. One white man can chase a hundred of 'em. I 've managed five hundred at a time. I 'll pay for burying all the niggers that are killed."

The conference resulted in a well-defined plan, to be put into operation the following day, by which the city government was to be wrested from the Republicans and their negro allies.

"And now," said General Belmont, "while we are cleansing the Augean stables, we may as well remove the cause as the effect. There are several negroes too many in this town, which will be much the better without them. There 's that yellow lawyer, Watson. He 's altogether too mouthy, and has too much business. Every nigger that gets into trouble sends for Watson, and white lawyers, with families to support and social positions to keep up, are deprived of their legitimate source of income."

"There 's that damn nigger real estate agent," blurted out McBane. "Billy Kitchen used to get most of the nigger business, but this darky has almost driven him to the poorhouse. A white business man is entitled to a living in his own profession and his own home. That nigger don't belong here nohow. He came from the North a year or two ago, and is hand in glove with Barber, the nigger editor, which is enough of itself to damn him. *He 'll* have to go!"

"How about the collector of the port?"

"We 'd better not touch him. It would bring the government down upon us, which we want to avoid. We don't need to worry about the nigger preachers either. They want to stay here, where the loaves and the fishes are. We can make 'em write letters to the newspapers justifying our course, as a condition of their remaining."

"What about Billings?" asked McBane. Billings was the white Republican mayor. "Is that skunk to be allowed to stay in town?"

"No," returned the general, "every white Republican officeholder ought to be made to go. This town is only big enough for Democrats, and negroes who can be taught to keep their place."

"What about the colored doctor," queried McBane, "with the hospital, and the diamond ring, and the carriage, and the other fallals?"

"I should n't interfere with Miller," replied the general decisively. "He 's a very good sort of a negro, does n't meddle with politics, nor tread on any one else's toes. His father was a good citizen, which counts in his favor. He 's spending money in the community too, and contributes to its prosperity."

"That sort of nigger, though, sets a bad example," retorted McBane. "They make it all the harder to keep the rest of 'em down."

" 'One swallow does not make a summer,' " quoted the general. "When we get things arranged, there 'll be no trouble. A stream cannot rise higher than its fountain, and a smart nigger without a constituency will no longer be an object of fear. I say, let the doctor alone."

"He 'll have to keep mighty quiet, though," muttered McBane discontentedly. "I don't like smart niggers. I 've had to shoot several of them, in the course of my life."

"Personally, I dislike the man," interposed Carteret, "and if I consulted my own inclinations, would say expel him with the rest; but my grievance is a personal one, and to gratify it in that way would be a loss to the community. I wish to be strictly impartial in this matter, and to take no step which cannot be entirely justified by a wise regard for the public welfare."

"What 's the use of all this hypocrisy, gentlemen?" sneered McBane. "Every last one of us has an axe to grind! The major may as well put an edge on his. We 'll never get a better chance to have things our way. If this nigger doctor annoys the major, we 'll run him out with the rest. This is a white man's country, and a white man's city, and no nigger has any business here when a white man wants him gone!"

Carteret frowned darkly at this brutal characterization of their motives. It robbed the enterprise of all its poetry, and put a solemn act of revolution upon the plane of a mere vulgar theft of power. Even the general winced.

"I would not consent," he said irritably, "to Miller's being disturbed."

McBane made no further objection.

There was a discreet knock at the door.

"Come in," said Carteret.

Jerry entered. "Mistuh Ellis wants ter speak ter you a minute, suh," he said.

Carteret excused himself and left the room.

"Jerry," said the general, "you lump of ebony, the sight of you reminds me! If your master does n't want you for a minute, step across to Mr. Brown's and tell him to send me three cocktails."

"Yas, suh," responded Jerry, hesitating. The general had said nothing about paying.

"And tell him, Jerry, to charge them. I 'm short of change to-day."

"Yas, suh; yas, suh," replied Jerry, as he backed out of the presence, adding, when he had reached the hall: "Dere ain' no change fer Jerry dis time, sho': I 'll jes' make dat *fo'* cocktails, an' de gin'l won't never know de diffe'nce. I ain' gwine 'cross de road fer nothin', not ef I knows it."

Half an hour later, the conspirators dispersed. They had fixed the hour of the proposed revolution, the course to be pursued, the results to be obtained; but in stating their equation they had overlooked one factor,—God, or Fate, or whatever one may choose to call the Power that holds the destinies of man in the hollow of his hand.

XXX

THE MISSING PAPERS

Mrs. Carteret was very much disturbed. It was supposed that the shock of her aunt's death had affected her health, for since that event she had fallen into a nervous condition which gave the major grave concern. Much to the general surprise, Mrs. Ochiltree had left no will, and no property of any considerable value except her homestead, which descended to Mrs. Carteret as the natural heir. Whatever she may have had on hand in the way of ready money had undoubtedly been abstracted from the cedar chest by the midnight marauder, to whose visit her death was immediately due. Her niece's grief was held to mark a deep-seated affection for the grim old woman who had reared her.

Mrs. Carteret's present state of mind, of which her nervousness was a sufficiently accurate reflection, did in truth date from her aunt's death, and also in part from the time of the conversation with Mrs. Ochiltree, one afternoon, during and after the drive past Miller's new hospital. Mrs. Ochiltree had grown steadily more and more childish after that time, and her niece had never succeeded in making her pick up the thread of thought where it had been dropped. At any rate, Mrs. Ochiltree had made no further disclosure upon the subject.

An examination, not long after her aunt's death, of the papers found near the cedar chest on the morning after the murder had contributed to Mrs. Carteret's enlightenment, but had not promoted her peace of mind.

When Mrs. Carteret reached home, after her hurried exploration of the cedar chest, she thrust into a bureau drawer the envelope she had found. So fully was her mind occupied, for several days, with the funeral, and with the excitement attending the arrest of Sandy Campbell, that she deferred the examination of the contents of the envelope until near the end of the week.

One morning, while alone in her chamber, she drew the envelope from the drawer, and was holding it in her hand, hesitating as to whether or not she should open it, when the baby in the next room began to cry.

The child's cry seemed like a warning, and yielding to a vague uneasiness, she put the paper back.

"Phil," she said to her husband at luncheon, "Aunt Polly said some strange things to me one day before she died,—I don't know whether she was quite in her right mind or not; but suppose that my father had left a will by which it was provided that half his property should go to that woman and her child?"

"It would never have gone by such a will," replied the major easily. "Your Aunt Polly was in her dotage, and merely dreaming. Your father would never have been such a fool; but even if he had, no such will could have stood the test of the courts. It would clearly have been due to the improper influence of a designing woman."

"So that legally, as well as morally," said Mrs. Carteret, "the will would have been of no effect?"

"Not the slightest. A jury would soon have broken down the legal claim. As for any moral obligation, there would have been nothing moral about the affair. The only possible consideration for such a gift was an immoral one. I don't wish to speak harshly of your father, my dear, but his conduct was gravely reprehensible. The woman herself had no right or claim whatever; she would have been whipped and expelled from the town, if justice—blind, bleeding justice, then prostrate at the feet of slaves and aliens—could have had her way!"

"But the child"—

"The child was in the same category. Who was she, to have inherited the estate of your ancestors, of which, a few years before, she would herself have formed a part? The child of shame, it was hers to pay the penalty. But the discussion is all in the air, Olivia. Your father never did and never would have left such a will."

This conversation relieved Mrs. Carteret's uneasiness. Going to her room shortly afterwards, she took the envelope from her bureau drawer and drew out a bulky paper. The haunting fear that it might be such a will as her aunt had suggested was now removed; for such an instrument, in the light of what her husband had said confirming her own intuitions, would be of no valid effect. It might be just as well, she thought, to throw the paper in the fire without looking at it. She wished to think as well as might be of her father, and she felt that her respect for his memory would not be strengthened by the knowledge that he had meant to leave his estate away from her; for her aunt's words had been open to the construction that she was to have been left destitute. Curiosity strongly prompted her to read the paper. Perhaps the will contained no such provision as she had feared, and it might convey some request or direction which ought properly to be complied with.

She had been standing in front of the bureau while these thoughts passed through her mind, and now, dropping the envelope back into the drawer mechanically, she unfolded the document. It was written on legal paper, in her father's own hand.

Mrs. Carteret was not familiar with legal verbiage, and there were several expressions of which she did not perhaps appreciate the full effect; but a very hasty glance enabled her to ascertain the purport of the paper. It was a will, by which, in one item, her father devised to his daughter Janet, the child of the woman known as Julia Brown, the sum of ten thousand dollars, and a certain plantation or tract of land a short distance from the town of Wellington. The rest and residue of his estate, after deducting all legal charges and expenses, was bequeathed to his beloved daughter, Olivia Merkell.

Mrs. Carteret breathed a sigh of relief. Her father had not preferred another to her, but had left to his lawful daughter the bulk of his estate. She felt at the same time a growing indignation at the thought that that woman should so have wrought upon her father's weakness as to induce him to think of leaving so much valuable property to her bastard,—property which by right should go, and now would go, to her own son, to whom by every rule of law and decency it ought to descend.

A fire was burning in the next room, on account of the baby,—there had been a light frost the night before, and the air was somewhat chilly. For the moment the room was empty. Mrs. Carteret came out from her chamber and threw the offending paper into the fire, and watched it slowly burn. When it had been consumed, the carbon residue of one sheet still retained its form, and she could read the words on the charred portion. A sentence, which had escaped her eye in her rapid reading, stood out in ghostly black upon the gray background:—

"All the rest and residue of my estate I devise and bequeath to my daughter Olivia Merkell, the child of my beloved first wife."

Mrs. Carteret had not before observed the word "first." Instinctively she stretched toward the fire the poker which she held in her hand, and at its touch the shadowy remnant fell to pieces, and nothing but ashes remained upon the hearth.

Not until the next morning did she think again of the envelope which had contained the paper she had burned. Opening the drawer where it lay, the oblong blue envelope confronted her. The sight of it was distasteful. The indorsed side lay uppermost, and the words seemed like a mute reproach:—

"The Last Will and Testament of Samuel Merkell."

Snatching up the envelope, she glanced into it mechanically as she moved toward the next room, and perceived a thin folded paper which had heretofore escaped her notice. When opened, it proved to be a certificate of marriage, in due form, between Samuel Merkell and Julia Brown. It was dated from a county in South Carolina, about two years before her father's death.

For a moment Mrs. Carteret stood gazing blankly at this faded slip of paper. Her father *had* married this woman!—at least he had gone through the form of marriage with her, for to him it had surely been no more than an empty formality. The marriage of white and colored persons was forbidden by law. Only recently she had read of a case where both the parties to such a crime, a colored man and a white woman, had been sentenced to long terms in the penitentiary. She even recalled the circumstances. The couple had been living together unlawfully,—they were very low people, whose private lives were beneath the public notice,—but influenced by a religious movement pervading the community, had sought, they said at the trial, to secure the blessing of God upon their union. The higher law, which imperiously demanded that the purity and prestige of the white race be preserved at any cost, had intervened at this point.

Mechanically she moved toward the fireplace, so dazed by

this discovery as to be scarcely conscious of her own actions. She surely had not formed any definite intention of destroying this piece of paper when her fingers relaxed unconsciously and let go their hold upon it. The draught swept it toward the fireplace. Ere scarcely touching the flames it caught, blazed fiercely, and shot upward with the current of air. A moment later the record of poor Julia's marriage was scattered to the four winds of heaven, as her poor body had long since mingled with the dust of earth.

The letter remained unread. In her agitation at the discovery of the marriage certificate, Olivia had almost forgotten the existence of the letter. It was addressed to "John Delamere, Esq., as Executor of my Last Will and Testament," while the lower left-hand corner bore the direction: "To be delivered only after my death, with seal unbroken."

The seal was broken already; Mr. Delamere was dead; the letter could never be delivered. Mrs. Carteret unfolded it and read:—

> MY DEAR DELAMERE,—I have taken the liberty of naming you as executor of my last will, because you are my friend, and the only man of my acquaintance whom I feel that I can trust to carry out my wishes, appreciate my motives, and preserve the silence I desire.
>
> I have, first, a confession to make. Inclosed in this letter you will find a certificate of marriage between my child Janet's mother and myself. While I have never exactly repented of this marriage, I have never had the courage to acknowledge it openly. If I had not married Julia, I fear Polly Ochiltree would have married me by main force,—as she would marry you or any other gentleman unfortunate enough to fall in the way of this twice-widowed man-hunter. When my wife died, three years ago, her sister Polly offered to keep house for me and the child. I would sooner have had the devil in the house, and yet I trembled with alarm,—there seemed no way of escape,—it was so clearly and obviously the proper thing.
>
> But she herself gave me my opportunity. I was on the point of consenting, when she demanded, as a condition

of her coming, that I discharge Julia, my late wife's maid. She was laboring under a misapprehension in regard to the girl, but I grasped at the straw, and did everything to foster her delusion. I declared solemnly that nothing under heaven would induce me to part with Julia. The controversy resulted in my permitting Polly to take the child, while I retained the maid.

Before Polly put this idea into my head, I had scarcely looked at Julia, but this outbreak turned my attention toward her. She was a handsome girl, and, as I soon found out, a good girl. My wife, who raised her, was a Christian woman, and had taught her modesty and virtue. She was free. The air was full of liberty, and equal rights, and all the abolition clap-trap, and she made marriage a condition of her remaining longer in the house. In a moment of weakness I took her away to a place where we were not known, and married her. If she had left me, I should have fallen a victim to Polly Ochiltree,—to which any fate was preferable.

And then, old friend, my weakness kept to the fore. I was ashamed of this marriage, and my new wife saw it. Moreover, she loved me,—too well, indeed, to wish to make me unhappy. The ceremony had satisfied her conscience, had set her right, she said, with God; for the opinions of men she did not care, since I loved her,—she only wanted to compensate me, as best she could, for the great honor I had done my handmaiden,—for she had read her Bible, and I was the Abraham to her Hagar, compared with whom she considered herself at a great advantage. It was her own proposition that nothing be said of this marriage. If any shame should fall on her, it would fall lightly, for it would be undeserved. When the child came, she still kept silence. No one, she argued, could blame an innocent child for the accident of birth, and in the sight of God this child had every right to exist; while among her own people illegitimacy would involve but little stigma.

I need not say that I was easily persuaded to accept this sacrifice; but touched by her fidelity, I swore to provide handsomely for them both. This I have tried to do by the will of which I ask you to act as executor. Had I left the child more, it might serve as a ground for attacking the will; my acknowledgment of the tie of blood is sufficient to justify a reasonable bequest.

I have taken this course for the sake of my daughter Olivia, who is dear to me, and whom I would not wish to make ashamed; and in deference to public opinion, which it is not easy to defy. If, after my death, Julia should choose to make our secret known, I shall of course be beyond the reach of hard words; but loyalty to my memory will probably keep her silent. A strong man would long since have acknowledged her before the world and taken the consequences; but, alas! I am only myself, and the atmosphere I live in does not encourage moral heroism. I should like to be different, but it is God who hath made us, and not we ourselves!

Nevertheless, old friend, I will ask of you one favor. If in the future this child of Julia's and of mine should grow to womanhood; if she should prove to have her mother's gentleness and love of virtue; if, in the new era which is opening up for her mother's race, to which, unfortunately, she must belong, she should become, in time, an educated woman; and if the time should ever come when, by virtue of her education or the development of her people, it would be to her a source of shame or unhappiness that she was an illegitimate child,—if you are still alive, old friend, and have the means of knowing or divining this thing, go to her and tell her, for me, that she is my lawful child, and ask her to forgive her father's weakness.

When this letter comes to you, I shall have passed to—the Beyond; but I am confident that you will accept this trust, for which I thank you now, in advance, most heartily.

The letter was signed with her father's name, the same signature which had been attached to the will.

Having firmly convinced herself of the illegality of the papers, and of her own right to destroy them, Mrs. Carteret ought to have felt relieved that she had thus removed all traces of her dead father's folly. True, the other daughter remained,—she had seen her on the street only the day before. The sight of this person she had always found offensive, and now, she felt, in view of what she had just learned, it must be even more so. Never, while this woman lived in the town, would she be able to throw the veil of forgetfulness over this blot upon her father's memory.

As the day wore on, Mrs. Carteret grew still less at ease. To herself, marriage was a serious thing,—to a right-thinking woman the most serious concern of life. A marriage certificate, rightfully procured, was scarcely less solemn, so far as it went, than the Bible itself. Her own she cherished as the apple of her eye. It was the evidence of her wifehood, the seal of her child's legitimacy, her patent of nobility,—the token of her own and her child's claim to social place and consideration. She had burned this pretended marriage certificate because it meant nothing. Nevertheless, she could not ignore the knowledge of another such marriage, of which every one in the town knew,—a celebrated case, indeed, where a white man, of a family quite as prominent as her father's, had married a colored woman during the military occupation of the state just after the civil war. The legality of the marriage had never been questioned. It had been fully consummated by twenty years of subsequent cohabitation. No amount of social persecution had ever shaken the position of the husband. With an iron will he had stayed on in the town, a living protest against the established customs of the South, so rudely interrupted for a few short years; and, though his children were negroes, though he had never appeared in public with his wife, no one had ever questioned the validity of his marriage or the legitimacy of his offspring.

The marriage certificate which Mrs. Carteret had burned dated from the period of the military occupation. Hence Mrs. Carteret, who was a good woman, and would not have done a dishonest thing, felt decidedly uncomfortable. She had destroyed the marriage certificate, but its ghost still haunted her.

Major Carteret, having just eaten a good dinner, was in a very agreeable humor when, that same evening, his wife brought up again the subject of their previous discussion.

"Phil," she asked, "Aunt Polly told me that once, long before my father died, when she went to remonstrate with him for keeping that woman in the house, he threatened to marry Julia if Aunt Polly ever said another word to him about the matter. Suppose he *had* married her, and had *then* left a will,—would the marriage have made any difference, so far as the will was concerned?"

Major Carteret laughed. "Your Aunt Polly," he said, "was a remarkable woman, with a wonderful imagination, which seems to have grown more vivid as her memory and judgment weakened. Why should your father marry his negro housemaid? Mr. Merkell was never rated as a fool,—he had one of the clearest heads in Wellington. I saw him only a day or two before he died, and I could swear before any court in Christendom that he was of sound mind and memory to the last. These notions of your aunt were mere delusions. Your father was never capable of such a folly."

"Of course I am only supposing a case," returned Olivia. "Imagining such a case, just for the argument, would the marriage have been legal?"

"That would depend. If he had married her during the military occupation, or over in South Carolina, the marriage would have been legally valid, though morally and socially outrageous."

"And if he had died afterwards, leaving a will?"

"The will would have controlled the disposition of his estate, in all probability."

"Suppose he had left no will?"

"You are getting the matter down pretty fine, my dear! The woman would have taken one third of the real estate for life, and could have lived in the homestead until she died. She would also have had half the other property,—the money and goods and furniture, everything except the land,—and the negro child would have shared with you the balance of the estate. That, I believe, is according to the law of descent and distribution."

Mrs. Carteret lapsed into a troubled silence. Her father *had* married the woman. In her heart she had no doubt of the validity of the marriage, so far as the law was concerned; if one marriage of such a kind would stand, another contracted under similar conditions was equally as good. If the marriage had been valid, Julia's child had been legitimate. The will she had burned gave this sister of hers—she shuddered at the word—but a small part of the estate. Under the law, which intervened now that there was no will, the property should have been equally divided. If the woman had been white,—but the woman had *not* been white, and the same rule of moral conduct did not, *could* not, in the very nature of things, apply, as between white people! For, if this were not so, slavery had been, not merely an economic mistake, but a great crime against humanity. If it had been such a crime, as for a moment she dimly perceived it might have been, then through the long centuries there had been piled up a catalogue of wrong and outrage which, if the law of compensation be a law of nature, must some time, somewhere, in some way, be atoned for. She herself had not escaped the penalty, of which, she realized, this burden placed upon her conscience was but another installment.

If she should make known the facts she had learned, it would mean what?—a division of her father's estate, a recognition of the legality of her father's relations with Julia. Such a stain upon her father's memory would be infinitely worse than if he had not married her. To have lived with her without marriage was a social misdemeanor, at which society in the old days had winked, or at most had frowned. To have married her was to have committed the unpardonable social sin. Such a scandal Mrs. Carteret could not have endured. Should she seek to make restitution, it would necessarily involve the disclosure of at least some of the facts. Had she not destroyed the will, she might have compromised with her conscience by producing it and acting upon its terms, which had been so stated as not to disclose the marriage. This was now rendered impossible by her own impulsive act; she could not mention the will at all, without admitting that she had destroyed it.

Mrs. Carteret found herself in what might be called, vulgarly, a moral "pocket." She could, of course, remain silent. Mrs. Carteret was a good woman, according to her lights, with a cultivated conscience, to which she had always looked as her mentor and infallible guide.

Hence Mrs. Carteret, after this painful discovery, remained for a long time ill at ease,—so disturbed, indeed, that her mind reacted upon her nerves, which had never been strong; and her nervousness affected her strength, which had never been great, until Carteret, whose love for her had been deepened and strengthened by the advent of his son, became alarmed for her health, and spoke very seriously to Dr. Price concerning it.

XXXI

THE SHADOW OF A DREAM

MRS. CARTERET awoke, with a start, from a troubled dream. She had been sailing across a sunlit sea, in a beautiful boat, her child lying on a bright-colored cushion at her feet. Overhead the swelling sail served as an awning to keep off the sun's rays, which far ahead were reflected with dazzling brilliancy from the shores of a golden island. Her son, she dreamed, was a fairy prince, and yonder lay his kingdom, to which he was being borne, lying there at her feet, in this beautiful boat, across the sunlit sea.

Suddenly and without warning the sky was overcast. A squall struck the boat and tore away the sail. In the distance a huge billow—a great white wall of water—came sweeping toward their frail craft, threatening it with instant destruction. She clasped her child to her bosom, and a moment later found herself struggling in the sea, holding the child's head above the water. As she floated there, as though sustained by some unseen force, she saw in the distance a small boat approaching over the storm-tossed waves. Straight toward her it came, and she had reached out her hand to grasp its side, when the rower looked back, and she saw that it was her sister. The recognition had been mutual. With a sharp movement of one oar the boat glided by, leaving her clutching at the empty air.

She felt her strength begin to fail. Despairingly she signaled with her disengaged hand; but the rower, after one mute, reproachful glance, rowed on. Mrs. Carteret's strength grew less and less. The child became heavy as lead. Herself floating in the water, as though it were her native element, she could no longer support the child. Lower and lower it sank,—she was powerless to save it or to accompany it,—until, gasping wildly for breath, it threw up its little hands and sank, the cruel water gurgling over its head,—when she awoke with a start and a chill, and lay there trembling for several minutes before she heard little Dodie in his crib, breathing heavily.

She rose softly, went to the crib, and changed the child's position to an easier one. He breathed more freely, and she went back to bed, but not to sleep.

She had tried to put aside the distressing questions raised by the discovery of her father's will and the papers accompanying it. Why should she be burdened with such a responsibility, at this late day, when the touch of time had well-nigh healed these old sores? Surely, God had put his curse not alone upon the slave, but upon the stealer of men! With other good people she had thanked Him that slavery was no more, and that those who once had borne its burden upon their consciences could stand erect and feel that they themselves were free. The weed had been cut down, but its roots remained, deeply imbedded in the soil, to spring up and trouble a new generation. Upon her weak shoulders was placed the burden of her father's weakness, her father's folly. It was left to her to acknowledge or not this shameful marriage and her sister's rights in their father's estate.

Balancing one consideration against another, she had almost decided that she might ignore this tie. To herself, Olivia Merkell,—Olivia Carteret,—the stigma of base birth would have meant social ostracism, social ruin, the averted face, the finger of pity or of scorn. All the traditional weight of public disapproval would have fallen upon her as the unhappy fruit of an unblessed union. To this other woman it could have had no such significance,—it had been the lot of her race. To them, twenty-five years before, sexual sin had never been imputed as more than a fault. She had lost nothing by her supposed illegitimacy; she would gain nothing by the acknowledgment of her mother's marriage.

On the other hand, what would be the effect of this revelation upon Mrs. Carteret herself? To have it known that her father had married a negress would only be less dreadful than to have it appear that he had committed some terrible crime. It was a crime now, by the laws of every Southern State, for white and colored persons to intermarry. She shuddered before the possibility that at some time in the future some person, none too well informed, might learn that her father had married a colored woman, and might assume that she, Olivia Carteret, or her child, had sprung from this shocking *mésalliance*,—a fate to which she would willingly have preferred death. No, this marriage must never be made known; the secret should remain buried forever in her own heart!

But there still remained the question of her father's property and her father's will. This woman was her father's child,—of that there could be no doubt, it was written in her features no less than in her father's will. As his lawful child,—of which, alas! there could also be no question,—she was entitled by law to half his estate. Mrs. Carteret's problem had sunk from the realm of sentiment to that of material things, which, curiously enough, she found much more difficult. For, while the negro, by the traditions of her people, was barred from the world of sentiment, his rights of property were recognized. The question had become, with Mrs. Carteret, a question of *meum* and *tuum*. Had the girl Janet been poor, ignorant, or degraded, as might well have been her fate, Mrs. Carteret might have felt a vicarious remorse for her aunt's suppression of the papers; but fate had compensated Janet for the loss; she had been educated, she had married well; she had not suffered for lack of the money of which she had been defrauded, and did not need it now. She had a child, it is true, but this child's career would be so circumscribed by the accident of color that too much wealth would only be a source of unhappiness; to her own child, on the contrary, it would open every door of life.

It would be too lengthy a task to follow the mind and conscience of this much-tried lady in their intricate workings upon this difficult problem; for she had a mind as logical as any woman's, and a conscience which she wished to keep void of offense. She had to confront a situation involving the element of race, upon which the moral standards of her people were hopelessly confused. Mrs. Carteret reached the conclusion, ere daylight dawned, that she would be silent upon the subject of her father's second marriage. Neither party had wished it known,—neither Julia nor her father,—and she would respect her father's wishes. To act otherwise would be to defeat his will, to make known what he had carefully concealed, and to give Janet a claim of title to one half her father's estate, while he had only meant her to have the ten thousand dollars named in the will.

By the same reasoning, she must carry out her father's will in respect to this bequest. Here there was another difficulty. The mining investment into which they had entered shortly after the birth of little Dodie had tied up so much of her property that it would have been difficult to procure ten thousand dollars immediately; while a demand for half the property at once would mean bankruptcy and ruin. Moreover, upon what ground could she offer her sister any sum of money whatever? So sudden a change of heart, after so many years of silence, would raise the presumption of some right on the part of Janet in her father's estate. Suspicion once aroused, it might be possible to trace this hidden marriage, and establish it by legal proof. The marriage once verified, the claim for half the estate could not be denied. She could not plead her father's will to the contrary, for this would be to acknowledge the suppression of the will, in itself a criminal act.

There was, however, a way of escape. This hospital which had recently been opened was the personal property of her sister's husband. Some time in the future, when their investments matured, she would present to the hospital a sum of money equal to the amount her father had meant his colored daughter to have. Thus indirectly both her father's will and her own conscience would be satisfied.

Mrs. Carteret had reached this comfortable conclusion, and was falling asleep, when her attention was again drawn by her child's breathing. She took it in her own arms and soon fell asleep.

"By the way, Olivia," said the major, when leaving the house next morning for the office, "if you have any business down town to-day, transact it this forenoon. Under no circumstances must you or Clara or the baby leave the house after midday."

"Why, what 's the matter, Phil?"

"Nothing to alarm you, except that there may be a little political demonstration which may render the streets unsafe. You are not to say anything about it where the servants might hear."

"Will there be any danger for you, Phil?" she demanded with alarm.

"Not the slightest, Olivia dear. No one will be harmed; but it is best for ladies and children to stay indoors."

Mrs. Carteret's nerves were still more or less unstrung from her mental struggles of the night, and the memory of her dream came to her like a dim foreboding of misfortune. As though in sympathy with its mother's feelings, the baby did not seem as well as usual. The new nurse was by no means an ideal nurse,—Mammy Jane understood the child much better. If there should be any trouble with the negroes, toward which her husband's remark seemed to point,—she knew the general political situation, though not informed in regard to her husband's plans,—she would like to have Mammy Jane near her, where the old nurse might be protected from danger or alarm.

With this end in view she dispatched the nurse, shortly after breakfast, to Mammy Jane's house in the negro settlement on the other side of the town, with a message asking the old woman to come immediately to Mrs. Carteret's. Unfortunately, Mammy Jane had gone to visit a sick woman in the country, and was not expected to return for several hours.

XXXII

THE STORM BREAKS

THE Wellington riot began at three o'clock in the afternoon of a day as fair as was ever selected for a deed of darkness. The sky was clear, except for a few light clouds that floated, white and feathery, high in air, like distant islands in a sapphire sea. A salt-laden breeze from the ocean a few miles away lent a crisp sparkle to the air.

At three o'clock sharp the streets were filled, as if by magic, with armed white men. The negroes, going about, had noted, with uneasy curiosity, that the stores and places of business, many of which closed at noon, were unduly late in opening for the afternoon, though no one suspected the reason for the delay; but at three o'clock every passing colored man was ordered, by the first white man he met, to throw up his hands. If he complied, he was searched, more or less roughly, for firearms, and then warned to get off the street. When he met another group of white men the scene was repeated. The man thus summarily held up seldom encountered more than two groups before disappearing across lots to his own home or some convenient hiding-place. If he resisted any demand of those who halted him— But the records of the day are historical; they may be found in the newspapers of the following date, but they are more firmly engraved upon the hearts and memories of the people of Wellington. For many months there were negro families in the town whose children screamed with fear and ran to their mothers for protection at the mere sight of a white man.

Dr. Miller had received a call, about one o'clock, to attend a case at the house of a well-to-do colored farmer, who lived some three or four miles from the town, upon the very road, by the way, along which Miller had driven so furiously a few weeks before, in the few hours that intervened before Sandy Campbell would probably have been burned at the stake. The drive to his patient's home, the necessary inquiries, the filling of the prescription from his own medicine-case, which he carried along with him, the little friendly conversation about the weather and the crops, and, the farmer being an intelligent and thinking man, the inevitable subject of the future of their race,—these, added to the return journey, occupied at least two hours of Miller's time.

As he neared the town on his way back, he saw ahead of him half a dozen men and women approaching, with fear written in their faces, in every degree from apprehension to terror. Women were weeping and children crying, and all were going as fast as seemingly lay in their power, looking behind now and then as if pursued by some deadly enemy. At sight of Miller's buggy they made a dash for cover, disappearing, like a covey of frightened partridges, in the underbrush along the road.

Miller pulled up his horse and looked after them in startled wonder.

"What on earth can be the matter?" he muttered, struck with a vague feeling of alarm. A psychologist, seeking to trace the effects of slavery upon the human mind, might find in the South many a curious illustration of this curse, abiding long after the actual physical bondage had terminated. In the olden time the white South labored under the constant fear of negro insurrections. Knowing that they themselves, if in the negroes' place, would have risen in the effort to throw off the yoke, all their reiterated theories of negro subordination and inferiority could not remove that lurking fear, founded upon the obscure consciousness that the slaves ought to have risen. Conscience, it has been said, makes cowards of us all. There was never, on the continent of America, a successful slave revolt, nor one which lasted more than a few hours, or resulted in the loss of more than a few white lives; yet never was the planter quite free from the fear that there might be one.

On the other hand, the slave had before his eyes always the fear of the master. There were good men, according to their lights,—according to their training and environment,—among the Southern slave-holders, who treated their slaves kindly, as slaves, from principle, because they recognized the claims of humanity, even under the dark skin of a human chattel. There was many a one who protected or pampered his negroes, as the case might be, just as a man fondles his dog,—because they were his; they were a part of his estate, an integral part of the entity of property and person which made up the aristocrat; but with all this kindness, there was always present, in the consciousness of the lowest slave, the knowledge that he was in his master's power, and that he could make no effectual protest against the abuse of that authority. There was also the knowledge, among those who could think at all, that the best of masters was himself a slave to a system, which hampered his movements but scarcely less than those of his bondmen.

When, therefore, Miller saw these men and women scampering into the bushes, he divined, with this slumbering race consciousness which years of culture had not obliterated, that there was some race trouble on foot. His intuition did not long remain unsupported. A black head was cautiously protruded from the shrubbery, and a black voice—if such a description be allowable—addressed him:—

"Is dat you, Doctuh Miller?"

"Yes. Who are you, and what 's the trouble?"

"What 's de trouble, suh? Why, all hell 's broke loose in town yonduh. De w'ite folks is riz 'gins' de niggers, an' say dey 're gwine ter kill eve'y nigger dey kin lay han's on."

Miller's heart leaped to his throat, as he thought of his wife and child. This story was preposterous; it could not be true, and yet there must be something in it. He tried to question his informant, but the man was so overcome with excitement and fear that Miller saw clearly that he must go farther for information. He had read in the Morning Chronicle, a few days before, the obnoxious editorial quoted from the Afro-American Banner, and had noted the comment upon it by the white editor. He had felt, as at the time of its first publication, that the editorial was ill-advised. It could do no good, and was calculated to arouse the animosity of those whose friendship, whose tolerance, at least, was necessary and almost indispensable to the colored people. They were living, at the best, in a sort of armed neutrality with the whites; such a publication, however serviceable elsewhere, could have no other effect in Wellington than to endanger this truce and defeat the hope of a possible future friendship. The right of free speech entitled Barber to publish it; a larger measure of common-sense would have made him withhold it. Whether it was the republication of this article that had stirred up anew the sleeping dogs of race prejudice and whetted their thirst for blood, he could not yet tell; but at any rate, there was mischief on foot.

"Fer God's sake, doctuh, don' go no closeter ter dat town," pleaded his informant, "er you 'll be killt sho'. Come on wid us, suh, an' tek keer er yo'se'f. We 're gwine ter hide in de swamps till dis thing is over!"

"God, man!" exclaimed Miller, urging his horse forward, "my wife and child are in the town!"

Fortunately, he reflected, there were no patients confined in the hospital,—if there should be anything in this preposterous story. To one unfamiliar with Southern life, it might have seemed impossible that these good Christian people, who thronged the churches on Sunday, and wept over the sufferings of the lowly Nazarene, and sent missionaries to the heathen, could be hungering and thirsting for the blood of their fellow men; but Miller cherished no such delusion. He knew the history of his country; he had the threatened lynching of Sandy Campbell vividly in mind; and he was fully persuaded that to race prejudice, once roused, any horror was possible. That women or children would be molested of set purpose he did not believe, but that they might suffer by accident was more than likely.

As he neared the town, dashing forward at the top of his horse's speed, he heard his voice called in a loud and agitated tone, and, glancing around him, saw a familiar form standing by the roadside, gesticulating vehemently.

He drew up the horse with a suddenness that threw the faithful and obedient animal back upon its haunches. The colored lawyer, Watson, came up to the buggy. That he was laboring under great and unusual excitement was quite apparent from his pale face and frightened air.

"What 's the matter, Watson?" demanded Miller, hoping now to obtain some reliable information.

"Matter!" exclaimed the other. "Everything 's the matter! The white people are up in arms. They have disarmed the colored people, killing half a dozen in the process, and wounding as many more. They have forced the mayor and aldermen to resign, have formed a provisional city government *à la française*, and have ordered me and half a dozen other fellows to leave town in forty-eight hours, under pain of sudden death. As they seem to mean it, I shall not stay so long. Fortunately, my wife and children are away. I knew you were out here, however, and I thought I 'd come out and wait for you, so that we might talk the matter over. I don't imagine they mean you any harm, personally, because you tread on nobody's toes; but you 're too valuable a man for the race to lose, so I thought I 'd give you warning. I shall want to sell you my property, too, at a bargain. For I 'm worth too much to my family to dream of ever attempting to live here again."

"Have you seen anything of my wife and child?" asked Miller, intent upon the danger to which they might be exposed.

"No; I did n't go to the house. I inquired at the drugstore and found out where you had gone. You need n't fear for them,—it is not a war on women and children."

"War of any kind is always hardest on the women and children," returned Miller; "I must hurry on and see that mine are safe."

"They 'll not carry the war so far into Africa as that," returned Watson; "but I never saw anything like it. Yesterday I had a hundred white friends in the town, or thought I had,—men who spoke pleasantly to me on the street, and sometimes gave me their hands to shake. Not one of them said to me today: 'Watson, stay at home this afternoon.' I might have been killed, like any one of half a dozen others who have bit the dust, for any word that one of my 'friends' had said to warn me. When the race cry is started in this neck of the woods, friendship, religion, humanity, reason, all shrivel up like dry leaves in a raging furnace."

The buggy, into which Watson had climbed, was meanwhile rapidly nearing the town.

"I think I 'll leave you here, Miller," said Watson, as they approached the outskirts, "and make my way home by a roundabout path, as I should like to get there unmolested. Home!—a beautiful word that, is n't it, for an exiled wanderer? It might not be well, either, for us to be seen together. If you put the hood of your buggy down, and sit well back in the shadow, you may be able to reach home without interruption; but avoid the main streets. I 'll see you again this evening, if we 're both alive, and I can reach you; for my time is short. A committee are to call in the morning to escort me to the train. I am to be dismissed from the community with public honors."

Watson was climbing down from the buggy, when a small party of men were seen approaching, and big Josh Green, followed by several other resolute-looking colored men, came up and addressed them.

"Dr. Miller," cried Green, "Mr. Watson,—we 're lookin' fer a leader. De w'ite folks are killin' de niggers, an' we ain' gwine ter stan' up an' be shot down like dogs. We 're gwine ter defen' ou' lives, an' we ain' gwine ter run away f'm no place where we 've got a right ter be; an' woe be ter de w'ite man w'at lays han's on us! Dere 's two niggers in dis town ter eve'y w'ite man, an' ef we 've got ter be killt, we 'll take some w'ite folks 'long wid us, ez sho' ez dere 's a God in heaven,—ez I s'pose dere is, dough He mus' be 'sleep, er busy somewhar e'se ter-day. Will you-all come an' lead us?"

"Gentlemen," said Watson, "what is the use? The negroes will not back you up. They have n't the arms, nor the moral courage, nor the leadership."

"We 'll git de arms, an' we 'll git de courage, ef you 'll come an' lead us! We wants leaders,—dat 's w'y we come ter you!"

"What 's the use?" returned Watson despairingly. "The odds are too heavy. I 've been ordered out of town; if I stayed, I 'd be shot on sight, unless I had a body-guard around me."

"We 'll be yo' body-guard!" shouted half a dozen voices.

"And when my body-guard was shot, what then? I have a wife and children. It is my duty to live for them. If I died, I should get no glory and no reward, and my family would be reduced to beggary,—to which they 'll soon be near enough as it is. This affair will blow over in a day or two. The white people will be ashamed of themselves to-morrow, and apprehensive of the consequences for some time to come. Keep quiet, boys, and trust in God. You won't gain anything by resistance."

" 'God he'ps dem dat he'ps demselves,' " returned Josh

stoutly. "Ef Mr. Watson won't lead us, will you, Dr. Miller?" said the spokesman, turning to the doctor.

For Miller it was an agonizing moment. He was no coward, morally or physically. Every manly instinct urged him to go forward and take up the cause of these leaderless people, and, if need be, to defend their lives and their rights with his own,—but to what end?

"Listen, men," he said. "We would only be throwing our lives away. Suppose we made a determined stand and won a temporary victory. By morning every train, every boat, every road leading into Wellington, would be crowded with white men,—as they probably will be any way,—with arms in their hands, curses on their lips, and vengeance in their hearts. In the minds of those who make and administer the laws, we have no standing in the court of conscience. They would kill us in the fight, or they would hang us afterwards,—one way or another, we should be doomed. I should like to lead you; I should like to arm every colored man in this town, and have them stand firmly in line, not for attack, but for defense; but if I attempted it, and they should stand by me, which is questionable,—for I have met them fleeing from the town,—my life would pay the forfeit. Alive, I may be of some use to you, and you are welcome to my life in that way,—I am giving it freely. Dead, I should be a mere lump of carrion. Who remembers even the names of those who have been done to death in the Southern States for the past twenty years?"

"I 'members de name er one of 'em," said Josh, "an' I 'members de name er de man dat killt 'im, an' I s'pec' his time is mighty nigh come."

"My advice is not heroic, but I think it is wise. In this riot we are placed as we should be in a war: we have no territory, no base of supplies, no organization, no outside sympathy,—we stand in the position of a race, in a case like this, without money and without friends. Our time will come,—the time when we can command respect for our rights; but it is not yet in sight. Give it up, boys, and wait. Good may come of this, after all."

Several of the men wavered, and looked irresolute.

"I reckon that 's all so, doctuh," returned Josh, "an', de way you put it, I don' blame you ner Mr. Watson; but all dem reasons ain' got no weight wid me. I 'm gwine in dat town, an' ef any w'ite man 'sturbs me, dere 'll be trouble,—dere 'll be double trouble,—I feels it in my bones!"

"Remember your old mother, Josh," said Miller.

"Yas, suh, I 'll 'member her; dat 's all I kin do now. I don' need ter wait fer her no mo', fer she died dis mo'nin'. I 'd lack ter see her buried, suh, but I may not have de chance. Ef I gits killt, will you do me a favor?"

"Yes, Josh; what is it?"

"Ef I should git laid out in dis commotion dat 's gwine on, will you collec' my wages f'm yo' brother, and see dat de ole 'oman is put away right?"

"Yes, of course."

"Wid a nice coffin, an' a nice fune'al, an' a head-bo'd an' a foot-bo'd?"

"Yes."

"All right, suh! Ef I don' live ter do it, I 'll know it 'll be 'tended ter right. Now we 're gwine out ter de cotton compress, an' git a lot er colored men tergether, an' ef de w'ite folks 'sturbs me, I should n't be s'prise' ef dere 'd be a mix-up;—an' ef dere is, me an *one* w'ite man 'll stan' befo' de jedgment th'one er God dis day; an' it won't be me w'at 'll be 'feared er de jedgment. Come along, boys! Dese gentlemen may have somethin' ter live fer; but ez fer my pa't, I 'd ruther be a dead nigger any day dan a live dog!"

XXXIII

INTO THE LION'S JAWS

The party under Josh's leadership moved off down the road. Miller, while entirely convinced that he had acted wisely in declining to accompany them, was yet conscious of a distinct feeling of shame and envy that he, too, did not feel impelled to throw away his life in a hopeless struggle.

Watson left the buggy and disappeared by a path at the roadside. Miller drove rapidly forward. After entering the town, he passed several small parties of white men, but escaped scrutiny by sitting well back in his buggy, the presumption being that a well-dressed man with a good horse and buggy was white. Torn with anxiety, he reached home at about four o'clock. Driving the horse into the yard, he sprang down from the buggy and hastened to the house, which he found locked, front and rear.

A repeated rapping brought no response. At length he broke a window, and entered the house like a thief.

"Janet, Janet!" he called in alarm, "where are you? It is only I,—Will!"

There was no reply. He ran from room to room, only to find them all empty. Again he called his wife's name, and was about rushing from the house, when a muffled voice came faintly to his ear,—

"Is dat you, Doctuh Miller?

"Yes. Who are you, and where are my wife and child?"

He was looking around in perplexity, when the door of a low closet under the kitchen sink was opened from within, and a woolly head was cautiously protruded.

"Are you *sho'* dat 's you, doctuh?"

"Yes, Sally; where are"—

"An' not some w'ite man come ter bu'n down de house an' kill all de niggers?"

"No, Sally, it 's me all right. Where is my wife? Where is my child?"

"Dey went over ter see Mis' Butler 'long 'bout two o'clock,

befo' dis fuss broke out, suh. Oh, Lawdy, Lawdy, suh! Is all de cullud folks be'n killt 'cep'n' me an' you, suh? Fer de Lawd's sake, suh, you won' let 'em kill me, will you, suh? I 'll wuk fer you fer nuthin', suh, all my bawn days, ef you 'll save my life, suh!"

"Calm yourself, Sally. You 'll be safe enough if you stay right here, I 've no doubt. They 'll not harm women,—of that I 'm sure enough, although I have n't yet got the bearings of this deplorable affair. Stay here and look after the house. I must find my wife and child!"

The distance across the city to the home of the Mrs. Butler whom his wife had gone to visit was exactly one mile. Though Miller had a good horse in front of him, he was two hours in reaching his destination. Never will the picture of that ride fade from his memory. In his dreams he repeats it night after night, and sees the sights that wounded his eyes, and feels the thoughts—the haunting spirits of the thoughts —that tore his heart as he rode through hell to find those whom he was seeking.

For a short distance he saw nothing, and made rapid progress. As he turned the first corner, his horse shied at the dead body of a negro, lying huddled up in the collapse which marks sudden death. What Miller shuddered at was not so much the thought of death, to the sight of which his profession had accustomed him, as the suggestion of what it signified. He had taken with allowance the wild statement of the fleeing fugitives. Watson, too, had been greatly excited, and Josh Green's group were desperate men, as much liable to be misled by their courage as the others by their fears; but here was proof that murder had been done,—and his wife and children were in the town. Distant shouts, and the sound of firearms, increased his alarm. He struck his horse with the whip, and dashed on toward the heart of the city, which he must traverse in order to reach Janet and the child.

At the next corner lay the body of another man, with the red blood oozing from a ghastly wound in the forehead. The negroes seemed to have been killed, as the band plays in circus parades, at the street intersections, where the example would be most effective. Miller, with a wild leap of the heart, had barely passed this gruesome spectacle, when a sharp voice commanded him to halt, and emphasized the order by covering him with a revolver. Forgetting the prudence he had preached to others, he had raised his whip to strike the horse, when several hands seized the bridle.

"Come down, you damn fool," growled an authoritative voice. "Don't you see we 're in earnest? Do you want to get killed?"

"Why should I come down?" asked Miller.

"Because we 've ordered you to come down! This is the white people's day, and when they order, a nigger must obey. We 're going to search you for weapons."

"Search away. You 'll find nothing but a case of surgeon's tools, which I 'm more than likely to need before this day is over, from all indications."

"No matter; we 'll make sure of it! That 's what we 're here for. Come down, if you don't want to be pulled down!"

Miller stepped down from his buggy. His interlocutor, who made no effort at disguise, was a clerk in a dry-goods store where Miller bought most of his family and hospital supplies. He made no sign of recognition, however, and Miller claimed no acquaintance. This man, who had for several years emptied Miller's pockets in the course of more or less legitimate trade, now went through them, aided by another man, more rapidly than ever before, the searchers convincing themselves that Miller carried no deadly weapon upon his person. Meanwhile, a third ransacked the buggy with like result. Miller recognized several others of the party, who made not the slightest attempt at disguise, though no names were called by any one.

"Where are you going?" demanded the leader.

"I am looking for my wife and child," replied Miller.

"Well, run along, and keep them out of the streets when you find them; and keep your hands out of this affair, if you wish to live in this town, which from now on will be a white man's town, as you niggers will be pretty firmly convinced before night."

Miller drove on as swiftly as might be.

At the next corner he was stopped again. In the white man who held him up, Miller recognized a neighbor of his own. After a short detention and a perfunctory search, the white man remarked apologetically:—

"Sorry to have had to trouble you, doctuh, but them 's the o'ders. It ain't men like you that we 're after, but the vicious and criminal class of niggers."

Miller smiled bitterly as he urged his horse forward. He was quite well aware that the virtuous citizen who had stopped him had only a few weeks before finished a term in the penitentiary, to which he had been sentenced for stealing. Miller knew that he could have bought all the man owned for fifty dollars, and his soul for as much more.

A few rods farther on, he came near running over the body of a wounded man who lay groaning by the wayside. Every professional instinct urged him to stop and offer aid to the sufferer; but the uncertainty concerning his wife and child proved a stronger motive and urged him resistlessly forward. Here and there the ominous sound of firearms was audible. He might have thought this merely a part of the show, like the "powder play" of the Arabs, but for the bloody confirmation of its earnestness which had already assailed his vision. Somewhere in this seething caldron of unrestrained passions were his wife and child, and he must hurry on.

His progress was painfully slow. Three times he was stopped and searched. More than once his way was barred, and he was ordered to turn back, each such occasion requiring a detour which consumed many minutes. The man who last stopped him was a well-known Jewish merchant. A Jew—God of Moses!—had so far forgotten twenty centuries of history as to join in the persecution of another oppressed race! When almost reduced to despair by these innumerable delays, he perceived, coming toward him, Mr. Ellis, the sub-editor of the Morning Chronicle. Miller had just been stopped and questioned again, and Ellis came up as he was starting once more upon his endless ride.

"Dr. Miller," said Ellis kindly, "it is dangerous for you on the streets. Why tempt the danger?"

"I am looking for my wife and child," returned Miller in desperation. "They are somewhere in this town,—I don't know where,—and I must find them."

Ellis had been horror-stricken by the tragedy of the afternoon, the wholly superfluous slaughter of a harmless people, whom a show of force would have been quite sufficient to overawe. Elaborate explanations were afterwards given for these murders, which were said, perhaps truthfully, not to have been premeditated, and many regrets were expressed. The young man had been surprised, quite as much as the negroes themselves, at the ferocity displayed. His own thoughts and feelings were attuned to anything but slaughter. Only that morning he had received a perfumed note, calling his attention to what the writer described as a very noble deed of his, and requesting him to call that evening and receive the writer's thanks. Had he known that Miss Pemberton, several weeks after their visit to the Sound, had driven out again to the hotel and made some inquiries among the servants, he might have understood better the meaning of this missive. When Miller spoke of his wife and child, some subtle thread of suggestion coupled the note with Miller's plight.

"I 'll go with you, Dr. Miller," he said, "if you 'll permit me. In my company you will not be disturbed."

He took a seat in Miller's buggy, after which it was not molested.

Neither of them spoke. Miller was sick at heart; he could have wept with grief, even had the welfare of his own dear ones not been involved in this regrettable affair. With prophetic instinct he foresaw the hatreds to which this day would give birth; the long years of constraint and distrust which would still further widen the breach between two peoples whom fate had thrown together in one community.

There was nothing for Ellis to say. In his heart he could not defend the deeds of this day. The petty annoyances which the whites had felt at the spectacle of a few negroes in office; the not unnatural resentment of a proud people at what had seemed to them a presumptuous freedom of speech and lack of deference on the part of their inferiors,—these things, which he knew were to be made the excuse for overturning the city government, he realized full well were no sort of justification for the wholesale murder or other horrors which might well ensue before the day was done. He could not approve the acts of his own people; neither could he, to a negro, condemn them. Hence he was silent.

"Thank you, Mr. Ellis," exclaimed Miller, when they had reached the house where he expected to find his wife. "This is the place where I was going. I am—under a great obligation to you."

"Not at all, Dr. Miller. I need not tell you how much I regret this deplorable affair."

Ellis went back down the street. Fastening his horse to the fence, Miller sprang forward to find his wife and child. They would certainly be there, for no colored woman would be foolhardy enough to venture on the streets after the riot had broken out.

As he drew nearer, he felt a sudden apprehension. The house seemed strangely silent and deserted. The doors were closed, and the venetian blinds shut tightly. Even a dog which had appeared slunk timidly back under the house, instead of barking vociferously according to the usual habit of his kind.

XXXIV

THE VALLEY OF THE SHADOW

MILLER knocked at the door. There was no response. He went round to the rear of the house. The dog had slunk behind the woodpile. Miller knocked again, at the back door, and, receiving no reply, called aloud.

"Mrs. Butler! It is I, Dr. Miller. Is my wife here?"

The slats of a near-by blind opened cautiously.

"Is it really you, Dr. Miller?"

"Yes, Mrs. Butler. I am looking for my wife and child,—are they here?"

"No, sir; she became alarmed about you, soon after the shooting commenced, and I could not keep her. She left for home half an hour ago. It is coming on dusk, and she and the child are so near white that she did not expect to be molested."

"Which way did she go?"

"She meant to go by the main street. She thought it would be less dangerous than the back streets. I tried to get her to stay here, but she was frantic about you, and nothing I could say would keep her. Is the riot almost over, Dr. Miller? Do you think they will murder us all, and burn down our houses?"

"God knows," replied Miller, with a groan. "But I must find her, if I lose my own life in the attempt."

Surely, he thought, Janet would be safe. The white people of Wellington were not savages; or at least their temporary reversion to savagery would not go as far as to include violence to delicate women and children. Then there flashed into his mind Josh Green's story of his "silly" mother, who for twenty years had walked the earth as a child, as the result of one night's terror, and his heart sank within him.

Miller realized that his buggy, by attracting attention, had been a hindrance rather than a help in his progress across the city. In order to follow his wife, he must practically retrace his steps over the very route he had come. Night was falling. It would be easier to cross the town on foot. In the dusk his own color, slight in the daytime, would not attract attention, and by dodging in the shadows he might avoid those who might wish to intercept him. But he must reach Janet and the boy at any risk. He had not been willing to throw his life away hopelessly, but he would cheerfully have sacrificed it for those whom he loved.

He had gone but a short distance, and had not yet reached the centre of mob activity, when he intercepted a band of negro laborers from the cotton compress, with big Josh Green at their head.

"Hello, doctuh!" cried Josh, "does you wan' ter jine us?"

"I 'm looking for my wife and child, Josh. They 're somewhere in this den of murderers. Have any of you seen them?"

No one had seen them.

"You men are running a great risk," said Miller. "You are rushing on to certain death."

"Well, suh, maybe we is; but we 're gwine ter die fightin'. Dey say de w'ite folks is gwine ter bu'n all de cullud schools an' chu'ches, an' kill all de niggers dey kin ketch. Dey 're gwine ter bu'n yo' new hospittle, ef somebody don' stop 'em."

"Josh—men—you are throwing your lives away. It is a fever; it will wear off to-morrow, or to-night. They 'll not burn the schoolhouses, nor the hospital—they are not such fools, for they benefit the community; and they 'll only kill the colored people who resist them. Every one of you with a gun or a pistol carries his death warrant in his own hand. I 'd rather see the hospital burn than have one of you lose his life. Resistance only makes the matter worse,—the odds against you are too long."

"Things can't be any wuss, doctuh," replied one of the crowd sturdily. "A gun is mo' dange'ous ter de man in front of it dan ter de man behin' it. Dey 're gwine ter kill us anyhow; an' we 're tired,—we read de newspapers,—an' we 're tired er bein' shot down like dogs, widout jedge er jury. We 'd ruther die fightin' dan be stuck like pigs in a pen!"

"God help you!" said Miller. "As for me, I must find my wife and child."

"Good-by, doctuh," cried Josh, brandishing a huge knife.

"'Member 'bout de ole 'oman, ef you lives thoo dis. Don' fergit de headbo'd an' de footbo'd, an' a silver plate on de coffin, ef dere 's money ernuff."

They went their way, and Miller hurried on. They might resist attack; he thought it extremely unlikely that they would begin it; but he knew perfectly well that the mere knowledge that some of the negroes contemplated resistance would only further inflame the infuriated whites. The colored men might win a momentary victory, though it was extremely doubtful; and they would as surely reap the harvest later on. The qualities which in a white man would win the applause of the world would in a negro be taken as the marks of savagery. So thoroughly diseased was public opinion in matters of race that the negro who died for the common rights of humanity might look for no meed of admiration or glory. At such a time, in the white man's eyes, a negro's courage would be mere desperation; his love of liberty, a mere animal dislike of restraint. Every finer human instinct would be interpreted in terms of savagery. Or, if forced to admire, they would none the less repress. They would applaud his courage while they stretched his neck, or carried off the fragments of his mangled body as souvenirs, in much the same way that savages preserve the scalps or eat the hearts of their enemies.

But concern for the fate of Josh and his friends occupied only a secondary place in Miller's mind for the moment. His wife and child were somewhere ahead of him. He pushed on. He had covered about a quarter of a mile more, and far down the street could see the signs of greater animation, when he came upon the body of a woman lying upon the sidewalk. In the dusk he had almost stumbled over it, and his heart came up in his mouth. A second glance revealed that it could not be his wife. It was a fearful portent, however, of what her fate might be. The "war" had reached the women and children. Yielding to a professional instinct, he stooped, and saw that the prostrate form was that of old Aunt Jane Letlow. She was not yet quite dead, and as Miller, with a tender touch, placed her head in a more comfortable position, her lips moved with a last lingering flicker of consciousness:—

"Comin', missis, comin'!"

Mammy Jane had gone to join the old mistress upon whose

memory her heart was fixed; and yet not all her reverence for her old mistress, nor all her deference to the whites, nor all their friendship for her, had been able to save her from this raging devil of race hatred which momentarily possessed the town.

Perceiving that he could do no good, Miller hastened onward, sick at heart. Whenever he saw a party of white men approaching,—these brave reformers never went singly,—he sought concealment in the shadow of a tree or the shrubbery in some yard until they had passed. He had covered about two thirds of the distance homeward, when his eyes fell upon a group beneath a lamp-post, at sight of which he turned pale with horror, and rushed forward with a terrible cry.

XXXV

"MINE ENEMY, O MINE ENEMY!"

THE PROCEEDINGS of the day—planned originally as a "demonstration," dignified subsequently as a "revolution," under any name the culmination of the conspiracy formed by Carteret and his colleagues—had by seven o'clock in the afternoon developed into a murderous riot. Crowds of white men and half-grown boys, drunk with whiskey or with license, raged through the streets, beating, chasing, or killing any negro so unfortunate as to fall into their hands. Why any particular negro was assailed, no one stopped to inquire; it was merely a white mob thirsting for black blood, with no more conscience or discrimination than would be exercised by a wolf in a sheepfold. It was race against race, the whites against the negroes; and it was a one-sided affair, for until Josh Green got together his body of armed men, no effective resistance had been made by any colored person, and the individuals who had been killed had so far left no marks upon the enemy by which they might be remembered.

"Kill the niggers!" rang out now and then through the dusk, and far down the street and along the intersecting thoroughfares distant voices took up the ominous refrain,—"Kill the niggers! Kill the damned niggers!"

Now, not a dark face had been seen on the street for half an hour, until the group of men headed by Josh made their appearance in the negro quarter. Armed with guns and axes, they presented quite a formidable appearance as they made their way toward the new hospital, near which stood a schoolhouse and a large church, both used by the colored people. They did not reach their destination without having met a number of white men, singly or in twos or threes; and the rumor spread with incredible swiftness that the negroes in turn were up in arms, determined to massacre all the whites and burn the town. Some of the whites became alarmed, and recognizing the power of the negroes, if armed and conscious of their strength, were impressed by the immediate necessity of overpowering and overawing them. Others, with appetites already whetted by slaughter, saw a chance, welcome rather than not, of shedding more black blood. Spontaneously the white mob flocked toward the hospital, where rumor had it that a large body of desperate negroes, breathing threats of blood and fire, had taken a determined stand.

It had been Josh's plan merely to remain quietly and peaceably in the neighborhood of the little group of public institutions, molesting no one, unless first attacked, and merely letting the white people see that they meant to protect their own; but so rapidly did the rumor spread, and so promptly did the white people act, that by the time Josh and his supporters had reached the top of the rising ground where the hospital stood, a crowd of white men much more numerous than their own party were following them at a short distance.

Josh, with the eye of a general, perceived that some of his party were becoming a little nervous, and decided that they would feel safer behind shelter.

"I reckon we better go inside de hospittle, boys," he exclaimed. "Den we 'll be behind brick walls, an' dem other fellows 'll be outside, an' ef dere 's any fightin', we 'll have de bes' show. We ain' gwine ter do no shootin' till we 're pestered, an' dey 'll be less likely ter pester us ef dey can't git at us widout runnin' some resk. Come along in! Be men! De gov'ner er de President is gwine ter sen' soldiers ter stop dese gwines-on, an' meantime we kin keep dem white devils f'm bu'nin' down our hospittles an' chu'ch-houses. W'en dey comes an' fin's out dat we jes' means ter pertect ou' prope'ty, dey 'll go 'long 'bout deir own business. Er, ef dey wants a scrap, dey kin have it! Come erlong, boys!"

Jerry Letlow, who had kept out of sight during the day, had started out, after night had set in, to find Major Carteret. Jerry was very much afraid. The events of the day had filled him with terror. Whatever the limitations of Jerry's mind or character may have been, Jerry had a keen appreciation of the danger to the negroes when they came in conflict with the whites, and he had no desire to imperil his own skin. He valued his life for his own sake, and not for any altruistic theory that it might be of service to others. In other words, Jerry was something of a coward. He had kept in hiding all day, but finding, toward evening, that the riot did not abate, and fearing, from the rumors which came to his ears, that all the negroes would be exterminated, he had set out, somewhat desperately, to try to find his white patron and protector. He had been cautious to avoid meeting any white men, and, anticipating no danger from those of his own race, went toward the party which he saw approaching, whose path would cross his own. When they were only a few yards apart, Josh took a step forward and caught Jerry by the arm.

"Come along, Jerry, we need you! Here 's another man, boys. Come on now, and fight fer yo' race!"

In vain Jerry protested. "I don' wan' ter fight," he howled. "De w'ite folks ain' gwine ter pester me; dey 're my frien's. Tu'n me loose,—tu'n me loose, er we all gwine ter git killed!"

The party paid no attention to Jerry's protestations. Indeed, with the crowd of whites following behind, they were simply considering the question of a position from which they could most effectively defend themselves and the building which they imagined to be threatened. If Josh had released his grip of Jerry, that worthy could easily have escaped from the crowd; but Josh maintained his hold almost mechanically, and, in the confusion, Jerry found himself swept with the rest into the hospital, the doors of which were promptly barricaded with the heavier pieces of furniture, and the windows manned by several men each, Josh, with the instinct of a born commander, posting his forces so that they could cover with their guns all the approaches to the building. Jerry still continuing to make himself troublesome, Josh, in a moment of impatience, gave him a terrific box on the ear, which stretched him out upon the floor unconscious.

"Shet up," he said; "ef you can't stan' up like a man, keep still, and don't interfere wid men w'at will fight!"

The hospital, when Josh and his men took possession, had been found deserted. Fortunately there were no patients for that day, except one or two convalescents, and these, with the attendants, had joined the exodus of the colored people from the town.

A white man advanced from the crowd without toward the main entrance to the hospital. Big Josh, looking out from a window, grasped his gun more firmly, as his eyes fell upon the man who had murdered his father and darkened his mother's life. Mechanically he raised his rifle, but lowered it as the white man lifted up his hand as a sign that he wished to speak.

"You niggers," called Captain McBane loudly,—it was that worthy,—"you niggers are courtin' death, an' you won't have to court her but a minute er two mo' befo' she 'll have you. If you surrender and give up your arms, you 'll be dealt with leniently,—you may get off with the chain-gang or the penitentiary. If you resist, you 'll be shot like dogs."

"Dat 's no news, Mr. White Man," replied Josh, appearing boldly at the window. "We 're use' ter bein' treated like dogs by men like you. If you w'ite people will go 'long an' ten' ter yo' own business an' let us alone, we 'll ten' ter ou'n. You 've got guns, an' we 've got jest as much right ter carry 'em as you have. Lay down yo'n, an' we 'll lay down ou'n,—we did n' take 'em up fust; but we ain' gwine ter let you bu'n down ou' chu'ches an' school'ouses, er dis hospittle, an' we ain' comin' out er dis house, where we ain' disturbin' nobody, fer you ter shoot us down er sen' us ter jail. You hear me!"

"All right," responded McBane. "You 've had fair warning. Your blood be on your"—

His speech was interrupted by a shot from the crowd, which splintered the window-casing close to Josh's head. This was followed by half a dozen other shots, which were replied to, almost simultaneously, by a volley from within, by which one of the attacking party was killed and another wounded.

This roused the mob to frenzy.

"Vengeance! vengeance!" they yelled. "Kill the niggers!"

A negro had killed a white man,—the unpardonable sin, admitting neither excuse, justification, nor extenuation. From time immemorial it had been bred in the Southern white consciousness, and in the negro consciousness also, for that matter, that the person of a white man was sacred from the touch of a negro, no matter what the provocation. A dozen colored men lay dead in the streets of Wellington, inoffensive people, slain in cold blood because they had been bold enough to question the authority of those who had assailed them, or frightened enough to flee when they had been ordered to stand still; but their lives counted nothing against that of a riotous white man, who had courted death by attacking a body of armed men.

The crowd, too, surrounding the hospital, had changed somewhat in character. The men who had acted as leaders in the early afternoon, having accomplished their purpose of overturning the local administration and establishing a provisional government of their own, had withdrawn from active participation in the rioting, deeming the negroes already sufficiently overawed to render unlikely any further trouble from that source. Several of the ringleaders had indeed begun to exert themselves to prevent further disorder, or any loss of property, the possibility of which had become apparent; but those who set in motion the forces of evil cannot always control them afterwards. The baser element of the white population, recruited from the wharves and the saloons, was now predominant.

Captain McBane was the only one of the revolutionary committee who had remained with the mob, not with any purpose to restore or preserve order, but because he found the company and the occasion entirely congenial. He had had no opportunity, at least no tenable excuse, to kill or maim a negro since the termination of his contract with the state for convicts, and this occasion had awakened a dormant appetite for these diversions. We are all puppets in the hands of Fate, and seldom see the strings that move us. McBane had lived a life of violence and cruelty. As a man sows, so shall he reap. In works of fiction, such men are sometimes converted. More often, in real life, they do not change their natures until they are converted into dust. One does well to distrust a tamed tiger.

On the outskirts of the crowd a few of the better class, or at least of the better clad, were looking on. The double volley described had already been fired, when the number of these was augmented by the arrival of Major Carteret and Mr. Ellis, who had just come from the Chronicle office, where the next day's paper had been in hasty preparation. They pushed their way towards the front of the crowd.

"This must be stopped, Ellis," said Carteret. "They are burning houses and killing women and children. Old Jane, good old Mammy Jane, who nursed my wife at her bosom, and has waited on her and my child within a few weeks, was killed only a few rods from my house, to which she was evidently fleeing for protection. It must have been by accident,—I cannot believe that any white man in town would be dastard enough to commit such a deed intentionally! I would have defended her with my own life! We must try to stop this thing!"

"Easier said than done," returned Ellis. "It is in the fever stage, and must burn itself out. We shall be lucky if it does not burn the town out. Suppose the negroes should also take a hand at the burning? We have advised the people to put the negroes down, and they are doing the job thoroughly."

"My God!" replied the other, with a gesture of impatience, as he continued to elbow his way through the crowd; "I meant to keep them in their places,—I did not intend wholesale murder and arson."

Carteret, having reached the front of the mob, made an effort to gain their attention.

"Gentlemen!" he cried in his loudest tones. His voice, unfortunately, was neither loud nor piercing.

"Kill the niggers!" clamored the mob.

"Gentlemen, I implore you"—

The crash of a dozen windows, broken by stones and pistol shots, drowned his voice.

"Gentlemen!" he shouted; "this is murder, it is madness; it is a disgrace to our city, to our state, to our civilization!"

"That 's right!" replied several voices. The mob had recognized the speaker. "It *is* a disgrace, and we 'll not put up with it a moment longer. Burn 'em out! Hurrah for Major Carteret, the champion of 'white supremacy'! Three cheers for the Morning Chronicle and 'no nigger domination'!"

"Hurrah, hurrah, hurrah!" yelled the crowd.

In vain the baffled orator gesticulated and shrieked in the effort to correct the misapprehension. Their oracle had spoken; not hearing what he said, they assumed it to mean encouragement and coöperation. Their present course was but the logical outcome of the crusade which the Morning Chronicle had preached, in season and out of season, for many months. When Carteret had spoken, and the crowd had cheered him, they felt that they had done all that courtesy required, and he was good-naturedly elbowed aside while they proceeded with the work in hand, which was now to drive out the negroes from the hospital and avenge the killing of their comrade.

Some brought hay, some kerosene, and others wood from a pile which had been thrown into a vacant lot near by. Several safe ways of approach to the building were discovered, and the combustibles placed and fired. The flames, soon gaining a foothold, leaped upward, catching here and there at the exposed woodwork, and licking the walls hungrily with long tongues of flame.

Meanwhile a desultory firing was kept up from the outside, which was replied to scatteringly from within the hospital. Those inside were either not good marksmen, or excitement had spoiled their aim. If a face appeared at a window, a dozen pistol shots from the crowd sought the spot immediately.

Higher and higher leaped the flames. Suddenly from one of the windows sprang a black figure, waving a white handkerchief. It was Jerry Letlow. Regaining consciousness after the effect of Josh's blow had subsided, Jerry had kept quiet and watched his opportunity. From a safe vantage-ground he had scanned the crowd without, in search of some white friend. When he saw Major Carteret moving disconsolately away after his futile effort to stein the torrent, Jerry made a dash for the window. He sprang forth, and, waving his handkerchief as a flag of truce, ran toward Major Carteret, shouting frantically:—

"Majah Carteret—*O* majah! It 's me, suh, Jerry, suh! I did n' go in dere myse'f, suh,—I wuz drag' in dere! I would n' do nothin' 'g'inst de w'ite folks, suh,—no, 'ndeed, I would n', suh!"

Jerry's cries were drowned in a roar of rage and a volley of shots from the mob. Carteret, who had turned away with Ellis, did not even hear his servant's voice. Jerry's poor flag of truce, his explanations, his reliance upon his white friends, all failed him in the moment of supreme need. In that hour, as in any hour when the depths of race hatred are stirred, a negro was no more than a brute beast, set upon by other brute beasts whose only instinct was to kill and destroy.

"Let us leave this inferno, Ellis," said Carteret, sick with anger and disgust. He had just become aware that a negro was being killed, though he did not know whom. "We can do nothing. The negroes have themselves to blame,—they tempted us beyond endurance. I counseled firmness, and firm measures were taken, and our purpose was accomplished. I am not responsible for these subsequent horrors,—I wash my hands of them. Let us go!"

The flames gained headway and gradually enveloped the burning building, until it became evident to those within as well as those without that the position of the defenders was no longer tenable. Would they die in the flames, or would they be driven out? The uncertainty soon came to an end.

The besieged had been willing to fight, so long as there seemed a hope of successfully defending themselves and their property; for their purpose was purely one of defense. When they saw the case was hopeless, inspired by Josh Green's reckless courage, they were still willing to sell their lives dearly. One or two of them had already been killed, and as many more disabled. The fate of Jerry Letlow had struck terror to the hearts of several others, who could scarcely hide their fear. After the building had been fired, Josh's exhortations were no longer able to keep them in the hospital. They preferred to fight and be killed in the open, rather than to be smothered like rats in a hole.

"Boys!" exclaimed Josh,—"men!—fer nobody but men would do w'at you have done,—the day has gone 'g'inst us. We kin see ou' finish; but fer my part, I ain' gwine ter leave dis worl' widout takin' a w'ite man 'long wid me, an' I sees my man right out yonder waitin',—I be'n waitin' fer him twenty years, but he won' have ter wait fer me mo' 'n 'bout twenty seconds. Eve'y one er you pick yo' man! We 'll open de do', an' we 'll give some w'ite men a chance ter be sorry dey ever started dis fuss!"

The door was thrown open suddenly, and through it rushed a dozen or more black figures, armed with knives, pistols, or clubbed muskets. Taken by sudden surprise, the white people stood motionless for a moment, but the approaching negroes had scarcely covered half the distance to which the heat of the flames had driven back the mob, before they were greeted with a volley that laid them all low but two. One of these, dazed by the fate of his companions, turned instinctively to flee, but had scarcely faced around before he fell, pierced in the back by a dozen bullets.

Josh Green, the tallest and biggest of them all, had not apparently been touched. Some of the crowd paused in involuntary admiration of this black giant, famed on the wharves for his strength, sweeping down upon them, a smile upon his face, his eyes lit up with a rapt expression which seemed to take him out of mortal ken. This impression was heightened by his apparent immunity from the shower of lead which less susceptible persons had continued to pour at him.

Armed with a huge bowie-knife, a relic of the civil war, which he had carried on his person for many years for a definite purpose, and which he had kept sharpened to a razor edge, he reached the line of the crowd. All but the bravest shrank back. Like a wedge he dashed through the mob, which parted instinctively before him, and all oblivious of the rain of lead which fell around him, reached the point where Captain McBane, the bravest man in the party, stood waiting to meet him. A pistol-flame flashed in his face, but he went on, and raising his powerful right arm, buried his knife to the hilt in the heart of his enemy. When the crowd dashed forward to wreak vengeance on his dead body, they found him with a smile still upon his face.

One of the two died as the fool dieth. Which was it, or was it both? "Vengeance is mine," saith the Lord, and it had not been left to Him. But they that do violence must expect to suffer violence. McBane's death was merciful, compared with the nameless horrors he had heaped upon the hundreds of helpless mortals who had fallen into his hands during his career as a contractor of convict labor.

Sobered by this culminating tragedy, the mob shortly afterwards dispersed. The flames soon completed their work, and this handsome structure, the fruit of old Adam Miller's industry, the monument of his son's philanthropy, a promise of good things for the future of the city, lay smouldering in ruins, a melancholy witness to the fact that our boasted civilization is but a thin veneer, which cracks and scales off at the first impact of primal passions.

XXXVI

FIAT JUSTITIA

BY THE LIGHT of the burning building, which illuminated the street for several blocks, Major Carteret and Ellis made their way rapidly until they turned into the street where the major lived. Reaching the house, Carteret tried the door and found it locked. A vigorous ring at the bell brought no immediate response. Carteret had begun to pound impatiently upon the door, when it was cautiously opened by Miss Pemberton, who was pale, and trembled with excitement.

"Where is Olivia?" asked the major.

"She is upstairs, with Dodie and Mrs. Albright's hospital nurse. Dodie has the croup. Virgie ran away after the riot broke out. Sister Olivia had sent for Mammy Jane, but she did not come. Mrs. Albright let her white nurse come over."

"I 'll go up at once," said the major anxiously. "Wait for me, Ellis,—I 'll be down in a few minutes."

"Oh, Mr. Ellis," exclaimed Clara, coming toward him with both hands extended, "can nothing be done to stop this terrible affair?"

"I wish I could do something," he murmured fervently, taking both her trembling hands in his own broad palms, where they rested with a surrendering trustfulness which he has never since had occasion to doubt. "It has gone too far, already, and the end, I fear, is not yet; but it cannot grow much worse."

The editor hurried upstairs. Mrs. Carteret, wearing a worried and haggard look, met him at the threshold of the nursery.

"Dodie is ill," she said. "At three o'clock, when the trouble began, I was over at Mrs. Albright's,—I had left Virgie with the baby. When I came back, she and all the other servants had gone. They had heard that the white people were going to kill all the negroes, and fled to seek safety. I found Dodie lying in a draught, before an open window, gasping for breath. I ran back to Mrs. Albright's,—I had found her much better to-day,—and she let her nurse come over. The nurse says that Dodie is threatened with membranous croup."

"Have you sent for Dr. Price?"

"There was no one to send,—the servants were gone, and the nurse was afraid to venture out into the street. I telephoned for Dr. Price, and found that he was out of town; that he had gone up the river this morning to attend a patient, and would not be back until to-morrow. Mrs. Price thought that he had anticipated some kind of trouble in the town to-day, and had preferred to be where he could not be called upon to assume any responsibility."

"I suppose you tried Dr. Ashe?"

"I could not get him, nor any one else, after that first call. The telephone service is disorganized on account of the riot. We need medicine and ice. The drugstores are all closed on account of the riot, and for the same reason we could n't get any ice."

Major Carteret stood beside the brass bedstead upon which his child was lying,—his only child, around whose curly head clustered all his hopes; upon whom all his life for the past year had been centred. He stooped over the bed, beside which the nurse had stationed herself. She was wiping the child's face, which was red and swollen and covered with moisture, the nostrils working rapidly, and the little patient vainly endeavoring at intervals to cough up the obstruction to his breathing.

"Is it serious?" he inquired anxiously. He had always thought of the croup as a childish ailment, that yielded readily to proper treatment; but the child's evident distress impressed him with sudden fear.

"Dangerous," replied the young woman laconically. "You came none too soon. If a doctor is n't got at once, the child will die,—and it must be a good doctor."

"Whom can I call?" he asked. "You know them all, I suppose. Dr. Price, our family physician, is out of town."

"Dr. Ashe has charge of his cases when he is away," replied the nurse. "If you can't find him, try Dr. Hooper. The child is growing worse every minute. On your way back you 'd better get some ice, if possible."

The major hastened downstairs.

"Don't wait for me, Ellis," he said. "I shall be needed here for a while. I 'll get to the office as soon as possible. Make up the paper, and leave another stick out for me to the last minute, but fill it up in case I 'm not on hand by twelve. We must get the paper out early in the morning."

Nothing but a matter of the most vital importance would have kept Major Carteret away from his office this night. Upon the presentation to the outer world of the story of this riot would depend the attitude of the great civilized public toward the events of the last ten hours. The Chronicle was the source from which the first word would be expected; it would give the people of Wellington their cue as to the position which they must take in regard to this distressful affair, which had so far transcended in ferocity the most extreme measures which the conspirators had anticipated. The burden of his own responsibility weighed heavily upon him, and could not be shaken off; but he must do first the duty nearest to him,—he must first attend to his child.

Carteret hastened from the house, and traversed rapidly the short distance to Dr. Ashe's office. Far down the street he could see the glow of the burning hospital, and he had scarcely left his own house when the fusillade of shots, fired when the colored men emerged from the burning building, was audible. Carteret would have hastened back to the scene of the riot, to see what was now going on, and to make another effort to stem the tide of bloodshed; but before the dread of losing his child, all other interests fell into the background. Not all the negroes in Wellington could weigh in the balance for one instant against the life of the feeble child now gasping for breath in the house behind him.

Reaching the house, a vigorous ring brought the doctor's wife to the door.

"Good-evening, Mrs. Ashe. Is the doctor at home?"

"No, Major Carteret. He was called to attend Mrs. Wells, who was taken suddenly ill, as a result of the trouble this afternoon. He will be there all night, no doubt."

"My child is very ill, and I must find some one."

"Try Dr. Yates. His house is only four doors away."

A ring at Dr. Yates's door brought out a young man.

"Is Dr. Yates in?"

"Yes, sir."

"Can I see him?"

"You might see him, sir, but that would be all. His horse was frightened by the shooting on the streets, and ran away and threw the doctor, and broke his right arm. I have just set it; he will not be able to attend any patients for several weeks. He is old and nervous, and the shock was great."

"Are you not a physician?" asked Carteret, looking at the young man keenly. He was a serious, gentlemanly looking young fellow, whose word might probably be trusted.

"Yes, I am Dr. Evans, Dr. Yates's assistant. I 'm really little more than a student, but I 'll do what I can."

"My only child is sick with the croup, and requires immediate attention."

"I ought to be able to handle a case of the croup," answered Dr. Evans, "at least in the first stages. I 'll go with you, and stay by the child, and if the case is beyond me, I may keep it in check until another physician comes."

He stepped back into another room, and returning immediately with his hat, accompanied Carteret homeward. The riot had subsided; even the glow from the smouldering hospital was no longer visible. It seemed that the city, appalled at the tragedy, had suddenly awakened to a sense of its own crime. Here and there a dark face, emerging cautiously from some hiding-place, peered from behind fence or tree, but shrank hastily away at the sight of a white face. The negroes of Wellington, with the exception of Josh Green and his party, had not behaved bravely on this critical day in their history; but those who had fought were dead, to the last man; those who had sought safety in flight or concealment were alive to tell the tale.

"We pass right by Dr. Thompson's," said Dr. Evans. "If you have n't spoken to him, it might be well to call him for consultation, in case the child should be very bad."

"Go on ahead," said Carteret, "and I 'll get him."

Evans hastened on, while Carteret sounded the old-fashioned knocker upon the doctor's door. A gray-haired negro servant, clad in a dress suit and wearing a white tie, came to the door.

"De doctuh, suh," he replied politely to Carteret's question, "has gone ter ampitate de ahm er a gent'eman who got one er his bones smashed wid a pistol bullet in de—fightin' dis atternoon, suh. He 's jes' gone, suh, an' lef' wo'd dat he 'd be gone a' hour er mo', suh."

Carteret hastened homeward. He could think of no other available physician. Perhaps no other would be needed, but if so, he could find out from Evans whom it was best to call.

When he reached the child's room, the young doctor was bending anxiously over the little frame. The little lips had become livid, the little nails, lying against the white sheet, were blue. The child's efforts to breathe were most distressing, and each gasp cut the father like a knife. Mrs. Carteret was weeping hysterically.

"How is he, doctor?" asked the major.

"He is very low," replied the young man. "Nothing short of tracheotomy—an operation to open the windpipe—will relieve him. Without it, in half or three quarters of an hour he will be unable to breathe. It is a delicate operation, a mistake in which would be as fatal as the disease. I have neither the knowledge nor the experience to attempt it, and your child's life is too valuable for a student to practice upon. Neither have I the instruments here."

"What shall we do?" demanded Carteret. "We have called all the best doctors, and none are available."

The young doctor's brow was wrinkled with thought. He knew a doctor who could perform the operation. He had heard, also, of a certain event at Carteret's house some months before, when an unwelcome physician had been excluded from a consultation,—but it was the last chance.

"There is but one other doctor in town who has performed the operation, so far as I know," he declared, "and that is Dr. Miller. If you can get him, he can save your child's life."

Carteret hesitated involuntarily. All the incidents, all the arguments, of the occasion when he had refused to admit the colored doctor to his house, came up vividly before his memory. He had acted in accordance with his lifelong beliefs, and had carried his point; but the present situation was different,—this was a case of imperative necessity, and every other interest or consideration must give way before the imminence of his child's peril. That the doctor would refuse the call, he did not imagine: it would be too great an honor for a negro to decline,—unless some bitterness might have grown out of the proceedings of the afternoon. That this doctor was a man of some education he knew; and he had been told that he was a man of fine feeling,—for a negro,—and might easily have taken to heart the day's events. Nevertheless, he could hardly refuse a professional call,—professional ethics would require him to respond. Carteret had no reason to suppose that Miller had ever learned of what had occurred at the house during Dr. Burns's visit to Wellington. The major himself had never mentioned the controversy, and no doubt the other gentlemen had been equally silent.

"I 'll go for him myself," said Dr. Evans, noting Carteret's hesitation and suspecting its cause. "I can do nothing here alone, for a little while, and I may be able to bring the doctor back with me. He likes a difficult operation."

It seemed an age ere the young doctor returned, though it was really only a few minutes. The nurse did what she could to relieve the child's sufferings, which grew visibly more and more acute. The mother, upon the other side of the bed, held one of the baby's hands in her own, and controlled her feelings as best she might. Carteret paced the floor anxiously, going every few seconds to the head of the stairs to listen for Evans's footsteps on the piazza without. At last the welcome sound was audible, and a few strides took him to the door.

"Dr. Miller is at home, sir," reported Evans, as he came in. "He says that he was called to your house once before, by a third person who claimed authority to act, and that he was refused admittance. He declares that he will not consider such a call unless it come from you personally."

"That is true, quite true," replied Carteret. "His position is a just one. I will go at once. Will—will—my child live until I can get Miller here?"

"He can live for half an hour without an operation. Beyond that I could give you little hope."

Seizing his hat, Carteret dashed out of the yard and ran rapidly to Miller's house; ordinarily a walk of six or seven minutes, Carteret covered it in three, and was almost out of breath when he rang the bell of Miller's front door.

The ring was answered by the doctor in person.

"Dr. Miller, I believe?" asked Carteret.

"Yes, sir."

"I am Major Carteret. My child is seriously ill, and you are the only available doctor who can perform the necessary operation."

"Ah! You have tried all the others,—and then you come to me!"

"Yes, I do not deny it," admitted the major, biting his lip. He had not counted on professional jealousy as an obstacle to be met. "But I *have* come to you, as a physician, to engage your professional services for my child,—my only child. I have confidence in your skill, or I should not have come to you. I request—nay, I implore you to lose no more time, but come with me at once! My child's life is hanging by a thread, and you can save it!"

"Ah!" replied the other, "as a father whose only child's life is in danger, you implore *me*, of all men in the world, to come and save it!"

There was a strained intensity in the doctor's low voice that struck Carteret, in spite of his own preoccupation. He thought he heard, too, from the adjoining room, the sound of some one sobbing softly. There was some mystery here which he could not fathom unaided.

Miller turned to the door behind him and threw it open. On the white cover of a low cot lay a childish form in the rigidity of death, and by it knelt, with her back to the door, a woman whose shoulders were shaken by the violence of her sobs. Absorbed in her grief, she did not turn, or give any sign that she had recognized the intrusion.

"There, Major Carteret!" exclaimed Miller, with the tragic eloquence of despair, "there lies a specimen of your handiwork! There lies *my* only child, laid low by a stray bullet in this riot which you and your paper have fomented; struck down as much by your hand as though you had held the weapon with which his life was taken!"

"My God!" exclaimed Carteret, struck with horror. "Is the child dead?"

"There he lies," continued the other, "an innocent child,—there he lies dead, his little life snuffed out like a candle, because you and a handful of your friends thought you must override the laws and run this town at any cost!—and there kneels his mother, overcome by grief. We are alone in the house. It is not safe to leave her unattended. My duty calls me here, by the side of my dead child and my suffering wife! I cannot go with you. There is a just God in heaven!—as you have sown, so may you reap!"

Carteret possessed a narrow, but a logical mind, and except when confused or blinded by his prejudices, had always tried to be a just man. In the agony of his own predicament,—in the horror of the situation at Miller's house,—for a moment the veil of race prejudice was rent in twain, and he saw things as they were, in their correct proportions and relations,—saw clearly and convincingly that he had no standing here, in the presence of death, in the home of this stricken family. Miller's refusal to go with him was pure, elemental justice; he could not blame the doctor for his stand. He was indeed conscious of a certain involuntary admiration for a man who held in his hands the power of life and death, and could use it, with strict justice, to avenge his own wrongs. In Dr. Miller's place he would have done the same thing. Miller had spoken the truth,—as he had sown, so must he reap! He could not expect, could not ask, this father to leave his own household at such a moment.

Pressing his lips together with grim courage, and bowing mechanically, as though to Fate rather than the physician, Carteret turned and left the house. At a rapid pace he soon reached home. There was yet a chance for his child: perhaps some one of the other doctors had come; perhaps, after all, the disease had taken a favorable turn,—Evans was but a young doctor, and might have been mistaken. Surely, with doctors all around him, his child would not be permitted to die for lack of medical attention! He found the mother, the doctor, and the nurse still grouped, as he had left them, around the suffering child.

"How is he now?" he asked, in a voice that sounded like a groan.

"No better," replied the doctor; "steadily growing worse. He can go on probably for twenty minutes longer without an operation."

"Where is the doctor?" demanded Mrs. Carteret, looking

eagerly toward the door. "You should have brought him right upstairs. There 's not a minute to spare! Phil, Phil, our child will die!"

Carteret's heart swelled almost to bursting with an intense pity. Even his own great sorrow became of secondary importance beside the grief which his wife must soon feel at the inevitable loss of her only child. And it was his fault! Would that he could risk his own life to spare her and to save the child!

Briefly, and as gently as might be, he stated the result of his errand. The doctor had refused to come, for a good reason. He could not ask him again.

Young Evans felt the logic of the situation, which Carteret had explained sufficiently. To the nurse it was even clearer. If she or any other woman had been in the doctor's place, she would have given the same answer.

Mrs. Carteret did not stop to reason. In such a crisis a mother's heart usurps the place of intellect. For her, at that moment, there were but two facts in all the world. Her child lay dying. There was within the town, and within reach, a man who could save him. With an agonized cry she rushed wildly from the room.

Carteret sought to follow her, but she flew down the long stairs like a wild thing. The least misstep might have precipitated her to the bottom; but ere Carteret, with a remonstrance on his lips, had scarcely reached the uppermost step, she had thrown open the front door and fled precipitately out into the night.

XXXVII

THE SISTERS

MILLER'S doorbell rang loudly, insistently, as though demanding a response. Absorbed in his own grief, into which he had relapsed upon Carteret's departure, the sound was an unwelcome intrusion. Surely the man could not be coming back! If it were some one else— What else might happen to the doomed town concerned him not. His child was dead,—his distracted wife could not be left alone.

The doorbell rang—clamorously—appealingly. Through the long hall and the closed door of the room where he sat, he could hear some one knocking, and a faint voice calling.

"Open, for God's sake, open!"

It was a woman's voice,—the voice of a woman in distress. Slowly Miller rose and went to the door, which he opened mechanically.

A lady stood there, so near the image of his own wife, whom he had just left, that for a moment he was well-nigh startled. A little older, perhaps, a little fairer of complexion, but with the same form, the same features, marked by the same wild grief. She wore a loose wrapper, which clothed her like the drapery of a statue. Her long dark hair, the counterpart of his wife's, had fallen down, and hung disheveled about her shoulders. There was blood upon her knuckles, where she had beaten with them upon the door.

"Dr. Miller," she panted, breathless from her flight and laying her hand upon his arm appealingly,—when he shrank from the contact she still held it there,—"Dr. Miller, you will come and save my child? You know what it is to lose a child! I am so sorry about your little boy! You will come to mine!"

"Your sorrow comes too late, madam," he said harshly. "My child is dead. I charged your husband with his murder, and he could not deny it. Why should I save your husband's child?"

"Ah, Dr. Miller!" she cried, with his wife's voice,—she never knew how much, in that dark hour, she owed to that resemblance—"it is *my* child, and I have never injured you. It is my child, Dr. Miller, my only child. I brought it into the world at the risk of my own life! I have nursed it, I have watched over it, I have prayed for it,—and it now lies dying! Oh, Dr. Miller, dear Dr. Miller, if you have a heart, come and save my child!"

"Madam," he answered more gently, moved in spite of himself, "my heart is broken. My people lie dead upon the streets, at the hands of yours. The work of my life is in ashes,—and, yonder, stretched out in death, lies my own child! God! woman, you ask too much of human nature! Love, duty, sorrow, *justice*, call me here. I cannot go!"

She rose to her full height. "Then you are a murderer," she cried wildly. "His blood be on your head, and a mother's curse beside!"

The next moment, with a sudden revulsion of feeling, she had thrown herself at his feet,—at the feet of a negro, this proud white woman,—and was clasping his knees wildly.

"O God!" she prayed, in tones which quivered with anguish, "pardon my husband's sins, and my own, and move this man's hard heart, by the blood of thy Son, who died to save us all!"

It was the last appeal of poor humanity. When the pride of intellect and caste is broken; when we grovel in the dust of humiliation; when sickness and sorrow come, and the shadow of death falls upon us, and there is no hope elsewhere,—we turn to God, who sometimes swallows the insult, and answers the appeal.

Miller raised the lady to her feet. He had been deeply moved,—but he had been more deeply injured. This was his wife's sister,—ah, yes! but a sister who had scorned and slighted and ignored the existence of his wife for all her life. Only Miller, of all the world, could have guessed what this had meant to Janet, and he had merely divined it through the clairvoyant sympathy of love. This woman could have no claim upon him because of this unacknowledged relationship. Yet, after all, she *was* his wife's sister, his child's kinswoman. She was a fellow creature, too, and in distress.

"Rise, madam," he said, with a sudden inspiration, lifting her gently. "I will listen to you on one condition. My child lies dead in the adjoining room, his mother by his side. Go in there, and make your request of her. I will abide by her decision."

The two women stood confronting each other across the body of the dead child, mute witness of this first meeting between two children of the same father. Standing thus face to face, each under the stress of the deepest emotions, the resemblance between them was even more striking than it had seemed to Miller when he had admitted Mrs. Carteret to the house. But Death, the great leveler, striking upon the one hand and threatening upon the other, had wrought a marvelous transformation in the bearing of the two women. The sad-eyed Janet towered erect, with menacing aspect, like an avenging goddess. The other, whose pride had been her life, stood in the attitude of a trembling suppliant.

"*You* have come here," cried Janet, pointing with a tragic gesture to the dead child,—"*you*, to gloat over your husband's work. All my life you have hated and scorned and despised me. Your presence here insults me and my dead. What are you doing here?"

"Mrs. Miller," returned Mrs. Carteret tremulously, dazed for a moment by this outburst, and clasping her hands with an imploring gesture, "my child, my only child, is dying, and your husband alone can save his life. Ah, let me have my child," she moaned, heart-rendingly. "It is my only one—my sweet child—my ewe lamb!"

"This was *my* only child!" replied the other mother; "and yours is no better to die than mine!"

"You are young," said Mrs. Carteret, "and may yet have many children,—this is my only hope! If you have a human heart, tell your husband to come with me. He leaves it to you; he will do as you command."

"Ah," cried Janet, "I have a human heart, and therefore I will not let him go. *My* child is dead—O God, my child, my child!"

She threw herself down by the bedside, sobbing hysterically. The other woman knelt beside her, and put her arm about her neck. For a moment Janet, absorbed in her grief, did not repulse her.

"Listen," pleaded Mrs. Carteret. "You will not let my baby die? You are my sister;—the child is your own near kin!"

"My child was nearer," returned Janet, rising again to her feet and shaking off the other woman's arm. "He was my son, and I have seen him die. I have been your sister for twenty-five years, and you have only now, for the first time, called me so!"

"Listen—sister," returned Mrs. Carteret. Was there no way to move this woman? Her child lay dying, if he were not dead already. She would tell everything, and leave the rest to God. If it would save her child, she would shrink at no sacrifice. Whether the truth would still further incense Janet, or move her to mercy, she could not tell; she would leave the issue to God.

"Listen, sister!" she said. "I have a confession to make. You *are* my lawful sister. My father was married to your mother. You are entitled to his name, and to half his estate."

Janet's eyes flashed with bitter scorn.

"And you have robbed me all these years, and now tell me that as a reason why I should forgive the murder of my child?"

"No, no!" cried the other wildly, fearing the worst. "I have known of it only a few weeks,—since my Aunt Polly's death. I had not meant to rob you,—I had meant to make restitution. Sister! for our father's sake, who did you no wrong, give me my child's life!"

Janet's eyes slowly filled with tears—bitter tears—burning tears. For a moment even her grief at her child's loss dropped to second place in her thoughts. This, then, was the recognition for which, all her life, she had longed in secret. It had come, after many days, and in larger measure than she had dreamed; but it had come, not with frank kindliness and sisterly love, but in a storm of blood and tears; not freely given, from an open heart, but extorted from a reluctant conscience by the agony of a mother's fears. Janet had obtained her heart's desire, and now that it was at her lips, found it but apples of Sodom, filled with dust and ashes!

"Listen!" she cried, dashing her tears aside. "I have but one word for you,—one last word,—and then I hope never to see your face again! My mother died of want, and I was brought up by the hand of charity. Now, when I have married a man who can supply my needs, you offer me back the money which you and your friends have robbed me of! You imagined that the shame of being a negro swallowed up every other ignominy,—and in your eyes I am a negro, though I am your sister, and you are white, and people have taken me for you on the streets,—and you, therefore, left me nameless all my life! Now, when an honest man has given me a name of which I can be proud, you offer me the one of which you robbed me, and of which I can make no use. For twenty-five years I, poor, despicable fool, would have kissed your feet for a word, a nod, a smile. Now, when this tardy recognition comes, for which I have waited so long, it is tainted with fraud and crime and blood, and I must pay for it with my child's life!"

"And I must forfeit that of mine, it seems, for withholding it so long," sobbed the other, as, tottering, she turned to go. "It is but just."

"Stay—do not go yet!" commanded Janet imperiously, her pride still keeping back her tears. "I have not done. I throw you back your father's name, your father's wealth, your sisterly recognition. I want none of them,—they are bought too dear! ah, God, they are bought too dear! But that you may know that a woman may be foully wronged, and yet may have a heart to feel, even for one who has injured her, you may have your child's life, if my husband can save it! Will," she said, throwing open the door into the next room, "go with her!"

"God will bless you for a noble woman!" exclaimed Mrs. Carteret. "You do not mean all the cruel things you have said,—ah, no! I will see you again, and make you take them back; I cannot thank you now! Oh, doctor, let us go! I pray God we may not be too late!"

Together they went out into the night. Mrs. Carteret tottered under the stress of her emotions, and would have fallen, had not Miller caught and sustained her with his arm until they reached the house, where he turned over her fainting form to Carteret at the door.

"Is the child still alive?" asked Miller.

"Yes, thank God," answered the father, "but nearly gone."

"Come on up, Dr. Miller," called Evans from the head of the stairs. "There 's time enough, but none to spare."

UNCOLLECTED STORIES

Dave's Neckliss

"HAVE some dinner, Uncle Julius?" said my wife.

It was a Sunday afternoon in early autumn. Our two women-servants had gone to a camp-meeting some miles away, and would not return until evening. My wife had served the dinner, and we were just rising from the table, when Julius came up the lane, and, taking off his hat, seated himself on the piazza.

The old man glanced through the open door at the dinner-table, and his eyes rested lovingly upon a large sugar-cured ham, from which several slices had been cut, exposing a rich pink expanse that would have appealed strongly to the appetite of any hungry Christian.

"Thanky, Miss Annie," he said, after a momentary hesitation, "I dunno ez I keers ef I does tas'e a piece er dat ham, ef yer 'll cut me off a slice un it."

"No," said Annie, "I won't. Just sit down to the table and help yourself; eat all you want, and don't be bashful."

Julius drew a chair up to the table, while my wife and I went out on the piazza. Julius was in my employment; he took his meals with his own family, but when he happened to be about our house at meal-times, my wife never let him go away hungry.

I threw myself into a hammock, from which I could see Julius through an open window. He ate with evident relish, devoting his attention chiefly to the ham, slice after slice of which disappeared in the spacious cavity of his mouth. At first the old man ate rapidly, but after the edge of his appetite had been taken off he proceeded in a more leisurely manner. When he had cut the sixth slice of ham (I kept count of them from a lazy curiosity to see how much he *could* eat) I saw him lay it on his plate; as he adjusted the knife and fork to cut it into smaller pieces, he paused, as if struck by a sudden thought, and a tear rolled down his rugged cheek and fell upon the slice of ham before him. But the emotion, whatever the thought that caused it, was transitory, and in a moment he continued his dinner. When he was through eating, he came out on the porch, and resumed his seat with the satisfied expression of countenance that usually follows a good dinner.

"Julius," I said, "you seemed to be affected by something, a moment ago. Was the mustard so strong that it moved you to tears?"

"No, suh, it wa'n't de mustard; I wuz studyin' 'bout Dave."

"Who was Dave, and what about him?" I asked.

The conditions were all favorable to story-telling. There was an autumnal languor in the air, and a dreamy haze softened the dark green of the distant pines and the deep blue of the Southern sky. The generous meal he had made had put the old man in a very good humor. He was not always so, for his curiously undeveloped nature was subject to moods which were almost childish in their variableness. It was only now and then that we were able to study, through the medium of his recollection, the simple but intensely human inner life of slavery. His way of looking at the past seemed very strange to us; his view of certain sides of life was essentially different from ours. He never indulged in any regrets for the Arcadian joyousness and irresponsibility which was a somewhat popular conception of slavery; his had not been the lot of the petted house-servant, but that of the toiling field-hand. While he mentioned with a warm appreciation the acts of kindness which those in authority had shown to him and his people, he would speak of a cruel deed, not with the indignation of one accustomed to quick feeling and spontaneous expression, but with a furtive disapproval which suggested to us a doubt in his own mind as to whether he had a right to think or to feel, and presented to us the curious psychological spectacle of a mind enslaved long after the shackles had been struck off from the limbs of its possessor. Whether the sacred name of liberty ever set his soul aglow with a generous fire; whether he had more than the most elementary ideas of love, friendship, patriotism, religion,—things which are half, and the better half, of life to us; whether he even realized, except in a vague, uncertain way, his own degradation, I do not know. I fear not; and if not, then centuries of repression had borne their legitimate fruit. But in the simple human feeling, and still more in the undertone of sadness, which pervaded his stories, I thought I could see a spark which, fanned by favoring breezes and fed by the memories of the past, might become in his children's children a glowing flame of sensibility, alive to every thrill of human happiness or human woe.

"Dave use' ter b'long ter my ole marster," said Julius; "he wuz raise' on dis yer plantation, en I kin 'member all erbout 'im, fer I wuz ole 'nuff ter chop cotton w'en it all happen'. Dave wuz a tall man, en monst'us strong: he could do mo' wuk in a day dan any yuther two niggers on de plantation. He wuz one er dese yer solemn kine er men, en nebber run on wid much foolishness, like de yuther darkies. He use' ter go out in de woods en pray; en w'en he hear de han's on de plantation cussin' en gwine on wid dere dancin' en foolishness, he use' ter tell 'em 'bout religion en jedgmen'-day, w'en dey would haf ter gin account fer eve'y idle word en all dey yuther sinful kyarin's-on.

"Dave had l'arn' how ter read de Bible. Dey wuz a free nigger boy in de settlement w'at wuz monst'us smart, en could write en cipher, en wuz alluz readin' books er papers. En Dave had hi'ed dis free boy fer ter l'arn 'im how ter read. Hit wuz 'g'in' de law, but co'se none er de niggers did n' say nuffin ter de w'ite folks 'bout it. Howsomedever, one day Mars Walker—he wuz de oberseah—foun' out Dave could read. Mars Walker wa'n't nuffin but a po' bockrah, en folks said he could n' read ner write hisse'f, en co'se he did n' lack ter see a nigger w'at knowed mo' d'n he did; so he went en tole Mars Dugal'. Mars Dugal' sont fer Dave, en ax' 'im 'bout it.

"Dave did n't hardly knowed w'at ter do; but he could n' tell no lie, so he 'fessed he could read de Bible a little by spellin' out de words. Mars Dugal' look' mighty solemn.

" 'Dis yer is a se'ious matter,' sezee; 'it 's 'g'in' de law ter l'arn niggers how ter read, er 'low 'em ter hab books. But w'at yer l'arn out'n dat Bible, Dave?'

"Dave wa'n't no fool, ef he wuz a nigger, en sezee:—

" 'Marster, I l'arns dat it 's a sin fer ter steal, er ter lie, er fer ter want w'at doan b'long ter yer; en I l'arns fer ter love de Lawd en ter 'bey my marster.'

"Mars Dugal' sorter smile' en laf' ter hisse'f, like he 'uz might'ly tickle' 'bout sump'n, en sezee:—

" 'Doan 'pear ter me lack readin' de Bible done yer much harm, Dave. Dat 's w'at I wants all my niggers fer ter know. Yer keep right on readin', en tell de yuther han's w'at yer be'n tellin' me. How would yer lack fer ter preach ter de niggers on Sunday?'

"Dave say he 'd be glad fer ter do w'at he could. So Mars Dugal' tole de oberseah fer ter let Dave preach ter de niggers, en tell 'em w'at wuz in de Bible, en it would he'p ter keep 'em fum stealin' er runnin' erway.

"So Dave 'mence' ter preach, en done de han's on de plantation a heap er good, en most un 'em lef' off dey wicked ways, en 'mence' ter love ter hear 'bout God, en religion, en de Bible; en dey done dey wuk better, en did n' gib de oberseah but mighty little trouble fer ter manage 'em.

"Dave wuz one er dese yer men w'at did n' keer much fer de gals,—leastways he did n' 'tel Dilsey come ter de plantation. Dilsey wuz a monst'us peart, good-lookin', gingybread-colored gal,—one er dese yer high-steppin' gals w'at hol's dey heads up, en won' stan' no foolishness fum no man. She had b'long' ter a gemman over on Rockfish, w'at died, en whose 'state ha' ter be sol' fer ter pay his debts. En Mars Dugal' had be'n ter de oction, en w'en he seed dis gal a-cryin' en gwine on 'bout bein' sol' erway fum her ole mammy, Aun' Mahaly, Mars Dugal' bid 'em bofe in, en fotch 'em ober ter our plantation.

"De young nigger men on de plantation wuz des wil' atter Dilsey, but it did n' do no good, en none un 'em could n' git Dilsey fer dey junesey,* 'tel Dave 'mence' fer ter go roun' Aun' Mahaly's cabin. Dey wuz a fine-lookin' couple, Dave en Dilsey wuz, bofe tall, en well-shape', en soopl'. En dey sot a heap by one ernudder. Mars Dugal' seed 'em tergedder one Sunday, en de nex' time he seed Dave atter dat, sezee:—

" 'Dave, w'en yer en Dilsey gits ready fer ter git married, I ain' got no rejections. Dey 's a poun' er so er chawin'-terbacker up at de house, en I reckon yo' mist'iss kin fine a frock en a ribbin er two fer Dilsey. Youer bofe good niggers, en yer neenter be feared er bein' sol' 'way fum one ernudder long ez I owns dis plantation; en I 'spec's ter own it fer a long time yit.'

*Sweetheart.

"But dere wuz one man on de plantation w'at did n' lack ter see Dave en Dilsey tergedder ez much ez ole marster did. W'en Mars Dugal' went ter de sale whar he got Dilsey en Mahaly, he bought ernudder han', by de name er Wiley. Wiley wuz one er dese yer shiny-eyed, double-headed little niggers, sha'p ez a steel trap, en sly ez de fox w'at keep out'n it. Dis yer Wiley had be'n pesterin' Dilsey 'fo' she come ter our plantation, en had nigh 'bout worried de life out'n her. She did n' keer nuffin fer 'im, but he pestered her so she ha' ter th'eaten ter tell her marster fer ter make Wiley let her 'lone. W'en he come ober to our place it wuz des ez bad, 'tel bimeby Wiley seed dat Dilsey had got ter thinkin' a heap 'bout Dave, en den he sorter hilt off aw'ile, en purten' lack he gin Dilsey up. But he wuz one er dese yer 'ceitful niggers, en w'ile he wuz laffin' en jokin' wid de yuther han's 'bout Dave en Dilsey, he wuz settin' a trap fer ter ketch Dave en git Dilsey back fer hisse'f.

"Dave en Dilsey made up dere min's fer ter git married long 'bout Christmas time, w'en dey 'd hab mo' time fer a weddin'. But 'long 'bout two weeks befo' dat time ole mars 'mence' ter lose a heap er bacon. Eve'y night er so somebody 'ud steal a side er bacon, er a ham, er a shoulder, er sump'n, fum one er de smoke-'ouses. De smoke-'ouses wuz lock', but somebody had a key, en manage' ter git in some way er 'nudder. Dey 's mo' ways 'n one ter skin a cat, en dey 's mo' d'n one way ter git in a smoke-'ouse,—leastways dat 's w'at I hearn say. Folks w'at had bacon fer ter sell did n' hab no trouble 'bout gittin' rid un it. Hit wuz 'g'in' de law fer ter buy things fum slabes; but Lawd! dat law did n' 'mount ter a hill er peas. Eve'y week er so one er dese yer big covered waggins would come 'long de road, peddlin' terbacker en w'iskey. Dey wuz a sight er room in one er dem big waggins, en it wuz monst'us easy fer ter swop off bacon fer sump'n ter chaw er ter wa'm yer up in de wintertime. I s'pose de peddlers did n' knowed dey wuz breakin' de law, caze de niggers alluz went at night, en stayed on de dark side er de waggin; en it wuz mighty hard fer ter tell *w'at* kine er folks dey wuz.

"Atter two er th'ee hund'ed er meat had be'n stole', Mars Walker call all de niggers up one ebenin', en tol' 'em dat de fus' nigger he cot stealin' bacon on dat plantation would git sump'n fer ter 'member it by long ez he lib'. En he say he 'd gin fi' dollars ter de nigger w'at 'skiver' de rogue. Mars Walker say he s'picion' one er two er de niggers, but he could n' tell fer sho, en co'se dey all 'nied it w'en he 'cuse em un it.

"Dey wa'n't no bacon stole' fer a week er so, 'tel one dark night w'en somebody tuk a ham fum one er de smoke-'ouses. Mars Walker des cusst awful w'en he foun' out de ham wuz gone, en say he gwine ter sarch all de niggers' cabins; w'en dis yer Wiley I wuz tellin' yer 'bout up'n say he s'picion' who tuk de ham, fer he seed Dave comin' 'cross de plantation fum to'ds de smoke-'ouse de night befo'. W'en Mars Walker hearn dis fum Wiley, he went en sarch' Dave's cabin, en foun' de ham hid under de flo'.

"Eve'ybody wuz 'stonish'; but dere wuz de ham. Co'se Dave 'nied it ter de las', but dere wuz de ham. Mars Walker say it wuz des ez he 'spected: he did n' b'lieve in dese yer readin' en prayin' niggers; it wuz all 'pocrisy, en sarve' Mars Dugal' right fer 'lowin' Dave ter be readin' books w'en it wuz 'g'in' de law.

"W'en Mars Dugal hearn 'bout de ham, he say he wuz might'ly 'ceived en disapp'inted in Dave. He say he would n' nebber hab no mo' conferdence in no nigger, en Mars Walker could do des ez he wuz a mineter wid Dave er any er de res' er de niggers. So Mars Walker tuk'n tied Dave up en gin 'im forty; en den he got some er dis yer wire clof w'at dey uses fer ter make sifters out'n, en tuk'n wrap' it roun' de ham en fasten it tergedder at de little een'. Den he tuk Dave down ter de blacksmif-shop, en had Unker Silas, de plantation blacksmif, fasten a chain ter de ham, en den fasten de yuther een' er de chain roun' Dave's neck. En den he says ter Dave, sezee:—

" 'Now, suh, yer 'll wear dat neckliss fer de nex' six mont's; en I 'spec's yer ner none er de yuther niggers on dis plantation won' steal no mo' bacon dyoin' er dat time.'

"Well, it des 'peared ez if fum dat time Dave did n' hab nuffin but trouble. De niggers all turnt ag'in' 'im, caze he be'n de 'casion er Mars Dugal' turnin' 'em all ober ter Mars Walker. Mars Dugal' wa'n't a bad marster hisse'f, but Mars Walker wuz hard ez a rock. Dave kep' on sayin' he did n' take de ham, but none un 'em did n' b'lieve 'im.

"Dilsey wa'n't on de plantation w'en Dave wuz 'cused er

stealin' de bacon. Ole mist'iss had sont her ter town fer a week er so fer ter wait on one er her darters w'at had a young baby, en she did n' fine out nuffin 'bout Dave's trouble 'tel she got back ter de plantation. Dave had patien'ly endyoed de finger er scawn, en all de hard words w'at de niggers pile' on 'im, caze he wuz sho' Dilsey would stan' by 'im, en would n' b'lieve he wuz a rogue, ner none er de yuther tales de darkies wuz tellin' 'bout 'im.

"W'en Dilsey come back fum town, en got down fum behine de buggy whar she b'en ridin' wid ole mars, de fus' nigger 'ooman she met says ter her,—

" 'Is yer seed Dave, Dilsey?'

" 'No, I ain' seed Dave,' says Dilsey.

" 'Yer des oughter look at dat nigger; reckon yer would n' want 'im fer yo' junesey no mo'. Mars Walker cotch 'im stealin' bacon, en gone en fasten' a ham roun' his neck, so he can't git it off'n hisse'f. He sut'nly do look quare.' En den de 'ooman bus' out laffin' fit ter kill herse'f. W'en she got thoo laffin' she up'n tole Dilsey all 'bout de ham, en all de yuther lies w'at de niggers be'n tellin' on Dave.

"W'en Dilsey started down ter de quarters, who should she meet but Dave, comin' in fum de cotton-fiel'. She turnt her head ter one side, en purten' lack she did n' seed Dave.

" 'Dilsey!' sezee.

"Dilsey walk' right on, en did n' notice 'im.

" '*Oh*, Dilsey!'

"Dilsey did n' paid no 'tention ter 'im, en den Dave knowed some er de niggers be'n tellin' her 'bout de ham. He felt monst'us bad, but he 'lowed ef he could des git Dilsey fer ter listen ter 'im fer a minute er so, he could make her b'lieve he did n' stole de bacon. It wuz a week er two befo' he could git a chance ter speak ter her ag'in; but fine'ly he cotch her down by de spring one day, en sezee:—

" 'Dilsey, w'at fer yer won' speak ter me, en purten' lack yer doan see me? Dilsey, yer knows me too well fer ter b'lieve I 'd steal, er do dis yuther wick'ness de niggers is all layin' ter me,—yer *knows* I would n' do dat, Dilsey. Yer ain' gwine back on yo' Dave, is yer?'

"But w'at Dave say did n' hab no 'fec' on Dilsey. Dem lies folks b'en tellin' her had p'isen' her min' 'g'in' Dave.

" 'I doan wanter talk ter no nigger,' says she, 'w'at be'n whip' fer stealin', en w'at gwine roun' wid sich a lookin' thing ez dat hung roun' his neck. I 's a 'spectable gal, *I* is. W'at yer call dat, Dave? Is dat a cha'm fer ter keep off witches, er is it a noo kine er neckliss yer got?'

"Po' Dave did n' knowed w'at ter do. De las' one he had pended on fer ter stan' by 'im had gone back on 'im, en dey did n' 'pear ter be nuffin mo' wuf libbin' fer. He could n' hol' no mo' pra'r-meetin's, fer Mars Walker would n' 'low 'im ter preach, en de darkies would n' 'a' listen' ter 'im ef he had preach'. He did n' eben hab his Bible fer ter comfort hisse'f wid, fer Mars Walker had tuk it erway fum 'im en burnt it up, en say ef he ketch any mo' niggers wid Bibles on de plantation he 'd do 'em wuss'n he done Dave.

"En ter make it still harder fer Dave, Dilsey tuk up wid Wiley. Dave could see him gwine up ter Aun' Mahaly's cabin, en settin' out on de bench in de moonlight wid Dilsey, en singin' sinful songs en playin' de banjer. Dave use' ter scrouch down behine de bushes, en wonder w'at de Lawd sen' 'im all dem tribberlations fer.

"But all er Dave's yuther troubles wa'n't nuffin side er dat ham. He had wrap' de chain roun' wid a rag, so it did n' hurt his neck; but w'eneber he went ter wuk, dat ham would be in his way; he had ter do his task, howsomedever, des de same ez ef he did n' hab de ham. W'eneber he went ter lay down, dat ham would be in de way. Ef he turn ober in his sleep, dat ham would be tuggin' at his neck. It wuz de las' thing he seed at night, en de fus' thing he seed in de mawnin'. W'eneber he met a stranger, de ham would be de fus' thing de stranger would see. Most un 'em would 'mence' ter laf, en whareber Dave went he could see folks p'intin' at him, en year 'em sayin':—

" 'W'at kine er collar dat nigger got roun' his neck?' er, ef dey knowed 'im, 'Is yer stole any mo' hams lately?' er 'W'at yer take fer yo' neckliss, Dave?' er some joke er 'nuther 'bout dat ham.

"Fus' Dave did n' mine it so much, caze he knowed he had n' done nuffin. But bimeby he got so he could n' stan' it no longer, en he 'd hide hisse'f in de bushes w'eneber he seed anybody comin', en alluz kep' hisse'f shet up in his cabin atter he come in fum wuk.

"It wuz monst'us hard on Dave, en bimeby, w'at wid dat ham eberlastin' en etarnally draggin' roun' his neck, he 'mence' fer ter do en say quare things, en make de niggers wonder ef he wa'n't gittin' out'n his mine. He got ter gwine roun' talkin' ter hisse'f, en singin' corn-shuckin' songs, en laffin' fit ter kill 'bout nuffin. En one day he tole one er de niggers he had 'skivered a noo way fer ter raise hams,—gwine ter pick 'em off'n trees, en save de expense er smoke-'ouses by kyoin' 'em in de sun. En one day he up'n tole Mars Walker he got sump'n pertickler fer ter say ter 'im; en he tuk Mars Walker off ter one side, en tole 'im he wuz gwine ter show 'im a place in de swamp whar dey wuz a whole trac' er lan' covered wid ham-trees.

"W'en Mars Walker hearn Dave talkin' dis kine er fool-talk, en w'en he seed how Dave wuz 'mencin' ter git behine in his wuk, en w'en he ax' de niggers en dey tole 'im how Dave be'n gwine on, he 'lowed he reckon' he 'd punish' Dave ernuff, en it mou't do mo' harm dan good fer ter keep de ham on his neck any longer. So he sont Dave down ter de blacksmif-shop en had de ham tuk off. Dey wa'n't much er de ham lef' by dat time, fer de sun had melt all de fat, en de lean had all swivel' up, so dey wa'n't but th'ee er fo' poun's lef'.

"W'en de ham had be'n tuk off'n Dave, folks kinder stopped talkin' 'bout 'im so much. But de ham had be'n on his neck so long dat Dave had sorter got use' ter it. He look des lack he 'd los' sump'n fer a day er so atter de ham wuz tuk off, en did n' 'pear ter know w'at ter do wid hisse'f; en fine'ly he up'n tuk'n tied a lighterd-knot ter a string, en hid it under de flo' er his cabin, en w'en nobody wuz n' lookin' he 'd take it out en hang it roun' his neck, en go off in de woods en holler en sing; en he allus tied it roun' his neck w'en he went ter sleep. Fac', it 'peared lack Dave done gone clean out'n his mine. En atter a w'ile he got one er de quarest notions you eber hearn tell un. It wuz 'bout dat time dat I come back ter de plantation fer ter wuk,—I had be'n out ter Mars Dugal's yuther place on Beaver Crick for a mont' er so. I had hearn 'bout Dave en de bacon, en 'bout w'at wuz gwine on on de plantation; but I did n' b'lieve w'at dey all say 'bout Dave, fer I knowed Dave wa'n't dat kine er man. One day atter I come back, me'n Dave wuz choppin' cotton tergedder, w'en Dave lean' on his hoe, en motion' fer me ter come ober close ter 'im; en den he retch' ober en w'ispered ter me.

" 'Julius', sezee, 'did yer knowed yer wuz wukkin' long yer wid a ham?'

"I could n' 'magine w'at he meant. 'G'way fum yer, Dave,' says I. 'Yer ain' wearin' no ham no mo'; try en fergit 'bout dat; 't ain' gwine ter do yer no good fer ter 'member it.'

" 'Look a-yer, Julius,' sezee, 'kin yer keep a secret?'

" 'Co'se I kin, Dave,' says I. 'I doan go roun' tellin' people w'at yuther folks says ter me.'

" 'Kin I trus' yer, Julius? Will yer cross yo' heart?'

"I cross' my heart. 'Wush I may die ef I tells a soul,' says I.

"Dave look' at me des lack he wuz lookin' thoo me en 'way on de yuther side er me, en sezee:—

" 'Did yer knowed I wuz turnin' ter a ham, Julius?'

"I tried ter 'suade Dave dat dat wuz all foolishness, en dat he ought n't ter be talkin' dat-a-way,—hit wa'n't right. En I tole 'im ef he 'd des be patien', de time would sho'ly come w'en eve'ything would be straighten' out, en folks would fine out who de rale rogue wuz w'at stole de bacon. Dave 'peared ter listen ter w'at I say, en promise' ter do better, en stop gwine on dat-a-way; en it seem lack he pick' up a bit w'en he seed dey wuz one pusson did n' b'lieve dem tales 'bout 'im.

"Hit wa'n't long atter dat befo' Mars Archie McIntyre, ober on de Wimbleton road, 'mence' ter complain 'bout somebody stealin' chickens fum his hen-'ouse. De chickens kep' on gwine, en at las' Mars Archie tole de han's on his plantation dat he gwine ter shoot de fus' man he ketch in his hen-'ouse. In less'n a week atter he gin dis warnin', he cotch a nigger in de hen-'ouse, en fill' 'im full er squir'l-shot. W'en he got a light, he 'skivered it wuz a strange nigger; en w'en he call' one er his own sarven's, de nigger tole 'im it wuz our Wiley. W'en Mars Archie foun' dat out, he sont ober ter our plantation fer ter tell Mars Dugal' he had shot one er his niggers, en dat he could sen' ober dere en git w'at wuz lef' un 'im.

"Mars Dugal' wuz mad at fus'; but w'en he got ober dere en hearn how it all happen', he did n' hab much ter say. Wiley wuz shot so bad he wuz sho' he wuz gwine ter die, so he up'n says ter ole marster:—

" 'Mars Dugal',' sezee, 'I knows I 's be'n a monst'us bad nigger, but befo' I go I wanter git sump'n off'n my mine. Dave did n' steal dat bacon w'at wuz tuk out'n de smoke-'ouse. *I* stole it all, en I hid de ham under Dave's cabin fer ter th'ow de blame on him—en may de good Lawd fergib me fer it.'

"Mars Dugal' had Wiley tuk back ter de plantation, en sont fer a doctor fer ter pick de shot out'n 'im. En de ve'y nex' mawnin' Mars Dugal' sont fer Dave ter come up ter de big house; he felt kinder sorry fer de way Dave had be'n treated. Co'se it wa'n't no fault er Mars Dugal's, but he wuz gwine ter do w'at he could fer ter make up fer it. So he sont word down ter de quarters fer Dave en all de yuther han's ter 'semble up in de yard befo' de big house at sun-up nex' mawnin'.

"Yearly in de mawnin' de niggers all swarm' up in de yard. Mars Dugal' wuz feelin' so kine dat he had brung up a bairl er cider, en tole de niggers all fer ter he'p deyselves.

"All de han's on de plantation come but Dave; en bimeby, w'en it seem lack he wa'n't comin', Mars Dugal' sont a nigger down ter de quarters ter look fer 'im. De sun wuz gittin' up, en dey wuz a heap er wuk ter be done, en Mars Dugal' sorter got ti'ed waitin'; so he up'n says:—

" 'Well, boys en gals, I sont fer yer all up yer fer ter tell yer dat all dat 'bout Dave's stealin' er de bacon wuz a mistake, ez I s'pose yer all done hearn befo' now, en I 's mighty sorry it happen'. I wants ter treat all my niggers right, en I wants yer all ter know dat I sets a heap by all er my han's w'at is hones' en smart. En I want yer all ter treat Dave des lack yer did befo' dis thing happen', en mine w'at he preach ter yer; fer Dave is a good nigger, en has had a hard row ter hoe. En de fus' one I ketch sayin' anythin' 'g'in' Dave, I 'll tell Mister Walker ter gin 'im forty. Now take ernudder drink er cider all roun', en den git at dat cotton, fer I wanter git dat Persimmon Hill trac' all pick' ober ter-day.'

"W'en de niggers wuz gwine 'way, Mars Dugal' tole me fer ter go en hunt up Dave, en bring 'im up ter de house. I went down ter Dave's cabin, but could n' fine 'im dere. Den I look' roun' de plantation, en in de aidge er de woods, en 'long de road; but I could n' fine no sign er Dave. I wuz 'bout ter gin up de sarch, w'en I happen' fer ter run 'cross a foot-track w'at look' lack Dave's. I had wukked 'long wid

Dave so much dat I knowed his tracks: he had a monst'us long foot, wid a holler instep, w'ich wuz sump'n skase 'mongs' black folks. So I follered dat track 'cross de fiel' fum de quarters 'tel I got ter de smoke-'ouse. De fus' thing I notice' wuz smoke comin' out'n de cracks; it wuz cu'ous, caze dey had n' be'n no hogs kill' on de plantation fer six mont' er so, en all de bacon in de smoke-'ouse wuz done kyoed. I could n' 'magine fer ter sabe my life w'at Dave wuz doin' in dat smoke-'ouse. I went up ter de do' en hollered:—

" 'Dave!'

"Dey did n' nobody answer. I did n' wanter open de do', fer w'ite folks is monst'us pertickler 'bout dey smoke-'ouses; en ef de oberseah had a-come up en cotch me in dere, he mou't not wanter b'lieve I wuz des lookin' fer Dave. So I sorter knock at de do' en call' out ag'in:—

" 'O Dave, hit 's me—Julius! Doan be skeered. Mars Dugal' wants yer ter come up ter de big house,—he done 'skivered who stole de ham.'

"But Dave did n' answer. En w'en I look' roun' ag'in en did n' seed none er his tracks gwine way fum de smoke-'ouse, I knowed he wuz in dere yit, en I wuz 'termine' fer ter fetch 'im out; so I push de do' open en look in.

"Dey wuz a pile er bark burnin' in de middle er de flo', en right ober de fier, hangin' fum one er de rafters, wuz Dave; dey wuz a rope roun' his neck, en I did n' haf ter look at his face mo' d'n once fer ter see he wuz dead.

"Den I knowed how it all happen'. Dave had kep' on gittin' wusser en wusser in his mine, 'tel he des got ter b'lievin' he wuz all done turnt ter a ham; en den he had gone en built a fier, en tied a rope roun' his neck, des lack de hams wuz tied, en had hung hisse'f up in de smoke-'ouse fer ter kyo.

"Dave wuz buried down by de swamp, in de plantation buryin'-groun'. Wiley did n' died fum de woun' he got in Mars McIntyre's hen-'ouse; he got well atter a w'ile, but Dilsey would n' hab nuffin mo' ter do wid 'im, en 't wa'n't long 'fo' Mars Dugal' sol' 'im ter a spekilater on his way souf,—he say he did n' want no sich a nigger on de plantation, ner in de county, ef he could he'p it. En w'en de een' er de year come, Mars Dugal' turnt Mars Walker off, en run de plantation hisse'f atter dat.

"Eber sence den," said Julius in conclusion, "w'eneber I eats ham, it min's me er Dave. I lacks ham, but I nebber kin eat mo' d'n two er th'ee poun's befo' I gits ter studyin' 'bout Dave, en den I has ter stop en leab de res' fer ernudder time."

There was a short silence after the old man had finished his story, and then my wife began to talk to him about the weather, on which subject he was an authority. I went into the house. When I came out, half an hour later, I saw Julius disappearing down the lane, with a basket on his arm.

At breakfast, next morning, it occurred to me that I should like a slice of ham. I said as much to my wife.

"Oh, no, John," she responded, "you should n't eat anything so heavy for breakfast."

I insisted.

"The fact is," she said, pensively, "I could n't have eaten any more of that ham, and so I gave it to Julius."

A Deep Sleeper

IT WAS four o'clock on Sunday afternoon, in the month of July. The air had been hot and sultry, but a light, cool breeze had sprung up, and occasional cirrus clouds overspread the sun, and for a while subdued his fierceness. We were all out on the piazza—as the coolest place we could find—my wife, my sister-in-law and I. The only sounds that broke the Sabbath stillness were the hum of an occasional vagrant bumble-bee, or the fragmentary song of a mocking-bird in a neighboring elm, who lazily trolled a stave of melody, now and then, as a sample of what he could do in the cool of the morning, or after a light shower, when the conditions would be favorable to exertion.

"Annie," said I, "suppose, to relieve the deadly dulness of the afternoon, that we go out and pull the big watermelon, and send for Colonel Pemberton's folks to come over and help us eat it."

"Is it ripe, yet?" she inquired sleepily, brushing away a troublesome fly that had impudently settled on her hair.

"Yes, I think so. I was out yesterday with Julius, and we thumped it, and concluded it would be fully ripe by tomorrow or next day. But I think it is perfectly safe to pull it to-day."

"Well, if you are sure, dear, we'll go. But how can we get it up to the house? It's too big to tote."

"I'll step round to Julius's cabin and ask him to go down with the wheelbarrow and bring it up," I replied.

Julius was an elderly colored man who worked on the plantation and lived in a small house on the place, a few rods from my own residence. His daughter was our cook, and other members of his family served us in different capacities.

As I turned the corner of the house I saw Julius coming up the lane. He had on his Sunday clothes, and was probably returning from the afternoon meeting at the Sandy Run Baptist Church, of which he was a leading member and deacon.

"Julius," I said, "we are going out to pull the big watermelon, and we want you to take the wheelbarrow and go with us, and bring it up to the house."

"Does yer reckon dat watermillun's ripe yit, sah?" said Julius. "Didn' 'pear ter me it went quite plunk enuff yistiddy fer ter be pull' befo' termorrer."

"I think it is ripe enough, Julius."

"Mawnin' 'ud be a better time fer ter pull it, sah, w'en de night air an' de jew's done cool' it off nice."

"Probably that's true enough, but we'll put it on ice, and that will cool it; and I'm afraid if we leave it too long, some one will steal it."

"I 'spec's dat so," said the old man, with a confirmatory shake of the head. "Yer takes chances w'en yer pulls it, en' yer takes chances w'en yer don't. Dey's a lot er po' w'ite trash roun' heah w'at ain' none too good fer ter steal it. I seed some un' 'em loafin' long de big road on mer way home fum chu'ch jes' now. I has ter watch mer own chicken-coop ter keep chick-'ns 'nuff fer Sunday eatin'. I'll go en' git de w'eelborrow."

Julius had a profound contempt for poor whites, and never let slip an opportunity for expressing it. He assumed that we shared this sentiment, while in fact our feeling toward this listless race was something entirely different. They were, like Julius himself, the product of a system which they had not created and which they did not know enough to resist.

As the old man turned to go away he began to limp, and put his hand to his knee with an exclamation of pain.

"What's the matter, Julius?" asked my wife.

"Yes, Uncle Julius, what ails you?" echoed her sweet young sister. "Did you stump your toe?"

"No, miss, it's dat mis'able rheumatiz. It ketches me now an' den in de lef' knee, so I can't hardly draw my bref. O Lawdy!" he added between his clenched teeth, "but dat do hurt. Ouch! It's a little better now," he said, after a moment, "but I doan' b'lieve I kin roll dat w'eelborrow out ter de watermillun-patch en' back. Ef it's all de same ter yo', sah, I'll go roun' ter my house en' sen' Tom ter take my place, w'iles I rubs some linimum on my laig."

"That'll be all right, Julius," I said, and the old man, hobbling, disappeared round the corner of the house. Tom was a lubberly, sleepy-looking negro boy of about fifteen, related to Julius's wife in some degree, and living with them.

The old man came back in about five minutes. He walked slowly, and seemed very careful about bearing his weight on the afflicted member.

"I sont 'Liza Jane fer ter wake Tom up," he said. "He's down in de orchard asleep under a tree somewhar. 'Liza Jane knows whar he is. It takes a minute er so fer ter wake 'im up. 'Liza Jane knows how ter do it. She tickles 'im in de nose er de yeah wid a broomstraw; hollerin' doan' do no good. Dat boy is one er de Seben Sleepers. He's wuss'n his gran'daddy used ter be."

"Was his grandfather a deep sleeper, Uncle Julius?" asked my wife's sister.

"Oh, yas, Miss Mabel," said Julius, gravely. "He wuz a monst'us pow'ful sleeper. He slep' fer a mont' once."

"Dear me, Uncle Julius, you must be joking," said my sister-in-law incredulously. I thought she put it mildly.

"Oh, no, ma'm, I ain't jokin'. I never jokes on ser'ous subjec's. I wuz dere w'en it all happen'. Hit wuz a monst'us quare thing."

"Sit down, Uncle Julius, and tell us about it," said Mabel; for she dearly loved a story, and spent much of her time "drawing out" the colored people in the neighborhood.

The old man took off his hat and seated himself on the top step of the piazza. His movements were somewhat stiff and he was very careful to get his left leg in a comfortable position.

"Tom's gran'daddy wuz name' Skundus," he began. "He had a brudder name' Tushus en' ernudder name' Cottus en' ernudder name' Squinchus." The old man paused a moment and gave his leg another hitch.

My sister-in-law was shaking with laughter. "What remarkable names!" she exclaimed. "Where in the world did they get them?"

"Dem names wuz gun ter 'em by ole Marse Dugal' McAdoo, wat I use' ter b'long ter, en' dey use' ter b'long ter. Marse Dugal' named all de babies w'at wuz bawn on de plantation. Dese young un's mammy wanted ter call 'em sump'n plain en' simple, like 'Rastus' er 'Cæsar' er 'George Wash'n'-ton;' but ole Marse say no, he want all de niggers on his place ter hab diffe'nt names, so he kin tell 'em apart. He'd done use' up all de common names, so he had ter take sump'n else. Dem names he gun Skundus en' his brudders is Hebrew names en' wuz tuk out'n de Bible."

"Can you give me chapter and verse?" asked Mabel.

"No, Miss Mabel, I doan know 'em. Hit ain' my fault dat I ain't able ter read de Bible. But ez I wuz a-sayin', dis yer Skundus growed up ter be a peart, lively kind er boy, en' wuz very well liked on de plantation. He never quo'lled wid de res' er de han's en' alluz behaved 'isse'f en' tended ter his wuk. De only fault he had wuz his sleep'ness. He'd haf ter be woke up ev'y mawnin' ter go ter his wuk, en' w'enever he got a chance he'd fall ersleep. He wuz might'ly nigh gittin' inter trouble mod'n once fer gwine ter sleep in de fiel'. I never seed his beat fer sleepin'. He could sleep in de sun er sleep in de shade. He could lean upon his hoe en' sleep. He went ter sleep walk'n' 'long de road oncet, en' mighty nigh bus't his head open 'gin' a tree he run inter. I did heah he oncet went ter sleep while he wuz in swimmin'. He wuz floatin' at de time, en' come mighty nigh gittin' drownded befo' he woke up. Ole Marse heared 'bout it en' ferbid his gwine in swimmin' enny mo', fer he said he couldn't 'ford ter lose 'im.

"When Skundus wuz growed up he got ter lookin' roun' at de gals, en' one er de likeliest un 'em tuk his eye. It was a gal name' Cindy, w'at libbed wid 'er mammy in a cabin by dey-se'ves. Cindy tuk ter Skundus ez much ez Skundus tuk ter Cindy, en' bimeby Skundus axed his marster ef he could marry Cindy. Marse Dugal' b'long' ter de P'isbytay'n Chu'ch en' never 'lowed his niggers ter jump de broomstick, but alluz had a preacher fer ter marry 'em. So he tole Skundus ef him en' Cindy would 'ten' ter dey wuk good dat summer till de crap was laid by, he'd let 'em git married en' hab a weddin' down ter de quarters.

"So Skundus en' Cindy wukked hahd as dey could till 'bout a mont' er so befo' layin' by, w'en Marse Dugal's brudder, Kunnel Wash'n'ton McAdoo, w'at libbed down in Sampson County, 'bout a hunderd mile erway, come fer ter visit Marse Dugal'. Dey wuz five er six folks in de visitin' party, en' our w'ite folks needed a new gal fer ter he'p wait on 'em. Dey picked out de likeliest gal dey could fine 'mongs' de fiel'-han's, en' 'cose dat wuz Cindy. Cindy wuz might'ly tickled fer ter be tuk in de house-sarvice, fer it meant better vittles en' better clo's en' easy wuk. She didn' seed Skundus quite as much, but she seed 'im w'eneber she could. Prospe'ity didn' spile Cindy; she didn' git stuck up en' 'bove 'sociatin' wid fiel'-han's, lack some gals in her place 'ud a done.

"Cindy wuz sech a handy gal 'roun' de house, en' her marster's relations lacked her so much, dat w'en dey visit wuz ober, dey wanted ter take Cindy 'way wid 'em. Cindy didn' want ter go en' said so. Her marster wuz a good-natured kind er man, en' would 'a' kep' her on de plantation. But his wife say no, it 'ud nebber do ter be lett'n' de sarvants hab dey own way, er dey soon wouldn' be no doin' nuthin' wid 'em. Ole marster tole 'er he done promus ter let Cindy marry Skundus.

" 'O, well,' sez ole Miss, 'dat doan' cut no figger. Dey's too much er dis foolishness 'bout husban's en' wibes 'mongs' de niggers now-a-days. One nigger man is de same as ernudder, en' dey'll be plenty un 'em down ter Wash'n'ton's plantation.' Ole Miss wuz a mighty smart woman, but she didn' know ev'ything.

" 'Well,' says ole Marse, 'de craps 'll be laid by in a mont' now, 'en den dey won't be much ter do fer ernudder mont' er six weeks. So we'll let her go down dere an' stay till cotton-pickin' time; I'll jes' len' 'er ter 'em till den. Ef dey wants ter keep 'er en' we finds we doan need 'er, den we'll talk furder 'bout sellin' 'er. We'll tell her dat we jes' gwine let her go down dere wid de chil'en a week er so en' den come back, en' den we won't hab no fuss 'bout it.'

"So dey fixed it dat erway, en' Cindy went off wid 'em, she 'spectin' ter be back in a week er so, en' de w'ite folks not hahdly 'lowin' she'd come back at all. Skundus didn' lack ter hab Cindy go, but he couldn' do nuthin'. He wuz wukkin' off in ernudder part er de plantation w'en she went erway, en' had ter tell her good-by de night befo'.

"Bimeby, w'en Cindy didn' come back in two or th'ee weeks, Skundus 'mence ter git res'less. En' Skundus wuz diff'ent f'um udder folks. Mos' folks w'en dey gits res'less can't sleep good, but de mo' res'lesser Skundus got, de mo' sleepier he 'peared ter git. W'eneber he wuz'n wukkin' er eatin', he'd be sleepin'. W'en de yuther niggers 'ud be skylarkin' 'roun' nights en' Sundays, Skundus 'ud be soun' asleep in his cabin. Things kep' on dis way fer 'bout a mont' atter Cindy went away, w'en one mawnin' Skundus didn't come ter wuk. Dey look' fer 'im 'roun' de plantation, but dey couldn' fin' 'im, en' befo' de day wuz gone, ev'ybody wuz sho' dat Skundus had runned erway.

"Cose dey wuz a great howdydo 'bout it. Nobody hadn' nebber runned erway fum Marse Dugal' befo', an' dey hadn' b'en a runaway nigger in de neighbo'hood fer th'ee er fo' years. De w'ite folks wuz all wukked up, en' dey wuz mo' ridin' er hosses en' mo' hitchin up er buggies d'n a little. Ole Marse Dugal' had a lot er papers printed en' stuck up on trees 'long de roads, en' dey wuz sump'n put in de noospapers—a free nigger f'um down on de Wim'l'ton Road read de paper ter some er our han's—tellin' all 'bout how high Skundus wuz, en' w'at kine er teef he had, en' 'bout a skyah he had on his lef' cheek, en' how sleepy he wuz, en' off'rin' a reward er one hunder' dollars fer whoeber 'ud ketch 'im. But none of 'em eber cotch 'im.

"W'en Cindy fus' went away she wuz kinder down in de mouf fer a day er so. But she went to a fine new house, de folks treated her well en' dere wuz sich good comp'ny 'mongs' her own people, dat she made up 'er min' she might 's well hab a good time fer de week er two she wuz gwine ter stay down dere. But w'en de time roll' on en' she didn' heared nothin' 'bout gwine back, she 'mence' ter git kinder skeered she wuz'n nebber gwine ter see her mammy ner Skundus no mo'. She wuz monst'us cut up 'bout it, an' los' 'er appetite en' got so po' en' skinny, her mist'ess sont 'er down ter de swamp fer ter git some roots fer ter make some tea fer 'er health. Her mist'ess sont her 'way 'bout th'ee o'clock en' Cindy didn' come back till atter sundown; en' she say she b'en lookin' fer de roots, dat dey didn' 'pear ter be none er dem kin' er roots fer a mile er so 'long de aidge er de swamp.

"Cindy 'mence' ter git better jes' ez soon as she begun ter drink de root-tea. It wuz a monst'us good med'cine, leas'ways in her case. It done Cindy so much good dat her mist'ess 'cluded she'd take it herse'f en' gib it ter de chil'en.

De fus' day Cindy went atter de roots dey wuz some lef' ober, en' her mist'ess tol' 'er fer ter use dat fer de nex' day. Cindy done so, but she tol' 'er mist'ess hit didn' hab no strenk en' didn' do 'er no good. So ev'y day atter dat Marse Wash'n'ton's wife 'ud sen' Cindy down by de aidge er de swamp fer ter git fresh roots.

" 'Cindy,' said one er de fiel'-han's one day, 'yer better keep 'way fum dat swamp. Dey's a ha'nt walkin' down dere.'

" 'Go way fum yere wid yo' foolishness,' said Cindy. 'Dey ain' no ha'nts. W'ite folks doan' b'lieve in sich things, fer I heared 'em say so; but yer can't 'spec' nothin' better fum fiel'-han's.'

"Dey wuz one man on de plantation, one er dese yer dandy niggers w'at 'uz alluz runnin' atter de wimmen folks, dat got ter pest'rin' Cindy. Cindy didn' paid no 'tention ter 'im, but he kep' on tryin' fer ter co't her w'en he could git a chance. Fin'ly Cindy tole 'im fer ter let her 'lone, er e'se sump'n' might happen ter 'im. But he didn' min' Cindy, en' one ebenin' he followed her down ter de swamp. He los' track un er, en' ez he wuz a-startin' back out'n de swamp, a great big black ha'nt 'bout ten feet high, en' wid a fence-rail in its han's jump out'n de bushes en' chase 'im cl'ar up in de co'n fiel'. Leas'ways he said it did; en' atter dat none er de niggers wouldn't go nigh de swamp, 'cep'n Cindy, who said it wuz all foolishness—it wuz dis nigger's guilty conscience dat skeered 'im—she hadn' seed no ha'nt en' wuz'n skeered er nuffin' she didn't see.

"Bimeby, w'en Cindy had be'n gone fum home 'bout two mont's, harves'-time come on, en' Marse Dugal' foun' hisse'f short er han's. One er de men wuz down wid de rheumatiz, Skundus wuz gone, en' Cindy wuz gone, en' Marse Dugal tole ole Miss dey wuz no use talkin', he couldn' 'ford ter buy no new han's, en' he'd ha' ter sen' fer Cindy, 'en put her in de fiel'; fer de cotton-crap wuz a monst'us big 'un dat year, en' Cindy wuz one er de bes' cotton-pickers on de plantation. So dey wrote a letter to Marse Wash'n'ton dat day fer Cindy, en' wanted Cindy by de 'een er de mont', en' Marse Wash'n'-ton sont her home. Cindy didn't 'pear ter wanter come much. She said she'd got kinder use' ter her noo home; but she didn' hab no mo' ter say 'bout comin' dan she did 'bout goin'. Howsomedever, she went down ter de swamp fer ter git roots fer her mist'ess up ter de las' day she wuz dere.

"W'en Cindy got back home, she wuz might'ly put out 'ca'se Skundus wuz gone, en' hit didn' 'pear ez ef anythin' anybody said ter 'er 'ud comfort 'er. But one mawnin' she said she'd dreamp' dat night dat Skundus wuz gwine ter come back; en' sho' 'nuff, de ve'y nex' mawnin' who sh'd come walkin' out in de fiel' wid his hoe on his shoulder but Skundus, rubbin' his eyes ez ef he hadn' got waked up good yit.

"Dey wuz a great 'miration mongs' de niggers, en' somebody run off ter de big house fer ter tell Marse Dugal'. Bimeby here come Marse Dugal' hisse'f, mad as a hawnit, a-cussin' en' gwine on like he gwine ter hurt somebody; but anybody w'at look close could' 'a' seed he wuz 'mos' tickled ter def fer ter git Skundus back ergin.

" 'Whar yer be'n run erway ter, yer good-fer-nuthin', lazy, black nigger?' sez 'e. 'I'm gwine ter gib yer fo' hunderd lashes. I'm gwine ter hang yer up by yer thumbs en' take ev'y bit er yer black hide off'n yer, en' den I'm gwine ter sell yer ter de fus' specilater w'at comes' long buyin' niggers fer ter take down ter Alabam'. W'at yer mean by runnin' er way fum yer good, kin' marster, yer good-fer-nuthin', wool-headed, black scound'el?'

"Skundus looked at 'im ez ef he didn' understan'. 'Lawd, Marse Dugal',' sez 'e, 'I doan' know w'at youer talkin' 'bout. I ain' runned erway; I ain' be'n nowhar.'

" 'Whar yer be'n fer de las' mon'?' said Marse Dugal'. 'Tell me de truf, er I'll hab yer tongue pulled out by de roots. I'll tar yer all ober yer en' set yer on fiah. I'll—I'll'— Marse Dugal' went on at a tarrable rate, but eve'ybody knowed Marse Dugal' bark uz wuss'n his bite.

"Skundus look lack 'e wuz skeered mos' ter def fer ter heah Marse Dugal' gwine on dat erway, en' he couldn' 'pear to un'erstan' w'at Marse Dugal' was talkin' erbout.

" 'I didn' mean no harm by sleep'n in de barn las' night, Marse Dugal',' sez 'e, 'en' ef yer'll let me off dis time, I won' nebber do so no mo'.'

"Well, ter make a long story sho't, Skundus said he had gone ter de barn dat Sunday atternoon befo' de Monday w'en he could't be foun', fer ter hunt aigs, en' wiles he wuz up dere de hay had 'peared so sof' en' nice dat he had laid down fer take a little nap; dat it wuz mawnin' w'en he woke en' foun' hisse'f all covered up whar de hay had fell over on 'im. A hen had built a nes' right on top un 'im, en' it had half-a-dozen aigs in it. He said he hadn't stop fer ter git no brekfus', but had jes' suck' one or two er de aigs en' hurried right straight out in de fiel', fer he seed it wuz late en' all de res' er de han's wuz gone ter wuk.

" 'Youer a liar,' said Marse Dugal', 'en' de truf ain't in yer. Yer b'en run erway en' hid in de swamp somewhar ernudder.' But Skundus swo' up en' down dat he hadn' b'en out'n dat barn, en' fin'lly Marse Dugal' went up ter de house en' Skundus went on wid his wuk.

"Well, yer mought know dey wuz a great 'miration in de neighbo'hood. Marse Dugal' sont fer Skundus ter cum up ter de big house nex' day, en' Skundus went up 'spect'n' fer ter ketch forty. But w'en he got dere, Marse Dugal' had fetched up ole Doctor Leach fum down on Rockfish, 'en another young doctor fum town, en' dey looked at Skundus's eyes en' felt of his wris' en' pulled out his tongue, en' hit 'im in de chis', en' put dey yeahs ter his side fer ter heah 'is heart beat; en' den dey up'n made Skundus tell how he felt w'en 'e went ter sleep en' how he felt w'en 'e woke up. Dey stayed ter dinner, en' w'en dey got thoo' talkin' en' eatin' en' drinkin', dey tole Marse Dugal' Skundus had had a catacornered fit, en' had be'n in a trance fer fo' weeks. En' w'en dey l'arned about Cindy, en' how dis yer fit had come on gradg'ly atter Cindy went away, dey 'lowed Marse Dugal' 'd better let Skundus en' Cindy git married, er he'd be liable ter hab some mo' er dem fits. Fer Marse Dugal' didn' want no fittified niggers ef 'e could he'p it.

"Atter dat, Marse Dugal' had Skundus up ter de house lots er times fer ter show 'im off ter folks w'at come ter visit. En' bein' as Cindy wuz back home, en' she en' Skundus wukked hahd, en' he couldn' 'ford fer ter take no chances on dem long trances, he 'lowed em ter got married soon ez cotton-pickin' wuz ober, en' gib 'em a cabin er dey own ter lib in down in de quarters. En' sho' 'nuff, dey didn' had no trouble keep'n' Skundus wak f'm dat time fo'th, fer Cindy turned out ter hab a temper of her own, en' made Skundus walk a chalk-line.

"Dis yer boy, Tom," said the old man, straightening out his leg carefully, preparatory to getting up, "is jes' like his gran'-daddy. I b'lieve ef somebody didn' wake 'im up he'd sleep till jedgmen' day. Heah 'e comes now. Come on heah wid dat w'eelborrow, yer lazy, good-fer-nuthin' rascal."

Tom came slowly round the house with the wheelbarrow, and stood blinking and rolling his eyes as if he had just emerged from a sound sleep and was not yet half awake.

We took our way around the house, the ladies and I in front, Julius next and Tom bringing up the rear with the wheelbarrow. We went by the well-kept grape-vines, heavy with the promise of an abundant harvest, through a narrow field of yellowing corn, and then picked our way through the watermelon-vines to the spot where the monarch of the patch had lain the day before, in all the glory of its coat of variegated green. There was a shallow concavity in the sand where it had rested, but the melon itself was gone.

Lonesome Ben

THERE had been some talk among local capitalists about building a cotton mill on Beaver Creek, a few miles from my place on the sand hills in North Carolina, and I had been approached as likely to take an interest in such an enterprise. While I had the matter under advisement it was suggested, as an inducement to my co-operation, that I might have the brick for the mill made on my place—there being clay there suitable for the purpose—and thus reduce the amount of my actual cash investment. Most of my land was sandy, though I had observed several outcroppings of clay along the little creek or branch forming one of my boundaries.

One afternoon in summer, when the sun was low and the heat less oppressive than it had been earlier in the day, I ordered Julius, our old colored coachman, to harness the mare to the rockaway and drive me to look at the clay-banks. When we were ready, my wife, who wished to go with me for the sake of the drive, came out and took her seat by my side.

We reached our first point of destination by a road running across the plantation, between a field of dark-green maize on the one hand and a broad expanse of scuppernong vines on the other. The road led us past a cabin occupied by one of my farm-hands. As the carriage went by at a walk, the woman of the house came to the door and curtsied. My wife made some inquiry about her health, and she replied that it was poor. I noticed that her complexion, which naturally was of a ruddy brown, was of a rather sickly hue. Indeed, I had observed a greater sallowness among both the colored people and the poor whites thereabouts than the hygienic conditions of the neighborhood seemed to justify.

After leaving this house our road lay through a cotton field for a short distance, and then we entered a strip of woods, through which ran the little stream beside which I had observed the clay. We stopped at the creek, the road by which we had come crossing it and continuing over the land of my neighbor, Colonel Pemberton. By the roadside, on my own land, a bank of clay rose in almost a sheer perpendicular for about ten feet, evidently extending back some distance into the low, pine-clad hill behind it, and having also frontage upon the creek. There were marks of bare feet on the ground along the base of the bank, and the face of it seemed freshly disturbed and scored with finger marks, as though children had been playing there.

"Do you think that clay would make good brick, Julius?" I asked the old man, who had been unusually quiet during the drive. He generally played with the whip, making little feints at the mare, or slapping her lightly with the reins, or admonishing her in a familiar way; but on this occasion the heat or some other cause had rendered him less demonstrative than usual.

"Yas, suh, I knows it would," he answered.

"How do you know? Has it ever been used for that purpose?"

"No, suh; but I got my reasons fer sayin' so. Ole Mars Dugal useter hab a brickya'd fu'ther up de branch—I dunno as yer noticed it, fer it's all growed ober wid weeds an' grass. Mars Dugal said dis yer clay wouldn' make good brick, but I knowed better."

I judged from the appearance of the clay that it was probably deficient in iron. It was of a yellowish-white tint and had a sort of greasy look.

"Well," I said, "we'll drive up to the other place and get a sample of that clay, and then we'll come back this way."

"Hold on a minute, dear," said my wife, looking at her watch, "Mabel has been over to Colonel Pemberton's all the afternoon. She said she'd be back at five. If we wait here a little while she'll be along and we can take her with us."

"All right," I said, "we'll wait for her. Drive up a little farther, Julius, by that jessamine vine."

While we were waiting, a white woman wearing a homespun dress and slat-bonnet, came down the road from the other side of the creek, and lifting her skirts slightly, waded with bare feet across the shallow stream. Reaching the claybank she stooped and gathered from it, with the aid of a convenient stick, a quantity of the clay which she pressed together in the form of a ball. She had not seen us at first, the bushes partially screening us; but when, having secured the clay, she turned her face in our direction and caught sight of us watching her, she hid the lump of clay in her pocket with a shamefaced look, and hurried away by the road she had come.

"What is she going to do with that, Uncle Julius?" asked my wife. We were Northern settlers, and still new to some of the customs of the locality, concerning which we often looked to Julius for information. He had lived on the place many years and knew the neighborhood thoroughly.

"She's gwineter eat it, Miss Annie," he replied, "w'en she gits outer sight."

"Ugh!" said my wife with a grimace, "you don't mean she's going to eat that great lump of clay?"

"Yas'm I does; dat's jes' w'at I means—gwineter eat eve'y bit un it, an' den come back bimeby fer mo'."

"I should think it would make them sick," she said.

"Dey gits use' ter it," said Julius. "Howsomeber, ef dey eats too much it does make 'em sick; an' I knows w'at I'm er-talkin' erbout. I doan min' w'at dem kinder folks does," he added, looking contemptuously after the retreating figure of the poor-white woman, "but w'eneber I sees black folks eat'n' clay of'n dat partic'lar clay-bank, it alluz sets me ter studyin' 'bout po' lonesome Ben."

"What was the matter with Ben?" asked my wife. "You can tell us while we're waiting for Mabel."

Old Julius often beguiled our leisure with stories of plantation life, some of them folk-lore stories, which we found to be in general circulation among the colored people; some of them tales of real life as Julius had seen it in the old slave days; but the most striking were, we suspected, purely imaginary, or so colored by old Julius's fancy as to make us speculate at times upon how many original minds, which might have added to the world's wealth of literature and art, had been buried in the ocean of slavery.

"W'en ole Mars Marrabo McSwayne owned dat place ober de branch dere, w'at Kunnel Pembe'ton owns now," the old man began, "he useter hab a nigger man name' Ben. Ben wuz one er dese yer big black niggers—he was mo'd'n six foot high an' black ez coal. He wuz a fiel'-han' an' a good wukker, but he had one little failin'—he would take a drap er so oncet in a w'ile. Co'se eve'ybody laks a drap now an' den, but it 'peared ter 'fec' Ben mo'd'n it did yuther folks. He didn' hab much chance dat-a-way, but eve'y now an' den he'd git holt er sump'n' somewahr, an' sho's he did, he'd git out'n de narrer road. Mars Marrabo kep' on wa'nin' 'm 'bout it, an' fin'lly he tol' 'im ef he eber ketch 'im in dat shape ag'in he 'uz gwineter gib 'im fo'ty. Ben knowed ole Mars Marrabo had a good 'memb'ance an' alluz done w'at he said, so he wuz monst'us keerful not ter gib 'm no 'casion fer ter use his 'memb'ance on him. An' so fer mos' a whole yeah Ben 'nied hisse'f an' nebber teched a drap er nuffin'.

"But it's h'ad wuk ter larn a ole dog new tricks, er ter make him fergit de ole uns, an' po' Ben's time come bimeby, jes' lak ev'ybody e'se's does. Mars Marrabo sent 'im ober ter dis yer plantation one day wid a bundle er cotton-sacks fer Mars Dugal,' an' wiles he wuz ober yere, de ole Debbil sent a' 'oman w'at had cas' her eyes on 'im an' knowed his weakness, fer ter temp' po' Ben wid some licker. Mars Whiskey wuz right dere an' Mars Marrabo wuz a mile erway, an' so Ben minded Mars Whiskey an' fergot 'bout Mars Marrabo. W'en he got back home he couldn' skasely tell Mars Marrabo de message w'at Mars Dugal' had sent back ter 'im.

"Mars Marrabo listen' at 'im 'temp' ter tell it; and den he says, kinder col' and cuttin'-like—he didn' 'pear ter get mad ner nuffin':

" 'Youer drunk, Ben.'

"De way his marster spoke sorter sobered Ben, an' he 'nied it of co'se.

" 'Who? Me, Mars Marrabo? *I* ain' drunk; no, marster, *I* ain' drunk. I ain' teched a drap er nuffin' sence las' Chris'mas, suh'.

" 'Youer drunk, Ben, an' don't you dare ter 'spute my wo'd, er I'll kill you in yo' tracks! I'll talk ter you Sad'day night, suh, w'en you'll be sober, an' w'en you'll hab Sunday ter 'flect over ou' conve'sation, an' 'nuss yo' woun's.'

"W'en Mars Marrabo got th'oo talkin' Ben wuz mo' sober dan he wuz befo' he got drunk. It wuz Wednesday w'en Ben's marster tol 'im dis, an' 'twix' den and Friday night Ben done a heap er studyin'. An' de mo' he studied de mo' he didn' lak de way Mars Marrabo talked. He hadn' much trouble wid Mars Marrabo befo,' but he knowed his ways, an' he knowed dat de longer Mars Marrabo waited to do a thing de wusser he got 'stid er gittin' better lak mos' folks. An' Ben fin'lly made up his min' he wa'n't gwineter take dat cow-hidin.' He 'lowed dat ef he wuz little, like some er de dahkies on de plantation, he wouldn' min' it so much; but he wuz so big dey'd be mo' groun' fer Mars Marrabo ter cover, an' it would hurt dat much mo.' So Ben 'cided ter run erway.

"He had a wife an' two chil'en, an' dey had a little cabin ter deyse'ves down in de quahters. His wife Dasdy wuz a good-lookin,' good-natu'd 'oman, an' 'peared ter set a heap er sto' by Ben. De little boy wuz name' Pete; he wuz 'bout eight er nine years ole, an' had already 'menced ter go out in de fiel' an' he'p his mammy pick cotton, fer Mars Marrabo wuz one er dese yer folks w'at wants ter make eve'y aidge cut. Dis yer little Pete wuz a mighty soople dancer, an' w'en his daddy would set out in de yahd an' pick de banjo fer 'im, Pete could teach de ole folks noo steps—dancin' jes seemed to come nachul ter 'im. Dey wuz a little gal too; Ben didn' pay much 'tention ter de gal, but he wuz monst'us fond er Dasdy an' de boy. He wuz sorry ter leab 'em, an' he didn' tell 'em nuffin' 'bout it fer fear dey'd make a fuss. But on Friday night Ben tuk all de bread an' meat dey wuz in de cabin an' made fer de woods.

"W'en Sad'day come an' Ben didn' 'pear, an' nobody didn' know nuffin' 'bout 'im, Mars Marrabo 'lowed of co'se dat Ben had runned erway. He got up a pahty an' tuk de dawgs out an' follered de scen' down ter de crick an' los' it. Fer Ben had tuk a go'd-full er tar 'long wid' 'im, an' w'en he got ter de crick he had 'n'inted his feet wid tar, an' dat th'owed de houns' off'n de scent. Dey sarched de woods an' follered de roads an' kep' watchin' fer a week, but dey couldn' fin' no sign er Ben. An' den Mars Marrabo got mo' stric', an' wuked his niggers hahder'n eber, ez ef he wanted ter try ter make up fer his loss.

"W'en Ben stahted out he wanted ter go ter de No'th. He didn' know how fur it wuz, bet he 'lowed he retch dar in fo' er five days. He knowed de No'th Stah, an' de fus night he kep' gwine right straight to'ds it. But de nex' night it was rainin,' an' fer two er th'ee nights it stayed cloudy, an' Ben couldn' see de No'th Stah. Howsomeber, he knowed he had got stahted right' an' he kep' gwine right straight on de same way fer a week er mo' 'spectin' ter git ter de No'th eve'y day, w'en one mawin' early, atter he had b'en walkin' all night, he come right smack out on de crick jes whar he had stahted f'om.

"Co'se Ben wuz monst'us disapp'inted. He had been wond'rin' w'y he hadn' got ter de No'th befo,' an' behol,' heah he wuz back on de ole plantation. He couldn' un'erstan' it at fus,' but he wuz so hongry he didn' hab time ter study 'bout nuffin' fer a little w'ile but jes' ter git sump'n' ter eat; fer he had done eat up de bread an' meat he tuk away wid 'im, an' had been libbin' on roas'n-ears an' sweet'n taters he'd slip out'n de woods an' fin' in co'n fiel's 'an 'tater-patches. He look 'cross de crick, an' seed dis yer clay-bank, an' he waded ober an' got all he could eat, an' den tuk a lump wid 'im, an' hid in de woods ag'in 'til he could study de matter ober some.

"Fus' he 'lowed dat he better gib hiss'ef up an' take his lammin.' But jes' den he 'membered de way Mars Marrabo looked at 'im an' w'at he said 'bout Sad'day night; an' den he 'lowed dat ef Mars Marrabo ketch 'im now, he'd wear 'im ter a frazzle an' chaw up de frazzle, so de wouldn' be nuffin' lef' un 'im at all, an' dat Mars Marrabo would make a' example an' a warnin' of 'im fer all de niggers in de naberhood. Fac' is Mars Marrabo prob'ly wouldn' a' done much ter 'im fer it 'ud be monst'us po' 'couragement fer runaway niggers ter come back, ef dey gwineter git killed w'en dey come. An' so Ben waited 'til night, an' den he went back an' got some mo' clay an' eat it an' hid hisse'f in de woods ag'in.

"Well, hit wuz quare 'bout Ben, but he stayed roun' heah fer a mont,' hidin' in de woods in de daytime, an' slippin' out nights an' gittin' clay ter eat an' water f'om de crick yanker ter drink. De water in dat crick wuz cl'ar in dem days, stidder bein' yallar lak it is now."

We had observed that the water, like that of most streams that take their rise in swamps, had an amber tint to which the sand and clay background of the bed of the stream imparted an even yellower hue.

"What did he do then, Julius?" asked my wife, who liked to hear the end of a story.

"Well, Miss, he made up his min' den dat he wuz gwineter

staht fer de No'th ag'in. But wiles he b'en layin' roun' in de woods he had 'mence ter feel monst'us lonesome, an' it 'peared ter him dat he jes' couldn' go widout seein' Dasdy an' little Pete. Fus' he 'lowed he'd go up ter de cabin, but he thought 'bout de dogs 'roun' de yahd, an' dat de yuther dahkies mought see 'im, and so he 'cided he'd better watch fer 'em 'til dey come long de road—it wuz dis yer same road—w'en he could come out'n de woods an' talk ter 'em. An' he eben 'lowed he mought 'suade 'em ter run erway wid 'im an' dey could all get ter de No'th, fer de nights wuz cl'ar now, an' he couldn' lose de No'th Stah.

"So he waited two er th'ee days, an' sho' nuff long come Dasdy one mornin,' comin' over to Mars Dugal's fer ter fetch some things fer her missis. She wuz lookin' kinder down in de mouf, fer she thought a heap er Ben, an' wuz monst'us sorry ter lose 'im, w'iles at de same time she wuz glad he wuz free, fer she 'lowed he'd done got ter de Norf long befo.' An' she wuz studyin' 'bout Ben, w'at a fine-lookin' man he wuz, an' wond'rin' ef she'd eber see 'im any mo.'

"W'en Ben seed her comin' he waited 'til she got close by, an' den he stepped out 'n de woods an' come face ter face wid her. She didn' 'pear to know who he wuz, an' seem kinder skeered.

" 'Hoddy, Dasdy honey,' he said.

" 'Huh!' she said, ''pears ter me you'er mighty fermilyer on sho't acquaintance.'

" 'Sho't acquaintance.' Why, doan' yer know me, Dasdy?'

" 'No. I doan know yer f'om a skeercrow. I never seed yer befo' in my life, an' nebber wants ter see yer ag'in. Whar did yer com f'om anyhow? Whose nigger is yer? Er is yer some low-down free nigger dat doan b'long ter nobody an' doan own nobody?'

" 'W'at fer you talk ter me like dat, honey? I's Ben, yo' Ben. Why doan you know yo' own man?'

"He put out his ahms fer ter draw her ter 'im, but she jes' gib one yell, an' stahted ter run. Ben wuz so 'stonish' he didn' know w'at ter do, an' he stood dere in de road 'til he heared somebody e'se comin', w'en he dahted in de woods ag'in.

"Po' Ben wuz so 'sturbed in his min' dat he couldn' hahdly

eat any clay dat day. He couldn' make out w'at wuz de matter wid Dasdy but he 'lowed maybe she'd heared he wuz dead er sump'n,' an' thought he wuz a ha'nt, an' dat wuz w'y she had run away. So he watch' by de side er de road, an' nex' mornin' who should come erlong but little Pete, wid a reed over his shoulder, an' a go'd-full er bait, gwine fishin' in de crick.

"Ben called 'im; 'Pete, *O* Pete! *Little* Pete.'

"Little Pete cocked up his ears an' listened. 'Peared lak he'd heared dat voice befo.' He stahted fer de woods fer ter see who it wuz callin' 'im, but befo' he got dere Ben stepped out an' retched fer im.

" 'Come heah, honey, an' see yo' daddy, who ain' seenyer fer so long.'

"But little Pete tuk one look at 'im, an' den 'menceter holler an squeal an' kick an' bite an' scratch. Ben wuz so 'stonish' dat he couldn' hol' de boy, who slipped out'n his han's an run to'ds de house ez fas' ez his legs would tote 'im.

"Po' Ben kep' gittin' wus an' wus mixed up. He couldn' make out fer de life er 'im w'at could be de matter. Nobody didn' 'pear ter wanter own 'im. He felt so cas' down dat he didn' notice a nigger man comin' long de road 'til he got right close up on 'im, an' didn' heah dis man w'en he said 'Hoddy' ter 'im.

" 'W'at's de matter wid yer?' said de yuther man w'en Ben didn' 'spon'. 'W'at jedge er member er de legislater er hotel-keeper does you b'long ter dat you can't speak ter a man w'en he says hoddy ter yer?'

"Ben kinder come ter hisse'f an' seed it wuz Primus, who b'long ter his marster an' knowed 'im as well as anybody. But befo' he could git de words out'n his mouf Primus went on talkin.'

" 'Youer de mos' mis'able lookin' merlatter I eber seed. Dem rags look lak dey be'n run th'oo a sawmill. My marster doan 'low no strange niggers roun' dis yer plantation, an' yo' better take yo' yaller hide 'way f'um yer as fas' as yo' kin.'

"Jes den somebody hollered on de yuther side er de crick, an' Primus stahted off on a run, so Ben didn' hab no chance ter say no mo' ter 'im.

"Ben almos' 'lowed he wuz gwine out'n' his min', he wuz

so 'stonished an' mazed at none er dese yer folks reco'nizin' 'im. He went back in de woods ag'in an' stayed dere all day, wond'rin' w'at he wuz gwineter do. Oncet er twicet he seed folks comin' 'long de road, an' stahted out ter speak ter 'em, but changed his min' an' slip' back ag'in.

"Co'se ef Mars Marrabo had been huntin' Ben he would 'a' foun' 'im. But he had long sence los' all hope er seein' im ag'in, an' so nobody didn' 'sturb Ben in de woods. He stayed hid a day er two mo' an' den he got so lonesome an' homesick fer Dasdy an' little Pete an' de yuther dahkies,—somebody ter talk ter—dat he jes' made up his min' ter go right up ter de house an' gib hisse'f up an' take his med'cine. Mars Marrabo couldn' do nuffin' mo' d'n kill 'im an' he mought's well be dead as hidin' in de woods wid nobody ter talk ter er look at ner nuffin'. He had jes' come out 'n de woods an' stahted up dis ve'y road, w'en who sh'd come 'long in a hoss 'n buggy but ole Mars Marrabo, drivin' ober ter dat yuther brickyahd youer gwinter see now. Ben run out 'n de woods, and fell down on his knees in de road right in front er Mars Marrabo. Mars Marrabo had to pull on de lines an' hol' de hoss up ter keep 'im f'um runnin' ober Ben.

" 'Git out'n de road, you fool nigger,' says Mars Marrabo, 'does yer wanter git run ober? Whose nigger is you, anyhow?'

" 'I's yo' nigger, Mars Marrabo; doan yer know Ben, w'at runned erway?'

" 'Yas, I knows my Ben w'at runned erway. Does you know whar he is?'

" 'Why, I's yo' Ben, Mars Marrabo. Doan yer know me, marster?'

" 'No, I doan know yer, yer yaller rascal! W'at de debbil yer mean by tellin' me sich a lie? Ben wuz black ez a coal an' straight ez an' arrer. Youer yaller ez dat clay-bank, an' crooked ez a bair'l-hoop. I reckon youer some 'stracted nigger, tun't out by some marster w'at doan wanter take keer er yer. You git off'n my plantation, an' doan show yo' clay-cullud hide aroun' yer no more, er I'll hab yer sent ter jail an' whip.'

"Mars Marrabo drove erway an' lef' po' Ben mo' dead 'n alive. He crep' back in de bushes an' laid down an' wep' lak a baby. He didn' hab no wife, no chile, no frien's, no marster—

he'd be'n willin' ernuff to git 'long widout a marster, w'en he had one, but it 'peared lak a sin fer his own marster ter 'ny 'im an' cas' 'im off dat-a-way. It 'peared ter 'im he mought jes' ez well be dead ez livin', fer he wuz all alone in de worl', wid nowhar ter go, an' nobody didn' hab nuffin' ter say ter 'im but ter 'buse 'im an' drive 'im erway.

"Atter he got ober his grievin' spell he 'mence ter wonder w'at Mars Marrabo meant by callin' 'im yaller, an' ez long ez nobody didn' seem ter keer whuther dey seed 'im er not, he went down by de crick in broad daylight, an' kneel down by de water an' looked at his face. Fus' he didn' reco'nize hisse'f an' glanshed back ter see ef dey wa'n't somebody lookin' ober his shoulder—but dey wa'n't. An' w'en he looked back in de water he seed de same thing—he wa'n't black no mo', but had turnt ter a light yaller.

"Ben didn' knowed w'at ter make er it fer a minute er so. Fus' he 'lowed he must hab de yaller fever, er de yaller janders, er sump'n lak dat'! But he had knowed rale dark folks ter hab janders befo', and it hadn't nebber 'fected 'em dat-a-way. But bimeby he got up o'ff'n 'is han's an' knees an' wuz stan'in' lookin' ober de crick at de clay-bank, an' wond'rin ef de clay he'd b'en eat'n' hadn' turnt 'im yaller w'en he heared sump'n say jes' ez plain ez wo'ds.

" 'Turnt ter clay! turnt ter clay! turnt ter clay!'

"He looked all roun', but he couldn' see nobody but a big bullfrog settin' on a log on de yuther side er de crick. An' w'en he turnt roun' an' sta'ted back in de woods, he heared de same thing behin' 'im.

" 'Turnt ter clay! turnt ter clay! turnt ter clay!'

"Dem wo'ds kep' ringin' in 'is yeahs 'til he fin'lly 'lowed dey wuz boun' ter be so, er e'se dey wouldn' a b'en tol' ter 'im, an' dat he had libbed on clay so long an' had eat so much, dat he must 'a' jes nach'ly turnt ter clay!"

"Imperious Caesar, turned to clay,
Might stop a hole to keep the wind away,"

I murmured parenthentically.

"Yas, suh," said the old man, "turnt ter clay. But you's mistook in de name, suh; hit wuz Ben, you 'member, not Caesar. Ole Mars Marrabo did hab a nigger name' Caesar, but dat wuz anudder one."

"Don't interrupt him, John," said my wife impatiently. "What happened then, Julius?"

"Well, po' Ben didn' know w'at ter do. He had be'n lonesome ernuff befo', but now he didn' eben hab his own se'f ter 'so'ciate wid, fer he felt mo' lak a stranger 'n he did lak Ben. In a day er so mo' he 'mence ter wonder whuther he wuz libbin' er not. He had hearn 'bout folks turnin' ter clay w'en dey wuz dead, an' he 'lowed maybe he wuz dead an' didn' knowed it, an' dat wuz de reason w'y eve'body run erway f'm 'im an' wouldn' hab nuffin' ter do wid 'im. An' ennyhow, he 'lowed ef he wa'n't dead, he mought's well be. He wande'ed roun' a day er so mo', an' fin'lly de lonesomeness, an' de sleepin' out in de woods, 'mongs' de snakes an' sco'pions, an' not habbin' nuffin' fit ter eat, 'mence ter tell on him, mo' an' mo', an' he kep' gittin' weakah an' weakah 'til one day, w'en he went down by de crick fer ter git a drink er water, he foun' his limbs gittin' so stiff hit 'uz all he could do ter crawl up on de bank an' lay down in de sun. He laid dere 'til he died, an' de sun beat down on 'im, an' beat down on 'im, an' beat down on 'im, fer th'ee er fo' days, 'til it baked 'im as ha'd as a brick. An' den a big win' come erlong an' blowed a tree down, an' it fell on 'im an' smashed 'im all ter pieces, an' groun' 'im ter powder. An' den a big rain come erlong, an' washed 'im in de crick, 'an eber sence den de water in dat crick's b'en jes' as yer sees it now. An dat wuz de een' er po' lonesome Ben, an' dat's de reason w'y I knows dat clay'll make brick an' w'y I doan nebber lak ter see no black folks eat'n it."

My wife came of a family of reformers, who could never contemplate an evil without seeking an immediate remedy. When I decided that the bank of edible clay was not fit for brickmaking, she asked me if I would not have it carted away, suggesting at the same time that it could be used to fill a low place in another part of the plantation.

"It would be too expensive," I said.

"Oh, no," she replied, "I don't think so. I have been talking with Uncle Julius about it, and he says he has a nephew who is out of employment, and who will take the contract for ten dollars, if you will furnish the mule and cart, and board him while the job lasts."

As I had no desire to add another permanent member to my household, I told her it would be useless; that if the people did not get clay there they would find it elsewhere, and perhaps an inferior quality which might do greater harm, and that the best way to stop them from eating it was to teach them self-respect, when she had opportunity, and those habits of industry and thrift whereby they could get their living from the soil in a manner less direct but more commendable.

The Dumb Witness

THE OLD Murchison place was situated on the Lumberton plank road, about two miles from my vineyard on the North Carolina sandhills. Old Julius, our colored coachman, had driven me over one spring morning to see young Murchison, the responsible manager of the property, about some walnut timber I wished to purchase from him for shipment. I had noticed many resources of the country that the easy-going Southerners had not thought of developing; and I took advantage of them when I found it convenient and profitable to do so.

We entered the lane leading to the house by passing between two decaying gateposts. This entrance had evidently once possessed some pretensions to elegance, for the massive posts had been faced with dressed lumber and finished with ornamental tops, some fragments of which still remained; and the one massive hinge, hanging by a slender rust-eaten nail, had been wrought into a fantastic shape. As we drove through the gateway, a green lizard scampered down from the top of one of the posts, where he had been sunning himself, and a rattlesnake lying in the path lazily uncoiled his motley brown length, and, sounding his rattle the meanwhile, wriggled slowly off into the rank grass and weeds.

The house stood well back from the road, on the crest of one of the regular undulations of the sandhill country. It was partly concealed, when approached from the road, by intervening trees and shrubbery, which had once formed a well ordered pleasaunce, but now grew in wild and tangled profusion, so that it was difficult to distinguish one bush or tree from another. The lane itself was partially overgrown, and the mare's fetlocks swept the dew from the grass, where it had not yet been dried by the morning sun.

As we drew nearer, the house stood clearly revealed. It was apparently of more ancient date than any I had seen in the neighborhood. It was a large two-story frame house, built in the colonial style, with a low-pitched roof, and a broad piazza along the front, running the full length of both stories and supported by huge round columns, and suggesting distantly, in its general effect, the portico of a Greek temple. The roof had sunk on one side, and the shingles were old and cracked and moss-grown; while several of the windows in the upper part of the house were boarded up, and others filled with sash from which the glass had apparently long since been broken.

For a space of several rods on each side of the house the ground was bare of grass and shrubbery, and scarcely less forbidding than the road we had traveled. It was rough and uneven, lying in little hillocks and hollows, as though it had been dug over at hazard, or explored by some vagrant drove of hogs. At one side, beyond this barren area, lay an enclosed kitchen garden, in which a few collards and okra-plants and tomato-vines struggled desperately against neglect and drought and poverty of soil.

A casual glance might have led one not informed to the contrary, to believe the place untenanted, so lonely and desolate did it seem. But as we approached we became aware of two figures on the long piazza. At one end of it, in a massive arm-chair of carved oak, a man was seated—apparently a very old man, for he was bent and wrinkled. His thin white hair hung down upon his shoulders. His face was of a high-bred and strongly marked type, with something of the hawk-like contour usually associated with extreme acquisitiveness. His eyes were turned toward the opposite end of the piazza, where a woman was also seated. She seemed but little younger than the man, and her face was enough like his, in a feminine way, to suggest that they might be related in some degree, unless this inference was negatived by the woman's complexion, which disclosed a strong infusion of darker blood. She wore a homespun frock and a muslin cap and sat bolt upright, with her hands folded on her lap, looking toward her *vis-à-vis* at the other end of the piazza.

As we drew up a short distance from the door, the old man rose, as we supposed, to come forward and greet us. But, instead of stopping at the steps and facing outward, he continued his course to the other end of the piazza and halted before the woman.

"Viney," he said, in a sharply imperative voice, "my uncle says you will tell me where he put the papers. I am tired of this nonsense. I insist upon knowing immediately."

The woman made no reply, but her faded eyes seemed to glow for a moment, like the ashes of a dying fire fanned by some random breath of air.

"Why do you not answer me?" he continued, with increasing vehemence. "I tell you I insist upon knowing. It is imperative that I should know, and know at once. My interests are suffering for every day's delay. The papers—where are the papers?"

Still the woman sat silent, though her figure seemed to stiffen as she leaned slightly toward him. He grew visibly more impatient at her silence, and began to threaten her.

"Tell me immediately, you hussy, or you will have reason to regret it. You take liberties that cannot be permitted. I will not put up with it," he said, shaking his fist as he spoke. "I shall have to have you whipped."

The slumbrous fire in the woman's eyes flamed up for a moment. She rose from her seat, and drawing herself up to her full height—she was a tall woman, though bowed somewhat with years—began to speak, I thought at first in some foreign tongue. But after a moment I knew that no language or dialect, at least none of European origin, could consist of such a discordant jargon, such a meaningless cacophony as that which fell from the woman's lips. And as she went on, pouring out a flood of sounds that were not words, and which yet seemed now and then vaguely to suggest words, as clouds suggest the shapes of mountains and trees and strange beasts, the old man seemed to bend like a reed before a storm, and began to expostulate, accompanying his words with deprecatory gestures.

"Yes, Viney, good Viney," he said in soothing tones, "I know it was wrong, and I've always regretted it—always from the very day I did it. But you shouldn't bear malice, Viney, it isn't Christian. The Bible says you should bless them that curse you, and do good to them that despitefully use you. But I was good to you before, Viney, and I was good to you afterwards, and I know you have forgiven me—good Viney, noble-hearted Viney!—and you are going to tell me. Now, *do* tell me where the papers are," he added, pleadingly, offering to take her hand, which lay on the arm of the chair.

She drew her hand away, as she muttered something in the

same weird tones she had employed before. The old man bent toward her, in trembling eagerness, but seemed disappointed.

"Try again, Viney," he said, "that's a good girl. Your old master thinks a great deal of you, Viney. He is your best friend."

Again she made an inarticulate response. He seemed to comprehend, and turning from her, came down the steps, muttering to himself, took up a spade that stood at one end of the steps, passed by us without seeming conscious of our presence, and hastening with tottering footsteps to one side of the yard began digging furiously.

I had been so much interested in this curious drama that I had forgotten for the time being the business that brought me there. The old woman, however, when the man had gone, rose from her seat and went into the house, without giving us more than a look.

"What's the matter with them, Julius?" I said, returning with a start to the world of reality.

The old man pointed to his head.

"Dey's bofe 'stracted, suh," he said, "out'n dey min'. Dey's be'n dat-a-way fer yeahs an' yeahs."

At that moment the young man of the house came out to the door, and greeted us pleasantly. He asked me to alight from the carriage and led me to the chair the old man had occupied. It was a massive oak affair, with carved arms and back and a wooden seat, and looked as though it might be of ancient make, perhaps an heirloom. I found young Murchison was a frank and manly young fellow, and quite capable of looking out for his own interests. I struck a bargain with him, on terms that were fair to both. When I had concluded my business and invited him to call and see me sometime, I got into the carriage, and Julius drove down the lane and out into the road again. In going out, we passed near the old man, who was still muttering to himself and digging rapidly, but with signs of weariness. He did not look up as we went by, but seemed entirely absorbed in his strange pursuit.

In the evening, after supper, Julius came up to the house. We sat out on the porch, my wife and her sister and Julius and I. We cut a large watermelon, and when Julius had eaten the half we gave to him, he told us the story of old man Murchison's undoing. The air was cool, the sky was clear, the stars shone with a brightness unknown in higher latitudes. The voices of the night came faintly from the distant woods, and there could have been no more romantic setting for the story of jealousy, revenge and disappointment which the old white-haired negro told us, in his own quaint dialect—a story of things possible only in an era which, happily, has passed from our history, as, in God's own time—and may it be soon!—it will from all the earth. Some of the facts in this strange story—circumstances of which Julius was ignorant, though he had the main facts correct—I learned afterwards from other sources, but I have woven them all together here in orderly sequence.

The Murchison family had occupied their ancestral seat on the sandhills for a hundred years or more. There were not many rich families in that part of North Carolina, and this one, by reason of its wealth and other things, was easily the most conspicuous in several counties. The first great man of the family, General Arthur Murchison, had won distinction in the war of independence, and during all the Revolutionary period had been one of the most ardent of the Carolina patriots. After peace was established he had taken high place in the councils of the State. Elected a delegate to the Constitutional Convention at Philadelphia in 1787, it was largely due to his efforts that North Carolina adopted the Federal Constitution the following year. His son became a distinguished jurist, whose name is still a synonym for legal learning and juridical wisdom in North Carolina. Roger Murchison, the son of Judge Murchison—the generations had followed one another rapidly in a country of warm skies and early marriages—was the immediate predecessor of Malcolm Murchison, the demented old man who was nominal owner of the estate at the time of my visit to the house.

In Roger Murchison the family may be said to have begun to decline from the eminence it had attained in the career of Judge Murchison. In the first place, Roger Murchison did not marry, thus seemingly indicating a lack of the family pride which would have made him wish to continue the name in the direct line. Again, though his career in college had been brilliant; though the wealth and standing of the family gave him social and political prestige; and though he had held high office under the State and National governments, he had never while in public life especially distinguished himself for eloquence or statesmanship, but had, on the contrary, enjoyed a life of ease and pleasure and had wasted what his friends thought rare gifts. He was fond of cards, of fast horses, of rare wines, and of gay society. It is not surprising, therefore, that he spent very little time on his property, preferring the life of cities to the comparative dullness of plantation life with such colorless distractions as a neighboring small town could offer.

He had inherited a large estate, including several plantations, and numerous slaves. During his frequent absences from home, in the last fifteen years of his life, he left his property under the management of a nephew, Malcolm Murchison, the orphan son of a younger brother, and his own prospective heir. Young Malcolm was a youth of unusual strength of character and administrative capacity, and even before he had attained his majority showed himself a better manager than his uncle had ever been. So well, indeed, did he manage the estate that his uncle left it for ten years practically in his hands, looking to him only for the means he required to lead his own life in other places. It is true he appeared periodically and assumed the role of proprietor, but Malcolm was the man to whom the community and the slaves looked as both the present and the future master.

Young Murchison kept bachelor's hall in the great house. The only women about the establishment were an old black cook, and the housekeeper, a tall, comely young quadroon—she had too a dash of Indian blood, which perhaps gave her straighter and blacker hair than she would otherwise have had, and also perhaps endowed her with some other qualities which found their natural expression in the course of subsequent events—if indeed her actions needed anything more than common human nature to account for them. The duties of young Murchison's housekeeper were not onerous; compared with a toiling field hand she led a life of ease and luxury. The one conspicuous vice of Malcolm Murchison was avarice. If he had other failings, they were the heritage of the period, and he shared them with his contemporaries of the same caste. Perhaps it was his avarice that kept him from marrying; it was cheaper to have his clothing and his table looked after by a slave than by a woman who would not have been content with her food and clothing. At any rate, for ten or fifteen years he remained single, and ladies never set foot in the Murchison house. Men sometimes called and smoked and drank, played cards, bought and sold produce or slaves, but the foot of a white woman had not touched the floor for fifteen years, when Mrs. Martha Todd came from Pennsylvania to the neighboring town of Patesville to visit a cousin living there, who had married a resident of the town.

Malcolm Murchison met Mrs. Todd while she was driving on the road one day. He knew her companion, in response to whose somewhat distant bow he lifted his hat. Attracted by the stranger's appearance, he made inquiries about her in the town, and learned that she was a widow and rich in her own right. He sought opportunities to meet her, courted her, and after a decent interval of hesitation on her part—she had only just put off mourning for her first husband—received her promise to be his wife.

He broke the news to his housekeeper by telling her to make the house ready for a mistress. The housekeeper had been in power too long to yield gracefully, or perhaps she foresaw and dreaded the future. Some passionate strain of the mixed blood in her veins—a very human blood—broke out in a scene of hysterical violence. She pleaded, remonstrated, raged. He listened calmly through it all—he had anticipated some such scene—and at the end said to her:

"You had better be quiet and obedient. I have heard what you have to say—this once—and it will be useless for you to repeat it, for I shall not listen again. If you are reasonable, I will send you to the other plantation. If not, I will leave you here, with your new mistress."

She was silent for the time being, but raged inwardly. The next day she stole away from home, went to the town, sought out the new object of Murchison's devotion, and told her something—just what she told no one but herself and the lady ever knew.

When Murchison called in the evening, Mrs. Todd sent down word that she was not at home. With the message came a note:

"I have had my wedded happiness spoiled once. A burnt

child dreads the fire—I do not care to go twice through the same experience. I have learned some things about you that will render it impossible for me ever to marry you. It is needless to seek an explanation."

He went away puzzled and angry. His housekeeper wore an anxious look, which became less anxious as she observed his frame of mind. He had been wondering where Mrs. Todd had got the information—he could not doubt what it was—that had turned her from him. Suddenly a suspicion flashed into his mind. He went away early the next morning and made investigations. In the afternoon he came home with all the worst passions of weak humanity, clad with irresponsible power, flaming in his eyes.

"I will teach you," he said to his housekeeper, who quailed before him, "to tell tales about your master. I will put it out of your power to dip your tongue in where you are not concerned."

There was no one to say him nay. The law made her his. It was a lonely house, and no angel of mercy stayed his hand.

About a week later he received a letter,—a bulky envelope. On breaking the seal, he found the contents to consist of two papers, one of which was a letter from a friend and political associate of his uncle. It was dated at Washington, and announced the death of his Uncle Roger as the result of an accident. A team of spirited horses had run away with him and thrown him out of the carriage, inflicting a fatal injury. The letter stated that his uncle had lingered for a day, during which he had dictated a letter to his nephew; that his body had been embalmed and placed in a vault, to await the disposition of his relatives or representatives. His uncle's letter was enclosed with the one above and ran as follows:

> "My dear Malcolm: This is the last communication I shall ever make to you, I am sorry to say—though I don't know that I ought to complain, for I have always been a philosopher, and have had a good time to boot. There must be an end to all things, and I cannot escape the common fate.
>
> "You have been a good nephew and a careful manager, and I have not forgotten the fact. I have left a will

in which you are named as my sole heir, barring some small provision for my sister Mary. With the will you will find several notes, and mortgages securing them, on plantations in the neighborhood—I do not need to specify, as they explain themselves; also some bonds and other securities of value and your grandmother's diamond necklace. I do not say here where they are, lest this letter might fall into the wrong hands; but your housekeeper Viney knows their hiding place. She is devoted to you and to the family—she ought to be, for she is of our blood—and she only knows the secret. I would not have told her, of course, had I not thought of just some such chance as this which has befallen me. She does not know the value of the papers, but simply that they are important.

"And now, Malcolm, my boy, goodbye. I am crossing the river and I reach back to clasp your hand once more—just once.

"Your dying Uncle,
"Roger Murchison"

Malcolm Murchison took this letter to Viney. She had been banished from the house to a cabin in the yard, where she was waited on by the old black cook. He felt a little remorseful as he looked at her; for, after all, she was a woman, and there had been excuses for what she had done; and he had begun to feel, in some measure, that there was no sufficient excuse for what he had done.

She looked at him with an inscrutable face as he came in, and he felt very uncomfortable under the look.

"Viney," he said, not unkindly, "I'm sorry I went so far, and I'm glad you're getting better."

Her expression softened, a tear rolled down her cheek, and he felt correspondingly relieved. It is so easy to forgive our own sins against others.

"Your old Master Roger is dead. I have just received a letter telling me how it happened. He was thrown from a buggy in a runaway and injured so badly that he died the same day. He had time to write me a letter, in which he says you can tell me where he put certain papers that you know about. Can you tell"—he remembered her condition—"can you show me where they are?"

A closer observer than Malcolm Murchison might have detected at this moment another change in the woman's expression. Perhaps it was in her eyes more than elsewhere; for into their black depths there sprang a sudden fire. Beyond this, however, and a slight quickening of her pulse, of which there was no visible manifestation, she gave no sign of special feeling; and even if these had been noticed they might have been attributed to the natural interest felt at hearing of her old master's death.

The only answer Viney made was to lift her hand and point it to her mouth.

"Yes, I know," he said hastily, "you can't tell me—not now at least, but you can surely point out the place to me."

She shook her head and pointed again to her mouth.

"Is it hidden in some place that you can't lead me to when you are able to get up?"

She nodded her head.

"Will it require words to describe it so that I can find it?"

Again she nodded affirmatively.

He reflected a moment. "Is it in the house?" he asked.

She shook her head.

"In the yard?"

Again she made a negative sign.

"In the barn?"

No.

"In the fields?"

No.

He tried for an hour, naming every spot he could think of as a possible hiding-place for the papers, but with no avail. Every question was answered in the negative.

When he had exhausted his ingenuity in framing questions he went away very much disappointed. He had been patiently waiting for his reward for many years, and now when it should be his, it seemed to elude his grasp.

"Never mind," he said, "we will wait until you are better, and then perhaps you may be able to speak intelligibly. In the meantime you shall not want for anything."

He had her removed to the house and saw that she received every attention. She was fed with dainty food, and such care as was possible was given to her wound. In due time it healed. But she did not even then seem able to articulate, even in whispers, and all his attempts to learn of her the whereabouts of the missing papers, were met by the same failure. She seemed willing enough, but unable to tell what he wished to know. There was apparently some mystery which only words could unravel.

It occurred to him more than once how simple it would be for her to write down the few words necessary to his happiness. But, alas! She might as well have been without hands, for any use she could make of them in that respect. Slaves were not taught to write, for too much learning would have made them mad. But Malcolm Murchison was a man of resources—he would have her taught to write. So he employed a teacher—a free colored man who had picked up some fragments of learning, and who could be trusted to hold his tongue, to teach Viney to read and write. But somehow she made poor progress. She was handicapped of course by her loss of speech. It was unfamiliar work too for the teacher, who would not have been expert with a pupil equipped with all the normal faculties. Perhaps she had begun too old; or her mind was too busily occupied with other thoughts to fix it on the tedious and painful steps by which the art of expression in writing is acquired. Whatever the reason, she manifested a remarkable stupidity while seemingly anxious to learn; and in the end Malcolm was compelled to abandon the attempt to teach her.

Several years passed in vain efforts to extract from Viney in some way the wished-for information. Meantime Murchison's affairs did not prosper. Several other relatives claimed a share in his uncle's estate; on the ground that he had died intestate. In the absence of the will, their claims could not be successfully disputed. Every legal means of delay was resorted to, and the authorities were disposed, in view of the remarkable circumstances of the case, to grant every possible favor. But the law fixed certain limits to delay in the settlement of an estate, and in the end he was obliged either to compromise the adverse claims or allow them to be fixed by legal process. And while certain of what his own rights were, he was compelled to see a large part of what was rightfully his go into hands where it would be difficult to trace or recover it if the will were found. Some of the estates against which he suspected the hidden notes and mortgages were held, were sold and otherwise disposed of. His worry interfered with proper attention to his farming operations, and one crop was almost a failure. The factor to whom he shipped his cotton went bankrupt owing him a large balance, and he fell into debt and worried himself into a fever. The woman Viney nursed him through it, and was always present at his side, a mute reproach for his cruelty, a constant reminder of his troubles. Her presence was the worst of things for him, and yet he could not bear to have her out of his sight; for in her lay the secret he longed for and which he hoped at some time in some miraculous way to extract from her.

When he rose from his sick-bed after an illness of three months, he was but the wreck of the strong man he had once been. His affairs had fallen into hopeless disorder. His slaves, except Viney, were sold to pay his debts, and there remained to him of the almost princely inheritance he had expected, only the old place on the sandhills and his slave, Viney, who still kept house for him. His mind was vacant and wandering, except on the one subject of the hidden will, and he spent most of the time in trying to extract from Viney the secret of its hiding-place. A young nephew came and lived with him and did what was necessary to hold the remnant of the estate together.

When the war came Viney was freed, with the rest of her brethren in bondage. But she did not leave the old place. There was some gruesome attraction in the scene of her suffering, or perhaps it was the home instinct. The society of humankind did not possess the same attraction for her as if she had not been deprived of the power of speech. She stayed on and on, doing the simple housework for the demented old man and his nephew, until the superstitious negroes and poor whites of the neighborhood said that she too shared the old man's affliction. Day after day they sat on the porch, when her indoor work was done, the old man resting in the carved oaken arm-chair, and she in her splint-bottom chair; or the old man commanding, threatening, expostulating, entreating her to try, just once more, to tell him his uncle's message—she replying in the meaningless inarticulate mutterings that we had heard; or the old man digging, digging furiously, and she watching him from the porch, with the same inscrutable eyes, though dulled somewhat by age, that had flashed upon him for a moment in the dimly lighted cabin where she lay on her bed of pain.

The summer following the visit I made to the old Murchison place I accompanied my wife North on a trip to our former home. On my return several weeks later I had occasion again to visit young Murchison, and drove over one morning to the house. As we drove up the lane I noticed a surprising change in the surroundings. A new gate had been hung, upon a pair of ugly cast-iron hinges. The grass in the path had been mowed, and the weeds and shrubs bordering it had been cut down. The neglected pleasure-garden had been reduced to some degree of order, and the ground around the house had been plowed and harrowed, and the young blades of grass were shooting up and covering the surface with a greenish down. The house itself had shared in the general improvement. The roof had been repaired and the broken windows mended, and from certain indications in the way of ladders and pails in the yard, I inferred that it was intended to paint the house. This however was merely a supposition, for house-painting is an art that languishes in the rural districts of the South.

Julius had been noticing my interest in these signs of prosperity, with a pleased expression that boded further surprises.

"What's been going on here, Julius?" I asked.

"Ole Mars Murchison done dead, suh—died las' mont', an' eve'ything goes ter young Mistah Roger. He's done 'mence' ter fix de ole place up. He be'n ober ter yo' place lookin' 'roun', an' he say he's gwineter hab his'n lookin' lak yo'n befo' de yeah's ober."

We stopped the rockaway in front of the house. As we drew up, an old woman came out of the front door, in whom I recognized one of the strange couple I had seen on the piazza on my former visit. She seemed intelligent enough, and I ventured to address her.

"Is Mr. Murchison at home?"

"Yas, suh," she answered, "I'll call 'im."

Her articulation was not distinct, but her words were intelligible. I was never more surprised in my life.

"What does this mean, Julius?" I inquired, turning to the old man, who was grinning and chuckling to himself in great glee at my manifest astonishment. "Has she recovered her speech?"

"She'd nebber lost it, suh. Ole Viney could 'a' talked all de time, ef she'd had a min' ter. Atter ole Mars Ma'colm wuz dead, she tuk an' showed Mistah Roger whar de will an' de yuther papers wuz hid. An' whar yer reckon dey wuz, zuh?"

"I give it up, Julius. Enlighten me."

"Dey wa'n't in de house, ner de yah'd, ner de ba'n, ner de fiel's. Dey wuz hid in de seat er dat ole oak a'm-cheer on de piazza yander w'at ole Mars Ma'colm be'n settin' in all dese yeahs."

The March of Progress

The colored people of Patesville had at length gained the object they had for a long time been seeking—the appointment of a committee of themselves to manage the colored schools of the town. They had argued, with some show of reason, that they were most interested in the education of their own children, and in a position to know, better than any committee of white men could, what was best for their children's needs. The appointments had been made by the county commissioners during the latter part of the summer, and a week later a meeting was called for the purpose of electing a teacher to take charge of the grammar school at the beginning of the fall term.

The committee consisted of Frank Gillespie, or "Glaspy," a barber, who took an active part in local politics; Bob Cotten, a blacksmith, who owned several houses and was looked upon as a substantial citizen; and Abe Johnson, commonly called "Ole Abe" or "Uncle Abe," who had a large family, and drove a dray, and did odd jobs of hauling; he was also a class-leader in the Methodist church. The committee had been chosen from among a number of candidates—Gillespie on account of his political standing, Cotten as representing the solid element of the colored population, and Old Abe, with democratic impartiality, as likely to satisfy the humbler class of a humble people. While the choice had not pleased everybody,—for instance, some of the other applicants,—it was acquiesced in with general satisfaction. The first meeting of the new committee was of great public interest, partly by reason of its novelty, but chiefly because there were two candidates for the position of teacher of the grammar school.

The former teacher, Miss Henrietta Noble, had applied for the school. She had taught the colored children of Patesville for fifteen years. When the Freedmen's Bureau, after the military occupation of North Carolina, had called for volunteers to teach the children of the freedmen, Henrietta Noble had offered her services. Brought up in a New England household by parents who taught her to fear God and love her fellow-men, she had seen her father's body brought home from a Southern battle-field and laid to rest in the village cemetery; and a short six months later she had buried her mother by his side. Henrietta had no brothers or sisters, and her nearest relatives were cousins living in the far West. The only human being in whom she felt any special personal interest was a certain captain in her father's regiment, who had paid her some attention. She had loved this man deeply, in a maidenly, modest way; but he had gone away without speaking, and had not since written. He had escaped the fate of many others, and at the close of the war was alive and well, stationed in some Southern garrison.

When her mother died, Henrietta had found herself possessed only of the house where she lived and the furniture it contained, neither being of much value, and she was thrown upon her own resources for a livelihood. She had a fair education and had read many good books. It was not easy to find employment such as she desired. She wrote to her Western cousins, and they advised her to come to them, as they thought they could do something for her if she were there. She had almost decided to accept their offer, when the demand arose for teachers in the South. Whether impelled by some strain of adventurous blood from a Pilgrim ancestry, or by a sensitive pride that shrank from dependence, or by some dim and unacknowledged hope that she might sometime, somewhere, somehow meet Captain Carey—whether from one of these motives or a combination of them all, joined to something of the missionary spirit, she decided to go South, and wrote to her cousins declining their friendly offer.

She had come to Patesville when the children were mostly a mob of dirty little beggars. She had distributed among them the cast-off clothing that came from their friends in the North; she had taught them to wash their faces and to comb their hair; and patiently, year after year, she had labored to instruct them in the rudiments of learning and the first principles of religion and morality. And she had not wrought in vain. Other agencies, it is true, had in time coöperated with her efforts, but any one who had watched the current of events must have been compelled to admit that the very fair progress of the colored people of Patesville in the fifteen years following emancipation had been due chiefly to the unselfish labors of Henrietta Noble, and that her nature did not belie her name.

Fifteen years is a long time. Miss Noble had never met Captain Carey; and when she learned later that he had married a Southern girl in the neighborhood of his post, she had shed her tears in secret and banished his image from her heart. She had lived a lonely life. The white people of the town, though they learned in time to respect her and to value her work, had never recognized her existence by more than the mere external courtesy shown by any community to one who lives in the midst of it. The situation was at first, of course, so strained that she did not expect sympathy from the white people; and later, when time had smoothed over some of the asperities of war, her work had so engaged her that she had not had time to pine over her social exclusion. Once or twice nature had asserted itself, and she had longed for her own kind, and had visited her New England home. But her circle of friends was broken up, and she did not find much pleasure in boarding-house life; and on her last visit to the North but one, she had felt so lonely that she had longed for the dark faces of her pupils, and had welcomed with pleasure the hour when her task should be resumed.

But for several reasons the school at Patesville was of more importance to Miss Noble at this particular time than it ever had been before. During the last few years her health had not been good. An affection of the heart similar to that from which her mother had died, while not interfering perceptibly with her work, had grown from bad to worse, aggravated by close application to her duties, until it had caused her grave alarm. She did not have perfect confidence in the skill of the Patesville physicians, and to obtain the best medical advice had gone to New York during the summer, remaining there a month under the treatment of an eminent specialist. This, of course, had been expensive and had absorbed the savings of years from a small salary; and when the time came for her to return to Patesville, she was reduced, after paying her traveling expenses, to her last ten-dollar note.

"It is very fortunate," the great man had said at her last

visit, "that circumstances permit you to live in the South, for I am afraid you could not endure a Northern winter. You are getting along very well now, and if you will take care of yourself and avoid excitement, you will be better." He said to himself as she went away: "It 's only a matter of time, but that is true about us all; and a wise physician does as much good by what he withholds as by what he tells."

Miss Noble had not anticipated any trouble about the school. When she went away the same committee of white men was in charge that had controlled the school since it had become part of the public-school system of the State on the withdrawal of support from the Freedmen's Bureau. While there had been no formal engagement made for the next year, when she had last seen the chairman before she went away, he had remarked that she was looking rather fagged out, had bidden her good-by, and had hoped to see her much improved when she returned. She had left her house in the care of the colored woman who lived with her and did her housework, assuming, of course, that she would take up her work again in the autumn.

She was much surprised at first, and later alarmed, to find a rival for her position as teacher of the grammar school. Many of her friends and pupils had called on her since her return, and she had met a number of the people at the colored Methodist church, where she taught in the Sunday-school. She had many friends and supporters, but she soon found out that her opponent had considerable strength. There had been a time when she would have withdrawn and left him a clear field, but at the present moment it was almost a matter of life and death to her—certainly the matter of earning a living—to secure the appointment.

The other candidate was a young man who in former years had been one of Miss Noble's brightest pupils. When he had finished his course in the grammar school, his parents, with considerable sacrifice, had sent him to a college for colored youth. He had studied diligently, had worked industriously during his vacations, sometimes at manual labor, sometimes teaching a country school, and in due time had been graduated from his college with honors. He had come home at the end of his school life, and was very naturally seeking the employment for which he had fitted himself. He was a "bright" mulatto, with straight hair, an intelligent face, and a well-set figure. He had acquired some of the marks of culture, wore a frock-coat and a high collar, parted his hair in the middle, and showed by his manner that he thought a good deal of himself. He was the popular candidate among the progressive element of his people, and rather confidently expected the appointment.

The meeting of the committee was held in the Methodist church, where, in fact, the grammar school was taught, for want of a separate school-house. After the preliminary steps to effect an organization, Mr. Gillespie, who had been elected chairman, took the floor.

"The principal business to be brought befo' the meet'n' this evenin'," he said, "is the selection of a teacher for our grammar school for the ensuin' year. Two candidates have filed applications, which, if there is no objections, I will read to the committee. The first is from Miss Noble, who has been the teacher ever since the grammar school was started."

He then read Miss Noble's letter, in which she called attention to her long years of service, to her need of the position, and to her affection for the pupils, and made formal application for the school for the next year. She did not, from motives of self-respect, make known the extremity of her need; nor did she mention the condition of her health, as it might have been used as an argument against her retention.

Mr. Gillespie then read the application of the other candidate, Andrew J. Williams. Mr. Williams set out in detail his qualifications for the position: his degree from Riddle University; his familiarity with the dead and living languages and the higher mathematics; his views of discipline; and a peroration in which he expressed the desire to devote himself to the elevation of his race and assist the march of progress through the medium of the Patesville grammar school. The letter was well written in a bold, round hand, with many flourishes, and looked very aggressive and overbearing as it lay on the table by the side of the sheet of small notepaper in Miss Noble's faint and somewhat cramped handwriting.

"You have heard the readin' of the application," said the chairman. "Gentlemen, what is yo' pleasure?"

There being no immediate response, the chairman continued:

"As this is a matter of consid'able importance, involvin' not only the welfare of our schools, but the progress of our race, an' as our action is liable to be criticized, whatever we decide, perhaps we had better discuss the subjec' befo' we act. If nobody else has anythin' to obse've, I will make a few remarks."

Mr. Gillespie cleared his throat, and, assuming an oratorical attitude, proceeded:

"The time has come in the history of our people when we should stand together. In this age of organization the march of progress requires that we help ourselves, or be left forever behind. Ever since the war we have been sendin' our child'n to school an' educatin' 'em; an' now the time has come when they are leavin' the schools an' colleges, an' are ready to go to work. An' what are they goin' to do? The white people won't hire 'em as clerks in their sto's an' factories an' mills, an' we have no sto's or factories or mills of our own. They can't be lawyers or doctors yet, because we have n't got the money to send 'em to medical colleges an' law schools. We can't elect many of 'em to office, for various reasons. There 's just two things they can find to do—to preach in our own pulpits, an' teach in our own schools. If it was n't for that, they 'd have to go on forever waitin' on white folks, like their fo'fathers have done, because they could n't help it. If we expect our race to progress, we must educate our young men an' women. If we want to encourage 'em to get education, we must find 'em employment when they are educated. We have now an opportunity to do this in the case of our young friend an' fellow-citizen, Mr. Williams, whose eloquent an' fine-lookin' letter ought to make us feel proud of him an' of our race.

"Of co'se there are two sides to the question. We have got to consider the claims of Miss Noble. She has been with us a long time an' has done much good for our people, an' we 'll never forget her work an' frien'ship. But, after all, she has been paid for it; she has got her salary regularly an' for a long time, an' she has probably saved somethin', for we all know she has n't lived high; an', for all we know, she may have had somethin' left her by her parents. An' then again, she 's white, an' has got her own people to look after her; they 've got all the money an' all the offices an' all the everythin',—all that they 've made an' all that we 've made for fo' hundred years, —an' they sho'ly would look out for her. If she don't get this school, there 's probably a dozen others she can get at the North. An' another thing: she is gettin' rather feeble, an' it 'pears to me she 's hardly able to stand teachin' so many child'n, an' a long rest might be the best thing in the world for her.

"Now, gentlemen, that 's the situation. Shall we keep Miss Noble, or shall we stand by our own people? It seems to me there can hardly be but one answer. Self-preservation is the first law of nature. Are there any other remarks?"

Old Abe was moving restlessly in his seat. He did not say anything, however, and the chairman turned to the other member.

"Brother Cotten, what is yo' opinion of the question befo' the board?"

Mr. Cotten rose with the slowness and dignity becoming a substantial citizen, and observed:

"I think the remarks of the chairman have great weight. We all have nothin' but kind feelin's fer Miss Noble, an' I came here to-night somewhat undecided how to vote on this question. But after listenin' to the just an' forcible arguments of Brother Glaspy, it 'pears to me that, after all, the question befo' us is not a matter of feelin', but of business. As a business man, I am inclined to think Brother Glaspy is right. If we don't help ourselves when we get a chance, who is goin' to help us?"

"That bein' the case," said the chairman, "shall we proceed to a vote? All who favor the election of Brother Williams—"

At this point Old Abe, with much preliminary shuffling, stood up in his place and interrupted the speaker.

"Mr. Chuhman," he said, "I s'pose I has a right ter speak in dis meet'n'? I *s'pose* I is a member er dis committee?"

"Certainly, Brother Johnson, certainly; we shall be glad to hear from you."

"I s'pose I 's got a right ter speak my min', ef I is po' an' black, an' don' weah as good clo's as some other members er de committee?"

"Most assuredly, Brother Johnson," answered the chairman, with a barber's suavity, "you have as much right to be heard as anyone else. There was no intention of cuttin' you off."

"I s'pose," continued Abe, "dat a man wid fo'teen child'n kin be 'lowed ter hab somethin' ter say 'bout de schools er dis town?"

"I am sorry, Brother Johnson, that you should feel slighted, but there was no intention to igno' yo' rights. The committee will be please' to have you ventilate yo' views."

"Ef it 's all be'n an' done reco'nized an' 'cided dat I 's got de right ter be heared in dis meet'n', I 'll say w'at I has ter say, an' it won't take me long ter say it. Ef I should try ter tell all de things dat Miss Noble has done fer de niggers er dis town, it 'd take me till ter-morrow mawnin'. Fer fifteen long yeahs I has watched her incomin's an' her outgoin's. Her daddy was a Yankee kunnel, who died fightin' fer ou' freedom. She come heah when we—yas, Mr. Chuhman, when you an' Br'er Cotten—was jes' sot free, an' when none er us did n' have a rag ter ou' backs. She come heah, an' she tuk yo' child'n an' my child'n, an' she teached 'em sense an' manners an' religion and book-l'arnin'. When she come heah we did n' hab no chu'ch. Who writ up No'th an' got a preacher sent to us, an' de fun's ter buil' dis same chu'ch-house we 're settin' in ternight? Who got de money f'm de Bureau to s'port de school? An' when dat was stop', who got de money f'm de Peabody Fun'? Talk about Miss Noble gittin' a sal'ry! Who paid dat sal'ry up ter five years ago? Not one dollah of it come outer ou' pockets!

"An' den, w'at did she git fer de yuther things she done? Who paid her fer teachin' de Sunday-school? Who paid her fer de gals she kep' f'm throwin' deyse'ves away? Who paid fer de boys she kep' outer jail? I had a son dat seemed to hab made up his min' ter go straight ter hell. I made him go ter Sunday-school, an' somethin' dat woman said teched his heart, an' he behaved hisse'f, an' I ain' got no reason fer ter be 'shame' er 'im. An' I can 'member, Br'er Cotten, when you did n' own fo' houses an' a fahm. An' when yo' fus' wife was sick, who sot by her bedside an' read de Good Book ter 'er, w'en dey wuz n' nobody else knowed how ter read it, an' comforted her on her way across de col', dahk ribber? An' dat ain' all I kin 'member, Mr. Chuhman! When yo' gal Fanny was a baby, an' sick, an' nobody knowed what was de matter wid 'er, who sent fer a doctor, an' paid 'im fer comin', an' who he'ped nuss dat chile, an' tol' yo' wife w'at ter do, an' save' dat chile's life, jes' as sho' as de Lawd has save' my soul?

"An' now, aftuh fifteen yeahs o' slavin' fer us, who ain' got no claim on her, aftuh fifteen yeahs dat she has libbed 'mongs' us an' made herse'f one of us, an' endyoed havin' her own people look down on her, aftuh she has growed ole an' gray wukkin' fer us an' our child'n, we talk erbout turnin' 'er out like a' ole hoss ter die! It 'pears ter me some folks has po' mem'ries! Whar would we 'a' be'n ef her folks at de No'th had n' 'membered us no bettuh? An' we had n' done nothin', neither, fer dem to 'member us fer. De man dat kin fergit w'at Miss Noble has done fer dis town is unworthy de name er nigger! He oughter die an' make room fer some 'spectable dog!

"Br'er Glaspy says we got a' educated young man, an' we mus' gib him sump'n' ter do. Let him wait; ef I reads de signs right he won't hab ter wait long fer dis job. Let him teach in de primary schools, er in de country; an' ef he can't do dat, let 'im work awhile. It don't hahm a' educated man ter work a little; his fo'fathers has worked fer hund'eds of years, an' we 's worked, an' we 're heah yet, an' we 're free, an' we 's gettin' ou' own houses an' lots an' hosses an' cows—an' ou' educated young men. But don't let de fus' thing we do as a committee be somethin' we ought ter be 'shamed of as long as we lib. I votes fer Miss Noble, fus', las', an' all de time!"

When Old Abe sat down the chairman's face bore a troubled look. He remembered how his baby girl, the first of his children that he could really call his own, that no master could hold a prior claim upon, lay dying in the arms of his distracted young wife, and how the thin, homely, and short-sighted white teacher had come like an angel into his cabin, and had brought back the little one from the verge of the grave. The child was a young woman now, and Gillespie had well-founded hopes of securing the superior young Williams for a son-in-law; and he realized with something of shame that this later ambition had so dazzled his eyes for a moment as to obscure the memory of earlier days.

Mr. Cotten, too, had not been unmoved, and there were

tears in his eyes as he recalled how his first wife, Nancy, who had borne with him the privations of slavery, had passed away, with the teacher's hand in hers, before she had been able to enjoy the fruits of liberty. For they had loved one another much, and her death had been to them both a hard and bitter thing. And, as Old Abe spoke, he could remember, as distinctly as though they had been spoken but an hour before, the words of comfort that the teacher had whispered to Nancy in her dying hour and to him in his bereavement.

"On consideration, Mr. Chairman," he said, with an effort to hide a suspicious tremor in his voice and to speak with the dignity consistent with his character as a substantial citizen, "I wish to record my vote fer Miss Noble."

"The chair," said Gillespie, yielding gracefully to the majority, and greatly relieved that the responsibility of his candidate's defeat lay elsewhere, "will make the vote unanimous, and will appoint Brother Cotten and Brother Johnson a committee to step round the corner to Miss Noble's and notify her of her election."

The two committeemen put on their hats, and, accompanied by several people who had been waiting at the door to hear the result of the meeting, went around the corner to Miss Noble's house, a distance of a block or two away. The house was lighted, so they knew she had not gone to bed. They went in at the gate, and Cotten knocked at the door.

The colored maid opened it.

"Is Miss Noble home?" said Cotten.

"Yes; come in. She 's waitin' ter hear from the committee."

The woman showed them into the parlor. Miss Noble rose from her seat by the table, where she had been reading, and came forward to meet them. They did not for a moment observe, as she took a step toward them, that her footsteps wavered. In her agitation she was scarcely aware of it herself.

"Miss Noble," announced Cotten, "we have come to let you know that you have be'n 'lected teacher of the grammar school fer the next year."

"Thank you; oh, thank you so much!" she said. "I am very glad. Mary"—she put her hand to her side suddenly and tottered—"Mary, will you—"

A spasm of pain contracted her face and cut short her

speech. She would have fallen had Old Abe not caught her and, with Mary's help, laid her on a couch.

The remedies applied by Mary, and by the physician who was hastily summoned, proved unavailing. The teacher did not regain consciousness.

If it be given to those whose eyes have closed in death to linger regretfully for a while about their earthly tenement, or from some higher vantage-ground to look down upon it, then Henrietta Noble's tolerant spirit must have felt, mingling with its regret, a compensating thrill of pleasure; for not only those for whom she had labored sorrowed for her, but the people of her own race, many of whom, in the blindness of their pride, would not admit during her life that she served them also, saw so much clearer now that they took charge of her poor clay, and did it gentle reverence, and laid it tenderly away amid the dust of their own loved and honored dead.

Two weeks after Miss Noble's funeral the other candidate took charge of the grammar school, which went on without any further obstacles to the march of progress.

Baxter's Procrustes

BAXTER'S PROCRUSTES is one of the publications of the Bodleian Club. The Bodleian Club is composed of gentlemen of culture, who are interested in books and book-collecting. It was named, very obviously, after the famous library of the same name, and not only became in our city a sort of shrine for local worshipers of fine bindings and rare editions, but was visited occasionally by pilgrims from afar. The Bodleian has entertained Mark Twain, Joseph Jefferson, and other literary and histrionic celebrities. It possesses quite a collection of personal mementos of distinguished authors, among them a paperweight which once belonged to Goethe, a lead pencil used by Emerson, an autograph letter of Matthew Arnold, and a chip from a tree felled by Mr. Gladstone. Its library contains a number of rare books, including a fine collection on chess, of which game several of the members are enthusiastic devotees.

The activities of the club are not, however, confined entirely to books. We have a very handsome clubhouse, and much taste and discrimination have been exercised in its adornment. There are many good paintings, including portraits of the various presidents of the club, which adorn the entrance hall. After books, perhaps the most distinctive feature of the club is our collection of pipes. In a large rack in the smoking-room—really a superfluity, since smoking is permitted all over the house—is as complete an assortment of pipes as perhaps exists in the civilized world. Indeed, it is an unwritten rule of the club that no one is eligible for membership who cannot produce a new variety of pipe, which is filed with his application for membership, and, if he passes, deposited with the club collection, he, however, retaining the title in himself. Once a year, upon the anniversary of the death of Sir Walter Raleigh, who, it will be remembered, first introduced tobacco into England, the full membership of the club, as a rule, turns out. A large supply of the very best smoking mixture is laid in. At nine o'clock sharp each member takes his pipe from the rack, fills it with tobacco, and then the whole club, with the president at the head, all smoking furiously, march in solemn procession from room to room, upstairs and downstairs, making the tour of the clubhouse and returning to the smoking-room. The president then delivers an address, and each member is called upon to say something, either by way of a quotation or an original sentiment, in praise of the virtues of nicotine. This ceremony—facetiously known as "hitting the pipe"—being thus concluded, the membership pipes are carefully cleaned out and replaced in the club rack.

As I have said, however, the *raison d'être* of the club, and the feature upon which its fame chiefly rests, is its collection of rare books, and of these by far the most interesting are its own publications. Even its catalogues are works of art, published in numbered editions, and sought by libraries and book-collectors. Early in its history it began the occasional publication of books which should meet the club standard,—books in which emphasis should be laid upon the qualities that make a book valuable in the eyes of collectors. Of these, age could not, of course, be imparted, but in the matter of fine and curious bindings, of hand-made linen papers, of uncut or deckle edges, of wide margins and limited editions, the club could control its own publications. The matter of contents was, it must be confessed, a less important consideration. At first it was felt by the publishing committee that nothing but the finest products of the human mind should be selected for enshrinement in the beautiful volumes which the club should issue. The length of the work was an important consideration,—long things were not compatible with wide margins and graceful slenderness. For instance, we brought out Coleridge's Ancient Mariner, an essay by Emerson, and another by Thoreau. Our Rubáiyát of Omar Khayyám was Heron-Allen's translation of the original MS. in the Bodleian Library at Oxford, which, though less poetical than FitzGerald's, was not so common. Several years ago we began to publish the works of our own members. Bascom's Essay on Pipes was a very creditable performance. It was published in a limited edition of one hundred copies; and since it had not previously appeared elsewhere and was copyrighted by the club, it was sufficiently rare to be valuable for that reason. The second publication of local origin was Baxter's Procrustes.

I have omitted to say that once or twice a year, at a meeting of which notice has been given, an auction is held at the Bodleian. The members of the club send in their duplicate copies, or books they for any reason wish to dispose of, which are auctioned off to the highest bidder. At these sales, which are well attended, the club's publications have of recent years formed the leading feature. Three years ago, number three of Bascom's Essay on Pipes sold for fifteen dollars;—the original cost of publication was one dollar and seventy-five cents. Later in the evening an uncut copy of the same brought thirty dollars. At the next auction the price of the cut copy was run up to twenty-five dollars, while the uncut copy was knocked down at seventy-five dollars. The club had always appreciated the value of uncut copies, but this financial indorsement enhanced their desirability immensely. This rise in the Essay on Pipes was not without a sympathetic effect upon all the club publications. The Emerson essay rose from three dollars to seventeen, and the Thoreau, being by an author less widely read, and by his own confession commercially unsuccessful, brought a somewhat higher figure. The prices, thus inflated, were not permitted to come down appreciably. Since every member of the club possessed one or more of these valuable editions, they were all manifestly interested in keeping up the price. The publication, however, which brought the highest prices, and, but for the sober second thought, might have wrecked the whole system, was Baxter's Procrustes.

Baxter was, perhaps, the most scholarly member of the club. A graduate of Harvard, he had traveled extensively, had read widely, and while not so enthusiastic a collector as some of us, possessed as fine a private library as any man of his age in the city. He was about thirty-five when he joined the club, and apparently some bitter experience—some disappointment in love or ambition—had left its mark upon his character. With light, curly hair, fair complexion, and gray eyes, one would have expected Baxter to be genial of temper, with a tendency toward wordiness of speech. But though he had occasional flashes of humor, his ordinary demeanor was characterized by a mild cynicism, which, with his gloomy pessimistic philosophy, so foreign to the temperament that should accompany his physical type, could only be accounted for upon the hypothesis of some secret sorrow such as I have suggested. What it might be no one knew. He had means and social position, and was an uncommonly handsome man. The fact that he remained unmarried at thirty-five furnished some support for the theory of a disappointment in love, though this the several intimates of Baxter who belonged to the club were not able to verify.

It had occurred to me, in a vague way, that perhaps Baxter might be an unsuccessful author. That he was a poet we knew very well, and typewritten copies of his verses had occasionally circulated among us. But Baxter had always expressed such a profound contempt for modern literature, had always spoken in terms of such unmeasured pity for the slaves of the pen, who were dependent upon the whim of an undiscriminating public for recognition and a livelihood, that no one of us had ever suspected him of aspirations toward publication, until, as I have said, it occurred to me one day that Baxter's attitude with regard to publication might be viewed in the light of effect as well as of cause,—that his scorn of publicity might as easily arise from failure to achieve it, as his never having published might be due to his preconceived disdain of the vulgar popularity which one must share with the pugilist or balloonist of the hour.

The notion of publishing Baxter's Procrustes did not emanate from Baxter,—I must do him the justice to say this. But he had spoken to several of the fellows about the theme of his poem, until the notion that Baxter was at work upon something fine had become pretty well disseminated throughout our membership. He would occasionally read brief passages to a small coterie of friends in the sitting-room or library,—never more than ten lines at once, or to more than five people at a time,—and these excerpts gave at least a few of us a pretty fair idea of the motive and scope of the poem. As I, for one, gathered, it was quite along the line of Baxter's philosophy. Society was the Procrustes which, like the Greek bandit of old, caught every man born into the world, and endeavored to fit him to some preconceived standard, generally to the one for which he was least adapted. The world was full of men and women who were merely square pegs in round holes, and *vice versa*. Most marriages were unhappy because the contracting parties were not properly mated. Religion was mostly superstition, science for the most part sciolism, popular education merely a means of forcing the stupid and repressing the bright, so that all the youth of the rising generation might conform to the same dull, dead level of democratic mediocrity. Life would soon become so monotonously uniform and so uniformly monotonous as to be scarce worth the living.

It was Smith, I think, who first proposed that the club publish Baxter's Procrustes. The poet himself did not seem enthusiastic when the subject was broached; he demurred for some little time, protesting that the poem was not worthy of publication. But when it was proposed that the edition be limited to fifty copies he agreed to consider the proposition. When I suggested, having in mind my secret theory of Baxter's failure in authorship, that the edition would at least be in the hands of friends, that it would be difficult for a hostile critic to secure a copy, and that if it should not achieve success from a literary point of view, the extent of the failure would be limited to the size of the edition, Baxter was visibly impressed. When the literary committee at length decided to request formally of Baxter the privilege of publishing his Procrustes, he consented, with evident reluctance, upon condition that he should supervise the printing, binding, and delivery of the books, merely submitting to the committee, in advance, the manuscript, and taking their views in regard to the bookmaking.

The manuscript was duly presented to the literary committee. Baxter having expressed the desire that the poem be not read aloud at a meeting of the club, as was the custom, since he wished it to be given to the world clad in suitable garb, the committee went even farther. Having entire confidence in Baxter's taste and scholarship, they, with great delicacy, refrained from even reading the manuscript, contenting themselves with Baxter's statement of the general theme and the topics grouped under it. The details of the bookmaking, however, were gone into thoroughly. The paper was to be of hand-made linen, from the Kelmscott Mills; the type blackletter, with rubricated initials. The cover, which was Baxter's own selection, was to be of dark green morocco, with a cap-and-bells border in red inlays, and doublures of maroon morocco with a blind-tooled design. Baxter was authorized to contract with the printer and superintend the publication. The whole edition of fifty numbered copies was to be disposed of at auction, in advance, to the highest bidder, only one copy to each, the proceeds to be devoted to paying for the printing and binding, the remainder, if any, to go into the club treasury, and Baxter himself to receive one copy by way of remuneration. Baxter was inclined to protest at this, on the ground that his copy would probably be worth more than the royalties on the edition, at the usual ten per cent, would amount to, but was finally prevailed upon to accept an author's copy.

While the Procrustes was under consideration, some one read, at one of our meetings, a note from some magazine, which stated that a sealed copy of a new translation of Campanella's Sonnets, published by the Grolier Club, had been sold for three hundred dollars. This impressed the members greatly. It was a novel idea. A new work might thus be enshrined in a sort of holy of holies, which, if the collector so desired, could be forever sacred from the profanation of any vulgar or unappreciative eye. The possessor of such a treasure could enjoy it by the eye of imagination, having at the same time the exaltation of grasping what was for others the unattainable. The literary committee were so impressed with this idea that they presented it to Baxter in regard to the Procrustes. Baxter making no objection, the subscribers who might wish their copies delivered sealed were directed to notify the author. I sent in my name. A fine book, after all, was an investment, and if there was any way of enhancing its rarity, and therefore its value, I was quite willing to enjoy such an advantage.

When the Procrustes was ready for distribution, each subscriber received his copy by mail, in a neat pasteboard box. Each number was wrapped in a thin and transparent but very strong paper, through which the cover design and tooling were clearly visible. The number of the copy was indorsed upon the wrapper, the folds of which were securely fastened at each end with sealing-wax, upon which was impressed, as a guaranty of its inviolateness, the monogram of the club.

At the next meeting of the Bodleian a great deal was said about the Procrustes, and it was unanimously agreed that no finer specimen of bookmaking had ever been published by the club. By a curious coincidence, no one had brought his copy with him, and the two club copies had not yet been received from the binder, who, Baxter had reported, was retaining them for some extra fine work. Upon resolution, offered by a member who had not subscribed for the volume, a committee of three was appointed to review the Procrustes at the next literary meeting of the club. Of this committee it was my doubtful fortune to constitute one.

In pursuance of my duty in the premises, it of course became necessary for me to read the Procrustes. In all probability I should have cut my own copy for this purpose, had not one of the club auctions intervened between my appointment and the date set for the discussion of the Procrustes. At this meeting a copy of the book, still sealed, was offered for sale, and bought by a non-subscriber for the unprecedented price of one hundred and fifty dollars. After this a proper regard for my own interests would not permit me to spoil my copy by opening it, and I was therefore compelled to procure my information concerning the poem from some other source. As I had no desire to appear mercenary, I said nothing about my own copy, and made no attempt to borrow. I did, however, casually remark to Baxter that I should like to look at his copy of the proof sheets, since I wished to make some extended quotations for my review, and would rather not trust my copy to a typist for that purpose. Baxter assured me, with every evidence of regret, that he had considered them of so little importance that he had thrown them into the fire. This indifference of Baxter to literary values struck me as just a little overdone. The proof sheets of Hamlet, corrected in Shakespeare's own hand, would be well-nigh priceless.

At the next meeting of the club I observed that Thompson and Davis, who were with me on the reviewing committee, very soon brought up the question of the Procrustes in conversation in the smoking-room, and seemed anxious to get from the members their views concerning Baxter's production, I supposed upon the theory that the appreciation of any book review would depend more or less upon the degree to which it reflected the opinion of those to whom the review should be presented. I presumed, of course, that Thompson and Davis had each read the book,—they were among the subscribers,—and I was desirous of getting their point of view.

"What do you think," I inquired, "of the passage on Social Systems?" I have forgotten to say that the poem was in blank verse, and divided into parts, each with an appropriate title.

"Well," replied Davis, it seemed to me a little cautiously, "it is not exactly Spencerian, although it squints at the Spencerian view, with a slight deflection toward Hegelianism. I should consider it an harmonious fusion of the best views of all the modern philosophers, with a strong Baxterian flavor."

"Yes," said Thompson, "the charm of the chapter lies in this very quality. The style is an emanation from Baxter's own intellect,—he has written himself into the poem. By knowing Baxter we are able to appreciate the book, and after having read the book we feel that we are so much the more intimately acquainted with Baxter,—the real Baxter."

Baxter had come in during this colloquy, and was standing by the fireplace smoking a pipe. I was not exactly sure whether the faint smile which marked his face was a token of pleasure or cynicism; it was Baxterian, however, and I had already learned that Baxter's opinions upon any subject were not to be gathered always from his facial expression. For instance, when the club porter's crippled child died Baxter remarked, it seemed to me unfeelingly, that the poor little devil was doubtless better off, and that the porter himself had certainly been relieved of a burden; and only a week later the porter told me in confidence that Baxter had paid for an expensive operation, undertaken in the hope of prolonging the child's life. I therefore drew no conclusions from Baxter's somewhat enigmatical smile. He left the room at this point in the conversation, somewhat to my relief.

"By the way, Jones," said Davis, addressing me, "are you impressed by Baxter's views on Degeneration?"

Having often heard Baxter express himself upon the general downward tendency of modern civilization, I felt safe in discussing his views in a broad and general manner.

"I think," I replied, "that they are in harmony with those

of Schopenhauer, without his bitterness; with those of Nordau, without his flippancy. His materialism is Haeckel's, presented with something of the charm of Omar Khayyám."

"Yes," chimed in Davis, "it answers the strenuous demand of our day,—dissatisfaction with an unjustified optimism,—and voices for us the courage of human philosophy facing the unknown."

I had a vague recollection of having read something like this somewhere, but so much has been written, that one can scarcely discuss any subject of importance without unconsciously borrowing, now and then, the thoughts or the language of others. Quotation, like imitation, is a superior grade of flattery.

"The Procrustes," said Thompson, to whom the metrical review had been apportioned, "is couched in sonorous lines, of haunting melody and charm; and yet so closely interrelated as to be scarcely quotable with justice to the author. To be appreciated the poem should be read as a whole,—I shall say as much in my review. What shall you say of the letter-press?" he concluded, addressing me. I was supposed to discuss the technical excellence of the volume from the connoisseur's viewpoint.

"The setting," I replied judicially, "is worthy of the gem. The dark green cover, elaborately tooled, the old English lettering, the heavy linen paper, mark this as one of our very choicest publications. The letter-press is of course De Vinne's best,—there is nothing better on this side of the Atlantic. The text is a beautiful, slender stream, meandering gracefully through a wide meadow of margin."

For some reason I left the room for a minute. As I stepped into the hall, I almost ran into Baxter, who was standing near the door, facing a hunting print of a somewhat humorous character, hung upon the wall, and smiling with an immensely pleased expression.

"What a ridiculous scene!" he remarked. "Look at that fat old squire on that tall hunter! I 'll wager dollars to doughnuts that he won't get over the first fence!"

It was a very good bluff, but did not deceive me. Under his mask of unconcern, Baxter was anxious to learn what we thought of his poem, and had stationed himself in the hall that he might overhear our discussion without embarrassing us by his presence. He had covered up his delight at our appreciation by this simulated interest in the hunting print.

When the night came for the review of the Procrustes there was a large attendance of members, and several visitors, among them a young English cousin of one of the members, on his first visit to the United States; some of us had met him at other clubs, and in society, and had found him a very jolly boy, with a youthful exuberance of spirits and a naïve ignorance of things American, that made his views refreshing and, at times, amusing.

The critical essays were well considered, if a trifle vague. Baxter received credit for poetic skill of a high order.

"Our brother Baxter," said Thompson, "should no longer bury his talent in a napkin. This gem, of course, belongs to the club, but the same brain from which issued this exquisite emanation can produce others to inspire and charm an appreciative world."

"The author's view of life," said Davis, "as expressed in these beautiful lines, will help us to fit our shoulders for the heavy burden of life, by bringing to our realization those profound truths of philosophy which find hope in despair and pleasure in pain. When he shall see fit to give to the wider world, in fuller form, the thoughts of which we have been vouchsafed this foretaste, let us hope that some little ray of his fame may rest upon the Bodleian, from which can never be taken away the proud privilege of saying that he was one of its members."

I then pointed out the beauties of the volume as a piece of bookmaking. I knew, from conversation with the publication committee, the style of type and rubrication, and could see the cover through the wrapper of my sealed copy. The dark green morocco, I said, in summing up, typified the author's serious view of life, as a thing to be endured as patiently as might be. The cap-and-bells border was significant of the shams by which the optimist sought to delude himself into the view that life was a desirable thing. The intricate blind-tooling of the doublure shadowed forth the blind fate which left us in ignorance of our future and our past, or of even what the day itself might bring forth. The black-letter type, with rubricated initials, signified a philosophic pessimism enlightened by the conviction that in duty one might find, after all, an excuse for life and a hope for humanity. Applying this test to the club, this work, which might be said to represent all that the Bodleian stood for, was in itself sufficient to justify the club's existence. If the Bodleian had done nothing else, if it should do nothing more, it had produced a masterpiece.

There was a sealed copy of the Procrustes, belonging, I believe, to one of the committee, lying on the table by which I stood, and I had picked it up and held it in my hand for a moment, to emphasize one of my periods, but had laid it down immediately. I noted, as I sat down, that young Hunkin, our English visitor, who sat on the other side of the table, had picked up the volume and was examining it with interest. When the last review was read, and the generous applause had subsided, there were cries for Baxter.

"Baxter! Baxter! Author! Author!"

Baxter had been sitting over in a corner during the reading of the reviews, and had succeeded remarkably well, it seemed to me, in concealing, under his mask of cynical indifference, the exultation which I was sure he must feel. But this outburst of enthusiasm was too much even for Baxter, and it was clear that he was struggling with strong emotion when he rose to speak.

"Gentlemen, and fellow members of the Bodleian, it gives me unaffected pleasure—sincere pleasure—some day you may know how much pleasure—I cannot trust myself to say it now—to see the evident care with which your committee have read my poor verses, and the responsive sympathy with which my friends have entered into my views of life and conduct. I thank you again, and again, and when I say that I am too full for utterance,—I 'm sure you will excuse me from saying any more."

Baxter took his seat, and the applause had begun again when it was broken by a sudden exclamation.

"By Jove!" exclaimed our English visitor, who still sat behind the table, "what an extraordinary book!"

Every one gathered around him.

"You see," he exclaimed, holding up the volume, "you fellows said so much about the bally book that I wanted to see what it was like; so I untied the ribbon, and cut the leaves with the paper knife lying here, and found—and found that there was n't a single line in it, don't you know!"

Blank consternation followed this announcement, which proved only too true. Every one knew instinctively, without further investigation, that the club had been badly sold. In the resulting confusion Baxter escaped, but later was waited upon by a committee, to whom he made the rather lame excuse that he had always regarded uncut and sealed books as tommy-rot, and that he had merely been curious to see how far the thing could go; and that the result had justified his belief that a book with nothing in it was just as useful to a book-collector as one embodying a work of genius. He offered to pay all the bills for the sham Procrustes, or to replace the blank copies with the real thing, as we might choose. Of course, after such an insult, the club did not care for the poem. He was permitted to pay the expense, however, and it was more than hinted to him that his resignation from the club would be favorably acted upon. He never sent it in, and, as he went to Europe shortly afterwards, the affair had time to blow over.

In our first disgust at Baxter's duplicity, most of us cut our copies of the Procrustes, some of us mailed them to Baxter with cutting notes, and others threw them into the fire. A few wiser spirits held on to theirs, and this fact leaking out, it began to dawn upon the minds of the real collectors among us that the volume was something unique in the way of a publication.

"Baxter," said our president one evening to a select few of us who sat around the fireplace, "was wiser than we knew, or than he perhaps appreciated. His Procrustes, from the collector's point of view, is entirely logical, and might be considered as the acme of bookmaking. To the true collector, a book is a work of art, of which the contents are no more important than the words of an opera. Fine binding is a desideratum, and, for its cost, that of the Procrustes could not be improved upon. The paper is above criticism. The true collector loves wide margins, and the Procrustes, being all margin, merely touches the vanishing point of the perspective.

The smaller the edition, the greater the collector's eagerness to acquire a copy. There are but six uncut copies left, I am told, of the Procrustes, and three sealed copies, of one of which I am the fortunate possessor."

After this deliverance, it is not surprising that, at our next auction, a sealed copy of Baxter's Procrustes was knocked down, after spirited bidding, for two hundred and fifty dollars, the highest price ever brought by a single volume published by the club.

The Doll

WHEN Tom Taylor, proprietor of the Wyandot Hotel barber shop, was leaving home, after his noonday luncheon, to return to his work, his daughter, a sprightly, diminutive brown maid, with very bright black eyes and very curly, black hair, thrust into his coat pocket a little jointed doll somewhat the worse for wear.

"Now, don't forget, papa," she said, in her shrill childish treble, "what's to be done to her. Her arms won't work, and her legs won't work, and she can't hold her head up. Be sure and have her mended this afternoon, and bring her home when you come to supper; for she's afraid of the dark, and always sleeps with me. I'll meet you at the corner at half-past six—and don't forget, whatever you do."

"No, Daisy, I'll not forget," he replied, as he lifted her to the level of his lips and kissed her.

Upon reaching the shop he removed the doll from his pocket and hung it on one of the gilded spikes projecting above the wire netting surrounding the cashier's desk, where it would catch his eye. Some time during the afternoon he would send it to a toy shop around the corner for repairs. But the day was a busy one, and when the afternoon was well advanced he had not yet attended to it.

Colonel Forsyth had come up from the South to attend a conference of Democratic leaders to consider presidential candidates and platforms. He had put up at the Wyandot Hotel, but had been mainly in the hands of Judge Beeman, chairman of the local Jackson club, who was charged with the duty of seeing that the colonel was made comfortable and given the freedom of the city. It was after a committee meeting, and about 4 in the afternoon, that the two together entered the lobby of the Wyandot. They were discussing the platforms to be put forward by the two great parties in the approaching campaign.

"I reckon, judge," the colonel was saying, "that the Republican party will make a mistake if it injects the Negro question into its platform. The question is primarily a local one, and if the North will only be considerate about the matter, and let us alone, we can settle it to our entire satisfaction. The Negro's place is defined by nature, and in the South he knows it and gives us no trouble."

"The Northern Negroes are different," returned the judge.

"They are just the same," rejoined the colonel. "It is you who are different. You pamper them and they take liberties with you. But they are all from the South, and when they meet a Southerner they act accordingly. They are born to serve and to submit. If they had been worthy of equality they would never have endured slavery. They have no proper self-respect; they will neither resent an insult, nor defend a right, nor avenge a wrong."

"Well, now, colonel, aren't you rather hard on them? Consider their past."

"Hard? Why, no, bless your heart! I've got nothing against the nigger. I like him—in his place. But what I say is the truth. Are you in a hurry?"

"Not at all."

"Then come downstairs to the barber shop and I'll prove what I say."

The shop was the handsomest barber shop in the city. It was in the basement, and the paneled ceiling glowed with electric lights. The floor was of white tile, the walls lined with large mirrors. Behind ten chairs, of the latest and most comfortable design, stood as many colored barbers, in immaculate white jackets, each at work upon a white patron. An air of discipline and good order pervaded the establishment. There was no loud talking by patrons, no unseemly garrulity on the part of the barbers. It was very obviously a well-conducted barber shop, frequented by gentlemen who could afford to pay liberally for superior service. As the judge and the colonel entered a customer vacated the chair served by the proprietor.

"Next gentleman," said the barber.

The colonel removed his collar and took his seat in the vacant chair, remarking, as he ran his hand over his neck, "I want a close shave, barber."

"Yes, sir; a close shave."

The barber was apparently about forty, with a brown complexion, clean-cut features and curly hair. Committed by circumstances to a career of personal service, he had lifted it by intelligence, tact and industry to the dignity of a successful business. The judge, a regular patron of the shop, knew him well and had often, while in his chair, conversed with him concerning his race—a fruitful theme, much on the public tongue.

"As I was saying," said the colonel, while the barber adjusted a towel about his neck, "the Negro question is a perfectly simple one."

The judge thought it hardly good taste in the colonel to continue in his former strain. Northern men might speak slightingly of the Negro, but seldom in his presence. He tried a little diversion.

"The tariff," he observed, "is a difficult problem."

"Much more complicated, suh, than the Negro problem, which is perfectly simple. Let the white man once impress the Negro with his superiority; let the Negro see that there is no escape from the inevitable, and that ends it. The best thing about the Negro is that, with all his limitations, he can recognize a finality. It is the secret of his persistence among us. He has acquired the faculty of evolution, suh—by the law of the survival of the fittest. Long ago, when a young man, I killed a nigger to teach him his place. One who learns a lesson of that sort certainly never offends again, nor fathers any others of his breed."

The barber, having lathered the colonel's face, was stropping his razor with long, steady strokes. Every word uttered by the colonel was perfectly audible to him, but his impassive countenance betrayed no interest. The colonel seemed as unconscious of the barber's presence as the barber of the colonel's utterance. Surely, thought the judge, if such freedom of speech were the rule in the South the colonel's contention must be correct, and the Negroes thoroughly cowed. To a Northern man the situation was hardly comfortable.

"The iron and sugar interests of the South," persisted the judge, "will resist any reduction of the tariff."

The colonel was not to be swerved from the subject, nor from his purpose, whatever it might be.

"Quite likely they will; and we must argue with them, for they are white men and amenable to reason. The nigger, on the other hand, is the creature of instinct; you cannot argue with him; you must order him, and if he resists shoot him, as I did.

"Don't forget, barber," said the colonel, "that I want a close shave."

"No, sir," responded the barber, who, having sharpened his razor, now began to pass it, with firm and even hand, over the colonel's cheek.

"It must have been," said the judge, "an aggravated case, to justify so extreme a step."

"Extreme, suh? I beg yo' pardon, suh, but I can't say I had regarded my conduct in that light. But it was an extreme case so far as the nigger was concerned. I am not boasting about my course; it was simply a disagreeable necessity. I am naturally a kind-hearted man, and don't like to kill even a fly. It was after the war, suh, and just as the reconstruction period was drawing to a close. My mother employed a Negro girl, the child of a former servant of hers, to wait upon her."

The barber was studying the colonel's face as the razor passed over his cheek. The colonel's eyes were closed, or he might have observed the sudden gleam of interest that broke through the barber's mask of self-effacement, like a flash of lightning from a clouded sky. Involuntarily the razor remained poised in midair, but, in less time than it takes to say it, was moving again, swiftly and smoothly, over the colonel's face. To shave a talking man required a high degree of skill, but they were both adepts, each in his own trade—the barber at shaving, the colonel at talking.

"The girl was guilty of some misconduct, and my mother reprimanded her and sent her home. She complained to her father, and he came to see my mother about it. He was insolent, offensive and threatening. I came into the room and ordered him to leave it. Instead of obeying, he turned on me in a rage, suh, and threatened me. I drew my revolver and shot him. The result was unfortunate; but he and his people learned a lesson. We had no further trouble with bumptious niggers in our town."

"And did you have no trouble in the matter?" asked the judge.

"None, suh, to speak of. There were proceedings, but they were the merest formality. Upon my statement, confirmed by that of my mother, I was discharged by the examining magistrate, and the case was never even reported to the grand jury. It was a clear case of self-defense."

The barber had heard the same story, with some details ignored or forgotten by the colonel. It was the barber's father who had died at the colonel's hand, and for many long years the son had dreamed of this meeting.

He remembered the story in this wise: His father had been a slave. Freed by the Civil War, he had entered upon the new life with the zeal and enthusiasm of his people at the dawn of liberty, which seem, in the light of later discouragements, so pathetic in the retrospect. The chattel aspired to own property; the slave, forbidden learning, to educate his children. He had worked early and late, had saved his money with a thrift equal to that of a German immigrant, and had sent his children regularly to school.

The girl—the barber remembered her very well—had been fair of feature, soft of speech and gentle of manner, a pearl among pebbles. One day her father's old mistress had met him on the street and, after a kindly inquiry about his family, had asked if she might hire his daughter during the summer, when there was no school. Her own married daughter would be visiting her, with a young child, and they wanted some neat and careful girl to nurse the infant.

"Why, yas ma'am," the barber's father had replied. "I reckon it might be a good thing fer Alice. I wants her ter be a teacher; but she kin l'arn things from you, ma'am, that no teacher kin teach her. She kin l'arn manners, ma'am, an' white folks' ways, and nowhere better than in yo' house."

So Alice had gone to the home of her father's former mistress to learn white folks' ways. The lady had been kind and gracious. But there are ways and ways among all people.

When she had been three weeks in her new employment her mistress's son—a younger brother of the colonel—came home from college. Some weeks later Alice went home to her father. Who was most at fault the barber never knew. A few hours afterward the father called upon the lady. There was a stormy interview. Things were said to which the ears of white ladies were unaccustomed from the lips of black men. The elder son had entered the room and interfered. The barber's father had turned to him and exclaimed angrily:

"Go 'way from here, boy, and don't talk ter me, or I'm liable ter harm you."

The young man stood his ground. The Negro advanced menacingly toward him. The young man drew his ready weapon and fatally wounded the Negro—he lived only long enough, after being taken home, to gasp out the facts to his wife and children.

The rest of the story had been much as the colonel had related it. As the barber recalled it, however, the lady had not been called to testify, but was ill at the time of the hearing, presumably from the nervous shock.

That she had secretly offered to help the family the barber knew, and that her help had been rejected with cold hostility. He knew that the murderer went unpunished, and that in later years he had gone into politics, and became the leader and mouthpiece of his party. All the world knew that he had ridden into power on his hostility to Negro rights.

The barber had been a mere boy at the time of his father's death, but not too young to appreciate the calamity that had befallen the household. The family was broken up. The sordid details of its misfortunes would not be interesting. Poverty, disease and death had followed them, until he alone was left. Many years had passed. The brown boy who had wept beside his father's bier, and who had never forgotten nor forgiven, was now the grave-faced, keen-eyed, deft-handed barber, who held a deadly weapon at the throat of his father's slayer.

How often he had longed for this hour! In his dreams he had killed this man a hundred times, in a dozen ways. Once, when a young man, he had gone to meet him, with the definite purpose of taking his life, but chance had kept them apart. He had imagined situations where they might come face to face; he would see the white man struggling in the water; he would have only to stretch forth his hand to save him; but he would tell him of his hatred and let him drown. He would see him in a burning house, from which he might rescue him; and he would call him murderer and let him burn!

He would see him in the dock for murder of a white man, and only his testimony could save him, and he would let him suffer the fate that he doubly deserved! He saw a vision of his father's form, only an hour before thrilling with hope and energy, now stiff and cold in death; while under his keen razor lay the neck of his enemy, the enemy, too, of his race, sworn to degrade them, to teach them, if need be, with the torch and with the gun, that their place was at the white man's feet, his heel upon their neck; who held them in such contempt that he could speak as he had spoken in the presence of one of them. One stroke of the keen blade, a deflection of half an inch in its course, and a murder would be avenged, an enemy destroyed!

For the next sixty seconds the barber heard every beat of his own pulse, and the colonel, in serene unconsciousness, was nearer death than he had ever been in the course of a long and eventful life. He was only a militia colonel, and had never been under fire, but his turbulent political career had been passed in a community where life was lightly valued, where hot words were often followed by rash deeds, and murder was tolerated as a means of private vengeance and political advancement. He went on talking, but neither the judge nor the barber listened, each being absorbed in his own thoughts.

To the judge, who lived in a community where Negroes voted, the colonel's frankness was a curious revelation. His language was choice, though delivered with the Southern intonation, his tone easy and conversational, and, in addressing the barber directly, his manner had been courteous enough. The judge was interested, too, in watching the barber, who, it was evident, was repressing some powerful emotion. It seemed very probable to the judge that the barber might resent this cool recital of murder and outrage. He did not know what might be true of the Negroes in the South, but he had been judge of a police court in one period of his upward career, and he had found colored people prone to sudden rages, when under the influence of strong emotion, handy with edged tools, and apt to cut thick and deep, nor always careful about the color of the cuticle. The barber's feelings were plainly stirred, and the judge, a student of human nature, was curious to see if he would be moved to utterance. It would have been no novelty—patrons of the shop often discussed race questions with the barber. It was evident that the colonel was trying an experiment to demonstrate his contention in the lobby above. But the judge could not know the barber's intimate relation to the story, nor did it occur to him that the barber might conceive any deadly purpose because of a purely impersonal grievance. The barber's hand did not even tremble.

In the barber's mind, however, the whirlwind of emotions had passed lightly over the general and settled upon the particular injury. So strong, for the moment, was the homicidal impulse that it would have prevailed already had not the noisy opening of the door to admit a patron diverted the barber's attention and set in motion a current of ideas which fought for the colonel's life. The barber's glance toward the door, from force of habit, took in the whole shop. It was a handsome shop, and had been to the barber a matter of more than merely personal pride. Prominent among a struggling people, as yet scarcely beyond the threshold of citizenship, he had long been looked upon, and had become accustomed to regard himself, as a representative man, by whose failure or success his race would be tested. Should he slay this man now beneath his hand, this beautiful shop would be lost to his people. Years before the whole trade had been theirs. One by one the colored master barbers, trained in the slovenly old ways, had been forced to the wall by white competition, until his shop was one of the few good ones remaining in the hands of men of his race. Many an envious eye had been cast upon it. The lease had only a year to run. Strong pressure, he knew, had been exerted by a white rival to secure the reversion. The barber had the hotel proprietor's promise of a renewal; but he knew full well that should he lose the shop no colored man would succeed him: a center of industry, a medium of friendly contact with white men, would be lost to his people—many a good turn had the barber been able to do for them while he had the ear—literally had the ear—of some influential citizen, or held some aspirant for public office by the throat. Of the ten barbers in the shop all but one were married, with families dependent upon them for support. One was sending a son to college; another was buying a home. The unmarried one was in his spare hours studying a profession, with the hope of returning to practice it among his people in a Southern State. Their fates were all, in a measure, dependent upon the proprietor of the shop. Should he yield to the impulse which was swaying him their livelihood would be placed in jeopardy. For what white man, while the memory of this tragic event should last, would trust his throat again beneath a Negro's razor?

Such, however, was the strength of the impulse against which the barber was struggling that these considerations seemed likely not to prevail. Indeed, they had presented themselves to the barber's mind in a vague, remote, detached manner, while the dominant idea was present and compelling, clutching at his heart, drawing his arm, guiding his fingers. It was by their mass rather than by their clearness that these restraining forces held the barber's arm so long in check—it was society against self, civilization against the primitive instinct, typifying, more fully than the barber could realize, the great social problem involved in the future of his race.

He had now gone once over the colonel's face, subjecting that gentleman to less discomfort than he had for a long time endured while undergoing a similar operation. Already he had retouched one cheek and had turned the colonel's head to finish the other. A few strokes more and the colonel could be released with a close shave—how close he would never know!—or, one stroke, properly directed, and he would never stand erect again! Only the day before the barber had read, in the newspapers, the account of a ghastly lynching in a Southern State, where, to avenge a single provoked murder, eight Negroes had bit the dust and a woman had been burned at the stake for no other crime than that she was her husband's wife. One stroke and there would be one less of those who thus wantonly played with human life!

The uplifted hand had begun the deadly downward movement—when one of the barbers dropped a shaving cup, which was smashed to pieces on the marble floor. Fate surely fought for the colonel—or was it for the barber? Involuntarily the latter stayed his hand—instinctively his glance went toward the scene of the accident. It was returning to the upraised steel, and its uncompleted task, when it was arrested by Daisy's doll, hanging upon the gilded spike where he had left it.

If the razor went to its goal he would not be able to fulfil his promise to Daisy! She would wait for him at the corner, and wait in vain! If he killed the colonel he himself could hardly escape, for he was black and not white, and this was North and not South, and personal vengeance was not accepted by the courts as a justification for murder. Whether he died or not, he would be lost to Daisy. His wife was dead, and there would be no one to take care of Daisy. His own father had died in defense of his daughter; he must live to protect his own. If there was a righteous God, who divided the evil from the good, the colonel would some time get his just deserts. Vengeance was God's; it must be left to Him to repay!

The jointed doll had saved the colonel's life. Whether society had conquered self or not may be an open question, but it had stayed the barber's hand until love could triumph over hate!

The barber laid aside the razor, sponged off the colonel's face, brought him, with a movement of the chair, to a sitting posture, brushed his hair, pulled away the cloths from around his neck, handed him a pasteboard check for the amount of his bill, and stood rigidly by his chair. The colonel adjusted his collar, threw down a coin equal to double the amount of his bill and, without waiting for the change, turned with the judge to leave the shop. They had scarcely reached the door leading into the hotel lobby when the barber, overwrought by the long strain, collapsed heavily into the nearest chair.

"Well, judge," said the colonel, as they entered the lobby, "that was a good shave. What a sin it would be to spoil such a barber by making him a postmaster! I didn't say anything to him, for it don't do to praise a nigger much—it's likely to give him the big head—but I never had," he went on, running his hand appreciatively over his cheek, "I never had a better shave in my life. And I proved my theory. The barber is the son of the nigger I shot."

The judge was not sure that the colonel had proved his theory, and was less so after he had talked, a week later, with the barber. And, although the colonel remained at the Wyandot for several days, he did not get shaved again in the hotel barber shop.

White Weeds

STUDENTS of Danforth University during the late Nineties may remember the remarkable events following the death of Professor Carson of that institution.

At three o'clock one afternoon Professor Carson left his own apartments in Merle Hall and crossed the university campus toward the president's house. It was obvious to the few students whom he encountered during his short walk that Professor Carson was deeply absorbed in thought, because, ordinarily a model of politeness, upon this occasion he either passed them as though unaware of their presence, or responded to their respectful salutations with a very palpable perfunctoriness. There was reason enough, the students knew, for a certain degree of preoccupation on the part of Professor Carson, but hardly sufficient to account for an agitation so extreme as not only to disturb his usually grave and composed countenance but to make him forget his punctilious manners. A man might well be absent-minded upon his wedding day, but he need not look as though he were under sentence of death and straining every effort to secure a reprieve. For Professor Carson, as everyone knew, was to be married at 7 o'clock in the evening to Miss Marian Tracy, by common consent of the university faculty and the student body the most beautiful woman of her years in Attica.

It was a noble campus that Professor Carson crossed. Founded by a wealthy merchant of a past generation, before the days of colossal and burdensome fortunes, the university had never been regarded as a medium of self-advertisement, but as the contribution of an enlightened philanthropist to the training of youth and the advancement of science. There was a broad quadrangular sweep of velvety turf, crossed by two intersecting avenues of noble elms, while distributed symmetrically around the square were a dozen stately stone buildings, some ivy-clad, others beginning already to show, though the institution was only fifty years old, the markings of frost and snow and sun and rain which in a strenuous Northern climate so soon simulate the mellowness of age.

Professor Carson found the president at home and was ushered into his presence. President Trumbull of Danforth University was a suave and learned gentleman of fifty, in whom a fine executive mind had not overborne a zeal for scholarship, in which he had achieved deserved renown before assuming the cares of administration. A more striking contrast than that between the two men it would be difficult to imagine; physically they were almost the antitheses of each other. Professor Carson was tall and slender with fair hair, which he wore much longer than most men; the president was sturdy and his hair dark, with a very slight sprinkling of white, and ruddy of complexion. The professor's forehead was high and narrow, the president's lower but broader. The president's eye was gray, keen and steady; the professor's blue, weak and wavering. The one was the face of a man of affairs, who welcomed responsibilities as a fit exercise for high powers; the other that of a man lacking resolution and prone, in the crises of life, to seek the support and direction of stronger minds. It was, indeed, Dr. Trumbull's well-known decision of character which had brought Professor Carson, torn by conflicting emotions, across the campus to the president's house. Both were men of striking appearance, not to say handsome men, Professor Carson's manner being marked by a certain distinction, accounted for in some measure by his consciousness that he was of an old and distinguished ancestry. He was deeply wedded to his work, and punctiliously conscientious in its performance; he was professor of mathematics, a science governed by exact rules and requiring little exercise of judgment or imagination. He had been connected with the school longer than President Trumbull and was loyal to its ideals and traditions, with the tenacity of a vine which has thrust its slender roots into the interstices of a rock.

President Trumbull was in his study, in company with his daughter Marcia, a handsome and intelligent child of twelve who sat beside a window reading, while her father wrote at his desk. At a glance from his visitor, the president, with another glance, dismissed Marcia. Professor Carson, murmuring a request for permission, closed the door of the room and sat, or rather sank into a chair near the president.

"Well, Professor Carson, what can I do for you? I see that you have something on your mind."

"Dr. Trumbull," said the other, "I am in the greatest trouble of my life."

"Bless me, Professor! What can it be? Nothing serious, I hope?"

"Serious is hardly the name for it—it is more than serious. It is a matter that concerns my whole future—almost a matter of life and death. As you know, I am—I was to be married tonight."

"Yes, and to an exceedingly beautiful and charming lady."

This statement was made in all sincerity, and not without a certain degree of regret. Dr. Trumbull was a widower of less than a year's standing. Had Professor Carson waited a while longer, he would not have been without a formidable rival.

"Exactly," said Professor Carson, extending his hand with a gesture unconsciously tragic, "and an hour ago I received this letter."

Dr. Trumbull took the letter, and as he read it an air of astonishment overspread his features.

"An extraordinary statement," he exclaimed, "most extraordinary! But surely it is not true—surely you cannot believe it?"

"I—don't—know what to believe. It is possible—most things are possible."

"But, my dear sir, this is an anonymous letter—the weapon of malice—the medium of slander."

"I know it, sir. In the ordinary affairs of life I should have tossed it into the fire. But this is a matter vital to my happiness. And there is always the possibility that someone might wish to tell another the truth, without seeming to do an unkind thing. An anonymous letter *might* be written with the best of motives."

"The method throws suspicion on the motive. Is there no clue to the writer? Have you any enemy?"

"None that I know of," replied Professor Carson promptly. "I don't know of a man in the world who should wish me other than well."

"Or a woman?"

"Or a woman," came the reply with equal promptness.

"It is more calculated to injure the lady than you," said the president reflectively. "*She* may have enemies."

"She is the soul of candor, and popular with her own sex."

"She is beautiful, and popular with the other sex—sufficient reasons why she might be the object of envy or malice."

"The letter is from another city. It is postmarked 'Drexel.' "

"Drexel is forty miles away," returned the president. "One might take the ten o'clock train from here, post the letter at Drexel, and be back here by twelve o'clock. The letter would be here for afternoon delivery."

Professor Carson examined the envelope.

"It was post-marked at Drexel at eleven o'clock. The receiving stamp shows it delivered at the post office here at 12:15. It reached me in the afternoon delivery. It is typewritten, so there is no penmanship to afford a clue."

"I have passed the point of concern about its origin," returned Professor Carson. "It is the fact itself that worries me. The mere suggestion is torture. If the statement be true, it means the ruin of my happiness. If it be false—and pray God it is—I have no time, before the hour set for the wedding, to ascertain the fact. I must decide now, with such light as I have. As my friend and superior in office, what would you advise me to do?"

"Why not ask the lady?"

"I could not do it. If it were true, I could not marry her."

"Nor, as I understand, would you wish to. And if it were false, your mind would be at ease."

"But if I should ask her, she might not marry me; and if it is false, I would not lose her for the world."

"You would trust her word?"

"Implicitly. She is too proud to lie."

"Then, my dear Professor Carson, if you feel that way. . . ."

"Then you would advise me?"

"Is it so important?" asked the president, perplexed. "The world would never know it, even if it were true."

"Someone knows it—if it be true," returned the other. "And then, I should wish to have children, and it is of them I should have to think—it would be criminal not to think of them. The time is so short that I don't know what to do nor where to turn. I thought you might advise me—you are so prompt, so resourceful. I should wish to adopt a course that would protect myself, and yet in no way reflect upon the lady, or upon the university, or impair my usefulness here."

"Such delicacy was to be expected of you, Professor Carson. If it were my own affair, I could decide it promptly, but unless I could put myself exactly in your place, as perhaps I should be unable to do, I should hesitate to advise a man upon a matter so vital. Your problem is a difficult one from your own point of view—perhaps from any man's. You are engaged to be married, within a few hours, to a most charming woman, in whose worth and worthiness you have had entire confidence. The wedding preparations are made, the guests invited. Even now, in all probability, the bride is dressing for the wedding. At this moment you receive an anonymous letter, purporting to convey information which, if true, renders the lady ineligible for marriage with you. I see but three courses open to you as a gentleman—and those who know you would expect you to consider the subject first from that point of view. You can take the letter to the lady, ask her frankly if the charge be true, and marry her or not, as she may answer. A less frank but at least forgivable step would be to postpone the marriage on account of sudden indisposition—you are looking far from well just now. If she confirmed the statement of the letter, you would have to make some such excuse, in order to spare her feelings. A third course, which a man—some men at least—who loved the lady well enough would follow, would be to throw the letter into the fire and marry her."

"But which do you think—" began Professor Carson desperately, "which do you think—"

"I think," said the president, interrupting him, "that you had better choose between the three. A gentleman of your character and antecedents can hardly fail to select a course consistent with—"

"With honor," murmured the poor professor. "Thank you, sir," he added with dignity, "I shall trouble you no further. But whatever course I decide upon, I may ask you to hold in strict confidence all that I have said, and the contents of this letter?"

"You need hardly ask it. It is not a matter to be repeated.

Whether the marriage take place or no, we should have no right to compromise the lady."

At 7 o'clock the same evening the marriage of Professor John Marshall Carson to Miss Marian Tracy took place at the latter's residence. Miss Tracy was alone in the world, having neither parents nor near relatives living. She had been a teacher in a ladies' seminary, and made her home with a distant connection who lived in the town. To the college world the event was a notable one. Professor Carson was, if not exactly popular, at least very highly esteemed by his colleagues. If he seemed at times to hold himself aloof from the other professors, his attitude was instinctively ascribed to a natural reserve rather than to undue self-esteem. If any new-fledged tutor or professor ever attempted to be familiar with the professor of mathematics, he was brought back to the conventional by a tact so delicate, a courtesy so refined, that no offense was taken, and respect took the place of what, at a ruder rebuff, might easily have been dislike. The wedding was attended by all of the professors and their wives, as well as by many of the townspeople.

The house was decorated for the wedding with red and white roses. Festoons of smilax ran from the chandeliers in the center to the corners of the rooms. The floors were covered with white canvas. Gorman and McAlee's orchestra, screened behind palms in the back hall, played a varied program of classical and popular music, ranging from Mendelssohn to ragtime. These details are mentioned because they are important to the remainder of the story. The bride,

> "Clothed in white samite,
> Mystic, wonderful,"

as Dr. Trumbull murmured when the vision dawned upon him—was radiant in the well-preserved beauty of thirty years, for Miss Tracy was no longer in her first youth. When she entered the front parlor upon the arm of her cousin, to the strains of the wedding march, there was not a man present who did not think Professor Carson an extremely lucky man. It was observed, however, by those who paid the bridegroom any attention, that he did not seem as happy as the occasion demanded; that the voice with which he spoke the irrevocable vows had not the vibrant ring that might be expected from the virile man united to his mate; that the hand which he gave to those who congratulated him was limp and cold; that while from time to time during the evening his eyes sought the bride's face with a look of longing, behind this lay a haunting distrust—that he seemed to be seeking something which he did not find; that at other times his manner was *distrait* and his smile forced; and that when the last guests were departing, his expression alternated between anticipation and dread. President Trumbull, the most distinguished guest, responded at the supper table to a toast in which he wished the couple every felicity. At no time during the evening did Professor Carson allude to the interview of the afternoon, nor did the president mention it to him then or thereafter. There had been no scandal, no sensation, and Dr. Trumbull had no disposition to pry into another's secrets.

If there were any lingering curiosity on Dr. Trumbull's part concerning which of the two possible courses open to him besides postponement of the marriage Professor Carson had adopted, it was not lessened by his observation of the married couple during the succeeding months. He went to Europe for the summer, but upon his return in the autumn to his duties, he met Professor Carson daily, in the routine of the university work, and the lady from time to time in the social life of which the university was the center. Only a few meetings were necessary to convince him that neither husband nor wife was happy. Professor Carson, at the end of what should have been a restful vacation, had visibly declined in health. Always slender, he had become emaciated. His natural gravity had developed into an almost sepulchral solemnity, his innate reserve into a well-nigh morbid self-absorption. The rare smile which had at times flickered upon his features seemed to have gone out forever.

His efforts to overcome this melancholy were at times very apparent. Mrs. Carson was fond of society, and they often went out together. On such occasions their bearing towards one another was perfect, of its kind. Professor Carson was the embodiment of chivalrous courtesy—a courtesy so marked that in the bearing of any other man toward his own wife it would have provoked a smile. The lady, in her demeanor toward her husband responded in a manner so similar as to seem at times ironical. In a free and familiar society of intimates they were, when together, conspicuous. The lady when alone could unbend; but Professor Carson after his marriage never appeared in society alone.

In spite, however, of this elaborate deference toward one another, more than one observer besides Dr. Trumbull suspected that their union was not one of perfect happiness. Dr. Trumbull wondered, more than once, whether Carson had asked her, before their marriage, the question suggested by the anonymous letter, and, receiving a negative answer, had had his faith shaken after marriage, or whether he had loyally burned the letter, but had been unable to divest himself of the hateful doubt it had engendered, which was slowly sapping his vitality. That some cause was producing this unfortunate result became more and more apparent, for before the next summer vacation came around, Professor Carson took to his bed, and, after a brief illness, was enrolled among the great majority.

The number of those who were interested in the Carsons' household was largely increased during the two days succeeding the professor's death. Announcement was duly made that the funeral services would take place on Saturday afternoon—Professor Carson had died on Thursday—and were to be conducted by old Dr. Burridge, rector emeritus of St. Anne's. This in itself was a novelty, for Dr. Burridge was purblind and hard of hearing, and rarely performed any priestly function except some service where sight and hearing were not prime essentials. Some surprise being expressed that Dr. McRae, the rector in charge, had not been requested to officiate, it was learned that Dr. Burridge would act by special request of the widow.

This, however, was a trivial preliminary. The real surprise began when those who entered the house shortly before the hour fixed for the service, found none of the customary trappings of woe, but on the contrary, a house decked as for a wedding ceremony. It required only a moment for those who had been present at Professor Carson's marriage a few months before to perceive with a sort of dazed wonder, that an effort had seemingly been made to reproduce, as near as the plan of the rooms would permit, the decorations upon that occasion. Roses, white and red, were banked in the corners; long streamers of smilax ran from the chandeliers to the corners of the room, and were twined around the stair railing. Where, at the wedding ceremony a floral altar had been reared, the body of Professor Carson, in immaculate evening dress, lay upon a bier, composed of a casket the sides of which were let down so as to resemble more a couch than the last narrow house of a mortal man.

The troubled wonder of the funeral guests was still further augmented when in the rear hall, behind a screen of palms. Gormand and McAlee's orchestra began to play Wagner's "O du mein holder Abendstern." For a moment, while the gathering audience were realizing that a band associated only with pleasure parties was playing music, which, while not exactly profane, was certainly not religious—for a few moments the audience was silent, and then the room was as murmurous with whispered comment as a wheat-field shaken by the wind.

One of the professors spoke to the undertaker, who was hovering, like a bird of prey, around the hall.

"What is the meaning," he asked, "of this extraordinary performance?"

"Don't ask me, sir. It is the widow's orders. I don't approve of it, sir, but business is business with me. It is the widow's orders, and, as the person chiefly interested, the widow's wishes are sacred."

While Dr. Burridge, in full canonicals, having taken his place before the bier, to which he was led by one of the ushers, was reading the first part of the beautiful Episcopal service for the burial of the dead, there was opportunity for those present to reach in some degree the frame of mind befitting so solemn an occasion. At that point, following the first lesson, where a hymn is sung or an anthem, the discomfort returned with even greater force when a hired quartet, which some of those present recognized as belonging to the neighboring town of Drexel, began to sing, to a soft accompaniment by the orchestra, not the conventional and the expected "Abide with Me" or "Lead, Kindly Light," but Graben Hoffman's exquisite love song, "Der schoenste Engel." As the words were German only a few understood them, but in the bosoms of the rest there was a vague intuition that the song was of a piece with the other unusual features of the occasion.

Good old Dr. Burridge, however, to whose dull hearing all music was the same, had neither seen nor heard anything to mar the solemnity of the service. He repeated the Creed, in which he was joined by those who were sufficiently collected, and added the fitting prayers. When he had concluded the portion of the service which could be performed at the home, and the undertaker had announced that the remainder of the service would take place at the cemetery, the guests instead of rising returned to their seats as though by a common premonition that there was something more to happen. Nor were they disappointed, for almost immediately the orchestra struck up the "Wedding March" from *Lohengrin*, and Mrs. Carson, clad not in widow's weeds but in bridal array, her face set in a tragic smile, entered the back parlor and moved in time to the music down the narrow lane which had been left between the chairs, and pausing before the bier took off her wedding ring and placed it in her dead husband's hand; took off her wreath of orange blossoms and laid it among the flowers by his side. Then, turning, she left the room by the side door. A few moments later, when the casket had been closed and the body was ready for sepulture, she came downstairs dressed in an ordinary street costume of dark cloth, took her place in the mourner's carriage, and followed the remains to the grave, by the side of which she stood like any ordinary spectator until ashes had been consigned to ashes, and dust to dust, after which she immediately entered her carriage and was driven away, leaving the mystified throng morally certain that nothing but a pronounced mental aberration on the part of Mrs. Carson could account for so extraordinary, not to say shocking a funeral. To more than one the mad scene in Hamlet occurred as at least a distant parallel, though no one of them had ever dreamed that the stately Mrs. Carson had loved her middle-aged husband so deeply as, like Ophelia, to go mad for love of him.

So paralyzed with amazement had been everyone at the funeral, and brief had been Mrs. Carson's appearances, that not anyone had uttered a word of condolence or spoken to her during the afternoon. That very night she left Attica. Her house was closed and her affairs settled by her distant cousin, and it was learned that she had gone abroad for an indefinite sojourn. By the will of Professor Carson, which was presented for probate shortly after his decease, he left to his widow the whole of his estate, which amounted to some $20,000 in money and securities.

A little more than a year after Professor Carson's death, at the close of the school year, Dr. Trumbull, accompanied by his daughter Marcia—he had been a widower now for three years—left home to spend the summer in Europe. A few weeks later, upon stepping aboard the steamer at Mainz for the trip down the Rhine, he saw seated upon the deck, at a little distance, a lady whose outlines, though her face was turned away, seemed familiar. Having seen his daughter comfortably seated and their hand baggage placed, he went over to the lady, who, upon his addressing her by name, looked up with a start, and then extended both her hands.

"Why, Dr. Trumbull, what a surprise! You are the last person whom I should have expected to see!"

"And, I suppose, the one whom it gives you the least pleasure to see?"

"By no means! Indeed, I am glad to see you. One's home friends are never so welcome as when one meets them in a foreign land."

"Yes, I believe it is understood that a mere bowing acquaintance at home becomes an intimate friend abroad."

"Now, doctor, I shall not follow your very palpable lead; you must take my friendship at its face value."

"My dear Mrs. Carson, I am only too glad to do so, and am sincerely delighted, on my part, that our paths have met."

The president's daughter, finding herself deserted, and recognizing Mrs. Carson, came over at this juncture, and was duly hugged and kissed.

"How tall you are growing, dear!" said the lady. "It is only about a year since I saw you, and you look three years older."

"My dresses are longer," said Marcia ingenuously. "Oh, I'm so glad we've met you. You know, I always liked you, Mrs. Carson, even before you were married."

"You dear child! And as for you, who could help loving

you? But, there, how selfish I am! In my pleasure at our meeting, I had forgotten all about Professor and Mrs. Gilman. I'm traveling with them, you know. Professor Gilman has had his 'sabbatical year,' and I've been with them ever since they came over last July. At school Mrs. Gilman was my dearest friend, and they have been very good to me."

"And you never give up your friends?"

"Never! So long as they are good to me. But excuse me a moment, and I will look them up."

She returned shortly with her friends. The two gentlemen were old acquaintances and former intimates. Professor Gilman, an authority on medieval history, had been a colleague of Dr. Trumbull's at Brown, many years before. After the exchange of cordial greetings, the ladies, accompanied by Marcia, went over to the side of the boat, leaving the gentlemen together.

They spoke of their work and their travels, and then the conversation turned on Mrs. Carson.

"She is looking well," said President Trumbull.

"A fine woman," returned Professor Gilman, "a woman of character, capable of forming a definite purpose, and of carrying it out; and yet not at all hard, and in some ways exceedingly feminine. My wife loves her dearly, and we have enjoyed having her with us."

"I never thought," said Dr. Trumbull, "that she was quite happy with Carson."

"Happy! Far from it! I suppose, after Carson's remarkable funeral, that all Attica imagined her out of her mind?"

"Her conduct was unusual, certainly, and in default of explanation, such a suspicion might really have seemed charitable."

"Did it ever occur to you that there might be a reasonable explanation, without that hypothesis?"

"Frankly, yes, though I could never have imagined what it was. I happened to know something of Carson's antecedents, and of certain events preceding his marriage, which I have thought might in some obscure way have accounted for Mrs. Carson's eccentric conduct upon that occasion. But the knowledge came to me in such a manner that I shall probably never know any more about it."

"Did it concern a letter?"

"Yes."

"An anonymous letter?"

"Yes."

"Then I know it already. Mrs. Carson is my wife's other self—even I play only second fiddle. They have no secrets from one another. I know that Mrs. Carson values your good opinion, and since you know so much, I imagine she would not be unwilling for you to know all the facts—if you could dream them, say. Indeed, you ought to know them."

It was a warm day. Their cigars were good. The ladies left them alone for half an hour. The steamer glided smoothly down the Rhine. Two gentlemen in middle life, upon their vacation, might have dozed and might have dreamed. At any rate, before the ladies rejoined them, each knew all that the other knew of Mrs. Carson's story, and what they did not know required no supernatural wisdom to divine it.

When, after the wedding, the guests had departed and the wedded pair were left alone, the bride observed that Professor Carson was ill at ease, and that his embarrassment was serious. For a while he wandered about the room. At length he sat down beside her and began to speak.

"Marian," he said, "I have a very painful duty to perform. This afternoon, only a few hours ago, I received through the mail an anonymous letter, containing a certain statement with reference to yourself."

To say that his wife was surprised is a mild statement. She was not a child, but a mature woman, and the inference seemed plain; a wedding, an anonymous letter upon the eve of it. That he had not believed the statement, whatever it had been, was apparent, for he had married her. But right upon the heels of this conviction came the first false note in her conception of Professor Carson's character—a doubt of his taste. She had considered him the flower of courtesy—had looked upon his chivalrous deference for women as a part of his Southern heritage. It was this attribute of his, which, more than anything else, had attracted her. That having loyally ignored such a letter, he should now tell her of it was hardly to have been expected of him.

"I could not believe the statement," he went on, "and

therefore, as honor required of me, I threw the letter into the fire, and fulfilled my contract."

Again the lady winced. It hardly required a sensitive mind to infer, from his language, that he had married her because of their previous engagement. His choice of words was at least unfortunate.

"I am sorry," she said with spirit, "that you should have felt under any compulsion."

"There was none," he replied, "except that of my love. And I did not believe the story."

"Then why mention it?"

"Because I must know," he replied, "and yet I dared not run the risk of losing you. Had I asked you the question before our marriage, your pride, which in my eyes is one of your greatest charms, might have made you refuse to marry me."

"Quite likely," she replied, with rising anger. "But, since you ignored the letter, and disbelieve the story, why, oh, why, do you tell me now?"

"Because," he said wildly, "because I love you, and because my happiness is so bound up in you, and because this charge is of such a nature, that I can never shake off its memory until I learn from your own lips that it is false. I know it is false—I am sure it is false—it must be false; but I want your lips to give it the lie. Whatever you say, I shall believe."

She was a woman, and for a moment curiosity replaced indignation.

"And what," she asked, "is this terrible charge which I must meet, this crime I must deny?"

"It is a monstrous calumny. Could anyone, looking at your fair face, at your clear eye, your frank and noble countenance, believe that one drop of Negro blood coursed through your veins? Preposterous!"

His words were confident, but his voice scarcely rang true, and she could read the lingering dread in his eyes. This, then, that some unknown person had said of her, was the offense with which she was charged!

She was silent. He watched her anxiously.

"Suppose," she answered with a forced smile, "suppose, for the sake of the argument, it had been true—what then?"

"Ah, dearest," he replied, reassured by her smile, and drawing nearer to her, while she retreated behind a convenient chair. "I should have suffered a severe shock. For the sake of the university, and to avoid scandal, I should have lived with you, had you been willing, and to the outer world we should have been husband and wife; but to ourselves the relationship would have existed in name only."

"And you married me," she said coldly, "with such a doubt in your mind, and with such a purpose, should the doubt be wrongly resolved? It seems scarcely fair to me. I might have answered yes."

He explained his state of mind, or at least endeavored to make it clear, plainly surprised that he should find it necessary; for to his mind, the mere statement of the fact was its own explanation.

His father had been a planter, with wide estates and numerous slaves. His mother had suffered deeply in her pride and her affections, because of some poor unfortunate of color. With his mother's milk he had drunk in a deadly antipathy to the thought of any personal relation between white people and black but that of master and servant. The period of his adolescence had coincided with the tense years during which the white South, beaten on the field, had sought in a fierce and unreasoning pride a refuge from the humiliation of defeat, and with equal unreason, but very humanly, had visited upon the black pawns in the game, who were near at hand, the hatred they felt for their conquerors. Most of this feeling Professor Carson had overcome, but this one thing was bred in the bone.

"It is part of me," he said. "Nothing could ever make me feel that the touch of a Negress was not pollution. Beside my mother's deathbed I swore a solemn vow that this sin should never be laid at my door."

His bride was not flattered by the suggestion. She, a Negress, to whom his vow might apply!

"How white," she asked, "must one be, to come within the protection of the code of Southern chivalry?"

"There are no degrees," he explained. "To me, and those who think like me, men and women are either white or black. Those who are not all white are all black. Were I married in fact to a woman even seemingly as white as you, yet not entirely white, I should feel guilty of mortal sin. I should lie awake at night, dreading lest my children should show traces of their descent from an inferior and degraded race. I should never know a moment's happiness."

"Pardon my curiosity," she said, "but this is interesting—at least. What, may I ask, was to have been—my attitude in this marriage? In this state there would have been no legal objection to our union. We are both Episcopalians, and our church looks upon divorce with disfavor. Was I to have submitted without protest to a plan which left me married, yet no wife?"

"It would have been for you to say," he replied. "I could not blame you for concealing your antecedents. For me to seek a divorce would have been to reveal your secret, which honor would scarcely have permitted, and the same reason, I imagined, might constrain you. But, let us thank heaven! I am spared the trial, and with your assurance that all is well we shall be happy all the rest of our lives."

He moved toward her to take her in his arms.

"You forget," she answered quickly, and still evading him, "that I have given you no such assurance."

Professor Carson turned white to the lips. She thought he would have fainted at her feet; he clutched the table beside him for support. She would have pitied him, had she despised him less.

"What," he faltered, "can it be possible?"

"I shall certainly not deny it," she replied.

And she never did. They lived together according to his program. He was never certain, and in his doubt he found his punishment. When he died, she yielded to a woman's weakness. She was not a widow, but a bride. She owed Professor Carson no affection and felt for him no regret. He had outraged her finest feelings, and she had stooped to a posthumous revenge, which had satisfied her mind, while it only mystified others; indeed, she had cared very little, at the time, for what others might think. That having known her, and loved her, and married her, a prejudice which reflected in no wise upon her character, her intelligence or her beauty could keep them apart, was the unpardonable sin. She must be loved for what she was.

"It is curious," said Dr. Trumbull, reflectively, "how the

fixed idea dominates the mind. Perfectly reasonable and logical and fair-minded upon every other topic, upon one pet aversion a man may skirt the edge of mania. Nature has set no impassable barrier between races. A system which, assuming the Negro race to be inferior, condemns Mrs. Carson, because of some remote strain of its blood, to celibacy and social ostracism, or throws her back upon the inferior race, is scarcely complimentary to our own. The exaggerated race feeling of men like Carson is more than a healthy instinct for the preservation of a type; it is more than a prejudice. It is an obsession."

"A disease," returned Professor Gilman. "In all probability, had she given Professor Carson the answer he wanted, it would never have satisfied him. The seed had been planted in his mind; it was sure to bring forth a harvest of suspicion and distrust. He would in any event have worried himself into a premature grave. His marriage, while the doubt existed, was a refinement of Quixotry—and of unconscious selfishness; to spare the feelings of the possible white woman, and to save her for himself, he deliberately contemplated the destruction of the happiness of the possible—Negress."

Across the deck, Dr. Trumbull studied the graceful contour of Mrs. Carson's figure, the fine lines of her profile. A widow, and yet no wife! It was interesting. It would be a brave man who would marry her—but surely she had never loved Carson.

Dr. Trumbull had always admired her, since he had known her. Had she been willing, and had she waited a little longer, she might have been spared the somewhat tragic interlude with Carson.

"I had always wondered," he said, reflectively, "which of the three courses open to Carson he adopted—to postpone the marriage—to burn the letter—or to ask her frankly whether its contents were true. It seems that he did all three—he asked whether or not the statement was true; he burned the letter and married her without mentioning it; and—he deferred the marriage—the real marriage. It was the order in which he did them that destroyed his happiness and shortened his life."

"And all," said Professor Gilman, "for nothing, absolutely

nothing. What malicious mind conceived and wrote the letter, Mrs. Carson never learned, but there was not a word of truth in it! Her blood is as entirely pure as Professor Carson's could have been. My wife knew her people, and her line of descent for two hundred years is quite as clear, quite as good, as that of most old American families. But here come the ladies."

"Oh, papa," cried Marcia, "you and Professor Gilman have been so busy talking that you have missed the most beautiful scenery—the Lorelei, and Bingen, and Ehrenbreitstein, and—oh, my! If it hadn't been for Mrs. Carson, who has been telling me all the legends, I shouldn't have known anything about them."

"I saw you with her and Mrs. Gilman, dear, and knew it was all right. Perhaps Mrs. Carson will show them to me—some other time."

The Kiss

MRS. CARTWRIGHT left the streetcar at the nearest corner, and walked the half of a city block that led to her own gateway, and up the flower-bordered flagged walk across the green lawn to the verandah where her two children, Talbot and Cecile, were playing, under the supervision of a white-capped nurse. They were beautiful children, fashionably dressed. It was a beautiful home, upon a beautiful street, and Mrs. Cartwright was a beautiful woman.

Beautiful, and young. She had been less than twenty when Eustace Cartwright had first met her. Her family had been poor, and in financial difficulties. Cartwright had rescued them from ruin, and, fascinated by Hilda's beauty and her wit, had taken her from an eight-room house in a shabby suburb, had bestowed his old and honored name upon her, and, after a summer in Switzerland, had brought her home to the handsome residence on Euclid Avenue which his grandfather had built forty years before. It was not in the latest style, but was possessed of a spaciousness, a dignity and a comfort which suited Cartwright's quiet, scholarly tastes.

They had been very happy for several years. Hilda's two children had occupied her mind and her time. She appreciated to the full her good fortune; never more than when, while driving in her carriage or her automobile, she passed her former friends on foot, or, when, while shopping, she saw them standing behind the counter. She wore the airs and graces of a fine lady in a manner to satisfy even her husband's friends, who had been not entirely certain that Cartwright had not stooped to marry her.

The serpent had entered Eden when Cartwright's nephew, Carroll Deane, the son of his only sister, became a member of the household, after the death of his mother, already a widow. Cartwright was fond of the handsome, blue-eyed youth, whose liveliness was in marked contrast to his own taciturn sedateness. He showered the boy with benefits, and found a keen pleasure in seeing him enjoy the things for which the elder man had never greatly cared. Carroll was a convenient escort for Hilda when Cartwright did not care to go to a ball or party, a function which Carroll seemed more willing to perform than most young men to wait upon their female relatives. The beauty of the two young people—their vivacity, their youthful zest for pleasure, their freedom of intercourse, brought about the old result. There was a fierce insurrection of primal passions, a few months of guilty pleasure, and then Carroll had gone away to college.

Carroll and Hilda corresponded during his absence. He came home for the Christmas holidays. He went away again, and the correspondence continued. He returned for the Easter vacation, and had left that morning, a day late, for the East. She had accompanied him to the station, on a streetcar, and they had parted with a handclasp and a few whispered words—their real parting had taken place, an hour before, at the house. She was conscious, when the train pulled out, of a loss, and yet of a relief. The mantle of deceit did not rest lightly upon her shoulders—she had not sinned without suffering.

She was glad, as she went up the walk that day, that Carroll was gone. She had quite decided to break off their affair. It was too wicked, too treacherous, too dangerous. Eustace had been easy to deceive, but once enlightened, was not the man to endure lightly such an offense at the hands of the objects of his own bounty. Carroll had agreed with her. He was going to Europe in June, to be gone all summer. They would write, now and then, friendly letters—that was all.

As an earnest of her reformation, which was to begin as soon as he had gone, she had given him his letters and demanded hers.

"I destroyed them," he said, "last night."

She was obliged to take his word, though she had not always found him truthful—light love is apt to take liberties with truth. A lingering doubt had assailed her at the railroad station.

"You are sure, dear," she said, "that you burnt my letters?"

"Quite sure," he returned. "I hated to, but we had agreed that it was best."

It was sweet to have him hate to; but it was best, and she felt relieved, and tried to be glad—that he had burnt her letters, and that he was gone, and that she would not see him again for many months, by which time it would be easy for them to meet as friends and relatives, and with no other thought.

This feeling had grown in strength during her return homeward on the streetcar. The sight of her beautiful home, the outward and visible sign of physical comfort and assured position; the merry greeting of her rosy-cheeked children—the pledges of her wifehood—strengthened her renewed sense of virtue and conjugal fidelity.

She had laid off the last of her wraps, together with the last lingering consciousness of her sins, and had entered upon her role of ideal wife, when the telephone bell rang. She was near the instrument and took down the receiver.

"Hello, is this East 897-B?"

"Yes, is that you, Eustace?"

"Yes, Hilda. I have bad news, Carroll's train met with an accident, about twenty miles out. Many were killed or injured."

Her heart stopped beating.

"And Carroll?" she breathed.

"Is among the killed."

She dropped the receiver and sat for a moment like one dazed. Then the instinct of self-preservation returned, and she picked up the receiver and placed it to her ear.

"Hello, hello, hello!" came her husband's voice. "Are you there, Hilda?"

"Yes—yes!"

"I thought they'd cut us off. I wanted to say that a relief train is leaving the Union Station in ten minutes, and I am going out on it. If he is dead, I will bring his body home. It is terrible—poor boy, just on the threshold of life—facing its struggles and its joys—my sister's only child, whom I loved as my own son."

Hilda had been thinking with lightning-like rapidity (an electric wave, it is said, would flash around the earth an incredible number of times a second, could it last so long). Carroll was dead, and he had not destroyed her letters—she knew instinctively that he had not destroyed them—and they were either on his person or in his luggage. Eustace would go to the scene of the wreck, and he would find them, and she would be disgraced and ruined. A wild thought seized her.

"Can I go with you?" she demanded anxiously.

She would go with him, and perhaps she could get the letters, so that Eustace would never see them.

"I don't think it necessary, dear. The scene would only harrow your feelings."

"I might be of some use," she insisted.

"You can be of more use in preparing for our reception. And you haven't time. I've barely five minutes to make the station, and it would take you twenty, if you had an automobile at the door."

She hung up the receiver, despair in her heart. Never before had her sin appeared so hideous. She felt a foreboding, not dim and distant, but vivid and imminent, that her punishment was at hand—that she would lose everything that made her life worth living. She would lose husband, children, home—her position, her good name—all the things for which women strive, and which few of whom attain in such full measure as they had come to her. She could not even retain the solace of guilty love—for her lover was dead—dead in his youth and his beauty and his sins, with the proofs of his treachery upon his person. She would have nothing left, except her beauty, and the flower of that was gone; nor was it a commodity that could go twice to such a market. She wished that she were dead.

But she took no steps to carry out the wish. Perhaps, after all, Carroll had destroyed the letters. They might have been lost in the wreck. Perhaps Eustace would not search Carroll's luggage. She would hope against hope—even against the cold fear which clutched her heart and told her there was no escape.

Cartwright returned home in the afternoon, bringing the body of his nephew. Hilda awaited her fate in agonized suspense. But there was nothing unusual in Cartwright's manner, unless it were an added gravity, for which the occasion was sufficient to account. Hilda had very little opportunity for conversation with him during the day—he was fully occupied with preparations for the funeral and with communications from and to friends of Carroll.

Carroll's trunk and valise had been brought to the house, and Hilda, during her husband's absence, examined their contents thoroughly. She found many souvenirs of their love—a lock of hair, a ring, half a dozen photographs, a ribbon, a glove, a stolen slipper—each with its tender associations. Had she been less anxious, she would have wept her eyes out, but even the tragedy of death faded in importance beside the tragedy of the life which would face her should Eustace find her letters.

She felt a measure of relief when she did not find them. Would she have felt more relieved at finding them? She did not know—there was always the possibility that Eustace might have found them first and read them. On the whole, she thought she would rather have found them; she would have destroyed them, and the chances were that her husband had not examined Carroll's luggage.

She even overcame her emotions enough to make sure that the letters were not upon Carroll's body. He must have destroyed them, as he had said. She had misjudged the poor boy. He had told the truth, and had made a sacrifice, for her sake. She would cherish a tender memory of him, for their love's sake.

The funeral took place next day. Eustace's manner reassured Hilda. Nothing was omitted which the dignity and position of the family required. Eustace wore a band of crepe upon his hat, and, with Hilda and the children in deep mourning, followed the body to the family vault in Lake View Cemetery.

Hilda felt greatly relieved when all was over. Her husband had shown no sign of suspicion. It was inconceivable that he could have done what he had that day, with knowledge of the dead youth's treachery. Hilda swore a silent and solemn oath that never again would she run such a risk—never again would she be tempted to deceive this loyal and courteous gentleman who had done so much for her. She would prove, by her devotion, how much she loved and respected him, and she would atone, so far as in her lay, for the wrong she had already done him. The atonement, of course, must be secret, as the sin had been. Confession would be worse than useless; it could do no one any good—it would not only destroy her husband's happiness but deprive her of opportunity for reparation.

She felt, as she sat opposite Eustace at dinner that night, a chastened gladness that Carroll was gone. He had, in a sense, deserved his fate, and she was free, from her sin and from its consequences—free to tread the straight and pleasant path of honest happiness by the side of a gentleman who loved her—free through no merit of her own, it was true, but by the decree of a kind fate which had spared her while taking her fellow sinner.

When the dessert was served, she rang for the nurse, who took the children away.

"Will you come into my study?" said Eustace, quietly, when they were gone. "I have something to say to you."

The color left her face, the light forsook her eyes. Her panoply of self-absolution and future immaculateness slipped, like a dropped garment, from her sinful soul and left it bare, as she rose mechanically and followed the accusing figure of her husband from the room.

His study lay across the hall. As she entered, he placed a chair for her, with formal courtesy. He then unlocked a drawer of his desk and took from it a bundle of letters, tied with narrow blue ribbon. She recognized the ribbon and remembered vividly when and from where it had been taken.

"These, I think" said Cartwright, in calm and even tones, "are yours—it is the law, I believe, that letters belong, first to the recipient, then to the writer. My interest, I think, was sufficient to justify my having read them—or some of them—enough of them. I now return them—to their lawful owner."

He put out his hand. She took the letters mechanically and laid them on her lap. An hour earlier, had she laid hands on them, she would have concealed them in her bosom. Now they had been read. Then they had been pregnant with immense possibilities—now they were dead—a spent rocket—dead as the body of her lover in the vault—dead as her hope for future happiness. They might lie on her lap, or on the floor, or in Eustace's desk, so far as he and she were concerned.

She heard him speaking, as though from a distance, and it was with an effort, at first, that she grasped the purport of his speech.

"Of course you realize, Hilda, what the result of this discovery must be. You can no longer be wife of mine, or I husband of yours. I have lost, at one blow, wife and nephew—both of whom I loved—what more I have lost I leave for you to imagine; you have a keen mind and a judgment riper than your years.

"I shall not attempt to fix or to distribute the blame for this deplorable affair which has worked my misfortune. Carroll is dead—as the result of his own folly, in all likelihood, for had he left yesterday, as he ought to have done, he would not have been a passenger upon the wrecked train. But you were the older of the two. You were a mother—you had your children to consider. And you were a wife, and held my honor in your hands."

He had not lifted his voice in the least, but upon her quivering conscience every word fell like the lash of a whip. She shrank together, and almost cowered before him, while her eyes sought the floor, but could get no further than the damning bundle of letters upon her lap.

"I shall not reproach you," he went on, "now or ever. When this interview is ended, I shall never mention the matter again—it will not be a pleasant subject. As I have said, you can no longer be my wife. But neither would I have you leave me. There are the children—I must consider them, if you did not; they must never, by any act of mine, have occasion to hold their mother in disrespect. Carroll was my sister's child; to blacken his memory would be to reflect upon her and upon all of us; nor do I care to become a subject of pity or ridicule."

She wondered vaguely, and dully, what he was going to—what he *could* do that would carry out his purpose and yet leave undone the things he did not wish to do.

"You will continue," he said, "that is, if my wishes prevail—to occupy your place in the household. To the world—to the servants even, there will be no change. If there should be at first some slight and inevitable constraint, and you think the servants might take notice, you can discharge them all and take on new ones who will know no past with which to compare our future. You will doubtless be glad to share with me the effort to keep the children in the dark—for their sakes?"

He seemed to wait for an answer, and she murmured something inarticulate which he apparently took for acquiescence.

"This, of course, will limit our intercourse. The house is large, and we need not interfere at all with one another. A very slight difference of arrangement will effect all the change that is necessary."

Her fingers were mechanically picking at the folds of her gown. The bundle of letters had slipped to the floor. Something within her shrank from what the life to which he condemned her might become. Nor had her husband ever seemed so noble, so worthy of love and respect as now when he sat in judgment upon her, and she had lost him.

Perhaps he noticed her change of expression.

"You shall be free," he said, "to come and go. I shall not interfere with your movements—except that I shall exercise a certain supervision over your company, for both our sakes. Upon formal occasions, when it is conventionally required, I will attend you—perhaps I have neglected my duty in that regard, and am myself to blame, in part, for what has happened.

"If you find life unendurable under these terms," he added, rising as though to dismiss her, "doubtless we can find a remedy. You could travel, or reside abroad, for your health. Or if you should wish, sometime, to seek a divorce—such things can be quietly arranged, with no scandal.

"And now, if there is nothing you wish to say, or ask, shall we terminate this painful interview?"

She rose, and with desperate effort, stepped firmly forward—had she faltered, he would, she knew, have offered her his arm—and she was unworthy to take it. He stooped, however, picked up the packet of letters, and, as he opened the door of the library with one hand, extended the bundle with the other.

"Permit me," he said, "you were leaving your letters."

How many lifetimes Hilda Cartwright lived in the next five years, she never stopped to figure out, but the time was long. From the very beginning she accepted, as a finality, the situation and her husband's terms. To the outside world, they were husband and wife, living in conventional harmony—if conjugal harmony be any longer conventional. If friends of their own social circle suspected anything between them, they were courteous enough not to mention it—to their faces; and when curiosity had nothing new to feed upon, it soon died away.

Their divided life was rendered easier by a gradual change in their habits. Cartwright had never cared a great deal for society, and Hilda began to go out less and less, until she became, in time, almost as much a recluse as her husband.

As the best atonement she could make for her offense, she sought to become what she imagined Eustace would have liked her to be, had she never disappointed him. She was a perfect housekeeper, an ideal mother. Such social duties as she still undertook were performed with effectiveness, grace and dignity, and Mrs. Cartwright became known as one of the most respected and admired of the younger matrons of her set. She was active in the work of her church, and a liberal contributor, both of time and money, to a number of good charities. Her benefactions fell like dew upon many a thirsty soul, because they felt in what she did the subtle sympathy with weakness or misfortune which comes only from those who have trod the same path.

Time dealt gently with her. She grew in the noble virtues which take their root in self-sacrifice. They left their impress upon her face, which became more beautiful with the passing years. At thirty she was in a young matronly prime which put her youthful and more immature beauty to the blush.

During all the years of her atonement, Cartwright had never, by a single word, recalled the subject of their estrangement. Nor were they much together, except in the presence of others. He was always courteous—too courteous, one shrewd lady said, for a man who loved his wife—and sometimes almost kind. But while Hilda loved him well enough to have thrown herself at his feet and placed his heel upon her neck, she was ever conscious of the impalpable barrier which separated them—a barrier as impenetrable as the shirt of chain mail which gentlemen of the romantic past wore under their silken doublets when dining with their friends. She did not attempt to pass this barrier—it would turn a smile, or a fond word, she felt instinctively, as surely as the steel jacket would stop a dagger-thrust. If he would ever change she did not know. If so, she would be there, beside him; if not, she must bear her punishment as best she could.

She knew he was not happy—and the knowledge was part, the greater part—of her punishment. Nor had he quite her resources to ward off unhappiness. Companionship was in large measure denied him. She had her children, nor did she realize, in her absorption, the extent to which she monopolized their society. He threw himself eagerly into affairs, and devoted himself, in his hours of relaxation, to the studies of which he was so fond.

But Hilda saw he was not happy, and, at last, that he was not well. His cheeks grew thinner, his hair was more than touched with gray, he lost some of the spring of life. Hilda watched him silently, with a yearning love, and with a growing fear. If he should die, it would be of unhappiness, and she would have murdered him as surely as though she had dropped poison in his cup.

In the spring of the fifth year of their estrangement, Cartwright fell ill. The doctor diagnosed the case as one of fever, possibly malignant, and ordered isolation and a trained nurse.

"I shall nurse him myself," said Hilda firmly.

"Impossible, madam. You will be liable to infection. And there are the children to consider."

"They can be sent away, if necessary," she declared. "For myself I do not care—and I am strong. I shall nurse him."

She could not be dissuaded, but took her place by Cartwright's bedside. At the height of the fever he became delirious, and said some things which tore her heart—not altogether with pain. She had a trained nurse to assist her, but at these times she sent the nurse out of the room.

He seemed to be mending, when, one morning, he took a turn for the worse. The doctor made a careful examination.

"Astonishing," he said, as he finished. "I never knew of such a combination. He has developed diphtheria, of a malignant type."

She knew what this implied. "Is there no hope?" she whispered hoarsely.

"None," he replied, "without a miracle—and the age of miracles is past. At his age, he could scarcely hope to recover even in good health; in his present weakened condition there is no power of resistance whatever—it is only a matter of a day or two. Meanwhile it is dangerous for you to be near him—you have denied yourself sleep and rest—you are in none too good condition yourself to resist disease."

"I shall stay beside him," she declared, "to the last moment. I wish to be near him when he—if he—recovers consciousness. If it were only for a moment, and I were away, I should never forgive myself."

He protested, but in vain. Finding she would stay, he gave her minute directions how to avoid infection.

"Above all things, guard your mouth. Don't let your lips touch anything—not even your hands—that could possibly convey the contagion. I think you are running an unnecessary risk, but willful woman—"

"Must have her way," said Hilda, closing the conversation.

The doctor went away, but returned in an hour, remained two, and went away again.

"I'll be back in another hour. He'll last till morning, perhaps."

While the doctor was gone, Cartwright opened his eyes and looked up at his wife. The nurse was asleep in the next room.

"Hilda," he said, "is it you, dear?"

"Yes, Eustace," she returned, dropping on her knees beside the bed and taking his thin hand in hers.

"I am ill, am I not, Hilda?"

"Yes, dear, you are very ill."

"I am going to die, Hilda. I haven't cared a great deal about living, for several years."

"Spare me, Eustace, and spare yourself. If you die, I shall not care to live."

His face lit up with a rare smile.

"Do you love me?" he whispered, with his failing breath.

"I would give my life for you—and give it twice for one word of love."

"One word, my darling—one word? I have loved you always—I have never ceased to love you, and I am dying of my love. I wish now that I could live, but I suppose it is too late. But kiss me, Hilda, before I die!"

Then bravely, and without a moment's hesitation, she took

her life into her hands and bent her face to his. He threw his arms, hot with fever, about her neck, and their lips met in a long, lingering caress.

They ought to have died, of course, and given their story a dramatic ending. But the doctor came back, an hour later, with a new culture which dissipated the gathering membrane.

They spent their new honeymoon in the Engadine—it was long before the war—and were as happy as chastened remorse, upon one side, and complete forgiveness, upon the other, and fervent love, upon both, would permit.

SELECTED ESSAYS

What Is a White Man?

THE FIAT having gone forth from the wise men of the South that the "all-pervading, all-conquering Anglo-Saxon race" must continue forever to exercise exclusive control and direction of the government of this so-called Republic, it becomes important to every citizen who values his birthright to know who are included in this grandiloquent term. It is of course perfectly obvious that the writer or speaker who used this expression—perhaps Mr. Grady of Georgia—did not say what he meant. It is not probable that he meant to exclude from full citizenship the Celts and Teutons and Gauls and Slavs who make up so large a proportion of our population; he hardly meant to exclude the Jews, for even the most ardent fire-eater would hardly venture to advocate the disfranchisement of the thrifty race whose mortgages cover so large a portion of Southern soil. What the eloquent gentleman really meant by this high-sounding phrase was simply the white race; and the substance of the argument of that school of Southern writers to which he belongs, is simply that for the good of the country the Negro should have no voice in directing the government or public policy of the Southern States or of the nation.

But it is evident that where the intermingling of the races has made such progress as it has in this country, the line which separates the races must in many instances have been practically obliterated. And there has arisen in the United States a very large class of the population who are certainly not Negroes in an ethnological sense, and whose children will be no nearer Negroes than themselves. In view, therefore, of the very positive ground taken by the white leaders of the South, where most of these people reside, it becomes in the highest degree important to them to know what race they belong to. It ought to be also a matter of serious concern to the Southern white people; for if their zeal for good government is so great that they contemplate the practical overthrow of the Constitution and laws of the United States to secure it, they ought at least to be sure that no man entitled to it by their own argument, is robbed of a right so precious as that of free citizenship; the "all-pervading, all conquering Anglo-Saxon" ought to set as high a value on American citizenship as the all-conquering Roman placed upon the franchise of his State two thousand years ago. This discussion would of course be of little interest to the genuine Negro, who is entirely outside of the charmed circle, and must content himself with the acquisition of wealth, the pursuit of learning and such other privileges as his "best friends" may find it consistent with the welfare of the nation to allow him; but to every other good citizen the inquiry ought to be a momentous one. What is a white man?

In spite of the virulence and universality of race prejudice in the United States, the human intellect long ago revolted at the manifest absurdity of classifying men fifteen-sixteenths white as black men; and hence there grew up a number of laws in different states of the Union defining the limit which separated the white and colored races, which was, when these laws took their rise and is now to a large extent, the line which separated freedom and opportunity from slavery or hopeless degradation. Some of these laws are of legislative origin; others are judge-made laws, brought out by the exigencies of special cases which came before the courts for determination. Some day they will, perhaps, become mere curiosities of jurisprudence; the "black laws" will be bracketed with the "blue laws," and will be at best but landmarks by which to measure the progress of the nation. But to-day these laws are in active operation, and they are, therefore, worthy of attention; for every good citizen ought to know the law, and, if possible, to respect it; and if not worthy of respect, it should be changed by the authority which enacted it. Whether any of the laws referred to here have been in any manner changed by very recent legislation the writer cannot say, but they are certainly embodied in the latest editions of the revised statutes of the states referred to.

The colored people were divided, in most of the Southern States, into two classes, designated by law as Negroes and mulattoes respectively. The term Negro was used in its ethnological sense, and needed no definition; but the term "mulatto" was held by legislative enactment to embrace all persons of color not Negroes. The words "quadroon" and "mestizo" are employed in some of the law books, tho not defined; but the term "octoroon," as indicating a person having one-eighth of Negro blood, is not used at all, so far as the writer has been able to observe.

The states vary slightly in regard to what constitutes a mulatto or person of color, and as to what proportion of white blood should be sufficient to remove the disability of color. As a general rule, less than one-fourth of Negro blood left the individual white—in theory; race questions being, however, regulated very differently in practice. In Missouri, by the code of 1855, still in operation, so far as not inconsistent with the Federal Constitution and laws, "any person other than a Negro, any one of whose grandmothers or grandfathers is or shall have been a Negro, tho all of his or her progenitors except those descended from the Negro may have been white persons, shall be deemed a mulatto." Thus the color-line is drawn at one-fourth of Negro blood, and persons with only one-eighth are white.

By the Mississippi code of 1880, the color-line is drawn at one-fourth of Negro blood, all persons having less being theoretically white.

Under the *code noir* of Louisiana, the descendant of a white and a quadroon is white, thus drawing the line at one-eighth of Negro blood. The code of 1876 abolished all distinctions of color; as to whether they have been re-enacted since the Republican Party went out of power in that state the writer is not informed.

Jumping to the extreme North, persons are white within the meaning of the Constitution of Michigan who have less than one-fourth of Negro blood.

In Ohio the rule, as established by numerous decisions of the Supreme Court, was that a preponderance of white blood constituted a person a white man in the eye of the law, and entitled him to the exercise of all the civil rights of a white man. By a retrogressive step the color-line was extended in 1861 in the case of marriage, which by statute was forbidden between a person of pure white blood and one having a visible admixture of African blood. But by act of legislature, passed in the spring of 1887, all laws establishing or permitting distinctions of color were repealed. In many parts of the state these laws were always ignored, and they would doubtless have been repealed long ago but for the sentiment of the southern counties, separated only by the width of the Ohio River from a former slave-holding state. There was a bill introduced in the legislature during the last session to re-enact the "black laws," but it was hopelessly defeated; the member who introduced it evidently mistook his latitude; he ought to be a member of the Georgia legislature.

But the state which, for several reasons, one might expect to have the strictest laws in regard to the relations of the races, has really the loosest. Two extracts from decisions of the Supreme Court of South Carolina will make clear the law of that state in regard to the color line.

> The definition of the term mulatto, as understood in this state, seems to be vague, signifying generally a person of mixed white or European and Negro parentage, in whatever proportions the blood of the two races may be mingled in the individual. But it is not invariably applicable to every admixture of African blood with the European, nor is one having all the features of a white to be ranked with the degraded class designated by the laws of this state as persons of color, because of some remote taint of the Negro race. The line of distinction, however, is not ascertained by any rule of law. . . . Juries would probably be justified in holding a person to be white in whom the admixture of African blood did not exceed the proportion of one-eighth. But it is in all cases a question for the jury, to be determined by them upon the evidence of features and complexion afforded by inspection, the evidence of reputation as to parentage, and the evidence of the rank and station in society occupied by the party. The only rule which can be laid down by the courts is that where there is a distinct and visible admixture of Negro blood, the individual is to be denominated a mulatto or person of color.

In a later case the court held: "The question whether persons are colored or white, where color or feature are doubtful, is for the jury to decide by reputation, by reception into society, and by their exercise of the privileges of the white man, as well as by admixture of blood."

It is an interesting question why such should have been, and should still be, for that matter, the law of South Carolina, and why there should exist in that state a condition of public opinion which would accept such a law. Perhaps it may be attributed to the fact that the colored population of South Carolina always outnumbered the white population, and the eagerness of the latter to recruit their ranks was sufficient to overcome in some measure their prejudice against the Negro blood. It is certainly true that the color-line is, in practice as in law, more loosely drawn in South Carolina than in any other Southern State, and that no inconsiderable element of the population of that state consists of these legal white persons, who were either born in the state, or, attracted thither by this feature of the laws, have come in from surrounding states, and, forsaking home and kindred, have taken their social position as white people. A reasonable degree of reticence in regard to one's antecedents is, however, usual in such cases.

Before the War the color-line, as fixed by law, regulated in theory the civil and political status of persons of color. What that status was, was expressed in the Dred Scott decision. But since the War, or rather since the enfranchisement of the colored people, these laws have been mainly confined—in theory, be it always remembered—to the regulation of the intercourse of the races in schools and in the marriage relation. The extension of the color-line to places of public entertainment and resort, to inns and public highways, is in most states entirely a matter of custom. A colored man can sue in the courts of any Southern State for the violation of his common-law rights, and recover damages of say fifty cents without costs. A colored minister who sued a Baltimore steamboat company a few weeks ago for refusing him first-class accommodation, he having paid first-class fare, did not even meet with that measure of success; the learned judge, a Federal judge by the way, held that the plaintiff's rights had been invaded, and that he had suffered humiliation at the hands of the defendant company, but that "the humiliation was not sufficient to entitle him to damages." And the learned judge dismissed the action without costs to either party.

Having thus ascertained what constitutes a white man, the good citizen may be curious to know what steps have been taken to preserve the purity of the white race. Nature, by some unaccountable oversight having to some extent neglected a matter so important to the future prosperity and progress of mankind. The marriage laws referred to here are in active operation, and cases under them are by no means infrequent. Indeed, instead of being behind the age, the marriage laws in the Southern States are in advance of public opinion; for very rarely will a Southern community stop to figure on the pedigree of the contracting parties to a marriage where one is white and the other is known to have any strain of Negro blood.

In Virginia, under the title "Offenses against Morality," the law provides that "any white person who shall intermarry with a Negro shall be confined in jail not more than one year and fined not exceeding one hundred dollars." In a marginal note on the statute-book, attention is called to the fact that "a similar penalty is not imposed on the Negro"—a stretch of magnanimity to which the laws of other states are strangers. A person who performs the ceremony of marriage in such a case is fined two hundred dollars, one-half of which goes to the informer.

In Maryland, a minister who performs the ceremony of marriage between a Negro and a white person is liable to a fine of one hundred dollars.

In Mississippi, code of 1880, it is provided that "the marriage of a white person to a Negro or mulatto or person who shall have one-fourth or more of Negro blood, shall be unlawful"; and as this prohibition does not seem sufficiently emphatic, it is further declared to be "incestuous and void," and is punished by the same penalty prescribed for marriage within the forbidden degrees of consanguinity.

But it is Georgia, the *alma genetrix* of the chain-gang, which merits the questionable distinction of having the harshest set of color laws. By the law of Georgia the term "person of color" is defined to mean "all such as have an admixture of Negro blood, and the term 'Negro,' includes mulattoes." This definition is perhaps restricted somewhat by another provision, by which "all Negroes, mestizoes, and their descendants, having one-eighth of Negro or mulatto blood in their veins, shall be known in this State as persons of color." A colored minister is permitted to perform the ceremony of marriage between colored persons only, tho white ministers are not forbidden to join persons of color in wedlock. It is further provided that "the marriage relation between white persons and persons of African descent is forever prohibited, and such marriages shall be null and void." This is a very sweeping provision; it will be noticed that the term "persons of color," previously defined, is not employed, the expression "persons of African descent" being used instead. A court which was so inclined would find no difficulty in extending this provision of the law to the remotest strain of African blood. The marriage relation is forever prohibited. Forever is a long time. There is a colored woman in Georgia said to be worth $300,000—an immense fortune in the poverty stricken South. With a few hundred such women in that state, possessing a fair degree of good looks, the color-line would shrivel up like a scroll in the heat of competition for their hands in marriage. The penalty for the violation of the law against intermarriage is the same sought to be imposed by the defunct Glenn Bill for violation of its provisions; i.e., a fine not to exceed one thousand dollars, and imprisonment not to exceed six months, or twelve months in the chain-gang.

Whatever the wisdom or justice of these laws, there is one objection to them which is not given sufficient prominence in the consideration of the subject, even where it is discussed at all; they make mixed blood a *prima-facie* proof of illegitimacy. It is a fact that at present, in the United States, a colored man or woman whose complexion is white or nearly white is presumed, in the absence of any knowledge of his or her antecedents, to be the offspring of a union not sanctified by law. And by a curious but not uncommon process, such persons are not held in the same low estimation as white people in the same position. The sins of their fathers are not visited upon the children, in that regard at least; and their mothers' lapses from virtue are regarded either as misfortunes or as faults excusable under the circumstances. But in spite of all this, illegitimacy is not a desirable distinction, and is likely to become less so as these people of mixed blood advance in wealth and social standing. This presumption of illegitimacy was once, perhaps, true of the majority of such persons; but the times have changed. More than half of the colored people of the United States are of mixed blood; they marry and are given in marriage, and they beget children of complexions similar to their own. Whether or not, therefore, laws which stamp these children as illegitimate, and which by indirection establish a lower standard of morality for a large part of the population than the remaining part is judged by, are wise laws; and whether or not the purity of the white race could not be as well preserved by the exercise of virtue, and the operation of those natural laws which are so often quoted by Southern writers as the justification of all sorts of Southern "policies"—are questions which the good citizen may at least turn over in his mind occasionally, pending the settlement of other complications which have grown out of the presence of the Negro on this continent.

Independent, May 30, 1889

The Future American

What the Race Is Likely to Become in the Process of Time

The future American race is a popular theme for essayists, and has been much discussed. Most expressions upon the subject, however, have been characterized by a conscious or unconscious evasion of some of the main elements of the problem involved in the formation of a future American race, or, to put it perhaps more correctly, a future ethnic type that shall inhabit the northern part of the western continent. Some of these obvious omissions will be touched upon in these articles; and if the writer has any preconceived opinions that would affect his judgment, they are at least not the hackneyed prejudices of the past—if they lead to false conclusions, they at least furnish a new point of view, from which, taken with other widely differing views, the judicious reader may establish a parallax that will enable him to approximate the truth.

The popular theory is that the future American race will consist of a harmonious fusion of the various European elements which now make up our heterogeneous population. The result is to be something infinitely superior to the best of the component elements. This perfection of type—no good American could for a moment doubt that it will be as perfect as everything else American—is to be brought about by a combination of all the best characteristics of the different European races, and the elimination, by some strange alchemy, of all their undesirable traits—for even a good American will admit that European races, now and then, have some undesirable traits when they first come over. It is a beautiful, a hopeful, and to the eye of faith, a thrilling prospect. The defect of the argument, however, lies in the incompleteness of the premises, and its obliviousness of certain facts of human nature and human history.

Before putting forward any theory upon the subject, it may be well enough to remark that recent scientific research has swept away many hoary anthropological fallacies. It has been demonstrated that the shape or size of the head has little or nothing to do with the civilization or average intelligence of a race; that language, so recently lauded as an infallible test of racial origin is of absolutely no value in this connection, its distribution being dependent upon other conditions than race. Even color, upon which the social structure of the United States is so largely based, has been proved no test of race. The conception of a pure Aryan, Indo-European race has been abandoned in scientific circles, and the secret of the progress of Europe has been found in racial heterogeneity, rather than in racial purity. The theory that the Jews are a pure race has been exploded, and their peculiar type explained upon a different and much more satisfactory hypothesis. To illustrate the change of opinion and the growth of liberality in scientific circles, imagine the reception which would have been accorded to this proposition, if laid down by an American writer fifty or sixty years ago: "The European races, as a whole, show signs of a secondary or derived origin; certain characteristics, especially the texture of the hair, lead us to class them as intermediate between the extreme primary types of the Asiatic and Negro races respectively." This is put forward by the author, not as a mere hypothesis, but as a proposition fairly susceptible of proof, and is supported by an elaborate argument based upon microscopical comparisons, to which numerous authorities are cited. If this fact be borne in mind it will simplify in some degree our conception of a future American ethnic type.

By modern research the unity of the human race has been proved (if it needed any proof to the careful or fair-minded observer), and the differentiation of races by selection and environment has been so stated as to prove itself. Greater emphasis has been placed upon environment as a factor in ethnic development, and what has been called "the vulgar theory of race," as accounting for progress and culture, has been relegated to the limbo of exploded dogmas. One of the most perspicuous and forceful presentations of these modern conclusions of anthropology is found in the volume above quoted, a book which owes its origin to a Boston scholar.

Proceeding then upon the firm basis laid down by science and the historic parallel, it ought to be quite clear that the future American race—the future American ethnic type—will be formed of a mingling, in a yet to be ascertained proportion, of the various racial varieties which make up the present population of the United States; or, to extend the area a little farther, of the various peoples of the northern hemisphere of the western continent; for, if certain recent tendencies are an index of the future it is not safe to fix the boundaries of the future United States anywhere short of the Arctic Ocean on the north and the Isthmus of Panama on the south. But, even with the continuance of the present political divisions, conditions of trade and ease of travel are likely to gradually assimilate to one type all the countries of the hemisphere. Assuming that the country is so well settled that no great disturbance of ratios is likely to result from immigration, or any serious conflict of races, we may safely build our theory of a future American race upon the present population of the country. I use the word "race" here in its popular sense—that of a people who look substantially alike, and are moulded by the same culture and dominated by the same ideals.

By the eleventh census, the ratios of which will probably not be changed materially by the census now under way, the total population of the United States was about 65,000,000, of which about seven million were black and colored, and something over 200,000 were of Indian blood. It is then in the three broad types—white, black and Indian—that the future American race will find the material for its formation. Any dream of a pure white race, of the Anglo-Saxon type, for the United States, may as well be abandoned as impossible, even if desirable. That such future race will be predominantly white may well be granted—unless climate in the course of time should modify existing types; that it will call itself white is reasonably sure; that it will conform closely to the white type is likely; but that it will have absorbed and assimilated the blood of the other two races mentioned is as certain as the operation of any law well can be that deals with so uncertain a quantity as the human race.

There are no natural obstacles to such an amalgamation. The unity of the race is not only conceded but demonstrated by actual crossing. Any theory of sterility due to race crossing may as well be abandoned; it is founded mainly on prejudice and cannot be proved by the facts. If it come from Northern or European sources, it is likely to be weakened by lack of knowledge; if from Southern sources, it is sure to be colored by prejudices. My own observation is that in a majority of cases people of mixed blood are very prolific and very long-lived. The admixture of races in the United States has never taken place under conditions likely to produce the best results but there have nevertheless been enough conspicuous instances to the contrary in this country, to say nothing of a long and honorable list in other lands, to disprove the theory that people of mixed blood, other things being equal, are less virile, prolific or able than those of purer strains. But whether this be true or not is apart from this argument. Admitting that races may mix, and that they are thrown together under conditions which permit their admixture, the controlling motive will be not abstract considerations with regard to a remote posterity, but present interest and inclination.

The Indian element in the United States proper is so small proportionally—about one in three hundred—and the conditions for its amalgamation so favorable, that it would of itself require scarcely any consideration in this argument. There is no prejudice against the Indian blood, in solution. A half or quarter-breed, removed from the tribal environment, is freely received among white people. After the second or third remove he may even boast of his Indian descent; it gives him a sort of distinction, and involves no social disability. The distribution of the Indian race, however, tends to make the question largely a local one, and the survival of tribal relation may postpone the results for some little time. It will be, however, the fault of the United States Indian himself if he be not speedily amalgamated with the white population.

The Indian element, however, looms up larger when we include Mexico and Central America in our fields of discussion. By the census of Mexico just completed, over eighty per cent of the population is composed of mixed and Indian races. The remainder is presumably of pure Spanish, or European blood, with a dash of Negro along the coast. The population is something over twelve millions, thus adding nine millions of Indians and Mestizos to be taken into account. Add several millions of similar descent in Central America, a million in Porto Rico, who are said to have an aboriginal strain, and it may safely be figured that the Indian element will be quite considerable in the future American race. Its amalgamation will involve no great difficulty, however; it has been going on peacefully in the countries south of us for several centuries, and is likely to continue along similar lines. The peculiar disposition of the American to overlook mixed blood in a foreigner will simplify the gradual absorption of these Southern races.

The real problem, then, the only hard problem in connection with the future American race, lies in the Negro element of our population. As I have said before, I believe it is destined to play its part in the formation of this new type. The process by which this will take place will be no sudden and wholesale amalgamation—a thing certainly not to be expected, and hardly to be desired. If it were held desirable, and one could imagine a government sufficiently autocratic to enforce its behests, it would be no great task to mix the races mechanically, leaving to time merely the fixing of the resultant type.

Let us for curiosity outline the process. To start with, the Negroes are already considerably mixed—many of them in large proportion, and most of them in some degree—and the white people, as I shall endeavor to show later on, are many of them slightly mixed with the Negro. But we will assume, for the sake of the argument, that the two races are absolutely pure. We will assume, too, that the laws of the whole country were as favorable to this amalgamation as the laws of most Southern States are at present against it; i.e., that it were made a misdemeanor for two white or two colored persons to marry, so long as it was possible to obtain a mate of the other race—this would be even more favorable than the Southern rule, which makes no such exception. Taking the population as one-eighth Negro, this eighth, married to an equal number of whites, would give in the next generation a population of which one-fourth would be mulattoes. Mating these in turn with white persons, the next generation would be composed one-half of quadroons, or persons one-fourth Negro. In the third generation, applying the same rule, the entire population would be composed of octoroons, or persons only one-eighth Negro, who would probably call themselves white, if by this time there remained any particular advantage in being so considered. Thus in three generations the pure whites would be entirely eliminated, and there would be no perceptible trace of the blacks left.

The mechanical mixture would be complete; as it would probably be put, the white race would have absorbed the black. There would be no inferior race to domineer over; there would be no superior race to oppress those who differed from them in racial externals. The inevitable social struggle, which in one form or another, seems to be one of the conditions of progress, would proceed along other lines than those of race. If now and then, for a few generations, an occasional trace of the black ancestor should crop out, no one would care, for all would be tarred with the same stick. This is already the case in South America, parts of Mexico and to a large extent in the West Indies. From a Negroid nation, which ours is already, we would have become a composite and homogeneous people, and the elements of racial discord which have troubled our civil life so gravely and still threaten our free institutions, would have been entirely eliminated.

But this will never happen. The same result will be brought about slowly and obscurely, and, if the processes of nature are not too violently interrupted by the hand of man, in such a manner as to produce the best results with the least disturbance of natural laws. In another article I shall endeavor to show that this process has been taking place with greater rapidity than is generally supposed, and that the results have been such as to encourage the belief that the formation of a uniform type out of our present racial elements will take place within a measurably near period.

Boston Evening Transcript, August 18, 1900

A Stream of Dark Blood in the Veins of the Southern Whites

I have said that the formation of the new American race type will take place slowly and obscurely for some time to come, after the manner of all healthy changes in nature. I may go further and say that this process has already been going on ever since the various races in the Western world have been brought into juxtaposition. Slavery was a rich soil for the production of a mixed race, and one need only read the literature and laws of the past two generations to see how steadily, albeit slowly and insidiously, the stream of dark blood has insinuated itself into the veins of the dominant, or, as a Southern critic recently described it in a paragraph that came under my eye, the "domineering" race. The Creole stories of Mr. Cable and other writers were not mere figments of the imagination; the beautiful octoroon was a corporeal fact; it is more than likely that she had brothers of the same complexion, though curiously enough the male octoroon has cut no figure in fiction, except in the case of the melancholy Honoré Grandissime, f. m. c.; and that she and her brothers often crossed the invisible but rigid color line was an historical fact that only an ostrich-like prejudice could deny.

Grace King's "Story of New Orleans" makes the significant statement that the quadroon women of that city preferred white fathers for their children, in order that these latter might become white and thereby be qualified to enter the world of opportunity. More than one of the best families of Louisiana has a dark ancestral strain. A conspicuous American family of Southwestern extraction, which recently contributed a party to a brilliant international marriage, is known, by the well-informed, to be just exactly five generations removed from a Negro ancestor. One member of this family, a distinguished society leader, has been known, upon occasion, when some question of the rights or privileges of the colored race came up, to show a very noble sympathy for her distant kinsmen. If American prejudice permitted her and others to speak freely of her pedigree, what a tower of strength her name and influence would be to a despised and struggling race!

A distinguished American man of letters, now resident in Europe, who spent many years in North Carolina, has said to the writer that he had noted, in the course of a long life, at least a thousand instances of white persons known or suspected to possess a strain of Negro blood. An amusing instance of this sort occurred a year or two ago. It was announced through the newspapers, whose omniscience of course no one would question, that a certain great merchant of Chicago was a mulatto. This gentleman had a large dry goods trade in the South, notably in Texas. Shortly after the publication of the item reflecting on the immaculateness of the merchant's descent, there appeared in the Texas newspapers, among the advertising matter, a statement from the Chicago merchant characterizing the rumor as a malicious falsehood, concocted by his rivals in business, and incidentally calling attention to the excellent bargains offered to retailers and jobbers at his great emporium. A counter-illustration is found in the case of a certain bishop, recently elected, of the African Methodist Episcopal Church, who is accused of being a white man. A colored editor who possesses the saving grace of humor, along with other talents of a high order, gravely observed, in discussing this rumor, that "the poor man could not help it, even if he were white, and that a fact for which he was in no wise responsible should not be allowed to stand in the way of his advancement."

During a residence in North Carolina in my youth and early manhood I noted many curious phases of the race problem. I have in mind a family of three sisters so aggressively white that the old popular Southern legend that they were the unacknowledged children of white parents was current concerning them. There was absolutely not the slightest earmark of the Negro about them. It may be stated here, as another race fallacy, that the "telltale dark mark at the root of the nails," supposed to be an infallible test of Negro blood, is a delusion and a snare, and of no value whatever as a test of race. It belongs with the grewsome superstition that a woman apparently white may give birth to a coal-black child by a white father. Another instance that came under my eye was that of a very beautiful girl with soft, wavy brown hair, who is now living in a Far Western State as the wife of a white husband. A typical case was that of a family in which the tradition of Negro origin had persisted long after all trace of it had disappeared. The family took its origin from a white ancestress, and had consequently been free for several generations. The father of the first colored child, counting the family in the female line—the only way it could be counted—was a mulatto. A second infusion of white blood, this time on the paternal side, resulted in offspring not distinguishable from pure white. One child of this generation emigrated to what was then the Far West, married a white woman and reared a large family, whose descendants, now in the fourth or fifth remove from the Negro, are in all probability wholly unaware of their origin. A sister of this pioneer emigrant remained in the place of her birth and formed an irregular union with a white man of means, with whom she lived for many years and for whom she bore a large number of children, who became about evenly divided between white and colored, fixing their status by the marriages they made. One of the daughters, for instance, married a white man and reared in a neighboring county a family of white children, who, in all probability, were as active as any one else in the recent ferocious red-shirt campaign to disfranchise the Negroes.

In this same town there was stationed once, before the war, at the Federal arsenal there located, an officer who fell in love with a "white Negro" girl, as our Southern friends impartially dub them. This officer subsequently left the army, and carried away with him to the North the whole family of his inamorata. He married the woman, and their descendants, who live in a large Western city, are not known at all as persons of color, and show no trace of their dark origin.

Two notable bishops of the Roman Catholic communion in the United States are known to be the sons of a slave mother and a white father, who, departing from the usual American rule, gave his sons freedom, education and a chance in life, instead of sending them to the auction block. Colonel T. W. Higginson, in his *Cheerful Yesterdays*, relates the story of a white colored woman whom he assisted in her escape from slavery or its consequences, who married a white man in the vicinity of Boston and lost her identity with the colored race. How many others there must be who know of similar instances! Grace King, in her "Story of New Orleans," to which I have referred, in speaking of a Louisiana law which required the public records, when dealing with persons of color, always to specify the fact of color, in order, so far had the admixture of races gone, to distinguish them from whites, says: "But the officers of the law could be bribed, and the qualification once dropped acted, inversely, as a patent of pure blood."

A certain well-known Shakspearean actress has a strain of Negro blood, and a popular leading man under a well-known manager is similarly gifted. It would be interesting to give their names, but would probably only injure them. If they could themselves speak of their origin, without any unpleasant consequences, it would be a handsome thing for the colored race. That they do not is no reproach to them; they are white to all intents and purposes, even by the curious laws of the curious States from which they derived their origin, and are in all conscience entitled to any advantage accompanying this status.

Anyone at all familiar with the hopes and aspirations of the colored race, as expressed, for instance, in their prolific newspaper literature, must have perceived the wonderful inspiration which they have drawn from the career of a few distinguished Europeans of partial Negro ancestry, who have felt no call, by way of social prejudice, to deny or conceal their origin, or to refuse their sympathy to those who need it so much. Pushkin, the Russian Shakspeare, had a black ancestor. One of the chief editors of the London *Times*, who died a few years ago, was a West Indian colored man, who had no interest in concealing the fact. One of the generals of the British army is similarly favored, although the fact is not often referred to. General Alfred Dodds, the ranking general of the French army, now in command in China, is a quadroon. The poet, Robert Browning, was of West Indian origin, and some of his intimate personal friends maintained and proved to their own satisfaction that he was partly of Negro descent. Mr. Browning always said that he did not know; that there was no family tradition to that effect; but if it could be demonstrated he would admit it freely enough, if it would reflect any credit upon a race who needed it so badly.

The most conspicuous of the Eurafricans (to coin a word) were the Dumas family, who were distinguished for three generations. The mulatto, General Dumas, won distinction in the wars under the Revolution. His son, the famous Alexandre Dumas *père*, has delighted several generations with his novels, and founded a school of fiction. His son, Alexandre *fils*, novelist and dramatist, was as supreme in his own line as his father had been in his. Old Alexandre gives his pedigree in detail in his memoirs; and the Negro origin of the family is set out in every encyclopædia. Nevertheless, in a literary magazine of recent date, published in New York, it was gravely stated by a writer that "there was a rumor, probably not well founded, that the author of *Monte-Cristo* had a very distant strain of Negro blood." If this had been written with reference to some living American of obscure origin, its point might be appreciated; but such extreme delicacy in stating so widely known a fact appeals to one's sense of humor.

These European gentlemen could be outspoken about their origin, because it carried with it no social stigma or disability whatever. When such a state of public opinion exists in the United States, there may be a surprising revision of pedigrees!

A little incident that occurred not long ago near Boston will illustrate the complexity of these race relations. Three light-colored men, brothers, by the name, we will say, of Green, living in a Boston suburb, married respectively a white, a brown and a black woman. The children with the white mother became known as white, and associated with white people. The others were frankly colored. By a not unlikely coincidence, in the course of time the children of the three families found themselves in the same public school. Curiously enough, one afternoon the three sets of Green children—the white Greens, the brown Greens and the black Greens—were detained after school, and were all directed to report to a certain schoolroom, where they were assigned certain tasks at the blackboards about the large room. Still more curiously, most of the teachers of the school happened to have business in this particular room on that particular afternoon, and all of them seemed greatly interested in the Green children.

"Well, well, did you ever! Just think of it! And they are all first cousins!" was remarked audibly.

The children were small, but they lived in Boston, and were, of course, as became Boston children, preternaturally intelligent for their years. They reported to their parents the incident and a number of remarks of a similar tenor to the one above quoted. The result was a complaint to the school authorities, and a reprimand to several teachers. A curious feature of the affair lay in the source from which the complaint emanated. One might suppose it to have come from the white Greens; but no, they were willing that the incident should pass unnoticed and be promptly forgotten; publicity would only advertise a fact which would work to their social injury. The dark Greens rather enjoyed the affair; they had nothing to lose; they had no objections to being known as the cousins of the others, and experienced a certain not unnatural pleasure in their discomfiture. The complaint came from the brown Greens. The reader can figure out the psychology of it for himself.

A more certain proof of the fact that Negro blood is widely distributed among the white people may be found in the laws and judicial decisions of the various States. Laws, as a rule, are not made until demanded by a sufficient number of specific cases to call for a general rule; and judicial decisions of course are never announced except as the result of litigation over contested facts. There is no better index of the character and genius of a people than their laws.

In North Carolina, marriage between white persons and free persons of color was lawful until 1830. By the Missouri code of 1855, the color line was drawn at one-fourth of Negro blood, and persons of only one-eighth were legally white. The same rule was laid down by the Mississippi code of 1880. Under the old *code noir* of Louisiana, the descendant of a white and a quadroon was white. Under these laws many persons currently known as "colored," or, more recently as "Negro," would be legally white if they chose to claim and exercise the privilege. In Ohio, before the Civil War, a person more than half-white was legally entitled to all the rights of a white man. In South Carolina, the line of cleavage was left somewhat indefinite; the color line was drawn tentatively at one-fourth of Negro blood, but this was not held conclusive.

"The term 'mulatto'," said the Supreme Court of that State in a reported case, "is not invariably applicable to every admixture of African blood with the European, nor is one having all the features of a white to be ranked with the degraded class designated by the laws of the State as persons of color, because of some remote taint of the Negro race. . . . The question whether persons are colored or white, where color or feature is doubtful, is for the jury to determine by reputation, by reception into society, and by their exercises of the privileges of a white man, as well as by admixture of blood."

It is well known that this liberality of view grew out of widespread conditions in the State, which these decisions in their turn tended to emphasize. They were probably due to the large preponderance of colored people in the State, which rendered the whites the more willing to augment their own number. There are many interesting color-line decisions in the reports of the Southern courts, which space will not permit the mention of.

In another article I shall consider certain conditions which retard the development of the future American race type which I have suggested, as well as certain other tendencies which are likely to promote it.

Boston Evening Transcript, August 25, 1900

A Complete Race-Amalgamation Likely to Occur

I HAVE endeavored in two former letters to set out the reasons why it seems likely that the future American ethnic type will be formed by a fusion of all the various races now peopling this continent, and to show that this process has been under way, slowly but surely, like all evolutionary movements, for several hundred years. I wish now to consider some of the conditions which will retard this fusion, as well as certain other facts which tend to promote it.

The Indian phase of the problem, so far at least as the United States is concerned, has been practically disposed of in what has already been said. The absorption of the Indians will be delayed so long as the tribal relations continue, and so long as the Indians are treated as wards of the Government, instead of being given their rights once for all, and placed upon the footing of other citizens. It is presumed that this will come about as the wilder Indians are educated and by the development of the country brought into closer contact with civilization, which must happen before a very great while. As has been stated, there is no very strong prejudice against the Indian blood; a well-stocked farm or a comfortable fortune will secure a white husband for a comely Indian girl any day, with some latitude, and there is no evidence of any such strong race instinct or organization as will make the Indians of the future wish to perpetuate themselves as a small and insignificant class in a great population, thus emphasizing distinctions which would be overlooked in the case of the individual.

The Indian will fade into the white population as soon as he chooses, and in the United States proper the slender Indian strain will ere long leave no trace discoverable by anyone but the anthropological expert. In New Mexico and Central America, on the contrary, the chances seem to be that the Indian will first absorb the non-indigenous elements, unless, which is not unlikely, European immigration shall increase the white contingent.

The Negro element remains, then, the only one which seems likely to present any difficulty of assimilation. The main obstacle that retards the absorption of the Negro into the general population is the apparently intense prejudice against color which prevails in the United States. This prejudice loses much of its importance, however, when it is borne in mind that it is almost purely local and does not exist in quite the same form anywhere else in the world, except among the Boers of South Africa, where it prevails in an even more aggravated form; and, as I shall endeavor to show, this prejudice in the United States is more apparent than real, and is a caste prejudice which is merely accentuated by differences of race. At present, however, I wish to consider it merely as a deterrent to amalgamation.

This prejudice finds forcible expression in the laws which prevail in all the Southern States, without exception, forbidding the intermarriage of white persons and persons of color—these last being generally defined within certain degrees. While it is evident that such laws alone will not prevent the intermingling of races, which goes merrily on in spite of them, it is equally apparent that this placing of mixed marriages beyond the pale of the law is a powerful deterrent to any honest or dignified amalgamation. Add to this legal restriction, which is enforced by severe penalties, the social odium accruing to the white party to such a union, and it may safely be predicted that so long as present conditions prevail in the South, there will be little marrying or giving in marriage between persons of different race. So ferocious is this sentiment against intermarriage, that in a recent Missouri case, where a colored man ran away with and married a young white woman, the man was pursued by a "posse"—a word which is rapidly being debased from its proper meaning by its use in the attempt to dignify the character of lawless Southern mobs—and shot to death; the woman was tried and convicted of the "crime" of "miscegenation"—another honest word which the South degrades along with the Negro.

Another obstacle to race fusion lies in the drastic and increasing proscriptive legislation by which the South attempts to keep the white and colored races apart in every place where their joint presence might be taken to imply equality; or, to put it more directly, the persistent effort to degrade the Negro to a distinctly and permanently inferior caste. This is undertaken by means of separate schools, separate railroad and street cars, political disfranchisement, debasing and abhorrent prison systems, and an unflagging campaign of calumny, by which the vices and shortcomings of the Negroes are grossly magnified and their virtues practically lost sight of. The popular argument that the Negro ought to develop his own civilization, and has no right to share in that of the white race, unless by favor, comes with poor grace from those who are forcing their civilization upon others at the cannon's mouth; it is, moreover, uncandid and unfair. The white people of the present generation did not make their civilization; they inherited it ready-made, and much of the wealth which is so strong a factor in their power was created by the unpaid labor of the colored people. The present generation has, however, brought to a high state of development one distinctively American institution, for which it is entitled to such credit as it may wish to claim; I refer to the custom of lynching, with its attendant horrors.

The principal deterrent to race admixture, however, is the low industrial and social efficiency of the colored race. If it be conceded that these are the result of environment, then their cause is not far to seek, and the cure is also in sight. Their poverty, their ignorance and their servile estate render them as yet largely ineligible for social fusion with a race whose pride is fed not only by the record of its achievements but by a constant comparison with a less developed and less fortunate race, which it has held so long in subjection.

The forces that tend to the future absorption of the black race are, however, vastly stronger than those arrayed against it. As experience has demonstrated, slavery was favorable to the mixing of races. The growth, under healthy civil conditions, of a large and self-respecting colored citizenship would doubtless tend to lessen the clandestine association of the two races; but the effort to degrade the Negro may result, if successful, in a partial restoration of the old status. But, assuming that the present anti-Negro legislation is but a temporary reaction, then the steady progress of the colored race in wealth and culture and social efficiency will, in the course of time, materially soften the asperities of racial prejudice and permit them to approach the whites more closely, until, in time, the prejudice against intermarriage shall have been overcome by other considerations.

It is safe to say that the possession of a million dollars, with the ability to use it to the best advantage, would throw such a golden glow over a dark complexion as to override anything but a very obdurate prejudice. Mr. Spahr, in his well-studied and impartial book on *America's Working People*, states as his conclusion, after a careful study of conditions in the South, that the most advanced third of the Negroes of that section has already, in one generation of limited opportunity, passed in the race of life the least advanced third of the whites. To pass the next third will prove a more difficult task, no doubt, but the Negroes will have the impetus of their forward movement to push them ahead.

The outbreaks of race prejudice in recent years are the surest evidence of the Negro's progress. No effort is required to keep down a race which manifests no desire nor ability to rise; but with each new forward movement of the colored race it is brought into contact with the whites at some fresh point, which evokes a new manifestation of prejudice until custom has adjusted things to the new condition. When all Negroes were poor and ignorant they could be denied their rights with impunity. As they grow in knowledge and in wealth they become more self-assertive, and make it correspondingly troublesome for those who would ignore their claims. It is much easier, by a supreme effort, as recently attempted with temporary success in North Carolina, to knock the race down and rob it of its rights once for all, than to repeat the process from day to day and with each individual; it saves wear and tear on the conscience, and makes it easy to maintain a superiority which it might in the course of a short time require some little effort to keep up.

This very proscription, however, political and civil at the South, social all over the country, varying somewhat in degree, will, unless very soon relaxed, prove a powerful factor in the mixture of the races. If it is only by becoming white that colored people and their children are to enjoy the rights and dignities of citizenship, they will have every incentive to "lighten the breed," to use a current phrase, that they may claim the white man's privileges as soon as possible. That this motive is already at work may be seen in the enormous extent to which certain "face bleachers" and "hair straighteners" are advertised in the newspapers printed for circulation among the colored people. The most powerful factor in achieving any result is the wish to bring it about. The only thing that ever succeeded in keeping two races separated when living on the same soil—the only true ground of caste—is religion, and as has been alluded to in the case of the Jews, this is only superficially successful. The colored people are the same as the whites in religion; they have the same standards and mediums of culture, the same ideals, and the presence of the successful white race as a constant incentive to their ambition. The ultimate result is not difficult to foresee. The races will be quite as effectively amalgamated by lightening the Negroes as they would be by darkening the whites. It is only a social fiction, indeed, which makes of a person seven-eighths white a Negro; he is really much more a white man.

The hope of the Negro, so far as the field of moral sympathy and support in his aspirations is concerned, lies, as always, chiefly in the North. There the forces which tend to his elevation are, in the main, allowed their natural operation. The exaggerated zeal with which the South is rushing to degrade the Negro is likely to result, as in the case of slavery, in making more friends for him at the North; and if the North shall not see fit to interfere forcibly with Southern legislation, it may at least feel disposed to emphasize, by its own liberality, its disapproval of Southern injustice and barbarity.

An interesting instance of the difference between the North and the South in regard to colored people, may be found in two cases which only last year came up for trial in two adjoining border States. A colored man living in Maryland went over to Washington and married a white woman. The marriage was legal in Washington. When they returned to their Maryland home they were arrested for the crime of "miscegenation"—perhaps it is only a misdemeanor in Maryland—and sentenced to fine and imprisonment, the penalty of extra-judicial death not extending so far North. The same month a couple, one white and one colored, were arrested in New Jersey for living in adultery. They were found guilty by the court, but punishment was withheld upon a promise that they would marry immediately; or, as some cynic would undoubtedly say, the punishment was commuted from imprisonment to matrimony.

The adding to our territories of large areas populated by dark races, some of them already liberally dowered with Negro blood, will enhance the relative importance of the non-Caucasian elements of the population, and largely increase the flow of dark blood toward the white race, until the time shall come when distinctions of color shall lose their importance, which will be but the prelude to a complete racial fusion.

The formation of this future American race is not a pressing problem. Because of the conditions under which it must take place, it is likely to be extremely slow—much slower, indeed, in our temperate climate and highly organized society, than in the American tropics and sub-tropics, where it is already well under way, if not a *fait accompli*. That it must come in the United States, sooner or later, seems to be a foregone conclusion, as the result of natural law—*lex dura, sed tamen lex*—a hard pill, but one which must be swallowed. There can manifestly be no such thing as a peaceful and progressive civilization in a nation divided by two warring races, and homogeneity of type, at least in externals, is a necessary condition of harmonious social progress.

If this, then, must come, the development and progress of all the constituent elements of the future American race is of the utmost importance as bearing upon the quality of the resultant type. The white race is still susceptible of some improvement; and if, in time, the more objectionable Negro traits are eliminated, and his better qualities correspondingly developed, his part in the future American race may well be an important and valuable one.

Boston Evening Transcript, September 1, 1900

Superstitions and Folk-Lore of the South

DURING a recent visit to North Carolina, after a long absence, I took occasion to inquire into the latter-day prevalence of the old-time belief in what was known as "conjuration" or "goopher," my childish recollection of which I have elsewhere embodied into a number of stories. The derivation of the word "goopher" I do not know, nor whether any other writer than myself has recognized its existence, though it is in frequent use in certain parts of the South. The origin of this curious superstition itself is perhaps more easily traceable. It probably grew, in the first place, out of African fetichism which was brought over from the dark continent along with the dark people. Certain features, too, suggest a distant affinity with Voodooism, or snake worship, a cult which seems to have been indigenous to tropical America. These beliefs, which in the place of their origin had all the sanctions of religion and social custom, became, in the shadow of the white man's civilization, a pale reflection of their former selves. In time, too, they were mingled and confused with the witchcraft and ghost lore of the white man, and the tricks and delusions of the Indian conjurer. In the old plantation days they flourished vigorously, though discouraged by the "great house," and their potency was well established among the blacks and the poorer whites. Education, however, has thrown the ban of disrepute upon witchcraft and conjuration. The stern frown of the preacher, who looks upon superstition as the ally of the Evil One; the scornful sneer of the teacher, who sees in it a part of the livery of bondage, have driven this quaint combination of ancestral traditions to the remote chimney corners of old black aunties, from which it is difficult for the stranger to unearth them. Mr. Harris, in his Uncle Remus stories, has, with fine literary discrimination, collected and put into pleasing and enduring form, the plantation stories which dealt with animal lore, but so little attention has been paid to those dealing with so-called conjuration, that they seem in a fair way to disappear, without leaving a trace behind. The loss may not be very great, but these vanishing traditions might furnish valuable data for the sociologist, in the future study of racial development. In writing, a few years ago, the volume entitled *The Conjure Woman*, I suspect that I was more influenced by the literary value of the material than by its sociological bearing, and therefore took, or thought I did, considerable liberty with my subject. Imagination, however, can only act upon data—one must have somewhere in his consciousness the ideas which he puts together to form a connected whole. Creative talent, of whatever grade, is, in the last analysis, only the power of rearrangement—there is nothing new under the sun. I was the more firmly impressed with this thought after I had interviewed half a dozen old women, and a genuine "conjure doctor;" for I discovered that the brilliant touches, due, I had thought, to my own imagination, were after all but dormant ideas, lodged in my childish mind by old Aunt This and old Uncle That, and awaiting only the spur of imagination to bring them again to the surface. For instance, in the story, "Hot-foot Hannibal," there figures a conjure doll with pepper feet. Those pepper feet I regarded as peculiarly my own, a purely original creation. I heard, only the other day, in North Carolina, of the consternation struck to the heart of a certain dark individual, upon finding upon his doorstep a rabbit's foot—a good omen in itself perhaps—to which a malign influence had been imparted by tying to one end of it, in the form of a cross, two small pods of red pepper!

Most of the delusions connected with this belief in conjuration grow out of mere lack of enlightenment. As primeval men saw a personality behind every natural phenomenon, and found a god or a devil in wind, rain, and hail, in lightning, and in storm, so the untaught man or woman who is assailed by an unusual ache or pain, some strenuous symptom of serious physical disorder, is prompt to accept the suggestion, which tradition approves, that some evil influence is behind his discomfort; and what more natural than to conclude that some rival in business or in love has set this force in motion?

Relics of ancestral barbarism are found among all peoples, but advanced civilization has at least shaken off the more obvious absurdities of superstition. We no longer attribute insanity to demoniac possession, nor suppose that a king's touch can cure scrofula. To many old people in the South, however, any unusual ache or pain is quite as likely to have been caused by some external evil influence as by natural causes. Tumors, sudden swellings due to inflammatory rheumatism or the bites of insects, are especially open to suspicion. Paralysis is proof positive of conjuration. If there is any doubt, the "conjure doctor" invariably removes it. The credulity of ignorance is his chief stock in trade—there is no question, when he is summoned, but that the patient has been tricked.

The means of conjuration are as simple as the indications. It is a condition of all witch stories that there must in some way be contact, either with the person, or with some object or image intended to represent the person to be affected; or, if not actual contact, at least close proximity. The charm is placed under the door-sill, or buried under the hearth, or hidden in the mattress of the person to be conjured. It may be a crude attempt to imitate the body of the victim, or it may consist merely of a bottle, or a gourd, or a little bag, containing a few rusty nails, crooked pins, or horsehairs. It may be a mysterious mixture thrown surreptitiously upon the person to be injured, or merely a line drawn across a road or path, which line it is fatal for a certain man or woman to cross. I heard of a case of a laboring man who went two miles out of his way, every morning and evening, while going to and from his work, to avoid such a line drawn for him by a certain powerful enemy.

Some of the more gruesome phases of the belief in conjuration suggest possible poisoning, a knowledge of which baleful art was once supposed to be widespread among the imported Negroes of the olden time. The blood or venom of snakes, spiders, and lizards is supposed to be employed for this purpose. The results of its administration are so peculiar, however, and so entirely improbable, that one is supposed to doubt even the initial use of poison, and figure it in as part of the same general delusion. For instance, a certain man "swelled up all over" and became "pieded," that is, pied or spotted. A white physician who was summoned thought that the man thus singularly afflicted was poisoned, but did not recognize the poison nor know the antidote. A conjure doctor, subsequently called in, was more prompt in his diagnosis. The man, he said, was poisoned with a lizard, which at that very moment was lodged somewhere in the patient's anatomy. The lizards and snakes in these stories, by the way, are not confined to the usual ducts and cavities of the human body, but seem to have freedom of movement throughout the whole structure. This lizard, according to the "doctor," would start from the man's shoulder, descend to his hand, return to the shoulder, and pass down the side of the body to the leg. When it reached the calf of the leg the lizard's head would appear right under the skin. After it had been perceptible for three days the lizard was to be cut out with a razor, or the man would die. Sure enough, the lizard manifested its presence in the appointed place at the appointed time; but the patient would not permit the surgery, and at the end of three days paid with death the penalty of his obstinacy. Old Aunt Harriet told me, with solemn earnestness, that she herself had taken a snake from her own arm, in sections, after a similar experience. Old Harriet may have been lying, but was, I imagine, merely self-deluded. Witches, prior to being burned, have often confessed their commerce with the Evil One. Why should Harriet hesitate to relate a simple personal experience which involved her in no blame whatever?

Old Uncle Jim, a shrewd, hard old sinner, and a palpable fraud, who did not, I imagine, believe in himself to any great extent, gave me some private points as to the manner in which these reptiles were thus transferred to the human system. If a snake or a lizard be killed, and a few drops of its blood be dried upon a plate or in a gourd, the person next eating or drinking from the contaminated vessel will soon become the unwilling landlord of a reptilian tenant. There are other avenues, too, by which the reptile may gain admittance; but when expelled by the conjure doctor's arts or medicines, it always leaves at the point where it entered. This belief may have originally derived its existence from the fact that certain tropical insects sometimes lay their eggs beneath the skins of animals, or even of men, from which it is difficult to expel them until the larvae are hatched. The chico or "jigger" of the West Indies and the Spanish Main is the most obvious example.

Old Aunt Harriet—last name uncertain, since she had borne those of her master, her mother, her putative father, and half a dozen husbands in succession, no one of which seemed to take undisputed precedence—related some very remarkable experiences. She at first manifested some reluctance to speak of conjuration, in the lore of which she was said to be well versed; but by listening patiently to her religious experiences—she was a dreamer of dreams and a seer of visions—I was able now and then to draw a little upon her reserves of superstition, if indeed her religion itself was much more than superstition.

"W'en I wuz a gal 'bout eighteen or nineteen," she confided, "de w'ite folks use' ter sen' me ter town ter fetch vegetables. One day I met a' ole conjuh man name' Jerry Macdonal', an' he said some rough, ugly things ter me. I says, says I, 'You mus' be a fool.' He didn' say nothin', but jes' looked at me wid 'is evil eye. W'en I come 'long back, dat ole man wuz stan'in' in de road in front er his house, an' w'en he seed me he stoop' down an' tech' de groun', jes' lack he wuz pickin' up somethin', an' den went 'long back in 'is ya'd. De ve'y minute I step' on de spot he tech', I felt a sha'p pain shoot thoo my right foot, it tu'n't under me, an' I fell down in de road. I pick' myself up an' by de time I got home, my foot wuz swoll' up twice its nachul size. I cried an' cried an' went on, fer I knowed I'd be'n trick' by dat ole man. Dat night in my sleep a voice spoke ter me an' says: 'Go an' git a plug er terbacker. Steep it in a skillet er wa'm water. Strip it lengthways, an' bin' it ter de bottom er yo' foot'.' I never didn' use terbacker, an' I laid dere, an' says ter myse'f, 'My Lawd, wa't is dat, wa't is dat!' Soon ez my foot got kind er easy, dat voice up an' speaks ag'in: 'Go an' git a plug er terbacker. Steep it in a skillet er wa'm water, an' bin' it ter de bottom er yo' foot.' I scramble' ter my feet, got de money out er my pocket, woke up de two little boys sleepin' on de flo', an' tol' 'em ter go ter de sto' an' git me a plug er terbacker. Dey didn' want ter go, said de sto' wuz shet, an' de sto' keeper gone ter bed. But I chased 'em fo'th, an' dey found' de sto' keeper an' fetch' de terbacker—dey sho' did. I soaked it in de skillet, an' stripped it 'long by degrees, till I got ter de en', w'en I boun' it under my foot an' roun' my ankle. Den I kneel' down an' prayed, an' next mawnin de swellin' wuz all gone! Dat voice wus de Spirit er de Lawd talkin' ter me, it sho' wuz! De Lawd have mussy upon us, praise his Holy Name!"

Very obviously Harriet had sprained her ankle while looking at the old man instead of watching the path, and the hot fomentation had reduced the swelling. She is not the first person to hear spirit voices in his or her own vagrant imaginings.

On another occasion, Aunt Harriet's finger swelled up "as big as a corn cob." She at first supposed the swelling to be due to a felon. She went to old Uncle Julius Lutterloh, who told her that some one had tricked her. "My Lawd!" she exclaimed, "how did they fix my finger?" He explained that it was done while in the act of shaking hands. "Doctor" Julius opened the finger with a sharp knife and showed Harriet two seeds at the bottom of the incision. He instructed her to put a poultice of red onions on the wound over night, and in the morning the seeds would come out. She was then to put the two seeds in a skillet, on the right hand side of the fire-place, in a pint of water, and let them simmer nine mornings, and on the ninth morning she was to let all the water simmer out, and when the last drop should have gone, the one that put the seeds in her hand was to go out of this world! Harriet, however, did not pursue the treatment to the bitter end. The seeds, once extracted, she put into a small phial, which she corked up tightly and put carefully away in her bureau drawer. One morning she went to look at them, and one of them was gone. Shortly afterwards the other disappeared. Aunt Harriet has a theory that she had been tricked by a woman of whom her husband of that time was unduly fond, and that the faithless husband had returned the seeds to their original owner. A part of the scheme of conjuration is that the conjure doctor can remove the spell and put it back upon the one who laid it. I was unable to learn, however, of any instance where this extreme penalty had been insisted upon.

It is seldom that any of these old Negroes will admit that he or she possesses the power to conjure, though those who can remove spells are very willing to make their accomplishment known, and to exercise it for a consideration. The only professional conjure doctor whom I met was old Uncle Jim Davis, with whom I arranged a personal interview. He came to see me one evening, but almost immediately upon his arrival a minister called. The powers of light prevailed over those of darkness, and Jim was dismissed until a later time, with a commission to prepare for me a conjure "hand" or good luck charm, of which, he informed some of the children about the house, who were much interested in the proceedings. I was very much in need. I subsequently secured the charm, for which, considering its potency, the small sum of silver it cost me was no extravagant outlay. It is a very small bag of roots and herbs, and, if used according to directions, is guaranteed to insure me good luck and "keep me from losing my job." The directions require it to be wet with spirits nine mornings in succession, to be carried on the person, in a pocket on the right hand side, care being taken that it does not come in contact with any tobacco. When I add that I procured, from an equally trustworthy source, a genuine graveyard rabbit's foot, I would seem to be reasonably well protected against casual misfortune. I shall not, however, presume upon this immunity, and shall omit no reasonable precaution which the condition of my health or my affairs may render prudent.

An interesting conjure story, which I heard, involves the fate of a lost voice. A certain woman's lover was enticed away by another woman, who sang very sweetly, and who, the jilted one suspected, had told lies about her. Having decided upon the method of punishment for this wickedness, the injured woman watched the other closely, in order to find a suitable opportunity for carrying out her purpose; but in vain, for the fortunate one, knowing of her enmity, would never speak to her or remain near her. One day the jilted woman plucked a red rose from her garden, and hid herself in the bushes near her rival's cabin. Very soon an old woman came by, who was accosted by the woman in hiding, and requested to hand the red rose to the woman of the house. The old woman, suspecting no evil, took the rose and approached the house, the other woman following her closely, but keeping herself always out of sight. When the old woman, having reached the door and called out the mistress of the house, delivered the rose as requested, the recipient thanked the giver in a loud voice, knowing the old woman to be somewhat deaf. At the moment she spoke, the woman in hiding reached up and caught her rival's voice, and clasping it tightly in her right hand, escaped unseen, to her own cabin. At the same instant the afflicted woman missed her voice, and felt a sharp pain shoot through her left arm, just below the elbow. She at first suspected the old woman of having tricked her through the medium of the red rose, but was subsequently informed by a conjure doctor that her voice had been stolen, and that the old woman was innocent. For the pain he gave her a bottle of medicine, of which nine drops were to be applied three times a day, and rubbed in with the first two fingers of the right hand, care being taken not to let any other part of the hand touch the arm, as this would render the medicine useless. By the aid of a mirror, in which he called up her image, the conjure doctor ascertained who was the guilty person. He sought her out and charged her with the crime which she promptly denied. Being pressed, however, she admitted her guilt. The doctor insisted upon immediate restitution. She expressed her willingness, and at the same time her inability to comply—she had taken the voice, but did not possess the power to restore it. The conjure doctor was obdurate and at once placed a spell upon her which is to remain until the lost voice is restored. The case is still pending, I understand; I shall sometime take steps to find out how it terminates.

How far a story like this is original, and how far a mere reflection of familiar wonder stories, is purely a matter of speculation. When the old mammies would tell the tales of Br'er Rabbit and Br'er Fox to the master's children, these in turn would no doubt repeat the fairy tales which they had read in books or heard from their parents' lips. The magic mirror is as old as literature. The inability to restore the stolen voice is foreshadowed in the *Arabian Nights*, when the "Open Sesame" is forgotten. The act of catching the voice has a simplicity which stamps it as original, the only analogy of which I can at present think being the story of later date, of the words which were frozen silent during the extreme cold of an Arctic winter, and became audible again the following summer when they had thawed out.

Modern Culture, May 1901

Charles W. Chesnutt's Own View of His New Story, The Marrow of Tradition

I HAVE been asked to make for this page a brief summary of the motive and chief points of my forthcoming novel, *The Marrow of Tradition.* The primary object of this story, as it should be of every work of fiction, is to entertain; and yet it belongs in the category of purpose novels, inasmuch as it seeks to throw light upon the vexed moral and sociological problems which grow out of the presence, in our Southern states, of two diverse races, in nearly equal numbers.

The title of the book fairly embodies the theme, which is an attempt to picture, through the medium of dramatic narrative, the atmosphere in which these problems must be worked out—an atmosphere of which the dominant note is Tradition.

Tradition made the white people masters, rulers, who absorbed all the power, the wealth, the honors of the community, and jealously guarded this monopoly, with which they claimed to be divinely endowed, by denying to those who were not of their caste the opportunity to acquire any of these desirable things.

Tradition, on the other hand, made the Negro a slave, an underling, existing by favor and not by right, his place the lowest in the social scale, to which, by the same divine warrant, he was hopelessly confined.

The old order has passed away, but these opinions, deeply implanted in the consciousness of two races, still persist, and *The Marrow of Tradition* seeks to show the efforts of the people of a later generation to adjust themselves in this traditional atmosphere to the altered conditions of a new era.

There is no subject of more vital interest to the student of history or of life than the upward struggle of a race, as there is no issue of greater importance to the nation than a right settlement of the race problem.

As to the story, it must speak for itself. It has several threads of interest, the chief incidents being concerned with the fate of the child of a proud old family related by an unacknowledged tie to the family of a colored doctor. The father of the child leads a reactionary political movement against the Negro, while the doctor is at the head of an enterprise for the education and uplifting of his people. There is a crime, followed by a threatened lynching. There is an episode of injury and revenge, another of wrong and forgiveness.

Among the characters are a typical old "mammy," a faithful servant who is willing to die for his master and an ideal old aristocrat who practically sacrifices his life to save that of his servant. The incidents of the race riot described in the story were studied from two recent outbreaks of that kind—one in Wilmington, N.C., and the other in New Orleans.

The political element of the story involves a fair statement, I believe, of the course and the underlying motives of the recent and temporarily successful movement for the disfranchisement of the colored race in the South, and particularly in North Carolina, where there was less excuse for it than in any other state where it has been carried through.

There is a love story with a happy ending. The book is not a study in pessimism, for it is the writer's belief that the forces of progress will in the end prevail, and that in time a remedy may be found for every social ill.

It may interest the readers of my previous books to learn that *The Marrow of Tradition* admits of an ending which is at the same time consistent with the canons of good art and satisfying to the emotions.

Cleveland World, October 20, 1901

The Disfranchisement of the Negro

THE RIGHT of American citizens of African descent, commonly called Negroes, to vote upon the same terms as other citizens of the United States, is plainly declared and firmly fixed by the Constitution. No such person is called upon to present reasons why he should possess this right: that question is foreclosed by the Constitution. The object of the elective franchise is to give representation. So long as the Constitution retains its present form, any State Constitution, or statute, which seeks, by juggling the ballot, to deny the colored race fair representation, is a clear violation of the fundamental law of the land, and a corresponding injustice to those thus deprived of this right.

For thirty-five years this has been the law. As long as it was measurably respected, the colored people made rapid strides in education, wealth, character and self-respect. This the census proves, all statements to the contrary notwithstanding. A generation has grown to manhood and womanhood under the great, inspiring freedom conferred by the Constitution and protected by the right of suffrage—protected in large degree by the mere naked right, even when its exercise was hindered or denied by unlawful means. They have developed, in every Southern community, good citizens, who, if sustained and encouraged by just laws and liberal institutions, would greatly augment their number with the passing years, and soon wipe out the reproach of ignorance, unthrift, low morals and social inefficiency, thrown at them indiscriminately and therefore unjustly, and made the excuse for the equally undiscriminating contempt of their persons and their rights. They have reduced their illiteracy nearly 50 per cent. Excluded from the institutions of higher learning in their own States, their young men hold their own, and occasionally carry away honors, in the universities of the North. They have accumulated three hundred million dollars worth of real and personal property. Individuals among them have acquired substantial wealth, and several have attained to something like national distinction in art, letters and educational leadership. They are numerously represented in the learned professions. Heavily handicapped, they have made such rapid progress that the suspicion is justified that their advancement, rather than any stagnation or retrogression, is the true secret of the virulent Southern hostility to their rights, which has so influenced Northern opinion that it stands mute, and leaves the colored people, upon whom the North conferred liberty, to the tender mercies of those who have always denied their fitness for it.

It may be said, in passing, that the word "Negro," where used in this paper, is used solely for convenience. By the census of 1890 there were 1,000,000 colored people in the country who were half, or more than half, white, and logically there must be, as in fact there are, so many who share the white blood in some degree, as to justify the assertion that the race problem in the United States concerns the welfare and the status of a mixed race. Their rights are not one whit the more sacred because of this fact; but in an argument where injustice is sought to be excused because of fundamental differences of race, it is well enough to bear in mind that the race whose rights and liberties are endangered all over this country by disfranchisement at the South, are the colored people who live in the United States to-day, and not the low-browed, man-eating savage whom the Southern white likes to set upon a block and contrast with Shakespeare and Newton and Washington and Lincoln.

Despite and in defiance of the Federal Constitution, to-day in the six Southern States of Mississippi, Louisiana, Alabama, North Carolina, South Carolina and Virginia, containing an aggregate colored population of about 6,000,000, these have been, to all intents and purposes, denied, so far as the States can effect it, the right to vote. This disfranchisement is accomplished by various methods, devised with much transparent ingenuity, the effort being in each instance to violate the spirit of the Federal Constitution by disfranchising the Negro, while seeming to respect its letter by avoiding the mention of race or color.

These restrictions fall into three groups. The first comprises a property qualification—the ownership of $300 worth or more of real or personal property (Alabama, Louisiana, Virginia and South Carolina); the payment of a poll tax

(Mississippi, North Carolina, Virginia); an educational qualification—the ability to read and write (Alabama, Louisiana, North Carolina). Thus far, those who believe in a restricted suffrage everywhere, could perhaps find no reasonable fault with any one of these qualifications, applied either separately or together.

But the Negro has made such progress that these restrictions alone would perhaps not deprive him of effective representation. Hence the second group. This comprises an "understanding" clause—the applicant must be able "to read, or understand when read to him, any clause in the Constitution" (Mississippi), or to read and explain, or to understand and explain when read to him, any section of the Constitution (Virginia); an employment qualification—the voter must be regularly employed in some lawful occupation (Alabama); a character qualification—the voter must be a person of good character and who "understands the duties and obligations of citizens under a republican [!] form of government" (Alabama). The qualifications under the first group it will be seen, are capable of exact demonstration; those under the second group are left to the discretion and judgment of the registering officer—for in most instances these are all requirements for registration, which must precede voting.

But the first group, by its own force, and the second group, under imaginable conditions, might exclude not only the Negro vote, but a large part of the white vote. Hence, the third group, which comprises: a military service qualification—any man who went to war, willingly or unwillingly, in a good cause or a bad, is entitled to register (Ala., Va.); a prescriptive qualification, under which are included all male persons who were entitled to vote on January 1, 1867, at which date the Negro had not yet been given the right to vote; a hereditary qualification (the so-called "grandfather" clause), whereby any son (Va.), or descendant (Ala.), of a soldier, and (N.C.) the descendant of any person who had the right to vote on January 1, 1867, inherits that right. If the voter wish to take advantage of these last provisions, which are in the nature of exceptions to a general rule, he must register within a stated time, whereupon he becomes a member of a privileged class of permanently enrolled voters not subject to any of the other restrictions.

It will be seen that these restrictions are variously combined in the different States, and it is apparent that if combined to their declared end, practically every Negro may, under color of law, be denied the right to vote, and practically every white man accorded that right. The effectiveness of these provisions to exclude the Negro vote is proved by the Alabama registration under the new State Constitution. Out of a total, by the census of 1900, of 181,471 Negro "males of voting age," less than 3,000 are registered; in Montgomery county alone, the seat of the State capital, where there are 7,000 Negro males of voting age, only 47 have been allowed to register, while in several counties not one single Negro is permitted to exercise the franchise.

These methods of disfranchisement have stood such tests as the United States Courts, including the Supreme Court, have thus far seen fit to apply, in such cases as have been before them for adjudication. These include a case based upon the "understanding" clause of the Mississippi Constitution, in which the Supreme Court held, in effect, that since there was no ambiguity in the language employed and the Negro was not directly named, the Court would not go behind the wording of the Constitution to find a meaning which discriminated against the colored voter; and the recent case of Jackson vs. Giles, brought by a colored citizen of Montgomery, Alabama, in which the Supreme Court confesses itself impotent to provide a remedy for what, by inference, it acknowledges *may* be a "great political wrong," carefully avoiding, however, to state that it is a wrong, although the vital prayer of the petition was for a decision upon this very point.

Now, what is the effect of this wholesale disfranchisement of colored men, upon their citizenship? The value of food to the human organism is not measured by the pains of an occasional surfeit, but by the effect of its entire deprivation. Whether a class of citizens should vote, even if not always wisely—what class does?—may best be determined by considering their condition when they are without the right to vote.

The colored people are left, in the States where they have been disfranchised, absolutely without representation, direct or indirect, in any law-making body, in any court of justice, in any branch of government—for the feeble remnant of voters left by law is so inconsiderable as to be without a shadow of power. Constituting one-eighth of the population of the whole country, two-fifths of the whole Southern people, and a majority in several States, they are not able, because disfranchised where most numerous, to send one representative to the Congress, which, by the decision in the Alabama case, is held by the Supreme Court to be the only body, outside of the State itself, competent to give relief from a great political wrong. By former decisions of the same tribunal, even Congress is impotent to protect their civil rights, the Fourteenth Amendment having long since, by the consent of the same Court, been in many respects as completely nullified as the Fifteenth Amendment is now sought to be. They have no direct representation in any Southern legislature, and no voice in determining the choice of white men who might be friendly to their rights. Nor are they able to influence the election of judges or other public officials, to whom are entrusted the protection of their lives, their liberties and their property. No judge is rendered careful, no sheriff diligent, for fear that he may offend a black constituency; the contrary is most lamentably true; day after day the catalogue of lynchings and anti-Negro riots upon every imaginable pretext, grows longer and more appalling. The country stands face to face with the revival of slavery; at the moment of this writing a federal grand jury in Alabama is uncovering a system of peonage established under cover of law.

Under the Southern program it is sought to exclude colored men from every grade of the public service; not only from the higher administrative functions, to which few of them would in any event, for a long time aspire, but from the lowest as well. A Negro may not be a constable or a policeman. He is subjected by law to many degrading discriminations. He is required to be separated from white people on railroads and street cars, and, by custom, debarred from inns and places of public entertainment. His equal right to a free public education is constantly threatened and is nowhere equitably recognized. In Georgia, as has been shown by Dr. Du Bois, where the law provides for a pro rata distribution of the public school fund between the races, and where the colored school population is 48 per cent. of the total, the amount of the fund devoted to their schools is only 20 per cent. In New Orleans, with an immense colored population, many of whom are persons of means and culture, all colored public schools above the fifth grade have been abolished.

The Negro is subjected to taxation without representation, which the forefathers of this Republic made the basis of a bloody revolution.

Flushed with their local success, and encouraged by the timidity of the Courts and the indifference of public opinion, the Southern whites have carried their campaign into the national government, with an ominous degree of success. If they shall have their way, no Negro can fill any federal office, or occupy, in the public service, any position that is not menial. This is not an inference, but the openly, passionately avowed sentiment of the white South. The right to employment in the public service is an exceedingly valuable one, for which white men have struggled and fought. A vast army of men are employed in the administration of public affairs. Many avenues of employment are closed to colored men by popular prejudice. If their right to public employment is recognized, and the way to it open through the civil service, or the appointing power, or the suffrages of the people, it will prove, as it has already, a strong incentive to effort and a powerful lever for advancement. Its value to the Negro, like that of the right to vote, may be judged by the eagerness of the whites to deprive him of it.

Not only is the Negro taxed without representation in the States referred to, but he pays, through the tariff and internal revenue, a tax to a National government whose supreme judicial tribunal declares that it cannot, through the executive arm, enforce its own decrees, and, therefore, refuses to pass upon a question, squarely before it, involving a basic right of citizenship. For the decision of the Supreme Court in the Giles case, if it foreshadows the attitude which the Court will take upon other cases to the same general end which will soon come before it, is scarcely less than a reaffirmation of the Dred Scott decision; it certainly amounts to this—that in spite of the Fifteenth Amendment, colored men in the United States have no political rights which the States are bound to respect. To say this much is to say that all privileges and immunities which Negroes henceforth enjoy, must be by favor of the whites; they are not *rights*. The whites have so declared; they proclaim that the country is theirs, that the Negro should be thankful that he has so much, when so much more might be withheld from him. He stands upon a lower footing than any alien; he has no government to which he may look for protection.

Moreover, the white South sends to Congress, on a basis including the Negro population, a delegation nearly twice as large as it is justly entitled to, and one which may always safely be relied upon to oppose in Congress every measure which seeks to protect the equality, or to enlarge the rights of colored citizens. The grossness of this injustice is all the more apparent since the Supreme Court, in the Alabama case referred to, has declared the legislative and political department of the government to be the only power which can right a political wrong. Under this decision still further attacks upon the liberties of the citizen may be confidently expected. Armed with the Negro's sole weapon of defense, the white South stands ready to smite down his rights. The ballot was first given to the Negro to defend him against this very thing. He needs it now far more than then, and for even stronger reasons. The 9,000,000 free colored people of to-day have vastly more to defend than the 3,000,000 hapless blacks who had just emerged from slavery. If there be those who maintain that it was a mistake to give the Negro the ballot at the time and in the manner in which it was given, let them take to heart this reflection: that to deprive him of it to-day, or to so restrict it as to leave him utterly defenseless against the present relentless attitude of the South toward his rights, will prove to be a mistake so much greater than the first, as to be no less than a crime, from which not alone the Southern Negro must suffer, but for which the nation will as surely pay the penalty as it paid for the crime of slavery. Contempt for law is death to a republic, and this one has developed alarming symptoms of the disease.

And now, having thus robbed the Negro of every political and civil *right*, the white South, in palliation of its course, makes a great show of magnanimity in leaving him, as the sole remnant of what he acquired through the Civil War, a very inadequate public school education, which, by the present program, is to be directed mainly towards making him a better agricultural laborer. Even this is put forward as a favor, although the Negro's property is taxed to pay for it, and his labor as well. For it is a well settled principle of political economy, that land and machinery of themselves produce nothing, and that labor indirectly pays its fair proportion of the tax upon the public's wealth. The white South seems to stand to the Negro at present as one, who, having been reluctantly compelled to release another from bondage, sees him stumbling forward and upward, neglected by his friends and scarcely yet conscious of his own strength; seizes him, binds him, and having bereft him of speech, of sight and of manhood, "yokes him with the mule" and exclaims, with a show of virtue which ought to deceive no one: "Behold how good a friend I am of yours! Have I not left you a stomach and a pair of arms, and will I not generously permit you to work for me with the one, that you may thereby gain enough to fill the other? A brain you do not need. We will relieve you of any responsibility that might seem to demand such an organ."

The argument of peace-loving Northern white men and Negro opportunists that the political power of the Negro having long ago been suppressed by unlawful means, his right to vote is a mere paper right, of no real value, and therefore to be lightly yielded for the sake of a hypothetical harmony, is fatally short-sighted. It is precisely the attitude and essentially the argument which would have surrendered to the South in the sixties, and would have left this country to rot in slavery for another generation. White men do not thus argue concerning their own rights. They know too well the value of ideals. Southern white men see too clearly the latent power of these unexercised rights. If the political power of the Negro was a nullity because of his ignorance and lack of leadership, why were they not content to leave it so, with the pleasing assurance that if it ever became effective, it would be because the Negroes had grown fit for its exercise? On the contrary, they have not rested until the possibility of its revival was apparently headed off by new State constitutions. Nor are they satisfied with this. There is no doubt that an effort will be made to secure the repeal of the Fifteenth Amendment, and thus forestall the development of the wealthy and educated Negro, whom the South seems to anticipate as a greater menace than the ignorant ex-slave. However improbable this repeal may seem, it is not a subject to be lightly dismissed; for it is within the power of the white people of the nation to do whatever they wish in the premises—they did it once; they can do it again. The Negro and his friends should see to it that the white majority shall never wish to do anything to his hurt. There still stands, before the Negro-hating whites of the South, the specter of a Supreme Court which will interpret the Constitution to mean what it says, and what those who enacted it meant, and what the nation, which ratified it, understood, and which will find power, in a nation which goes beyond seas to administer the affairs of distant peoples, to enforce its own fundamental laws; the specter, too, of an aroused public opinion which will compel Congress and the Courts to preserve the liberties of the Republic, which are the liberties of the people. To wilfully neglect the suffrage, to hold it lightly, is to tamper with a sacred right; to yield it for anything else whatever is simply suicidal. Dropping the element of race, disfranchisement is no more than to say to the poor and poorly taught, that they must relinquish the right to defend themselves against oppression until they shall have become rich and learned, in competition with those already thus favored and possessing the ballot in addition. This is not the philosophy of history. The growth of liberty has been the constant struggle of the poor against the privileged classes; and the goal of that struggle has ever been the equality of all men before the law. The Negro who would yield this right, deserves to be a slave; he has the servile spirit. The rich and the educated can, by virtue of their influence, command many votes; can find other means of protection; the poor man has but one, he should guard it as a sacred treasure. Long ago, by fair treatment, the white leaders of the South might have bound the Negro to themselves with hoops of steel. They have not chosen to take this course, but by assuming from the beginning an attitude hostile to his rights, have never gained his confidence, and now seek by foul means to destroy where they have never sought by fair means to control.

I have spoken of the effect of disfranchisement upon the colored race; it is to the race as a whole, that the argument of the problem is generally directed. But the unit of society in a republic is the individual, and not the race, the failure to recognize this fact being the fundamental error which has beclouded the whole discussion. The effect of disfranchisement upon the individual is scarcely less disastrous. I do not speak of the moral effect of injustice upon those who suffer from it; I refer rather to the practical consequences which may be appreciated by any mind. No country is free in which the way upward is not open for every man to try, and for every properly qualified man to attain whatever of good the community life may offer. Such a condition does not exist, at the South, even in theory, for any man of color. In no career can such a man compete with white men upon equal terms. He must not only meet the prejudice of the individual, not only the united prejudice of the white community; but lest some one should wish to treat him fairly, he is met at every turn with some legal prohibition which says, "Thou shalt not," or "Thus far shalt thou go and no farther." But the Negro race is viable; it adapts itself readily to circumstances; and being thus adaptable, there is always the temptation to

> "Crook the pregnant hinges of the knee,
> Where thrift may follow fawning."

He who can most skillfully balance himself upon the advancing or receding wave of white opinion concerning his race, is surest of such measure of prosperity as is permitted to men of dark skins. There are Negro teachers in the South—the privilege of teaching in their own schools is the one respectable branch of the public service still left open to them—who, for a grudging appropriation from a Southern legislature, will decry their own race, approve their own degradation, and laud their oppressors. Deprived of the right to vote, and, therefore, of any power to demand what is their due, they feel impelled to buy the tolerance of the whites at any sacrifice. If to live is the first duty of man, as perhaps it is the first instinct, then those who thus stoop to conquer may be right. But is it needful to stoop so low, and if so, where lies the ultimate responsibility for this abasement?

I shall say nothing about the moral effect of disfranchisement upon the white people, or upon the State itself. What slavery made of the Southern whites is a matter of history. The abolition of slavery gave the South an opportunity to emerge from barbarism. Present conditions indicate that the spirit which dominated slavery still curses the fair section over which that institution spread its blight.

And now, is the situation remediless? If not so, where lies the remedy? First let us take up those remedies suggested by the men who approve of disfranchisement, though they may sometimes deplore the method, or regret the necessity.

Time, we are told, heals all diseases, rights all wrongs, and is the only cure for this one. It is a cowardly argument. These people are entitled to their rights to-day, while they are yet alive to enjoy them; and it is poor statesmanship and worse morals to nurse a present evil and thrust it forward upon a future generation for correction. The nation can no more honestly do this than it could thrust back upon a past generation the responsibility for slavery. It had to meet that responsibility; it ought to meet this one.

Education has been put forward as the great corrective—preferably industrial education. The intellect of the whites is to be educated to the point where they will so appreciate the blessings of liberty and equality, as of their own motion to enlarge and defend the Negro's rights. The Negroes, on the other hand, are to be so trained as to make them, not equal with the whites in any way—God save the mark!—this would be unthinkable!—but so useful to the community that the whites will protect them rather than lose their valuable services. Some few enthusiasts go so far as to maintain that by virtue of education the Negro will, in time, become strong enough to protect himself against any aggression of the whites; this, it may be said, is a strictly Northern view.

It is not quite clearly apparent how education alone, in the ordinary meaning of the word, is to solve, in any appreciable time, the problem of the relations of Southern white and black people. The need of education of all kinds for both races is wofully apparent. But men and nations have been free without being learned, and there have been educated slaves. Liberty has been known to languish where culture had reached a very high development. Nations do not first become rich and learned and then free, but the lesson of history has been that they first become free and then rich and learned, and oftentimes fall back into slavery again because of too great wealth, and the resulting luxury and carelessness of civic virtues. The process of education has been going on rapidly in the Southern States since the Civil War, and yet, if we take superficial indications, the rights of the Negroes are at a lower ebb than at any time during the thirty-five years of their freedom, and the race prejudice more intense and uncompromising. It is not apparent that educated Southerners are less rancorous than others in their speech concerning the Negro, or less hostile in their attitude toward his rights. It is their voice alone that we have heard in this discussion; and if, as they state, they are liberal in their views as compared with the more ignorant whites, then God save the Negro!

I was told, in so many words, two years ago, by the Superintendent of Public Schools of a Southern city that "there was no place in the modern world for the Negro, except under the ground." If gentlemen holding such opinions are to instruct the white youth of the South, would it be at all surprising if these, later on, should devote a portion of their leisure to the improvement of civilization by putting under the ground as many of this superfluous race as possible?

The sole excuse made in the South for the prevalent injustice to the Negro is the difference in race, and the inequalities and antipathies resulting therefrom. It has nowhere been declared as a part of the Southern program that the Negro, when educated, is to be given a fair representation in government or an equal opportunity in life; the contrary has been strenuously asserted; education can never make of him anything but a Negro, and, therefore, essentially inferior, and not to be safely trusted with any degree of power. A system of education which would tend to soften the asperities and lessen the inequalities between the races would be of inestimable value. An education which by a rigid separation of the races from the kindergarten to the university, fosters this racial antipathy, and is directed toward emphasizing the superiority of one class and the inferiority of another, might easily have disastrous, rather than beneficial results. It would render the oppressing class more powerful to injure, the oppressed quicker to perceive and keener to resent the injury, without proportionate power of defense. The same assimilative education which is given at the North to all children alike, whereby native and foreign, black and white, are taught side by side in every grade of instruction, and are compelled by the exigencies of discipline to keep their prejudices in abeyance, and are given the opportunity to learn and appreciate one another's good qualities, and to establish friendly relations which may exist throughout life, is absent from the Southern system of education, both of the past and as proposed for the future. Education is in a broad sense a remedy for all social ills; but the disease we have to deal with now is not only constitutional but acute. A wise physician does not simply give a tonic for a diseased limb, or a high fever; the patient might be dead before the constitutional remedy could become effective. The evils of slavery, its injury to whites and blacks, and to the body politic, were clearly perceived and acknowledged by the educated leaders of the South as far back as the Revolutionary War and the Constitutional Convention, and yet they made no effort to abolish it. Their remedy was the same —time, education, social and economic development;—and yet a bloody war was necessary to destroy slavery and put its spirit temporarily to sleep. When the South and its friends are ready to propose a system of education which will recognize and teach the equality of all men before the law, the potency of education alone to settle the race problem will be more clearly apparent.

At present even good Northern men, who wish to educate the Negroes, feel impelled to buy this privilege from the none too eager white South, by conceding away the civil and political rights of those whom they would benefit. They have, indeed, gone farther than the Southerners themselves in approving the disfranchisement of the colored race. Most Southern men, now that they have carried their point and disfranchised the Negro, are willing to admit, in the language of a recent number of the Charleston *Evening Post*, that "the attitude of the Southern white man toward the Negro is incompatible with the fundamental ideas of the republic." It remained for our Clevelands and Abbotts and Parkhursts to assure them that their unlawful course was right and justifiable, and for the most distinguished Negro leader to declare that "every revised Constitution throughout the Southern States has put a premium upon intelligence, ownership of property, thrift and character." So does every penitentiary sentence put a premium upon good conduct; but it is poor consolation to the one unjustly condemned, to be told that he may shorten his sentence somewhat by good behavior. Dr. Booker T. Washington, whose language is quoted above, has, by his eminent services in the cause of education, won deserved renown. If he has seemed, at times, to those jealous of the best things for their race, to decry the higher education, it can easily be borne in mind that his career is bound up in the success of an industrial school; hence any undue stress which he may put upon that branch of education may safely be ascribed to the natural zeal of the promoter, without detracting in any degree from the essential value of his teachings in favor of manual training, thrift and character-building. But Mr. Washington's prominence as an educational leader, among a race whose prominent leaders are so few, has at times forced him, perhaps reluctantly, to express himself in regard to the political condition of his people, and here his utterances have not always been so wise nor so happy. He has declared himself in favor of a restricted suffrage, which at present means, for his own people, nothing less than complete loss of representation—indeed it is only in that connection that the question has been seriously mooted; and he has advised them to go slow in seeking to enforce their civil and political rights, which, in effect, means silent submission to injustice. Southern white men may applaud this advice as wise, because it fits in with their purposes; but Senator McEnery of Louisiana, in a recent article in the *Independent*, voices the Southern white opinion of such acquiescence when he says: "What other race would have submitted so many years to slavery without complaint? *What other race would have submitted so quietly to disfranchisement?* These facts stamp his [the Negro's] inferiority to the white race." The time to philosophize about the good there is in evil, is not while its correction is still possible, but, if at all, after all hope of correction is past. Until then it calls for nothing but rigorous condemnation. To try to read any good thing into these fraudulent Southern constitutions, or to accept them as an accomplished fact, is to condone a crime against one's race. Those who commit crime should bear the odium. It is not a pleasing spectacle to see the robbed applaud the robber. Silence were better.

It has become fashionable to question the wisdom of the Fifteenth Amendment. I believe it to have been an act of the highest statesmanship, based upon the fundamental idea of this Republic, entirely justified by conditions; experimental in its nature, perhaps, as every new thing must be, but just in principle; a choice between methods, of which it seemed to the great statesmen of that epoch the wisest and the best, and essentially the most just, bearing in mind the interests of the freedmen and the Nation, as well as the feelings of the Southern whites; never fairly tried, and therefore, not yet to be justly condemned. Not one of those who condemn it, has been able, even in the light of subsequent events, to suggest a better method by which the liberty and civil rights of the freedmen and their descendants could have been protected. Its abandonment, as I have shown, leaves this liberty and these rights frankly without any guaranteed protection. All the education which philanthropy or the State could offer as a *substitute* for equality of rights, would be a poor exchange; there is no defensible reason why they should not go hand in hand, each encouraging and strengthening the other. The education which one can demand as a right is likely to do more good than the education for which one must sue as a favor.

The chief argument against Negro suffrage, the insistently proclaimed argument, worn threadbare in Congress, on the platform, in the pulpit, in the press, in poetry, in fiction, in impassioned rhetoric, is the reconstruction period. And yet the evils of that period were due far more to the venality and indifference of white men than to the incapacity of black voters. The revised Southern constitutions adopted under reconstruction reveal a higher statesmanship than any which preceded or have followed them, and prove that the freed voters could as easily have been led into the paths of civic righteousness as into those of misgovernment. Certain it is that under reconstruction the civil and political rights of all men were more secure in those States than they have ever been since. We will hear less of the evils of reconstruction, now that the bugaboo has served its purpose by disfranchising the Negro. It will be laid aside for a time while the nation discusses the political corruption of great cities; the scandalous conditions in Rhode Island; the evils attending reconstruction in the Philippines, and the scandals in the postoffice department—for none of which, by the way, is the Negro charged with any responsibility, and for none of which is the restriction of the suffrage a remedy seriously proposed. Rhode Island is indeed the only Northern State which has a property qualification for the franchise!

There are three tribunals to which the colored people may justly appeal for the protection of their rights: the United States Courts, Congress and public opinion. At present all three seem mainly indifferent to any question of human rights under the Constitution. Indeed, Congress and the Courts merely follow public opinion, seldom lead it. Congress never enacts a measure which is believed to oppose public opinion; —your Congressman keeps his ear to the ground. The high, serene atmosphere of the Courts is not impervious to its voice; they rarely enforce a law contrary to public opinion, even the Supreme Court being able, as Charles Sumner once put it, to find a reason for every decision it may wish to render; or, as experience has shown, a method to evade any question which it cannot decently decide in accordance with public opinion. The art of straddling is not confined to the political arena. The Southern situation has been well described by a colored editor in Richmond: "When we seek relief at the hands of Congress, we are informed that our plea involves a legal question, and we are referred to the Courts. When we appeal to the Courts, we are gravely told that the question is a political one, and that we must go to Congress. When Congress enacts remedial legislation, our enemies take it to the Supreme Court, which promptly declares it unconstitutional." The Negro might chase his rights round and round this circle until the end of time, without finding any relief.

Yet the Constitution is clear and unequivocal in its terms,

and no Supreme Court can indefinitely continue to construe it as meaning anything but what it says. This Court should be bombarded with suits until it makes some definite pronouncement, one way or the other, on the broad question of the constitutionality of the disfranchising Constitutions of the Southern States. The Negro and his friends will then have a clean-cut issue to take to the forum of public opinion, and a distinct ground upon which to demand legislation for the enforcement of the Federal Constitution. The case from Alabama was carried to the Supreme Court expressly to determine the constitutionality of the Alabama Constitution. The Court declared itself without jurisdiction, and in the same breath went into the merits of the case far enough to deny relief, without passing upon the real issue. Had it said, as it might with absolute justice and perfect propriety, that the Alabama Constitution is a bold and impudent violation of the Fifteenth Amendment, the purpose of the lawsuit would have been accomplished and a righteous cause vastly strengthened.

But public opinion cannot remain permanently indifferent to so vital a question. The agitation is already on. It is at present largely academic, but is slowly and resistlessly, forcing itself into politics, which is the medium through which republics settle such questions. It cannot much longer be contemptuously or indifferently elbowed aside. The South itself seems bent upon forcing the question to an issue, as, by its arrogant assumptions, it brought on the Civil War. From that section, too, there come now and then, side by side with tales of Southern outrage, excusing voices, which at the same time are accusing voices; which admit that the white South is dealing with the Negro unjustly and unwisely; that the Golden Rule has been forgotten; that the interests of white men alone have been taken into account, and that their true interests as well are being sacrificed. There is a silent white South, uneasy in conscience, darkened in counsel, groping for the light, and willing to do the right. They are as yet a feeble folk, their voices scarcely audible above the clamor of the mob. May their convictions ripen into wisdom, and may their numbers and their courage increase! If the class of Southern white men of whom Judge Jones of Alabama, is so noble a representative, are supported and encouraged by a righteous public opinion at the North, they may, in time, become the dominant white South, and we may then look for wisdom and justice in the place where, so far as the Negro is concerned, they now seem well-nigh strangers. But even these gentlemen will do well to bear in mind that so long as they discriminate in any way against the Negro's equality of right, so long do they set class against class and open the door to every sort of discrimination, there can be no middle ground between justice and injustice, between the citizen and the serf.

It is not likely that the North, upon the sober second thought, will permit the dearly-bought results of the Civil War to be nullified by any change in the Constitution. So long as the Fifteenth Amendment stands, the *rights* of colored citizens are ultimately secure. There were would-be despots in England after the granting of Magna Charta; but it outlived them all, and the liberties of the English people are secure. There was slavery in this land after the Declaration of Independence, yet the faces of those who love liberty have ever turned to that immortal document. So will the Constitution and its principles outlive the prejudices which would seek to overthrow it.

What colored men of the South can do to secure their citizenship to-day, or in the immediate future, is not very clear. Their utterances on political questions, unless they be to concede away the political rights of their race, or to soothe the consciences of white men by suggesting that the problem is insoluble except by some slow remedial process which will become effectual only in the distant future, are received with scant respect—could scarcely, indeed, be otherwise received, without a voting constituency to back them up,—and must be cautiously made, lest they meet an actively hostile reception. But there are many colored men at the North, where their civil and political rights in the main are respected. There every honest man has a vote, which he may freely cast, and which is reasonably sure to be fairly counted. When this race develops a sufficient power of combination, under adequate leadership,—and there are signs already that this time is near at hand,—the Northern vote can be wielded irresistibly for the defense of the rights of their Southern brethren.

In the meantime the Northern colored men have the right

of free speech, and they should never cease to demand their rights, to clamor for them, to guard them jealously, and insistently to invoke law and public sentiment to maintain them. He who would be free must learn to protect his freedom. Eternal vigilance is the price of liberty. He who would be respected must respect himself. The best friend of the Negro is he who would rather see, within the borders of this republic one million free citizens of that race, equal before the law, than ten million cringing serfs existing by a contemptuous sufferance. A race that is willing to survive upon any other terms is scarcely worthy of consideration.

The direct remedy for the disfranchisement of the Negro lies through political action. One scarcely sees the philosophy of distinguishing between a civil and a political right. But the Supreme Court has recognized this distinction and has designated Congress as the power to right a political wrong. The Fifteenth Amendment gives Congress power to enforce its provisions. The power would seem to be inherent in government itself; but anticipating that the enforcement of the Amendment might involve difficulty, they made the supererogatory declaration. Moreover, they went further, and passed laws by which they provided for such enforcement. These the Supreme Court has so far declared insufficient. It is for Congress to make more laws. It is for colored men and for white men who are not content to see the blood-bought results of the Civil War nullified, to urge and direct public opinion to the point where it will demand stringent legislation to enforce the Fourteenth and Fifteenth Amendments. This demand will rest in law, in morals and in true statesmanship; no difficulties attending it could be worse than the present ignoble attitude of the Nation toward its own laws and its own ideals—without courage to enforce them, without conscience to change them, the United States presents the spectacle of a Nation drifting aimlessly, so far as this vital, National problem is concerned, upon the sea of irresolution, toward the maelstrom of anarchy.

The right of Congress, under the Fourteenth Amendment, to reduce Southern representation can hardly be disputed. But Congress has a simpler and more direct method to accomplish the same end. It is the sole judge of the qualifications of its own members, and the sole judge of whether any member presenting his credentials has met those qualifications. It can refuse to seat any member who comes from a district where voters have been disfranchised; it can judge for itself whether this has been done, and there is no appeal from its decision.

If, when it has passed a law, any Court shall refuse to obey its behests, it can impeach the judges. If any president refuse to lend the executive arm of the government to the enforcement of the law, it can impeach the president. No such extreme measures are likely to be necessary for the enforcement of the Fourteenth and Fifteenth Amendments—and the Thirteenth, which is also threatened—but they are mentioned as showing that Congress is supreme; and Congress proceeds, the House directly, the Senate indirectly, from the people and is governed by public opinion. If the reduction of Southern representation were to be regarded in the light of a bargain by which the Fifteenth Amendment was surrendered, then it might prove fatal to liberty. If it be inflicted as a punishment and a warning, to be followed by more drastic measures if not sufficient, it would serve a useful purpose. The Fifteenth Amendment declares that the right to vote *shall not* be denied or abridged on account of color; and any measure adopted by Congress should look to that end. Only as the power to injure the Negro in Congress is reduced thereby, would a reduction of representation protect the Negro; without other measures it would still leave him in the hands of the Southern whites, who could safely be trusted to make him pay for their humiliation.

Finally, there is, somewhere in the Universe a "Power that works for righteousness," and that leads men to do justice to one another. To this power, working upon the hearts and consciences of men, the Negro can always appeal. He has the right upon his side, and in the end the right will prevail. The Negro will, in time, attain to full manhood and citizenship throughout the United States. No better guaranty of this is needed than a comparison of his present with his past. Toward this he must do his part, as lies within his power and his opportunity. But it will be, after all, largely a white man's conflict, fought out in the forum of the public conscience. The Negro, though eager enough when opportunity offered, had comparatively little to do with the abolition of slavery, which was a vastly more formidable task than will be the enforcement of the Fifteenth Amendment.

The Negro Problem, 1903

The Courts and the Negro

THE FUNCTION of courts in the organization of modern society is to protect rights,—to pass upon disputes between man and man or between the individual and the State; and then, by their mandate, to set in motion the arm of the executive to prevent or punish a wrong or to enforce a right. Obviously if this great power be not rightly exercised, if it be swayed by prejudice or class interest, justice will not be done.

The rights of citizens of the United States are embodied in constitutions and statutes. But these, at best, are mere declarations of principles, which, in the complex and shifting nature of society, it is left for courts to apply to the particular instance. And in so doing courts often give to constitutions and statutes constructions which have the effect of greatly enlarging or narrowing their scope and sometimes, as I shall show, of even altering the whole course of government on matters of the most vital consequence. If public opinion acquiesce in these interpretations, they remain the law; if not, the legislature assumes to correct them by new statute, and the process is thus begun all over again. Nowhere, in the history of our jurisprudence, has this power of courts been more strongly exerted than in the matter of Negro rights, and nowhere has it been more swayed by prejudice and class interest. We are taught, and properly taught, to hold our courts in high respect. As a rule this is not difficult. But courts are made up of human beings. Under wigs and gowns and titles and deferential formulas, judges are simply men, and subject, as other men, to every human frailty. I shall endeavor to trace, of course in an inadequate and sketchy way and subject to correction by those better informed in the principles and practice of the law and the progress of our jurisprudence, the history of Negro rights as affected by the decisions of the Supreme Court of the United States. This can be done most effectively by reference to a few leading cases. For the Court rarely reverses itself, and has followed the prevailing public opinion so closely, in its interpretation of the Constitution and laws applying to the Negro, that its decisions have seldom been disturbed by legislative enactment.

The historic antebellum cause was, of course, the Dred Scott decision. Dred Scott was returned to slavery, and citizenship of the United States was denied to Negroes, thus repealing so far as it applied to them, Article 4 Section 2 of the Constitution: "The citizens of each State shall be entitled to all privileges and immunities of citizens of the several States." Of this decision the venerable Justice Harlan said, in his dissenting opinion in the Civil Rights Cases (109 U.S.): "It is said that the case of Dred Scott vs. Sandford overruled the action of two generations, virtually inserted a new clause in the Constitution, changed its character, and made a new departure in the workings of the federal government." Thus vast and portentous is the power resting in the hands of nine men who hold their office for life and are directly responsible to no one. This decision was purely a political one and deserved the outburst of indignation which greeted it and did so much to bring about the ultimate abolition of slavery.

How different was the attitude of Lord Mansfield in the parallel English case! A Negro who had been in England was sought to be returned to a British colony as a slave. He claimed his freedom. Lord Mansfield might have made a similar ruling to that of the Supreme Court, with much better warrant, for there was no written constitution to restrain him, and by custom Negro slaves had often been brought into England by their masters and returned to the colonies. But the English jurist seized his opportunity to recognize a principle which enlarged human rights. The Supreme Court chose to give a narrow and strained interpretation of the law and thereby restrict human rights.

I think it is exceedingly unfortunate for the Negro that the seat of government should be located in the South. Inevitably the administration, the courts, the whole machinery of government takes its tone from its environment. The influence of social life upon government is well known—it has always been the power behind the throne. The fate of nations has more often been settled in clubs and parlors than in courts and parliaments. The influence of Southern customs and Southern caste which is and always has been enthroned at Washington, has colored the attitude of presidents and congressmen and judges toward the Negro. To men living in a community where by law all men are denied the suffrage, it does not seem such an enormity that the Negro elsewhere should be left without it. To men living in a community where service and courtesy in public places is in large measure denied the Negro, there seems no particular enormity in separate car laws and similar iniquities. Had the capital of this nation been left at Philadelphia or established in Boston or New York, the Negro would long since, in my opinion, have had his rights enlarged and recognized. Justice Mansfield lived in a free country. Justice Taney lived in Maryland, and the Supreme Court sat in Washington.

The Dred Scott decision, with all its implications, remained the law until it was overturned by revolution, and the effort made to fix, by the Constitution, the rights of the colored race to equal citizenship. Certainly the language of the amendments is plain enough to bear that interpretation; and certainly that was the intent of those who drew them and promoted their passage. But they were, after all, mere statements of principles, not difficult of application in the North, but involving social revolution in the South. It was necessary to embody them in federal and state statutes, and then, in order to render them effective, to enforce their application.

The Thirteenth Amendment abolished slavery and by implication extended to the former slaves the rights as well as the status of free men. The Fourteenth Amendment extended citizenship of the United States in terms to all persons born or naturalized in the country and subject to its jurisdiction; forbade the making or enforcement of any law which abridged the privileges or immunities of citizens or which should deprive any person of life, liberty or property without due process of law or deny to any person within its jurisdiction the equal protection of the laws.

One of the earliest federal statutes intended to carry into effect the principles of the Thirteenth and Fourteenth Amendments was the Civil Rights bill of 1866, by which were fixed the rights of Negroes in the courts, their right to contract, to sue, to be parties, to testify, and their full and equal benefit of all laws and proceedings for the security of persons and property as is enjoyed by white citizens. In general these rights have been respected, so far as statutes and Supreme Court decisions are concerned, although the right to contract in marriage, and certain other rights, have been limited under the principle of police power in the State.

In the case of Virginia vs. Rives, 100 U.S. 313 (1879) it was held by the Supreme Court:

> The Fourteenth Amendment was ordained to secure equal rights to all persons, and extends its protection to races and classes, and prohibits any state legislation which has the effect of denying to any race or class, or to any individual, the equal protection of the laws. The plain object of this amendment, as well as of the statutes enacted prior thereto, was to place the negro race, with respect to its civil rights, upon the same level with the white. They made the rights and responsibilities, civil and criminal, of the two races exactly the same.

Such a statement would seem both comprehensive and conclusive. But a moment of reflection will show that it is neither. What constitutes race? When are rights equal or unequal? What is a denial of the equal protection of the laws? What are civil rights? What are civil and criminal responsibilities, and when are they the same, and exactly the same?

The answers of the Supreme Court to these questions, as they have come up, generally in cases based on the Fourteenth Amendment, have fixed, for the present at least, the legal status of colored citizens.

When it became clear that in the former slave states civil rights, as Charles Sumner and the men of his school defined them, were to be denied the Negro in spite of the Fourteenth Amendment, the Civil Rights Act of 1875 was enacted. It was not long before numerous cases involving this law were presented to the Supreme Court, and in 1883 (109 U.S.) five cases were considered together. By the opinion of the Court, sections 1 and 2 of the civil rights act were held unconstitutional, section 1 giving full and equal enjoyment to all citizens of the accommodations of inns, public conveyances and places of public amusement, and section 2 providing a penalty. It was held that these things were subject to regulation by the State only and that Congress had no power to legislate except as to State action which is subversive of the fundamental rights specified in the amendment, and that therefore the Fourteenth Amendment had no application. In this case Justices Bradley and Harlan filed dissenting opinions. Justice Harlan based his argument upon Article IV., Section 2, of the Constitution, heretofore quoted, and maintained that no State could deny privileges and immunities to colored persons on the ground that they were extended only to whites, and that the majority opinion, to the effect that the nation, in the absence of State laws, adverse to such rights and privileges, might not interfere for their protection and security, is a denial to Congress of the power by appropriate legislation to enforce one of the provisions of the Fifteenth Amendment. And quoting what I have already said in reference to the effect of the Dred Scott decision in changing the character of the Constitution, he expressed the fear that the decision in the Civil Rights Cases would mark the opening of an era in which the rights to freedom and American citizenship cannot receive from the nation efficient protection. These were prophetic words.

In the course of the opinion of the Court, Justice Bradley said, very truly:

> When a man has emerged from slavery and by the aid of beneficent legislation has shaken off the inseparable concomitants of that state, there must be some stage in the progress of his elevation when he takes the rank of a mere citizen, and ceases to be the special favorite of the law, and when his rights as a citizen or a man are to be protected in the ordinary modes by which other men's rights are protected.

There is nothing to indicate, except the well known facts of the situation, whether or not this perfectly correct statement was made with jocular intent. Certainly there is such a stage, but it was obvious then that the Negro had not yet reached it. And Justice Harlan further says: "The opinion proceeds upon grounds entirely too narrow and artificial. I cannot resist the conclusion that the substance and spirit of the recent amendments to the Constitution have been sacrificed to a subtle and ingenious verbal criticism."

In the Civil Rights decision the Court did not hold that the things complained of were not deprivations of rights, but merely that they were not attributable to any action of the State. For it is the *State* which is prohibited by the Fourteenth Amendment from denying to any person within its jurisdiction the equal protection of the laws, and this amendment has been held not violated until the denial of the rights has some State sanction or authority. I do not recall whether this argument was made or not, but why would it not have been a good one, in that case, and in cases which are made under civil rights laws of the Northern States? Railroad companies are creatures of the State. Whatever powers they exercise are derived from the State and to that extent they are the agents of the State, and the State is responsible for their acts. Similar reasoning would apply to inns and common carriers, labor unions and other bodies, either chartered by the State or enjoying special benefits by statute or by common law.

But to my mind the most important and far reaching decision of the Supreme Court upon the question of civil rights is that in the case of Plessy vs. Ferguson, a case which came from Louisiana in 1895. (163 U.S., 537.) The opinion is a clear and definite approval of the recognition by State laws, of color distinctions, something which had theretofore been avoided in civil rights cases. It establishes racial caste in the United States as firmly as though it were established by act of Congress. To the opinion Mr. Justice Harlan dissented with his usual vigor, and Justice Brewer did not hear the argument or participate in the decision. The Court cited the passage quoted by me from a former decision:

> The Fourteenth Amendment was ordained to secure equal rights to all persons, and extends its protection to races and classes, and prohibits any State legislation which has the effect of denying to any race or class, or to any individual, the equal protection of the laws, and made the rights of the two races exactly the same.

And then the Court stabbed in the back, and to death, this ideal presentment of rights, in the following language, and threw its bleeding corpse to the Negro,—the comprehensive Negro, black, brown, yellow and white—the plaintiff in that case, which involved the separate car law of Louisiana, was seven-eighths white and showed no sign of the darker blood—as that court's definition of his civil status:

> But in the nature of things it [the Fourteenth Amendment] could not have been intended to abolish distinctions based upon color or to enforce social, as distinguished from political, equality, or a commingling of the two races upon terms unsatisfactory to either. If the two races are to meet on terms of social equality, it must be the result of natural affinities, a mutual appreciation of each other's merits and a voluntary consent of individuals. When the government, therefore, has secured for each of its citizens equal rights before the law and equal opportunities for improvement and progress, it has accomplished the end for which it was organized, and performed all the functions respecting social advantages with which it is endowed. Legislation is powerless to eradicate racial instincts or to abolish distinctions based upon physical differences. If the civil and political rights of both races be equal, one cannot be inferior to the other civilly or politically. If one race be inferior to the other socially, the Constitution of the United States cannot put them upon the same plane.
>
> A statute which implies merely a legal distinction between the white and colored races—a distinction which is founded in the color of the two races and which must always exist so long as men are distinguished from the other race by color—has no tendency to destroy the legal equality of the two races or reestablish a state of involuntary servitude.

When it was suggested in the argument that to sustain such discriminating laws might justify separate cars for people with red hair or aliens, or require people to walk on different sides of the street, or require colored men's houses to be in separate blocks, the Court in the opinion, said that such regulations must be reasonable. And the Court held: "In determining the question of reasonableness, it is at liberty to act with reference to the usages, customs and traditions of the people, with a view to the promotion of their comfort and the preservation of the public peace and good order."

It is obvious where this leaves the Negro, and it is difficult to see where the 14th Amendment has any application.

The opinion in Plessy vs. Ferguson is, to my mind, as epoch making as the Dred Scott decision. Unfortunately, it applies to a class of rights which do not make to the heart and conscience of the nation the same direct appeal as was made by slavery, and has not been nor is it likely to produce any such revulsion of feeling.

Another extract from the opinion makes one wonder whether the Court was merely playing with the subject:

> We consider the underlying failure of the plaintiff's argument to consist in the assumption that the enforced separation of the races stamps the colored race with the badge of inferiority. If this be so, it is not by reason of anything found in the act itself, but solely because the colored race chooses to put that construction upon it.

I presume that hanging might be pleasant if a man could only convince himself that it would not be painful, nor disgraceful, nor terminate his earthly career. It is perhaps true that some Negroes—I suspect very few people of mixed blood—have seemed to accept this reasoning. But I have never been able to see how a self-respecting colored man can approve of any discriminating legislation. To do so is to condone his own degradation, and accept an inferior citizenship. If discrimination must of necessity be submitted to, it should meet no better reception than silence. Protest were better still.

I need not suggest the far-reaching effect of this decision. The colored people of the South have been, it would seem, as completely segregated as the business of daily life will permit. Perhaps the lowest depths of race hatred have not been sounded, but a more humiliating, insulting and degrading system is hardly conceivable under even a nominally free government. And under Plessy vs. Ferguson there is no reason why any Northern State may not reproduce in its own borders the conditions in Alabama and Georgia. And it may be that the Negro and his friends will have to exert themselves to save his rights at the North.

The latest, and since Plessy vs. Ferguson, the most serious blow delivered by the Supreme Court to Negro rights—it was in fact a restriction of the rights of white men, and involved the Negro only indirectly—is that of Berea College vs. Kentucky (1908). A recent statute of Kentucky forbade the receiving of both white and Negro races as pupils for instruction in any institution of learning. (Ky. Acts 1904, ch. 85, page 181.) Berea College was indicted and fined for a violation of this statute. The case was appealed to the Kentucky Court of Appeals. (123 Ky. 209, 94 S.W. 623.) There were other sections of the statute, some of which the court found unconstitutional; but it affirmed the judgment below, sustaining the constitutionality of the section upon which it was based, the principal ground of the decision being that the original charter of Berea College had been conditioned upon the right of the legislature to revoke or alter it, and that the statute of Kentucky was in effect an amendment of the charter which did not defeat or substantially impair the object of the grant, the object of the grant being "to give instruction to all who might apply, and promote the cause of Christ." The Supreme Court of the United States accepted the decision of the Kentucky Court on the ground that the judgment being a non-federal ground, fairly construed, sustained the decision, and that the decision by a State court of the extent and limitation of the powers conferred by the State upon one of its own corporations is of a purely local nature. The Court did not consider the statute as a whole, but only the section above referred to.

Justice Harlan, dissenting, said:

> In my judgment the Court should directly meet and decide the broad question presented by the section. It should adjudge whether the statute, as a whole, is or is not unconstitutional, in that it makes it a crime against the state to maintain or operate a private institution of learning where white and black pupils are received, at the same time, for instruction. . . . I am of opinion that in its essential parts, the statute is an arbitrary invasion of the rights of liberty and property guaranteed by

the Fourteenth Amendment against hostile state action, and is, therefore, void.

Since this decision Berea College, the attitude of which in the matter was scarcely heroic, though perhaps justified by the law of self-preservation, has set aside certain moneys and promoted the collection of a fund to establish a school which should provide for colored students the advantages formerly offered by Berea College, and since then the Jim Crow annex of that institution has been dodging injunctions and protests, seeking a place to lay its woolly head and to rest its tired feet. All honor to Justice Harlan. There is no more inspiring spectacle than this grand old man, ever steadfast to right and justice, fighting unwearyingly, never yielding, and almost always defeated, for the principles which were so dearly bought by the Civil War. I know nothing with which to compare it except the staunchness of the *New York Evening Post* and the *Independent*, which, with a few individuals, amid all the ruck of concession and compromise have kept alight the torch of liberty against the day when in the language of the decision in the Civil Rights Cases, the Negro shall "take the rank of a mere citizen . . . and when his rights as a citizen or a man are to be protected in the ordinary modes by which other men's rights are protected"—the time when the colored race shall have gained sufficient strength to protect itself, or until the democratic spirit now so nearly dead in the nation shall have become again a vivifying flame. I hope they may live to see the day.

THE RIGHT TO VOTE.

The Fifteenth Amendment provided that "the right of citizens of the United States to vote shall not be denied or abridged by the United States, on account of race, color or previous condition of servitude," and Congress was given power in the Amendment to enforce by appropriate legislation its provisions.

The right of colored men to vote on equal terms with white men as provided by the Fifteenth Amendment, has never been denied in terms by any State, but in effect disfranchisement is general throughout the South. A few individuals are permitted to vote, but the race is disfranchised; and the race, and not the individual, is the social unit. It was easily within the power of the government to strangle the movement for disfranchisement at its birth. It would have been as easy for the Department of Justice to work up a case involving disfranchisement, as it was to work up the recent cases against peonage, and to have them taken to the Supreme Court in the ordinary course. And the Court might have held, as it did in cases involving the right to sit on juries, that the action of State officers charged with the execution of the law was as much a violation of the Constitution as an act of the legislature. But on the contrary, it took the narrow view, and held that so long as the State did not discriminate in terms against Negroes as such, there was no violation of the constitutional provision,—though in effect it might disfranchise the race.

In the case of Giles vs. Harris (189 U.S. 475), where a Negro was refused the right to register, the Court did not find that a wrong had not been done, but, assuming, for the sake of the argument that the facts claimed were true and that the Constitution had been disregarded, declared itself impotent to enforce any mandate it might make in that behalf and referred the plaintiff to Congress for relief. To this decision Justices Brewer, Brown and Harlan dissented. Other cases have been before the Court, but it has steadily refused to face the main issue and has entrenched itself behind a hedge of technicalities. It will require, in all probability, some such extreme measure as that proposed, the other day, in Maryland, to force a decision; and there are those who have so little confidence in the majority of the Court as at present constituted, where similar questions are involved, as to be glad the question was not put up to them until there is some greater assurance of an effective public demand to back up a right decision. There is little more that the States can do, within the limit of the Fourteenth Amendment as now construed, to further defeat Negro rights. For the Supreme Court to repeal, by judicial construction, the uniform application of the Fourteenth and Fifteenth Amendments, would be a calamity indeed.

Speech, c. 1908

Post-Bellum—Pre-Harlem

My first book, *The Conjure Woman*, was published by the Houghton Mifflin Company in 1899. It was not, strictly speaking, a novel, though it has been so called, but a collection of short stories in Negro dialect, put in the mouth of an old Negro gardener, and related by him in each instance to the same audience, which consisted of the Northern lady and gentleman who employed him. They are naive and simple stories, dealing with alleged incidents of chattel slavery, as the old man had known it and as I had heard of it, and centering around the professional activities of old Aunt Peggy, the plantation conjure woman, and others of that ilk.

In every instance Julius had an axe to grind, for himself or his church, or some member of his family, or a white friend. The introductions to the stories, which were written in the best English I could command, developed the characters of Julius's employers and his own, and the wind-up of each story reveals the old man's ulterior purpose, which, as a general thing, is accomplished.

Most of the stories in *The Conjure Woman* had appeared in the *Atlantic Monthly* from time to time, the first story, "The Goophered Grapevine," in the issue of August, 1887, and one of them, "The Conjurer's Revenge," in the *Overland Monthly*. Two of them were first printed in the bound volume.

After the book had been accepted for publication, a friend of mine, the late Judge Madison W. Beacom, of Cleveland, a charter member of the Rowfant Club, suggested to the publishers a limited edition, which appeared in advance of the trade edition in an issue of one hundred and fifty numbered copies and was subscribed for almost entirely by members of the Rowfant Club and of the Cleveland bar. It was printed by the Riverside Press on large hand-made linen paper, bound in yellow buckram, with the name on the back in black letters on a white label, a very handsome and dignified volume. The trade edition was bound in brown cloth and on the front was a picture of a white-haired old Negro, flanked on either side by a long-eared rabbit. The dust-jacket bore the same illustration.

The name of the story teller, "Uncle" Julius, and the locale of the stories, as well as the cover design, were suggestive of Mr. Harris's Uncle Remus, but the tales are entirely different. They are sometimes referred to as folk tales, but while they employ much of the universal machinery of wonder stories, especially the metamorphosis, with one exception, that of the first story, "The Goophered Grapevine," of which the norm was a folk tale, the stories are the fruit of my own imagination, in which respect they differ from the Uncle Remus stories which are avowedly folk tales.

Several subsequent editions of *The Conjure Woman* were brought out; just how many copies were sold altogether I have never informed myself, but not enough for the royalties to make me unduly rich, and in 1929, just thirty years after the first appearance of the book, a new edition was issued by Houghton Mifflin Company. It was printed from the original plates, with the very handsome title page of the limited edition, an attractive new cover in black and red, and a very flattering foreword by Colonel Joel Spingarn.

Most of my books are out of print, but I have been told that it is quite unusual for a volume of short stories which is not one of the accepted modern classics to remain on sale for so long a time.

At the time when I first broke into print seriously, no American colored writer had ever secured critical recognition except Paul Laurence Dunbar, who had won his laurels as a poet. Phillis Wheatley, a Colonial poet, had gained recognition largely because she was a slave and born in Africa, but the short story, or the novel of life and manners, had not been attempted by any one of that group.

There had been many novels dealing with slavery and the Negro. Harriet Beecher Stowe, especially in *Uncle Tom's Cabin*, had covered practically the whole subject of slavery and race admixture. George W. Cable had dwelt upon the romantic and some of the tragic features of racial contacts in Louisiana, and Judge Albion W. Tourgée, in what was one of the best sellers of his day, *A Fool's Errand*, and in his

Bricks Without Straw, had dealt with the problems of reconstruction.

Thomas Dixon was writing the Negro down industriously and with marked popular success. Thomas Nelson Page was disguising the harshness of slavery under the mask of sentiment. The trend of public sentiment at the moment was distinctly away from the Negro. He had not developed any real political or business standing; socially he was outcast. His musical and stage successes were still for the most part unmade, and on the whole he was a small frog in a large pond, and there was a feeling of pessimism in regard to his future.

Publishers are human, and of course influenced by the opinions of their public. The firm of Houghton Mifflin, however, was unique in some respects. One of the active members of the firm was Francis J. Garrison, son of William Lloyd Garrison, from whom he had inherited his father's hatred of slavery and friendliness to the Negro. His partner, George H. Mifflin, was a liberal and generous gentleman trained in the best New England tradition. They were both friendly to my literary aspirations and became my personal friends.

But the member of their staff who was of most assistance to me in publishing my first book was Walter Hines Page, later ambassador to England under President Wilson, and at that time editor of the *Atlantic Monthly*, as well as literary adviser for the publishing house, himself a liberalized Southerner, who derived from the same part of the South where the stories in *The Conjure Woman* are located, and where I passed my adolescent years. He was a graduate of Macon College, a fellow of Johns Hopkins University, had been attached to the staff of the *Forum* and the *New York Evening Post*, and was as broad-minded a Southerner as it was ever my good fortune to meet.

Three of the *Atlantic* editors wrote novels dealing with race problems—William Dean Howells in *An Imperative Duty*, Bliss Perry in *The Plated City*, and Mr. Page in *The Autobiography of Nicholas Worth.*

The first of my conjure stories had been accepted for the *Atlantic* by Thomas Bailey Aldrich, the genial auburn-haired poet who at that time presided over the editorial desk. My relations with him, for the short time they lasted, were most cordial and friendly.

Later on I submitted to Mr. Page several stories of post-war life among the colored people which the *Atlantic* published, and still later the manuscript of a novel. The novel was rejected, and was subsequently rewritten and published by Houghton Mifflin under the title of *The House Behind the Cedars.* Mr. Page, who had read the manuscript, softened its rejection by the suggestion that perhaps a collection of the conjure stories might be undertaken by the firm with a better prospect of success. I was in the hands of my friends, and submitted the collection. After some omissions and additions, all at the advice of Mr. Page, the book was accepted and announced as *The Conjure Woman*, in 1899, and I enjoyed all the delights of proof-reading and the other pleasant emotions attending the publication of a first book. Mr. Page, Mr. Garrison and Mr. Mifflin vied with each other in helping to make our joint venture a literary and financial success.

The book was favorably reviewed by literary critics. If I may be pardoned one quotation, William Dean Howells, always the friend of the aspiring author, in an article published in the *Atlantic Monthly* for May, 1900, wrote:

> The stories of *The Conjure Woman* have a wild, indigenous poetry, the creation of sincere and original imagination, which is imparted with a tender humorousness and a very artistic reticence. As far as his race is concerned, or his sixteenth part of a race, it does not greatly matter whether Mr. Chesnutt invented their motives, or found them, as he feigns, among his distant cousins of the Southern cabins. In either case the wonder of their beauty is the same, and whatever is primitive and sylvan or campestral in the reader's heart is touched by the spells thrown on the simple black lives in these enchanting tales. Character, the most precious thing in fiction, is faithfully portrayed.

Imagine the thrill with which a new author would read such an encomium from such a source!

From the publisher's standpoint, the book proved a modest success. This was by no means a foregone conclusion, even assuming its literary merit and the publisher's imprint, for reasons which I shall try to make clear.

I have been referred to as the "first Negro novelist," meaning, of course, in the United States; Pushkin in Russia and the two Dumas in France had produced a large body of popular fiction. At that time a literary work by an American of acknowledged color was a doubtful experiment, both for the writer and for the publisher, entirely apart from its intrinsic merit. Indeed, my race was never mentioned by the publishers in announcing or advertising the book. From my own viewpoint it was a personal matter. It never occurred to me to claim any merit because of it, and I have always resented the denial of anything on account of it. My colored friends, however, with a very natural and laudable zeal for the race, with which I found no fault, saw to it that the fact was not overlooked, and I have before me a copy of a letter written by one of them to the editor of the *Atlanta Constitution*, which had published a favorable review of the book, accompanied by my portrait, chiding him because the reviewer had not referred to my color.

A woman critic of Jackson, Mississippi, questioning what she called the rumor as to my race, added, "Some people claim that Alexander Dumas, author of *The Count of Monte Cristo* and *The Three Musketeers*, was a colored man. This is obviously untrue, because no Negro could possibly have written these books"—a pontifical announcement which would seem to settle the question definitely, despite the historical evidence to the contrary.

While *The Conjure Woman* was in the press, the *Atlantic* published a short story of mine called "The Wife of His Youth" which attracted wide attention. James MacArthur, at that time connected with the *Critic*, later with *Harper's*, in talking one day with Mr. Page, learned of my race and requested leave to mention it as a matter of interest to the literary public. Mr. Page demurred at first on the ground that such an announcement might be harmful to the success of my forthcoming book, but finally consented, and Mr. MacArthur mentioned the fact in the *Critic*, referring to me as a "mulatto."

As a matter of fact, substantially all of my writings, with the exception of *The Conjure Woman*, have dealt with the problems of people of mixed blood, which, while in the main the same as those of the true Negro, are in some instances and in some respects much more complex and difficult of treatment, in fiction as in life.

I have lived to see, after twenty years or more, a marked change in the attitude of publishers and the reading public in regard to the Negro in fiction. The development of Harlem, with its large colored population in all shades, from ivory to ebony, of all degrees of culture, from doctors of philosophy to the lowest grade of illiteracy; its various origins, North American, South American, West Indian and African; its morals ranging from the highest to the most debased; with the vivid life of its cabarets, dance halls, and theatres; with its ambitious business and professional men, its actors, singers, novelists and poets, its aspirations and demands for equality—without which any people would merit only contempt—presented a new field for literary exploration which of recent years has been cultivated assiduously.

One of the first of the New York writers to appreciate the possibilities of Harlem for literary purposes was Carl Van Vechten, whose novel *Nigger Heaven* was rather severely criticized by some of the colored intellectuals as a libel on the race, while others of them praised it highly. I was prejudiced in its favor for reasons which those who have read the book will understand. I found it a vivid and interesting story which presented some new and better types of Negroes and treated them sympathetically.

The Negro novel, whether written by white or colored authors, has gone so much farther now in the respects in which it was criticized that *Nigger Heaven*, in comparison with some of these later productions, would be almost as mild as a Sunday School tract compared to *The Adventures of Fanny Hill.* Several of these novels, by white and colored authors alike, reveal such an intimate and meticulous familiarity with the baser aspects of Negro life, North and South, that one is inclined to wonder how and from what social sub-sewers they gathered their information. With the exception of one or two of the earlier ones, the heroine of the novel is never chaste, though for the matter of that few post-Victorian heroines are, and most of the male characters are likewise weaklings or worse.

I have in mind a recent novel, brilliantly written by a gifted black author, in which, to my memory, there is not a single decent character, male or female. These books are written primarily for white readers, as it is extremely doubtful whether a novel, however good, could succeed financially on its sales to colored readers alone. But it seems to me that a body of twelve million people, struggling upward slowly but surely from a lowly estate, must present all along the line of its advancement many situations full of dramatic interest, ranging from farce to tragedy, with many admirable types worthy of delineation.

Caste, a principal motive of fiction from Richardson down through the Victorian epoch, has pretty well vanished among white Americans. Between the whites and the Negroes it is acute, and is bound to develop an increasingly difficult complexity, while among the colored people themselves it is just beginning to appear.

Negro writers no longer have any difficulty in finding publishers. Their race is no longer a detriment but a good selling point, and publishers are seeking their books, sometimes, I am inclined to think, with less regard for quality than in the case of white writers. To date, colored writers have felt restricted for subjects to their own particular group, but there is every reason to hope that in the future, with proper encouragement, they will make an increasingly valuable contribution to literature, and perhaps produce chronicles of life comparable to those of Dostoievsky, Dumas, Dickens or Balzac.

The Colophon, February 1931

CHRONOLOGY

NOTE ON THE TEXTS

NOTES

Chronology

1858 Born Charles Waddell Chesnutt on June 20 in Cleveland, Ohio, the first child of Ann Maria (Sampson) Chesnutt and Andrew Jackson Chesnutt. (Both parents are from Fayetteville, North Carolina, and were among the 465 free blacks recorded as living there by the 1850 U.S. census. Mother, b. 1832, is the daughter of Chloe Sampson, of mixed race, and possibly Henry E. Sampson, a white slaveholder. Father, b. 1833, is the son of Anna M. Chesnutt, of mixed race, and probably Waddell Cade, a white landowner in Fayetteville. Parents left North Carolina in 1856 with small group of free blacks who traveled north by wagon train and were married in Cleveland on July 26, 1857.) Father works as driver-conductor for horse-car line. Soon after Chesnutt's birth, family moves to Oberlin, Ohio, where father works as a wheelwright's assistant.

1860 Brother Lewis born January 16 in Oberlin. Family returns to Cleveland and father resumes working as a horse-car driver.

1861–65 Brother Andrew born. Sister is born and dies in infancy. Father serves as teamster with the Union army.

1866 Family moves to Fayetteville, where father opens grocery store on Gillespie Street with support from Waddell Cade.

1866–70 Sisters Clara and Mary are born.

1867 Chesnutt begins attending Howard School, public school for black children built with Freedmen's Bureau funds on land purchased by his father and six other African-American men.

1868–70 Father is elected county justice of the peace and commissioner on the Republican ticket and serves until Democrats win elections in 1870.

1871 Sister Lillian born. Mother dies, and her first cousin, Mary Ochiltree, moves in with family to care for younger children. (She will later marry Chesnutt's father, and they will have several children.)

1872 Father's grocery store fails, and family moves to farm outside of Fayetteville. Chesnutt becomes pupil-teacher at Howard School under principal Robert Harris.

1873–76 Becomes assistant in 1873 to Cicero Harris, principal of the Peabody School in Charlotte, North Carolina, and Robert Harris's brother. Spends summers teaching in rural schools in North and South Carolina. Begins writing journal (will keep it intermittently through 1882). Studies Latin, German, algebra, and history on his own, and reads Byron, Cowper, Burns, Dickens, and Stowe's *Uncle Tom's Cabin*. Starts learning shorthand and to play the organ. Sends money to his father to help support family.

1877 Becomes assistant principal of the State Colored Normal School established at Fayetteville to train African-American schoolteachers.

1878 Marries Susan W. Perry, age 19, a teacher at the Howard School and the daughter of Edwin Perry, proprietor of the barber shop in the Fayetteville Hotel, on June 6.

1879 Daughter Ethel born in April. Visits Washington, D.C., during summer in unsuccessful attempt to find job as a stenographer.

1880 Reads Albion Tourgée's novel *A Fool's Errand*. Becomes friends with J. W. Davis, minister of the Fayetteville A.M.E. Zion Church, and has extensive conversations with George Haigh, a white bookseller. Declines Republican nomination for town commissioner, possibly to avoid repercussions against the Normal School. Studies rhetoric and takes French and German lessons from Emil Neufeld, a German Jewish immigrant; reads Goethe's *Faust*. Continues to study stenography and records speech by Frederick Douglass for the *Raleigh Sentinel* in October. Becomes principal of the Normal School following the death of Robert Harris. Daughter Helen born in December. Family moves into its own home.

1881–82 Becomes organist, choirmaster, and Sunday school superintendent at Fayetteville A.M.E. Zion Church. Reads

Molière's *George Dandin*, Thackeray's *Vanity Fair*, and Shakespeare. Studies Greek. Writes satiric verse "A Perplexed Nigger." Visits New York and Cleveland in summer of 1882.

1883 Resigns as principal of the Normal School in May. Moves to New York City, where he works as a reporter for the Dow, Jones and Company news agency and writes column of Wall Street news for the *New York Mail and Express*. Son Edwin is born in Fayetteville in September. Leaves New York in November and moves to Cleveland, where he works in the accounting department of the Nickel Plate Railroad Company.

1884 Rents house on Wilcutt Avenue in April and brings wife and children to Cleveland. (Family later moves to house on Ashland Avenue.)

1885 Transfers to legal department of Nickel Plate Railroad, where he works as a stenographer. Begins studying law with company counsel Samuel Williamson, a former judge of the county common pleas court. Sells short story "Uncle Peter's House" to the S. S. McClure syndicate, and it is published in the *Cleveland News and Herald* in December 1885. (Will sell seven other stories to the McClure syndicate that appear in newspapers, 1886–88.)

1886 Begins publishing stories in *Family Fiction*. Family moves to house on Florence Street.

1887 Passes Ohio bar examination with the highest grade in his group. Works at law firm of Henderson, Kline, and Tolles as a stenographer. Begins publishing sketches and anecdotes in humor magazines *Tid-Bits* ("A Soulless Corporation") and *Puck*. "The Goophered Grapevine" appears in the August *Atlantic Monthly* (the first fiction by an African-American to be published there). Chesnutts become members of the Cleveland Social Circle, an exclusive social club of "better-educated people of color."

1888 "Po' Sandy" published in May *Atlantic Monthly*. Builds successful business as a court reporter but is unable to find clients for law practice. Sister Lillian comes to live with family and help with stenography work.

1889 Begins correspondence with George Washington Cable and participates in his "Open Letter Club," forum for circulating letters and essays on racial questions. Visits Cable in Northampton, Massachusetts. Declines offer to become Cable's secretary. Leaves Henderson, Kline, and Tolles and sets up his own stenographic office. Family moves into newly built house at 64 Brenton Street and begins attending Emmanuel Episcopal Church. Publishes essay "What Is a White Man?" (New York *Independent*, May 30) and short stories "The Conjurer's Revenge" (*Overland Monthly*, June), "Dave's Neckliss" (*Atlantic Monthly*, October), and "The Sheriff's Children" (*Independent*, November 7) . Writes "Rena Walden," story that later becomes novel *The House Behind the Cedars.*

1890 Daughter Dorothy born in December.

1891 Publishes essay "A Multitude of Counselors" in the *Independent*, April 2. Proposal for collection of stories is rejected by Houghton, Mifflin.

1893 "A Deep Sleeper" published in magazine *Two Tales* in March. Visits Chicago World's Fair. Declines to invest $2,500 in Albion Tourgée's proposed journal *The National Citizen.*

1896 Visits Paris and travels through England in late summer.

1897 Walter Hines Page, editor of *Atlantic Monthly* and an editor at Houghton, Mifflin, accepts "The Wife of His Youth" (published July 1898) and "The March of Progress" (eventually published in *Century*, January 1901). Houghton, Mifflin rejects novel *Mandy Oxendine* (published in 1997). Daughters Ethel and Helen enter Smith College in Northampton, Massachusetts. At Page's request, Chesnutt sends him copies of 20 published and unpublished stories. Visits Boston and meets Page in the fall.

1898 Novel "A Business Career" rejected by Houghton, Mifflin. After Page proposes publishing a collection of conjure tales, Chesnutt sends him six new stories in May.

1899 *The Conjure Woman* published by Houghton, Mifflin in March. Chesnutt begins giving public lectures and readings. Visits Boston in August and arranges publication of a second story collection. Meets with M. A. DeWolfe Howe, editor of the Beacon Biographies of Eminent Americans, and proposes writing a biography of Frederick Douglass for the series. Closes stenographic business on September 30 and sets up literary office at home, intending to become a full-time writer and lecturer. *Frederick Douglass* published by Smith, Maynard on November 27; *The Wife of His Youth and Other Stories of the Color Line* published by Houghton, Mifflin, November 29.

1900 Reviews Booker T. Washington's *The Future of the American Negro* for *The Critic.* Meets William Dean Howells in New York in February and is pleased when Howells praises his stories in an essay published in the May *Atlantic Monthly. Southern Workman* publishes stories "Lonesome Ben" (March) and "Tobe's Tribulations" (November). Novel "The Rainbow Chasers" is rejected by Houghton, Mifflin in March and by Robert Underwood Johnson of the *Century* in April. Publishes "The Future American," controversial three-part essay on racial amalgamation, in the *Boston Evening Transcript*, August 18–September 1. Works on *The Marrow of Tradition*, novel inspired by November 1898 riot in Wilmington, North Carolina, during which white supremacists overthrew the city government and killed an estimated 20 African-Americans. Novel *The House Behind the Cedars* published by Houghton, Mifflin on October 27. Brothers Lewis and Andrew (Jack) establish a successful photography studio in Cleveland.

1901 Makes southern lecture tour, February–March, visiting Wilmington and meeting with Booker T. Washington at Tuskegee. Publishes articles based on his trip in the *Boston Evening Transcript* and the *Cleveland Leader.* Writes to the Macmillan Company in April to protest its publication of *The American Negro* by William Hannibal Thomas, which Chesnutt describes as racially defamatory; the book is soon withdrawn from sale. Essay "Superstitions and Folk-Lore of the South" appears in *Modern Culture* in May. Daughters Ethel and Helen graduate from Smith, and Ethel begins teaching at Tuskegee. Chairs Committee on Colored Troops for the 35th National Encampment of the Grand Army of the Republic in

Cleveland, and gives speech at memorial service for President William McKinley in September. *The Marrow of Tradition* published by Houghton, Mifflin in late October. Sales are disappointing, and Chesnutt establishes new stenographic firm.

1902 Applies to join Rowfant Club, an exclusive Cleveland bibliophile society, but is vetoed by some of its members on racial grounds. Ethel returns to Cleveland and marries Edward Williams, a librarian at Western Reserve University, and Helen begins teaching in the Cleveland public schools. (She will eventually teach Latin at Central High School, where Langston Hughes will be one of her students.)

1903 Contributes "The Disfranchisement of the Negro" to *The Negro Problem: A Series of Articles by Representative American Negroes of Today*, a collection that also includes essays by W.E.B. Du Bois and Booker T. Washington. Corresponds with Du Bois. Novel "Evelyn's Husband," depicting love triangle among white upper-class Bostonians, is rejected by McClure, Phillips. Grandson Charles Waddell Chesnutt Williams born.

1904 Family moves to new house at 1668 (later renumbered 9719) Lamont Avenue. Story "Baxter's Procrustes" published in June *Atlantic Monthly*. Novel *The Colonel's Dream* accepted by Walter Hines Page, now at Doubleday, Page, after being rejected by Houghton, Mifflin.

1905 Accepts membership on Committee of Twelve, organized by Booker T. Washington for "the advancement of the interests of the Negro race." Delivers lecture "Race Prejudice: Its Causes and Its Cure" before the Boston Historical and Literary Association. Son Edwin graduates from Harvard College. *The Colonel's Dream* published by Doubleday, Page in September. Becomes member of the Cleveland Council of Sociology, a civic improvement group. Attends 70th birthday party for Mark Twain held at Delmonico's in New York City.

1906 Delivers "The Age of Problems," speech advocating racial equality, to the Cleveland Council of Sociology.

1908 Criticizes several Supreme Court decisions in speech "The Courts and the Negro." Addresses annual conference of the Niagara Movement, founded by Du Bois in 1905 to seek political and economic rights for blacks.

1910 Addresses May meeting of the National Negro Committee, which reorganizes itself as the National Association for the Advancement of Colored People; Chesnutt becomes a member of its General Committee. Hospitalized in June after suffering a minor stroke. Declines to endorse public statement by Du Bois attacking Booker T. Washington. Accepts election as member of the Rowfant Club.

1912 Story "The Doll" published by Du Bois in *The Crisis*, April. Becomes member of Cleveland Chamber of Commerce. Tours Europe with Helen in summer, traveling through Belgium, the Netherlands, Germany, Switzerland, Italy, France, and England, where they visit composer Samuel Coleridge-Taylor.

1913 Persuades Cleveland mayor Newton Baker to oppose bill prohibiting interracial marriage in Ohio (bill is defeated). Awarded LL.D. degree by Wilberforce University. Daughter Dorothy graduates from Western Reserve University (she will work as a juvenile court probation officer before becoming a schoolteacher). Delivers speech during centenary celebration of the battle of Lake Erie in which he describes the role of black sailors and soldiers in the War of 1812.

1914 Helps establish Playhouse Settlement (later called Karamu House), social settlement house in the Central Avenue district of Cleveland. Buys automobile and learns to drive.

1915 Skids on hill and crashes car in February; accident kills a young female passenger and injures his wife. Edwin graduates from dental school at Northwestern and opens practice in Chicago. Supports woman suffrage in "Women's Rights," article published in August *Crisis*. Successfully protests plan by Ohio agricultural official to arrange screening of D. W. Griffith's film *The Birth of a Nation* for youth excursion group.

1916 Attends conference on racial issues held at Amenia, New York, estate of Joel Spingarn.

1917 Enlists Chamber of Commerce in successful attempt to have *The Birth of a Nation* banned in Cleveland. Becomes member of National Arts Club. Protests harsh treatment of black soldiers in southern training camps.

1918 Forms business partnership with Helen C. Moore, a white stenographer who becomes office manager of Chesnutt & Moore.

1920 Falls ill with appendicitis and peritonitis. Father dies.

1921 Novel *Paul Marchand, F.M.C.* is rejected by Houghton, Mifflin and Alfred Knopf (published in 1999). *The House Behind the Cedars* is serialized in the *Chicago Defender*.

1922 Signs protest against American occupation of Haiti.

1923 Supports protest against attempt by Harvard University to exclude black students from its freshman dormitories and dining halls.

1924 Dorothy marries John Slade. Film adaptation of *The House Behind the Cedars*, produced and directed by Oscar Micheaux, is released (Micheaux will release another version, *Veiled Aristocrats*, in 1932). Conjure tale "The Marked Tree" appears in *The Crisis*, December 1924–January 1925.

1925 Grandson John Chesnutt Slade born. Builds summer house at Idlewild, resort near Baldwin, Michigan.

1926 Corresponds with Carl Van Vechten, who had praised Chesnutt's work in his novel *Nigger Heaven*.

1927 New edition of *The Conjure Woman* published by Houghton, Mifflin.

1928 Appears before Senate committee to oppose the Shipstead Anti-Injunction bill because of the racially exclusive practices of labor unions. Awarded Spingarn Medal by the NAACP. Completes novel *The Quarry* (published in 1999).

1930 Publishes "The Negro in Cleveland" in *Clevelander*, November.

1931 "Post-Bellum—Pre-Harlem" published in *The Colophon* and reprinted in *The Crisis.*

1932 Dies at home at 5:30 P.M. on November 15 of arteriosclerosis complicated by hypertension. Buried in Lake View Cemetery after funeral service at Emmanuel Episcopal Church.

Note on the Texts

This volume contains two collections of short stories by Charles W. Chesnutt, *The Conjure Woman* (1899) and *The Wife of His Youth and Other Stories of the Color Line* (1899); two of Chesnutt's novels, *The House Behind the Cedars* (1900) and *The Marrow of Tradition* (1901); nine stories not collected by Chesnutt; and a selection of seven essays published between 1889 and 1931.

Three stories collected in *The Conjure Woman* were first published in periodicals between 1887 and 1889: "The Goophered Grapevine" (*Atlantic Monthly*, August 1887), "Po' Sandy" (*Atlantic Monthly*, May 1888), and "The Conjurer's Revenge" (*Overland Monthly*, June 1889). These stories are connected by the recurring figure of Uncle Julius, a former slave whose tales of conjuration, drawn from folklore and rendered in dialect, are told to a northern couple who have recently moved to North Carolina. Although Chesnutt wrote, in a letter dated September 26, 1889, "I think I have about used up the old Negro who serves as mouthpiece, and I shall drop him in future stories, as well as much of the dialect," Uncle Julius continued to appear in stories written between 1889 and 1896, including "Dave's Neckliss," "A Deep Sleeper," "Lonesome Ben," and "The Dumb Witness." These stories differ from the earlier Uncle Julius tales because they do not feature conjuration and the fantastic elements in them are less prominent.

The seven Uncle Julius stories were among the works of short fiction that Chesnutt submitted to Houghton, Mifflin in October 1897. Walter Hines Page, a senior member of the firm and an editor at the *Atlantic Monthly*, rejected the proposed collection and suggested that Chesnutt seek another publisher. He then added: "There is yet a possibility of Mssrs. Houghton, Mifflin and Company's doing something for you along this line—if you had enough 'conjure' stories to make a book, even a small book. I cannot help feeling that that would succeed. All the readers who have read your stories agree on this—that 'The Goophered Grapevine' and 'Po' Sandy,' and the one or two others that have the same original quality that these show, are stories that are sure to live—in fact, I know of nothing so good of their kind anywhere. For myself, I venture unhesitatingly the prediction of a notable and lasting success with them, but the trouble at present is there are only about three of these stories which have this quality unmixed with other qualities. If you could produce five or six more like these, I think I am safe in making you a double promise—first, of magazine publication, and then the collection, I think would make a successful book."

Chesnutt responded to Page's letter by writing six "conjure" stories in April and May of 1898. Four of these stories, "The Gray Wolf's Ha'nt," "Mars Jeems's Nightmare," "Sis' Becky's Pickaninny," and "Hot-Foot Hannibal," were included in the collection, titled *The Conjure Woman*, along with "The Goophered Grapevine," "Po' Sandy," and "The Conjurer's Revenge." Chesnutt made a few changes in wording in "Po' Sandy" and significantly revised "The Goophered Grapevine" and "The Conjurer's Revenge" for inclusion in *The Conjure Woman*. He added several paragraphs to the opening of "The Goophered Grapevine," while leaving Julius's tale as it originally appeared in the 1887 *Atlantic Monthly* version of the story; also, in a letter accompanying the six new stories, Chesnutt told Page of his intention to revise "The Conjurer's Revenge," writing that the story "has a good deal of extraneous matter in it, and is a trifle coarse here and there. I shall rewrite it at once, as I think it was checked by your house as suitable for book publication." "Hot-Foot Hannibal" was published in the *Atlantic Monthly* in January 1899; the three other 1898 stories that were included in the collection first appeared in *The Conjure Woman*, published by Houghton, Mifflin in March 1899. Chesnutt did not subsequently revise *The Conjure Woman* after the 1899 Houghton, Mifflin edition, the text of which is printed here.

In July 1899, Chesnutt wrote to Page inquiring whether Houghton, Mifflin would be interested in bringing out a second collection of short stories "along the line of 'The Wife of His Youth,'" a story published in *Atlantic Monthly* in July 1898 that had received favorable attention from critics. Houghton, Mifflin quickly agreed to the proposal, announcing a forthcoming book of Chesnutt stories in the September 1899 issue of *Bookman*. For the volume, Chesnutt submitted nine stories written between 1887 and the summer of 1898; in an accompanying letter, Chesnutt said, "I should like to hope that the stories, while written to depict life as it is, in certain aspects that no one has ever before attempted to adequately describe, may throw a light upon the great problem on which the stories are strung; for the backbone of this volume is not a character, like Uncle Julius in *The Conjure Woman*, but a subject, as indicated in the title—*The Color Line*."

Three of the stories in *The Wife of His Youth and Other Stories of the Color Line* first appeared in periodicals: "The Sheriff's Children" (*Independent*, November 7, 1889), "The Wife of His Youth" (*At-*

lantic Monthly, July 1898), and "The Bouquet" (*Atlantic Monthly*, November 1899). The other six, "Her Virginia Mammy," "A Matter of Principle," "Cicely's Dream," "The Passing of Grandison," "Uncle Wellington's Wives," and "The Web of Circumstance" first appeared in *The Wife of His Youth and Other Stories of the Color Line*, published by Houghton, Mifflin late in 1899. (These stories had been written at various times: "The Web of Circumstance," for example, was one of the stories Chesnutt had unsuccessfully submitted to Houghton, Mifflin in 1891 for possible book publication, and "The Bouquet," "A Matter of Principle," and "Uncle Wellington's Wives" were among the pieces sent to the publisher along with some of the "conjure" stories in 1897.) Chesnutt did not revise the stories after their publication in this collection. The text printed here is taken from the 1899 Houghton, Mifflin edition.

The House Behind the Cedars began as "Rena," an unpublished short story that Chesnutt wrote in 1889, revised at least three times between 1889 and 1891, and had expanded into a short novel by 1895. In the latter half of the 1890s, Chesnutt continued work on the manuscript, which was submitted to Houghton, Mifflin in 1899 and rejected. After Doubleday & McClure expressed interest in a newly revised version of "Rena Walden," Houghton, Mifflin decided to have a second look at the novel. In a letter to his wife dated January 27, 1900, Chesnutt wrote that although Doubleday & McClure was "real anxious to publish *Rena*," he would not accept its offer until he met with Houghton, Mifflin, adding, "I don't need to worry about getting publishers at present." In March 1900, Chesnutt agreed to publish the book, which was soon retitled *The House Behind the Cedars*, with Houghton, Mifflin. In October 1900 Chesnutt told his daughters that he had "finished reading the proofs of *The House Behind the Cedars*, which has been improved by the process." *The House Behind the Cedars* was published by Houghton, Mifflin, in late 1900, and the text of this edition is printed here.

Much of *The Marrow of Tradition* is based on an outbreak of violence against African-Americans in Wilmington, North Carolina, that took place in the wake of the election of November 1898. Chesnutt visited Wilmington early in 1901 to undertake research for the novel, which was written during the spring and early summer of that year. In July 1901 he sent his completed typescript to Houghton, Mifflin; in a letter enclosed with it, Chesnutt wrote that the novel was "entirely sincere" and "certainly a much better book" than the others he had written. *The Marrow of Tradition* was published in October 1901 by Houghton, Mifflin and was not subsequently revised by Chesnutt. The text printed here is taken from the 1901 edition.

This volume prints nine stories that were not collected by

Chesnutt, including the four Uncle Julius stories submitted to Houghton, Mifflin in 1897 that were not included in *The Conjure Woman.* Three of these were published in periodicals: "Dave's Neckliss" (*Atlantic Monthly*, October 1889), "A Deep Sleeper" (*Two Tales*, March 11, 1893), and "Lonesome Ben" (*Southern Workman*, March 1900). For the present volume, the texts printed here of these stories are taken from their periodical publications. "The Dumb Witness" was not published during Chesnutt's lifetime. The version that appears in *The Conjure Woman and Other Conjure Tales*, edited by Richard Brodhead (Raleigh-Durham: Duke University Press, 1993), is based on two drafts of the story in the Charles Waddell Chesnutt Papers at the Fisk University Library. The earlier and more complete of these drafts is a 21-page typescript which is missing its second page; the other typescript version, comprised of eight pages, represents a later stage of revision but is fragmentary and incomplete. The Duke edition is a composite text based on these typescripts, following the later typescript wherever it exists and using the first typescript for the remainder of the story. "The Dumb Witness" was revised and incorporated with an altered ending into Chapters 19 and 35 of Chesnutt's novel *The Colonel's Dream* (1905). The text printed here is that of the independent story in *The Conjure Woman and Other Conjure Tales.*

Three of the five remaining uncollected stories were published in periodicals: "The March of Progress" (*Century*, January 1901), "Baxter's Procrustes" (*Atlantic Monthly*, June 1904), and "The Doll" (*The Crisis*, April 1912). The texts printed here are taken from their periodical publications. "White Weeds" was submitted with "The Doll" and "Baxter's Procrustes" to *Atlantic Monthly* in early 1904; but, like "The Doll," it was not accepted for publication by that magazine. It is not clear when "The Kiss" was written, but a reference in the story's final paragraph to "the war" suggests that it was completed after 1914. Neither "White Weeds" nor "The Kiss" was published during Chesnutt's lifetime. They first appeared in *The Short Fiction of Charles W. Chesnutt* (Washington D.C.: Howard University Press, 1974), edited by Sylvia Lyons Render. The texts of both stories as printed here are taken from *The Short Fiction of Charles W. Chesnutt.*

The texts of the seven essays included in this volume come from *Charles W. Chesnutt: Essays and Speeches*, edited by Joseph R. McElrath Jr., Robert C. Leitz III, and Jesse S. Crisler (Stanford: Stanford University Press, 1999). Six of these essays were published during Chesnutt's lifetime, and the editors of *Charles W. Chesnutt: Essays and Speeches* take the texts of "What Is a White Man?" (*Independent*, May 30, 1889), "Superstitions and Folk-Lore of the South" (*Modern*

Culture, May 1901), "Charles W. Chesnutt's Own View of His New Story, *The Marrow of Tradition*" (Cleveland *World*, October 20, 1901), and "Post-Bellum—Pre-Harlem" (*The Colophon*, February 1931) from the periodical versions. "The Future American" was published in three parts in the *Boston Evening Transcript* on August 18, August 25, and September 1, 1900. The text presented in *Charles W. Chesnutt: Essays and Speeches* is based on the newspaper version and incorporates emendations taken from a typescript in the Fisk University Library that was made after the newspaper publication of the essay. "The Disfranchisement of the Negro" was published in *The Negro Problem* (New York: James Pott & Co., 1903). The text in *Charles W. Chesnutt: Essays and Speeches* is taken from Chesnutt's corrected copy of the galley proof, now in the library of the Western Reserve Historical Society, and includes the emendation of a reading present in both the corrected galley and the published text: at 877.26, the editors change "Jackson vs. Giles" to "Jackson W. Giles," the name of the plantiff in *Giles* v. *Harris*. The present volume does not incorporate this emendation, as explained in the notes. "The Courts and the Negro" was not published during Chesnutt's lifetime. The text in *Charles W. Chesnutt: Essays and Speeches* is taken from an undated typescript in the Fisk University Library that was signed by Chesnutt and contains his handwritten emendations. An additional emendation was made by the editors of *Charles W. Chesnutt: Essays and Speeches*: at 898.6, "Reeves" was changed to "Rives," the correct name of the appellant in *Virginia* v. *Rives*. (In presenting texts taken from typescript sources, the editors of *Charles W. Chesnutt: Essays and Speeches* also made emendations in the punctuation of quotations and the placement of periods and commas in relation to closing parentheses and quotation marks.)

This volume presents the texts of the original printings chosen for inclusion here, but it does not attempt to reproduce nontextual features of their typographic design. The texts are presented without change, except for the correction of typographical errors. Spelling, punctuation, and capitalization are often expressive features and are not altered, even when inconsistent or irregular. The following is a list of typographical errors corrected, cited by page and line number: 120.30, *joi*; 132.12, be would; 166.2, negro. I; 166.33, May/be; 193.7, here."; 217.15, 'oman,; 235.19, trucks; 398.3, interest?; 579.36, "while; 747.24, ' pear; 748.19, monst' us; 749.31, 'fom; 750.25, 'pears; 751.25, "W'at's; 751.26, 'spon'.; 751.26, "W'at; 753.15, yaller.'

Notes

In the notes below, the reference numbers denote page and line of this volume (the line count includes chapter headings). No note is made for material included in standard desk references such as Webster's *Collegiate*, *Biographical*, and *Geographical* dictionaries. Biblical quotations are keyed to the King James Version. Quotations from Shakespeare are keyed to *The Riverside Shakespeare*, ed. G. Blakemore Evans (Boston: Houghton Mifflin, 1974). For further biographical information than is contained in the Chronology, see Frances Richardson Keller, *An American Crusade: The Life of Charles Waddell Chesnutt* (Provo: Brigham Young University Press, 1978); William L. Andrews, *The Literary Career of Charles W. Chesnutt* (Baton Rouge: Louisiana State University Press, 1980); Helen M. Chesnutt, *Charles Waddell Chesnutt: Pioneer of the Color Line* (Chapel Hill: University of North Carolina Press, 1952); Curtis W. Ellison and E. W. Metcalf Jr., *Charles W. Chesnutt: A Reference Guide* (Boston: G. K. Hall, 1977); Joseph R. McElrath Jr., and Robert C. Leitz III, editors, *To Be an Author: Letters of Charles W. Chesnutt, 1889–1905* (Princeton: Princeton University Press, 1997); Richard Brodhead, editor, *The Journals of Charles W. Chesnutt* (Durham: Duke University Press, 1993); and Joseph R. McElrath Jr., Robert C. Leitz III, and Jesse S. Crislers, editors, *Charles W. Chesnutt: Essays and Speeches* (Stanford: Stanford University Press, 1999).

THE CONJURE WOMAN

5.1 *Goophered*] Goopher (also "goofer" or "guffer") is a word of African origin, etymologically akin to Mende "ngafa" (spirit, ghost), Ewe "gafe" (shrine of a god), Fon "kafo" (iron fetish), or the Ki-Kongo verb "kufwa" (to die); it denotes a curse or spell as well as the conjurer who performs it. Other English-language derivatives of the word include "goofer dust" (graveyard dirt), "goofed" (high on marijuana), "goofing" (making a mistake), "goofy," and "goofball."

5.2–6.26 SOME YEARS AGO . . . fallen into desuetude.] The story's opening was expanded to create a frame for the collection *The Conjure Woman*. The first publication of "The Goophered Grapevine" in *Atlantic Monthly* (August 1887) began with the following paragraph:

> About ten years ago my wife was in poor health, and our family doctor, in whose skill and honesty I had implicit confidence, advised a change of

climate. I was engaged in grape-culture in northern Ohio, and decided to look for a locality suitable for carrying on the same business in some Southern State. I wrote to a cousin who had gone into the turpentine business in central North Carolina, and he assured me that no better place could be found in the South than the State and neighborhood in which he lived: climate and soil were all that could be asked for, and land could be bought for a mere song. A cordial invitation to visit him while I looked into the matter was accepted. We found the weather delightful at that season, the end of the summer, and were most hospitably entertained. Our host placed a horse and buggy at our disposal, and himself acted as guide until I got somewhat familiar with the country.

5.33 Patesville] The setting for many of Chesnutt's works, Patesville is based on Fayetteville, North Carolina.

10.1 buckrahs] White men.

10.9 spring guns] Device set to fire when a trespasser trips a wire attached to the trigger.

12.37 So Henry 'n'int his head wid de sap] In an 1899 interview (Pauline Carrington Bouvé, "An Aboriginal Author: The Work and Personality of Charles W. Chesnutt," *Boston Transcript*, August 22, 1899), Chesnutt described the man on whom Uncle Henry was based as follows:

> My father-in-law had made enough to buy one of the old Southern houses—a town house it was—but there was a great garden around it. One day an old colored man came to work in this garden, and as he leaned on his hoe he told me of an old man who had anointed his bald head with scuppernong grape-juice which had the remarkable effect of producing a luxuriant crop of hair. This hair grew with the rising sap of the scuppernong vines and fell away periodically with the shrivelling of the grapes, occasioning a yearly repetition of the anointing process. That was the foundation of "The Goophered Grapevine."

15.33 manyo] manure.

31.11 hardened my heart] See Exodus 7:13.

51.38 tu'n-row] Turnrow, a furrow made in soil by a plow.

53.9 mou'ners' bench] Mourners' bench, a bench or seat set apart at religious revival meetings for mourners and those who have not been baptized.

81.14 temper' de win' ter de sho'n ram] In Laurence Sterne's *A Sentimental Journey* (1768), a character observes that "God tempers the wind . . . to the shorn lamb."

81.23 colloguin'] Colloguing: conferring secretly, or conspiring.

86.20 Lethe] Mythological river in Hades whose water wiped out all memory of the past.

THE WIFE OF HIS YOUTH AND OTHER STORIES OF THE COLOR LINE

101.1 *The Wife of His Youth*] See Proverbs 5:18–20: "Let thy fountain be blessed: and rejoice with the wife of thy youth. Let her be as the loving hind and pleasant roe; let her breasts satisfy thee at all times; and be thou ravished always with her love. And why wilt thou, my son, be ravished with a strange woman, and embrace the bosom of a stranger?"

101.33–34 a pillar of cloud by day and of fire by night] See Exodus 13:21.

102.23 Groveland] The setting of many of Chesnutt's works, Groveland was modeled upon his birthplace, Cleveland, Ohio.

103.5–6 Mrs. Molly Dixon] In an interview with Max Bennett Thrasher (*Boston Evening Transcript*, September 4, 1901), Chesnutt reported that the manuscript of the story was one year old when he realized that it "lacked the element of conflicting interest" and "saw that there ought to be another woman in it, by contrast with whom the little old black wife should be made more striking."

104.12–13 'With malice . . . for all,'] From Abraham Lincoln's second inaugural address, March 4, 1865.

104.29–30 "A Dream of Fair Women."] Alfred Tennyson's poem about devoted and loyal women was first published in 1832; the quoted lines come from the section on Helen. The 1866 edition, illustrated by John Everett Millais, carried as frontispiece an image of Cleopatra that portrayed her in accordance with Tennyson's description as "a queen, with swarthy cheeks."

104.32–35 "At length I saw . . . divinely fair."] "A Dream of Fair Women," lines 85–89.

105.1–2 "O sweet pale . . . Margaret."] Tennyson's "Margaret" (1832), lines 1–2. In a subsequent stanza, contrasting Margaret with her sister Adeline, Tennyson writes: "Your hair is darker, and your eyes / Touch'd with a somewhat darker hue."

105.8–19 "She seem'd . . . Upon her perfect lips."] Tennyson, "Sir Launcelot and Queen Guinevere" (1842), lines 23–27, 40–45.

108.4 slave marriage] Slave marriages were not legally binding.

112.5–7 'This above all . . . false to any man.'] Shakespeare, *Hamlet*, I, iii, 78–80.

117.8–9 Yet we are all made after God's own image] See Genesis 1:27.

131.27 "bummers"] Foraging soldiers from Sherman's army.

152.7–8 Many had called, but none had been chosen.] See Matthew 20:16.

156.34 pedigree of . . . Pushkin] The Russian writer Alexander Pushkin (1799–1837) was the great-grandson, on his mother's side, of Abram Hannibal, an Abyssinian nobleman who was purchased as a slave by Peter the Great; Pushkin recounted the traditions associated with his ancestor in the novella *The Negro of Peter the Great* (1827).

156.34–35 Dumas's] Alexandre Dumas (1802–1870), French dramatist and novelist, was the grandson of the marquis Antoine-Alexandre Davy de la Pailleterie, a general in the French army, and Marie Cessette Dumas, a woman of African descent with whom he lived in San Domingo.

158.2 the leopard can change his spots] See Jeremiah 13:23: "Can the Ethiopian change his skin, or the leopard his spots? Then may ye also do good, that are accustomed to do evil."

168.10–11 For of one blood God made all the nations] See Acts 17:26.

177.22–23 Pharaoh's daughter . . . bulrushes] See Exodus 2:5–6.

183.18 Junonian] Resembling Juno, the supreme goddess of the ancient Romans.

188.12 Fugitive Slave Law] The Fugitive Slave Law was passed by Congress in September 1850.

203.32 North Star] A comic inversion of the meaning of the North Star in slave narratives where it leads the runaway slave to freedom.

203.34–35 Mr. Simms] William Gilmore Simms (1806–1870), southern historical novelist whose works included *The Yemassee* (1835) and *Woodcraft* (1854).

204.11 fatted calf] See Luke 15:27.

205.9 fleshpots of Egypt] See Exodus 16:3.

207.40 land flowing with milk and honey] See Deuteronomy 27:3.

225.32 For a' that an' a' that] See Robert Burns, "Is There for Honest Poverty" (1795), lines 9–13: "What tho' on hamely fare we dine, / Wear hodden grey, an' a' that? / Gie fools their silks, and knaves their wine— / A man's a man for a' that! / For a' that, and an' a' that."

239.35 Confederate Memorial Day] Any of several days in southern states commemorating servicemen of the Confederacy; in North Carolina, May 10.

259.30 nolled] Ended, from the legal term *nolle prosequi*, the formal notice by a prosecutor that a prosecution will be terminated.

THE HOUSE BEHIND THE CEDARS

272.8–10 'Man dat is bawn er 'oman . . . lack as a flower.'] See Job 14:1–2.

272.10–11 'De days . . . three-sco' an' ten'] See Psalm 90:10.

272.29 "Tippecanoe and Tyler too."] Slogan in the 1840 presidential campaign of Whig candidates William Henry Harrison and John Tyler, referring to Harrison's command of American troops in a battle fought in 1811 with Indians along the Tippecanoe River in northern Indiana.

274.28 Phryne] Greek courtesan of the 4th century B.C. who was a model for representations of Aphrodite by the sculptor Praxiteles (whose mistress she was said to be) and the painter Apelles. She (or another person of the same name) was tried for impiety; her defender, the orator Hyperides, achieved her acquittal by tearing her dress in order to display her beauty to the judges. The anecdote was popularized by Jean-Léon Gérôme's widely reproduced painting "Phryne Before the Areopagus" (1861). (The name "Phryne," meaning toad, was an indication of sallow complexion.)

278.35–36 "Imperious Caesar . . . the wind away,"] Shakespeare, *Hamlet*, V, i, 213–14.

295.27 Shylock's bond] "A pound of flesh, to be by him cut off / Nearest the merchant's heart": Shakespeare, *The Merchant of Venice*, IV, i, 232–33.

299.12–13 Ashby-de-la-Zouch] Town where the tournament is held in Walter Scott's novel *Ivanhoe* (1819).

299.17 Pentelic marble] A superior marble quarried in ancient times from Mount Pentelikon in Greece.

302.1–2 six Rebeccas and eight Rowenas] In *Ivanhoe*, the hero's affections are torn between the Jewish physician's daughter Rebecca and the Saxon noblewoman Rowena, whom he eventually marries.

318.8–9 "The sins . . . upon the children,"] See Exodus 34:6–7.

321.32 "Let the dead past bury its dead."] See Luke 9:60 and also Matthew 8:22.

358.18 Warwick the Kingmaker] Richard Neville (1428–1471), Earl of Warwick, known as "the Kingmaker" for his role in the War of the Roses. Warwick was the hero of the popular novel *The Last of the Barons* (1843) by Edward Bulwer-Lytton.

358.22–23 "She should have . . . instead of Rowena,"] See note 302.1–2.

373.17 Witch of Endor] Female sorcerer who at the command of Saul, the first king of Israel, brought up the dead Samuel "out of the earth"; see 1 Samuel 28:7–14.

374.2–375.2 Among the books were . . . the roc's leg.] The passage amounts to a catalogue of some of Chesnutt's own favorite books and authors.

374.7 Clarissa Harlowe] Heroine of the epistolary novel (1748) by Samuel Richardson.

374.9 Roderick Random] Hero of the comic maritime novel (1748) by Tobias Smollett.

374.38 Sophia] Heiress loved by the hero in Henry Fielding's *Tom Jones* (1749).

374.38–39 Eugene Aram] Novel (1832) by Edward Bulwer-Lytton.

374.39–40 Richard the Lion-heart . . . tent] In Walter Scott's *The Talisman* (1825).

374.40 Gil Blas] Hero of the picaresque novel (1715–26) by Alain-René Le Sage.

375.6 Tree of Knowledge] See Genesis 2:9–3:12.

375.8 heirs of the ages] See Tennyson's *Locksley Hall* (1842): "I the heir of all the ages, in the foremost files of time."

379.12 Dred Scott] In *Dred Scott* v. *Sandford* (1857) the U.S. Supreme Court ruled that Congress could not prohibit slavery in federal territories, and that free Negroes were not citizens of the United States. Chief Justice Roger B. Taney wrote the opinion of the court in the case.

379.29 "One touch . . . whole world kin,"] Shakespeare, *Troilus and Cressida*, III, iii, 175.

392.3–4 "to him that hath shall be given"] Cf. Matthew 13:12: "For whosoever hath, to him shall be given, and he shall have more abundance: but whosoever hath not, from him shall be taken away even that he hath." See also Mark 4:25 and Luke 8:18.

410.9 Nimrod] Son of Cush and a "mighty hunter"; see Genesis 10:8–9.

425.26 the shadow of the Ethiopian] The phrase is taken from George Washington Cable, *The Grandissimes: A Story of Creole Life* (1879–80).

THE MARROW OF TRADITION

464.1–3 I like you . . . tradition's shown.] The fourth line of the stanza reads: "And all that history, much that fiction weaves."

483.28 the widow's cruse] The cruse with which the widow succored the prophet Elijah was to remain full of oil "until the day that the Lord sendeth rain upon the earth"; see 1 Kings 17:9–16.

483.30 Fortunatus's purse] In medieval legend, a purse that is inexhaustible.

488.40 Fusion ticket] The Fusion alliance won the North Carolina state elections in 1894 and 1896.

489.24 Gin'l Belmont an' Cap'n McBane] Chesnutt modeled his characters on the white supremacists who planned the 1898 Wilmington riot, condensing the "Secret Nine" who called for the re-establishment of "Anglo-Saxon rule and honest government in North Carolina" to the "Secret Three" of *The Marrow of Tradition*. General Belmont was inspired by Alfred Moore Waddell (who may have been related to Chesnutt's paternal grandfather), and Captain McBane was drawn after Mike Dowling, the organizer of the Red Shirts, the terrorist arm of the Wilmington Democrats.

495.19 Ham] Noah's son Ham, the putative forefather of Africans according to extensively elaborated Biblical interpretations prevalent in the antebellum period and after. In Genesis 9:18, Ham is described as "the father of Canaan"; in verse 25 of the same chapter, one of Ham's sons is cursed by Noah in terms that were sometimes interpreted as a justification of slavery: "Cursed be Canaan; a servant of servants shall he be unto his brethren."

512.5 Procrustes] Mythical highwayman of Attica, said to have tied his victims to a bed, fitting them to its length by stretching them out or cutting off their legs.

512.31–32 'Blessed are the meek . . . inherit the earth.'] See Matthew 5:5.

519.7 *aut Cæsar, aut nullus*] Either Cæsar or no one.

522.19 Pontius Pilate] See Matthew 27:24.

531.30–532.10 The article was . . . a profound sensation.] The article described is based on "Mrs. Felton's Speech," an editorial by African-American journalist Alex Manly, published on August 18, 1898, in the *Wilmington Record*, of which Manly was editor. In 1897 the Georgia-born feminist and temperance journalist Rebecca Latimer Felton said: "If it takes lynching to protect a woman's dearest possession from drunken, ravenous beasts . . . then I say lynch a thousand a week if it becomes necessary." In his response, Manly wrote that white women "are not any more particular in the matter of clandestine meetings with colored men than the white men with colored women" and that when "the woman's infatuation or the man's boldness brings attention to them . . . the man is lynched for rape. Every negro lynched is called a Big Burly Black Brute, when, in fact, many of those who have been dealt with had white men for their fathers, and were not only not black and burly, but were sufficiently attractive for white girls of culture and refinement to fall in love with them, as is very well known to all."

534.31 Barber] Modeled on Alex Manly; see note 531.30–532.10.

552.32 Mosaic law of revenge] See Exodus 21:23–25.

553.8–9 'forgive our enemies . . . that curse us] See Matthew 5:44.

554.15 "Vengeance is mine, I will repay,"] See Romans 12:19.

564.27 Esau sold his birthright] See Genesis 25:29–34.

576.40 Hall Caine's] Hall Caine (1853–1931), popular British novelist whose works included *The Deemster* (1887) and *The Manxman* (1894).

645.16–17 Mr. Hyde . . . Dr. Jekyll] See Robert Louis Stevenson, *The Strange Case of Dr. Jekyll and Mr. Hyde* (1886).

651.8–9 grandfather clause] See Chesnutt's discussion of this issue, pages 876–77 in this volume.

653.12 *moujik*] Russian peasant.

654.27–29 no permanent place . . . except under the ground] In his essay "The Disfranchisement of the Negro" (885.18–25 in this volume), Chesnutt reports that he heard this from "the Superintendent of Public Schools of a Southern city."

659.6 Augean stables] One of Hercules' legendary twelve labors was the cleansing of the stables of king Augeas of Elis, which held 3,000 oxen and had not been cleaned in thirty years; Hercules accomplished the task by diverting a river.

667.28–29 Abraham to her Hagar] Hagar was the concubine of Abraham, the slave of his wife Sarah, and the mother of his son Ishmael. See Genesis 16:1–16, 21:9–20, and 25:12–13.

668.15–16 I should like . . . we ourselves!] See Psalm 100:3.

675.1 *mésalliance*] Misalliance.

675.15 *meum* and *tuum*] Mine and yours.

678.3 THE Wellington riot] Chesnutt drew on the November 1898 Wilmington riot, though he sets the riot in his novel before the election, whereas the historical event took place after election day.

704.26 Vengeance is mine] See note 554.15.

705.2 FIAT JUSTITIA] Let justice be done.

712.5–6 as you have sown, so may you reap] See Galatians 6:7.

712.11 the veil . . . in twain] See Mark 15:27–28: "And the veil of the temple was rent in twain from the top to the bottom."

717.36–37 apples of Sodom] Strabo, Tacitus, and Josephus describe them as beautiful externally and filled with ashes.

UNCOLLECTED STORIES

753.34–35 "Imperious Caesar . . . wind away,"] See note 278.35–36.

756.28 pleasaunce] Pleasure ground or garden of an estate.

758.33–34 bless them that curse you] See note 553.8–9.

781.2 PROCRUSTES] See note 512.5.

781.9 Joseph Jefferson] Popular American actor (1829–1905), best known for his performances in Dion Boucicault's *Rip Van Winkle.*

782.32 Rubáiyát of Omar Khayyám] Poems ascribed to Persian mathematician and astronomer Omar Khayyam (1048–1131); the English adaptation by Edward FitzGerald (1859) became widely popular toward the end of the 19th century.

786.2 doublures] Ornamental linings on the inner side of a book cover.

788.10–11 Spencerian] In the manner of social Darwinist essayist Herbert Spencer (1820–1903), whose main work is *The Synthetic Philosophy* (1896).

789.1–2 Nordau] Max Nordau (1849–1923), Hungarian author whose *Degeneration* (1895) was widely influential.

789.2 Haeckel's] Ernst Haeckel (1834–1919), German zoologist and Darwinian evolutionist.

803.14 Vengeance was God's] See note 554.15.

809.29–30 "Clothed . . . Mystic, wonderful,"] See Tennyson's "Morte d'Arthur," line 31; the reference is to the arm that holds the sword Excalibur.

810.7 *distrait*] Preoccupied, pensive, inattentive.

812.12–13 Wagner's . . . Abendstern."] Aria from Richard Wagner's opera *Tannhäuser* (1845), III, ii: "Oh you my lovely evening star."

812.38 "Abide with Me". . . "Lead, Kindly Light,"] "Abide with Me" (1861), hymn by John Henry Newman and William Henry Monk; "Lead, Kindly Light" (1868), hymn by John Henry Newman and John Bacchus Dykes.

812.39 "Der schoenste Engel."] Song ("The Most Beautiful Angel") by German composer Gustav Heinrich Graben-Hoffmann (1820–1900).

813.14 "Wedding March" from *Lohengrin*] The Bridal Song chorus "Treulich geführt, ziehet dahin" (Faithful and true, we lead ye forth) from Wagner's opera *Lohengrin*, III, 1.

SELECTED ESSAYS

837.9 Mr. Grady] Henry Wodfin Grady (1850–1889), editor of the *Atlanta Constitution* and advocate of a "new" South.

841.22 Dred Scott] See 379.12 (and note) and 896.3–19.

842.34 *alma genetrix*] Fostering progenitor.

843.15 colored woman in Georgia] Amanda Eubanks, of Rome, Georgia.

843.21 Glenn Bill] Bill passed by the Georgia House of Reprsentatives in 1887 that imposed criminal penalties on teachers and administrators who failed to segregate their schools. The bill failed to pass the state senate, though the state legislature did pass a bill cutting state funding to Atlanta University.

843.28 *prima-facie*] Legal presumption of fact.

843.35 The sins of their fathers] See note 318.8–9.

846.15–19 "The European races . . . respectively."] From William Z. Ripley's *The Races of Europe* (1899).

851.7–8 Creole stories of Mr. Cable] George Washington Cable (1844–1925) explored Creole life in *Old Creole Days* (1879), *Madame Delphine* (1881), and *The Grandissimes* (1879–80).

851.16 Grace King's] New Orleans author (1851–1932) whose stories were collected in *Monsieur Motte* (1888) and *Balcony Stories* (1893); the work referred to here and at 853.32–38 is *New Orleans: The Place and the People* (1895).

851.32 distinguished American man of letters] The novelist Albion W. Tourgée (1838–1905), author of *A Fool's Errand* (1879) and *Bricks Without Straw* (1880), was appointed U.S. consul in Bordeaux, France, in 1897.

853.27 T. W. Higginson] Thomas Wentworth Higginson (1823–1911), Unitarian minister who led the 1st South Carolina Volunteers in the Civil War, an experience described in *Army Life in a Black Regiment* (1870); his memoir *Cheerful Yesterdays* appeared in 1898.

854.17 Pushkin] See note 156.34.

854.22 Alfred Dodds] Alfred Amédée Dodds (1842–1922), French military officer who played a leading role in French colonial expansion in West Africa.

854.32 Dumas family] See note 156.34–35. Alexandre Dumas *fils* (1824–1895), wrote such novels as *The Lady of the Camillas.*

860.21 Mr. Spahr] Charles Barzillai Spahr (1860–1904) published *America's Working People* in 1899–1900.

862.32–33 *lex dura, sed tamen lex*] The law is hard, but is still the law.

864.5 "goopher,"] See note 5.1.

864.31–32 Mr. Harris] Joel Chandler Harris (1848–1908), Georgia-born writer famous for his Uncle Remus tales, the first of which were collected in *Uncle Remus; His Songs and Sayings* (1881).

867.38 chico or "jigger"] Small tropical fly or tick that burrows into the skin.

870.16–17 genuine graveyard rabbit's foot] See Chesnutt's story "Sis' Becky's Pickaninny," page 58.

871.36 words which were frozen] The episode occurs in the fourth book (1552–53) of François Rabelais' *Gargantua and Pantagruel.*

877.26 Jackson vs. Giles] The case was *Giles* v. *Harris* (1903); Jackson W. Giles was the appellant.

879.38 Dred Scott] See note 379.12.

883.23–24 "Crook the pregnant . . . follow fawning."] See Shakespeare, *Hamlet*, III, ii, 61–62.

896.3–4 Dred Scott] See note 379.12 and pages 841 and 879.

896.20 Lord Mansfield] William Murray, First Earl of Mansfield (1705–1793), chief justice of the King's Bench of Great Britain, 1756–88. In 1772 he ruled in *Somerset's Case* that James Somersett, a slave brought to England from Virginia, should be freed because there was no positive law in England supporting slavery.

899.5–6 Justices Bradley . . . dissenting opinion] Justice Joseph Bradley wrote the opinion of the court; Justice John Marshall Harland wrote the sole dissenting opinion.

899.15 Fifteenth Amendment] The protection of the privileges and immunities of national citizenship is a provision of the Fourteenth Amendment.

905.17 Giles vs. Harris] See note 877.26.

907.6 Mr. Harris's] See note 864.31–32.

907.22 Joel Spingarn] Joel Elias Spingarn (1875–1939), Columbia University professor of comparative literature, critic, and editor who in 1914 established the annual Spingarn Medal for outstanding African-Americans.

908.3 Thomas Dixon] North Carolina–born Baptist minister and lyceum lecturer (1864–1946) best known for his novels idealizing the Ku Klux Klan, including the trilogy *The Leopard's Spots* (1902), *The Clansman* (1905), and *The Traitor* (1907). D. W. Griffith filmed *The Clansman* as *The Birth of a Nation* in 1915.

908.4 Thomas Nelson Page] Virginia-born writer who cultivated a nostalgic picture of antebellum plantation life in the story collection *In Ole Virginia* (1887) and other works. His novel *Red Rock* (1897) was an attack on Reconstruction.

910.2–3 Pushkin . . . two Dumas in France] See notes 156.34–35 and 854.32.

911.19–20 Carl Van Vechten] Critic, novelist, and photographer (1880–1924) closely associated with the Harlem Renaissance; his novels include *Peter Whiffle* (1922), *The Tattooed Countess* (1924), and *Nigger Heaven* (1926).

911.23–24 for reasons . . . will understand] *Nigger Heaven* contains a passage praising Chesnutt's writing, and a lengthy plot summary of his story "A Matter of Principle."

911.31 *The Adventures of Fanny Hill*] Erotic novel by John Cleland (1710–1789), originally published under the title *Memoirs of a Woman of Pleasure* (1748–49).

Library of Congress Cataloging-in-Publication Data

Chesnutt, Charles Waddell, 1858–1932.
[Selections. 2001]
Stories, novels, & essays / Charles W. Chesnutt.
p. cm. — (Library of America ; 131)
Includes bibliographical references.
Contents: The conjure woman — The wife of his youth and other stories of the color line — The house behind the cedars — The marrow of tradition — Uncollected stories — Selected essays.
ISBN 1–931082–06–5 (alk. paper)
1. African Americans—Fiction. 2. African Americans. I. Title: Stories, novels, and essays. II. Title: Conjure woman. III. Title: Wife of his youth and other stories of the color line. IV. Title: House behind the cedars. V. Title: Marrow of tradition. VI. Title. VII. Series.
PS1292.C6 A6 2002
813′.4—dc21

2001038120

THE LIBRARY OF AMERICA SERIES

The Library of America fosters appreciation and pride in America's literary heritage by publishing, and keeping permanently in print, authoritative editions of its best and most significant writing. An independent nonprofit organization, it was founded in 1979 with seed money from the National Endowment for the Humanities and the Ford Foundation.

1. Herman Melville, *Typee, Omoo, Mardi* (1982)
2. Nathaniel Hawthorne, *Tales and Sketches* (1982)
3. Walt Whitman, *Poetry and Prose* (1982)
4. Harriet Beecher Stowe, *Three Novels* (1982)
5. Mark Twain, *Mississippi Writings* (1982)
6. Jack London, *Novels and Stories* (1982)
7. Jack London, *Novels and Social Writings* (1982)
8. William Dean Howells, *Novels 1875–1886* (1982)
9. Herman Melville, *Redburn, White-Jacket, Moby-Dick* (1983)
10. Nathaniel Hawthorne, *Collected Novels* (1983)
11. Francis Parkman, *France and England in North America*, vol. I (1983)
12. Francis Parkman, *France and England in North America*, vol. II (1983)
13. Henry James, *Novels 1871–1880* (1983)
14. Henry Adams, *Novels, Mont Saint Michel, The Education* (1983)
15. Ralph Waldo Emerson, *Essays and Lectures* (1983)
16. Washington Irving, *History, Tales and Sketches* (1983)
17. Thomas Jefferson, *Writings* (1984)
18. Stephen Crane, *Prose and Poetry* (1984)
19. Edgar Allan Poe, *Poetry and Tales* (1984)
20. Edgar Allan Poe, *Essays and Reviews* (1984)
21. Mark Twain, *The Innocents Abroad, Roughing It* (1984)
22. Henry James, *Essays, American & English Writers* (1984)
23. Henry James, *European Writers & The Prefaces* (1984)
24. Herman Melville, *Pierre, Israel Potter, The Confidence-Man, Tales & Billy Budd* (1985)
25. William Faulkner, *Novels 1930–1935* (1985)
26. James Fenimore Cooper, *The Leatherstocking Tales*, vol. I (1985)
27. James Fenimore Cooper, *The Leatherstocking Tales*, vol. II (1985)
28. Henry David Thoreau, *A Week, Walden, The Maine Woods, Cape Cod* (1985)
29. Henry James, *Novels 1881–1886* (1985)
30. Edith Wharton, *Novels* (1986)
31. Henry Adams, *History of the United States during the Administrations of Jefferson* (1986)
32. Henry Adams, *History of the United States during the Administrations of Madison* (1986)
33. Frank Norris, *Novels and Essays* (1986)
34. W. E. B. Du Bois, *Writings* (1986)
35. Willa Cather, *Early Novels and Stories* (1987)
36. Theodore Dreiser, *Sister Carrie, Jennie Gerhardt, Twelve Men* (1987)
37. Benjamin Franklin, *Writings* (1987)
38. William James, *Writings 1902–1910* (1987)
39. Flannery O'Connor, *Collected Works* (1988)
40. Eugene O'Neill, *Complete Plays 1913–1920* (1988)
41. Eugene O'Neill, *Complete Plays 1920–1931* (1988)
42. Eugene O'Neill, *Complete Plays 1932–1943* (1988)
43. Henry James, *Novels 1886–1890* (1989)
44. William Dean Howells, *Novels 1886–1888* (1989)
45. Abraham Lincoln, *Speeches and Writings 1832–1858* (1989)
46. Abraham Lincoln, *Speeches and Writings 1859–1865* (1989)
47. Edith Wharton, *Novellas and Other Writings* (1990)
48. William Faulkner, *Novels 1936–1940* (1990)
49. Willa Cather, *Later Novels* (1990)
50. Ulysses S. Grant, *Personal Memoirs and Selected Letters* (1990)

51. William Tecumseh Sherman, *Memoirs* (1990)
52. Washington Irving, *Bracebridge Hall, Tales of a Traveller, The Alhambra* (1991)
53. Francis Parkman, *The Oregon Trail, The Conspiracy of Pontiac* (1991)
54. James Fenimore Cooper, *Sea Tales: The Pilot, The Red Rover* (1991)
55. Richard Wright, *Early Works* (1991)
56. Richard Wright, *Later Works* (1991)
57. Willa Cather, *Stories, Poems, and Other Writings* (1992)
58. William James, *Writings 1878–1899* (1992)
59. Sinclair Lewis, *Main Street & Babbitt* (1992)
60. Mark Twain, *Collected Tales, Sketches, Speeches, & Essays 1852–1890* (1992)
61. Mark Twain, *Collected Tales, Sketches, Speeches, & Essays 1891–1910* (1992)
62. *The Debate on the Constitution: Part One* (1993)
63. *The Debate on the Constitution: Part Two* (1993)
64. Henry James, *Collected Travel Writings: Great Britain & America* (1993)
65. Henry James, *Collected Travel Writings: The Continent* (1993)
66. *American Poetry: The Nineteenth Century,* Vol. 1 (1993)
67. *American Poetry: The Nineteenth Century,* Vol. 2 (1993)
68. Frederick Douglass, *Autobiographies* (1994)
69. Sarah Orne Jewett, *Novels and Stories* (1994)
70. Ralph Waldo Emerson, *Collected Poems and Translations* (1994)
71. Mark Twain, *Historical Romances* (1994)
72. John Steinbeck, *Novels and Stories 1932–1937* (1994)
73. William Faulkner, *Novels 1942–1954* (1994)
74. Zora Neale Hurston, *Novels and Stories* (1995)
75. Zora Neale Hurston, *Folklore, Memoirs, and Other Writings* (1995)
76. Thomas Paine, *Collected Writings* (1995)
77. *Reporting World War II: American Journalism 1938–1944* (1995)
78. *Reporting World War II: American Journalism 1944–1946* (1995)
79. Raymond Chandler, *Stories and Early Novels* (1995)
80. Raymond Chandler, *Later Novels and Other Writings* (1995)
81. Robert Frost, *Collected Poems, Prose, & Plays* (1995)
82. Henry James, *Complete Stories 1892–1898* (1996)
83. Henry James, *Complete Stories 1898–1910* (1996)
84. William Bartram, *Travels and Other Writings* (1996)
85. John Dos Passos, *U.S.A.* (1996)
86. John Steinbeck, *The Grapes of Wrath and Other Writings 1936–1941* (1996)
87. Vladimir Nabokov, *Novels and Memoirs 1941–1951* (1996)
88. Vladimir Nabokov, *Novels 1955–1962* (1996)
89. Vladimir Nabokov, *Novels 1969–1974* (1996)
90. James Thurber, *Writings and Drawings* (1996)
91. George Washington, *Writings* (1997)
92. John Muir, *Nature Writings* (1997)
93. Nathanael West, *Novels and Other Writings* (1997)
94. *Crime Novels: American Noir of the 1930s and 40s* (1997)
95. *Crime Novels: American Noir of the 1950s* (1997)
96. Wallace Stevens, *Collected Poetry and Prose* (1997)
97. James Baldwin, *Early Novels and Stories* (1998)
98. James Baldwin, *Collected Essays* (1998)
99. Gertrude Stein, *Writings 1903–1932* (1998)
100. Gertrude Stein, *Writings 1932–1946* (1998)
101. Eudora Welty, *Complete Novels* (1998)
102. Eudora Welty, *Stories, Essays, & Memoir* (1998)
103. Charles Brockden Brown, *Three Gothic Novels* (1998)
104. *Reporting Vietnam: American Journalism 1959–1969* (1998)
105. *Reporting Vietnam: American Journalism 1969–1975* (1998)
106. Henry James, *Complete Stories 1874–1884* (1999)
107. Henry James, *Complete Stories 1884–1891* (1999)

108. *American Sermons: The Pilgrims to Martin Luther King Jr.* (1999)
109. James Madison, *Writings* (1999)
110. Dashiell Hammett, *Complete Novels* (1999)
111. Henry James, *Complete Stories 1864–1874* (1999)
112. William Faulkner, *Novels 1957–1962* (1999)
113. John James Audubon, *Writings & Drawings* (1999)
114. *Slave Narratives* (2000)
115. *American Poetry: The Twentieth Century,* Vol. 1 (2000)
116. *American Poetry: The Twentieth Century,* Vol. 2 (2000)
117. F. Scott Fitzgerald, *Novels and Stories 1920–1922* (2000)
118. Henry Wadsworth Longfellow, *Poems and Other Writings* (2000)
119. Tennessee Williams, *Plays 1937–1955* (2000)
120. Tennessee Williams, *Plays 1957–1980* (2000)
121. Edith Wharton, *Collected Stories 1891–1910* (2001)
122. Edith Wharton, *Collected Stories 1911–1937* (2001)
123. *The American Revolution: Writings from the War of Independence* (2001)
124. Henry David Thoreau, *Collected Essays and Poems* (2001)
125. Dashiell Hammett, *Crime Stories and Other Writings* (2001)
126. Dawn Powell, *Novels 1930–1942* (2001)
127. Dawn Powell, *Novels 1944–1962* (2001)
128. Carson McCullers, *Complete Novels* (2001)
129. Alexander Hamilton, *Writings* (2001)
130. Mark Twain, *The Gilded Age and Later Novels* (2002)
131. Charles W. Chesnutt, *Stories, Novels, and Essays* (2002)
132. John Steinbeck, *Novels 1942–1952* (2002)

This book is set in 10 point Linotron Galliard,
a face designed for photocomposition by Matthew Carter
and based on the sixteenth-century face Granjon. The paper is
acid-free Ecusta Nyalite and meets the requirements for permanence
of the American National Standards Institute. The binding
material is Brillianta, a woven rayon cloth made by
Van Heek-Scholco Textielfabrieken, Holland.
The composition is by The Clarinda
Company. Printing and binding by
R.R.Donnelley & Sons Company.
Designed by Bruce Campbell.